THE CAMBRIDGE HISTORY OF INI

THE CHINGGISID .

GW01561158

This volume centres on the history and legacy of the Mongol World Empire founded by Chinggis Khan and his sons, including its impact upon the modern world. An international team of scholars examines the political and cultural history of the Mongol Empire, its Chinggisid successor states, and the non-Chinggisid dynasties that came to dominate Inner Asia in its wake. Geographically, it focuses on the continental region from East Asia to Eastern Europe. Beginning in the twelfth century, the volume moves through to the establishment of Chinese and Russian political hegemony in Inner Asia from the sixteenth to the nineteenth centuries. Contributors use recent research and new approaches that have revitalized Inner Asian studies to highlight the world-historical importance of the regimes and states formed during and after the Mongol conquest. Their conclusions testify to the importance of a region whose modern fate has been overshadowed by Russia and China.

Nicola Di Cosmo is Henry Luce Foundation Professor of East Asian Studies in the School of Historical Studies at the Institute for Advanced Study, Princeton. His recent publications include *Ancient China and its Enemies: The Rise of Nomadic Powers in East Asian History* (2002), *Manchu-Mongol Relations on the Eve of the Qing Conquest* (2003) and *The Diary of a Manchu Soldier in Seventeenth-Century China* (2006).

Allen J. Frank is an independent scholar. He has published widely on the history of Islam in Imperial Russia and in the Central Asian Soviet successor states. His previous publications include *Islamic Historiography and 'Bulghar' Identity among the Tatars and Bashkirs of Russia* (1998), *Muslim Religious Institutions in Imperial Russia* (2001) and *An Islamic Biographical Dictionary of the Eastern Kazakh Steppe, 1770–1912* (as co-editor, 2005).

Peter B. Golden is Professor of History and Academic Director of the Center for Middle Eastern Studies at Rutgers University. Among his publications are *An Introduction to the History of the Turkic Peoples* (1992; Turkish editions 2002, 2006), *Nomads and their Neighbours in the Russian Steppe* (2003) and *The World of the Khazars: New Perspectives* (as co-editor, 2007).

THE CAMBRIDGE HISTORY OF INNER ASIA

THE CHINGGISID AGE

*

Edited by
NICOLA DI COSMO
ALLEN J. FRANK
and
PETER B. GOLDEN

CAMBRIDGE
UNIVERSITY PRESS

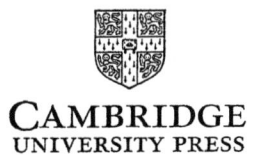

CAMBRIDGE
UNIVERSITY PRESS

University Printing House, Cambridge CB2 8BS, United Kingdom

Cambridge University Press is part of the University of Cambridge.

It furthers the University's mission by disseminating knowledge in the pursuit of education, learning and research at the highest international levels of excellence.

www.cambridge.org
Information on this title: www.cambridge.org/9781107492059

© Cambridge University Press 2009

This publication is in copyright. Subject to statutory exception and to the provisions of relevant collective licensing agreements, no reproduction of any part may take place without the written permission of Cambridge University Press.

First published 2009
First paperback edition 2015

A catalogue record for this publication is available from the British Library

Library of Congress Cataloguing in Publication data
The Cambridge history of medieval Inner Asia : the Chinggisid Age / edited by Nicola Di Cosmo, Allen Frank, and Peter B. Golden.
p. cm.
Includes bibliographical references and index.
ISBN 978-0-521-84926-5 (hardback)
1. Asia, Central – History. 2. Asia, Central – Civilization. 3. Mongols – Asia, Central – History. I. Di Cosmo, Nicola, 1957– II. Frank, Allen J., 1964– III. Golden, Peter B. IV. Title.

DS329.4.C36 2009
958.02 – dc22

2009014240

ISBN 978-0-521-84926-5 Hardback
ISBN 978-1-107-49205-9 Paperback

Cambridge University Press has no responsibility for the persistence or accuracy of URLs for external or third-party internet websites referred to in this publication, and does not guarantee that any content on such websites is, or will remain, accurate or appropriate.

Contents

List of figure and maps *viii*
List of contributors *ix*
Note on transliteration *xii*
List of abbreviations *xiii*
Maps *xviii*

Introduction *1*
NICOLA DI COSMO, ALLEN J. FRANK
and PETER B. GOLDEN

PART ONE
THE RISE OF THE CHINGGISIDS

1 · Inner Asia *c.* 1200 *9*
PETER B. GOLDEN

2 · The Mongol age in Eastern Inner Asia *26*
PETER JACKSON

3 · The Mongols in Central Asia from Chinggis Khan's invasion to the rise of Temür: the Ögödeid and Chaghadaid realms *46*
MICHAL BIRAN

4 · The Jochid realm: the western steppe and Eastern Europe *67*
ISTVÁN VÁSÁRY

PART TWO
LEGACIES OF THE MONGOL CONQUESTS

5 · Institutional development, revenues and trade *89*
ARSENIO PETER MARTINEZ

6 · Migrations, ethnogenesis *109*
PETER B. GOLDEN

7 · Islamization in the Mongol Empire *120*
DEVIN DEWEESE

8 · Mongols as vectors for cultural transmission *135*
THOMAS T. ALLSEN

PART THREE
CHINGGISID DECLINE: 1368–*c.* 1700

9 · The eastern steppe: Mongol regimes after the Yuan (1368–1636) *157*
VERONIKA VEIT

10 · Temür and the early Timurids to *c.* 1450 *182*
BEATRICE FORBES MANZ

11 · The later Timurids *c.* 1450–1526 *199*
STEPHEN DALE

PART FOUR
NOMADS AND SETTLED PEOPLES IN INNER ASIA AFTER THE TIMURIDS

12 · Uzbeks, Qazaqs and Turkmens *221*
YURI BREGEL

13 · The western steppe: Volga-Ural region, Siberia and the Crimea *237*
ALLEN J. FRANK

14 · Eastern Central Asia (Xinjiang): 1300–1800 *260*
JAMES MILLWARD

15 · The Chinggisid restoration in Central Asia: 1500–1785 *277*
R.D. McCHESNEY

16 · The western steppe: the Volga-Ural region, Siberia and the Crimea under Russian rule *303*
CHRISTIAN NOACK

PART FIVE
NEW IMPERIAL MANDATES AND THE END OF THE CHINGGISID ERA (18th–19th CENTURIES)

17 · The Qing and Inner Asia: 1636–1800 *333*
NICOLA DI COSMO

18 · The Qazaqs and Russia *363*
ALLEN J. FRANK

19 · Russia and the peoples of the Volga-Ural region: 1600–1850 *380*
ALLEN J. FRANK

20 · The new Uzbek states: Bukhara, Khiva and Khoqand: *c.* 1750–1886 *392*
YURI BREGEL

Bibliography *412*
Index *466*

Figure and maps

Figure

Genealogy of the Chaghadaid Rulers (up to 1347) 45

Maps

1 Inner Asia *c.* 1250 xviii
2 The Mongol Empire xx
3 Central Asia in the time of Timur xxii
4 Central Asia in the fifteenth and sixteenth centuries xxiii
5 Manchuria and Eastern Mongolia in *c.* 1600 xxiv
6 Central Asia in the seventeenth century xxv
7 Inner Mongolia under the Qing Dynasty xxvi
8 Outer Mongolia under the Qing Dynasty xxvii
9 Central Asia in the eighteenth century xxvii

Contributors

Thomas T. Allsen is Professor Emeritus, The College of New Jersey. His publications include *The Royal Hunt in Eurasian History* (2006), *Culture and Conquest in Mongol Eurasia* (2001), *Commodity and Exchange in the Mongol Empire* (1997) and *Mongol Imperialism: the Policies of the Grand Qan Möngke in China, Russia, and the Islamic Lands, 1251–1259* (1987).

Michal Biran is Associate Professor at the Institute of Asian and African Studies at the Hebrew University of Jerusalem. Her main publications include *Chinggis Khan* (2007), *The Qara Khitai Empire in Eurasian History: Between China and the Islamic World* (2005), *Mongols, Turks, and Others: Eurasian Nomads and the Sedentary World*, co-edited with Reuven Amitai-Preiss (2005) and *Qaidu and the Rise of the Independent Mongol State in Central Asia* (1997).

Yuri Bregel is Professor Emeritus of Central Eurasian Studies at Indiana University, Bloomington. His major works include *Khorezmskie Turkmeny v XIX veke* (1961), *Dokumenty arkhiva khivinskikh khanov po istorii i etnografii karakalpakov* (1967) and *An Historical Atlas of Central Asia* (2003). He is also the editor of the text (1988) and translation (1999) of the *Firdaws al-Iqbal* of Shir Muhammad Mirab Munis and Muhammad Riza Mirab Agahi.

Stephen F. Dale is Professor of South Asian and Islamic History at Ohio State University. He is the author of *The Garden of the Eight Paradises: Babur and the Culture of Empire, 1483–1530* (2004), *Indian Merchants and Eurasian Trade, 1600–1750* (1994) and *Islamic Society on the South Asian Frontier: the Mappilas of Malabar, 1498–1922* (1980).

Devin DeWeese is Professor of Central Eurasian Studies at Indiana University, Bloomington. His publications include *Islamization and Native Religion in the Golden Horde: Baba Tükles and Conversion to Islam in Historical and Epic Tradition* (1994).

Nicola Di Cosmo is the Henry Luce Foundation Professor of East Asia Studies at the School of Historical Studies, Institute for Advanced Study, Princeton. His publications include *Diary of a Manchu Soldier in Seventeenth-Century China* (2006), *A Documentary History of Manchu–Mongol Relations (1616–1626)*, co-authored with Dalizhabu Bao (2003), *Political Frontiers, Ethnic Boundaries and Human Geographies in Chinese History*, co-edited with Don J. Wyatt (2003), *Ancient China and its Enemies: the Rise of Nomadic Power in East Asian History* (2002) and *Warfare in Inner Asian History (500–1800)*, editor (2002).

ALLEN J. FRANK is an independent scholar who lives in Takoma Park, Maryland. His publications include *Muslim Religious Institutions in Imperial Russia: the Islamic World of Novouzensk District and the Kazakh Inner Horde, 1780–1910* (2001) and *Islamic Historiography and 'Bulghar' Identity among the Tatars and Bashkirs of Russia* (1998).

PETER B. GOLDEN is Professor of Central Eurasian History and Academic Director of the Center for Middle Eastern Studies at Rutgers University. His publications include *The World of the Khazars: New Perspectives*, co-edited with Haggai Ben-Shammai and András Róna-Tas (2007), *Türk Halkları Tarihine Giriş*, trans. Osman Karatay (2007), an expanded second edition of the Turkish translation of his *An Introduction to the History of the Turkic Peoples* (1992), *Hazarlar ve Musevîlik* (The Khazars and Judaism), a collection of essays with C. Zuckerman and A. Zajączkowski, edited and translated by Osman Karatay (2005), *Nomads and their Neighbours in the Russian Steppe: Turks, Khazars and Qipchaqs* (2003), *The King's Dictionary. The Rasulid Hexâglot*, editor (2000), *Nomads and Sedentary Societies in Medieval Eurasia* (1998) and *Khazar Studies*, 2 vols. (1980).

PETER JACKSON is Professor of Medieval History at Keele University. His main publications include *The Mongols and the West, 1221–1410* (2005), *The Delhi Sultanate: a Political and Military History* (1999) and *The Mission of Friar William of Rubruck: his Journey to the Court of the Great Khan Mongke, 1253–1255*, translated and co-edited with David Morgan (1990).

BEATRICE FORBES MANZ is Professor of History at Tufts University, Massachusetts. Her previous publications include *Power, Politics and Religion in Timurid Iran* (2007), *The Rise and Rule of Tamerlane* (1989) and as editor, *Central Asia in Historical Perspective* (1994) and *Studies on Chinese and Islamic Central Asia* (1995).

ARSENIO PETER MARTINEZ is Emeritus Associate Professor of Middle Eastern–Islamic Studies at the State University of New York and of Social Sciences at the City University of New York. He has published extensively on Persian sources on Inner Asian history. In addition to numerous translations, his publications include *'The Wealth of Ormus and of Ind': the Interregional Trade in Bullion, Intergovernmental Arbitrage, and Currency Manipulation in the Il-Khanate, 1304–1350* (1995–7), and *Changes in Chancery Language and Language Changes in General in the Middle East with Particular Reference to Iran in the Arab and Mongol Periods* (1987–91).

R. D. MCCHESNEY is Professor Emeritus of Middle Eastern Studies and History at New York University and director of the Afghanistan Digital Library. His recent publications include *Central Asia: Foundations of Change* (1997) and *Waqf in Central Asia* (1991). He is the editor and translator of Fayz Muhammad, *Kabul under Siege: an Inside Account of the 1929 Uprising* (1999).

JAMES MILLWARD is Professor of Intersocietal History in the Department of History and School of Foreign Service at Georgetown University. His research has focused on Chinese–Inner Asian relations and, in particular, the Xinjiang region. He is author of *Beyond the Pass: Economy, Ethnicity and Empire in Qing Central Asia, 1759–1864* (1998) and *Eurasian Crossroads: a History of Xinjiang* (2007).

Christian Noack is Lecturer for East European History (including Russia) at the National University of Ireland, Maynooth. Among his publications are *Muslimischer Nationalismus im Russischen Reich. Nationsbildung und Nationalbewegung bei Tataren und Baschkiren, 1860–1917* (2000).

István Vásáry is Professor of Turkic and Central Asian Studies at the Loránd Eötvös University (Budapest) and former Ambassador of the Republic of Hungary to Turkey (1991–6) and Iran (1999–2003). His recent books include *Cumans and Tatars: Oriental Military in the Pre-Ottoman Balkans, 1185–1361* (2005); *Turks, Tatars and Russians in the 13th–16th Centuries* (2007); *Eski İç Asya Tarihi* (Turkish translation of his *Pre-Mongol Inner Asia*) (1993, in Hungarian) and *The Golden Horde* (1986) and *Chancellery of the Golden Horde* (1987) (both in Hungarian).

Veronika Veit is Professor of Mongolian Studies at the Rheinische Friedrich Wilhelms-Universität Bonn. Her works include *Petitions of Grievances, 18th to Early 20th Century*, in collaboration with S. Rasidondug (1975), *The Four Qans of Qalqa, according to the Iledkel sastir of 1795* (1990, in German) and *The Role of Women in the Altaic World* (2007), as editor.

Note on transliteration

Arabic and Persian terms, including names and titles, have been transliterated according to the system used in the *International Journal of Middle Eastern Studies*. Russian has been transliterated according to the Library of Congress system. For Chinese, the *pinyin* transliteration system has been adopted. Turkic names and terms have been transliterated according to the system used in the *Encyclopaedia of Islam* with the usual exceptions (e.g. č is rendered as ch). Terms of Mongolian origin have been transliterated normally in accordance with Nicholas Poppe's *Grammar of Written Mongolian* except for č, γ, ǰ, š which are rendered respectively as ch, gh, j, sh. The letter q has been rendered as kh in terms and names around and after 1600 for consistency with more common forms of transliteration. Many Mongol names also appear in Turkicized form, in particular when a people or political unit has adopted a name of Mongol origin (e.g. Turk. *Chaghatay* for Mong. *Chaghadai* and hence *Chaghatayid* for *Chaghadaid*, Turk. *Noghay*, the name of a Turko-Mongolian people, from Mong. *Noghai*). Both forms will be indicated in the Index. Certain forms (e.g. Qara Khitai rather than Qara Qitai) which do not conform to this schema have become generally used in the scholarly literature and are employed here. For Manchu the system of Jerry Norman's *Manchu–English Lexicon* has been followed. Common renderings of place names, personal names and titles have been left in their usual English form.

Abbreviations

AEMAe	*Archivum Eurasiae Medii Aevi*. Wiesbaden.
AOH	*Acta Orientalia Academiae Scientiarum Hungaricae*. Budapest.
Bar Hebraeus/Budge	Bar Hebraeus, *The Chronography of Gregory Abu'l-Faraj 1225–1286, the Son of Aaron, the Hebrew Physician Commonly Known as Bar Hebraeus*, trans. E. A. W. Budge. London, 1932.
Bartol'd, *Sochineniia*	Vasilii V. Bartol'd, *Sochineniia*. Moscow: Izdatel'stvo Vostochnoi Literatury, 1963–77. 9 vols.
al-Bīrūnī, *Āthār*	al-Bīrūnī, *Al-Āthār al-Bāqiyya ʿan Qurūn al-Khāliyya: Chronologie Orientalischer Völker*, ed. C. E. Sachau. Leipzig: Brockhaus, 1878, reprint Leipzig: Brockhaus and Otto Harrassowitz, 1923, reprint Publications of the Institute for the History of Arabic-Islamic Science. Islamic Mathematics and Astronomy 30, Frankfurt am Main, 1998.
BSOAS	*Bulletin of the School of Oriental and African Studies*. London.
CAJ	*Central Asiatic Journal*. Wiesbaden.
CHChina, VI	Dennis Twitchett and Herbert Franke, eds., *The Cambridge History of China*, vol. VI, *Alien Regimes and Border States, 907–1368*. Cambridge: Cambridge University Press, 1994.
CHEIA	Denis Sinor, ed., *The Cambridge History of Early Inner Asia*. Cambridge: Cambridge University Press, 1990.
CHIran, V	John A. Boyle *et al.*, eds., *The Cambridge History of Iran*, vol. V, *The Saljuq and Mongol Periods*. Cambridge: Cambridge University Press, 1968.
CHIran, VI	Peter Jackson and Laurence Lockhart, eds., *The Cambridge History of Iran*, vol. VI, *The Timurid and Safavid Periods*. Cambridge: Cambridge University Press, 1986.

CMCT	*Chiu Man Chiu Tang. The Old Manchu Archives*, vols. I–II, ed. N. Kanda, J. Matsumura and H. Okada. Tokyo: The Toyo Bunko, 1972–5.
Dūghlāt/Ross	Dūghlāt, Haidar, *A History of the Moghuls of Central Asia being the Tarikh-i Rashidi of Mirza Muhammad Haidar, Dughlāt*, ed. N. Elias, trans. E. Denison Ross, 2nd edn. London, 1898; reprint London Curzon Press, and New York: Barnes and Noble, 1972.
Dūghlāt/Thackston	Dūghlāt, Muḥammad Ḥaydar, *Mirza Haydar Dughlat's Tarikh-i-Rashidi: A History of the Khans of Moghulistan*, trans. W. M. Thackston. Cambridge, Mass.: Harvard University, Press, 1996; Sources of Oriental Languages and Literatures 38; Central Asian Sources, III.
EI[1]	*Encyclopaedia of Islam*, 1st edn. Leiden: Brill, 1913–36.
EI[2]	*Encyclopaedia of Islam*, 2nd edn. Leiden: Brill, 1960–2002.
HJAS	*Harvard Journal of Asiatic Studies*. Cambridge, Mass.
HUS	*Harvard Ukrainian Studies*. Cambridge, Mass.
Ibn al-Athīr/Tornberg	Ibn al-Athīr, *Al-Kāmil fīal-Ta'rīkh*, ed. C. J. Tornberg. Beirut, 1965–6, pagination differs from the Leiden, 1851–76 edn. 12 vols.
Ibn Baṭṭūṭa/Defrémery	*Voyages d'Ibn Baṭṭūṭa*, ed. and trans. Charles Defrémery and B. R. Sanguinetti. Paris: L'Imprimirie Nationale, 1969. 4 vols.
Ibn Baṭṭūṭa/Gibb	Ibn Baṭṭūṭa, *The Travels of Ibn Baṭṭūṭa*, trans. Hamilton A. R. Gibb. Cambridge, Mass.: The Hakluyt Society, 1958–94. 4 vols.
Ibn Khaldūn	Ibn Khaldūn, ʿAbd al-Raḥmān, *Kitāb al-ʿibar*. Beirut: Dār al-Kitāb al-Lubnānī, 1957. 7 vols. Reprint Beirut: Dār al-Kitāb al-Lubnānī, 1983–6. 14 vols.
Ibn Khaldūn/*Muqaddima*	Ibn Khaldūn, *The Muqaddima (Muqaddimatu 'l-ʿalamati 'bni Khaldun)*. Beirut, 1886.
Ibn al-Nafīs	Ibn al-Nafīs, *The Theologus Autodidactus of Ibn al-Nafīs*, trans. Max Meyerhof and Joseph Schacht. Oxford: Clarendon Press, 1968.
IVRUz	Institut vostokovedeniia Akademii nauk Respubliki Uzbekistana (Institute of Oriental Studies of the Academy of Sciences of the Republic of Uzbekistan).
JAOS	*Journal of the American Oriental Society.*
JRAS	*Journal of the Royal Asiatic Society.*
al-Juvainī/Boyle	al-Juvaini, ʿAṭā-malik, *The History of the World-Conqueror*, trans. E. J. Boyle. Cambridge, Mass.: Harvard University Press, 1958. Reprint Seattle: University of Washington Press, 1997. 2 vols.
al-Juvainī/Qazvīnī	al-Juvainī, *Ta'rīkh-i Jahān-Gushā*, ed. M. Qazvīnī. Leiden and London, 1912, 1916, 1937. 3 vols.

Jūzjānī / Ḥabībī	Minhāj al-Dīn al-Jūzjānī, *Ṭabaqāt-i Nāṣirī*, ed. ʿA. Ḥabībī. Tehran, 1363 / 1984.
JWH	*Journal of World History.*
Kāšγarī / Dankoff	Maḥmūd al-Kāšγarī, *Compendium of the Turkic Dialects (Dīwān Luγāt al-Turk)*, ed. and trans. R. Dankoff in collaboration with J. Kelly. Cambridge, Mass., 1982–5. 3 vols.
Khvāndamīr / Thackston	Khvāndamīr, *Ḥabību' siyar* [*sic*], ed. and trans. Wheeler M. Thackston. Cambridge, Mass.: Department of Near Eastern Languages and Civilizations, Harvard University, 1994. 3 vols.
Mengda beilu / Wang	Zhao Hong, *Mengda beilu*, in Wang Guowei, ed., *Menggu shiliao sizhong*. Taibei: Zhengzhong shuju, 1975.
Mengda beilu / Olbricht, Pinks	*Meng-ta Pei-lu und Hei-Ta Shih-Lüeh*, intro. by Erich Haenisch and Yao Tsʿung-wu, trans. and commentary by Peter Olbricht and Elisabeth Pinks. Asiatische Forschungen 56. Wiesbaden: Otto Harrassowitz, 1980.
Munzavī, *Ganj-bakhsh*	Munzavī, Aḥmad, ed., *Fihrist-i nuskhahā-yi khaṭṭī-i Kitābkhānah-i Ganj-bakhsh*, vol. IV. Islamabad: Markaz-i Taḥqīqāt-i Fārsī-yi Īrān va Pākistān, 1982.
MWLD	*Manwen laodang [Manbun Rōtō] Tongki fuka hergei-i dangse. The Secret Chronicles of the Manchu Dynasty 1607–1637 A.D.* Trans. and annotated by Kanda Nobuo *et al.* Tokyo: The Toyo Bunko, 1955–63. 7 vols.
Nakhchivānī, *Dastūr*	Nakhchivānī, Muḥammad b. Hindūshāh, *Dastūr al-kātib fī taʿyīn al-marātib (Rukovodstvo dlia pistsa pri opredelenii stepenei)*, ed. A. A. Ali-zade. Moscow: Nauka, GRVL, 1976; Pamiatniki literatury narodov Vostoka, Teksty, Bol'shaia seriia 9. 2 vols. in 3.
Al-Nasawī / Buniiatov	Shihāb al-Dīn Muḥammad al-Nasawī, *Sīrat al-Sulṭān Jalāl al-Dīn Mankburnī (Zhizneopisanie sultana Dzhalal ad-Dina Mankburny)*, ed. and Russian trans. Z. M. Buniiatov. Moscow: Vostochnaia Literatura, 1996.
ONS	*Oriental Numismatic Society.* London.
PSRL	*Polnoe sobranie russkikh letopisei*. St Petersburg / Petrograd / Leningrad, 1846– . 43 vols. to date.
Qarshī	Qarshī, Jamāl, *Mulkhaqāt al-ṣurāḥ*, in V. V. Bartol'd, *Turkestan v epokhu mongol'skogo nashestviia, vol. I (texts).* St Petersburg: Tipografiia imperatorskoi akademii nauk, 1900, pp. 128–52.
Qāshānī	Qāshānī, Abū al-Qāsim ʿAbdallāh b. ʿAlī, *Taʾrīkh-i Uljaytū*, ed. Mahin Hambly. Tehran: Bangah-i tarjumah wa-nashr-i kitāb, 1969.
QGZ / Taskin	Ye Lungli, *Qidan guozhi: Istoriia gosudarstva kidanei (tsidan' gochzhi)*, trans. V. S. Taskin. Moscow, 1979.

QTZWHSL	*Qing Taizu Wuhuangdi Shilu*. In *Qing shi lu*, vol. II. Beijing: Zhonghua shuju, 1985.
Qutadghu Bilig	Yūsuf Khaṣṣ Ḥājib, *Kutadgu Bilig*, ed. R. R. Arat. Ankara, 1979.
Qutadghu Bilig/Eng.	R. Dankoff, trans., *Wisdom of Royal Glory*. Chicago, 1983.
Rashīd al-Dīn/ʿAli-zāde *et al.*	Rashīd al-Dīn, *Jāmiʿ al-Tavārīkh*, ed. ʿA. ʿA. ʿAli-zāde, A. A. Romaskevich and L. A Khetagurov. Baku: Nashariyyāt -i farhangistān-i ʿulūm-i jumhūri-i sosiyālīstī-i Adharbayjān, 1957; Moscow: Nauka, 1965/68, 1980. 3 vols.
Rashīd al-Dīn/Blochet	Rashīd al-Dīn, Faḍlallāh, *Jāmiʿ al-tavārīkh*, vol. II, ed. Edgar Blochet, E. J. W. Gibb Memorial Series 18. London and Leiden: Luzac and Brill, 1911.
Rashīd al-Dīn/Boyle	Rashīd al-Dīn, Faḍlallāh Abū al-Khayr, *The Successors of Genghis Khan*, ed. and trans. John A. Boyle. New York and London: Columbia University Press, 1971.
Rashīd al-Dīn/Jahn	Rashīd al-Dīn, *Tāʾrīkh-i Mubārak-i Ghāzānī*, ed. Karl Jahn. Gibb Memorial Series 14. London: Lusac & Co., 1940.
Rashīd al-Dīn/Karīmī	Rashīd al-Dīn, *Jāmiʿ al-Tavāarīkh*, ed. Barman Karīmī. Tehran: Iqbāl, 1338/1959. 2 vols.
Rashīd al-Dīn/Rawshan and Mūsavī	Rashīd al-Dīn, Faḍlallāh, *Jāmiʿ al-Tavārīkh*, ed. M. Rawshan and M. Mūsavī. Tehran, 1373/1994. 4 vols.
Rashīd al-Dīn/Thackston	*Rashiduddin Fazlullah's Jamiʿuʾt-tawarikh. Compendium of Chronicles*, trans. Wheeler M. Thackston. Sources of Oriental Languages and Literatures: Central Asian Sources 4. Cambridge, Mass.: Harvard University Press, 1998–9. 3 vols.
Secret History/de Rachewiltz	Igor de Rachewiltz, *The Secret History of the Mongols: a Mongolian Epic Chronicle of the Thirteenth Century*. Brill's Inner Asian Library 7. Leiden: Brill, 2004. 2 vols.
Shāmī/Tauer	Shāmī, Niẓām al-Dīn (1937, 1956) *Histoire des conquêtes de Tamerlan intitulée Ẓafarnāma, par Niẓāmuddīn Shāmī*, ed. Felix Tauer. Prague: Oriental Institute, 1937, 1956. 2 vols. (Vol. II contains additions made by Ḥāfiẓ-i Abrū.)
Simnānī, *Opera minora*	ʿAlāʾuddawla Simnānī, *Opera minora*, ed. W. M. Thackston, Jr. Cambridge, Mass.: Harvard University, Office of the University Publisher, 1988; Sources of Oriental Languages and Literatures, 10, ed. Şinasi Tekin and Gönül Alpay Tekin, Islamic Sources 2.
Simnānī, *al-ʿUrwa*	Simnānī, ʿAlāʾ al-Dawla, *al-ʿUrva li-ahl al-khalva va'l-jalva*, ed. Najīb Māyil Haravī. Tehran: Intishārāt-i Mawlā, 1362/1983.
SR	*Slavic Review*.

SVR	*Sobranie vostochnykh rukopisei Akademii nauk Uzbekskoi SSR*; vol. III, ed. A. A. Semenov. Tashkent: Fan, 1955; vol. IX, ed. A. Urunbaev and L. M. Epifanova. Tashkent: Fan, 1971.
Tavakkulī, *Ṣafvat al-ṣafā*	Ibn Bazzāz Ardabīlī, 'Tavakkulī'. *Ṣafvat al-ṣafā*, ed. Ghulām-riẓā Ṭabāṭabā'ī-Majd. Tabriz, 1373/1994.
al-ʿUmarī/India	al-ʿUmarī, Aḥmad b. Yaḥya ibn Faḍlallāh, *A Fourteenth Century Arab Account of India under Sultan Muhammad Bin Tughluq. Being English Translation of the Chapters on India from Shihāb al-Dīn al-ʿUmarī's Masālik al-abṣār fi-mamālik al-amṣār*, ed. Iqtidar H. Siddiqi and Qazi M. Ahmad. Aligarh: Siddiqi Pub. House, 1972.
al-ʿUmarī/Lech	al-ʿUmarī, *Das mongolische Weltreich: al-ʿUmarī's Darstellung der mongolischen Reiche in seinem Werk Masālik al-abṣār fī mamālik al-amṣār*, ed. and trans. Klaus Lech. Wiesbaden: Otto Harrassowitz, 1968. Asiatische Forschungen 22.
Vaṣṣāf	Vaṣṣāf, ʿAbd Allāh b. Faḍl Allāh, *Taʾrīkh-i Vaṣṣāf (Tajziyat al-amṣār va-tazjiyat al-aʿṣār)* (reprint Tehran: Shamsī 1338 S/1959–60 of facs. edn. Bombay, 1269 H/1852–3. Reprint Tehran: Ibn-i Sina, 1338/1959).
Yazdī/ʿAbbāsī	Yazdī, Sharaf al-Dīn ʿAlī, *Ẓafarnāma*, ed. Muḥammad ʿAbbāsī. Tehran: Amīr Kabīr, sh. 1336/1957. 2 vols.
YS	Song Lian, *Yuan shi* [The Official History of the Yuan]. Beijing: Zhonghua shuju, 1976. 15 vols.
Yule, *Cathay*	H. Yule, *Cathay and the Way Thither.* Works Issued by the Hakluyt Society, Series II, vol. XXXVII. Reprint Nendeln/Liechtenstein: Kraus Reprint Limited, 1967.

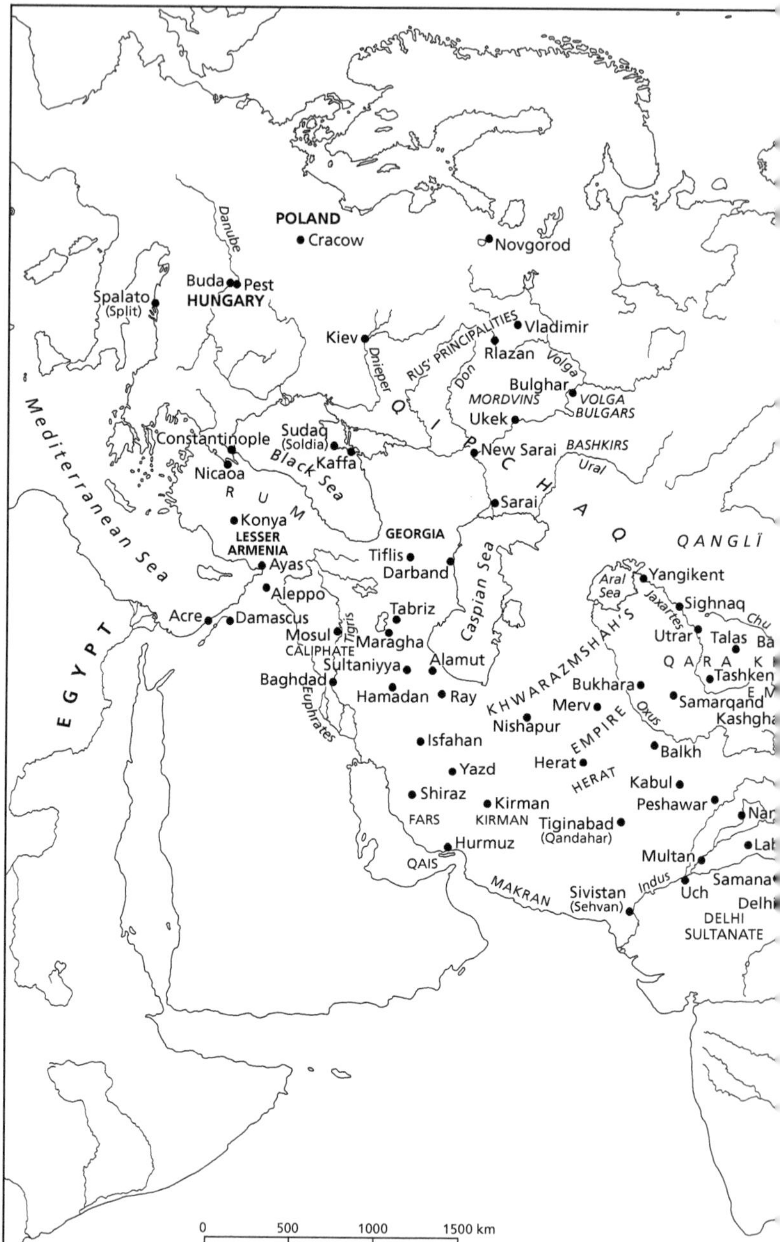

Map 1 Inner Asia *c.* 1250

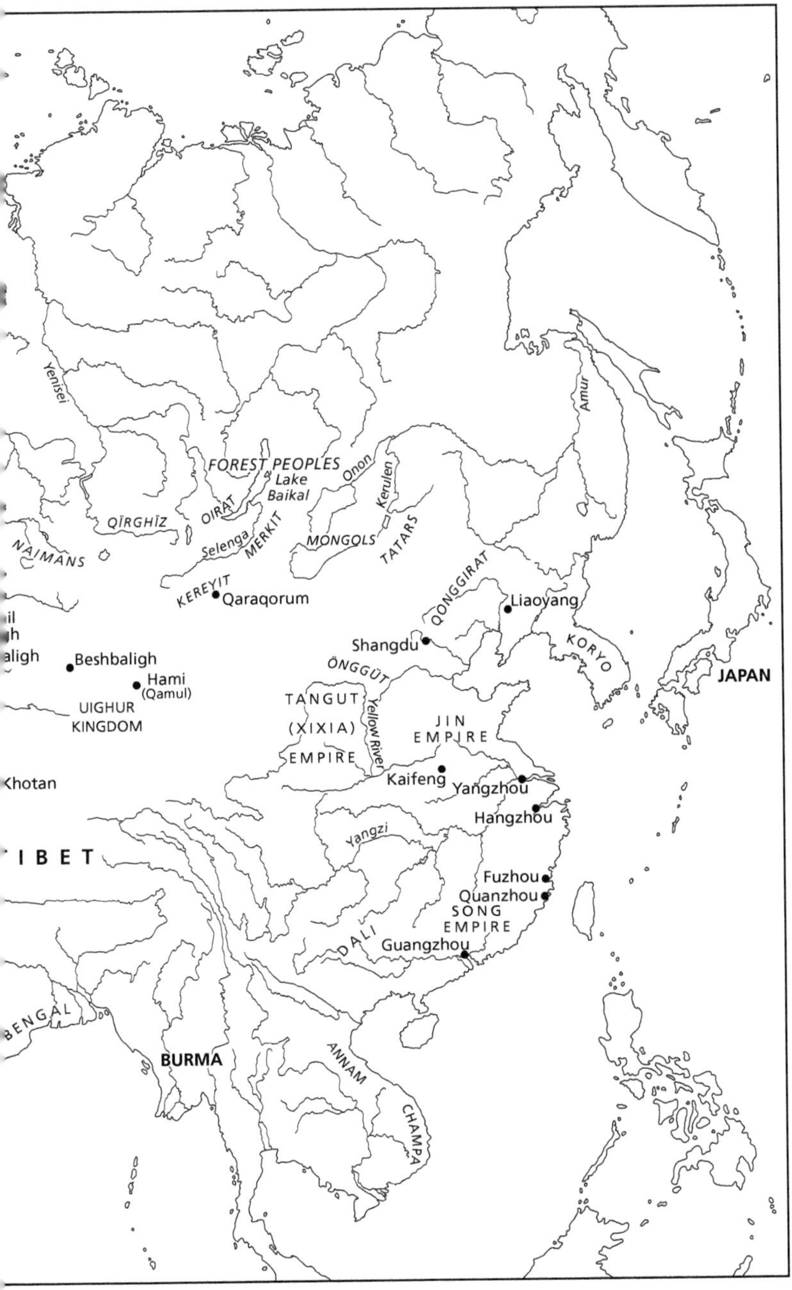

FOREST PEOPLES
Lake Baikal
Onon
Kerulen
Yenisei
Amur
QÏRGHÏZ
OIRAT
Selenga
MERKIT
MONGOLS
TATARS
NAIMANS
KEREYIT
Qaraqorum
QONGGIRAT
Liaoyang
Shangdu
KORYO
ÖNGGÜT
JAPAN
Beshbaligh
Hami (Qamul)
UIGHUR KINGDOM
TANGUT (XIXIA) EMPIRE
Yellow River
JIN EMPIRE
Kaifeng
Yangzhou
Hangzhou
Khotan
Yangzi
IBET
Fuzhou
Quanzhou
SONG EMPIRE
DALI
Guangzhou
BENGAL
BURMA
ANNAM
CHAMPA

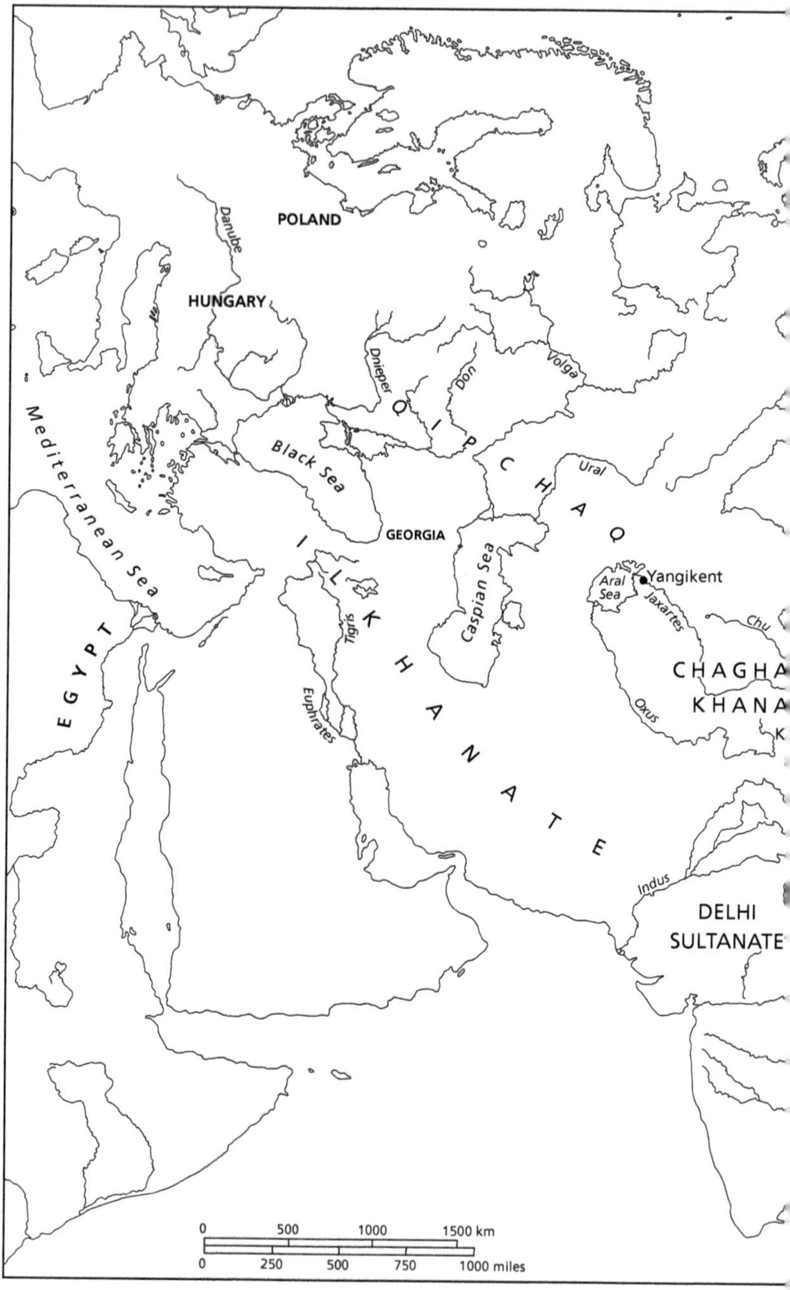

Map 2 The Mongol Empire

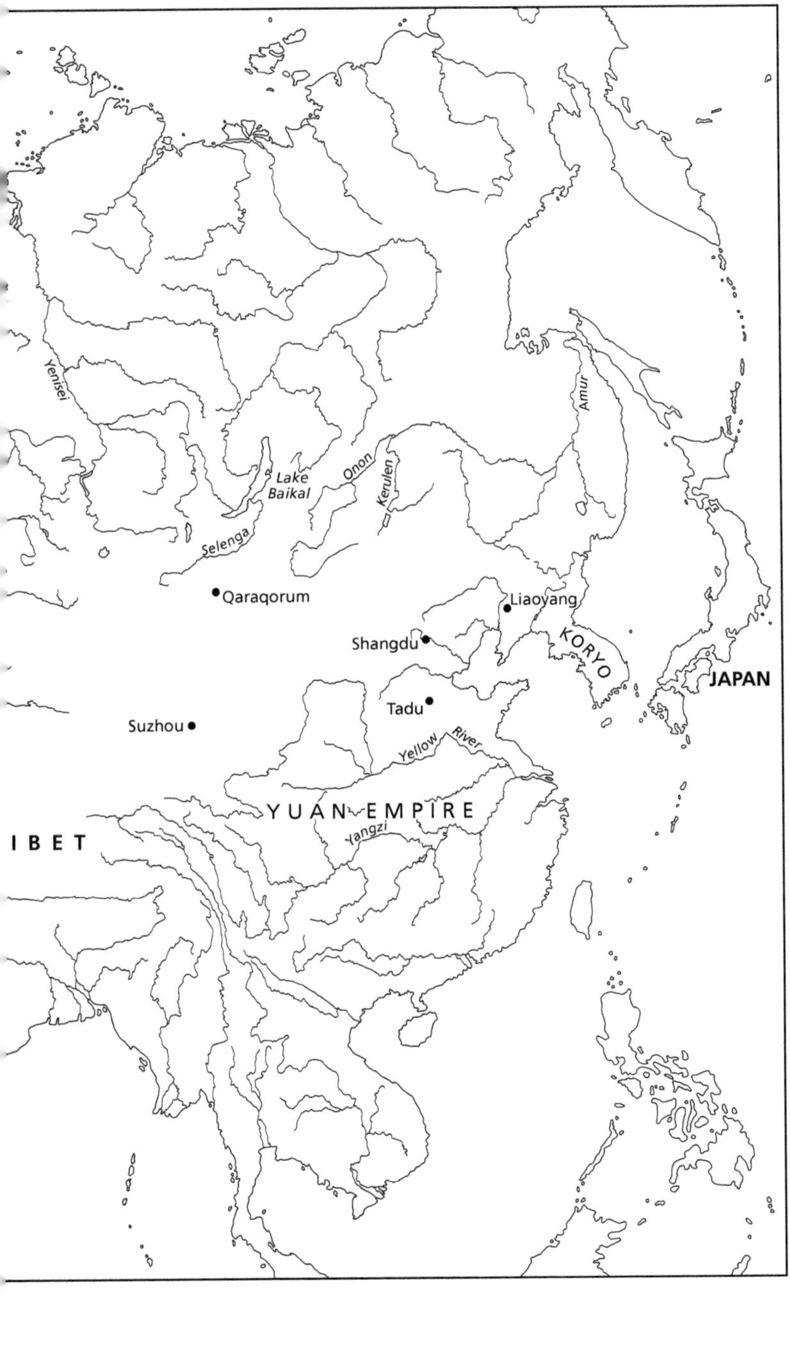
Yenisei
Lake
Baikal
Selenga
Onon
Kerulen
Amur
Qaraqorum
Liaoyang
Shangdu
KORYO
JAPAN
Tadu
Suzhou
Yellow River
YUAN EMPIRE
Yangzi
IBET

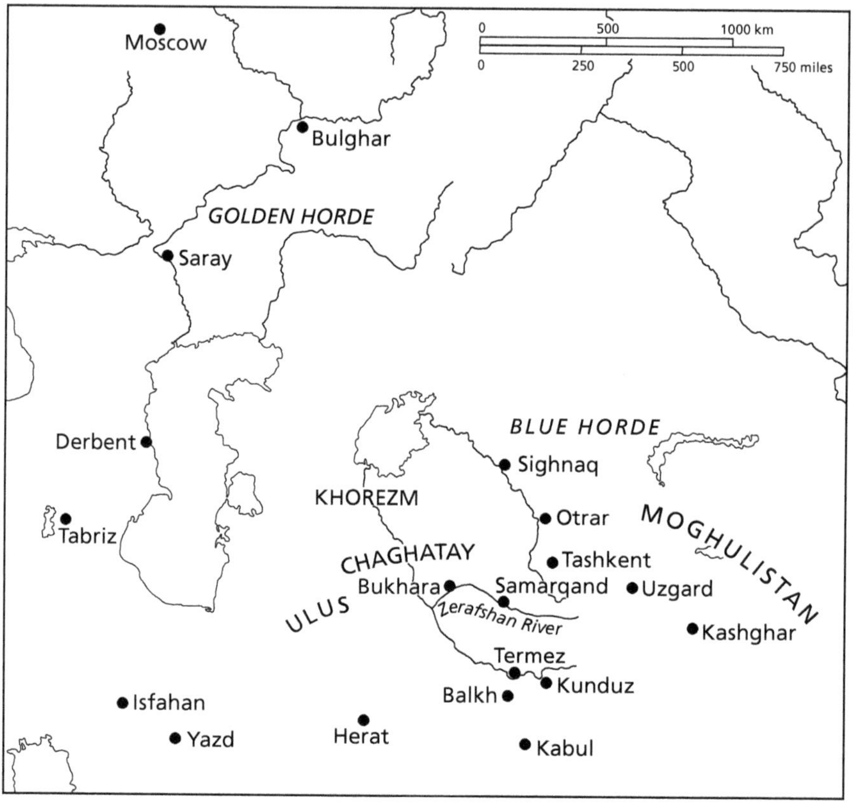

Map 3 Central Asia in the time of Timur

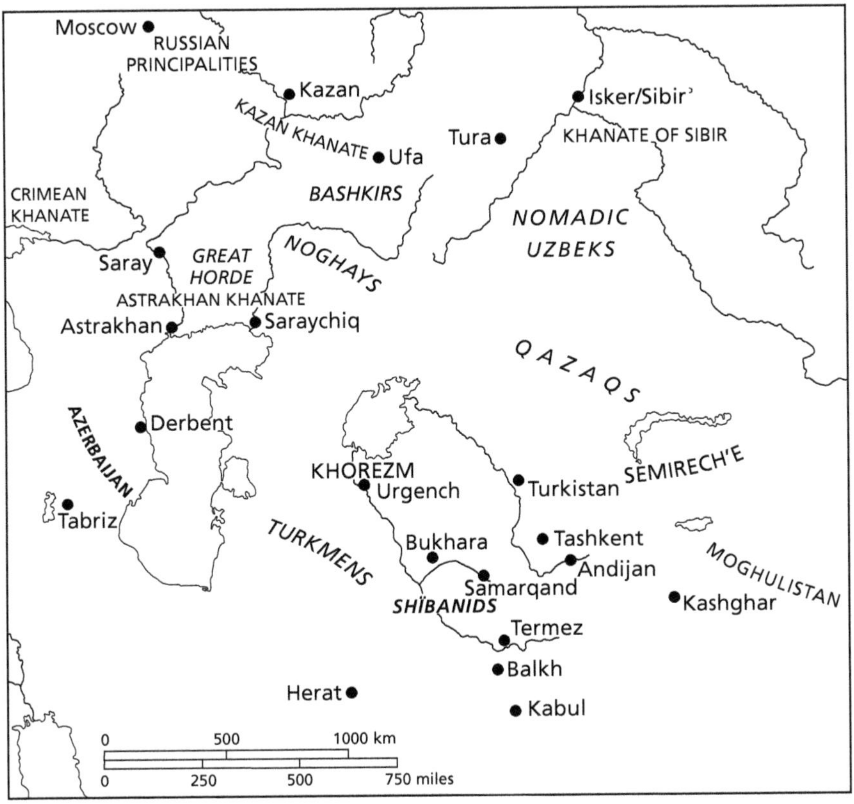

Map 4 Central Asia in the fifteenth and sixteenth centuries

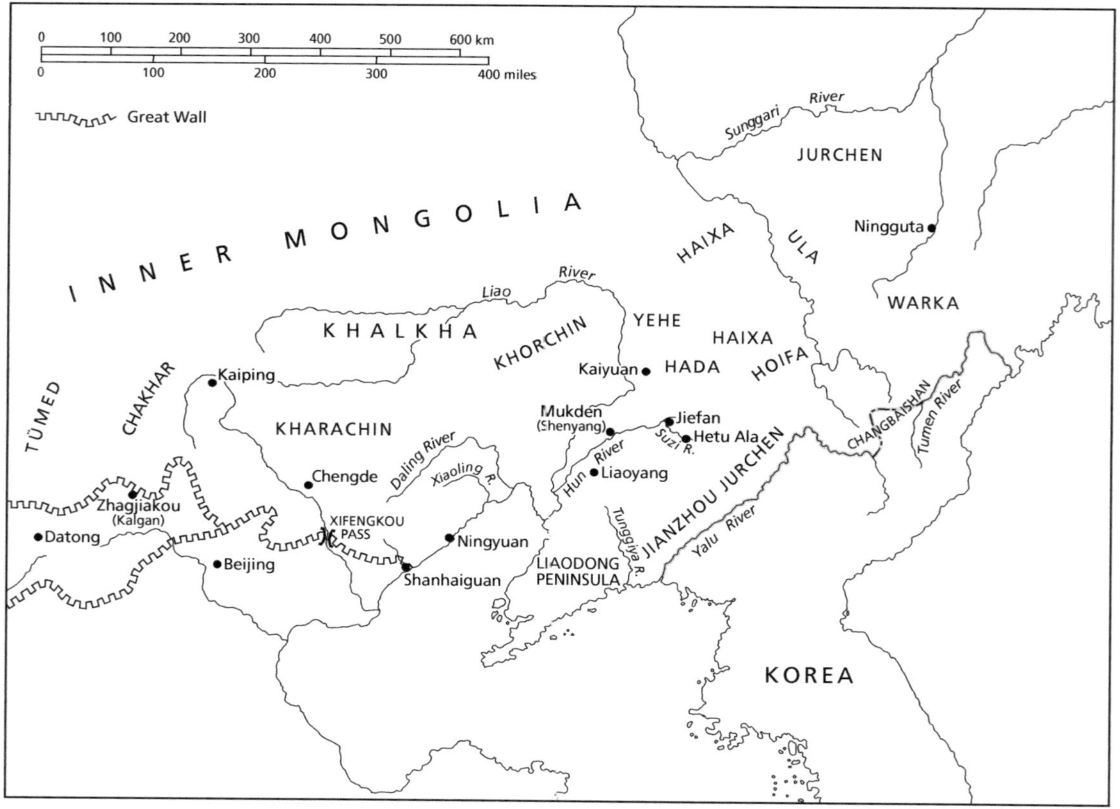

Map 5 Manchuria and Eastern Mongolia in *c.* 1600

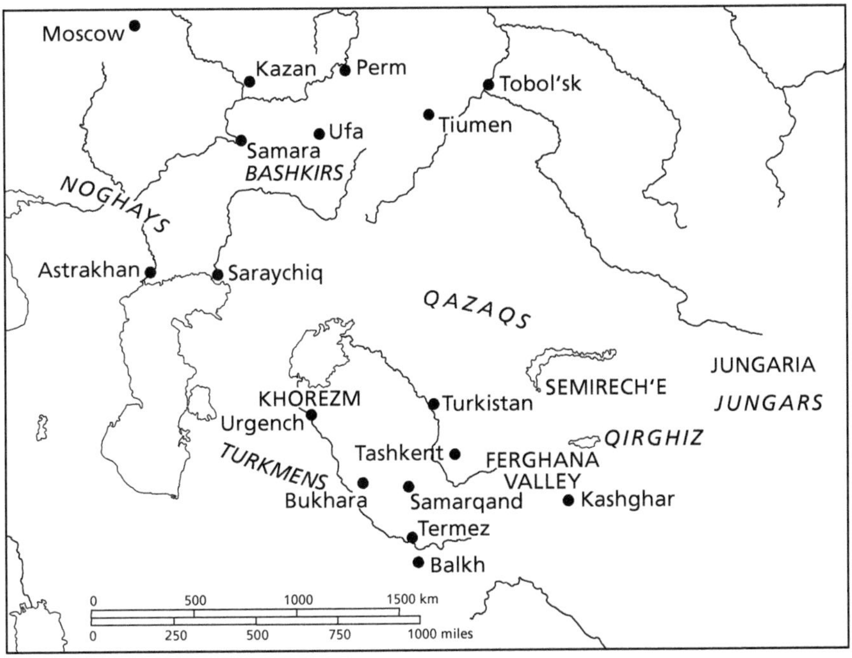

Map 6 Central Asia in the seventeenth century

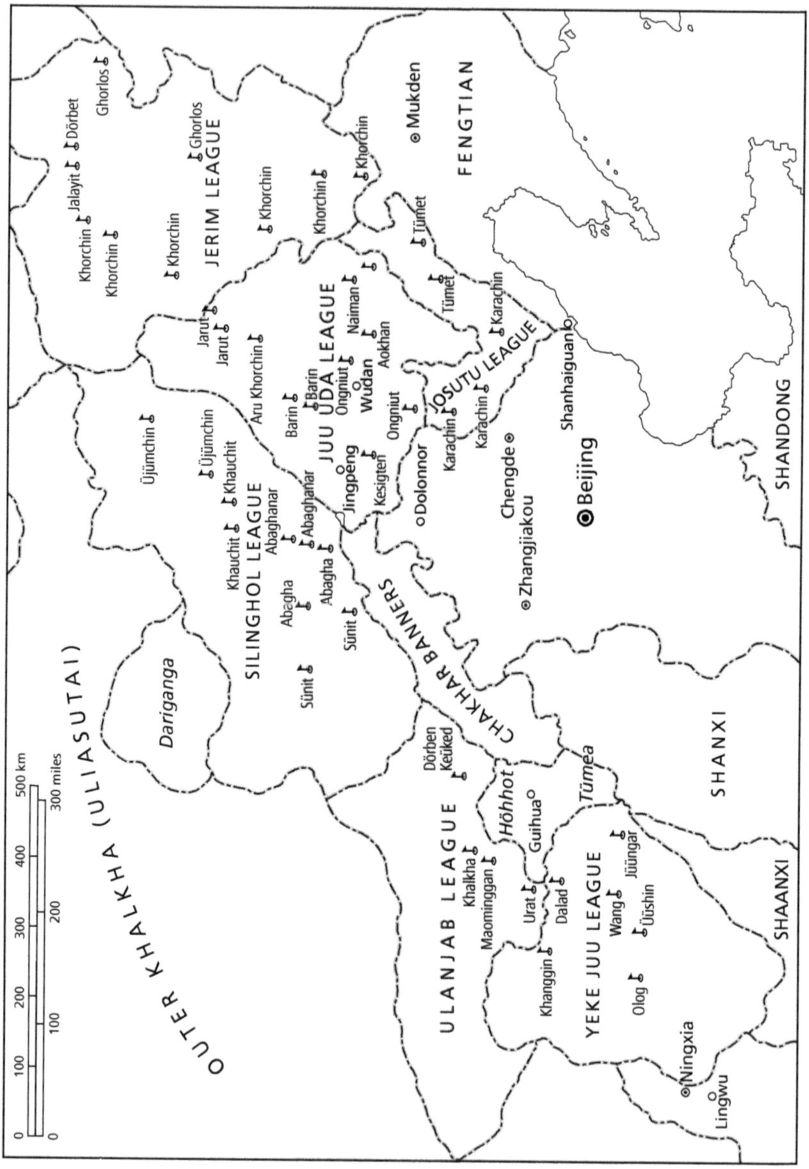

Map 7 Inner Mongolia under the Qing Dynasty

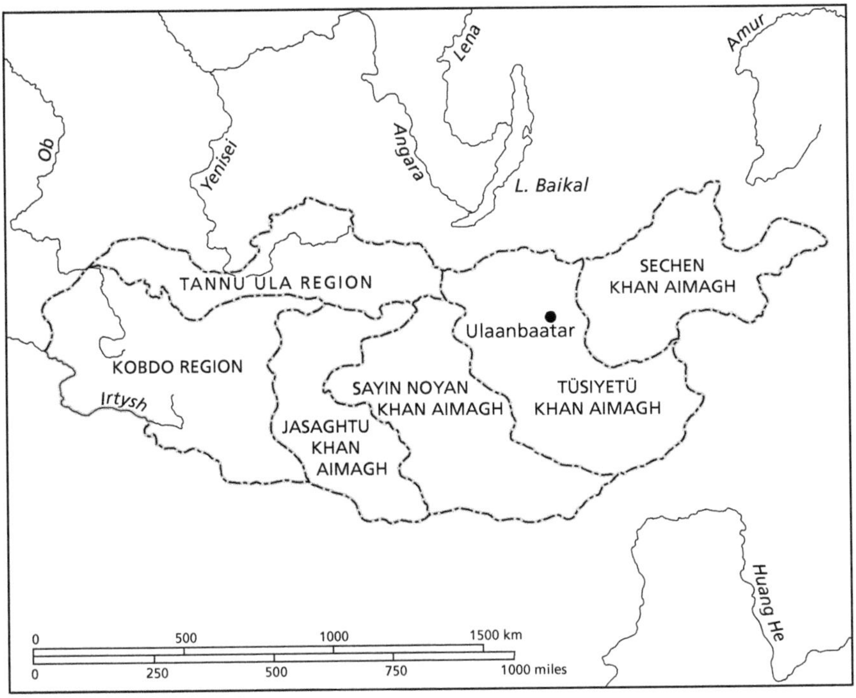

Map 8 Outer Mongolia under the Qing Dynasty

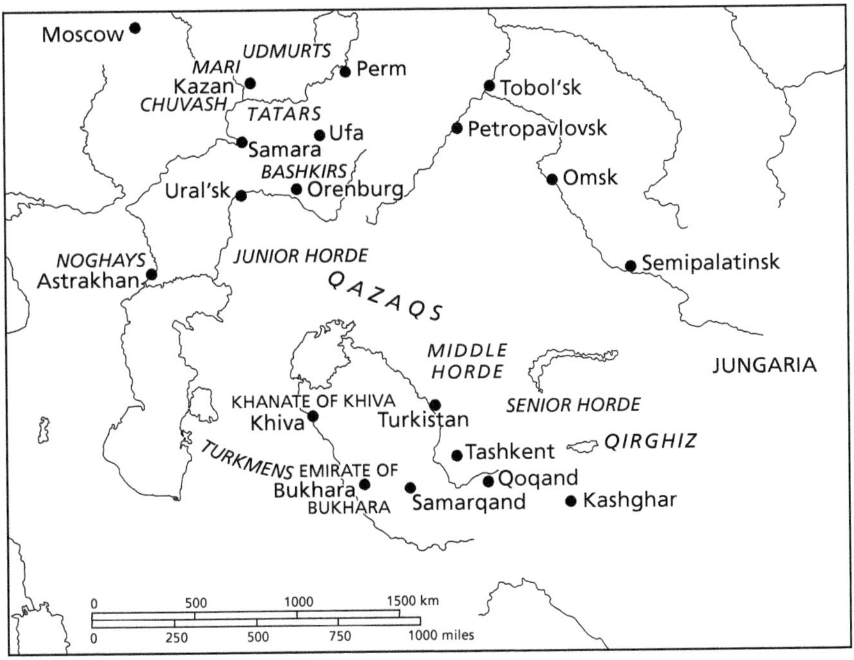

Map 9 Central Asia in the eighteenth century

Introduction

NICOLA DI COSMO, ALLEN J. FRANK
AND PETER B. GOLDEN

The vast expanse of land that forms the physical setting for the Chinggisid era in Inner Asian history extends from the forests of Manchuria in the east to the steppelands west of the Volga River stretching to the Black Sea. The forest and taiga zones of Siberia constitute the northern boundaries while the agrarian-sedentary world of China, the Islamic world and Christian Eastern Europe frame the region from the south and west. With the exception of the oasis city-states, many of them fabled connecting links in the Silk Road, much of this region consists of grassy prairies, the steppe, bounded by forest-steppe zones in the north and interspersed with deserts and semi-deserts in the south.

The history of this region from antiquity to modern times has primarily centred on the interaction of the nomadic world of the steppes with the much smaller Uralic or Palaeo-Siberian forest populations to the north, the settled, largely Iranian-speaking populations of the oasis city-states to the south and the larger states, often empires, south and later north of the steppe zone. The rise of the Chinggisid Mongol Empire was, in many respects, a culminating point in a long line of nomad-based polities with roots and political traditions going back to the Xiongnu (third century BCE–mid-second century CE). It was the most complex of these polities. The Steppe Imperial Tradition, like Roman political traditions in Europe, provided an ideology, in a number of variants, accepted across the Inner Asian nomadic world and a template for governance. In the aftermath of the Türk and then Uighur Empires, there was a sense of *translatio imperii*, perhaps increasingly muted as time passed. Some sense of the continuity of steppe imperial tradition was probably known to the Mongols of Chinggis Khan's day if only from their Uighur advisers and bookmen – although Mongolic peoples had been part of the Türk Empire. Above all, this tradition consisted of a ruling clan brought to power by conquest. In the Chinggisid era this clan was called the *altan urugh* ('Golden Clan'), led by a supreme, heavenly mandated ruler, the *Qaghan* (later *Qa'an*, *Khan* 'emperor'), a title of unknown origin used by Turkic and Mongolic peoples. The Qaghan's person was sacred and his rule was legitimated by military (and diplomatic) success, giving tangible evidence of his possession of charisma, heaven-sent good fortune. After Chinggis, it was expected that ruling houses in Inner Asia would derive from his descendants. The Qaghan's power was also manifested in his establishment of the *törü* (also *töre*), the body of legal practices according to which the ruler was to govern. The Mongol *jasagh* (Turkicized as *yasa*) has been compared with *törü* although the correspondence remains debated.

The Mongol state was primarily based, in the initial stage of its formation, on a military hierarchy that included increasingly larger units from tens to hundreds, thousands and tens of thousands headed by a progressively smaller aristocratic elite, culminating in the family of the Qaghan and his most valued military leaders, known as *nöküd* (sing. *nökür*) 'boon companions', men who had left their clan and tribal affiliations and pledged loyalty to their overlord. Various institutions upon which the military aristocratic state was modelled, such as the *comitatus*, the bodyguard, and the decimal organization of the army, can be traced back to Inner Asian precedents, and are derived from a political culture that encompasses Inner Asian imperial history, in particular that of the Xiongnu, Türk, Uighur, Khazar and Khitan empires. As in other Inner Asian political formations, the Mongol state was multi-ethnic and inclusive of a wide range of Turkic- and Mongolic-speaking nomads as well as other peoples.

Its emergence had a profound impact on the social organization of the Mongol and Turkic population of Mongolia, as it was preceded by an extended period of internal wars that transformed traditional group identities and continued to manipulate them well into the imperial period. Generally speaking, the militarization of the population of Mongolia led to the formation of a more cohesive and powerful aristocracy coalescing eventually around the person of the Qaghan and reorganized into vertical hierarchies that drew power and authority from their control of military units and appanages of land.

Also along traditional Inner Asian lines, this military aristocracy established a personal bond of allegiance to the Qaghan and aimed at its own reproduction as a military caste. It is in the superimposition of a thick military-aristocratic layer upon traditional nomadic society that one can locate the major impetus for the series of wars and the expansionist drive that is characteristic of the first phase of the Mongol conquests. The imperial system required, in order to survive, the concentration of extensive sources of wealth in the hands of the top echelons of the state. This need, combined with the economic imbalance between resources that could be generated by a reduced productive base and the large military establishment it was supposed to support, produced enormous pressure for the acquisition of external resources. The early campaigns of Chinggis Khan aimed at establishing control over international trade and at exacting tribute from neighbouring states, primarily the Tangut state of the Western Xia, and the Jurchen Jin dynasty ruling in North China.

The Mongol conquests of the early and mid-thirteenth century shattered the Turko-nomadic world, breaking down and then reconfiguring its earlier tribal structures. It brought new waves of Turkic groupings into Central and Western Inner Asia as well as the Near East, advancing Turkicization in all those regions.

As the Mongols began to impose their rule upon the settled populations of China, Iran, Central Asia and Russia, different forms of accommodation allowed them to integrate within their system of government various forms of administration based on pre-existing models of civil bureaucracy and social organization. The syncretistic nature of the Mongol governments established over extensive sedentary populations produced varieties of Mongol rule that cannot be assimilated to a single model, except possibly for the common trait that people identifying themselves as Mongols retained an overwhelming presence in the military apparatus of each state, with attendant privileges and high social status. Also, their major and minor courts across the different Mongol states remained remarkably open to multiple cultural influences, and the circulation of ideas, technologies, material goods, religions and even foods and entertainment benefited from the eclectic taste and multicultural environment that Mongol leaders generally favoured. The Mongols, of course, made choices as to what they accepted and what they rejected, a matter that was made painfully clear to Christian missionaries who attempted to convert Mongols but were far less successful than Buddhist monks and Muslim mullahs. Religion eventually became a major source of inspiration for radical changes in the ruling ideology of the Mongols throughout each of their *uluses* (states).

The Mongol world empire created a *pax* across Eurasia that, after the initial devastations of the conquest, revived economies and stimulated trade. It produced the outlines of an 'interlocking set of institutions … or world networks'.[1] The Chinggisid policy of identifying talented individuals among their subject populations and moving them to areas in which they could best serve Chinggisid interests gave far greater opportunities for cultural exchange between East and West. Thus, a Mongol official, Bolad Agha, with a history

1 Adshead, 1993, p. 4.

of service in Yuan China, came to Iran and was a major source for Rashīd ad-Dīn's *Jāmi' at-Tavārīkh*, an extraordinary 'world history' as seen from the vantage point of this Ilkhanid official.[2] In addition to the exchange and transfer of knowledge, intellectual capital, what S. A. M. Adshead has termed 'the basic information circuit',[3] this also included religions, long a staple of Silk Road intercourse. The Mongols abroad in Western and Central Inner Asia as well as in Iran all became Islamicized as well as largely Turkicized. It is under the aegis of the Chinggisids that Islam, with a strong nativized Ṣūfī influence, becomes the dominant religion of the Eurasian pastoral nomadic world – outside of Mongolia.

There was also the transfer of technology, in particular technology that related to the implements of war. This included the initial spread of gunpowder weaponry, which played so critical a role in shaping the modern world. At the same time, the spread of disease across the Old World was facilitated by the relative ease with which people and goods moved across Eurasia and thence into the southern Mediterranean world as well. This 'microbian common market', to use Adshead's pithy phrase,[4] was fully manifested in the Black Death that struck Europe and the Mediterranean Islamic world in the mid-fourteenth century.

The Chinggisid era in world history was a major step towards Eurasian integration and expanded that world or a larger world-consciousness to realms in North Africa and Southern Arabia, beyond the range of Mongol control. Multi-language dictionaries and grammars were composed within and outside the Chinggisid realms, from Korea, China, India, Russia and the Crimea to Yemen and Egypt. In many respects the Mongol Empire was the culminating point in pre-Modern World systems.[5] When the system began to fragment in the Timurid era, Europe embarked on its 'voyages of discovery' attempting to create other links with East, South and South-eastern Asia, ushering in the Modern World system.[6]

The political significance of the Chinggisids in Inner Asia remained evident long after Chinggisid dynasts had lost their grip on the region's nomadic and sedentary states. Chinggisid legitimacy was an important political force for the region's non-Chinggisid dynasties. Some, like Temür (Tamerlane),

2 Allsen, 1994b.
3 Adshead, 1993, p. 4.
4 Adshead, 1993, p. 4.
5 Abu-Lughod, 1989.
6 European shortages in gold and silver as well as competition along the trade routes were also major motivating forces, see Frank, A.G., 1998, pp. 56–8.

maintained puppet Chinggisid khans. Temür, at most, styled himself their 'son-in-law'. Subsequently, others often retained Chinggisid rulers as vassals, as the Ottomans did with the Crimean khans, or as the Russians did with the Kasimov khanate, and its Chinggisid vassals among the Qazaqs. Indeed, the sixteenth century witnessed the appropriation of the Chinggisid dynastic hierarchy by Muscovite dynasts, who had been erstwhile vassals of the Golden Horde. Chinggisid legitimacy remained a force to conjure with. At the same time, the hegemony of Chinggisid legitimacy elicited challenges from non-Chinggisid rulers, particularly among nomadic political challengers to the khans of the Golden Horde. Beginning in the fifteenth century non-Chinggisids began to invoke Islamic political legitimacy to obtain political support among Muslim nomads. This process first became evident in the Noghay Horde, and was also evident in sixteenth-century Siberia and among the Qazaqs and in Central Asia in the eighteenth century. The political development of Chinggisid successor states also came to have a strong influence on the development of ethnic identity in Inner Asia, particularly among the steppe nomads, where Chinggisid-dominated nomadic confederations became 'tribal' confederations claiming common ancestry. This process was closely linked to Islamic legends of origin, especially among the Qazaqs and Siberian Tatars, but the role of Chinggisid politics in these developments cannot be dismissed.

In Mongolia itself, the conversion of Altan Khan to Buddhism in the mid-sixteenth century brought to a head a process of gradual affirmation of a principle of 'caesaropapism' between the temporal power of the khan and the spiritual power of Tibetan Buddhist hierarchies that can be traced back to the Mongols, at the very least, to the sodality between Qubilai Khan and the Tibetan hierarch 'Phags-pa. After the defeat of the Mongols in China in 1368 and the failure of the Northern Yuan dynasty to 'reimperialize' the Mongol armies and peoples, fissiparous tendencies set in that could not be overcome, causing repeated failures to unify the Mongols into a new imperial formation. Migratory movements caused by trade opportunities with China led to a substantial increment of the Mongol population along the Chinese northern border, which became a fulcrum of economic and political revival.

In the political culture of Mongolia, the principle of Chinggisid legitimation was gradually diminished by the close political relations established by various tribes (or ethno-political groups) with Tibetan sects, whose support was virtually indispensable for advancing political claims. Non-Chinggisid rulers were thus able to propose themselves as potential rulers and challengers of rightful Chinggisid heirs. The rise of the Manchus, the 'imperialization' of most of the Mongols under a Qing banner, and the utter destruction of the Zunghars effectively closed the door to any possibility of re-creating a unified Mongol empire.

With the expansion of the Russian and Qing empires and the increasing inability of the nomads to compete militarily with the 'gunpowder empires', the nomads were brought within the orbits of their imperial neighbours. Preferential Chinggisid access to positions of political authority continued to be recognized at the local level within the territorial-administrative divisions created by the Manchus, but this was within the framework and bureaucratic structure of the Qing state. In time, the Qing and especially the Russian Empire sought to exert greater control over their still mobile and occasionally recalcitrant subjects in the steppe and mould them into more obedient servants of the state.

PART ONE

★

THE RISE OF THE CHINGGISIDS

I

Inner Asia *c*. 1200

PETER B. GOLDEN

Neighbours of the steppe

The steppe, extending from the Danube to Manchuria, has been uncharitably termed the 'inhospitable land of the barbarian'.[1] These 'barbarians' were largely pastoral nomads whose neighbours viewed them as avaricious and violent marauders. In the west, this nomadic world was framed by Hungary and Rus', the latter an increasingly divided state contested by rival branches of the Riurikid ruling house. Both states included steppe lands and pastoral nomadic populations that had taken service with the Hungarian and Rus' rulers. South of the steppe lands and the fabled Silk Road cities of its southern rim (Samarqand, Bukhara, Kashghar) were the petty states of the Balkans, the fading Byzantine Empire, the Seljukid state of Rūm (Anatolia), Georgian-dominated Transcaucasia, and the fragmented ʿAbbāsid Caliphate and post-Seljuk polities of the Near East. In the east, China was also politically divided. In the north-west were the Tanguts (Chin. Xixia, 1038–1227) in Ningxia, Shaanxi and Gansu, extending to Inner Mongolia and Xinjiang. They spoke a language related to or a branch of Tibeto-Burmese.[2] South of the Yangtze River was the ethnically Chinese Southern Song state (1127–1279), with its capital at Hangzhou. The Manchu-Tungusic Jurchen dominated the north-east, its ruling elite moving between five capitals (including Beijing). In 1125, the Jurchen had toppled the Khitan-Liao dynasty (907–1125), another Inner Asian people of Mongolic, or perhaps 'para-Mongolic', ethno-linguistic affiliations[3] and took the Chinese dynastic name Jin ('Golden', 1115–1234).[4] In Inner Asia, the Jin ruler was called *Altan Khan* (Mongolic 'Golden Khan'). Like their Liao predecessors, the Jin ruled over a 'dual-administration empire',[5]

1 Meserve, 1982.
2 See Dunnell, 1994, pp. 154–8; Dunnell, 1996, pp. 3–7, 27 ff.; Kychanov, 1968, pp. 11–51, 57–64.
3 'Para-Mongolic' languages 'were collaterally related to Proto-Mongolic', see Janhunen, 2003b, and Janhunen, 1996, pp. 146 ff.
4 Vorob'ev, 1975, pp. 19–51; Franke, 1990; Franke, 1994a, pp. 215 ff.; Chan, 1991.
5 Di Cosmo, 1999, pp. 32–3.

employing separate administrations for nomadic and sedentary populations. The Tangut realm was also a 'complex mix'.[6] Variants of dual administration may have been employed by the Qarakhanids, Khwārazmshāhs[7] and perhaps the Qara Khitai (1125–1212) in realms that encompassed the steppe and settled world.[8] Virtually all of the sedentary states around the steppe were afflicted by political instability.

Everywhere, the nomads were uneasy neighbours. Yūsuf Khaṣṣ Ḥājib, a Qarakhanid official, in his *Qutadhghu Bilig* (1069), a mirror for princes, warned that they should be treated cautiously for they were not only 'unmannerly and impudent . . . despicable and ignorant bumpkins',[9] but dangerous. The plaint of the Rus' chroniclers that nomad raiders killed and enslaved peaceful tillers of the soil[10] was one that could be echoed across the steppe-sedentary frontier. Even in the early modern era, as the Russian Empire advanced into the steppes, the populations of the Russo-Ukrainian borderlands were the second greatest source of slaves in the world after Africa.[11]

The western zone: the Volga-Ural region and the Qïpchaq steppe

Spanning the western and central zones, from the Danube to Khwārazm (Khorezm), Kazakhstan and Siberia, lay the Qïpchaq steppe (Pers. *Dasht-i Qipchāq*), the domain of the Cuman-Qïpchaq-Qanglï tribes. Deriving largely from the earlier Kimek union centred in Western Siberia, this was an acephalous confederation of chieftaincies, divided into regional groupings, which had established its supremacy here in the first half of the eleventh century. By 1200, certain lineages (such as the Sharuqanids) had begun to achieve regional dominance, but none could claim supreme authority. We know little of their internal history. Ibn Khaldūn briefly mentions old feuds between two Qïpchaq tribes,[12] giving us a glimpse of tribal rivalries. The Qïpchaq groups had carefully integrated themselves into the surrounding state systems, forging close politico-military and marital ties with competing Rus' princely factions, as well as with the Georgian and Khwārazmian ruling houses. Although largely

6 See Dunnell, 1996, pp. 7–8, 145–56; and Kychanov, 1968, pp. 108 ff.
7 On Qarakhanid administration, see Genç, 1981, and Necef, 2005, pp. 235 ff. On the Khwārazmshāh state, see Buniiatov, 1986, pp. 88–107.
8 Biran, 2005, pp. 128–31.
9 *Kutadgu Bilig*, pp. 58–59, lines 439–53; Dankoff, 1983, pp. 184–5.
10 *PSRL*, I, c. 277.
11 Khodarkovsky, 2002, p. 22.
12 Ibn Khaldūn, 1983–6, X, p. 805.

speaking dialects of north-western (Qïpchaq) Turkic, this was a polyethnic union. Some of the tribes, such as the Ölberli and Qitan-opa, originated in a Mongolic milieu. Others, such as the Baya'ut/Bayawut, had branches in both the Turkic and Mongolic worlds.[13] In the western zone, proto-towns developed around the chieftains' principal camps. In Central Inner Asia, the Qïpchaqs used Jand and Sïghnaq as their urban centres.[14]

Volga Bulgharia, Muslim in religion and Oghuro-Turkic in origin, was the dominant, commerce-oriented polity of the Middle Volga and neighbouring forest-steppe zone. A rival of the Rus' state in its pursuit of the products of the northern forests (especially furs), it was the main channel of those goods to Khwārazm, on the Oxus, in modern Western Uzbekistan and thence to the larger Islamic world. After the fall of Khazaria (*c.* 965–9) it also became a commercial intermediary between Rus' and the Muslim lands. The Volga Bulghars, assimilating Volga Finnic groupings, by the early thirteenth century were advancing into the neighbouring Ugrian territories ('Yugra' of the Rus' sources) as well. On the eve of the Mongol invasions, a conflict with Rus' was looming as each side sought advantages in the contested Finno-Ugric forest zone.[15]

The central zone: Western and Eastern Turkestan

The Qara Khitai

At the beginning of the thirteenth century, the Qara Khitai state (1125–1218) was, nominally, the dominant power here. However, control over the 'vassal' Khwārazmshāhs and Qarakhanids was problematic.[16] Yelü Dashi, a scion of the Liao house, retreating with his followers via Mongolia and Uighur Gaochang (Qocho), *c.* 1130–1, came to the Irtysh and Emil regions. Here, he established the Qara Khitai Empire and styled himself *Gürkhan* ('universal emperor'), a title hitherto not used in Inner Asia. Turko-Mongolian *qara* 'black' could be used to denote 'north' or 'great'. 'Black Khitai' is a variant of Qara Qitan/Qara Khitan used prior to 1125 by the Khitan. Chinese dynastic histories subsequently recognized them as the Western Liao (*Xi Liao*).[17] The transfer of the Liao state, with its rich mix of Inner Asian and Chinese traditions (including Chinese and Khitan-Liao writing systems)[18] as well as Buddhist religion to

13 Golden, 1992a, pp. 277–82, and Golden, 2003.
14 Baypakov, 2001, p. 145.
15 Petrukhin and Raevskii, 2004, pp. 347–58; Khuzin, 1997, pp. 101–10; Golden, 1992a, pp. 253–8.
16 Barthold, 1977, pp. 322–80; Bosworth, 1968, pp. 4–11, 14–15, 52, 140–6; Golden, 1990, chap. 13.
17 Biran, 2005, pp. 1, 19–41, 215–17; Wittfogel and Feng, 1949, pp. 619–74; and Pikov, 1989, pp. 53 ff.
18 Biran, 2005, pp. 127–8.

Muslim Irano-Turkic Central Inner Asia, was an extraordinary event. Neither Buddhism (which was patronized by the dynasty) nor Nestorian Christianity, which had long-standing communities across Inner Asia, could claim a dominant status. Nonetheless, the presence of Nestorian Christians amongst the Qara Khitai and the victory of the latter over the Seljuks (1141) may have served as one of the elements contributing to the Prester John tales of a Christian ruler who would defeat the Muslims.[19] Even more extraordinary was the survival of the Qara Khitai state, in no small measure a consequence of the political fragmentation of the region and of the Khitans' robust martial skills and organizational abilities.[20]

By 1143, the *Gürkhan*'s state stretched from the Altai to Transoxania, including much of South Kazakhstan, Uzbekistan, Tajikistan and parts of Xinjiang. Assessments of the Qara Khitai interlude in Inner Asian history have varied.[21] Influenced by Chinese culture, they, nevertheless, adhered to the Steppe Imperial Tradition, which had an appeal to the local Turkic nomads. They also brought some Liao governmental practices with them, but a complete picture of Qara Khitai administration remains elusive. Often, they appear to have adjusted to the local patterns, both Turko-nomadic and sedentary Irano-Muslim. They were not the template on which the later Chinggisid regime was modelled.[22]

The Qara Khitai capital was at Quz Ordu, in the Chu River Valley, at or near Balāsāghūn, the earlier Qarakhanid centre (near Tokmak in Kyrgyzstan),[23] but ruling over a mix of Turkic pastoralists and settled Iranian and Turkic groupings, they remained overwhelmingly nomadic. Islam was the religion of most of their sedentary subjects and some of the Turkic nomads. Mindful of their numerical inferiority, Qara Khitai rule tended to be relatively light and non-intrusive, often operating through vassal regimes (Khwārazmshāhs, Qarakhanids) that were allowed to keep the trappings of their rule. The Qara Khitai amply exploited their previous association with China, which enjoyed great prestige in the Turko-nomadic and Muslim world. The aura of China,

19 Dunlop, 1944, pp. 279–81; Adshead, 1993, p. 50; Biran, 2005, pp. 176–80 (on Qara Khitai religious communities). The Mongols used similar propaganda in the West, see Jackson, 2005, p. 48.

20 Biran, 2005, pp. 146–60, the Qara Khitai army may have had 80,000–100,000 troops.

21 E.g. Pikov, 1989, p. 161, calls them a 'parasitical' nomadic state that weakened the region and retarded political unification thereby facilitating the Mongol conquest. Agadzhanov, 1991, pp. 176–82, declares that they left no 'appreciable traces', but that the Mongols 'borrowed' some forms of governance from them.

22 Biran, 2005, pp. 128–31, 211. Morgan, 1986a, pp. 49–51, however, suggests more direct 'institutional borrowing'.

23 Biran, 2005, p. 104. The Qarakhanids had two capitals, Quz Ordu and Kashghar. The former appears to have had a higher status, see Kotchnev, 2001, p. 51.

together with their Inner Asian roots and traditions, mitigated pressures to convert to Islam.[24]

Distracted by rebellious vassals, the Qara Khitai apparently underestimated the brewing conflict in Mongolia which began to wash over their state in the late twelfth century. The increase of nomadic elements, always a disruptive force, added to their woes. The last ruler, Yelü Zhilugu (1178–1211), was deposed by his son-in-law, Güchülük, the Naiman prince to whom he had given a royal bride and refuge from Chinggis Khan in 1208. Zhilugu became 'emperor emeritus' until his death in 1213. The state fell to the Mongols five years later.[25]

The later Qarakhanids

The Qarakhanids (992–1211), divided into western and eastern Turkestanian sub-realms by the 1030s,[26] had long been a fading power over whom the Seljuks, Qara Khitai and Khwārazmshāhs (only in the early thirteenth century) had exercised varying degrees of dominion. Domestically, they battled unruly tribesmen and disgruntled urban populations. The famed cities of Bukhara, Samarqand, Tashkent and Kashghar as well as the developed regions of Ferghana were part of their realm. In keeping with Turkic notions of the collective sovereignty of the ruling house, the Qarakhanids tended to divide their territory into appanages which, unintentionally, allowed for more independent urban development, particularly on the part of leadership stemming from the scribal (*kātib*)-*ʿulamāʾ* class.[27] As a consequence, in cities like Bukhara, they increasingly faced rivals for *de facto* local authority from among powerful *raʾīs*es (town leaders) or *khaṭīb*s (Friday preachers). Families such as the Burhānids (*āl-i Burhān*)[28] held the title *Ṣadr* (lit. Arab. 'chest, heart, front part' hence 'leader' of the community). Brought to prominence in the early twelfth century by the Seljuks, they had consolidated their status by the time of the Qara Khitai conquest, carefully manoeuvring between their various overlords. A Burhānid served as a tax-collector for the Qara Khitai in the turbulent years of the early thirteenth century.[29] Western Qarakhanid domestic troubles and the mounting hostility towards the Qara Khitai gave Muḥammad Khwārazmshāh opportunities for intervention.

24 Biran, 2005, pp. 100, 203; Bosworth, 1968, pp. 146 ff.
25 Biran, 2005, pp. 64–5, 70–1, 74–86.
26 See Kotchnev, 2001, pp. 52–66, for the most recent genealogy of the Qarakhanids.
27 Mouminov, 2001, p. 132.
28 Pritsak, 1950, pp. 81–96.
29 Barthold, 1977, pp. 234, 326, 353–4; Bosworth, 1968, p. 137; Mouminov, 2001, pp. 135–6; Biran, 2005, p. 72.

Important tribal groupings, such as the Qarluqs, who had played a key role in the genesis of the Qarakhanid state, appear to have been reluctant and occasionally rebellious tributaries of the Qara Khitai in the latter half of the twelfth and early thirteenth centuries. Qara Khitai pressures had forced some of them out of Transoxania. They nomadized in a region extending from south-eastern Kazakhstan to Eastern Turkestan and subdivided into distinct polities. Almalïq (or Almalïgh, near Kulja in Xinjiang) and Qayalïq (or Qayalïgh, in south-eastern Kazakhstan) were associated with the eastern Qarluqs and although ruled by Muslims had Nestorian Christian and Buddhist populations.[30]

The Khwārazmshāh state

Khwārazm was a major Islamic intellectual centre that had also preserved many elements of its ancient culture.[31] On the eve of the Mongol conquests, the Khwārazmshāhs were an expanding regional power with an army estimated at 170,000 troops.[32] Ruled by a Seljuk-installed *ghulām* ('slave-soldier') dynasty, the Turkic Anushteginids (1077–1231), their military might rested, sometimes precariously, on Qïpchaq soldiery from the surrounding steppes. The Khwārazmshāh Atsïz (1127–56), a restless Seljuk subject, submitted to Qara Khitai rule following the latter's victory over the Seljuks at the Qatwan Steppe in 1141. Cautious and opportunistic vassals of their new overlords,[33] by the late twelfth to early thirteenth centuries, the Khwārazmshāhs were seeking to extend their authority in Inner Asia, further into Iran and had ambitions on Caliphal Baghdad itself.

Khwārazm was a familiar blend of a Turkic military elite ruling an Iranian agrarian and urban population that was already undergoing Turkicization. The ruling house, although intermarried with the eastern Qïpchaq-Qanghlï, in particular with the Bayawut (or Baya'ut) tribe, never succeeded in fully managing their frequently wayward kinsmen who served in important administrative and military positions. Tergen Khatun, the imperious Bayawut

30 Bartol'd, *Dvenadtsat' lektsii* in his *Sochineniia* V, pp. 108, 110–11; Golden, 1992a, p. 294; Kadyrbaev, 1990, pp. 22–4; Biran, 2005, pp. 39–40, 54, 74.

31 Cf. al-Bīrūnī, *Āthār*, pp. 235–9, on Khwārazmian festivals; Bartol'd, *Dvenadtsat' lektsii* in his *Sochineniia* V, pp. 119–21, considers the pre-Chinggisid Turko-Khwārazmian symbiosis an important stage in the development of subsequent Inner Asian Turkic literary traditions.

32 Kafesoğlu, 1956, p. 179.

33 İl-Arslan (1156–72), son of Atsïz, paid an annual tribute to the Qara Khitai, and his son, Tekish, who gained his throne with Qara Khitai aid, warned his son to maintain Qara Khitai goodwill, al-Juvainī / Qazvīnī, II, pp.16–20; al-Juvainī / Boyle, I, pp. 289–93; Jūzjānī / Ḥabībī, pp. 300, 302; Biran, 2005, pp. 41–4, 60 ff.

wife[34] of the Khwārazmshāh Tekish (1172–1200), meddled in state affairs to the advantage of her relatives and often to the disadvantage of her son Muḥammad (1200–20), constituting an uneasy diarchy.[35] In 1207, Muḥammad gained possession of Bukhara – but only as a Qara Khitai tribute-paying vassal. In 1210, however, he captured the *Tayangu*, the Qara Khitai military commander, at the Battle of the Ilamish steppe,[36] which, although militarily inconclusive, had considerable psychological importance. The Qara Khitai appeared to be weakening. By 1211–12, the *Gürkhan*'s domestic problems combined with the debility of the local Qarakhanids, allowed Muḥammad to claim dominion in much of Transoxania, Eastern and Central Iran.[37] Khwārazmian control of the region, however, was tenuous. The Qïpchaqs were too unpredictable. The Ghūrids (*c.* 1000–1215), in Afghanistan and Northern India, one-time Seljuk and Ghaznavid vassals, became formidable competitors in Eastern Iran. Muḥammad, exploiting Ghūrid internecine strife in the early thirteenth century, eventually established his authority there.[38] Despite the seeming military power at his disposal, his state ultimately rested on an insecure base and would be swept away with remarkable ease by the Mongols in 1220.[39]

Ethno-linguistic processes in Turkestan

Western Turkestan had since the tenth century become part of what has aptly been termed 'Turko-Persia'. This was a region in which Turkic-speaking nomadic elites had become rulers of regions whose hitherto mostly Soghdian-speaking populations, in particular those located in now important Islamic urban centres such as Bukhara and Samarqand, had largely adopted

34 *Tergen Khatun* is a title often used for women of tribal royalty, Barthold, 1977, p. 337 n. 2; Clauson, 1972, pp. 544–5. Jūzjānī/Ḥabībī, I, pp. 300–1, says she was called *khudāvanda-i Jahān* 'Queen of the World' and in a jealous rage almost killed her husband. For contradictory notices on her tribal affiliations, see al-Nasawī/Buniiatov, Arab, pp. 32, 51–2, Russian, pp. 65, 82 (who praises her as a stateswoman); al-Juvainī /Qazvīnī, II, p. 109, al-Juvainī/Boyle, II, p. 378. Other accounts hint at Qara Khitai connections, see discussion in Biran, 2005, pp. 144–5. There was also a Baya'ut tribe among the Mongols (see Rashīd al-Dīn/Rawshan and Mūsavī, I, pp. 179–81), early supporters of Chinggis Khan.

35 Barthold, 1977, p. 379; Buniiatov, 1986, p. 128.

36 According to al-Juvainī/Qazvīnī, II, pp. 74–81; al-Juvainī/Boyle, I, pp. 341–9, Muḥammad executed the *Tayangu*. Jūzjānī/Ḥabībī, pp. 307–8, says that he converted to Islam and was a source of information on the Qara Khitai for Khwārazm. Ibn al-Athīr/Tornberg, XII, p. 267, reports the capture of the *Tayangu* and that he was well treated.

37 Biran, 2005, pp. 70–80, on Qara Khitai–Khwārazmian relations during this crucial period. See also Barthold, 1977, pp. 349 ff.; Kafesoğlu, 1956, pp. 73 ff.; Buniiatov, 1986, pp. 38–62, 70–87, 128–55.

38 Jūzjānī/Ḥabībī, pp. 301–2, 305–8, 318 ff.; al-Juvainī/Qazvīnī, II, pp. 47 ff.; al-Juvainī/Boyle, I, 315 ff.; Bosworth, 1977, pp. 68–9, 113–31; Buniiatov, 1986, pp. 63–75; Nizami, 1998.

39 Bartol'd, *Dvenadtsat' lektsii* in his *Sochineniia*, V, pp. 116 ff.; Kafesoğlu, 1956, pp. 233 ff.; Buniiatov, 1986, pp. 128 ff.

Neo-Persian, a process that had been going on for centuries.[40] The languages of administration and higher culture were Persian and Arabic. Persian had revived under the Sāmānids (819–1005) and was widely employed in the polities ruled by Turkic elites. This Turko-Persian political and literary culture spread with various Turkic dynasties westwards to Asia Minor and subsequently into South Asia.[41] The impact of Turkic on the languages of Western Turkestan prior to the eleventh century does not seem to have been appreciable, outside of some political terminology, itself of complex and often non-Turkic origin. This was because the Turkic nomads were still largely steppe-dwellers.[42] By the eleventh century, as is clear from the comments of the Qarakhanid lexicographer, Maḥmūd Kāshgharī (writing *c.* 1077), there was considerable linguistic interaction taking place. Kāshgharī denigrates 'Turks' who have become bilingual or mixed with Iranian-speaking urban populations. He points to cities, such as Balāsāghūn, Ṭirāz (Talas) and Isbījāb, in which Soghdian was spoken alongside Turkic. This marked the final stages of the process by which Soghdians were being either Turkicized or Persianized.[43]

The situation with Khwārazmian, another north-eastern Iranian language, is more complicated. Persian was the language of government administration under the Turkic Khwārazmshāhs, but the native Khwārazmian tongue continued to be spoken by the bulk of the capital city's population. Outlying towns in the Syr Darya region of Khwārazmian (or Soghdian) origin had Turkic-speaking populations by the eleventh century.[44] The latest Khwārazmian texts date to the thirteenth and fourteenth centuries by which time the region was largely Turkicized. However, it is possible that Khwārazmian may have continued on as a vernacular for some time after that.[45]

Eastern Turkestan, whose oasis city-states often changed overlords, had Tokharian and Eastern Iranian (Khotanese Saka) populations, amongst which were Soghdian and Indian commercial colonies. Indic languages had been

40 On the rise of Neo-Persian (Fārsi, Tajik, Darī), see Frye, 1975, pp. 144, 168–74, 200–3. Soghdian continued to be spoken, for a time, in some of the more outlying cities (e.g. Balāsāghūn) and survives today only in the Yaghnobi language in Tajikistan. Modern Uzbek scholars suggest that Turkic-speakers, arriving in the region since 'ancient times', comprised the majority of the population of Central Inner Asia, sedentary and nomadic, by the ninth–tenth centuries, see Shāniyāzov, 2001, pp. 257–8.

41 Canfield, 1991b, pp. 6, 12–13; Shāniyāzov, 2001, pp. 305, 323 (on Turko-Persian/Tajik bilingualism, a long-standing feature of Central Inner Asia).

42 Bregel, 1991, pp. 55–6.

43 Kāšγarī/Dankoff, I, pp. 83–4, 115; Krippes, 1991, pp. 76, 78.

44 Bartol'd, *Dvenadtsat' lektsii* in his *Sochineniia*, V, pp. 116–17, dates Turkicization to the eleventh–thirteenth centuries; Buniiatov, 1986, pp. 93–100. Khwārazmian wazīrs were invariably non-Turks.

45 Bregel, 1991, pp. 59–60; Edel'man, 2000, p. 95.

used in the chancelleries of important cities such as Khotan, Kucha and Kroran (Kroraina, Chin. Loulan). Soghdian had made considerable inroads as a commercial *lingua franca* and eventually as the administrative language in the north while Khotanese dominated in the south, dying out sometime after the Qarakhanid conquest *c.* 1007. Tokharian was an important language of the courts.[46] Kāshgharī comments that the Khotanese, maintaining their own language and alphabet, spoke Turkic poorly. He did not consider them 'Turks' (a term he used with some elasticity) and held the same opinion of the Kanjakī who lived in villages near Turkic-speaking Kashghar, but continued to use a language related to Khotanese Saka.[47]

The large-scale influx of Uighurs into Eastern Turkestan after the fall of their empire in Mongolia (840) was the decisive factor in the Turkicization of the region. While other polities of the Uighur diaspora succumbed to more powerful neighbours, the realm of the *Ïduq-qut* (or *Ïdïqut* 'heaven-sent' ruler) with its principal urban centres in Beshbalïq and Qocho, persevered into the early thirteenth century, albeit under Qara Khitai overlordship. Uighur assimilation of the local Tokharian and Iranian-speaking peoples was still very much in progress in Kāshgharī's time. He reports that the Uighurs speak a 'pure Turkic' but also use another language 'among themselves',[48] a clear indication of bilingualism in an assimilating population. Turkicization, not unexpectedly, seems to have advanced from the north to the south. Many of the Uighurs, having sedentarized, became important elements in the cross-Eurasian trade networks, the bearers of cultures, religions and script systems to neighbouring nomadic peoples, including the Mongols.[49]

The Qïrghïz

The Qïrghïz of the Yenisei had formed a powerful Qaghanate, recognized as such by the Türk Empire, which often sought to bring them into submission. In 840, they destroyed the Uighur Qaghanate, but did not establish their centre in Mongolia. In their northern homeland, they were part of the larger Muslim trading network and were one of the sources of the *khutu* horn[50] (ivory tusks apparently extracted from finds of long-extinct mammoths).

46 Tremblay, 2001, pp. 24, 35, 148 n. 244. On the region's complex ethno-political history, see Tremblay, 2001, pp. 29–46, and Litvinskii, 1992. Resistance to Qarakhanid rule continued into the 1030s, see Necef, 2005, pp. 204–6, 296; Kitapçı, 2004, pp. 200–2.

47 Kāšγarī / Dankoff, I, pp. 83–5; Tremblay, 2007.

48 Kāšγarī / Dankoff, I, p. 83.

49 Semënov, 1978, pp. 32–4, 38–9; Dalai, 1983, pp. 150–6; Allsen, 1983, pp. 266–7; and de Rachewiltz, 1983, pp. 283–6, 288, 290, 295; Kadyrbaev, 1993, pp. 55, 66 ff., 88–9, 120–1.

50 *Ḥudūd al-ʿĀlam*, 1962, pp. 79–81, *Ḥudūd al-ʿĀlam*, 1970, pp. 96–7.

Their subsequent history is obscure. At one point, they may have controlled regions that extended from Lake Baikal to the Qarluq borders of Transoxania and extended into the Altai, Tuva and north-western Mongolia.[51] After some resistance, they appear to have become vassals of the Qara Khitai, but the extent of the latter's dominion here is unclear. Naiman warfare with the Kereyit touched the Qïrghïz borders.[52]

The Qïrghïz exercised some authority over what the Mongols called 'Forest Peoples', some of whom were Turkic, others Mongolic and yet others very probably Uralic or even Palaeo-Siberian. Rashīd al-Dīn notes of the Urasut, Telengüt and 'Kushtemī' (Küshtem[i]/Keshtim[i], Mong. Kesdim [Keshtim]), who were 'Forest Peoples' living in or around Qïrghïz-controlled areas, that they were like the Mongols and were skilful practitioners of Mongol medicine.[53] In the early thirteenth century, the Qïrghïz polity consisted of two regions, which Rashīd al-Dīn calls 'Qīrghīz' and 'Kim Kimchī'ūt' (Kem-Kemji'üt) which bordered on Mongolia. He reports that it has 'many towns and villages and many steppe-dwellers',[54] i.e. an area of both agricultural and pastoral nomadic economies.[55] In 1207, as part of Jochi's campaign against the 'Forest Peoples' (extending as far west as the 'Bajigit', probably the Magyars of modern Bashkiria who had remained in the east) the leaders of the 'Tümen Kirgisut', Yedi Inal, Aldï Er and Örebek Digin, submitted to Chinggis Khan.[56]

The eastern zone: Mongolia and its peoples

Mongolic- and Turkic-speakers had been interacting over millennia.[57] These cultural influences were reinforced during periods in which Turkic peoples formed major states in Mongolia (the Türk and Uighur empires) and subsequently when Turkic peoples (especially the Uighurs) provided important cultural advisers and bureaucratic cadres in states created by Mongolic or 'para-Mongolic' peoples (such as the Khitan). Many of the peoples in Mongolia (e.g. the Tatars, Kereyit, Naimans and Mergits/Merkits) on the eve of the foundation

51 Kyzlasov, 1984, pp. 72–8.
52 Kyzlasov, 1984, pp. 81–3; Biran, 2005, pp. 15, 36, 41, 46, 57; Rashīd al-Dīn/Rawshan and Mūsavī, I, p. 126.
53 Rashīd al-Dīn/Rawshan and Mūsavī, I, p. 106.
54 Rashīd al-Dīn/Rawshan and Mūsavī, I, p. 143. Kem is an old name of the Yenisei River, the original heartland of the Qïrghïz state.
55 Savinov, 1984, pp. 89–103 (who also discusses the complexities of Qïrghïz ethnogenesis and migrations).
56 *Secret History*/de Rachewiltz, I, pp. 163, 850, 853, II, p. 1047; Rashīd al-Dīn/Rawshan and Mūsavī, I, pp. 143–4. They were part of a revolt of the Forest Peoples in 1218–19 which was suppressed.
57 Schönig, 2005.

of the Chinggisid Empire were either of Turkic or mixed Turko-Mongolian origins or spoke Mongolic languages distinct from that of the Mongol tribe.[58]

Juvainī depicts Mongolia in the period just prior to Chinggis Khan's rise to power as impoverished, anarchic and caught up in constant warfare.[59] Our sources enumerate nearly fifty tribal entities in the region. The emergence of the Chinggisid Empire was, in many respects, a culminating point in a long line of Turkic and Mongolic nomad-based polities with surprisingly durable political traditions going back to the Xiongnu of Mongolia.[60] The Chinggisid realm was the most complex and successful of these polities.

The Tatars

The dominant force in Mongolia into the latter half of the twelfth century was the Tatar tribal union which, according to Rashīd al-Dīn, consisted of six distinct groupings each with its own army and chief. Of these, the Tutuqli'ut were the most esteemed.[61] The Tatar central habitat (*yurt*) was Büyür or Büyir Nur (Būyūr Nāw'ūr) in East Mongolia, but they had numerous 'tribes and branches' totalling some 70,000 households.[62] Turkic, Chinese, Soghdian, Khotanese Saka and Persian sources mention them from at least the eighth century and Tatar groupings were present in a number of locales in Mongolia, South Siberia and Gansu-East Turkestan. Tatars had been part of the Türk state and interacted closely with the Uighurs, Qïrghïz and Khitan. With the fall of the Liao, they came under the sway of the Jin, to whom they had earlier been major suppliers of horses. Although noted for their history of internecine strife, they sometimes policed the unruly steppe tribes for the Jin, which resulted in a long-standing enmity with the Mongols. On occasion, they also rose up against the *Altan Khan*. As a consequence of their power and special relationship with the Jin, their ethnonym had become a collective term for the steppe peoples to the north of China.[63]

The Mongols

The core groupings of the Mongol (*Mongghol*) tribe were originally one of the forest peoples, a hunting-fishing folk of South Siberia–Eastern Mongolia and

58 Bartol'd, *Dvenadtsat' lektsii* in his *Sochineniia*, V, pp. 125–6; Janhunen, 1996, pp. 159 ff.
59 al-Juvainī/Qazvīnī, I, p. 15; al-Juvainī/Boyle, I, p. 21.
60 Khazanov, 2003, pp. 42–3.
61 Rashīd al-Dīn/Rawshan and Mūsavī, I, p. 79. The name derives from Turk. *tutuqlïgh* 'tutuq, a title ultimately of Chinese origin (Clauson, 1972, p. 453: *totok*) among the early Türks.
62 Rashīd al-Dīn/Rawshan and Mūsavī, I, pp. 76–9.
63 Golden, 'Tatar' *EI*[2], X, pp. 370–1; Bailey, 1985, pp. 92–4; Kljaštornyj, 1992; Kliashtornyi and Savinov, 2005, pp. 142–8; Biran, 2005, pp. 25, 31–2; Viktorova, 1980, pp. 160–4.

the north-western Manchurian borderlands.[64] Although there is no conclusive evidence to indicate that they were part of the Khitan state or directly influenced by it,[65] the influx of Mongolic-speaking peoples into Mongolia during the Liao era probably had an impact on them. Before the twelfth century, the name was not widely known and the composition of the early Mongols is never fully delineated in the sources. Indeed, the first attestation of their ethnonym is uncertain and it, in all likelihood, did not gain prominence until Chinggis Khan began his programme of state formation.[66] While still containing forest-dwelling components (the *hoi-yin irgen* noted in the *Secret History* and by Rashīd al-Dīn), by the twelfth century the Mongols appear as predominantly steppe nomads who had, sometime earlier, come to the upper Onon Kerulen and Tola rivers. Although there was antagonism between steppe- and forest-dweller, the dividing line was not always clear.[67]

Genealogy

The two Mongol subdivisions, the *Niru'un* ('backbone') and *Dürlükin*,[68] claimed descent from a 'grey wolf' (*börte chino*) and 'fallow deer' (*qo'ai maral*),[69] animals long familiar to Inner Asian ethnogonic myths. Temüjin, the future Chinggis Khan, was born (mid-1160s?)[70] into the Kiyat subgrouping of the Borjigit lineage whose ancestress, like those of the other leading Mongol clans, was the quasi-legendary Alan Gho'a (late tenth–early eleventh centuries?).[71] His family

64 Bold, 2001, p. 82, places them 'southeast of Lake Baikal as far as the Khentii Mountains'. For current theories, see Kychanov, 1980, and Kychanov, 1997, pp. 174–7, who locates the early Mongols around the Great Khingan Mountains and southern Argun River.

65 Janhunen, 1996, p. 158, considers them a 'marginal' grouping, 'a small and peripheral tribe' of western Manchuria, perhaps with early close connections with the Khitan, but completely overshadowed by the latter.

66 Identified by Hambis, 1970, p. 126, and Taskin, 1984, pp. 56–7, 139, 141, 364, 365, with the *Mengwu / Mengwa* among the Shiwei, a grouping of Mongolic peoples, noted in the mid-tenth century *Jiu Tangshu*. Viktorova, 1980, pp. 161–2, questions this identification. See also Geley, 1979, pp. 59–98.

67 Rashīd al-Dīn/Rawshan and Mūsavī, I, p. 54, 106–7; *QGZ*/Taskin, p. 305; Vladimirtsov, 1934 in Vladimirtsov, 2002, pp. 328–30, 334; Ratchnevsky, 1992, pp. 6–7, 14. They borrowed much of their vocabulary for pastoral nomadism from Turkic, Kychanov, 1997, pp. 177–8.

68 Perhaps also *Törülkin* from *törülki* 'native', Togan, 1998, pp. 125–6, 133.

69 *Altan Tobchi*, see Lubsan, 1973, p. 53.

70 Ratchnevsky, 1992, pp. 15–19. His birth-name was Temüjin. He was given the title 'Chinggis Khan' in 1206 after his unification of the tribes of Mongolia.

71 Mong. *Alan Ghuu-a* (*Gho'a* 'beautiful' not to be confused with *qo'ai* 'fallow'), *Secret History*/de Rachewiltz, I, pp. 1, 244–5, 249–50; Kychanov, 1997, pp. 177–9; Viktorova, 1980, pp. 168, 171, 179–83; Kyzlasov, 1984, pp. 78–81; Vladimirtsov, 1922 and 1934 in Vladimirtsov, 2002, pp. 148, 342–4. Of Alan Gho'a's five children, two were the progeny of her husband, Dobun-mergen. The Borjigit stemmed from her youngest son, Bodonchar, one of the three children that were 'miraculously' born to the widowed Alan Gho'a through divine intervention.

had a *quda* relationship (a term denoting in-law ties) with the Qonggirat (or Onggirat), whose women were famous for their beauty.[72]

Political emergence: the Qamugh Mongghol Ulus

Under Qabul Khan (1130s), the Mongols began to coalesce into an important regional force with complex politico-marital ties within the tribal network of Mongolia. Not all the Mongol clans, it has been noted, necessarily participated in this state-building endeavour.[73] In 1147, the Jin had to recognize the Mongol chieftain as a ruler and buy him off with grain, cattle and territorial concessions.[74] The Tatars, acting on behalf of the Jin as well as in their own interests, cut short the further progress of the *Qamugh Mongghol Ulus* ('State of all the Mongols'). One of Qabul's kinsmen and successors, Hambaghai (*c.* 1160?), was captured by the Tatars and met a grisly end at the hands of the Jin (nailed to some kind of torture device), as did one of Qabul's sons and other local chieftains. Hambaghai died calling for his people to avenge him. In the early 1160s, the Tatars defeated the Mongol Qutula Khan[75] and the various factions became embroiled in internal conflicts exacerbated by Jin raids. All of this furthered the Tatar–Mongol blood feud leading subsequently to the near extermination, in 1202, of the Tatars by Temüjin.[76]

The Kereyit

West of the Mongols were the Kereyit 'people' (*irgen*), consisting of seven major subdivisions,[77] on the Tola, Orkhon and Kerulen rivers, controlling much

72 *Secret History*/de Rachewiltz, I, pp. 14–15, 326; Rashīd al-Dīn/Rawshan and Mūsavī, I, pp. 97, 157–9, the Qonggirat had close marital ties with the Kürlä'üt, Ilchigin and Barghut who also had *anda* and *quda* ties with the Mongols; Pelliot and Hambis, 1951, I, pp. 402 ff.; Vladimirtsov, 1934 in Vladimirtsov, 2002, p. 343, on *quda* relationships.

73 Munkuev, 1977, p. 379. How much of this pre-Chinggisid history was a back projection by the Mongols of the imperial age, who were anxious to show that their state of the early thirteenth century had deeper roots, remains unclear, see discussion in Geley, 1979, pp. 65, 69–74, 84.

74 Kychanov, 1980, pp. 146–7. For an overview of the literature on the Mongols of the thirteenth century, see Sinor, 1989.

75 Chinggis Khan's father, Yisügei Ba'atur, was a grandson of Qabul Khan and nephew of Qutula Khan, see *Secret History*/de Rachewiltz, I, p. 10; Rashīd al-Dīn/Rawshan and Mūsavī, I, pp. 218 ff.; Ratchnevsky, 1992, pp. 9 ff.; Vladimirtsov, 1922 in Vladimirtsov, 2002, pp. 148, 168.

76 *Secret History*/de Rachewiltz, I, pp. 10–13; Rashīd al-Dīn/Rawshan and Mūsavī, I, pp. 76–83, 186–7, 223 ff. (on Qabul Khan and his successors), 262 (tale of the torture of Ambaghai [Hambaqai]); Sandag, 1977, p. 26; Golden, 'Tatar', *EI*², X, p. 371; Kychanov, 1997, pp. 179–81.

77 Togan, 1998, p. 63; Rashīd al-Dīn/Rawshan and Mūsavī, I, pp. 111–12, 114–15, who lists five and ranks the Kirāyit (*Kereyit*) among the 'tribes of the Turks' (used here generically) who have their own political leadership, but are not closely tied to the other 'Turkic' and 'Mongol' tribes except 'in form and tongue'.

of Central-Eastern Mongolia and stretching southwards towards the Gobi Desert. They appear to have migrated here from the Irtysh-Altai zone. Their close political and marital ties with the Naiman, who aided their recovery, *c.* 1140, from setbacks administered by the Tatars, their rivals in Eastern Mongolia, subsequently turned rancorous. Although probably Mongol-speaking in their majority, the Kereyit ruling group may have been of Turkic origin or profoundly influenced by Turkic groupings, in particular the Uighurs. Their khans were developing special military and personal guard units, indicative of an increasingly sophisticated political structure and wider ambitions in Mongolia.[78]

Nestorian Christian missionaries converted them *c.* 1007[79] and some of their khans bore Christian names. By the latter half of the twelfth century, following a fratricidal struggle, To'oril (Turk. Toghrïl), the oldest son of Qurjaquz (Kyriakos) Buyruq[80] Khan, had established his authority, helped in this by Yisügei Ba'atur, the father of Chinggis Khan. They became sworn blood-brothers (*anda*), a very important relationship among the steppe peoples and one that the young Temüjin would exploit as To'oril continued to face domestic challenges. To'oril was later given the title *Ong Khan* (from Chinese *wang* 'king, prince') by the Jin and he played an important role in Temüjin's rise to power.[81] Rashīd al-Dīn mentions 'another Mongol book' which has some details of their early history and of Qurjaquz's centre in 'Orta Balghasun'.[82]

The Mergit (Merkit)[83]

The Mergit union, also called Uduyut Mergit, were, according to Rashīd al-Dīn, a 'kind of Mongol' (*ṣinf ī az Mughūl*) consisting of at least four bellicose

78 Rashīd al-Dīn/Rawshan and Mūsavī, I, pp. 112–25 (places them on the 'Onan and Kilūrān' i.e. Kerulen); Togan, 1998, pp. 11, 62 ff.; Ratchnevsky, 1992, pp. 2–4.

79 Bar Hebraeus/Budge, p. 184; Dunlop, 1944, pp. 277–9.

80 An old Turkic title (Clauson, 1972, pp. 387–8), perhaps pronounced *Buyiruq* or *Buyuruq* in Mongol.

81 *Secret History*/de Rachewiltz, I, p. 57; Bartol'd, 'Obrazovanie imperii Chingiz-khana' in his *Sochineniia*, V, p. 257; Vladimirtsov, 1922 in Vladimirtsov, 2002, pp. 146, 154; Ratchnevsky, 1992, pp. 31–3, 50–1; Togan, 1998, pp. 70 ff.

82 Rashīd al-Dīn/Rawshan and Mūsavī, I, pp. 112–24; Viktorova, 1980, pp. 5, 168–70; *Secret History*/de Rachewiltz, I, pp. 394–5, 553–4, 564, 629–30; Togan, 1998, pp. 60–71. Qurjaquz was the son of Murghuz/Marghuz (Marcus), whom Togan, pp. 66–8, identifies with Sariq Khan. The text of Rashīd al-Dīn/Rawshan and Mūsavī, I, pp. 90–3, is ambiguous. Marghuz was captured by the Tatar Nāw'ūr Buyruq Khan, sent off to the 'Jurchah' (Jurchens, i.e. Jin) and suffered the same form of cruel death as the Mongol Hambaghai. Marghuz's wife slaughtered the Tatar Nāw'ūr at a banquet, Rashīd al-Dīn/Rawshan and Mūsavī, I, pp. 115–16.

83 The proper form, noted in the most recent, critical edition of Rashīd al-Dīn/Rawshan and Mūsavī, I, p. 93, is *Mirgīt*, i.e. *Mergit*, cf. Modern Mong. *Merget*, *Merged* sing. *mergen* 'good marksman, learned sage' (Lessing *et al.*, 1982, p. 537). See also Pelliot and Hambis, 1951, I, pp. 227–8, 273–4. *Merkit* is the form most commonly used in European languages.

subgroupings without a strong central authority. Their principal leader by the late twelfth century was Toqto'a Beki (Tūqtā Bīkī).[84] They were located south of Lake Baikal and north-northwest of the Kereyit and Mongols, near the Selenge and Orkhon rivers. They had a feud with the Mongols that arose from an instance of bride kidnapping.[85] Typical of peoples whose economy spanned the forest and steppe, they also hunted, trapped, fished and perhaps practised some agriculture.[86]

The Naiman

The Naiman, who in the latter part of the twelfth century shifted from Qara Khitai to Jin allegiance,[87] were the dominant power in north-western Mongolia, between the Khangai and Altai, with territory extending from the area of the later Chinggisid capital Qara Qorum (located on the Orkhon River, the traditional political centre since the Türk era) westwards to the Irtysh. Here, they bordered on the territory of the Qïpchaq-Qanghï, with whom there were political ties. Some Naiman were steppe-dwellers, others lived in the mountains. Their northern neighbours were the Turkic Qïrghïz of the Yenisei. Beyond them were other 'peoples of the forest' (such as the Shibir and Kesdim or Keshtim). In the east, they bordered with the Kereyit of Ong Khan with whom there was 'constant strife and hostility'.[88] Although *Naiman* means 'eight' in Mongol, indicating perhaps the number of clans or subgroupings that constituted their union, the question of their ethno-linguistic affiliations, Turkic or Mongolic, remains unclear. Buddhism and Nestorian Christianity were known among them.[89] In the latter part of the twelfth century their leader was Inanch Bilge Bögü Khan who was barely able to contain the rivalry between his sons Tayang and Buyruq. They perished in Chinggis Khan's wars that united the tribes of Mongolia. Güchülük, the surviving Naiman prince,

84 Rashīd al-Dīn/Rawshan and Mūsavī, I, pp. 93–7. *Secret History*/de Rachewiltz, I, pp. 30, 32–4, 73 ff. The *Secret History*/de Rachewiltz (pp. 32–4) sometimes refers to three of these groupings (one of them the 'Uduyit Merkit') as 'The Three Merkit'. *Beki* denoted a chief shaman and leader, Vladimirtsov, 1934 in Vladimirtsov, 2002, pp. 345–6.

85 *Secret History*/de Rachewiltz, I, pp. 11–12. Temüjin's father kidnapped his mother, Hö'elün, from a Mergit.

86 *Secret History*/de Rachewiltz, I, pp. 39–40 (Mergit warned by 'some fishermen, sable catchers and wild animal hunters'), 74 (Ong Khan, captured by the Mergit, pounds grain for them, implying some agriculture), II, pp. 305, 527. Ratchnevsky, 1992, p. 5, says that they also rode reindeer.

87 Biran, 2005, pp. 46, 76 n. 127.

88 Rashīd al-Dīn/Rawshan and Mūsavī, I, pp. 125–6; *Secret History*/de Rachewiltz, I, p. 164, II, pp. 849–55; Pelliot and Hambis, 1951, I, p. 209.

89 Bartol'd, *Dvenadtsat' lektsii* in his *Sochineniia*, V, p. 125; *Secret History*/de Rachewiltz, I, pp. 518, 553, 582, 682. They have been identified with the Sekiz Oghuz ('Eight Oghuz') noted in mid-eighth-century Uighur inscriptions, Ratchnevsky, 1992, pp. 1–2.

as was noted previously, fled to the Qara Khitai in 1208.[90] Their Uighur scribe and seal-keeper, Tatar Tonga, was brought into Mongol service, introducing literacy to his new masters.[91]

The Oirat (Oyirat)

The *Dörben* ('Four') *Oirat* were north of the Mergit on the Senggür Müren, neighbouring with other, northern forest hunting-fishing peoples.[92] A liminal Mongolic people, Oirat Mongol differed from the other Mongolic dialects. Some accounts view them as a distinct people. Their leaders were politically powerful shamans who held the title *beki* ('strong'). The Mongols had *anda* and marital ties with them. At the time of Chinggis Khan's rise to power their leader was Qutuqa Beki.[93]

The Önggüt

The Önggüt were a Turkic people living in the Ordos region and beyond in Inner Mongolia where they had been resident for many centuries. Like many others in Mongolia, Christianity had come to them brought by Nestorian missionaries. They, the Uighurs and Kereyit, were possible sources for some of the Turkic political and cultural influences so clearly in evidence among the peoples in Mongolia. In the early thirteenth century, their leader was Alaqush who bore the title *Tegin Quri*. The Önggüt were subjects of the Jin who had settled them to guard the Great Wall. Alaqush early on submitted to Chinggis Khan and was, accordingly, held in favour by him. This did not prevent his murder by rival factions. His nephew and successor, Shigü, in whose name Alaqush had been killed, nonetheless, married a daughter of Chinggis Khan and retained his favour.[94]

90 Rashīd al-Dīn/Rawshan and Mūsavī, I, pp. 126–30; al-Juvainī/Qazwīnī, I, p. 46; al-Juvainī/Boyle, I, pp. 61–2; Biran, 2005, pp. 65, 75–6.

91 Vladimirtsov, 1922 in Vladimirtsov, 2002, p. 171.

92 Rashīd al-Dīn/ʿAlī-zāde *et al.*, I/1, p. 204, has *Sekiz Müren* (Turk. *Sekiz* 'eight' + Mong. *müren* 'river'), Rashīd al-Dīn/Rawshan and Mūsavī, I, pp. 99, 103–9: the Barqut, Quri, Tö'eles, Tumat, Bulghachin, Keremüjin, Urasut, Telengüt, 'Kushtami' (Mong. Kesdim), the 'Forest Uriyangqat' (to be distinguished from the Uriyangqat), all of whom lived near the Qïrghïz. Rashīd al-Dīn (Rashīd al-Dīn/Rawshan and Mūsavī, I, pp. 106, 152) regards some of the Uriyangqat as 'Mongols' and others as not. See also *Secret History*/de Rachewiltz, I, pp. 134, 247, II, p. 787.

93 Rashīd al-Dīn/Rawshan and Mūsavī, I, pp. 99–100; *Secret History*/de Rachewiltz, I, p. 527, II, p. 849.

94 *Secret History*/de Rachewiltz, I, pp. 112, 134, II, pp. 656, 669, 685; Barthol'd, 1968a, p. 108. Rashīd al-Dīn/Rawshan and Mūsavī, I, pp. 130–2, says that they were protectors of the Great Wall for the Altan Khan and derives their name from Mongol **öngü* which he claims is the Mongol name for the wall. The Önggüt have also been identified with the Bai Dada ('White Tatars') of the Chinese sources; *Mengda beilu*/Olbricht, Pinks, p. 6.

These were the major power blocs in Mongolia on the eve of the rise of the Mongol Empire. They were connected by a complex web of marital and blood-brotherhood ties and divided by ongoing feuds and rivalries.[95] The Jin, working through their Tatar proxies, attempted to exploit this in keeping with the time-honoured policy of divide and rule. This required a very delicate balancing of groups, for the Tatars harboured their own ambitions and had to be kept in check as well. It was this explosive situation that Chinggis Khan manipulated to his own ends.

95 Jagchid, 1988, pp. 56–7.

2

The Mongol age in Eastern Inner Asia

PETER JACKSON

The origins of the Mongols

The overthrow of the Khitan-Liao Empire (907–1125) by a Manchurian people, the Jurchen, created a power vacuum in what is now Mongolia. The Khitan had controlled the steppe region through a network of garrisons. The Jurchen, who now supplanted them as the Jin dynasty (1123–1234), devoted their energies to further conquests in North China at the expense of the indigenous Song Empire. They abandoned the strongpoints in the steppe for a more southerly line of fortification, beyond which they were content to wield an indirect influence by playing off the tribes one against the other. Apart from the increasingly sinicized Jurchen-Jin, three more or less sophisticated powers bordered the Mongolian steppes. Khitan fugitives had created a new empire in the west, known as the Qara ('Black') Khitai, which dominated Central Asia for almost a century (*c.* 1130–1218): its ruler, a member of the defunct Liao dynasty who bore the title *Gürkhan* ('world-ruler'), exercised hegemony over a number of Muslim states as far as Khwārazm (Khorezm) on the lower Oxus River. To the east lay the principality of the Uighurs, a semi-sedentarized Turkish people who occupied the oasis towns of the Tarim Basin and the northern Tian Shan range and whose ruler (entitled *Ïduq-qut*) paid tribute to the Qara Khitai. The Uighurs' southern neighbour was the empire of the Xixia (*c.* 982–1227), ruled by a people possibly of Tibetan stock, whom the Mongols called the Tangu'ut (Tangut). Each of these states maintained relations with tribes in Mongolia proper; but none of them was capable of active intervention in its tangled politics.

The Mongols (*Mengwu*) first surface in Chinese sources of the Tang period (618–907) as a relatively insignificant people some distance beyond the empire's northern frontiers.[1] By the late twelfth century they nomadized between the Onon and Kerulen rivers. There is some slight evidence for the emergence of

1 Ratchnevsky, 1966.

a 'Great Mongol state' (*Da Menggu guo*) in the second quarter of the twelfth century; though it may well have represented merely a transient confederacy, misunderstood by sedentary Chinese observers.[2] Whatever the case, the uniform depiction of the Mongols prior to the rise of Chinggis Khan, as found in thirteenth-century sources, is one of a poor and politically fragmented tribe, greatly inferior to its steppe neighbours. Some of these powers – the Naiman, in the Altai and Upper Irtysh region, and the Kereyit (Kerait), in the basin of the Orkhon and Tu'ula rivers – were pastoralists, rearing horses, sheep, cattle and goats. The Naiman and the Kereyit were each ruled by a single khan belonging to an established dynasty, apparently of Turkish origin; influenced, in all probability, by the Uighurs and by the Qara Khitai Empire, they already possessed a rudimentary bureaucracy. The Önggüt, a semi-sedentarized tribe speaking a Turkish dialect and dwelling north of the great loop in the Yellow River with their centre at Tiande (Marco Polo's 'Tenduc'), were more exposed to the influence of the Jurchen-Jin. The politically less advanced tribes tended to be forest peoples (*hoi-yin irgen*) whose livelihood was based on hunting and fishing, like the Qïrghïz of the upper Yenisei, the Oirat (Oyirat), west of Lake Baikal, and the aggressive Merkit, in the forests along the lower Selenge, though the last-named at least were in military terms a match for the Mongols. Some tribes, of course, practised a mixed economy, and pastoralist groups which had forfeited their herds, as did the clan of the future Chinggis Khan following his father's death, had in any case to adapt temporarily to a forest-type lifestyle.

Possibly the most renowned of the Mongols' neighbours were the Tatars, whose pasturelands lay to the east, around the Külün Nor and the Büyür Nor. Their name appears to have served, both in the Islamic world and in China, as a convenient label for all the peoples of the eastern steppe, in particular those who were not Turkish.[3] For the great majority of Muslim authors who report the arrival of the Mongols in Western Asia, the conquerors are 'Tatars'. Chao Hung, an ambassador from Song China who visited the Mongol military headquarters in the north in 1221, writes of the 'Black Tatars', the 'White Tatars' (i.e. probably the Önggüt), who were more cultured, and the 'Wild Tatars', who were poor and good for nothing but riding, and ascribes Chinggis Khan and his Mongols to the first of these groups.[4]

The *Secret History* (*Mongghol'un niucha tobcha'an*), the only surviving source to emanate directly from the Mongols and dating from *c.* 1228, just after Chinggis

2 Geley, 1979.
3 Kljaštornyj, 1992.
4 *Mengda beilu* / Olbricht, Pinks, p. 3.

Khan's death, introduces us to a world in which the basic components were the loosely structured tribe (*irgen*), or more often merely the clan or lineage (*obogh*). This was a world characterized by endemic feuding and raids in which the livestock of neighbouring clans or tribes were looted and individuals or even whole clans were carried off as prisoners. Those enslaved included both womenfolk, who were a means of perpetuating well-established exogamous traditions, and males who were employed by their new masters in a menial capacity. Such 'long-standing serfs' (*ötegü bo'ul*) might in time rise to positions of responsibility, though less often than free warriors who moved between tribes in order to attach themselves to a successful war-leader as his sworn retainers (*nököd*; sing. *nökör*). This reminds us that a tribe was not a group possessed of a common ancestry, but comprised disparate elements whose unity was purely political. Tribal genealogies represent *ex post facto* attempts to illustrate and legitimize longer-term conjunctions amid an otherwise constantly shifting pattern of alliances.

Chinggis Khan's early career

The origins and rise of Temüchin (Chinggis Khan) can be reconstructed from the *Secret History* and from the alternative tradition found in the *Altan Debter* ('Golden Book'). This is a lost Mongol chronicle dating from *c.* 1285, which is available in a Chinese translation, *Sheng-wu chin-zheng lu*, and was also later used by the Persian historian Rashīd al-Dīn (1303–4). When the boy was nine, his father, a chief of the Kiyat branch of the Borjigit clan named Yesügei, was poisoned by the Tatars in retaliation for having long before abducted and married Temüchin's mother Hö'elün. The widow along with the young Temüchin and his siblings were abandoned by Yesügei's kinsmen and the rest of the clan, and wandered for some years in circumstances of great hardship, surviving on fish, game and whatever else they could find. The *Secret History* gives Yesügei a distinguished genealogy that includes allegedly powerful khans, but modern efforts to identify these dynasts with the rulers of the earlier twelfth-century 'Great Mongol' polity are less than persuasive. Indeed, the envoy Chao Hung would insinuate that Chinggis Khan's Tatars called their empire 'the Great Mongol state' (*Da Menggu guo*) purely in order to connect themselves with an illustrious past and bolster their imperial pretensions.[5]

In time Temüchin was able to claim Börte, daughter of the chief of the Qonggirat and the bride originally secured for him by Yesügei, and used

5 *Mengda beilu* / Olbricht, Pinks, pp. 16–17.

her dowry, a sable coat, as a means of entering the service of his father's blood-brother (*anda*), To'oril, the khan of the Kereyit. Under To'oril's aegis, and with the aid of his own *anda*, Jamuqa, chief of the Jajirat, he gradually amassed a significant military retinue, warring alongside his benefactor at different times against the Merkit (who had temporarily abducted his wife Börte), the Tatars and the Naiman. The chronology of these campaigns is difficult to establish on the basis of the frequently unreliable dating in the *Secret History* and of the fragmentary material in Chinese sources. The Jurchen-Jin government in North China was always ready to intervene diplomatically in such conflicts as a means of insuring its steppe frontier. Having traditionally favoured the Tatars, in *c.* 1196 it switched its support to their enemies: To'oril was granted the Chinese title *wang* ('prince'), as a result of which he became known to posterity as Ong Khan, while Temüchin, who may have spent as many as ten years prior to this in North China as a guest of the Jin,[6] was given the less elevated rank of *ja'ut-quri*, tantamount to recognition as part of the Jin regime's network of client princes. With Jin encouragement, the allies attacked and largely exterminated the Tatars (1202).

From our sources it is possible to draw a picture of Temüchin as a charismatic leader, skilled at enlisting and retaining the loyalties of his followers, whether by well-chosen rewards or by consistently sharing the hardships they endured on his behalf. But his rise was by no means a linear progression. The nadir of his fortunes came in *c.* 1202, when he was left alone at Lake Baljuna with only a score of devoted adherents, whose participation in the so-called 'Baljuna covenant' would later earn them the highest status and privileges. And when it suited him, he was capable of breaking the alliances he formed with peers and patrons alike. Both Jamuqa and To'oril came to regret their association with him. Jamuqa was the first to move into the ranks of the opposition. Elected *Gürkhan* of at least a section of the Mongols in 1201, he was overthrown with the less than wholehearted assistance of To'oril. The latter, who had been pressured into adopting Temüchin as his heir, was finally induced by a jealous son to break with his protégé: defeated in battle, he was killed while fleeing into the territory of his Naiman enemies (1203). Next Temüchin, at the head of the Mongol clans and the newly subjugated Kereyit, turned on the Merkit and the Naiman. The Merkit, like the Tatars, were overthrown; the khan of the Naiman, Buyiruq, was defeated and killed (1204), and his people were likewise absorbed. In 1206 an assembly (*quriltai*) of Temüchin's kinsfolk and *nököd* and the tribal and clan chiefs who had accepted

6 For this obscure phase in Chinggis Khan's life, see Ratchnevsky, 1992, pp. 49–50.

his leadership acclaimed him as emperor, in the words of the *Secret History*, over 'the people of the felt-walled tents'.[7] It was at this gathering, if not before, that he assumed the style of Chinggis Khan[8] by which he is generally known.

The conquests in China and Western Asia

Chinggis Khan's first attack on a sedentary power was directed against the Xixia (Tangut) kingdom, whose ruler submitted in 1210 and agreed to pay tribute and supply troops for the Mongol campaigns. The victory gave the Mongols an alternative, north-western, means of access to the Jin Empire, which was now overtly hostile to this new steppe power. Chinggis Khan embarked on war against the Jurchen-Jin in 1211. In 1215, while his general Jebe took their eastern capital, Dong-jing (present-day Liaoyang), Chinggis Khan in person captured the imperial capital, Zhongdu (close to the site of modern Beijing), abandoned by the Jin emperor for the more southerly city of Kaifeng. During the next few years the conqueror was distracted by developments further west, and operations in North China were conducted by his able commander Muqali (d. 1223), who served as viceroy of the conquered regions with the Chinese title of *guo-wang* ('prince of the realm').

Although Chinggis Khan had unified the steppe pastoralists of Mongolia, a number of his enemies were still at large to the west. By 1206 the Naiman prince Güchülük (Küchülüg), son of Buyiruq, and the Merkit chief, Toqto'a Beki, had established themselves on the Irtysh.[9] From *c.* 1207 Chinggis Khan's eldest son, Jochi, was engaged in the reduction of the 'forest peoples' – the Qïrghïz, the Oirat, the Buriat (Buyirat/Buirat) – whose territory intervened. With the cooperation of the Oirat chief Quduqa Beki, Toqto'a Beki was overtaken and killed in battle in 1208–9, and his sons, who had entered the Uighur dominions, were first expelled in a joint campaign by the Mongols and the Uighur *Ïduq-qut* and shortly afterwards all but eliminated on the Jem River. The only surviving son would be killed by Jochi on the Yenisei in *c.* 1218.

Güchülük, for his part, found a welcome in the Qara Khitai Empire, where he married the *Gürkhan*'s daughter, but then, at the head of a significant force of Naiman and Merkit fugitives, turned against him, allying with the Qara Khitai's erstwhile subordinate, the Muslim shah of Khwārazm ʿAlāʾ al-Dīn Muḥammad bin Tekish. In *c.* 1211 he deposed his father-in-law and seized the throne himself. Güchülük's subsequent hostilities with his former ally, the Khwārazmshāh,

7 *Secret History*/de Rachewiltz, I, pp. 133, 135 (§§ 202, 203).
8 On this title, see de Rachewiltz, 1989.
9 For what follows, see Buell, 1992.

did not mean that Chinggis Khan could afford to ignore his presence. Jebe, sent west to destroy him, was welcomed alike by the Uighur *Ïduq-qut*, who was already tributary to Chinggis Khan, and by the *Gürkhan*'s Muslim subjects in towns like Kashghar and Khotan, whom Güchülük had persecuted. Güchülük was hunted down and killed somewhere in the Pamir region (*c.* 1218).

Although the Khwārazmshāh Muḥammad had in 1209 clashed with the Mongol forces in pursuit of the fleeing Merkit, their common hostility towards Güchülük for a time gave rise to friendly relations with Chinggis Khan. But the shah rapidly grew apprehensive regarding his new eastern neighbour, and the execution of a group of merchant-envoys from Mongol territory, who were suspected of espionage, by the Khwārazmian governor of Uṭrār furnished a *casus belli*. Chinggis Khan prepared a formidable army, which included the Uighur *Ïduq-qut* and the Muslim Turkish princes of Almalïq (Almalïgh) and Qayalïq (Qayalïgh), previously subject to the Qara Khitai. Muḥammad, who greatly distrusted his military commanders, made no attempt to oppose the invaders in the field, but distributed his forces as garrison troops among several different strongpoints. In the course of a seven-year campaign (1218–24), the Mongols avenged the murder of their envoys by wrecking the principal cities of the shah's provinces of Transoxania, Khwārazm and Khurāsān. The Khwārazmshāh's son and effective successor, Jalāl al-Dīn, maintained a relatively brief and futile opposition to Mongol armies in present-day Afghanistan, until a defeat by Chinggis Khan on the banks of the Indus (1221) compelled him to flee into India. Muḥammad himself had died earlier that year as an abject fugitive on an island in the Caspian Sea. Jebe and Sübe'etei, who had been sent in pursuit, pushed on through northern Persia and the Caucasus into the Pontic-Caspian steppes (1222–3), where they crushed the Qïpchaq (Polovtsy) and their allies among the southern Rus' princes, prior to rejoining the conqueror on his homeward march.

When Chinggis Khan returned to Mongolia in *c.* 1225, he was intent on the suppression of the Xixia kingdom, whose ruler had neglected to provide troops for the campaign against Khwārazm and had further withdrawn his forces from Muqali's command in North China. These were Chinggis Khan's final operations. He died in August 1227, just a matter of weeks before his generals overwhelmed the Xixia capital and put the ruler to death.

Chinggis Khan had allegedly determined the succession in *c.* 1218, prior to the seven-year campaign. Subordinating the claims of both his eldest son Jochi, who had been born following the release of his mother from captivity among the Merkit and whose legitimacy was consequently suspect, and the second, Chaghadai, whose relations with Jochi were extremely strained, he settled upon his third son, Ögödei, who had a reputation for mildness and compromise and was acceptable to his brothers. It was not until 1229, however, that a *quriltai* on the Kerulen enthroned Ögödei as *qaghan*. The two-year interval might suggest friction, though both Chaghadai and the fourth son, Tolui, appear to have cooperated loyally with the new sovereign; Jochi had predeceased his father.

During the first years of his reign (1229–41) Ögödei concentrated upon the war against the Jurchen-Jin, ably seconded by Tolui, who died on campaign in North China in 1232. The Jin Empire finally succumbed in 1234, and within less than twelve months the Mongols commenced hostilities against the Song, who had rashly collaborated with them against their hated rival. Following the *quriltai* of 1229 fresh forces had been sent into the western steppe, to attack the Qïpchaq and the Volga Bulghars, and to Persia, to continue its reduction and to hunt down the still active Khwārazmian elements. But it was only in 1235 that a new *quriltai* in Mongolia determined on a large-scale expedition to the west. This campaign (1236–42) was nominally headed by Jochi's son Batu and accompanied by several princes representing the other branches of the imperial dynasty, including Ögödei's eldest son Güyük and Tolui's eldest son Möngke. The Mongols destroyed the Volga Bulghars (1237), subdued or annihilated the Mordvins, the Burṭās and the Qïpchaq (1238–9), and sacked a number of towns in Rus' (1237–8, 1240), before ravaging Poland, Moravia and Hungary (1241–2). They withdrew from Europe, in all probability, because they had exhausted the available grasslands, because their immediate task was accomplished, and because the *qaghan*'s death required the princes and generals to assemble in Mongolia for the election of a successor.

Yet again a sovereign's death inaugurated a protracted interregnum. During the campaign in the western steppes, Batu and Güyük had quarrelled violently, and Batu's deliberate procrastination delayed Güyük's election as *qaghan* for five years. At one point Chinggis Khan's youngest brother, Temüge, attempted to seize the throne, but was prevented and executed after Güyük's accession. Güyük's brief reign (1246–8) witnessed no operations of any significance, and his premature death in April 1248 averted a major civil war, since he was moving westwards at the head of a large army with the aim of attacking his cousin and rival Batu. Despite the opposition of Ögödei's divided descendants, Batu was instrumental in securing the transfer of the imperial dignity to the Toluid branch, in the person of Möngke (1251–9). Those of Ögödei's line who resisted, and those of Chaghadai's descendants who supported them, were executed or exiled and deprived of their domains. Under the new regime the Jochids in the far west and the Toluids in Eastern Asia were paramount. There is evidence that at this juncture the *Secret History* was 'doctored' in order to suggest that Chinggis Khan had envisaged the replacement of Ögödei's progeny by that of Tolui.[10] But a rival tradition that the princes had sworn to maintain the dignity of the *qaghan* in Ögödei's family would persist.[11]

Reasons for the rapid emergence of the Mongol state

The military strength of nomadic societies – the impressive mobility of steppe cavalry, the hardiness borne of the pastoralist lifestyle, the discipline bred by participation in the annual winter hunt for game – furnishes only a partial explanation for the Mongols' success. So, too, do Chinggis Khan's unquestionable talents as a military commander and his capacity for welding the nomads into a more cohesive and more disciplined force. In both the Far East and Western Asia, the Mongols amply profited from certain weaknesses in the seemingly formidable powers with which they had to deal.

The Jin Empire, though by far the strongest of these, was past its prime, enervated by a series of disputed successions. The Qara Khitai Empire was destabilized by the influx of nomadic Naiman and Merkit and had forfeited the tribute formerly extracted from client states like the Uighur principality and Khwārazm. The Khwārazmshāh's bitter quarrel with the ʿAbbasid Caliph undermined any claim he might have made to be fighting a Holy War on behalf of Islam, particularly given his failure to protect Güchülük's Muslim subjects and their recovery of religious freedom at Mongol hands. Much of his territory, moreover, had been acquired only in recent years – Transoxania in 1212 and present-day Afghanistan in 1215–16 – and there had been no time to absorb it.

In their war against the Jurchen-Jin, the invaders further benefited greatly from the assistance of disaffected elements whose territory constituted an important buffer-zone between Mongol and Jin territory. The multi-ethnic Jüyin peoples rebelled against the Jin in 1207 and went over to the Mongols. The Önggüt ruler, who had entered into friendly relations with Temüchin as early as 1203, likewise gave him military support: his murder at the instigation of the Jin had little impact, since his successor continued his pro-Mongol policy.[12] Control of the Sino-Mongolian frontier zone gave Chinggis Khan a springboard for repeated attacks upon Jin territory proper. Further east, in the

10 Allsen, 1987, pp. 39–42.
11 References in Jackson, 2005a, p. 114 n. 7.
12 Buell, 1979a.

Liaodong region of Manchuria, the Khitan prince Yelü Liuge revolted against the Jin and gave his allegiance to Chinggis Khan (1212); though he later asserted his independence. Among other Khitans who joined the Mongols was the future minister Yelü Chucai. In addition, the Jin suffered from the desertion to the Mongols of several ethnic Chinese, and even Jurchen, commanders with their regiments. Of the 100,000 troops under Muqali's command in 1217, 77,000 were Khitan, Jurchen and Chinese auxiliaries, who were vital to the continued success of the Mongol general's operations.[13] Chinese experts in siege warfare (including the operation of incendiary, and perhaps even explosive, devices) accompanied Chinggis Khan on his expedition against the Khwārazmshāh.[14] From a relatively early date, therefore, the Mongol armies of conquest were composed of both steppe and sedentary elements and drew on Chinese military techniques.

Mongol governance

Steppe polities were notoriously fragile, and measures were required to counteract the centrifugal tendencies that had bedevilled earlier confederacies. On a negative level, this was achieved through the drastic action against tribes, such as the Tatars, the Kereyit, the Merkit and the Naiman, that had mounted the strongest resistance: the survivors were systematically redistributed among different military units so that any vestigial tribal loyalties might be rendered ineffective. Even tribes that had submitted to the conquerors more or less readily, and were as a consequence initially left intact, were nevertheless placed under military commanders from other tribes and later broken up. By this means new organisms came into being, owing an allegiance to the imperial dynasty that transcended and superseded the old tribal and clan affiliations.[15]

But it was also necessary to forge a more enduring state structure. Much of what we are told of the *quriltai* of 1206 relates to matters of organization and authority; and the majority of Chinggis Khan's enactments (Mong. *jasagh*; Turk. *yasa*) that have come down to us are concerned with military discipline: penalties for deserting a military unit, for fleeing during battle, for halting to plunder while the enemy remained undefeated, and so on. The Persian historian Juvainī, writing *c.* 1260 and our principal source for these regulations, also mentions the abolition of 'reprehensible customs', apparently referring

13 Allsen, 1994a, p. 358.
14 Allsen, 2002a, pp. 268–9, 277–9.
15 Golden, 2000, especially pp. 22–6.

to strict prohibitions against crimes such as theft.[16] Chinggis Khan laid the foundations for a supra-tribal judicial institution by appointing as chief judge (*yeke jarghuchi*) his adopted son, Shigi Qutuqu.

From Ögödei's reign the empire had a centre of sorts, Qaraqorum, on the upper Orkhon River, which acquired its first permanent buildings in *c.* 1235.[17] It had served Chinggis Khan as his base-camp before his departure for the west in *c.* 1218. Even under his successors, when it contained a palace, storehouses and part at least of the imperial treasury, it was in no sense a fixed capital, but simply one among a number of halting-places in the annual imperial itinerary. Ögödei nevertheless attempted to stimulate agriculture in the vicinity.[18] He further introduced the *yam* or network of postal relay stations that linked up the most important regions of the empire. Thus, so Rashīd al-Dīn tells us, thirty-seven such stations linked Qaraqorum with northern China.[19]

These measures could be described as the *sine qua non* of governing an empire on horseback. But the Mongol Empire, as one of its most distinguished servitors allegedly warned, could not be so governed;[20] and here, as in the military sphere, the mediatory role of representatives of the conquered sedentary peoples was pivotal. As early as *c.* 1204 Temüchin had recruited the former keeper of the Naiman khan's seal, a Uighur named Tata Tong-a, under whose guidance the Mongols adopted the Uighur script and began for the first time to produce documents in Mongolian. The Önggüt served as a vehicle for the transmission of Chinese ideas to the Mongols. The Mongol debt to the Qara Khitai Empire, which comprised both nomadic and sedentary elements and can accordingly be seen in some important respects as a precursor of their own, is uncertain; but there is widespread agreement that they borrowed from the Qara Khitai the office of *basqaq* (called in Mongolian *darugha*/*darughachi*), the 'resident' appointed to supervise the conduct of a client sedentary ruler, to oversee the collection of tribute and to requisition auxiliary forces.[21] Officers of East Asian origin were used in order to govern the recent conquests in Central Asia: thus the Khitan Yelü Ahai and his son Yelü Mian-sige were successively *basqaqs* of the Bukhara region.[22] But personnel were also transferred in the opposite direction: Chinggis Khan took back

16 On Chinggis Khan's *yasas*, see al-Juvainī/Qazvīnī, I, pp. 16–25; trans. al-Juvainī/Boyle, I, pp. 23–34; and cf., most importantly, Morgan, 1986a, pp. 163–76; de Rachewiltz, 1993.
17 Pelliot, 1925, p. 374.
18 al-Juvainī/Qazvīnī, I, pp. 169–70; al-Juvainī/Boyle, I, p. 213.
19 Rashīd al-Dīn/Rawshan and Mūsawī, I, p. 671; Rashīd al-Dīn/Thackston, II, pp. 328–9.
20 The Khitan Yelü Chucai, quoted in Morgan, 1982, p. 135.
21 Morgan, 1982, pp. 129–30. But cf. Endicott-West, 1989a, pp. 35 and 151 n. 55.
22 Buell, 1979b, pp. 124–6, 131–41.

east with him in 1223 a Muslim Turk from Ürgench in Khwārazm, Maḥmūd Yalawāch ('the envoy'), to govern the former Jin capital of Zhongdu. Maḥmūd and his son Mas'ūd were the two Muslims 'adept in the laws and customs of cities' whom, according to the *Secret History*,[23] the conqueror consulted following the reduction of Transoxania, in all probability from a desire to learn about urban taxation.

Already Temüchin had on one occasion levied taxation on his nomadic followers in order to relieve To'oril/Ong Khan at a time of particular hardship.[24] This levy, known as *qubchur*, persisted into the imperial era, when it was extended to the sedentary populations as a poll-tax. In each region the imposition of taxation was heralded by the census, first introduced to the sedentary conquests (to the best of our knowledge) in north China in 1234 and completed in 1236.[25] The *qubchur* was imposed in addition to the existing (non-Mongol) taxes traditionally paid by the sedentary peoples to their previous rulers and termed generically *qalan*.[26] These included both agricultural taxes, like the *kharāj* in Muslim lands, and commercial imposts, known under the collective designation *tamgha*. The *qubchur*, which was haphazard in character, caused considerable hardship and was deeply resented. The nomadic conquerors took some time to appreciate the danger that they might permanently damage the economy of the subject territories and thereby impair the tax-paying capacity of the population. Yet in large measure the momentum of the conquests reflects the *qaghans'* ability to tap an impressively broad resource base and extract a significant proportion of the sedentary wealth of their dominions.

The ideology of a world-empire

One obvious means of keeping the nascent empire in being was to absorb the nomads' energies in continued expansion. It is uncertain at what stage the Mongols embraced the notion of world-conquest. The Hungarian Dominican Friar Julian, reporting back from a reconnaissance mission in 1236–7, refers to the Mongols' aim of reducing the whole world, and dates it from Chinggis Khan's overthrow of the Khwārazmian Empire.[27] The earliest direct evidence similarly emanates from Christian Europe. The ideology of world-dominion found expression in the Mongol ultimatums to independent powers, of which the earliest to survive are those addressed to the Pope and brought back by his

23 *Secret History*/de Rachewiltz, I, pp. 194–5 (§ 263).
24 *Secret History*/de Rachewiltz, I, p. 74 (§ 151).
25 Abramowski, 1976, pp. 128, 131; Allsen, 1981, p. 35.
26 See Smith, 1970.
27 Dörrie, 1956, p. 172.

envoys in 1247–8: they leave the recipient in no doubt that he is now subject to the Mongols by virtue of Heaven's mandate. By this juncture, at least, the Mongols believed that the mandate had been issued to Chinggis Khan in person.[28]

Notions of imperial sway had been current among the steppe nomads for centuries, and were presumably transmitted to the Mongols by their Uighur and Khitan aides.[29] It was perhaps in keeping with this ideological background that Chinggis Khan in *c.* 1218 chose to set out from Qaraqorum, which lay in the centre of the sacred *refugium* of the Turks in the Orkhon Valley. Yet these imperial traditions – like the few details about Heaven's mandate to Chinggis Khan that are furnished in the *Secret History* – focused only on hegemony over the nomads, and did not encompass the sedentary world. But by 1223, when Chinggis Khan began his return march to Mongolia, he had already been drawn into an imperial role beyond the steppe by the need to eliminate fugitives like Güchülük who threatened to create a new power-base from which to challenge him; and he had left in place a rudimentary administration for the conquered regions of both the Jin and the Khwārazmian empires. David Morgan's contention that the Mongols came to believe in a programme of world-conquest only when they discovered that they were in fact conquering the world[30] may well be close to the truth. The development is probably to be dated to Chinggis Khan's own lifetime. This is not only supported by the testimony of Friar Julian, cited above, but is also implicit in the claim by Song envoys, visiting the Mongol imperial court in 1237, that the conqueror had ordered his family to complete the destruction of the Jin before resuming the subjugation of the Qïpchaq steppe.[31]

The *ulus*

In its ideological aspects – as in its territorial extent, its deployment of specialist administrative personnel from the sedentary world and its capacity to extract the wealth of its sedentary subjects – the Mongol Empire represented a significant advance on its Inner Asian precursors. But this should not be overstated. In time-honoured steppe fashion, the conquests were regarded as the property of the entire dynasty; and although presided over by a *qaghan* the empire was in effect run as a family firm. At different stages during his lifetime Chinggis Khan allotted an appanage (*ulus*) to each of the princes and princesses

28 Voegelin, 1941; de Rachewiltz, 1973.
29 Allsen, 1996.
30 Morgan, 1989, p. 200.
31 *Mengda beilu* / Olbricht and Pinks, p. 209.

of the imperial family, as also to certain of the Mongol generals. Juvainī tells us only about the appanages conferred on the four sons of the conqueror's principal wife Börte. He indicates that these territories radiated outwards from the centre of the empire according to the age of the son concerned. Thus Jochi, who in *c.* 1208 had received the recently subjected 'forest peoples', notably the Qïrghïz and the Oirat,[32] was subsequently given 'the territory extending from Qayalïq and Khwārazm to the furthest limits of Saqsīn and Bulghar and as far on that side as the hooves of Tatar horses had penetrated'. Chaghadai, as the second son, was granted the lands from the Uighur territory as far as Samarqand and Bukhara, while the domain of Ögödei, the third, lay to the east, in the region of Emil and the Qobaq River. Nothing specific is said about the appanage of Tolui, the youngest son, who remained, we are told, with his father.[33] As the 'hearth-prince' (*ot-chigin*), he was to inherit Chinggis Khan's original territory on the Onon and the Kerulen. The effect of these dispositions was to create extensive spheres of influence within the empire.

Symptomatic of the collegial character of the imperial enterprise was the composition of its armies and of the regional civil-military administrations. Whether raised for large-scale campaigns beyond the borders or left as garrison forces (*tammachi*) in recently conquered territory, the troops comprised contingents supplied by the various branches of the dynasty.[34] Unlike the steppe regions, the conquered sedentary territories, China and Persia, were not assigned as princely *ulus*es, but remained part of the '*ulus* of the centre', i.e. those territories under the direct administration of the *qaghan*'s own officials and military commanders. Nevertheless, even here members of the dynasty were granted revenues and sometimes entire urban populations as their appanages (Mong. *qubi*; Chin. *touxia*; *fendi*). In the course of a general distribution of the population of the vanquished Jin Empire in 1236, for instance, the *qaghan* Ögödei gave Chaghadai the inhabitants of the city of Taiyuan and Tolui's widow Sorqaqtani those of Zhengding.[35] And the regional governments – 'joint satellite administrations', to use the term coined by Professor Paul Buell – established in northern China, Turkestan and (in 1246) Persia similarly included not merely the *qaghan*'s own representatives but also those of the other Chinggisid lines.[36] The reigns of Chinggis Khan's first three successors were marked by the *qaghans*' attempts to intensify their authority

32 *Secret History*/de Rachewiltz, I, pp. 164–5 (§ 239).
33 al-Juvainī/Qazvīnī, I, pp. 31–2; al-Juvainī/Boyle, I, pp. 42–3 (greatly modified).
34 Aubin, 1969.
35 Allsen, 2001b.
36 Buell, 1979b, pp. 141–7.

over the appanages and by the equally strenuous efforts of the princes both to extend their holdings and to gain direct access to the sedentary revenues that they had been granted.

Möngke appears to have planned both a modification of the existing appanages and a fresh allocation. In some degree this was facilitated by the pruning of the lines of Ögödei and Chaghadai, who had opposed his accession; but it was also made possible by the fresh campaigns which Möngke launched against external powers in order to cement the cracks in the imperial edifice. From 1252–3 his second brother Qubilai was in command of the war with the Song, and there is some slight evidence that the *qaghan* intended Qubilai to rule over the Chinese conquests as his own *ulus*. At the same time their third brother, Hülegü, was placed at the head of another large army (again including Chinese siege experts), with the aim of reducing the still independent regions of Persia and Iraq. Whether Möngke intended Hülegü, too, to preside over his own *ulus* in south-west Asia is by no means certain: Rashīd al-Dīn is equivocal, claiming that this was the *qaghan*'s secret purpose but that he publicly ordered Hülegü to return to Mongolia once his task was completed.[37] Here in Western Asia, the changes came at the expense of Möngke's allies, for Hülegü's arrival curtailed the influence that the Jochids had hitherto enjoyed. Hülegü's forces sacked Baghdad and overthrew the ʿAbbasid Caliphate (1258). The Mongols were only halted at ʿAyn Jālūt (1260) in Palestine by the Egyptian Mamlūks. The victory was actually obtained over a rump force, since Hülegü had withdrawn into Azerbaijan with the bulk of his army. That he proved unable to avenge this reverse is due largely to developments within the Mongol world.

The disintegration of the unitary Mongol Empire

Möngke's death on campaign in China in July 1259 was followed by the almost simultaneous elections, at rival *quriltais* in China and Mongolia respectively, of Qubilai and of their youngest brother, Arigh Böke (1260); and for the first time a disputed succession gave rise to full-blown civil war. This soon spread to Central Asia, where each of the claimants attempted to instal his own candidate in Chaghadai's *ulus*, and even further west, since Hülegü, based in northern Persia, acknowledged Qubilai as *qaghan*, while Berke, the head of the Jochid *ulus*, supported Arigh Böke. Victory in the Far East went to Qubilai, who enjoyed access to the superior resources of China and was able to withhold grain

37 Rashīd al-Dīn/Rawshan and Mūsawī, II, p. 977; Rashīd al-Dīn/Thackston, III, p. 479 (modified). Cf. Allsen, 1987, pp. 47–51, and Jackson, 1999b, p. 29.

shipments from his hard-pressed brother. Despite moving from Mongolia to Central Asia in a vain attempt to establish a new power-base, Arigh Böke was obliged to submit (1264), and died soon afterwards.

The greater part of the empire had effectively split apart into four autonomous khanates, though Chinggisid descent continued to be indispensable to legitimacy. Of these powers, only the Ilkhanate, the domain of Hülegü and his successors in Persia, acknowledged the *qaghan*. The Jochids acquiesced in his sovereignty merely intermittently, and he was unable, in the longer term, to impose his authority on the Mongols of Central Asia. Here between 1268 and 1271 Ögödei's grandson Qaidu successfully welded together a confederacy of princes of the lines of Ögödei and Chaghadai, nominating the Chaghadayid khans himself, and created a state that extended from the Aral Sea and the lower Syr Darya as far as the Uighur territories and even, on occasions, Mongolia. The Mongol world did not recognize the authority of a *qaghan* again until 1303–4, when Qaidu's son Chapar and the Chaghadayids submitted to Qubilai's grandson and successor, Temür; though in the event this new-found amity did not last.

The effect of these upheavals was to halt the Mongol advance in Europe and the Near East, where in practice, albeit not in theory, the programme of world-dominion had to be shelved. Only in the Far East did the empire continue to expand. Korea, which had paid tribute intermittently since 1219, was fully incorporated as a client kingdom early in the 1270s; Tibet was brought within the *qaghan*'s sphere of influence around the same time. Qubilai enjoyed his greatest triumph in China, which had become his power-base. During the conflict with his brother, he had resided at Shangdu (the 'Xanadu' of Marco Polo and of Coleridge's celebrated poem) in northern China, which remained the 'summer capital' even after the construction in 1266 of a new capital at Zhongdu, renamed Dadu and known to the Mongols as Khanbaligh ('the Khan's city'). Qaidu's defiance did not prevent the *qaghan* from completing the reduction of the Song (1276–9). Prior to this, at the instigation of his Chinese advisers, he had adopted for his regime the dynastic style of Yuan (1271). Yet the prince who thus became the first Mongol emperor of China, and the first to unite the country under 'barbarian' rule, was equally the first *qaghan* not accepted by his kinsfolk throughout the empire.

Eastern Inner Asia in the later imperial era

The progeny of Chinggis Khan's younger brothers, Jochi Qasar, Qachi'un and Temüge Otchigin, commanding 'the troops of the left hand', governed appanages in Eastern Mongolia and Manchuria. In the civil war of 1260–4, these princes had supported Qubilai. But the *qaghan*'s policy of centralization and his steady encroachment on their domains provoked in 1287 a formidable rebellion headed by Temüge's descendant Nayan. The insurgents were in contact with Qaidu, though he proved unable to come to their aid. In the course of a major engagement in which Qubilai personally commanded his forces, they suffered a crushing defeat; they were executed, and their territories and dependants were redistributed among other members of the imperial dynasty.[38] Although Nayan's son Toqto'a seems to have inherited his father's property and received from a later *qaghan* the title of Prince of Liao,[39] his power was greatly reduced. The episode marked the end of the semi-autonomous *ulus* in the Far East. Qubilai incorporated Manchuria as the province of Liaoyang into the system administered from Khanbaligh.

Qubilai's fruitless efforts to bring the Central Asian Mongols to heel, and his conflict with Qaidu, will be examined in the next chapter. Here it should be noted simply that the struggle extended to Mongolia and other eastern regions, where the *qaghan* enjoyed greater success than in Turkestan. In maintaining contact with Mongolia, the key region – apart from those of Qubilai's own capitals at Shangdu and Dadu – was the former Tangut state (Chin. *Hexi*; Mong. *Qashi*), with its capital at Ningxia.[40] During Qubilai's lifetime this territory was the appanage of the *qaghan*'s second son Mangghala; and following Temür's accession it was conferred on Mangghala's son Ananda. Ananda converted to Islam and imposed his new faith on the troops under his command, numbering, according to Rashīd al-Dīn, nearly 150,000.[41] These forces were an integral part of the defence system that Temür maintained against the attacks of Qaidu and the Chaghadayid princes. Ananda came to grief in 1307, when he was summoned to Khanbaligh by the dowager empress, Bulughan, to be a candidate for the imperial throne in opposition to Temür's nephew Qaishan. The bid failed, and he and his supporters were arrested and executed by the victor.[42] But his appanage seems to have passed to his son Örüg-Temür.

Qubilai was able to set in motion the reconstruction of the Yenisei region in the 1260s. But this territory was devastated twice, first in 1277–8 by a band of rebel princes who had mutinied against his son Nomuqan, and then in 1289 by Qaidu, profiting from the *qaghan*'s absorption with the suppression of Nayan. On this occasion Qaidu also occupied Qaraqorum. The value of

38 Jackson, 1999b, pp. 33–5.
39 Rashīd al-Dīn/Rawshan and Mūsawī, II, p. 913; Rashīd al-Dīn/Thackston, II, p. 448.
40 Dardess, 1972–3, pp. 143–6.
41 Rashīd al-Dīn/Rawshan and Mūsawī, II, pp. 950–1; Rashīd al-Dīn/Thackston, II, p. 465.
42 Vaṣṣāf, 1959, pp. 498–501; Dardess, 1973, pp. 13–15.

his achievement was surely more emblematic than economic, but it doubtless constituted a severe blow to the old *qaghan*'s pride, since here lay the burial-places of his illustrious predecessors, notably Chinggis Khan himself. Qaidu's forces were not expelled until 1293. The *qaghan* does not seem to have persisted in his efforts to hold the Yenisei region, but in 1307 his great-grandson, the *qaghan* Qaishan, incorporated most of Mongolia, as Lingbei province, into the network of Chinese provincial administration. The territory would give the later Yuan emperors remarkably little trouble. An attempted revolt by the prince Alghui Temür in 1361 was suppressed without difficulty, and Mongolia would serve as the refuge and headquarters of the *qaghan* Toghan Temür when the Yuan finally abandoned China seven years later.

The impact of Mongol rule upon the subject peoples

Like other steppe peoples, the Mongols practised what has generally been labelled 'shamanism', involving veneration of ancestors and contact with the spirits of the dead. The religious specialist, the shaman (Turk. *qam*; Mong. *böge*), enters into an ecstatic state, makes contact with the spirit world and is able in consequence to offer guidance on the affairs of this life. But the nomads seem also to have viewed all faiths as equally valid approaches to the numinous. The imperial regime could be characterized as one of religious pluralism. The Nestorian form of Christianity had been present in Mongolia since at least the eleventh century, particularly among the Tatars, the Kereyit and the Önggüt. Some members of the Chinggisid dynasty became associated with particular faiths: Batu's son Sartaq (d. 1256–7), for instance, was said to have been baptized a Christian, and his uncle and successor, Berke, is everywhere described as a practising Muslim. Nevertheless, Chinggis Khan had allegedly enjoined his descendants not to distinguish between the different religions. The *qaghans* and their kinsfolk, who valued holy men from the various confessional groups for their skills in magic and healing, accordingly made gifts to religious foundations and exempted the 'religious classes' from the head-tax (though not from imposts on any economic activity in which they engaged), from military service and from forced labour.[43]

This is not to credit the Mongol rulers with toleration. Our sources depict Mongol law as impinging harshly on the subject population where their religious practices contravened steppe custom. Thus a Rus' prince was compelled to marry his brother's widow in accordance with the levirate that obtained in

43 Jackson, 2005b, pp. 262–8.

the steppe. We are most fully informed about the clash with Islamic practice. Muslim ablutions, for example, were forbidden because they ran counter to the prohibition against washing in running water; and the Muslim slaughter-ritual because it was at variance with the nomads' method of killing animals for food. During Ögödei's reign, his brother Chaghadai acquired a reputation as an especially determined upholder of Mongol laws, primarily at the Muslims' expense. It is difficult to see how these prohibitions could have been enforced at a distance from the steppe, among urban populations. Yet a generation later the *qaghan* Qubilai, who had taken umbrage at Muslim attitudes, forbade Muslims in China to observe either their ablutions or the slaughter-ritual for a period of seven years or so (1280–7); it is also noteworthy that he enforced the levirate among the Chinese population for some time after 1271.[44] Generally speaking, Mongol courts (*jarghu*) applied a law that sometimes bore heavily on their Chinese subjects, though under Qubilai's fourteenth-century successors, codes were drawn up that gave greater prominence to the laws of the conquered.[45]

Inner Asia's entry into contact with Europe

The Mongol Empire has justifiably been described as 'the largest continuous land empire that has so far existed'.[46] At the point of its disintegration into a number of khanates in *c.* 1261, it extended from Korea to the frontiers of the Christian West in Livonia, Poland and Hungary and in northern Syria. As a consequence, the Mongols' homeland was brought into contact with more distant regions of the world than any of its steppe predecessors, and became for some decades the hub of a system that embraced most of the Old World. Qaraqorum contained a colony of European Christian slaves carried off from Hungary in 1241: one of them, the Parisian silversmith Guillaume Bucher, constructed for Möngke a silver fountain that spewed forth different alcoholic beverages. But for the first time Inner Asia also now entered into diplomatic contact with the Christian West. An embassy from Pope Innocent IV, headed by the Franciscan Friar Giovanni del Pian di Carpine (John of Plano Carpini), and designed to deflect the Mongols from further assaults on Europe, travelled via Batu's *ordo* as far as the court of the *qaghan* Güyük in Mongolia (1246). A few years later rumours that there were Christians in the Mongol imperial dynasty and the high command prompted another Franciscan, William of

44 Ratchnevsky, 1970; Birge, 1995, pp. 107–46.
45 Ratchnevsky, 1993.
46 Morgan, 1986a, p. 5.

Rubruck, to visit Mongolia as the earliest missionary from the Latin Christian world (1253–5). At this juncture Western merchants had probably penetrated no further east than the Crimea, but the Venetians Niccolò and Maffeo Polo travelled to Qubilai's court in the early 1260s, and Niccolò's son, the more famous Marco Polo, spent the period 1274–91 in the *qaghan*'s service. Unlike the Western merchants who followed them during the first half of the fourteenth century, the Polos reached China overland, probably by way of the Gansu corridor.

Although the Latin world maintained diplomatic relations with the Ilkhans, after Carpini no other Catholic embassy is known to have reached the Far East prior to the Franciscan Giovanni di Montecorvino (d. 1328), who arrived at the *qaghan* Temür's court at Khanbaligh in *c.* 1295 primarily in order to spread the Gospel. This was likewise one of the functions of the Franciscan Giovanni di Marignolli, who carried a letter from Pope Benedict XII to the *qaghan* Toghan Temür in 1338. The monk Rabbān Ṣawma, of the Önggüt tribe, who accompanied his friend and pupil, the Nestorian Catholicos Mar Yabhallaha III, from Mongolia to Persia and went on to visit the Papal Curia and the French and English kings as the Ilkhan's ambassador in 1287–8, was very probably the first native of the Far East to travel to Western Europe on diplomatic business.

Montecorvino's missionary efforts began auspiciously with the conversion of the Nestorian Christian prince of the Önggüt, Körgüz ('George'), who allowed him to build a church near Tiande (Tenduc) that was excavated in the last century. The prince had his infant son baptized as John in the friar's honour, but on his untimely death at the hands of the Chaghadayid Mongols in 1298, his brothers took their nephew and people back into the Nestorian fold, and Montecorvino's work was undone. Thereafter his efforts were of necessity confined to Khanbaligh, and the Franciscans who joined him in 1307 at the behest of Pope Clement V similarly restricted their activities to China. It is in any case a moot point what Catholic baptism meant to Mongolian neophytes, as opposed to those who administered it. Only too easily were the interest of individual Mongol princes in magic and healing, together with the privileges extended to 'holy men', misinterpreted as signs of especial favour towards one particular religion. Even as he gave his support to Montecorvino, Körgüz himself is known to have endowed a Confucian temple near his residence.[47] The Franciscan missionary drive remained still-born even prior to the advent of the Ming; it had been completely forgotten by the time the Jesuit Matteo Ricci reached China in 1583.

47 Ch'en, 1966, pp. 53–7.

Genealogy of the Chaghadayid Rulers (up to 1347)

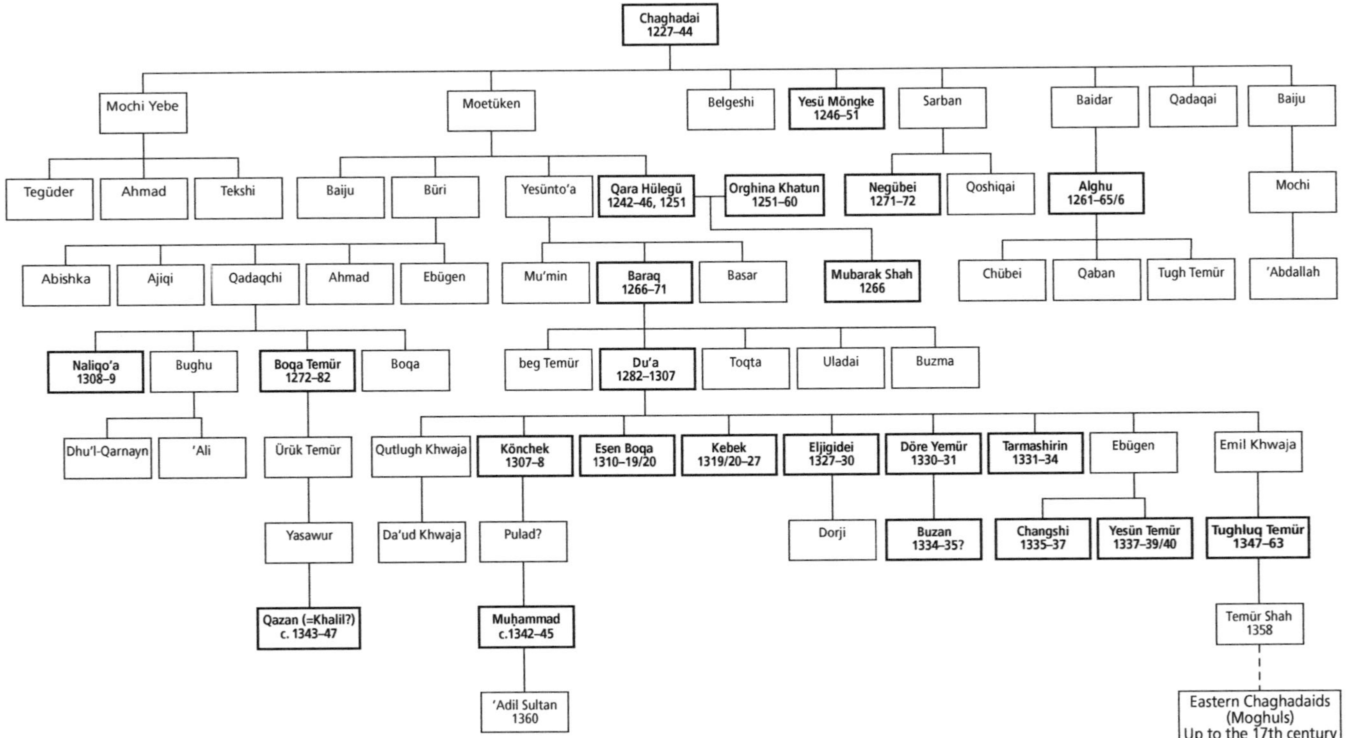

3

The Mongols in Central Asia from Chinggis Khan's invasion to the rise of Temür: the Ögödeid and Chaghadaid realms

MICHAL BIRAN

Chinggis's campaign into the Muslim world of Central Asia,[1] a watershed in the region's history, completed his transformation from a successful nomadic chieftain on the fringes of China to a world-conqueror on an unparalleled scale. The speedy annihilation of the Qara Khitai and Khwārazm (Khorezm) Shāh realms not only drastically enlarged the territories and manpower under Chinggis's control, but also bolstered his public image as someone predestined by Heaven to conquer the entire world. Moreover, these conquests closely exposed him to Muslim sedentary culture, different from that of China, which for centuries had been the major reference point for the nomads of Mongolia, thereby greatly enlarging the stock of administrative, military and cultural tools at his disposal. As for Central Asia, much of the region's subsequent political culture, ethnic composition and concepts of legitimacy and law go back to Chinggis Khan. Yet the century and a half that followed the Mongol conquest was far from being the region's golden age. Moreover, the history of Chinggisid Central Asia, largely associated with the Chaghadaid khanate, is less studied in comparison with contemporary Mongol states or with other periods of Central Asian history, because of the paucity of written sources. This chapter reviews the political history of Central Asia under the Mongols up to 1347 and then briefly discusses major economic and cultural-religious phenomena.

Political history

The United Empire up to Alghu's reign (1220s–1260s)

When Chinggis Khan apportioned appanages to his sons, Chaghadai (Turk. Chaghatay) received the land stretching from Uighuria to the Oxus, roughly

1 'Central Asia' here refers to the area between the Oxus and the eastern border of modern Xinjiang.

equivalent to modern Uzbekistan, Tajikistan, Kyrgyzstan, parts of South Kazakhstan and southern Xinjiang. Chaghadai resided in the vicinity of Almalïq (or Almalïgh) (near modern Kulja in north-west Xinjiang) on the Ili River. Ögödei, Chinggis's nominated heir, received a smaller adjacent region between Emil and Qobaq in Zungharia (north-east Xinjiang and South Kazakhstan), but as *qaghan* he ruled from Qara Qorum. Both the Ögödeid and Chaghadaid realms had been under Qara Khitai rule for most of the century preceding the Mongol invasion. This highly cosmopolitan and multilingual territory had enjoyed relative stability and prosperity for most of the second half of the twelfth century. Yet, even at its height, the region, unlike Iran or China, lacked an established imperial tradition and a strong sedentary basis. Its peaceful conditions were severely disturbed in the early thirteenth century by the deterioration of the Qara Khitai ruling house, the struggle between the Khwārazm Shāh and the Qara Khitai and the repercussions of the rise of Chinggis Khan in Mongolia, developments which caused the Qara Khitai to lose control of both Uighuria and Transoxania.[2]

The Mongol conquest of Central Asia was surprisingly benign in its eastern part: the Uighurs voluntarily submitted to Chinggis in 1209, becoming major cultural brokers for the nascent empire, and the Qarluqs of Qayalïq and Almalïq followed them in 1211. In 1218 when Jebe was sent to annihilate Güchülük, the Naiman prince who had usurped the Qara Khitai throne and threatened Chinggis's hegemony in Mongolia, he pursued and killed the prince, but did not severely harm Semirech'e and the Tarim Basin, incorporating most of the Qara Khitai troops into Mongol armies. The Mongol conquest of Transoxania, then under the Khwārazm Shāh, was, however, extremely harsh. Yet it was speedy: less than a year after the Mongols crossed the Jaxartes in the autumn of 1219 they already ruled the whole province, and Transoxania's successful restoration had already begun in earnest by Chinggis's time.[3] However, as one of the first regions that became part of the Mongol realm, Central Asia's resources – human and material – continued to be channelled for the benefit of the ever-expanding empire, often at the expense of local interests.

Chaghadai, an expert on Mongol law (*jasaq* or *yasa*) and rituals, remained in Mongol Central Asia. He was infamous for his harshness, which reportedly cost him the Qaghanate. Nonetheless, Chaghadai fully accepted the authority of his younger brother Ögödei, who succeeded Chinggis in 1229. He was highly respected as Chinggis's oldest living son (Jochi had died in 1227) and

2 See Biran, 2005.
3 See Jackson's chapter in this volume. For the conquest and restoration see Biran, 2007, pp. 47–70.

retained his own court and guard, but the close supervision of the *qaghan*'s representatives in the sedentary regions of his realm was often a source of tension. In 1238, when the Bukharan population headed by Maḥmūd Ṭarabī, a sieve-maker adept in magic, revolted against Mongol financial demands, Chaghadai took no part in its suppression, leaving it to the *qaghan*'s troops; the city was saved from savage Mongol reprisals by the intervention of Maḥmūd Yalawāch, the *qaghan*'s chief administrator in Turkestan. Shortly afterwards, Chaghadai fell into a dispute with Maḥmūd, after ordering the transfer of certain Transoxanian lands subject to the *qaghan* to another man. Maḥmūd complained to Ögödei, who forgave his brother, added the contested territories to Chaghadai's private appanages, and transferred Maḥmūd to China, while entrusting Turkestan's sedentary regions to Maḥmūd's son, Masʿūd Beg.[4] After Ögödei's death, Chaghadai quarrelled with the *qaghan*'s governor in Khurāsān, Körgüz, later executed in the Chaghadaid court. As early as 1242, Chaghadaid princes competed with Batu, khan of the Golden Horde, and with the representatives of Töregene, Ögödei's wife and the regent after his death (1241–6), for authority in Khurāsān.[5]

Chaghadai died around 1244,[6] and was succeeded by his grandson Qara Hülegü, whose father, Mö'etüken, Chinggis's favourite, had died during the Mongol siege of Bamiyan (1221). Although Qara Hülegü had been designated heir apparent by Chinggis Khan, Chaghadai and Ögödei, when Güyük took power in 1246, he deposed him in favour of Yesü Möngke, Chaghadai's oldest living son and Güyük's friend, who, however, excelled mostly in drinking. With Güyük's death (1248) most Chaghadaids supported the Ögödeids and opposed the accession of Tolui's son, Möngke (1251–9). The Toluid usurpation therefore badly harmed the Central Asian Mongols: the Ögödeid *ulus* was completely dissolved, most Ögödeids were either executed or exiled from Central Asia, their army redistributed among the other imperial branches and their territories mostly incorporated into the *qaghan*'s realm. Only a few minor princes who had supported Möngke received small and widely separated appanages. The Chaghadaids retained their *ulus* status but their ranks were also thinned: leading princes and commanders were either executed or exiled. Yesü Möngke was deposed in favour of Qara Hülegü, who had supported Möngke, but he died before reaching Turkestan, and was replaced by his widow, Orghina, Chinggis's granddaughter, who acted as a regent for their infant

4 al-Juvainī/Boyle, pp. 107–14; Rashīd al-Dīn/Boyle, p. 156; Allsen, 'Maḥmūd Yalavač', in de Rachewiltz *et al.* 1993, p. 124.
5 Harawī, 1994, pp. 127–8; Rashīd al-Dīn/Boyle, pp. 189–90; Jackson, 1992, p. 344.
6 Qarshī, p. 138.

son Mubārak Shāh. Chaghadaid weakness was quickly manipulated by the Jochids, who extended their control to Transoxania and Western Turkestan. The two defeated *ulus*es were thus reduced to varying degrees of impotency.[7]

The struggle between Qubilai and Arigh Böke, which followed Möngke's death (1259), gave the deprived *ulus*es of Central Asia a chance to restore their fortunes. The Toluid contenders tried to secure a Chaghadaid alliance, each appointing his protégé to the *qaghan*'s office: Qubilai sent Abishqa, Chaghadai's great-grandson who had been raised in China, to marry Orghina, but Arigh Böke engineered Abishqa's death before he reached Turkestan. He then appointed his supporter, Alghu, Chaghadai's grandson from Baidar, to head the *ulus*. In 1261 Arigh Böke sent Alghu to organize supply shipments from Central Asia to Mongolia. Taking advantage of the Golden Horde's preoccupation with the Ilkhanate in the early 1260s, Alghu (r. 1261–6) took over the former Chaghadaid territories and much more at the expense of the Golden Horde, the Ögödeids and the *qaghan*. Soon afterwards, in 1263, he switched his support to Qubilai, thereby largely facilitating the latter's victory. As a reward, Qubilai confirmed Alghu's rule over the territory stretching from the Altai to the Oxus, including the former Ögödeid realm as well. Even before that, Alghu gained the alliance of Orghina, who married him, and of Masʿūd Beg, the experienced administrator of Central Asia.[8] Yet before the Chaghadaids could fully benefit from Alghu's achievements, Ögödei's grandson, Qaidu, appeared on the scene and gained control over Central Asia.

The reign of Qaidu: 1271–1301[9]

Qaidu (1236–1301) was born to Ögödei's son Kashi and grew up in Ögödei's *ordu*. Too young to be involved in the succession disputes of 1251, in 1252 Möngke assigned him the city of Qayalïq, in South Kazakhstan, not far from Alghu's base in Almalïq. Qaidu might have begun striving for the Ögödeid cause during Möngke's reign, but the Qubilai–Arigh Böke conflict certainly permitted him to attempt the restoration of the fortunes of the Ögödeid *ulus*. His first rival was Alghu, who, after joining Qubilai, attacked Qaidu, as part of his attempt to impose his rule on Central Asia. Qaidu turned to the Golden Horde for help. With its assistance he managed to vanquish Alghu once, but was badly defeated in his second attempt, and was saved only by Alghu's death (early 1266).

The vacuum in Central Asia following Alghu's demise in close proximity to the deaths of Ilkhan Hülegü (1265) and Berke, khan of the Golden Horde

7 Allsen, 1987, pp. 30–4.
8 Barthold, 1977, pp. 488–92; Liu Yingsheng, 2006, pp. 143–70.
9 This section is mainly based on Biran, 1997.

(1267), as well as Qubilai's preoccupation in China, enabled Qaidu to expand his realm eastwards. Refusing Qubilai's appeals to appear at court, he took Talas and Almalïq and raided the Uighur capital Beshbalïq (near modern Turfan), which was under Qubilai's dominion. The *qaghan*, aware of the potential threat to his legitimacy from an Ögödeid rebel, reacted in 1268, and his army pushed back Qaidu first from Almalïq and then from Talas, where he became once more involved in Chaghadaid politics.

After Alghu's death, Orghina, in March 1266, enthroned her son Mubārak Shāh, without the *qaghan*'s approval. A few months later, however, he was deposed by his cousin, Baraq (r. 1266–71), who had grown up in Qubilai's *ordu*. Around 1263, Qubilai, hoping to use him against Qaidu, complied with Baraq's request to return to Central Asia. Although Baraq quickly turned against Qubilai, he had his own reasons for attacking Qaidu, fearing that after losing Talas he would aim at Transoxania. In 1268 Baraq soundly defeated Qaidu near the Jaxartes, but was unable to overcome the combined forces of Qaidu and the Golden Horde. He fled westwards and was busily pillaging Bukhara and Samarqand when Qaidu's emissaries offered peace. The princes set up a *quriltai* in the spring of 1269 at Talas, where they decided that two-thirds of Transoxania's revenues would devolve to Baraq and one-third to Qaidu and Möngke Temür, the Golden Horde khan (r. 1267–81). They agreed to defend the interests of Transoxania's sedentary population, whose administration was entrusted to Masʿūd Beg. The princes divided among them Transoxania's troops and artisans, formerly subject to the *qaghan*, and assigned pasturelands. From then on, the Mongols of Central Asia did not recognize the *qaghan*'s authority.

Dissatisfied with his lot, Baraq planned to invade Khurāsān, then under Ilkhanid rule, which he defined as his ancestors' appanage. After lengthy preparations, in early 1270 Baraq crossed the Oxus and established himself in Khurāsān, but when the troops of Ilkhan Abaqa (r. 1265–81) met him near Herat in July 1270 he suffered a crushing defeat, facilitated by the betrayal of Qaidu's troops who had deserted before the battle. Baraq fled to Transoxania and died soon afterwards (August 1271). Most of his troops joined Qaidu and less than a month after Baraq's demise, Qaidu was enthroned as *qaghan* at Talas. Apart from being the Ögödeid khan, he was also empowered to appoint the head of the Chaghadaid *ulus*. The Battle of Herat thus led to the accession of Qaidu and to the loss of independence of the Chaghadaid *ulus*.

This did not happen without opposition: the sons of both Baraq and Alghu rebelled against Qaidu, as did his newly appointed Chaghadaid Khan, Negübei b. Sarban b. Chaghadai (r. 1271–2). Qaidu executed Negübei and enthroned

Boqa-Temür (r. 1272–82), grandson of Mö'etüken's son Büri, whose family later challenged the Chaghadaid throne on several occasions. Abaqa tried to exploit the Central Asian upheavals: in 1273 his troops invaded Bukhara, reducing it to ashes before returning to Iran. The sons of Baraq and Alghu pillaged the city again in 1276. Conciliation between Baraq's sons and Qaidu was reached only in 1282, when Qaidu appointed Baraq's son, Du'a, as the Chaghadaid Khan (r. 1282–1307). The close cooperation between the two, which lasted until Qaidu's death, enabled Du'a to reorganize the Chaghadaid *ulus*. Alghu's sons, however, moved into the *qaghan*'s service, and garrisoned Hexi (the former Tangut region) up to the mid- to late fourteenth century.[10]

Another important advantage that Qaidu gained from Baraq's defeat in 1270 was the alliance of Masʿūd Beg. The latter and his sons served Qaidu and his family until the early 1300s, and with their blessing supervised the gradual rehabilitation of their sedentary territories.

Aware of Qaidu's achievements, and annoyed by his repeated refusals to acknowledge his authority, in 1271 Qubilai sent a coalition of lesser Toluid princes under his son Nomuqan to Almalïq against Qaidu, adding his senior general An Tong in 1275. Simultaneously Qubilai tried to assert his control of the Tarim Basin and of Uighuria, hoping to use these regions to support Nomuqan's force. This certainly endangered Qaidu, but in 1276 the princes that accompanied Nomuqan rebelled against him. They raided Mongolia, sent Nomuqan and An Tong to Qaidu and asked for his support. Qaidu dispatched Nomuqan to the Golden Horde and refrained from joining the princes, being busy fighting against Alghu's sons in Bukhara. Yet Qubilai's preoccupation with both this rebellion and the final assault on Song China (1276–9) enabled Qaidu to complete his takeover of Central Asia without a threat from the east. Moreover, after Qubilai had subdued the rebellion in 1282, many troops – and several fugitive princes – joined Qaidu, thereby greatly increasing his power. Around the same time Qaidu regained Almalïq, the old Chaghadaid capital. All this contributed to Du'a's willingness to accept Qaidu's leadership.

The 1280s and 1290s marked the apogee of Qaidu's state. During this period the Central Asian Mongols continuously harassed Yuan China, taking over the Tarim Basin and parts of Uighuria and obliging Qubilai to abandon the area in which he had heavily invested during the previous decades. They also supported other rebellions against Qubilai such as the 'Bry-Gung rebellion in Tibet in 1285 and that of Nayan, a descendant of Chinggis's brother, Otchigin, in Manchuria in 1287. While Qubilai fought in Manchuria, Qaidu and Du'a

10 For this Chaghadaid branch, see Liu Yingsheng, 2006, pp. 475–80.

invaded Mongolia, taking over Qara Qorum in 1289. Qubilai rushed troops to defend the original Mongol capital and the Central Asian princes evacuated it a few months later, but up to 1293 they continued to hold sway over large parts of Western Mongolia. Even after Yuan garrisons regained their control of the Yenisei area, Qaidu's forces were still able to threaten Qubilai's revenues in Mongolia, and they also continued their creeping annexation of Uighuria.

From the late 1280s onwards, Qaidu and Du'a's troops had also been active in other borderlands of Central Asia. Beginning in 1288 they invaded the Ilkhanate, taking over parts of Khurāsān. Here, too, they supported rebels, sending in the early 1290s troops to the aid of Nauruz, the rebellious Ilkhanid governor in Khurāsān. When Nauruz tried to assert his independence, however, Qaidu's troops were quick to defeat him, thereby facilitating his subsequent surrender to the future Ilkhan Ghāzān in 1294. Ilkhanid turncoats who had joined Qaidu during Nauruz's rebellion were, nonetheless, instrumental in future invasions from Central Asia: in 1295, when Chaghadaid forces reached Khurāsān and Māzandarān, and in 1300–1 when they reached further westwards, into Fars and Kirmān. Qaidu did not take part in these raids, leaving this front to his son Sarban, but Du'a was often dominant on the Khurāsāni border. Unlike the Yuan frontier, where many clashes between the invaders and Yuan army took place, the Ilkhans mostly refrained from meeting the Central Asian troops in battle, being more interested in their other fronts against the Golden Horde and the Mamlūks.

The invasions into Iran were connected with another direction of Chaghadaid expansion: southwards, towards Afghanistan and India. As early as 1262, Alghu attempted to seize the Ghazna region, the appanage of the Qara'unas (or Negüderi), a hitherto independent Mongol group, originating in a Golden Horde garrison, who had occupied large parts of present-day Afghanistan.[11] In the early 1270s the region was subject to the Ilkhanate, and Ilkhan Abaqa installed there the deposed Chaghadaid Khan, Mubārak Shāh, who had found refuge in his realm and who remained in this office at least until 1279. In the 1290s Nauruz, while in Qaidu's service, was described as commander of the Negüderids, and his return to the Ilkhanate must have badly harmed Central Asian interests. Yet, in the mid- to late 1290s, the Chaghadaids renewed their control of Ghazna, and the area was entrusted to Du'a's son, Qutlugh Khwāja, who acted in coordination with Sarban further north. From then on Ghazna remained part of the Chaghadaid realm, and was also a base for several invasions, both into Iran, as described earlier, and into the rich

11 On the Qara'unas, see Aubin, 1969.

Delhi Sultanate. The earliest recorded operation in India is dated to 1297–8 when Qaidu's generals invaded the Panjab, in what seems to have been one of many – and not always successful – small-scale raids of the Central Asian Mongols into the region. In 1299–1300 Qutlugh Khwāja's forces posed a greater threat. Advancing directly on Delhi, they defeated the Sultan's army, withdrawing, with much booty, mainly because Qutlugh Khwāja was fatally wounded. Chaghadaid pressure in this direction continued after his (and Qaidu's) death.

Qaidu's relations with the Golden Horde were relatively friendly, although Möngke Temür had never received his share from the Talas agreement. From his death and throughout Noghai's era (1280–99)[12] the Horde was beset by internal rivalries and temporarily renounced the remnants of its authority in Central Asia. In the late thirteenth century, however, Qaidu and Du'a were involved with their northern neighbours, the White Horde, descendants of Jochi's eldest son Orda, who were theoretically subject to the Golden Horde. Qaidu and Du'a tried to elevate their own candidate onto the throne of the White Horde, but his opponent, building on the improved relations between the new Golden Horde khan Toqto'a (r. 1290–1312) and the *qaghan*, tried around 1298 to ally the Golden Horde, the Yuan and the Ilkhanate against the Central Asian Mongols. This coalition never materialized but the threat forced Qaidu to station a considerable force on his northern frontier.

Even before that, the need to divide the Central Asian troops between various fronts, in the mid- to late 1290s, resulted in a series of defeats at the hands of the Yuan, where the new *qaghan*, Qubilai's grandson, Temür (r. 1295–1307), strengthened the border defences and attracted defectors from Qaidu's troops. In late 1298 Du'a set out to redress these setbacks and, taking Yuan border commanders by surprise, captured Temür's son-in-law, Körgüz, who commanded a garrison west of the Yenisei. The enraged Temür decided to eliminate the Central Asian menace. In 1300 a huge Yuan force under the newly appointed garrison commander, Qaishan (Temür's subsequent heir), moved to the Altai region to face Qaidu. The decisive battle took place in September 1301 south of the Altai and involved most of the troops of Qaidu and Du'a. After a fierce struggle Qaidu won the day but his death shortly afterwards enabled the Yuan to portray it as their victory.

Qaidu was the real founder of the Mongol state in Central Asia. Under his rule it asserted its independence from the *qaghan* and achieved a certain political and economic stability. Yet Qaidu was never strong enough to dismantle the Chaghadaids who retained their separate army and *ulus* inside his

12 For Noghai, a Jochid prince who acted as a joint ruler with the Golden Horde's khans, see Vásáry's chapter in this volume.

state. Their special position led to the collapse of the Ögödeid state soon after Qaidu's demise.

The return of the Chaghadaids: Du'a's house and its competitors up to the rise of the emirs (1301–1347)

With Qaidu's death the Chaghadaids resumed their independence under Du'a, yet the annihilation of the Ögödeids and its repercussions undermined the khanate's stability. On his death-bed, Qaidu ordered his sons to heed the advice of Du'a. Using his position as king-maker, the latter did not enthrone Qaidu's designated heir, his son Orus, but Qaidu's older but less competent son, Chapar. Despite certain Ögödeid resistance, in the spring of 1303 Chapar was solemnly enthroned in Emil. Soon afterwards, Du'a led a dramatic shift in the political orientation of the Central Asian Mongols and pursued peace with the Yuan. He explained his move in terms of Chinggisid unity, aspirations to continue Mongol expansion, securing the empire's trade routes and relieving the Chaghadaid army and subjects. More salient reasons were the fear of a joint Mongol attack on Central Asia, which the White Horde again proposed in 1302–3, and Du'a's wish to free himself of Ögödeid control.

Temür gladly accepted Du'a's peace proposal. Unlike Qaidu, Du'a posed no threat to the *qaghan*'s legitimacy, the economic and military advantages of appeasing the northern border were clear enough, and after three decades of Qaidu's activity the Yuan had already given up its control of Central Asia. In late 1304 Du'a and Chapar surrendered to Temür, thereby creating a global peace in the Mongol world, which included also the settlement of other inter-Mongol conflicts.[13] Du'a indeed used the peace for continuing the expansion into India, the only non-Mongol front open for the Chaghadaids. In 1303 and 1305 Chaghadaid troops threatened Delhi, in coordination with the Qara'unas. Smaller-scale raids continued in the next years as well, but the conflicts between Ögödeids and Chaghadaids, which became apparent in the attackers' ranks, enabled the Delhi Sultanate to defeat the invaders who retreated to Ghazna.[14]

Ironically, in Central Asia the general peace merely marked the beginning of bloody warfare between the Ögödeids and the Chaghadaids. Chapar failed to reap any benefit from the peace he had promoted: not only was he treated as Du'a's equal, he also had to give up some of his territory to the Chaghadaids. Chaghadaid attempts to replace the Ögödeids in Central Asia opened a series of skirmishes in Transoxania, Talas and, most importantly, on the Yuan

13 Biran, 1997, pp. 70–5.
14 Vaṣṣāf, pp. 510, 517; Jackson, 1999a, pp. 222–31.

frontier, where Orus, Qaidu's chosen heir, was stationed with Qaidu's crack troops. Only with Yuan help were the Chaghadaids able to win. In June 1306, a joint force of Du'a and the Yuan commander in the Altai, the future *qaghan*, Qaishan (r. 1308–11), whom Du'a had manipulated to believe that Orus had plotted against him, badly defeated Orus. Many of his troops, including leading princes in Qaidu's entourage, defected to the *qaghan*, and thus a considerable part of the Ögödeid army was absorbed by Yuan garrisons. The Yuan took over the Irtysh and the Altai regions, formerly under Chapar. In 1307 these regions together with most of Mongolia were organized into Yuan Lingbei province, which became home for a huge nomadic population formerly under Qaidu. Simultaneously other supporters of Qaidu were beaten on various fronts and surrendered either to the Ilkhanate or to the Golden Horde. In late 1306 the desperate Chapar therefore surrendered to Du'a. The latter assigned him an appanage and a salary but continued splitting the Ögödeid ranks, deposing Chapar in favour of another, but otherwise unknown, son of Qaidu, Yanchichar, and giving special rights to Güyük's grandson. Only Du'a's demise in early 1307 temporarily prevented the complete dissolution of the Ögödeid *ulus*.[15]

Du'a was succeeded by his son Könchek (r. 1307–8). Könchek continued Du'a's policies of expansion into India and curtailment of Ögödeid power, and was challenged by the demands of the new Yuan *qaghan*, who saw himself eligible for a share of the taxes of core Chaghadaid territories – Talas, Tashkent and Samarqand,[16] though this probably never materialized. After Könchek's untimely death, the throne was taken by Naliqo'a (r. 1308–9), brother of Böke Temür, the Chaghadaid khan who had preceded Du'a, and a Muslim. Opposition began among his immediate family, and gained force because of his pro-Muslim policies and his non-Du'aid descent. The opposition rallied around Du'a's son, Kebek, who with the help of Naliqo'a's Du'aid commanders managed to arrange his assassination during a banquet (*toy*) in 1308/9.

These struggles gave Qaidu's sons a last chance to regain power. In 1309 they attacked Kebek, who had just concluded his war with Naliqo'a. Recruiting the whole Chaghadaid army and some Ögödeid collaborators, Kebek managed to beat them, and in 1310 Chapar (with Yanchichar who died en route) therefore submitted to the Yuan. Chapar's arrival into the Yuan court, a journey that Qaidu refused to make since 1264, was solemnly celebrated in Dadu, where Chapar received Qaidu's frozen revenues from his Chinese appanages and the title Prince of Running (in Henan) which he passed on to his son

15 Vaṣṣāf, pp. 510–12; Qāshānī, pp. 33–6, 54; Biran, 1997, pp. 73–7.
16 *YS*, ch. 22, pp. 502–3.

and grandson. The year 1310 also marked the end of the Ögödeid state: Qaidu's domains south and west of the Altai were taken over by the Yuan, whereas most of the remaining Ögödeid territory was annexed to the Chaghadaid Khanate. Ögödeid princes served in the ranks of the Yuan, the Chaghadaids and even the Ilkhanate, but they no longer had their own polity, leaving Mongol rule in Central Asia to the Chaghadaids.[17]

After defeating Chapar, in 1309 Kebek orchestrated the enthronement of his older brother, Esen-Boqa (r. *c.* 1309/10–1319/20), who was called from Afghanistan. As a reward, Esen-Boqa let Kebek choose the khanate's best warriors for his personal guard and sent him westwards to administer Ferghana and Transoxania.[18] Another brother was sent to assert Chaghadaid control over the Qara'unas and the Indian frontier. Yet the main challenge to Esen-Boqa's reign came from the east. After the Yuan took over Chapar's realm, the winter and summer pastures of several Chaghadaid princes came under Yuan control, and the proximity of Yuan and Chaghadaid troops in Uighuria and the Altai created multiple opportunities for conflict. The simultaneous attempts of the Yuan to limit the volume of trade from Central Asia added to the tension. After his negotiation with Yuan garrison commanders over pasture rights failed in 1312 and his commander in Afghanistan suffered a defeat at the hands of the Ilkhan Öljeitü (r. 1305–16), Esen-Boqa feared a joint Yuan–Ilkhanid coalition. He detained Yuan and Ilkhanid diplomatic missions and contacted the new Golden Horde khan, Özbek (r. 1312–42). The latter, however, chose to side with the *qaghan* and may even have sent a considerable military force against the Chaghadaids. In 1314 Esen-Boqa twice attacked Yuan border commanders but lost. To compensate for the defeat, he sent Kebek to invade Khurāsān. Kebek vanquished the Ilkhanid troops, and Esen-Boqa joined him in Khurāsān. Yuan garrisons, now strengthened by Qaidu's former troops, took advantage of his absence. In 1316 they penetrated deeply into the Chaghadaid realm, reaching as far as Talas and the Issyk Kul and plundering Esen-Boqa's household. The Yuan soon withdrew, but they improved their positions on the borders and retook Qara Khojo, the Uighur capital. Small-scale warfare on the Yuan–Chaghadaid frontier continued until the end of Esen-Boqa's reign in 1319–20.[19]

Simultaneously, Kebek's achievements in the west also evaporated due to the defection of Prince Yasawur to the Ilkhanate. Yasawur, a grandson

17 Liu Yingsheng, 1986; Biran, 1997, pp. 69–80.
18 Qāshānī, pp. 149–50; Naṭanzī, p. 107; Vaṣṣāf, pp. 518–20; Kato, 1991, p. 103.
19 al- ʿUmarī/Lech, p. 79; Yuan Jue, n.d., ch. 34, pp. 512–13; Qāshānī, pp. 202–5; Liu Yingsheng, in Amitai-Preiss and Biran, 2005, pp. 339–53.

of Buqa-Temür, hence a non-Du'aid, had been the senior Chaghadaid commander in Transoxania prior to Kebek's arrival, and the two were often at odds, especially during the 1315 invasion of Khurāsān. In 1316, after a Yuan victory and elaborate negotiations with Öljeitü, Yasawur plundered Transoxania and crossed the Oxus accompanied by a *tümen* of his personal troops and by other princes and soldiers, some 30,000–40,000 warriors and their families. Ilkhan Öljeitü gladly appointed him over Khurāsān, a nomination confirmed by Öljeitü's heir, Abū Saʿīd (r. 1316–35). Yasawur had difficulty in asserting his authority, especially over the Kartid dynasty of Herat, but he had grand aspirations that included Iran and Iraq. In 1319, taking advantage of Abū Saʿīd's internal and external difficulties, Yasawur revolted against him. Abū Saʿīd turned to the Chaghadaids for help and Kebek, who in early 1320 inherited Esen-Boqa's throne, was happy to comply. In the spring of 1320 Kebek's troops executed Yasawur, winning back most of his emirs and offspring who returned to Transoxania.[20] Kebek, whose reign marked the zenith of the Chaghadaid khanate, also won over the Qara'unas in Afghanistan and in 1321–2 renewed Chaghadaid invasions into India. In 1322, allied with Özbek, he invaded Khurāsān, provoking an Ilkhanid retaliatory attack on Kebek's brother and commander in Afghanistan, Tarmashirin, in 1326. Tarmashirin was badly routed, but Ghazna remained in Chaghadaid hands.

Since his accession Kebek pursued peace with the Yuan, aware of the economic advantages of such a move, but he had first to quell the opposition of his emirs in the east who preferred to continue raiding. In 1323, Kebek was finally able to submit to the Yuan, thereby establishing tribute relations which continued for several decades. As part of the deal, Kebek may have regained Uighuria, since a Mongol document from Turfan cites his orders.[21] Kebek's main interest, however, remained in the west, and he is famous more for shaping the *ulus*'s internal affairs than for his active foreign policy. Unlike his predecessors, he took up residence in Transoxania, building a capital in Qarshī (Turk. 'palace'), near Nakhshab, and strove to restore agriculture, trade and urban life in his war-ravaged territories. He minted new coins, which bore his name (*Kebeks*, hence *kopeika* in Russian), and launched a new administrative division of the khanate into *tümens*, areas supporting 10,000 soldiers, assigning appanages to his emirs and taking great pains to limit their powers, thereby earning a reputation as a just ruler.[22]

20 Kempiners, 1985, esp. 64; Kato, 1991.
21 Cerensodnom and Taube, 1993, p. 183; Franke, 1962, pp. 404, 406.
22 For example, Ibn Baṭṭūṭa/Gibb, pp. 557–8; Naṭanzī, 1957, pp. 107–8, 110–11; Yazdī, 1972, pp. 181–2; Kato, 1991, pp. 111–15.

In 1327, Kebek was succeeded by his brother Eljigidei (r. 1327–30), an experienced soldier who was favourably disposed to both Buddhism and Christianity. He returned to Almalïq and was more interested in the eastern zone of his state. In 1328–9 he was involved in a Yuan *coup d'etat*, accompanying Qoshila, the eldest son of Qaishan (Yuan Wuzong r. 1308–11) who since 1317 had found refuge among the Chaghadaids from his uncles, and now coveted the Yuan throne. Despite the failure of his protégé, who was enthroned in Mongolia in early 1329 only to be poisoned by his brother and heir several months later, Eljigidei retained very friendly relations with the Yuan. Simultaneously, Eljigidei's brother and viceroy in Afghanistan, Tarmashirin, raided Delhi and gathered huge spoils before returning to Ghazna.

Eljigidei was succeeded by his brother Döre Temür (r. 1330–1), who was soon replaced by another brother, Tarmashirin (r. 1331–4). Like Kebek, Tarmashirin resided in Transoxania and promoted agriculture and trade. Unlike Kebek, he was a devout Muslim who actively disseminated Islam among his troops (many of them already Muslims), and used his conversion to facilitate diplomatic and trade relations with Mamlūk Egypt and the Delhi Sultanate. Tarmashirin maintained friendly relations with the Yuan, but, perhaps afraid of his eastern commanders, he refrained from visiting the eastern part of his realm and did not convene the traditional *toy*. This attitude, which the eastern emirs saw as abrogating the *yasa*, combined with his Muslim and pro-sedentary policies and his unfortunate family position – he was the last in a long line of lateral successors to Du'a, which meant that the lineal descendants of the former khans all had a potentially good claim for the throne – led to his swift fall. In 1334 Tarmashirin's nephew, Buzan, son of Döre Temür, headed the rebellion of the eastern emirs that deposed Tarmashirin.[23]

With Tarmashirin's fall the khanate entered into a confused period, in which even the identity of the reigning khan is not always clear, a fact that attests to the growing impotency of the khans *vis-à-vis* the emirs.[24] The period is characterized by bitter succession struggles, including an Ögödeid usurpation; by rulers with different religious and geographical orientations; by the growing interest of the Golden Horde in Central Asia; and by the broadening of Chaghadaid authority in Khurāsān. This, however, mainly favoured the emirs of the Qara'unas, one of whom eventually deposed the khan in 1347.

Some sources acknowledge Buzan as khan but there were certainly other pretenders (including even a Toluid candidate). The realm was then taken by

23 *YS*, ch. 31, pp. 696–701; Biran, 2002b, pp. 742–52.

24 The classical account of this period is Barthold, 1956–62, I, pp. 51–4, 134–8; also Manz, 1989, pp. 21–57; Liu Yingsheng, 2006, pp. 430–50.

Changshi (r. 1335–early 1337), Du'a's grandson from his son Ebügen. A devout Buddhist who also favoured Christianity, Changshi moved back to Almalïq, but was killed by his brother Yesün-Temür (r. early 1337–9 or 1340) less than two years after his accession. Muslim sources describe Yesün-Temür as a madman, famous for cutting off his mother's breasts, but a Mongolian document from Turfan shows that he had an active administration, and the many coins bearing his name indicate that his authority prevailed in both Almalïq and Transoxania.[25] Epidemics, which inflicted the Issyk Kul region in 1338–9, might have contributed to the deterioration of his rule, and in 1339 or 1340 he was deposed by the Ögödeid ʿAlī Sultan, son of Ürük Temür. This usurper was quickly deposed by the Chaghadaid emirs, and is famous mainly as a fanatic Muslim who persecuted the Christians in Almalïq.[26] These upheavals encouraged the Golden Horde to interfere in Central Asia, and only Özbek's death in 1342 put an end to a huge campaign.[27] In the early 1340s there were again, apparently, several candidates to the Chaghadaid throne including Muḥammad Pulād (or Muḥammad b. Pulād) b. Könchek b. Du'a, and Khalīl Sultan b. Yasawur who may have ruled simultaneously. Numismatic evidence attests that a certain Muḥammad ruled in Almalïq in 1345, and that Khalīl reigned in Bukhara in 1342–3. Khalīl may have been identical with Qazan, son of Yasawur, who according to most Muslim historical sources succeeded Muḥammad around 1343. Khalīl and Qazan both resided in Transoxania, but while Khalīl is mentioned only by Ibn Baṭṭūṭa and in hagiographic sources (as a dervish who might have been the teacher of Bahāʾal-Dīn Naqshband), Qazan is described in the Timurid sources as a 'bad last ruler' – an evil tyrant whose whims alienated his emirs. We have no alternative evidence to balance this view.[28] Under Qazan the Chaghadaids strengthened their hold on Khurāsān, benefiting from the collapse of the Ilkhanate (1335). Most of the new Khurāsāni territories came under the Qara'unas emir, Qazghan, who in 1347, on his second attempt, succeeded in deposing Qazan. With Qazghan's accession real power in Transoxania shifted from the khanate to the emirs, although he and his heirs continued to appoint puppet khans – Ögödeids and Chaghadaids.[29]

Simultaneously with Qazghan's accession, the eastern emirs enthroned Tughluq Temür (1347–63), an acclaimed grandson of Du'a through a minor

25 Aubin, 1976, p. 24; Fedorov, 2001; Fedorov, 2002; Cerensodnom and Taube, 1993, p. 181.
26 Ghaffārī, 1964, p. 198; Rashīd al-Dīn/Boyle, p. 28; *Shajarat al-atrāk* fol. 114b; Yule, 1967, pp. 31–2, 212.
27 al-Shujāʿī, 1985, II, pp. 214, 234.
28 Paul, 1990, pp. 284–91.
29 On Qazaghan see, for example, Aubin, 1976, pp. 23ff.; Naṭanzī, 1957, pp. 113–17; Khvāndamīr/Thackston, vol. 3/1, pp. 91–3, 380–3.

son, in Aqsu. Tughluq Temür, famed for bringing Islam to Moghulistan, invaded Transoxania in 1360 and 1361 and held it until his death in an attempt to revive the integrated Chaghadaid khanate,[30] but with the rise of Tamerlane (1370), who defeated Qazghan's grandson, Ḥusayn, the division between the *Ulus Chaghatay*, as the Turko-Mongolian nomads in Transoxania called themselves, and the eastern Chaghadaids in Moghulistan, became a reality. This political division, the roots of which are evident at least from Kebek's time, characterized Central Asia in earlier periods as well. In Transoxania the emirs continued to appoint puppet khans (mostly Ögödeids) well into Tamerlane's reign, while in the east, after a short period of dominion by the emirs, real power was regained by the Moghul Khans, who reigned until the late seventeenth century.[31]

Economy and administration

The Mongol state in Central Asia was divided into nomad and sedentary realms. The nomads were organized in decimal military units and subject to princes or commanders. Under Qaidu there was a strict distinction between his army and the Chaghadaid units. The Chaghadaids also kept the *keshig* (guard), which retained its core functions of guarding and serving the ruler. Khans and princes had their own guards and these units sometimes preserved their identity after the death of their leader.[32] Already under Qaidu, the khan usually commanded the Yuan front while princes led other fronts, notably Transoxania (facing the Ilkhanate) and Afghanistan (facing India and leading the Qara'unas). The princes who manned these posts were often leading candidates for the throne. When Kebek moved westwards he had difficulty in asserting his authority on the Yuan frontier. Tarmashirin did not have a loyal commander in the east, and from his reign onwards the Qara'unas were subject not to a prince but to an emir. The growing power of the Qara'unas' emir culminated in Qazghan's taking over Transoxania in 1347.

Probably from Qaidu's time and certainly from Kebek's the khanate was divided into *tümens* (Mong. '10,000'), an area the revenues from which were required to support one *tümen* of troops. The *tümen* commanders were responsible

30 Moghulistan (literally: land of the Mongols) was the name for the eastern Chaghadaid territories, comprising modern Kyrgyzstan, South Kazakhstan and most of Xinjiang; on Tughluq Temür see Dūghlāt/Thackston, I, pp. 6–14; Kim Hodong, in Amitai-Preiss and Morgan, 1999, pp. 299–304.

31 See the chapters by Manz and Millward in this volume.

32 Ibn Baṭṭūṭa/Gibb, pp. 557–8; Rashīd al-Dīn/Boyle, pp. 148, 155, 257, 313–15; al-Juvainī/Boyle, p. 273; Manz, 1989, pp. 34, 83, 164–5; Ando, 1992, pp. 89–90; Biran, 1997, pp. 81–92.

for the collection of taxes in their regions, but it is hard to determine the relationship, if any, between military and administrative *tümens*.[33]

Throughout the period under discussion, the Mongols remained nomads, living from pastoralism, hunting, raiding – and taxes – although supplementary agriculture is also attested. In the 1320s Transoxanian Mongol emirs owned villages, gardens and mills, and were generally more willing to live next to sedentaries than their kinsmen in Semirech'e.[34]

The sedentary sector in Central Asia was under the Yalawāch family throughout the thirteenth century, first under the *qaghans* and later under Alghu and Qaidu. Beneath these administrators, many local dynasties remained in power (in Almalïq, Uṭrār, Talas, Shāsh, Khojend, Ferghana, Tirmidh and Khotan). *Ṣadrs* (religious leaders) held prominent positions in other cities (Kashghar, Bukhara).[35]

After Qaidu's death the Chaghadaids had to establish their own administration. This was based on the Khans' guard, and, under Tarmashirin, was headed by four functionaries: the Khan's deputy (an emir); the vizier; the chamberlain and the seal-keeper.[36] *Shiḥnas* (governors) were stationed in cities, and, at least in Turfan, there was a complicated hierarchy of tax-collectors and postal station supervisors.[37]

Documents from Turfan describe a complicated taxation system, the main components of which were *alïm birïm* – a general tax which included land tax and commercial imports (*tamgha*); and *qalan* (labor tax). Additional taxes included the *qubchur* (poll-tax), and various demands for the maintenance of the postal system (for which most of the *qalan* labor was also assigned). While Chinese paper money was in use in Uighuria, most business was conducted there by barter and taxes were paid in kind (wine, leather, cotton, wheat).[38] In the rest of the Chaghadaid realm, however, most taxes were paid in cash. Already in the 1220s the Mongols sought to revive the Central Asian monetary economy, and under Möngke (1251–9) wide-scale minting of gold, silver and copper coins resumed in Almalïq. In 1271, concurrently with Qaidu's enthronement, Masʿūd Beg implemented a currency reform in Central Asia, minting coins with a high percentage of silver. After the stabilization of Qaidu's rule in 1281–2, these coins proliferated in various mints in Transoxania and Ferghana

33 Biran, 1997, pp. 99–100; Matsui, 2005, p. 79.
34 Naṭanzī, 1957, pp. 107–8; Qāshānī, p. 208; Chekhovich, 1965, pp. 58, 65, 67, 68, 75, 83, 84, 107; Manz, 1983.
35 Biran, 1997, pp. 98–9.
36 Ibn Baṭṭūṭa / Gibb, pp. 557–8.
37 Qāshānī, p. 205; Weiers, 1967; Dang, 2004, pp. 15–22. It is uncertain how typical was the situation in Turfan for the khanate's other areas.
38 Matsui, 2005, pp. 72–9; Liu Yingsheng, 1995, p. 209.

as well as in Almalïq and Kashghar. Although the coins were anonymous and not uniform in iconography, their identical weight, purity and basic design suggest a central supervision on minting.[39] Further reform was introduced by Kebek, who was the first khan to mint coins in his own name. Following the reforms of Ghāzān in early fourteenth-century Iran, Kebek minted silver coin (*dīnār*) equivalent to six smaller silver coins (*dirhams*) with a new weight, which resulted in a developed monetary economy in Transoxania in the mid-fourteenth century.[40]

Due to its central location, the Chaghadaid khanate had a major role in the commerce of the Silk Routes at least during the united empire period. Most of the *ortaq*s (merchant 'partners' of Mongol princes) were either Central Asian Muslims or Uighurs. They must have kept contacts in their original hometowns, thereby creating commercial networks which spread throughout the empire. Later, although the frequent wars and political upheavals harmed commercial interests and shifted much of the East–West trade to maritime routes, the khans actively endeavoured to promote trade, for example when Qaidu and Du'a built the city of Andijan to serve as Ferghana's mercantile centre, and commercial interests influenced their political posture, especially with regard to their relations with the Yuan. Trade flourished especially in the 1320s and 1330s, when rapprochement with the Yuan resulted in regular tribute missions to China, and opened the Silk Routes for European and Muslim traders. After Tarmashirin's conversion we find Iraqi, Syrian and Indian traders active in Transoxania, often heading towards China or to the Golden Horde.[41] Central Asian exports included agricultural products (fruits, grains), animals (horses, camels, tigers, leopards), jade, jewels, furs, medicinal herbs, textile, wine and slaves, and there existed a commercial infrastructure of loans, hospices, road maintenance, post-stations and load animals for hire.[42]

While the khans maintained workshops and the region continued to produce textiles, jewellery and weapons, artisanship under the Chaghadaids did not seem to match its pre-Mongol level, mainly due to the transfer of the region's best artisans to Mongolia and China in the united empire period and afterwards.

39 Davidovich, 1970a, pp. 64–5; Biran, 1997, p. 101.
40 Davidovich and Dani, 1998, in Asimov and Bosworth, 1998, pp. 406–8; al-ʿUmarī / Lech, p. 47; al-ʿUmarī / India, pp. 48–9; Ibn Baṭṭūṭa / Gibb, pp. 542–69.
41 Allsen, 1989; see for example, 45, ch. 51, p. 3568; 53, p. 3592; 59, p. 3752; 62, p. 3987; 65, p. 4204; 73, p. 4635; Ibn Baṭṭūṭa / Gibb, pp. 546–8; al-ʿUmarī / Lech, p. 41; al-ʿUmarī / India, pp. 48–9; Yule, 1967, pp. 31, 147, 212.
42 E.g. al-ʿUmarī / India, p. 49; al-ʿUmarī / Lech, pp. 47–8; Ibn Baṭṭūṭa / Gibb, pp. 542–69; *YS*, ch. 24 pp. 550, 551, 555; ch. 27, pp. 620, 629; ch. 28, pp. 631–2; *Jing shi dadian, zhan chi*, 1960, ch. 19420, pp. 2, 14; Liu Yingsheng, 1995, pp. 202, 209; Dang, 2004.

Agriculture suffered both from the constant wars and from the multitude of pastoralists, though there were also successful attempts at recovery supported by the khans. Agriculture was restored in Transoxania after the original Mongol conquest; after Qaidu's stabilization (in the 1280s and 1290s), and under Kebek and Tarmashirin (1320s and 1330s), this time with only partial success. Uighur agriculture revived mainly in the fourteenth century, but in Semirech'e many agricultural lands became pasture in the 1250s, and the mid-fourteenth-century wars led to the complete decline of the region's agriculture and urban centres.[43]

Culture and religion

The Mongols in Central Asia remained nomads throughout the period under discussion. They maintained mobile courts and welcomed their guests in lavish golden tents. Even when Kebek built a new capital in Qarshī it was a city of tents. The mobile courts included the usual Mongol amalgamation of experts of various origins: physicians, astronomers, scholars, poets, merchants and military specialists. Hunting remained a popular and respected activity of the khans, and women held a central place in Chaghadaid politics and patronage.[44]

Chaghadaid chancellery in Turfan was written in Mongolian at least until 1369, and the rare use of a 'Phags-Pa seal there suggests Yuan influence.[45] Already in Chaghadai's time, however, his court was called *ulugh ev* (Turk. 'Great House'), the khans Kebek and Tarmashirin spoke Turkic, and Turkic appeared on Chaghadaid seals.[46] Most Chaghadaid coins bore Arabic legends, and monumental inscriptions were written in Arabic and Persian.[47]

Chaghadai was famous as an expert in Mongol rituals and customary law (the *jasaq* or *yasa*). His erudition in ritual, especially the fire cult, made him the patron of shamans in later Mongolian folklore.[48] His zealousness in enforcing Mongol norms (sometimes colliding with Muslim ones) earned him an anti-Islamic reputation, although Muslims – often adept in magic no less than

43 Barthold, 1956–62, I, pp. 52–3; Biran, 1997, pp. 102–3; Chekhovich, 1965, pp. 40, 41, 42, 94; Ibn Baṭṭūṭa / Gibb, pp. 567, 571–2, 574, 590.

44 For example, Waley, 1931, pp. 97, 110, 116, 120; *YS*, ch. 151, p. 3581; Rashīd al-Dīn / Boyle, pp. 143, 149–51, 154; al-Juvainī / Boyle, pp. 272–6; Khvāndamīr / Thackston, pp. 44, 46; Ibn Baṭṭūṭa / Gibb, pp. 557–8; Naṭanzī, 1957, p. 110; Biran, 1997, pp. 2, 94, 97; O'Kane, 2004.

45 Ligeti, 1972, pp. 208–37; Franke, 1962, p. 407.

46 al-Juvainī / Boyle, pp. 504, 507, 536, 538, 563, 586, 612; Ibn Baṭṭūṭa / Gibb, p. 557; Franke, 1962, p. 407.

47 O'Kane, 2004, pp. 277–8; Babajanov, 1999.

48 Birtalan, 2005, p. 308.

in Muslim law – held important posts in his court.[49] Despite this reputation and several cases of Muslim or Buddhist zealousness, Qaidu and most Chaghadaid khans were tolerant towards the main religions in their realm: Islam, Buddhism and Christianity. Several khans (Du'a, Eljigidei, Changshi, Yesün-Temür) favoured Buddhism, and even after his Islamization Tughluq Temür is said to have asked for a Buddhist teacher from Tibet. Mongolian documents from Turfan, most of which are Buddhist texts, suggest the popularity of Buddhism among the Mongols in this region. Buddhist monasteries were exempted from labour taxes (as was the rule in China) and sometimes also from land and sales taxes.[50] Chaghadai himself was said to have been baptized, and several later khans (Eljigidei, Changshi) showed favour towards Christian missionaries and conducted diplomatic relations with the Pope.[51]

Chaghadaid Islamization was a gradual process, which began in the west and moved eastwards. As in the other Mongol khanates, contact with Muslim elements, mainly in the army and among the local population, as well as Sufi missionary activity were the main stimulators of conversion, though it took longer to root Islam among the *yasa*-adherent Chaghadaids than among other Mongols in West Asia. Tarmashirin is credited with bringing Islam to Mongol Transoxania, and his pro-Muslim policies certainly contributed to the khanate's Muslim character, although many emirs, several princes and ephemeral khans, and rank-and-file Mongols had embraced Islam before his rise. It took a few more decades before the Sufis established Islam in Moghulistan under Tughluq Temür and his heirs.[52] The few remaining Chaghadaid monuments – the mausoleum of Tughluq Temür in Almalïq and that of Bayan-Quli Khan (Qazghan's puppet khan, 1348–58) in Bukhara – date from the Muslim period and are obviously influenced by Ilkhanid style.[53]

The Chaghadaid subject population was mostly Muslim, although there were also considerable Buddhist and Christian communities. Uighuria was predominantly Buddhist and smaller Buddhist communities existed in Khotan, Kashghar and Qayalïq.[54] Although the Uighurs maintained close connections with Buddhists in Yuan China, Mongolian versions of the Alexander romance and of an Arabic divination book unearthed in Turfan suggest that Western cultural influence reached even the most eastern Chaghadaid realm.[55]

49 Khvāndamīr/Thackston, pp. 44, 46; al-Juvainī/Boyle, pp. 272–6.
50 Naṭanzī, 1957, p. 114; Ligeti, 1972, pp. 115–83; Matsui, 2005, pp. 72, 76; Roerich, 1949–53, II, p. 504; Jackson, 1992, p. 345.
51 Yule, 1967, pp. 31–2, 34–5, 81–8, 213–14; Ryan, 1998, pp. 364–8.
52 Biran, 2002b; Kim, 1999; Li Yixin, 1998.
53 O'Kane, 2004, pp. 277–88; Babajanov, 1999, pp. 197–207.
54 Liu Yingsheng, 2006, pp. 555–64.
55 Ligeti, 1972, pp. 184–207.

Nestorian communities were scattered in Central Asia mainly in Semirech'e and Samarqand and later in Almalïq. The Issyk Kul community was eliminated in 1338–9 due to a combination of epidemics, ʿAlī Sultan's massacres and a gradual process of Islamization, but tomb inscriptions attest a Nestorian presence in Almalïq up to the mid- to late 1360s.[56] The Catholic mission flourished in Central Asia in the 1320s and 1330s despite Tarmshirin's conversion. It began as a by-product of the mission in China and established bishoprics in Almalïq (mid-1320s) and Samarqand (1329). The Almalïq bishop and his companions were massacred in 1339 by ʿAlī Sultan, and attempts at revival – like those of the Nestorians – evaporated after the Islamization of the eastern khanate.[57]

We have more information on the culture of Chaghadaid Muslim subjects: although the main feature of the Chaghadaid period is the outward migration of scholars, certain scholarly activity continued inside the khanate. Before Chaghadaid Islamization, local Muslim dynasties in Almalïq, Khojend and Tirmidh recruited Muslim scholars; the Jaxartes region became more prominent with its centre in Sïghnaq; and Bukhara retained some of its pre-Mongol prestige through scholars such as Shams al-aiʾmāʾ Kārdārī (d. 1246), Ḥāfiẓ al-Dīn al-Kabīr (d. 1296) and the Maḥbūbī *ṣadrs* (attested till 1346).[58] Among the Bukharan colleges, one was built by Möngke's wife and another by Masʿūd Beg, and after Tarmashirin's conversion his emir established many colleges in Ghazna. Law as well as hadith, Qur'an, Arabic grammar and belle-lettres (*adab*) were taught in the colleges, and scientific activity in the fields of astronomy, mathematics, medicine, poetry and philology also continued.[59] Transoxania retained some scholarly prestige, at least in comparison to India: around the 1330s the Delhi Sultan Muḥammad b. Tughluq tried to attract Transoxanian scholars to his realm, and was willing to invest heavy sums of money to this end.[60]

Individual Sufis were active among the Chaghadaids, and are credited with Tughluq Temür's conversion. Chaghadaid Bukhara was a centre of thriving Sufi activity, mainly of the Kubravī order. Among the disciples of Najm al-Dīn Kubrā (d. 1220), the lines of Sayf al-Dīn Bākharzī and Bābā Kamāl Jandī were particularly active. Bākharzī (d. 1261), famous for converting the Golden Horde khan Berke (1257–67), held an important *waqf* in Bukhara, which

56 Niu Ruji 2007; Liu Yingsheng, 2006, pp. 543–54.

57 Ryan, 1998, pp. 371–3.

58 For example, Qarshī, pp. 140–3; Sakhāwī, 1966, II, pp. 194–5; al-Dhahabī, 1982–96, LVII, pp. 138–9, 266; LVIII, p. 78; LIX, p. 97; LX, pp. 178–9.

59 For example, al-Juvainī/Boyle, pp. 84–5; Sakhāwī, 1966, pp. 194–5; Muʿīn al-Fuqarāʾ, 1960, pp. 21, 31, 33, 36–7, 40, 53–4, 55, 56, 64, 71, 75; al-Dhahabī, 1982–96, LVII, p. 266; LVIII, pp. 116, 122; LIX, p. 57; LX, pp. 178–9; Brockelman, 1938, pp. 257, 297.

60 al-ʿUmarī/India, pp. 48–9.

originated in a grant from Möngke's wife. It remained under the administration of his family until the mid-fourteenth century, accumulated considerable economic power, and some of its riches were used for the purchase, conversion and manumission of slaves. Bābā Kamāl Jandī (d. 1273), whose student was the sheikh of Masʿūd Beg, was active in the Jaxartes region and beyond, among nomads and sedentaries. Bukharan Kubrāwī Sufis reached India, Kashmir, China and the Volga region and were a major agent of cross-cultural contacts in the khanate.[61]

The different economic and cultural orientations of the khanate's western and eastern realms contributed to its dissolution in 1347. Squeezed between stronger and richer Mongol khanates and plagued by internal strife and political instability, enhanced by its two competing *ulus*es, the record of the Chaghadaid khanate is less illustrious than that of its neighbours. Still, the name Chaghadai retained a certain prestige, attested by the fact that the Turko-Mongolian nomads in Transoxania continued to call themselves *Ulus Chaghatay* even under Tamerlane and his heirs, when Central Asia did reach one of its zeniths. It is thus not a coincidence that *Chaghatay* was also the name given to the eastern Turkic literary language that flourished in the region from the fifteenth century onwards.

61 Kim, 1996; DeWeese, 1988; DeWeese, 1994b.

4

The Jochid realm: the western steppe and Eastern Europe

ISTVÁN VÁSÁRY

According to the regulations of the *yasa*, the Mongol legal code based on Chinggis Khan's ordinances, the entire empire was the property of the Khan's family, and its members divided up this property according to set principles. Every new conquest necessitated the division of the added spoils. Chinggis's first wife, Börte, bore four male children and Chinggis 'envisioned each of them as a ruler and called them the four *külügs* [pillars]',[1] dividing up the empire between them during his lifetime. The youngest son, Tolui, was the 'guardian of the hearth' (Mong. *otchigin*), and thus received the ancient central Mongol regions along the Tola, Onon and Kerulen rivers as his inheritance. The third son, Ögödei, received the territory from Lake Balkhash westwards along the Imil and Irtysh rivers. The second son, Chaghadai (later Cha'adai), whose name is better known in its Turkic form, Chaghatay, became the official guardian of the *yasa*, and received the former centre of the Qara Khitai territory along the Ili, Chu and Talas rivers (today's Semirech'e) and later the Transoxania and Kashghar regions also came under his authority. Finally, Chinggis awarded the area of the Irtysh River and the Altai Mountains to his first-born son, Jochi, with the command to conquer the western steppe, the Dasht-i Qipchāq, as well.[2]

Jochi died unexpectedly in 1227, half a year before his father. According to Rashīd al-Dīn, Jochi had nearly forty sons, among whom the chronicler mentions fourteen by name.[3] Four of them later founded their own dynasties: Orda, Batu (whose position as Jochi's heir had been confirmed by Chinggis), Shiban (or Sheiban) and Toqa-Temür.[4] Orda refused to succeed his father in

1 Rashīd al-Dīn/Thackston, I, p. 147 = Rashīd al-Dīn/Rawshan and Mūsavī, I, p. 301.
2 Rashīd al-Dīn/Thackston, II, p. 359 = Rashīd al-Dīn/Rawshan and Mūsavī, II, p. 731.
3 Rashīd al-Dīn/Thackston, II, p. 348 = Rashīd al-Dīn/Rawshan and Mūsavī, II, pp. 709–10.
4 For Chinggisid genealogies, the best source is Rashīd al-Dīn's work and two hitherto unpublished works: the *Shuʿab-i panjgāne* of the same Rashīd al-Dīn and its Timurid continuation, the *Muʿizz al-ansāb*. The frequent references to the Istanbul MS of the former and the Paris MS of the latter in the scholarly literature cannot substitute for a reliable edition of both works. For Shiban's line see Sultanov, 2002.

favour of his younger brother, the second-born Batu, but he played an important role as the leader of the left-wing forces while Batu led the right wing. Orda's authority was acknowledged also by the Great Khan Möngke, in whose decrees Orda's name had precedence.[5]

The appanage empires, which Chinggis designated as his sons' territories, were called *ulus* in Mongol. The empire which was established in the western part of the Eurasian steppe and Eastern Europe during Batu's reign, though noted many times in both Russian and Muslim sources as 'Jochi's *ulus*', came to be called the 'Golden Horde' in Russian (*Zolotaia Orda*) from the sixteenth century onwards and hence, in modern historical scholarship.[6] Where did this name come from?

The word *ordu* (variant *orda*) was a common and ancient word in the Turko-Mongolian world, originally denoting the 'royal camp, the place where the royal tent was set up'.[7] This residence of the Great Khan was often referred to with the attribute 'gold', as the works of Rashīd al-Dīn and Plano Carpini clearly attest.[8] It seems most probable that later the khans of the individual *ulus*es, as a result of the weakening of the Great Khan's central authority, took over more and more attributes of the Great Khan and thus the residence of Batu and his descendants also became a 'Golden Horde'. The Russians could have borrowed this designation to denote the entire appanage empire.

The western campaign, 1236–1241

The *quriltai* held in 1235 decided upon a large western campaign which took place the following year. To all intents and purposes, therefore, the Golden Horde was 'born' in 1236. The conquest of the Qïpchaq steppe and Eastern Europe was a gigantic endeavour for which the entire armed forces of the empire were put in motion. Batu was the military leader, but representatives of every branch of Chinggis's family went off to battle by his side. Sübötei (Sübe'etei), the renowned military leader, who had already plundered Eastern Europe from 1221 to 1223, also participated in the expedition.[9]

In Europe the Hungarian Dominican monk Julianus was the first to hear about Mongol plans for the great European campaign. The Dominicans

5 See n. 3.
6 On the Russian term *Zolotaia Orda*, see Mitroshkina, 1968; Bogatova, 1970.
7 Clauson, 1972, p. 203; Doerfer, 1963–75, II, p. 452.
8 *Ordū-yi buzurg-i zarrīn* 'the great golden tent' in Rashīd al-Dīn/Rawshan and Mūsavī, I, p. 536 (somewhat misinterpreted in Rashīd al-Dīn/Thackston, II, p. 260). *Orda aurea* in Plano Carpini (*Ystoria Mongalorum*, IX.32): Wyngaert, 1929, I, p. 118.
9 Rashīd al-Dīn/Thackston, II, p. 325 = Rashīd al-Dīn/Rawshan and Mūsavī, I, pp. 665–6.

appeared on Hungarian soil in 1221 and their primary task was to proselytize the Cumans.[10] An important Cuman group under the leadership of Prince Baibars (Barts in the Hungarian sources) became baptized and acknowledged the supremacy of the Hungarian Crown in 1227. As a result of this success, Robert, Archbishop of Esztergom, founded a bishopric for the Cuman mission whose centre was the Moldavian city of Milkó (Milcov).[11] Another goal of Hungarian church policy was to convert the pagan Eastern Hungarians in the Volga region. Therefore, four monks of the Dominican order, one of them was Brother Julianus, set out on a journey in the spring of 1235 to find and convert the Eastern Hungarians whose territory was called *Magna Hungaria* in the Latin sources. Julianus found some of the Eastern Hungarians in 1236 not far from Volga Bulgharia, and while staying among them, he learned that Tatar forces were encamped five days away (probably in the region of the Ural River) and that they were preparing to move against the Germans. A second Dominican mission in 1237 was not able to reach the Volga Hungarians as it had to stop at the borders of the Suzdal' Principality. While here they learned that the Tatars had destroyed the country of the Volga Bulghars at the end of 1236 and intended to campaign against the Russian principalities.[12]

The first stop for the Mongol forces was Riazan'. The ancient Russian city fell in December 1237, followed by Kolomna and Moscow. The next victim was Vladimir, the seat of the Grand Prince during this period. Iurii Vsevolodovich fled the city, however, which the Tatars occupied in February 1237. Meanwhile, the second ruling city of the Vladimir principality, Suzdal', also became the prey of another Tatar force. After these events, the north Russian cities succumbed one after another: Rostov Velikii, Iaroslavl', Pereiaslavl' Zalesskii, Tver', among the more important ones. Spring floods and showers put a temporary stop to further Tatar raids, allowing Novgorod and all of north-east Rus' to avoid the torments of a Tatar siege and occupation. Batu and his troops turned southwards and occupied Kozel'sk and Kaluga. One part of the Mongol forces devastated the Mordvin lands as well as the nearby cities of Kliaz'ma, Murom and Gorokhovets, while the other part, proceeding southwards, took Pereiaslavl' and Chernigov. In 1238 the Tatars essentially conquered Cumania west of the Dnieper while at the end of December they ravaged once again the harbour city of Sudak (Soldaia) in the Crimea. In December

10 On the Dominican missions, see Altaner, 1924; for the Dominicans in thirteenth-century Hungary, see Pfeiffer, 1913.

11 For these events, see Makkai, 1936; Pashuto, 1966.

12 Among the many editions of the so-called 'Report of Riccardus' and the 'Letter of Julianus', see esp. Dörrie, 1956.

1240, Kiev, the ancient capital city of Rus', fell to them. Though the Grand Prince had moved northwards to Vladimir and Suzdal' during the preceding century, the city remained the centre of the Russian Church and the symbol of Russian statehood. After this, the westernmost Russian principalities, Galicia (Galich / Halych) and Lodomeria (Vladimir), quickly fell in turn.[13]

The road to Central and Western Europe now stood open. Batu had planned long ago to attack Hungary since the Tatars were extremely angry at King Béla IV who had spread his nominal authority over the Cumans as far as the Dnieper, and had accepted the fleeing Cumans into his country. Batu made his decision and the Tatar forces quickly rushed towards Poland, Moravia and Hungary from three directions.

The Polish and Hungarian campaigns, 1241

One contingent of the Tatar forces under the leadership of Qaidu and Baidar moved in the direction of Cracow and inflicted a decisive defeat against a Polish force at Chmielnik. After this they proceeded along the Oder and, by crossing Upper Silesia, burned and destroyed the important city of Breslau (today's Wrocław in Poland). Continuing further northwards the conquerors met a force at Liegnitz (modern Legnica in Poland) led by Duke Henry II of Silesia and the very best of the German and Polish cavalry units fell on the field of battle on 9 April 1241, two days before the troops of King Béla IV of Hungary suffered a crushing defeat on the plains of Muhi.[14] Now the road into the heart of the German territories lay open before the Tatars. Germany was spared, as the troops of Qaidu and Baidar rushed through Moravia and hurried to unite with their brethren in Hungary.

Simultaneously with the Polish and Moravian campaign, another Tatar force under Batu crossed the Carpathians, while a third group, under Qadan's authority, entered Transylvania. The most reliable contemporary accounts of these Tatar onslaughts are linked to the names of Rogerius, a clergyman of Italian origin (d. 1266) who resided in Nagyvárad and Thomas, Archdeacon of Spalato (d. 1268). They offer faithful and genuine eyewitness accounts of the Tatar conquest of Hungary in their respective works, the *Carmen miserabile* and the *Historia Salonitanorum Ponticifum*.[15] The Hungarians were ill-prepared

13 The best sources for the Russian campaign are the Russian annals edited in the series *PSRL*. For a narrative of these events, see Spuler, 1965, pp. 16–20; Grekov and Iakubovskii, 1950, pp. 207–17.

14 For the Polish campaign, see Spuler, 1965, pp. 22–3.

15 Szentpétery, 1937–8, II, pp. 543–88, and Gombos, 1937–43, III, pp. 2232–44.

to defend against the Tatars; moreover, the sharp antagonisms between the king and the nobles had paralysed even any preliminary actions. The most obvious cause of the internal conflicts was the invitation to the Cumans. The latter, with their prince Köten at their head, requested asylum in Hungary in 1239, and King Béla IV, led by both religious and military motives, gladly accepted them. The appearance of Cuman masses created huge tensions in Hungarian society since the Cumans, the bulk of whom were nomadic pastoralists, were unable to adapt themselves to a feudal society based on peasant agriculture.

On receiving the news that the Tatars had already destroyed the Russian lands and crossed the Carpathian Mountains, King Béla IV sent his palatine, Dénes, to defend the Verecke Pass which was called the Russian Gate. It was here that a part of the Hungarian population had crossed over the mountains in AD 896 and from where the Mongol invasion was now threatening. By March 1241, the Tatars tore apart the Hungarian defences at the Verecke Pass. The king waited on the left bank of the Danube, in Pest, for the troops of his nobles and clergy as well as the Cumans who had been called into battle. While the main Tatar force under Batu had broken into the country over the Verecke Pass, the southern force overran the Cuman lands in what are now Moldavia and Wallachia. Their northern wing, under the leadership of Great Khan Ögödei's son, Qadan, crossed the Carpathians, and soon captured the Transylvanian Saxon city of Radna. Meanwhile, at the end of March the great military leader Sübötei guided the main part of the southern Tatar force across the Ojtoz Pass into Transylvania. Finally, Tolui's son Böjek and his soldiers plundered Wallachia and the Szörény (Severin) Banate whence they would be able to enter Hungary at any time from the south. The situation of the King of Hungary was hopeless since not even a larger and more disciplined force would have been able to break free from the approaching Tatar pincers.

Under the shadow of the growing Tatar threat, the nobles and the people alike started to look for scapegoats and found them in the Cumans. Finally, the people of Buda, both German and Hungarian, slaughtered Köten and his entourage. When the Cuman troops heard about the murder of their ruler, they headed south to Bulgaria, burning villages as they moved. The moment of the decisive battle was approaching. This occurred in the Muhi Plain, at the confluence of the Sajó and Hernád rivers, on 11 April 1241. The cream of the Hungarian high clergy and nobility perished on the battlefield. Rogerius and Thomas of Spalato both paint a shocking picture of the destruction.[16] The

16 Szentpétery, 1937–8, II, pp. 569–71; Gombos, 1937–43, III, pp. 2235–8.

king had a narrow escape and fled to western Hungary in order to meet up with his wife at the Austrian border. Later, Béla IV fled to Zagreb, and then to Spalato (Split) in Dalmatia.

Meanwhile, Qadan continued to decimate Transylvania. The Tatars ravaged and burned Nagyvárad, one of medieval Hungary's most important cities. After the victory at Muhi, Batu's force moved against Pest and butchered the city's population. At the end of April, the Tatar forces having ravaged Poland, Moravia and Upper Hungary arrived from the north. The winter of 1241/2 was so harsh that the Danube completely froze over and the Tatars were able to cross over the ice, sealing the fate of Transdanubia. Batu's force immediately captured Esztergom, the royal residence and wealthiest city of Hungary, by siege and then raced across the Pannonian hills destroying everything in their path.

While Batu's force remained in Transdanubia, Qadan's troops set off to pursue Béla IV, who in March 1214 had left Spalato for Trau (Trogir). The Tatars, having failed to persuade the defenders of Trau to surrender, went to Cattaro (Kotor) which, in their fury, they burned to the ground. After this, they moved through Serbian lands to Bulgaria where Qadan's army united with the Tatar forces leaving Hungary. King Béla returned to Hungary only after he was certain that the Tatars had actually left his devastated country.

There are two reasons why Qadan's force left Dalmatia so quickly. First, it was unable to accomplish its main goal of capturing King Béla. Second, Batu had issued an order to retreat because news had arrived that the Great Khan, Ögödei, had died during the final days of 1241. The dreadful storm had finally left. After a period of destruction lasting one and a half years, Hungary was freed from the immediate danger of Tatar occupation.

Batu, the king-maker and empire-builder

Batu and his forces moved eastwards to attend the election of the new Great Khan. With Chaghatay's death in 1242, Chinggis's last son had left the scene and none of the grandchildren enjoyed as much authority as Batu. He became the Grey Eminence in the election for Great Khan and the empire's policies. Though Batu was an adversary of the entire Ögödei branch and often flaunted their authority, for the time being he was unable to come out against them openly. As a consequence, Ögödei's widow, the regent Döregene, triumphed and her son, Güyük, was chosen to be Great Khan in 1246. Plano Carpini, who was an eyewitness to this important event, wrote in detail about the *quriltai* which assembled near the source of the Orkhon River.[17] But Güyük soon died, and Batu's choice fell on Tolui's son, Möngke, who was elected Great Khan in 1250. The Ögödeid and Chaghatayid branches thus fell from power, suffering bloody repressions. The Ögödeids never recovered while the Chaghatayids were only later able to come back to life again in Central Asia.

Where were the lands of the Golden Horde? Its central part was the huge steppe, the Dasht-i Qipchāq, country of the former Cuman confederation. The borders of this region spread from the Irtysh River in Siberia in the east through south-west Siberia, the Kazak steppe, and the south Russian plain up to the Dniester River although the conquerors nomadized even further to the west. In the south the possessions of the Golden Horde included the Crimean Peninsula, the ancient agricultural and urban communities in the northern foothills of the Caucasus Mountains, as well as the northern part of Khwārazm (Khorezm) stretching westwards from the Aral Sea. The northern border extended to the Russian principalities while in the north-east the former Volga Bulghar state became part of the Golden Horde. If we look at its ethnic composition, it is striking that the Mongols, from the beginning, were in the minority with respect to the different Turkic (Cuman-Qïpchaq and Bulghar) elements, and by the end of the thirteenth century they had become completely assimilated into the Turkic population. Besides the dominant Turkic element, Iranians lived in the North Caucasus and Khwārazm while smaller Greek, Armenian, Jewish and Italian communities resided in the Crimea. The borders of the Golden Horde, especially in the east and the south, were rather fluid and in later periods often changed. Thus, the Tatar state of the Golden Horde, organized by the Mongols, was an empire with a Turkic majority, the successor of the Dasht-i Qipchāq nomads.

The huge Mongol world-empire fragmented in the 1260s, largely following the pre-conquest political and cultural frameworks. China and Iran, ruled by Mongol dynasties, became independent. The nomadic Mongols settled down in these areas of ancient civilizations and their descendants learned much about the art of statecraft. Within a hundred years the conquered peoples and cultures were able to absorb the conquerors and their culture. This was not the case, however, in the Golden Horde. Although the Tatars lost their ethnicity quite quickly, the Turkic population, in which the Tatars were assimilated, also followed nomadic traditions and cultures. Unlike China and Iran, the Mongol conquerors here were less able to rely on sedentary traditions of

17 Carpini, *Ystoria Mongalorum*, IX.28–45: Wyngaert, 1929, I, pp. 116–26.

administration and culture. It is significant that the Golden Horde remained a Tatar state much longer and that the Russians suffered under Tatar authority much longer than either China or Iran. We can also say that it was the Russians' historical misfortune that the Tatars did not settle more directly in the Russian principalities but placed their centre in the steppe region further to the south. The nomad Tatar, after he had collected tribute and then plundered and set fire to a village, returned to the steppe world. The civilizing influence of the Russians, therefore, scarcely reached the Tatars of the Golden Horde while the Russians, on the other hand, suffered heavily from the influence of the Tatars.[18]

Khan Batu chose the lower course of the Volga River as the centre of his *ulus* and encamped with his troops and herds in nomad fashion on the left bank of the river. From January to August the herdsmen moved up the river to approximately where modern Saratov is located while from August to December they headed down the river to the huge delta region in the area of modern Astrakhan. Their summer camps reached even further to the north while their winter camps extended into the region of the Caspian Sea.[19] In the early 1250s Batu founded a city, Sarai on the Volga Delta, which became the capital of the Golden Horde. Scholarly literature sometimes denoted this city as 'Old' Sarai in order to differentiate it from another town called New Sarai (*Sarai al-jadīd*) in the sources. According to common opinion the former one must have been located in the vicinity of modern Astrakhan in the Selitrennoe gorodishche while New Sarai lay near Tsarevskoe gorodishche in the Volgograd region.[20]

The Lower Volga region played an especially important role as a meeting point of international caravan and water routes. Both Batu and his successors encouraged the region's primarily Muslim traders by granting them every type of privilege. Consequently, urban life tied to trade also prospered during Batu's reign.[21] The Muslim East, therefore, was slowly able to revive from the destruction caused by the Tatar conquerors and even historians, such as

18 The most important studies of Tatar–Russian relations and the Tatar impact on Russian history are: Vernadsky, 1953; Halperin, 1985; Halperin, 1986; Ostrowski, 1998.

19 Plano Carpini (*Ystoria Mongalorum*, IX.13: Wyngaert, 1929, I, p. 108) describes in an exact manner how the Mongol lords nomadized along the rivers Dnieper, Don, Volga and Yayik (Ural).

20 Egorov, 1985, pp. 112–17. Recently this opinion has been questioned by I. V. Evstratov, V. G. Rudakov, E. Iu. Goncharov and others, inasmuch as they state that both Sarai and Sarai al-jadīd refer to Selitrennoe gorodishche. Consequently there was only one capital Sarai, while Tsarevskoe gorodishche can be identified with another town called Gulistān. There is a strong case for both views, and this requires further discussion, see Goncharov, 2003 (with further literature).

21 For the towns and settlements of the Golden Horde, see Egorov, 1985.

the Persian Jūzjānī, who were not sympathetic to the Mongols, acknowledged that Batu was a just ruler and a friend of the Muslims.[22] Tatar posterity labelled him *Sayin* Khan 'the good khan' which was the traditional posthumous title of deceased Mongol rulers.[23]

Berke Khan: the expansion of Islam

When Batu died in 1255 (or 1256), his oldest son, Sartaq, was in Great Khan Möngke's court in Qaraqorum. The Great Khan installed him as heir to his father's *ulus* but Sartaq died while returning home. Ulaghchi, Batu's youngest son, succeeded him but he too quickly passed away so that in 1257, Batu's younger brother, Berke, became khan. It was he who, on his older brother's orders, had called together the *quriltai* in 1251 which had confirmed the installation of Möngke as Great Khan. Berke was an experienced leader who, by the time that he ascended the throne, was not a young man.

Khan Berke, who probably adopted Islam before he ascended the throne, decided the destiny of his empire. The fact that the Golden Horde became a Muslim state was the most decisive event of Berke's reign. His conversion paved the way for Islam, but during his reign only a thin upper stratum of Mongol nomadic society adopted the religion of the Prophet.[24] Khan Berke was an energetic and talented ruler whom, along with his older brother Batu, we can view as a true founder of the Golden Horde. Batu created the framework of the empire while Berke organized the Golden Horde into an actual state.

The programme of consolidation, which had begun during Batu's reign, was continued under Berke. An important phase in this process was the census, which was ordered by Great Khan Möngke in 1257 and instituted throughout the empire in order to organize the collection of taxes.[25] The Tatar officials who conducted the census and collected the taxes, called *basqaqs* in Turkic and *darughas* in Mongol,[26] encountered opposition everywhere in the Russian principalities. In Rostov, Vladimir, Suzdal' and Iaroslavl' they were assassinated but soon the Russians were obliged to accept the Tatar dictates, as did also Prince Daniil of Galich whose land, Galicia and Lodomeria, had been pacified. All of the Russian principalities were irrevocably placed under the Tatars' control.[27]

22 Jūzjānī / Ḥabībī, II, p. 176.
23 Boyle, 1970.
24 For Berke's conversion, see Vásáry, 1990, pp. 230–52.
25 Allsen, 1987.
26 Vásáry, 1976; Vásáry, 1978; Ostrowski, 1998, pp. 38–45.
27 Spuler, 1965, pp. 34–5.

Warfare against Mongol-led Persia took up Berke's reign. Great Khan Möngke decided to bring about the final subjugation of the Muslim Near East and China. He sent his younger brother, Hülegü, to completely crush the Iranian Muslim world while sending his other younger brother, Qubilai, to the east to press for China's total submission. Both campaigns were empire-wide undertakings and perhaps the last such endeavours in the history of the Mongol world-empire. From the beginning, the relationship between Hülegü and his cousin, Berke, was strained. After the capture of Baghdad the Golden Horde and the newly developed Iranian Tatar state openly challenged one another. Although Azerbaijan had completely come under Hülegü's rule, a hundred-year-long struggle broke out between the Jochids and the Hülegüids for actual control of the territory. The Golden Horde found a natural ally in Mamlūk Egypt in its struggle against Mongol-led Persia. The Golden Horde and Mamlūk Egypt had every reason to become allies since they had a common enemy and a common Muslim faith. Sultan Baybars, the solidifier of Mamlūk authority, sent his first envoy to Berke Khan in 1261, and the exchange of envoys became systematic between Egypt and the Golden Horde thereafter. In the long run, the Golden Horde was unsuccessful in obtaining Azerbaijan, which would remain from this time forward in the hands of the Ilkhans of Iran.[28]

After the death of Great Khan Möngke in 1259, his brother, Arigh Böke, was chosen in Qaraqorum to be Great Khan while his other brother, Qubilai, who was ruling in China, also claimed the office. Hülegü supported Qubilai while Berke backed Arigh Böke. The struggle was decided only in 1260 with Qubilai's victory. He was then acknowledged by everyone as Great Khan. The Mongol world-empire entered a new period under his reign, since he moved his capital to China and quickly merged the title of Emperor of China with that of Great Khan. So Qubilai actually had no more voice in the workings of the distant Golden Horde.

Noghai and his era

Mengü-Temür (1267–80), a descendant of Batu and Berke's successor, continued the framework created by his predecessors. The Golden Horde was not only *de facto* independent, as it had been during the reigns of Berke and Batu, but also *de jure*. As an expression of sovereignty, Mengü-Temür was the first

28 There is an extensive literature on the political history of the Golden Horde–Ilkhanid Iran–Mamlūk Egypt triangle, see especially Amitai-Preiss, 1995; Zakirov, 1966.

Khan of the Golden Horde to mint coins *in his own name* in Qïrïm, Bulghar, Sarai and Khwārazm.[29]

During Mengü-Temür's reign the Italian colonies of the Crimea were founded. The Crimea played an important role in the Levant trade of the Middle Ages, functioning primarily as transit markets for goods such as silks and spices arriving from the eastern caravan routes, as well as slaves. The centre of this trade was the Genoese city of Caffa (today's Feodosiia) which experienced its golden age during the thirteenth to fifteenth centuries. As a possession of the Golden Horde, the Tatar rulers of the Crimean cities took their profit from this trade. The ancient rivalry between the two Italian city-states of Genoa and Venice continued in the Crimea. When the Genoese finally succeeded in pushing the Venetians out of Caffa, the Venetians obtained territory in the city of Tana (in the location of today's Azov in Russia), on the Don estuary and where they were able to construct their trading houses.[30]

Mengü-Temür's younger brother, Tudā-Mengü, followed him on the throne (r. 1280–7). Tudā-Mengü, a pious Muslim who only felt comfortable among dervishes and sheikhs, was a weak ruler, and the powerful emir Noghai actually ran affairs. Ultimately, Tudā-Mengü voluntarily abdicated in favour of his nephew Töle-Bugha.

Increasing political anarchy which already characterized the years of Tudā-Mengü's reign, only deepened with Töle-Bugha's accession to the throne. Emir Noghai, himself a Jochid, now came into full power. From the 1260s to his demise in 1300 (during the reign of Toqta, r. 1290–1312), Noghai dominated the Golden Horde to such an extent that the period has been termed 'Noghai and his era'.[31] Although he himself was a Jochid prince, formally he was only a 'leader of ten thousand' (*tümen begi*) who directly ruled the empire's western part which encompassed regions stretching from the Don River westwards. Only at the end of his life, did he adopt the khanal title, but he was considered a usurper.[32]

29 For these coins, see Ağat, 1976, pp. 54–5. Silver and copper coins were minted already during Berke's reign (1257–67) in Qïrïm and Bulghar, with no date and name, only the title 'Pādshāh-i islām Nāṣir al-Dunyā wa'l-Dīn' was written on them, and Berke's *tamgha* was added as a distinctive sign of the ruler (for these coins see www.zeno.ru/showgallery.php?cat=1249, accessed on 11 August 2007).

30 The contemporary Latin and Italian translations of Tatar letters of privilege given to the Venetians and Genoese in the Crimea between 1333 and 1381, are valuable historical sources. For their editions, see von Hammer-Purgstall, 1840, pp. 517–22; de Mas Latrie, 1868; Thomas and Pedrelli, 1880, 1899, I, pp. 243–4, 261–3, 311–13, II, pp. 24–5; Desimoni, 1887. For modern studies of these charters, see Vásáry, 2007; Grigor'ev and Grigor'ev, 2002.

31 See Veselovskii, 1922.

32 Vásáry, 2005, pp. 88–91.

Noghai distinguished himself in the Persian campaign of the 1260s. In 1265, he intervened in the Byzantine–Bulgar conflict in the Balkans and eventually married Euphrosyne, the daughter of the Byzantine Emperor. Thereafter, Noghai and his Tatars were systematic players in the power struggles between Byzantium and Bulgaria. It is impossible to understand Bulgarian history in the 1280s and 1290s without acknowledging the role of Noghai's Tatars.[33]

Khan Toqta (in Mongol Toqto'a), raised to the throne with Noghai's help, proved to be an energetic and capable ruler. His struggle against political anarchy ultimately led to conflict with Noghai. The final showdown occurred in 1300 at Kügenlik. Toqta was victorious and Noghai died on the battlefield.[34]

After Noghai's death, the Golden Horde never again acquired the influence he had exercised in the Balkans, Bulgaria and the Byzantine Empire. In the fourteenth century, the Ottomans, who were approaching the Balkans from Anatolia, gained control here while the Tatars' sphere of influence reached only to the Lower Danube.

The Golden Age: Toqta, Özbek and Janïbek

After defeating Noghai, Toqta could direct all of his energy towards empire-building. He strengthened central authority and promoted trade and urban culture. During the long reign of his successor, Özbek (1312–42), the Golden Horde attained its most illustrious period. An energetic ruler able to keep a tight rein on centrifugal forces in a favourable international situation, Özbek, a Muslim from his youth unlike his predecessor Toqta, also promoted the Islamization process initiated by Berke in the Golden Horde. As a result, Islam, at least among the ruling groups, truly took root, and the Golden Horde became a part of the Islamic world.[35] The relatively tolerant religious policy of the earlier Tatar rulers continued under Özbek Khan and the non-Muslim communities, especially the Orthodox and the Catholics, were able to live undisturbed for the most part. The Russian Orthodox Church received a general tax exemption from the Tatar Khans in 1267 during Mengü-Temür's reign and the later khans renewed these privileges.[36] In Sarai there was an Orthodox bishopric for the Russians living in the Tatar capital, but the Russian Church never conducted missionary activity among the Tatars.[37] On the other hand,

33 Vernadskii, 1927; Vásáry, 2005, pp. 71–98.

34 Tizengauzen, 1884, I, pp. 90–1, 113–14 (Baibars). Cf. also Vásáry, 2005, p. 91.

35 For the Islamization process, see DeWeese, 1994a.

36 For an edition of the *khanskie iarlyki*, see *Pamiatniki russkogo prava*, 1952–63, III, pp. 364–491. For their evaluation, see Grigor'ev, 2004.

37 For the Russian Church in the Golden Horde, especially in Sarai, see Poluboiarinova, 1978, pp. 22–34.

Catholic missionary orders, especially the Franciscans, were very active and their main centres were in the Crimea and in Sarai. But the hopes of the Papacy and the Franciscans to Christianize the Tatars, of course, were unfounded and remained unrealized.[38]

Under Özbek, the Golden Horde was more attentive towards Eastern Europe and the Russians in particular. Among the Russian princes, the Grand Prince of Vladimir was the most important figure. The bestowal of this princely title belonged to the jurisdiction of the Khan of the Golden Horde. The investiture of the grand princely title was a constant source of corruption among the Russian princes and an effective means of Tatar control. The khan's support meant immense power for the holder of the grand princely title over his fellow princes. In the 1320s, the new Prince of Moscow, Ivan Kalita, gained the grand princely title and began a new period in Russian–Tatar relations. The Grand Prince of Moscow acquired the right to collect the taxes owed to the Tatars from his fellow Russian princes, and as a result, his own authority and wealth grew. This economic revival of north-eastern Russia paved the way for the political rise of Muscovy in the coming centuries.[39]

Despite the external glitter of the reign of Özbek's son Janïbek (r. 1342–57), an attentive observer would have been able to sense the signs of decline beneath the surface. The century-old dream of obtaining Azerbaijan was realized during the last year of his reign in 1357, largely because a weakened Iran was no longer capable of holding it, not because the Golden Horde had become more powerful. The direct line of the Iranian Chinggisids, the descendants of Hülegü, ended with the death of the last Ilkhan, Abū Saʿīd in 1335. A long period of anarchy ensued. Janïbek only briefly enjoyed the great triumph of his life. He minted money in his own name in Tabrīz and rushed back to Sarai. En route he died, and his son Berdibek succeeded him.[40]

The period of decay and chaos (*bulghaq*), 1359–1380

Berdibek (r. 1357–9) obtained his father's throne in all likelihood by murder, and shortly afterwards he himself was killed. After Berdibek's murder, the Golden Horde fell into total anarchy and did not constitute a unified political state for the next twenty years. More than twenty-five khans succeeded

38 There is an extensive literature on the Catholic missions among the Mongols, see Pelliot, 1922–3; Pelliot, 1924; Pelliot, 1931; Richard, 1977.

39 Ostrowski, 1998, pp. 108–32.

40 Tizengauzen, 1884, I, pp. 372–3, 388–9 (Ibn Khaldūn), II, pp. 230–1, 101–2 (Taʾrīkh-i Shaikh Uvais); Iudin, Baranova and Abuseitova, 1992, pp. 134–5, 107–8. For Janïbek's reign, see Spuler, 1965, pp. 99–109.

one another (even the exact number cannot be determined from the sources) between 1359 and 1380. Intrigue, murder and usurpation became commonplace.[41]

Coins issued by the Tatar rulers illustrate more faithfully than written sources the entangled political relationships of the period. The struggle noticeably raged around the political centre Sarai. For example during the year 762 AH/AD 11 November 1360–30 October 1361, silver coins had been minted in Sarai al-jadīd with the names of the following six (!) khans: Maḥmūd Khiḍr, Temür-khoja, ʿAbdullāh, Keldibek, Ordu-Melik and Murīd.[42] Thus, within a period of a single year, the capital city had changed hands at least six times.

The East European peoples, especially the Lithuanians and the Russians, made use of this political chaos. The territory of the Golden Horde shrank in both the west and east. In 1362, at Sinie Vody (today's Siniukha River, a left-side tributary of the Bug), the Lithuanians defeated the Tatars, and finally tore Podolia away from the Golden Horde. Later, in 1365–70, the Lithuanians wrenched Kiev out of Tatar hands and a Lithuanian duke began to rule there as well.[43]

In the early 1360s, North Khwārazm with its city of Ürgench broke away from the Golden Horde as the Ṣūfī Dynasty, stemming from the Turkicized Mongolian Qongrat tribe, took over power.[44] The Volga Bulghar territories and the region of the Moksha River with the small city of Narovchat as its centre were able to live their own lives under the rule of petty monarchs who called themselves independent khans. In the Golden Horde's central regions, two power groups fought against one another. Emir Mamai, himself a non-Chinggisid warlord and king-maker, dominated from the Volga westwards, including the North Caucasus and the Crimea. The khans and candidate khans of the Blue Horde continued to rule the Volga and its left-bank territories, including Sarai and its environs. It was natural that during these years of anarchy it was more important for the Russians to build good relations with the warlord Mamai than with the constantly changing khans in Sarai.

During Dmitrii Ivanovich's reign (later called Dmitrii Donskoi, r. 1362–89) Moscow's moral and economic strength was constantly on the rise, although its two main opponents, the principalities of Tver' and Riazan', continued to follow their own independent policies. In 1378, Dmitrii's forces stopped

41 For a good attempt at clarifying the obscure data of the period, see Grigor'ev, 1983.

42 Ağat, 1976, pp. 160–1.

43 Spuler, 1965, pp. 116–19.

44 Grekov and Iakubovskii, 1950, p. 283. For the Ṣūfī coins minted in Khwārazm and dated in the 760s–781 AH, see www.zeno.ru/showgallery.php?cat=1260, accessed on 11 August 2007.

the Tatar cavalry in the vicinity of the Vozha River as they were moving towards Moscow. Emir Mamai wanted to avenge this defeat, and succeeded in getting the Lithuanian forces of Grand Duke Jagiello of Lithuania and the Russian troops of Prince Oleg of Riazan' to join him. Meanwhile, the Russian troops of Prince Dmitrii assembled near Moscow at Kolomna. The Russian Church fully supported Dmitrii, and Sergei of Radonezh, who would later be canonised as a saint, gave his personal blessing for the battle. The allied Russian forces moving southwards, crossed the Don and met the Tatar forces on the field of Kulikovo. Here, in September 1380, the Russians gained their first important victory over the Tatars since their defeat on the Kalka in 1223.[45]

The psychological impact of the battle was greater for the destiny of the Russian people than were its actual results. The Tatar state, in the years after Kulikovo, quickly revived. If we examine the significance of Kulikovo internally from the point of view of the Tatars, the event for them was less negative as it was positive for the Russians. We can say, therefore, that Kulikovo did more good for the Russians than it harmed the Tatars.

The Blue Horde and Toqtamïsh

After more than twenty years of anarchy a capable new khan emerged in the person of Toqtamïsh who originated from the territory of the Blue Horde. The Tatars called the territories to the west of the Ural River the *Aq Orda* 'White Horde', and the region situated between the Ural and the Irtysh rivers the *Kök Orda* 'Blue Horde'.[46] The two Hordes did not have a common name, if the term *Dzhuchiev ulus* 'Jochi's *ulus*', which was used by the Russians, is not some type of translation of a Tatar expression. From the beginning, Batu acknowledged his older brother, the first-born Orda, as the Khan of the Blue Horde. The latter, however, was not independent but in military terms composed the left wing of Jochi's entire *ulus*, i.e. the Golden Horde.[47]

45 On Ivan Donskoi and Kulikovo, with the patriotic tone characteristic of both imperial and Marxist Russian historiography, see Grekov and Iakubovskii, 1950, pp. 289–94.

46 There is considerable confusion concerning the terms 'Blue Horde' and 'White Horde' dating back to the Persian historians, especially Muʿīn al-Dīn Naṭanzī (*fl.* 1410s), who used the term *Aq Orda* for the Left Wing (see Aubin, 1957, pp. 68–102). The standard histories of the Golden Horde by von Hammer-Purgstall, Spuler and Grekov and Iakubovskii, and a legion of works reiterating their views claimed that the Blue Horde was the western branch (Right Hand) and the White Horde the eastern branch (Left Hand). But the investigations of the past thirty–forty years, which I am currently inclined to accept, have made it plausible that the actual designation was just the opposite. For these views see: Fedorov-Davydov, 1968; Iudin, 1983 in Iudin, Baranova and Abuseitova, 1992.

47 Allsen, 1987, pp. 5–40.

In essence, today's Kazak steppe, the eastern part of the former Dasht-i Qipchāq, made up the main territory of the nomads of the Blue Horde, but the old cultural centre along the middle and lower course of the Syr Darya River, where Sïghnaq became the residence of the khans, also belonged to them.

The Blue Horde, as Orda's descendants, had their own khans although they had to obey the Batuid khans of the White Horde ruling in Sarai. They therefore did not have the right to mint coins and had to participate in the campaigns of the Golden Horde. Mubārak-khoja was the first khan to mint coins in the Blue Horde in 768 and 769 AH (1366–8), a sign of the independence of Sïghnaq.[48] Urus Khan, who took power in Sïghnaq in 1368, ruled in a completely independent manner.[49] Meanwhile, his young relative (probably nephew), Toqtamïsh, who earlier fled to Emir Timur in Samarqand, became a powerful pretender to his throne. Timur himself was not a Chinggisid but originated from the Turko-Mongol Barlas tribe and during this period, while acting as the ruler of Transoxania, was a subordinate of the Chaghatayids. Timur gladly supported Toqtamïsh who subsequently became the Khan of the Blue Horde and minted coins in his own name in the capital city, Sïghnaq in 780 AH (1378–9). After the Russian victory over Mamai's forces at Kulikovo, Toqtamïsh crushed Mamai's troops along the Kalka River. Mamai escaped to the Crimean city of Caffa where he was killed by the Genoese in 1382.

The Blue and the White Hordes were once again united under one ruler, as in the reigns of Özbek and Janïbek. The victorious new khan saw that the time had finally arrived to bring Russian principalities back into submission. Toqtamïsh's Tatars moved straight for Moscow. Grand Prince Dmitrii Ivanovich, the victor of the Don, was forced to leave Moscow for Kostroma with his treasury and the Tatars plundered Moscow and burned it down. Toqtamïsh, in the blink of an eye, had crushed the Russian hopes, which had been raised after the Battle of Kulikovo. Moscow would need another hundred years to be able to finally overthrow the Tatar Yoke.[50]

Having reprimanded the Russians, Toqtamïsh speedily regained possession of Khwārazm and again minted coins in his own name from 1381 onwards.[51]

48 Vásáry, in Schamiloglu and Kocaoğlu, 2009 (in press).
49 With Mubārak-khoja and Urus, the lineage of Toqa-Temür, Jochi's thirteenth son, came to power in the eastern Dasht-i Qipchāq. The Ordaids, together with the Batuids, became extinct on the male line by the 1360s (cf. Vásáry, in Schamiloglu and Kocaoğlu, 2009, in press), but some insist on the Ordaid descent of Urus (cf. Sultanov, 2001, pp. 140–4).
50 Grekov and Iakubovskii, 1950, pp. 316–29.
51 For these coins see www.zeno.ru/showgallery.php?cat=1259, accessed on 11 August 2007.

Afterwards, he crossed the Caucasus into Azerbaijan in order to annex this territory, which had been lost since Janïbek's death in 1357 and had fallen into the hands of the Turko-Mongol Jalairid dynasty. In 1386, he captured the capital city of Tabrīz, amidst horrible destruction.[52]

A clash between Toqtamïsh and his patron, Timur, seemed unavoidable and imminent. In 1387, Timur reoccupied Khwārazm while exacting terrible revenge on its capital city, the 'disloyal' Ürgench. Henceforth, he would be looking for an occasion to settle accounts with the disloyal Khan Toqtamïsh.

The fight of Toqtamïsh and Timur

In the winter of 1391 Timur organized a large campaign against Toqtamïsh. He set out from Samarqand, pursuing Toqtamïsh who moved across the endless steppe apparently to avoid a battle. Timur finally caught up with him in the region of Samara along the Qundurcha River as it flows into the Volga north of this city. Toqtamïsh's troops suffered a complete defeat, and Timur's force obtained a huge amount of booty.[53] But it was not a crushing blow.

The fleeing Toqtamïsh's feverish political activities gained him Poland and Lithuania as allies. He recovered and in 1394, after crossing Derbent, he attacked Timur's territories in Persia and Shirvan. Timur, now seeking to finish off Toqtamïsh, crossed the Caucasus from the south and set up camp along the Terek River. In April 1395, Timur again defeated the Golden Horde's huge forces and Toqtamïsh fled to the Volga with Timur in pursuit. Timur then destroyed the large city of Ükek (opposite today's Saratov), but Toqtamïsh was able to slip away and fled northwards to Volga Bulgharia.

Timur now realised that Toqtamïsh represented a potential danger to him as long as he was alive and that he needed to crush the Golden Horde. His cavalry first swept into the western part of the Golden Horde from where they proceeded northwards in the direction of the Russian cities. After the destruction of the city of Yelets, he moved on Azaq, the wealthy trading city on the estuary of the Don. Timur spared only the Muslim inhabitants, but plundered the city and burned it down. Afterwards, he pillaged the mountainous regions of Daghestan and moved against Hājji-Tarkhan, the trading city on the Volga Delta (next to modern Astrakhan). In the winter of 1395, his troops, having

52 Tizengauzen, 1941, II, pp. 226–7, 97–8 (Zayn al-Dīn's *Zayl-i Ta'rīkh-i guzīda-yi Ḥamdallāh Mustavfī Qazvīnī*). Cf. also Grekov and Iakubovskii, 1950, pp. 330–2.

53 For a narrative of the campaign against the Qïpchaq steppe, see Shāmī/Tauer, I, pp. 117–25. Cf. also Grekov and Iakubovskii, 1950, pp. 354–61.

crossed the frozen Volga, entered the city and razed it to the ground. Sarai, the capital of the Golden Horde, came next.[54]

Azaq, Hājji-Tarkhan, Sarai and Ürgench, the capital of Khwārazm which was destroyed in 1388, constituted a significant part of one of the central sections of the trade route linking China and Inner Asia with Europe. This was the caravan route whose trade constituted the main economic strength of the Golden Horde. Thus, Timur not only shattered the Golden Horde, but also that section of the Eurasian trade served by these cities. Although they were rebuilt, they were never able to regain their former greatness, wealth and lustre. Toqtamïsh's two defeats brought about a decisive change in the life of Eastern Europe. The Soviet historian A. Iakubovskii, following S. Solov'ev, rightly states that Timur, though unintentionally, rendered a huge service to the Russians, since it was primarily they who profited from the enfeeblement of the Golden Horde.[55]

In 1396, Timur left behind charred and smouldering ruins on the plains of the Golden Horde. Toqtamïsh became a refugee and Temür-Qutlugh (r. 1397–1400), one of Urus Khan's grandsons, became the new Khan. In the realm of foreign affairs, Temür-Qutlugh, a political opponent of Toqtamïsh from the beginning, was, of course, loyal to Timur, who had bridled the Golden Horde.

During Temür-Qutlugh's reign and the first two decades of the fifteenth century, Edigü, whom we can consider the third great king-maker of the Golden Horde, similar to Noghai and Mamai, emerged. His name became a hallmark of the period much more than the names of the khans who alternated one another. Edigü, the chief of the Turko-Mongol Manghït tribe, the core of the later Noghay Tatars, became an epic hero in Noghay and Tatar folklore.[56]

Meanwhile, Toqtamïsh had fled to Grand Prince Vitautas (Witold) of Lithuania, who was ruling his country from Kiev. Vitautas settled a part of Toqtamïsh's Tatars in the region of Vilnius (Wilno) in Trakai (Troki). These Tatar settlements in Lithuania and Poland have remained intact up to today. Scarcely numbering several thousand and assimilated by the Polish and Belorussian surroundings, nonetheless they have preserved their Muslim heritage in the Białystok region of today's Poland, as well as in certain parts of

54 For a narrative of Timur's second campaign against Toqtamïsh, see Shāmī/Tauer, I, pp. 157–66. Cf. also Grekov and Iakubovskii, 1950, pp. 361–73.

55 A. Iakubovskii, in Grekov and Iakubovskii, 1950, p. 373.

56 For Edigü and the Manghïts, see Trepavlov, 2001b, pp. 51–89. For Edigü as an epic hero of the Noghay Tatars, see Schmitz, 1996.

Lithuania and Belorussia.[57] Toqtamïsh's Tatars as auxiliary troops became part of Vitautas's force, and the united Lithuanian force crossed the Dnieper and set up camp on one of its left-bank tributaries, the Vorskla. But the Lithuanian–Tatar coalition was not able to break Temür-Qutlugh's Golden Horde, and in August 1399, Vitautas was forced to flee. It was only now that Toqtamïsh finally disappeared from the arena of history. The defeated ruler fled to the north-east corner of Jochi's *ulus* in Western Siberia, where he became a helpless exile. However, a couple of weeks before Timur's death in 1405, Toqtamïsh's envoys unexpectedly arrived in Asia at the court of the great ruler. He granted Toqtamïsh pardon in the hope of utilizing his one-time protégé against Edigü of the Golden Horde. But Timur suddenly passed away in 1405, and Toqtamïsh also died in 1406 in the Siberian city of Tümen (today's Tiumen'). Thus ended three decades of drama between these two great friends and deadly enemies.

With Toqtamïsh's demise the possibility of the resuscitation of the one-time glory of a unified Golden Horde dwindled. The Tatars still represented a power factor in the history of fifteenth- and sixteenth-century Central Asia and Eastern Europe; but after the era of Edigü, the Golden Horde disintegrated into regional polities, the so-called Khanates of Kazan, Kasimov, the Crimea, Astrakhan and Sibir (Siberia), and the Noghay Horde.

57 See Kryczyński, 2000; Borawski and Dubiński, 1986.

PART TWO

★

LEGACIES OF THE MONGOL CONQUESTS

5

Institutional development, revenues and trade

ARSENIO PETER MARTINEZ

Institutional development

Contrasting degrees of institutional development can be seen in the two Toluid khanates, that is the Hülegüid (Ilkhanid) and the Yuan realms, and in the Jochid or Golden Horde khanate. All three began as conquering, occupying, essentially predatory, hierarchical tribal confederations. But, while the Toluid khanates did, or at least began to, evolve into true states directly managing their human and physical resources, the Jochid polity remained an emergent state that failed to evolve beyond its universal formative phase. The Ögödeid and Chaghatayid khanates began to undergo an evolution similar to that in the Toluid (ie. khanates), but the large proportion in their domains of steppe to sown and of pastoral-nomadic to agrarian-urban populations aborted their developments as states.

The slowing of Mongol expansion and the achievement of relative stability by the 1260s allowed interregional trade to resume. This was encouraged by Mongol rulers because it offered revenues and consumer goods, which they could distribute to insure the loyalty of their commanderies. Their degree of dependence on trade revenues varied. That of the Jochids was initially nearly total, but even after the Russian principalities began to produce substantial tributes, the commercial revenues remained crucial because these were entirely in cash and commodities used as money. However, in both Toluid khanates the ruling elite took over control of the uppermost levels of existing bureaucratic administrations, since the administrators' own survival dictated that they serve the new rulers. In China, the disruption entailed by the Mongol conquest was mitigated by the country's vastness. Devastation was confined to the area north of the Yangtze. The Song south and Nan-Chao were spared devastation because when they came under the Mongol's rule, these already had a bureaucracy made up of Khitan and other Sinicized elements, who would be loyal to them and were superimposed on their native counterparts in the new domains. This essentially traditional bureaucracy with its rich repertory of policies based on a millennial experience gave the Mongols effective control of the population and economic production throughout China, since the lower administrative echelons had a considerable commonality of interests with the population and consequently enjoyed a degree of cooperation that usually obviated any need to call in troops. Also the possibility of upward mobility, though limited, within the administration secured the loyalty of the lower, to the upper, echelons. A similar situation obtained under the Hülegüids, especially in Iraq and south Iran, which suffered less than Khurāsān, Qūhistān and Azerbaijan. In the parts of Iran spared devastation and in east-central Anatolia, where the administration of the Rūm-Saljūqid state was progressively and mostly absorbed peacefully before the end of the thirteenth century,[1] many administrators trained in the pre-Mongol regimes survived. These included experienced statesmen such as Ibn al-ʿAlqamī from the Caliphate, the *Ṣāḥib Atā* Fakhr al-Dīn ʿAlī and Muʿīn al-Dīn the *Parvāna* from the Rūm-Saljūqids, Nāsir al-Dīn Ṭūsī from the Assassins of Alamūt, the Juvainīs who had served the Khwārazm Shāh, and Ṣaʿd al-Daula and the incomparable Rashīd al-Dīn, who rose under the Ilkhans. Moreover, they collaborated with exceptionally capable Chinggisid rulers, such as Hülegü, Arghūn and Ghāzān, and talented commanders such as Samāghār, Ṭaghāchār, Nauruz and Chūbān in implementing a wide array of economic policies: the revalidation of land titles and the institution of a thirty-year moratorium on antiquated or questionable title deeds; the creation of cleruchies for the soldiery and assarts; the procurement of young male and female slaves for agricultural colonization; the reorganization of the state's arms and armaments manufactories and of arms procurement from contractual suppliers; a banning of interest-bearing loans to procurers of arms and supplies and to tax-farmers, which eliminated the speculation that had been spawned by government borrowing and by reliance on private credit by tax-farmers and purveyors to purchase government contracts corruptly in the first place and which ultimately led to a consolidation of all tax-farms into a *regie* analogous to Wang Anshi's centralization of finances to curb bureaucratic abuse; the restoration of the previously debased silver and gold coinages; the maintenance and exploitation of the silver currency through *battā* or *bikār*, that is scheduled depreciations or weakenings of the silver currency that culminated in periodic restrengthenings and recoinages, a practice copied from South India. This also produced an abolition of vassal issues and standardization of the empire's coinage and of all weights and dry and liquid

1 Nevertheless the process was remarked and deeply resented, most notably by the near contemporary historians al-Aq-Sarāyī and Ibn Bībī. See Martinez, 1987–91, pp. 107 ff., especially 110 ff. and 115.

measures. Non-official access to the postal relay was restricted. Similarly, they eliminated abuses in billeting, and effected a streamlining of the commissary, wardrobe and stables of the royal encampment (*ordu*), and the households of the dowager princesses. Of the latter there must have been a goodly number, given the male Chinggisids' proclivity to procreate and their tendency to die young from the effects of excessive indulgence, especially when campaigning was no longer continuous. The attempt to introduce fiduciary, paper currency borrowed from China was ill-fated. We know of no comparable legislation in the Jochid, Ögödeid or Chaghatayid appanages.

As Ibn Khaldūn pointed out, in regimes established by nomadic conquerors revenue crises led to a spread of dissatisfaction within the military establishment and tribal aristocracy that was regularly their undoing. Moreover, the Mongol polities were more prone to disputed successions and consequently instability and fragmentation than other, contemporary monarchies, because succession in the former was based on tanistry and was therefore more susceptible to disagreement than succession through primogeniture. Thus, with the contraction of trade and general economic reversal which all of the appanages underwent, fragmentation between the 1330s and the 1360s occurred as commanders of provincial garrisons usurped sovereignty, seized control of local revenues, paid their men, and lived another day.

In the fourteenth century, revenue crises were due ultimately to an alteration in the solar constant. This contracted and cooled the equatorial torrid zone, reduced inter- and intrazonal atmospheric circulation, and drew the globe's latitudinal weather zones closer to the equator. With the descent of the Westerlies, the northern temperate latitudes experienced heavier precipitation and lower temperatures year round. Starting in the first decades of the century, colder, wetter weather reduced seed-yields, raised grain prices, and produced widespread alimentary stress. When grain crops failed in 1315 and 1316, the resulting subsistence crisis affected both urban and rural areas in the British Isles and north-western Europe and as far east as Poland. The resulting mortality lowered stress for a time, but as the new weather patterns intensified, wide sections of the population developed chronic nutritional deficiencies that compromised immune systems and raised general morbidity. This accounts partly for the virulence of the Black Death near mid-century. In China, a series of natural disasters, beginning with catastrophic floods in the Yangtze Valley in 1332 caused by wetter weather, killed seven million people, produced widespread famine and by mid-century led to spreading banditry, which mutated into a xenophobic rebellion under a former monk. He reunified the country, became the first Ming emperor, and pushed the Mongols back to the steppe in 1368.

Unchecked growth of the demand on revenues was exacerbated by the assimilation of the conquerors to the conquered, which was rapid in all of the appanages except China, where the Mongols were relegated to permanent cantonments. In a reversed situation, however, many upper-class native elements in China assimilated to, and became integrated with, the middle and upper levels of the military establishment through intermarriage. The demand was caused by the attraction of the generality of the former to the material standards of the latter's middle and upper classes who, given the former's privileged position, were their social peers. Another cause was the realization by the conquerors' rank and file that the power of their superiors derived from an exploitation of the conquered that was possible only with their own collaboration. However, the burden on revenues was generated primarily by demographic expansion within the military establishment and Mongol aristocracy, among whom high birth rates were the result of the pronatalistic cultural complex, if not ethos, of militaristic societies, which strenuously discouraged non-coital sex, as well as extra-conjugal sex, especially if polygyny was practicable.[2]

Polygyny, moreover, was the primary factor causing assimilation. Warrior societies inured to frequent, if not constant, campaigning and high mortality rates needed constant manpower-replacement and therefore valued high birth rates. These, given the pre-modern rates of infant mortality, required large proportions of female to male parents. Moreover, social attitudes meant that Mongol women were in high demand and brought their families high dowries. The rank and file of the military, therefore, depending on the rung they occupied, procured their wives, concubines and serving girls from the non-Mongol auxiliaries of even lower status than themselves, their captives or the slave market. This social reality explains the common ethno-linguistic transformations of pastoral nomadic conquerors: Turkic-speaking elements in the Magyar-led union to Uralic-speaking Hungarians;[3] Bulghars, who were also Turkic, into speakers of South-Slavic, both in the seventh to ninth or tenth centuries; Mongols to Turkic-speaking, Muslim Tatars in the thirteenth and fourteenth centuries.

In China the demand for increased revenues is unmistakable. A rising incidence of taxation on the populace after Qubilai and the unpopular reforms of

2 The Mongol lexis that entered Persian, enriching it with a nuanced vocabulary it had previously lacked in this respect, is replete with terms of censure for slovenliness and loose sexual mores among females and a lack of self-discipline, alertness and resourcefulness among males, as well as terms associating sexuality with dirt. It was used by female caregivers to promote the internalization of role expectations in their charges and control their behaviour. See Martinez, 1987–91, pp. 132 ff.

3 See Halasi-Kun, 1986 [1988], pp. 37–8.

Bayan and Toghtu under Toghan Temür in the early and middle decades of the fourteenth century – abolition of the examination system, the segregation of all classes by ethnicity, and fiscal decentralization, which probably merely forestalled, and in its effects was already tantamount to, rebellion and usurpation – were essentially reactions to mounting deficits and a worsening of the financial crisis. In the Ilkhanate, Abū Saʿīd incompetently or irresponsibly aggravated factionalism. When he died in 1335 it broke up into a number of successor states and was invaded by the Jochids, who had never given up their claim to Arrān and Azerbaijan. The Jochid appanage itself underwent its *Velikaia Zamiatnia,* or 'Great Trouble', shortly after the death of Janïbek in 1357, when again incompetence and a disputed succession led to almost twenty years of civil war and the transfer of a weakened polity from the descendants of Batu to those of Orda. It recovered partially under Toqtamïsh, endured Temür's attacks and regained a measure of stability temporarily. The Mongol–Tatar polity which now constituted the Golden Horde was fatally weakened when it lost its western domains to the Girāyids in the third decade of the fifteenth century, but it survived around Sarāi into the 1480s. The Chaghatayid *ulus* was titularly reconstituted under Temür's tutelage, but abolished when he or his descendants assumed legal, as well as *de facto,* sovereignty.

By the mid-fourteenth century the conquerors in the Golden Horde had assimilated in language and religion to the more numerous surviving, basically pastoral-nomadic military elements like themselves who had been left by the earlier steppe polities. They had defeated, but not expelled, these, since the Mongols had the good sense to incorporate them into their own military establishment as subaltern auxiliaries. However, assimilation entailed Islamization and widened the cultural distinction between conqueror and conquered. Moreover, since the relationship between tax-payers and collectors hardly conduced to amicability, the restriction of the Golden Horde's involvement in its *regime foncier* to collection enforcement created a mutual apprehensiveness among the conquerors and the East Slavic population. It is significant that the agrarian masses of the latter in Eastern Russia were termed *krestiane* (from *khrestiane/khristiane* 'Christians'), which became the ordinary word for 'peasants' in Russian, as opposed to Ukrainian, Ruthenian *seliane,* etc., for it was doubtless deprecatingly used by tax-collectors who were quite conscious of confessional and other differences. A similar development is reflected in the development of *villanus* into 'villain' and 'villein' in English and the Romance languages.

The social system in the eastern steppe had become more elaborate in the century before the conquests, when the recently arrived Mongols found themselves surrounded by enemies and survival depended on strong leadership and strict obedience. There is no explicit statement in the sources, but vassalage apparently became compulsory for all Mongols, as in France during the Viking raids, when every Christian freeman not in holy orders bound himself to a lord. The universality of this division into lord and vassal underlies the dispositions in Chinggis's will, which apportioned army units of ten-thousands and thousands of warriors as *tammas* (probably 'bailment, *precarium*') and granted them and, incidentally, the lands they had conquered and occupied, as appanages (sing. *qubi* 'fief', or *ömchü/emchi* (Pers. *īnjū*) 'inheritance, share of property') to his sons, brothers, *nököd*, etc. Both the conquered and the military rank-and-file were the property or vassals of the Chinggisid dynasty and the Mongol aristocracy to whom they were allocated, but allocation was temporary and there were reallocations of troops from one appanage to another and permanent deportations of conquered subjects to the dominions of the paramount ruler. Two such deportations are known to have occurred. The first was ordered by Möngke in 1252 and was conducted in the Russian lands in the mid- to later 1250s. The second was carried out in Russia in 1275 and ordered by Qubilai, who needed troops for his conquest of the Song, in 1272 or 1273. The number of deportees was sizeable and their descendants were represented among the bodyguard of Togh Temür (Wenzong, 1328–32). With the destruction of the Chinggisids' unity, most of these sub-appanages were reassigned to local commanders and aristocrats or merged with the ruler's personal troops.

Given their social structure and culture, it is not surprising that the Mongols widened class differences. This was particularly true in rural society, into which they introduced debt-slavery in both the Ilkhanate and the Golden Horde, where the original Cossacks were at least in part fugitives from enslavement. Whereas there was an absolute ban in Islamic law on the enslavement of Muslims, the *kufr* or 'infidelity' (etymologically 'paganism') of non-Muslims and the right of Muslim warriors waging the *jihad* to the persons and property of non-Muslims, who were not protected by treaty, left them subject to enslavement. Furthermore, for the Altaic and other North and East Asian peoples, as Riasanovsky noted, the enslavement of insolvent members of the community, anti-social elements and defeated enemies was normal. As in Rome where slavery was an alternative to capital punishment, penal servitude was one of five standard punishments in China, included in the dynastic codes from the time of the Sui and the Tang. Already under the Zhou, captives and convicts with their descendants comprised one of the two categories of slave labourers. Balazs has estimated that under the Wei and Jurchen in North China not only were slaves more numerous than free peasants, but there was a tendency to assimilate the latter to the former, as in the late and sub-Roman periods, when we read in Justinian's legislation *servus aut colonus ... servus vel colonus ... servus qui quasi colonus in agro erat*. As for the Mongols, Rashīd al-Dīn assures us that in the Chinggisid civil wars 'they would capture one another's children and sell them to merchants. Moreover, out of poverty many of them would sell their own children.' The practice, he says, was extended to 'poor wretches' (*mudbirān*) who had contracted debts, originally with Mongols and Uighurs. Unable to repay, they fell into 'the degradation of captivity' (*dhill-i asīrī*) together with their wives and children. Similarly deleterious was the institution by Ghāzān Khan, in his effort to safeguard the caravan routes, of collective responsibility (*ʿuḥda*, a calque on *homologia*), but only in rural areas, because it would have been 'impractical, impossible [to enforce]' (*mutaʿadhdhar*) in urban districts. This was modelled on the *Baojia* (lit. 'guarantee-family'), studied by Brian McKnight, which in essence held the people of a rural district liable for any crimes committed locally and had been copied by the neo-Confucians from the Legalists.

The Mongol appanages, like other conquest states, begged the question of legitimacy. They existed by right of conquest or divine mandate, for which their existence was sufficient vindication. With cultural assimilation a retroactive legitimacy was sought through the patronage of Lamaism in the Yuan, and Islam in the other appanages. In the former the policy was ineffective given the practical Chinese approach to religion. In the latter it succeeded because institutional Islam, embodied in its legal-judicial quasi-clergy, though symbiotic with the regime, had become autonomous since before the close of the third Islamic century and supported any regime that respected its autonomy. In fact, popular resistance was normally impossible because everywhere the conquered upper classes relied on Mongol support, while the non-military and non-criminal majority of the conquered population was effectively precluded from the use of arms and dissident elements in the military were physically marginalized. Until the mid-fourteenth-century crisis, the lower classes could offer no effective resistance because they were leaderless, while the conquerors remained united. Even when the 'Great Trouble' came belatedly to Russia, the princes did not throw off the 'Mongol Yoke' because they needed the Horde's support against the expansive Polish-Lithuanian state with its superior army, which had adopted the tactics of its traditional enemies, the Teutonic Order. Successful insurrection was possible only when it was fomented and led by dissidents within a regime's own military establishment or if the latter was divided into two or more fairly equal rival groups. Then, rebellions did break out as the conquered population coalesced under previously marginalized, violent elements. This happened in Khurāsān in the later 1330s under the Sarbadars; in China in the 1350s.

In Russia the impossibility of effective resistance caused a withdrawal of disaffected elements from both nomadic and sedentary populations into inaccessible, defensible areas. Initially this may have been permitted because it served the regime's purposes by separating potential rebel leaders from their natural following. Thus, marginal elements from both societies joined during this period to form outlaw Qazaq or Cossack bands. The term connotes 'a vagabond, undisciplined person' and apparently comes from the Mongol *ghasaghan* 'obstinacy, refractoriness' or *ghazighu* 'perverse, deviant', the extended forms of which connote 'departure from custom, violation of the law, anomie, nonconformity'.[4] Comparable developments were common on the frontiers of the other Mongol appanages and similar, originally nomadic polities, with the sedentary world: the *Arab*s or '[unsubmitted] bedouins' of the Ḥafṣid state; the Oirats along the Syrian marches, who defected from the Ilkhans to the Mamlūks; the *qarāʾūnās* or 'base-born [Mongols]' also termed *nigūdārīyān* or 'nomads' (sg. Mong. *negüder*) of the Indo-Iranian marches; the *Türkmen* that is 'big' or 'real Turks' and *atrāk-i ūch* and the *atrāk-i Qaramān* or 'Turks of the Byzantine and Cilician-Armenian frontier lands' in the Aegean hinterlands and along the Taurus in Anatolia, one of whose groups, comprising tribesmen and refugees (Ar.-Turk. sg. *jalāʾ-lī*) who were victims of an emigration (*jalāʾ-i waṭan*), forced by fiscal oppression in the vassal Rum-Saljūqid state, would absorb the other groups and evolve into the Ottoman state. Even within the appanages when governments were weak, as in the Ilkhanate before Ghāzān's consolidation of power, 'runaway slaves... Mongols, Muslims, renegades, Kurds, Lur, Shol, Syrian *bedouins*, low-lifes, petty-criminals, some villagers and dwellers of outlying areas' (*ghulāmān-i gurīkhta... Mughul u Tāzīk u murtadd u Kurd u Shul u Shāmī... va runūd u aubāsh... ba'ḍi rustā'īhā wa aṭrāf-nishīnān*)[5] would join up with brigands in the Zagros and pose serious problems.

Revenues

Revenues were initially perceived in the appanages through taxes and corvées that went back to pre-conquest Mongolia. Society there had been organized along well-articulated class lines, with clans of aristocratic status, which were royal, agnatic and related to royalty by marriage and ties of *andalal*

4 See also discussion of this term in chapter 12, nn. 15, 16 of this volume.
5 Rashīd al-Dīn/Jahn, p. 277.

or 'sworn-brotherhood' and *nökürlel* that is 'companion-' or 'retainership', as well as with commoner (*qaraju*) tribes, clans and individuals that might themselves be of rich (*bayan*), client-servant, vassal or slave (*boghol/bo'ol*) status. Property was either private or communal and consisted of herds, agricultural land and pasture, vassals or serfs, and slaves, including armourers attached to tribal chiefs and other individuals or families. Private property not held by aristocrats or exempted persons was taxable (*albatu*). Communal property was also subject to taxation, usually in the form of a tithe levied on herds, manufactures and, in marginal lands between the steppe and the sown, on crops. The tax was apportioned among owning clans and families by councils composed of their chiefs or headmen. So long as the apportionment remained valid *de jure* or *de facto*, communal property, though subject to rotation and periodic redistribution, was, in the short term in effect, private. Aristocratic or royal revenues consisted of quasi-feudal taxes owed by the rest of society. In his decree (*yarlīgh*) ordering the creation of cleruchies (*iqṭāʿāt*) for the soldiery, Ghāzān Khan listed four categories of traditional Mongol imposts, which he had either abolished or mitigated. These are (1) a levy on herd animals (*qobchūr/qopchūr-i mawāshī*); (2) service in manning the imperial postal system (*bastan-i yāmhā-yi buzurg*); (3) 'the harsh burdens' imposed by Chinggis Khan's code (*aʿbāʾ-yi yāsāq-i sakht*); and (4) corvées or personal duties or services (*qalānāt*). These categories probably embrace most of the same levies as the five more specific ones extracted by Vladimirtsov[6] from two seventeenth-century works, the Khalkha code and Sagang Sechen's *Erdeni-yin Tobchi*, namely (1) levies on livestock and livestock products, especially meat, milk, and fermented milk or *koumiss* (*alban qobchi'ur, sigüsün*); (2) service in the feudal lord's household, especially the gathering of dry dung for use as fuel (*argal tegekü*); (3) service in the lord's retinue, especially on large hunts or battues (*ayan alba*); (4) participation in the lord's courier or postal service or the supply of mounts for the same (*ulagha sigüsün*); and (5) court attendance, both as a witness or as a member of the jury (*siqagha*).

From the viewpoint of the Persian sources, the earliest of which is the *risāla* or treatise on royal finances by Nāsir al-Dīn Ṭūsī (d. 1274), the Mongols' revenues came under four classes, if we omit treasure troves, gifts and the like: (1) Tolls, customs, and other taxes and escort or protection charges levied on interregional trade whether originating or terminating in, or in transit through, their territories. Since these were monetary taxes, not taxes in kind, they were easily perceived, allocated and transmitted. In the Golden Horde

6 Vladimirtsov, 1948, pp. 211 ff.

and Ilkhanid sources as well as Pegolotti's manual these are termed *tamghās* (Ital. sg. *tamunga/tamenga/camunoca*),[7] where it also designates a tax or requisition. (2) Booty, including slaves, and tribute from agrarian societies under indirect rule, whose rulers were reduced to vassal status. Āq-Sarāyī tells us that when Hülegü divided the Rūm-Saljūqid kingdom between ʿIzz al-Dīn Kai Kāʾūs II and Rukn al-Dīn Qïlïch Arslan IV in 1259, just after the fall of Baghdad, he imposed a tribute of '200,000 silver *dirhams*, 500 [pieces of] *nacchi* or brocade and Italian *cammocche*, 3,000 hats trimmed with gold filigree, 500 horses and 500 mules'.[8] (3) The *qob[i]chūr* or tax usually assessed as a tithe on the nomads' herds. Only members of the Chinggisid aristocracy, families allied by marriage, and individuals originally of lower status, who probably distinguished themselves by their valour or other service and were designated as *tarkhans*, were exempted. (4) Taxes, mainly in kind, from agrarian and artisanal production on directly administered lands. After Ghāzān Khan's reforms, which fully remonetized the Ilkhanate's economy, we can add to these numerous cash charges for services performed by the state, such as coinage and weighing merchandise, or on the use of services provided or supervised by the state, such as brokerage, the sale of wine in taverns, and the use of brothels and bathhouses. Thus, the fourteenth-century satirist, ʿUbaid-i Zākānī, defines '*ḥammāmī* bathhouse-keeper' as 'the collector of the fornication [*actually* sodomy] tax' (*tamghājī-yi jumāʿ*). When an economy was still under-monetized, so that commutation was impossible, as in Russia during the period of initial expansion, corvées were especially important. Except to the extent that commanders who became landlords were legally liable for agrarian taxes, at least in theory, the military population and the clergy, which in China included the Confucian scholarly class with their certified dependants, were largely exempted from taxation. In Russia this feature of Mongol policy was very significant, because it allowed the Orthodox Church to amass extraordinary wealth and power.

During the conquests troops foraged in their decimal units, but they were still essentially autarkic, since they were usually followed at a safe distance by herds brought out from Mongolia, which were supplemented by captured animals. As the front moved forward, tribute collection behind the lines passed from lower-unit to higher-ranking Mongol or allied commanders. With pacification, fiscal administration was gradually removed from the commandery and subsidies in kind were simultaneously introduced for the rank and file. The task fell to civilian administrators, many of whom were Uighurs,

7 A term encountered earlier as *thamga-* in Khotanese Saka, see Bailey, 1979, p. 147b.
8 al-Aq-Sarāyī, p. 62.

Khotanese, Kashmiris and Tibetans, who were designated by the Sino-Turko-Mongolian terms *bitikchī* 'scribe, clerk' and *bakhshī* 'commissary clerk' (from Chin. *boshi* 'teacher, master') in the Chaghatayid *ulus*, from which the usage passed to India, so that in Urdu/Hindustani *bakhshī* meant 'battalion paymaster'. Although supplies were eventually supplemented by donatives first in trade goods, but later in cash, they continued to be termed *taghar* (Mong. 'a sack of grain, dried lentils, pulse, etc.', properly 'a carpet, sack, or bag made of coarse wool'). The first sign of this development is Ögödei's appointment of Maḥmūd Yalawāch to organize the fiscal administration of Uighuria and Transoxania. Over time the military establishment, or that part on whose support the rulers depended, invariably moved from autarky to near total dependence on subsidies, while the politically connected among the commanderies gravitated towards remunerated governmental appointments with their opportunities for peculation, extortion and acquisition of land. Both Juvainī and Rashīd al-Dīn bitterly and scathingly complained of the corrupt collaboration of Mongol and locally recruited administrators.[9] In China, where Central and West Asian Muslims were initially employed in the highest echelons and Persian was used in the fiscal-finance bureaus, corruption was even more rampant until Qubilai took drastic action.

By contrast, the Jochids were content just to protect agriculture from their own pastoral-nomadic military establishment. They separated the *regime foncier*'s basic functions: the management of agriculture and extractive industries and the collection and accounting of revenues in kind and cash. They delegated the former to the vassal Russian princes; they consigned the latter to contractors. Though physical work was doubtless assigned to Russian servants or slaves, for the first three or four generations after the conquest accountancy was kept in the hands of clerks. Most were Sarts or Muslims from Central Asia who were accompanied by Mongol or allied *darughas* or *basqaqs*, Turkic and Mongolian terms meaning 'oppressors' or 'enforcers'. Tax-farming developed further in the Jochid than in the other appanages, as fiscal contractors joined with merchants, the richest of whom were the *ortaqs*, that is the 'business partners' of Mongol princes, aristocrats and senior commanders. Originally tax-farms were obtained through competitive bidding, but with time tax-rates came to be based on increments projected onto an existing base and were probably negotiated between syndicates of farmers and fiscal officials. 'Supplemental' levies were also added and their management was progressively consolidated until it was a logical step when in 1327 or 1328 the farming of all

9 al-Juvainī/Qazvīnī, I, pp. 4 ff.; Rashīd al-Dīn/Jahn, pp. 313 ff.

the Russian revenues together with the title of Grand Prince was conferred on Ivan I (r. 1325–40) of Moscow. This, of course, was the beginning of the reunification of Russia. The operation of the tax-farms, which now passed from Muslim to native Christian hands, was greatly facilitated by a progressive commutation of taxes in kind into cash revenues as a result of a general monetization of the Horde's and the Russian principalities' economies that was the result of a shift in interregional trade to the Golden Horde in the second quarter of the fourteenth century. A similar monetization had occurred in the final decades of the thirteenth century in the Ilkhanate as the West's India trade shifted to it from Egypt. This monetarization facilitated the implementation of Ghāzān Khan's fiscal agrarian reforms.

Trade

The grand trade of the High and later Middle Ages was between the Latin West and South India, the East Indies and, to a lesser extent, China. Oriental luxuries were always in demand by the wealthier classes in the West, but it had little that was in demand in the East and its chronically imbalanced Oriental trade had contracted sharply since Roman times as many European sources of silver became exhausted. In the earlier Middle Ages, the volume / value of goods exchanged remained generally low. However, the opening of rich silver mines first near Goslar towards the close of the tenth century, then at other sites in central Germany and lands to the east and south, and ultimately at other sites throughout Europe, especially in Sardinia, allowed the West's external trade to be balanced again with exported silver. In the eleventh, twelfth and thirteenth centuries silver production and this trade expanded concomitantly. Moreover, silver appreciated as it moved eastwards, because silver, which was abundant in relation to gold in the West, was relatively scarce in relation to gold in the East, especially in South India, where, along with West and South-East Africa, most of the gold was mined or washed in the Middle Ages. Gold similarly appreciated as it moved in the opposite direction.

There were four types of commodities: (1) expensive goods, mostly with little bulk or weight and therefore low transportation costs and high profit margins, so called *spezierie* or 'spices', that is aromatics, condiments, dyes, drugs, silks and other luxury fabrics, gems, jewellery, etc., mainly from India, the Indies and China, and furs from Russia; (2) bullion, though this was normally classed with the foregoing; (3) lower-cost, bulkier items for which there was broad demand, or industrial raw materials, which can be subdivided into (a) grain, lumber, ferrous metals, wax and non-luxury cloth, and (b) transportable, non-perishable or preserved foodstuffs (edible oils, sugar, wine, dried fruit, salted fish and caviar, etc.), and (4) slaves. Spices, gems and bullion were the most profitable commodities; the profitability of the others was lower, but varied considerably as demand and supply fluctuated independently. All four appanages participated in the first two types; the last two were the specialty of the Golden Horde.

Revenues from trade were precarious. These depended on the security of its routes and hence on the ability of governments to maintain security and protect traders and their wares. Failure to provide this forced traders to seek alternate routes. Also, commerce depended on profitability and therefore on the difference between the cost of goods and their transportation to the merchant, as well as his own expenses, on the one hand, and his sales revenues, on the other. The former could be controlled to an extent; the latter too often could not, as these depended on effective demand, which underwent periodic cyclical, and thus short-term minor, crises as the result of rises in grain prices caused by adverse weather and poor harvests. Moreover, socio-political, economic and even climatic changes produced major, systemic and structural crises that were enduring.

In the thirteenth and fourteenth centuries, East–West trade went by three routes, a mainly maritime, southern route through Egypt, with low transportation costs but high taxes and charges; a largely maritime, middle route with an overland stage between the Asiatic coast of the Mediterranean and the Persian Gulf, where higher transportation costs were offset by reduced charges; and a northerly, mainly overland route across Eurasia to China, India, etc. This route could begin in either the Black Sea or Mediterranean ports and its first overland leg went through either the Ilkhanate or the Golden Horde. The Ilkhanid overland route had been taken first by Marco Polo's father and uncle. On the second journey with Marco they had planned to go by sea, but, on learning in Hormuz that the sea route was blocked (probably by a Malay attack on Ceylon), they proceeded overland. Indeed, the Ilkhanid leg was the one preferred on the overland route down to the 1330s, after which traffic shifted to the Pontic ports.[10] In the period under consideration, all three routes

10 This is established by the rise in importance of the mints in north-eastern Persia during the first third of the fourteenth century. Between 1258 and 1297–8, they accounted for only 5 per cent of the total Ilkhanid mint output in gold and silver, all of their output being in silver. Between 1298–9 and 1333–4, they accounted for 13.2 per cent of total, 21.7 per cent of gold, and 6.5 per cent of all silver issued. Between 1334–5 and 1355–6, the same per cents were 3.7, 0 and 4.5. See Martinez, 1984, Tables VII–IX, pp. 140 ff. Similarly all thirty-nine Ilkhanid gold and silver specimens from Astarābād, Dāmgjān, Simnān, Shahristān, Jājarm, Jurjān, Sabzivār, Khabūhān, Isfarāyin, Nīshāpūr, Ṭūs and Bahrzan in the Album, 2001 and Lane-Poole, 1877, 1881, 1890–1 catalogues were issued between

were used, but each one or each leg more than the others in different sub-periods. Thus the polities along the routes saw expansions and contractions in their revenues and different degrees of monetization accordingly. They went through times during which rising and high monetary revenues from trade allowed them to consolidate control of their military establishments and rationalize their fiscal-financial operations, and other times when declining revenues loosened that control, forcing a return to less efficient collections and payments. This led to their fragmentation and decline or demise. The first route was under Mamlūk, the second under Ilkhanid, control. The western leg of the third, was under either Ilkhanid or Jochid control.

As the Ilkhanate's trade and trade revenues, which were calculated as percentages of merchandise value, fell, the resulting factionalism at the death of Abu Saʿīd in 1335 made its trade routes unsafe; the resulting boycott of its routes caused its fragmentation. Part of its trade shifted to Egypt. Venice negotiated 'modifications' of the papal ban on trade with the Mamlūks, obtained 'a concession of grace' and in 1345 after a suspension of twenty-two years resumed regular sailings to Alexandria (*concessio gratiae navium pro viaggio Alexandriae*)[11] of the convoys of armed galleys built, owned and leased by the state for the *muda* or regular, scheduled crossing between two points.[12] The main beneficiary, however, was the Golden Horde, with which Venice and Genoa hastily resolved a quarrel that had led to war with the Horde, since it offered access to both China and India.

The trade of the Golden Horde flowed through the ports of the Euxine on the Crimea and at the mouth of the Don. With the fall of Constantinople to the Fourth Crusade (1204), Venice claimed as her share 'a quarter and a half' (3/8) of the Byzantine Empire and took *inter alia* the southern coast of the Crimea, called Gothia, the chief ports of which were Soldaia (Sughdaq, Sughdaia) and Caffa. However, with the recapture of Constantinople by the Greeks (1261), the Venetians were replaced by Michael Palaeologus' (r. 1261–82) Genoese allies, who had demanded exclusive rights to the navigation and commerce of the Euxine. He admitted them and their Pisan rivals, who established a factory, Porto Pisano, near the mouth of the Don, and for a while excluded

the reigns of Arghūn and Tughā Temür, or between 1283–4 and almost certainly only as late as the early 1340s. (The last dated specimen was issued in Jājarm in 1342–3.) Of these thirty-nine, ten are gold. Between 1300–01 and 1332–3, of thirty-three specimens, ten are gold; between 1328–9 and 1332–3, of ten specimens, seven are gold, which indicates the exportation of gold from the Delhi Sultanate into Central Asia.

11 Thomas and Pedrelli, 1880, I, p. 277, no. 144.

12 The term is the Ar. *muʿdā*, a ferrying between two opposite coasts from *ʿdw* 'to lie opposite; to oppose, be hostile'.

the Venetians. The great student of Genoa's Black Sea trade, George Bratianu, dates the foundation of the Genoese colony at Caffa to 1265. Be that as it may, a few years later Mëngü Temür gave Caffa to a relative, Uran Temür, who sold it to the Genoese. Somewhat later Palaeologus concluded a treaty of peace with Venice, which allowed her access to the Euxine.

The fortune of Caffa was made with the treaties concluded in 1263 by Baibars with Michael Palaeologus and Berke and by the enlightened toleration of the Mongol rulers. The second treaty caught the Ilkhanate between two hostile neighbours, who would henceforth coordinate their policy and check further Ilkhanid expansion. The first allowed Egyptian merchants free passage through the straits and laid the foundation for the rich trade in slaves between Egypt and the Horde, including boys and youths to be trained as Mamlūks, a trade in which the Genoese and Egyptian merchants collaborated, despite an intensification of the papal embargo.

The commerce of the Pontic ports was basically two separate trades. That with Egypt was part of the trade between the Euxine and Mediterranean regions, which went back to the time of Greek colonization. The other was the overland trade between the West and East and South Asia in *spezierie*, especially silk. This second trade had opened for a century or two in the last century BC and again during the sixth century. It opened a third time following the establishment of peace among the warring appanages with the final defeat of the Ögödeids and flourished during the earlier and middle decades of the fourteenth century. It never exceeded the first trade in volume, but it did in value, since its margin of profit was much higher. The rise and fall of the revenues it generated determined the balance of centripetal and centrifugal forces in the Golden Horde.

Interestingly, before the rise of the overland Eurasian trade, the Genoese developed a triangular trade, for which they developed the Rūm-Saljūqid ports on the Black Sea, notably Samsun, Sinop and 'Vatiza' as early as the 1270s, in which they sold silver in the Ilkhanate to procure goods that would either be resold in the West and to the ruling elite in the Golden Horde or more likely to the court for redistribution to the commanderies, as was the case with the luxury fabrics and the fancy hats demanded by Hülegü in Anatolia. With the proceeds from the resale of these in Soldaia, not Caffa, the Genoese purchased in the Crimea the goods that they re-exported throughout the Mediterranean. Thus, even the few notarial acts from Caffa, Soldaia, etc. published by Bratianu reveal the commodities of the Crimean trade well before the fourteenth century: imports of luxury goods from the West and the Ilkhanate, most notably silk from Mosul and Gilan (*seta gaieli*, *fardelum unum sete guieli, qui est menarum quinquaginta* (cf. Pegolotti's *seta ghella*)), gold thread, buckram, Lombard cloth, velvets or velours, 'five bales of cloth from Rheims' (*balletas quinque telarum de Rens*), the same Cretan, Greek and Italian wines that also appear prominently in Pegolotti's section on Tana, as well as silver in coin and bars.[13] Apart from slaves, exports consisted of wax, linen, salted sturgeon and other fish, caviar,[14] and, of course, grain, wheat, barley and millet, on which Constantinople and Pera and other cities in Greece and the Archipelago soon became entirely dependent.

The importance of the Pontic trade for Venice, and the troubles that beset it, are reflected in the succession of diplomatic negotiations and agreements that Venice conducted with the Jochids and their governors as well as with her traditional rival Genoa. Four treaties were concluded, one with Özbek (r. 1312–42), two with Janïbek, one with Berdibek, in 1333, 1342, 1347 and 1358, at the same time as a *privilegium* was obtained from the 'lord' or governor of Soldaia guaranteeing Venetians fair treatment there and in two other ports in return for their indemnifying an Armenian *ortāq* of the still-powerful Taydūla Khātūn, once the favourite wife of Janïbek's father, Özbek. A similar agreement had been concluded with an earlier governor of Soldaia in 1356. Finally, an embassy was sent to Toqtamïsh in 1383 demanding restitution and security for Venetian merchants, and pointedly reminding him of how beneficial Venice's commerce was for him and his subjects (*multum accomoda et utilis suo imperio et suis*).[15] The deliberations of the Venetian Senate (*consilium rogatorum* or the *pregadi*) between 1344 and 1348 contain frequent references to 'the business of Tana' and 'matters in those parts', that is Janïbek's dominions.[16]

13 Bratianu, 1929, pp. 190, 239 ff., 244, 321 and especially pp. 306–7. Pegolotti, 1936, pp. 24–5, 208, 297, 300. The silver bar was termed *grivna*, 'torque', in Russian, since the Vikings, like the Celts, had bent and elongated it so that it could be worn about the neck. In Cumano-Qïpchaq, the bar was termed *sem* or *som* from Pers. *sēm/sīm*. The term became *sommo* in Italian.

14 The sturgeon and caviar most likely came from the Caspian, where Marco Polo already noted the presence of Genoese shipping, and were transshipped to the Black Sea via the Kuban River. That route was far more convenient for bulky sturgeon carcasses than the mountainous and much longer one from the Anatolian ports on the Mediterranean or Black Seas to the Caspian. By contrast, silk from Gilan was procured in Tabriz, even though Gilan, protected by the Alborz, was *de facto* an independent state prior to Uljaitu's conquest and annexation of the country. Polo, 1903, I, p. 52; Bratianu, 1927, pp. 276–7. The significance of the port of 'Lo Copa' was signalled by Lopez and Raymond, 1955, p. 244n.

15 Thomas and Pedrelli, 1880, II, p. 111.

16 Thomas and Pedrelli, 1880, I, pp. 320–41 (no. 170). To these we may add the notices of consultations and agreements between Venice and Genoa at the highest levels recorded in the *Regesti* of the *Libri Commemoriali*, see Pedrelli, 1876–96 (9 June and 18 June 1344), VI, p. 19; (10 June), II, 2, 21, 22; (2 July 1345), pp. 138–9, 144, 147–8 (nos. 125, 129, 152, 164 and 169).

The troubles culminated in Venice's military and diplomatic alliance with her arch-rival Genoa and Janïbek's failed siege of Caffa, during which his men catapulted the corpse of a plague victim into the city, from which Black Death was allegedly introduced into the West.

Trade was severely disrupted, permanently diminished and transformed as was the rest of economic and social life by the Black Death. In the West the plague killed workers but left intact the other means of production – land, liquid and fixed capital, and natural resources. Despite legal attempts by the upper classes to push down wages, the new scarcity of labour raised real wages in the West and kept them high in relation to grain and other staple prices until late in the fifteenth century. It also concentrated wealth among survivors at all levels of society. At the same time, because the silver, or rather billon, currency held by the majority of the population appreciated in relation to the liquid assets of the wealthy which were held in depreciated gold, overall patterns of effective demand moved away from cheap staples and very costly *spezierie* towards better-quality foodstuffs and beverages that were middling in price and caused producers to shift from grains to meat and dairy products, with the result that in large areas that had specialized in the cultivation of wheat or rye to a degree that verged on monoculture, landlords and small farmers now found it more profitable to raise or produce livestock, wine and ale, cheese and similar foods rather than grain. Consequently, the market for cheap grains had now to be filled by imports, the primary sources of which were the regions north and north-west of the Euxine. Thus, at the same time as the Pontic emporia lost much, probably most, of their transit trade in *spezierie* between the Latin West and Asia, their trade actually grew in grains, lumber, wax, salted fish, caviar and, of course, slaves who were needed to fill the labour force and could now be afforded by a larger proportion of the urban population. What was lost in margins of profit was largely made up for in volume. Thus, as trade contracted everywhere else after the 1320s, it continued to grow in the Black Sea and along the Trans-Eurasian overland route, but only until mid-century.

The scarcity and expensiveness of labour in the West and the improvement in the purchasing power of large sections of the urban population caused a revival of the slave trade, which now flourished as at no time since the West in the eighth, ninth and tenth centuries had balanced its temporarily revived eastern trade with the as yet non-Christianized Slavs who were caught by Christian soldiers and dealers along the eastern marches of the Carolingian Empire and whose self-designation became attached to the commodity they embodied. The recrudescence of slavery is reflected in the abundance of surnames in Italy such as Russo, Tartaro, Schiavo, Schiavone, Schiavetto, Schiavino,[17] etc., all of which, together with their plural forms, would have been borne by persons transported through the Pontic ports, apparently in great quantity, since the slave trade's profitability was depressed by oversupply.[18]

Two factors have been traditionally associated with the decline of the overland Eurasian trade. One, according to Beazeley, was the disappearance of 'the last semblance of a universal empire . . . a central power able to ensure order and safe transit' to European traders. The other was a confessional hostility to Westerners that was exacerbated by the cultural assimilation of the Mongol conquerors' descendants. Thus, Beazeley goes on to associate 'the infusion of Moslem bigotry into the Turko-Tatar mind' and the emergence of 'an Orient so anarchic and so perilous as the Upper Asia of the fifteenth century'.[19]

Reality, however, was more complex. The overland trade in costly *spezierie* – spices, silks, condiments, aromatics, gold, pearls, etc. – had contracted and the huge profits it generated, together with the great trading houses that realized them, such as the Peruzzi and Pegolotti's Bardi, had disappeared. But trading in slaves, sugar, furs, grains, wax, salted fish, all from the northern Pontic ports, thrived, in large part because these products were relatively so cheap

17 'Russo', which, after 'Rossi', is the second most widely used surname in modern Italy, occurs today in 3,168 communes (municipalities) and in numbers over 500 in Naples, Rome, Turin, Palermo with great concentrations in Lombardy, Piedmont and all of the *Mezzogiorno*; 'Schiavo' in 567 communes, with concentrations in the lower Po just west of Venice, Campania and around Milan; 'Tartari' in 184 communes, virtually all in northern Italy, with a large concentration around Bologna, but smaller ones in the Veneto and Liguria, as well as Lombardy and Piedmont; 'Tartaro' in 113 communes in the areas just mentioned, but also in the south. Other names given to slaves would have been 'Greco' and 'Turco', which could easily have been given to some slaves from the Pontic area, 'Saraceno' and 'Moro', which would have been applied to any Maghrebi or African. 'Greco' occurs in 2,227 communes mainly in the south and Lombard and Piedmont, 'Turco' in 842 communes, with concentrations in Liguria, Piedmont, Lombardy, the Veneto, Campania, Apulia and Calabria; 'Moro' in 1,432 communes, with concentrations in the Veneto and Lombardy, and 'Saraceno' in 226 communes mainly in the south, Lombardy and Piedmont. See 'L'Italia dei Cognomi' (www.gens.labo.net/en/cognomi/). Concentrations about Milan, Turin, Rome and, to a lesser extent, Bologna, would be explained by the availability of employment in these centres for lower-class men, since male descendants of slaves would not easily have transcended the class into which they were born in a conservative, patriarchal society, such as the Italian, with social and legal institutions developed for the preservation of family property and status across the generations. Concentrations in the south, especially Campania (*Terra di Lavoro*) and Sicily, point to demesne or plantation slavery.

18 The Franciscan Bartolomea di Giano (Bartholomaeus de Jano), writing from his friary in Constantinople in December 1438, states that reliable witnesses have informed him that 1,000 youths could currently be bought at Tana, Caffa or Mavro Castro (Akkerman) for ten, six, or even four florins. Thirty or more slave ships arrived yearly at Constantinople and their human cargoes were not a hundredth of the available supply, see *Epistola de crudelitate Turcorum* in Migne, 1866, cols. 1055 ff.

19 Beazeley, 1897–1906, III, p. 376.

and because patterns of consumption in the West had changed. Indeed, this trade contributed to the improving living standards of a growing urban middle class that we see throughout the fifteenth century and to the continuing deflation or stability of food-staple and commodity prices in silver in France and especially England, where the price and wage data are the fullest and most reliable.[20] Europe may no longer have demonetized and exported silver in exchange for imported gold that would be resold to speculators, as it did between the 1270s and the start of the 1330s, but it did continually export more silver than it produced because these staples from the northern Pontic ports were attractively priced and in great demand. Silver production in the West did decline after about 1300, but it hardly ceased, and technological innovations actually led to an initially modest, but cumulative, increase, which culminated in a 'boom in mining and metallurgy' by the end of the fifteenth century in Germany.[21] Yet not merely did Western silver supplies not increase, but they continued to dwindle. Clearly the West was continually demonetizing and exporting its circulating silver, or rather billon, stocks faster than its mines could produce new silver.

The change in the types of commodities traded and the profit margins these made possible was crucial. Whereas the high revenues from the trade in *spezierie* had gone to Jochid and other ruling elites, who provided escorts to, and whose tax-collectors dealt directly with, the caravans in which the Italians had travelled, profits from the trade in slaves, grain, etc. now went to the Muslim and *dhimmi* traders, most notably Armenian compradores, that supplied the Italians, who were in effect themselves relegated to their 'factories'. Moreover, the Muslim traders' attitudes and behaviour were no longer controlled by Mongol nobility. These had readily seen the potential benefits of, and encouraged, Western penetration, but their authority had been severely damaged by the sharp fall off in commercial revenues under Janïbek and the consequent internal divisions that followed his inability to reward loyalty on the same wide scale as before and his death or murder. The natural leaders of the Muslim burghers were the *ulema*, who prescribed and reinforced their followers' values and *Weltanschauung*, which did not accord believers and

20 See Lord Beveridge's twenty-year average prices of wheat in grains of silver in Postan and Habakkuk, 1966–89, II, pp. 166 and 205 (1st edn; pp. 215 and 255, 2nd edn), which may be compared to David L. Farmer's yearly average prices in Thirsk, 1967–2000, and III, pp. 502–98. Cf. also the course of construction of agricultural wages, Table 5.12, p. 593, and Appendix H, pp. 515–20 and the decline and then stability of important commodity prices, Appendix G, pp. 512–16. D'Avenel's data for French wheat prices has been conveniently converted into decennial averages by Abel, 1986, p. 304.

21 See Neff, 1987, pp. 723–39.

non-believers equal worth on the basis of a common creation, humanity or utilitarian advantage. Italian participation in the Pontic trade continued until the Ottomans expelled the Genoese from Caffa in 1475, but well before that point the same sharp cleavage developed that had long existed in the southern and eastern ports of the Mediterranean between Western exporters and their indigenous Muslim partners and counterparts, who monopolized inland commerce and the India trade beyond.

6

Migrations, ethnogenesis

PETER B. GOLDEN

Ethnogenesis: clan, tribe and state organization in Inner Asia

In Inner Asia, the nomads were organized hierarchically in lineages, clans and tribes defined by descent, real or fictive, from a common patrilineal ancestor. Although sharing a common name, territory, culture, language and political interests,[1] tribes were fractious and prone to internal power struggles. The indigenous terminology for these entities was fluid and as a consequence often appears less than precise in the Arabic, Persian and even native sources that describe them.[2] Expanding clans could become tribe-like in power and authority.[3] Tribes often formed loose, polyethnic unions, potential states depending on their response to interaction with neighbouring sedentary states.[4]

1 Pershits and Traide, 1986, pp. 144–6; Di Cosmo, 1999, p. 18 n. 60; Barfield, 1990, pp. 164–5.
2 On the Turkic terminology, see Golden, 2001, pp. 21–5; Clauson, 1972, pp. 96, 121–2, 152–3, 214–15, 306; Tenishev, 1997, pp. 307–9, 316–18, 323–4, cf. *urugh/uruq* 'progeny, descendants of a common ancestor, clan'; *oghush* perhaps 'family' in the early period and then a unit less than a clan or tribe (later 'clan, clansmen, tribe'); *bodh* (later *boy*) 'clan' (later 'also branch of a tribe, tribe'); *bodhun* 'tribal union, people'; *oba* 'clan, tribe'; *kün* 'people, persons, slaves'; *ulush* 'people, tribe, country, state'; *el/il* 'tribal union, country, state, empire'. In Mongol, fundamental units were the *obogh, obugh, ovogh, omogh* 'family, clan, tribe', or 'joint patrilineal descent group' with a 'traceable genealogical relationship' *aimagh* 'tribe'; *yasutan* 'belonging to some tribe or people, nation, people'; *irgen* 'people'; *ulus* 'people, nation, state, empire'. Shared descent from a common male ancestor was expressed by *yasun* 'bone'. The *oboghs* joined to form an *irgen* or *ulus*, see Lessing *et al.*, 1982, pp. 414, 430, 598, 873; Luvsandendev and Tsedendamba, 2001, I, p. 67, II, pp. 279, 454, IV, p. 470. Mongol social structure and the changes produced by the formation of the Chinggisid Empire are discussed in Vladimirtsov, 1934 in Vladimirtsov, 2002, pp. 295–488. Many of these terms are not easily defined. Thus, Geley, 1979, p. 60, after pointing to the complex ways in which this key social unit *obogh* could be formed, opts for the neutral 'named social group' as perhaps the best way to render this term. For a critique of the tribe and kinship paradigm, see Sneath, 2007, who views 'aristocrathi orders' as the social-political units around which steppe polities were shaped.
3 See *Secret History*/de Rachewiltz, I, p. 249; Vladimirtsov, 1934 in Vladimirtsov, 2002, pp. 341 ff.; Allsen, 1994a, pp. 324–5; Kychanov, 1997, pp. 181–2.
4 Khazanov, 2003, pp. 26–9, 36–9; Barfield, 1990, p. 166.

In nomad-based empires, the ruling clan, having achieved power by conquest, exercised a collective sovereignty over the realm. This gave rise to a succession system based on tanistry, which produced frequent throne struggles as any member of the ever-growing imperial house[5] could claim supreme power.[6] Attempts to regulate the ever-present possibility of internecine strife by establishing systems based on variants of collateral fraternal succession ultimately failed. Among some peoples, electoral councils (e.g. Mongol *quriltais*) confirmed power. Within the ruling clan, favour was usually given to princes born of noble mothers.[7]

Alongside the ruling clan at the summit of power was the tribe from which it sprang. Beneath it was a hierarchy of the core tribes of the founder-union and those tribes that had voluntarily submitted. Lower in rank were other pastoral nomadic tribes, hunting-trapping forest tribes and settled peoples added on in a process of conquest and superstratification. Subject tribes sometimes retained their original leadership, but more often than not conquered rulers or chieftains were replaced by members of the royal house or other trusted lineages. Tribal aristocracies (e.g. the Turkic *begs*) existed, but their role in a highly mobile society was much more limited than that of landed or service aristocracies in the sedentary world. At the bottom of the social scale were slaves.[8] When nomad-based states collapsed, the tribes re-established new polities under another ruling clan or returned to simpler forms of union, awaiting a catalyst to regroup into more complex polities.[9]

The ethnonym of the ruling tribe became the political name of its subject peoples.[10] The names *Türk*, *Tatar* and *Mongol* (*Mongghol*, rendered in Arabic and Persian as *Mughūl*) spread in this fashion. Imperial neighbours also promoted the ethnonymic use of these all-embracing politiconyms.[11] Rashīd al-Dīn (d. 1318), who gained much information from Mongol informants,[12] such as

5 By the time of his death (1227), Chinggis Khan had about 100 living descendants. His sons (e.g. Jochi had forty sons) and grandsons were equally prolific, see Abuseitova *et al.*, 2001, pp. 167, 171.

6 Fletcher, 1979–80, pp. 237–40; Fletcher, 1986, 36–8; Barfield, 1989, pp. 27–8, 138; Trepavlov, 1993, pp. 102–10.

7 A son of the Türk Qaghan Muqan (553–72) was prevented from attaining the Qaghanate because of his mother's 'low birth'. However, Ashina, the eponymous founder of the Türk royal house, was the son of a concubine, see Liu Mau-tsai, 1958, I, pp. 6, 43; Drompp, 1991, p. 98. Among the Mongols, seniority could also play a role, Vladimirtsov, 1934 in Vladimirtsov, 2002, pp. 345–7.

8 Khazanov, 2003, p. 37; Pritsak, 1952, pp. 52–4; Eberhard, 1970, pp. 113–17; Golden, 1982, pp. 49–51.

9 Golden, 1987–91; Khazanov, 2003, p. 42.

10 See Németh, 1991, pp. 54 ff. on the system of Turkic tribal names.

11 See Golden, 2001, pp. 13–20; Geley, 1979, p. 72.

12 Allsen, 1994b.

Bolad Agqha, who had previously served the Chinggisid administration in China and reflected what the Mongols and other 'steppe-dwellers' thought of their past, uses *Turk* as a generic for Turko-Mongolian steppe-dwellers. He also reports that *Tatar* and then *Mughūl* became the designation of the other 'Turkic groupings (*aṣnāf*) regardless of their different divisions and names'.[13] *Mughūl* acquired a number of meanings: ethnic Mongols, Turkicized Mongols, especially the nomads of 'Moghulistan' (the eastern part of the Chaghadaid *ulus* – south-eastern Kazakhstan, Kyrgyzstan, Eastern Turkestan), who maintained older steppe culture, and ultimately (in the fifteenth to seventeenth centuries) it became a generic for the Inner Asian nomads of the now fragmented Chinggisid realms.[14] Tales of the common origin of the Turks and Mongols were widespread.[15]

The impact of the conquests

Mongol expansion sparked the last of a series of westward migrations of Turkic peoples,[16] fixing the geographical configurations in which we find them today[17] and adding Mongolic elements (present earlier as well), in substantial numbers in some regions. It completed the Mongolization of Mongolia, a process already underway since the early tenth-century Khitan conquests.[18] Some of the great Transoxanian cities (such as Bukhara) remained largely Iranian in speech, but the rest of the region was overwhelmingly Turkicized. Today, nearly 89 per cent of the indigenous population is Turkic-speaking.[19] In the Chinggisid states west of Mongolia, Turkic became the *lingua franca* and increasingly the language of state.[20] The conquests brought new waves of Turks into the Near East, furthering the Turkicization of much of Anatolia

13 Rashīd al-Dīn / Rawshan and Mūsavī, I, pp. 39–41 (the chapter bears the title: 'Concerning the tribes (*aqwām*) of the Turks who in this day are called Mughūl, but in ancient times each had their own name'), pp. 77–8. Chinese sources used *Dada* (Tatar) similarly for a number of steppe peoples. Pers. *aṣnāf* 'Arab. ṣinf, pl. *aṣnāf*, which I am rendering as 'groupings', could denote 'a sort, species, or 'a part or portion or constituent of anything', see Lane, 1968, p. 1735 who ranks it smaller in size than *jins* (p. 470) 'a genus, kind or generical class', see also Dozy, 1968, I, p. 849: ṣinf 'famille, tribe, nation'.

14 See Abuseitova *et al.*, 2001, p. 194; Kim, 1999.

15 Rashīd al-Dīn / Rawshan and Mūsavī, I, pp. 47, 147; Dobrovits, 1994.

16 Although increasing the numbers of Turkic speakers west of Mongolia, the geographical alignment of the Qïpchaq (North-western), Siberian (North-eastern), Turkī (South-eastern) and Oghuz (South-western) Turkic groupings to each other did not essentially change, Golden, 1992a, pp. 291 ff.

17 Soviet nation-building completed the process, see Hagen, 2003; Edgar, 2004.

18 Bartol'd, *Dvenadtsat' lektsii* in his *Sochineniia*, V, p. 86; Golden, 1992a, pp. 184–5.

19 Bregel, 1991, pp. 54, 60.

20 Bartol'd, *Istoriia turetsko-mongol'skikh narodov* in his *Sochineniia*, V, pp. 211, 213.

and Azerbaijan.[21] Throughout their domain, the Mongols moved skilled subjects around the empire, increasing opportunities for cultural and linguistic exchange.[22]

Chinggisid armies incorporated newly subjugated Mongolic and Turkic tribes,[23] employing the most common form of polity formation in the steppe: superstratification.[24] In contrast to earlier steppe empires which absorbed intact the conquered tribes, Chinggis Khan broke up or decimated rival tribal unions such as the Tatars, Mergits, Naimans and Kereyits in Mongolia, a policy that was extended to the Tanguts (Xixia) of Gansu (1227)[25] and the Qïpchaq-Qanglï. The Mongols, particularly concerned about resistance from other steppe peoples, dealt harshly with them. Thus, in the campaign of 1221, conquered Qïpchaq-Qanglï were denationalized by being forced to cut their hair according to Mongol fashion and then distributed among the Mongol military formations.[26] The survivors of these wars, Mongolic and Turkic, were scattered among the Chinggisid armies of Inner Asia subsequently giving rise to clans or retribalized groupings bearing these names among post-conquest Turkic peoples.[27] A similar fate awaited lesser tribes (including Mongols)[28] that were melded into larger military units of diverse ethnic and tribal origins. Their names (e.g. Jalayir, Barulas) became sub-unit or clan names. The dispersal and the allotment of the tribesmen (and others) to the personal armies of Chinggisid princes became the norm. Polyglot units consisting of 'Uighurs, Qarluqs, Türkmen, Kāshgharīs and Kucheans' were not unknown.[29]

Another consideration in the conquest of the steppe peoples was strategic. It is estimated that in the early thirteenth century Inner Asia contained as much as half of the world's total equine population. This was under the control of the nomads. Thus, subjugation of the latter brought rich dividends in human and equine resources. Mongol soldiers went into combat with ten

21 Golden, 1992a, pp. 283–308.
22 See al-Juvainī/Qazvīnī, I, pp. 95, 101; al-Juvainī/Boyle, I, pp. 122, 128; Allsen, 1997b, pp. 35–6, and Allsen, 2001a.
23 See al-Juvainī/Qazvīnī, I, p. 63; al-Juvainī/Boyle, I, p. 82; Kadyrbaev, 1990, pp. 45–6.
24 Déer, 1938, pp. 10–16; Pritsak, 1988.
25 The *Secret History*/de Rachewiltz, I, pp. 125–6, reports that he distributed the surviving Mergit 'here and there, down to the last one'. Kychanov, 1968, pp. 315–30; Allsen, 1997a, pp. 17–18.
26 Rashīd al-Dīn/ Rawshan and Mūsavī, I, pp. 492, 500–03; Allsen, 1987, pp. 190 ff.
27 Sultanov, 1982, pp. 15, 31; Pishchulina, 1977, p. 233; Golden, 1992a, pp. 291–2, 299–300; Kuzeev, 1974, pp. 181–2, 222–8, 233, 311–12, 360, 466–8.
28 Morgan, 1986a, p. 89. Early allies were absorbed as units, maintaining some tribal identity. Vladimirtsov, 1934 in Vladimirtsov, 2002, pp. 424–9, on the transformation of the Mongol clan (*obogh*) into quasi-military formations (*otogh*).
29 Rashīd al-Dīn/Rawshan and Mūsavī, I, p. 74.

to twenty horses per trooper,[30] appearing, thus, to have limitless numbers of men and horses.

Chinggis Khan sought to replace the centrifugalism of the tribes, whose loyalties fluctuated with a leader's success and generosity, with obedient servitors of his dynasty, the *Altan Urugh* ('Golden Clan'). The *nökürs*, Chinggis's companions in arms who had left their clans and tribes for service with him, were the chief force of this new dynamic[31] and formed the *keshig*, his personal guard.[32] Whether there were Liao (Khitan) or Kereyit precedents for this is unclear.[33] Internecine strife and social stratification in Mongol society may have already created the preconditions for Chinggis Khan's programme. The clans had grown large and were already breaking up. Their chieftains had *nökürs* as well as hereditary servitors (*ötegü boghol* 'bound vassals').[34] Chinggis simply applied these structures to an empire, often stripping the tribes of their traditional leadership and distributing them among his armies.[35] In return for submission, servitors could advance through a meritocratic system and receive rewards directly from the state.[36] Under the Chinggisids, the elite (of whatever origin) became the *nökürs* and the subject tribes the *ötegü boghol/bo'ol*.[37] The Chinggisid ideology appealed to 'those who live behind felt walls' (the nomads) and their 'ethnic unity' deriving from the shared heritage of the Steppe Imperial Tradition and genealogical notions.[38]

Chinggisid willingness to move individuals and groups to parts of the empire where they were needed would have ethnic consequences, particularly among the Turkic peoples. After the death of the Grand Qaghan Möngke in 1259, the Mongol Empire began to fragment along the lines already apportioned by

30 Adshead, 1993, p. 61.
31 On *nökür* 'friend, companion', the personal retinue of the chief, see Németh, 1952; Vladimirtsov, 1934 in Vladimirtsov, 2002, pp. 385 ff.; Ratchnevsky, 1992, p. 13.
32 Hsiao, 1978, pp. 34–5; Allsen, 1987, pp. 99–100; Farquhar, 1990, pp. 2, 245; Morgan, 1986a, p. 90.
33 Wittfogel and Feng, 1949, pp. 540–1; Barfield, 1989, pp. 174–5; Bartol'd, *Dvenadtsat' lektsii* in his *Sochineniia*, V, pp. 135–6; Togan, 1998, pp. 11, 75, 108–21; Biran, 2005, pp. 114, 202.
34 See Vladimirtsov, 1934 in Vladimirtsov, 2002, pp. 354 ff.; Rashīd al-Dīn/Rawshan and Mūsavī, I, pp. 66, 225, 321; Kychanov, 1997, pp. 181–3; Golden, 2000, pp. 24–5.
35 Khazanov, 1984, p. 239; Morgan, 1986a, p. 90, concludes that Chinggis Khan created 'an artificial tribal system' with primary loyalty directed to the Chinggisid house and the military unit. The Khitans also moved peoples and tribes, see Wittfogel and Feng, 1949, pp. 46–50, 86 ff., 193; Jagchid, 1981, pp. 71, 83–4.
36 Togan, 1998, pp. 8, 11–12, 137–40, 146. Previously, tribal elites took the lion's share of the spoils of war.
37 Vladimirtsov, 1934 in Vladimirtsov, 2002, pp. 394–5; Togan, 1998, p. 117.
38 The Mongols separated the western Qïpchaqs from their Iranian Alano-As allies by saying that 'we and you are of one kind [*jins*], the As are foreign to us', Ibn al-Athīr/Tornberg, XII, pp. 385–6; Rashīd al-Dīn/Rawshan and Mūsavī, I, p. 534; Trepavlov, 1993, pp. 57–8.

Chinggis Khan to his four sons from Börte, his senior wife: the *ulus*es of the Jochids, Chaghadaids, Ögödeids and Toluids. In the new political order, power could only be held by a member of the *Altan Urugh*.[39] The technically subordinate domain (Ilkhanate) in Iran founded by the Toluid Hülegü (d. 1265) was functionally at the same level as the *ulus*es of Inner Asia.[40]

Ethnic processes in the *Ulus* of Jochi

The Turkicization of the invading Mongols (whose armies already contained Turkic elements) struck contemporary observers. A Mamlūk historian, al-ʿUmarī (d. 1348/9), commenting on the Qïpchaq steppe, reports that although the Mongols made the Qïpchaqs their subjects, 'all [of them] became like the Qibjāq, as if they were of one stock [*jins wāḥid*], because the Mughūl lived in the land of the Qibjāq and [because] of their marital ties with them and their community in their land'.[41] The relatively small numbers of Mongols who settled in the Jochid *ulus* undoubtedly furthered the process. While Mongol was the state and chancellery language,[42] Qïpchaq Turkic became the *lingua franca*.[43]

The Jochid realm, with its administrative centres (Saray, Saray-Berke)[44] on the lower Volga, encompassed lands from the Danube to Western Siberia, Kazakhstan and the borders of Transoxania. Initially, it was also called the *Ulugh Ulus* (Russ. *bol'shaia orda* 'great horde'). By the sixteenth century, it came to be known as the 'Golden Horde'. It consisted of a number of major units, including the 'Blue Horde' (*Kök Orda*), 'White Horde' (*Aq Orda*) and 'Grey Horde' (*Boz Orda*), the precise delineations of which remain debated, and numerous smaller units.[45]

39 al-Juvainī / Qazvīnī, I, p. 31; al-Juvainī / Boyle, I, pp. 42–3; Barthold, 1977, pp. 392–3; Jackson, 1978, and Jackson, 1999b; Allsen 1997a, pp. 1–23; Abuseitova *et al.*, 2001, pp. 168 ff.

40 See Allsen, 1991. By the late thirteenth to early fourteenth centuries, the Mongol elite in Iran had been Islamized and linguistically Turkicized or Persianized, see Martinez, 1987–91.

41 al-ʿUmarī / Lech (Arabic), p. 73.

42 Spuler, 1965, pp. 285–7; Grigor'ev, 1981.

43 Spuler, 1965, pp. 288–90; Schmieder, 1994, p. 141. Khwārazmian Turkic, with strong Qarluq–Qarakhanid elements, also influenced the culture and language of the Volga zone, Caferoğlu, 1964, II, pp. 107 ff. On the literature, both translations and original works, in Khwārazmian-Qïpchaq and Qïpchaq, see Ercilasun, 2004, pp. 373–404, and Turan, 2007, pp. 681–96. On acculturation and Turkicization in the neighbouring Ilkhanid state, see Martinez, 1986 [1988], pp. 213–16.

44 Fedorov-Davydov, 1994, pp. 10–12, 20–4.

45 Allsen, 1985–7; Iudin, 1983 reprinted in Iudin, Baranova and Abuseitova, 1992, pp. 14–56; Abuseitova et al., 2001, p. 173; Kliashtornyi and Sultanov, 1992, pp. 189–95; Golden, 1992a, pp. 297–9.

The Pontic-Volga-Ural nomads were overwhelmingly Qïpchaq Turkic-speaking. The one exception was the Islamic Volga Bulghar people in the Middle Volga-Kama region who had retained their Bulgharo-Oghuric speech (into the fourteenth century) or had become to varying degrees bilingual, speaking both Bulgharic and Qïpchaq.[46] The Chinggisid invasion swept away the Volga Bulghar state and expanded Qïpchaqization. Some Bulgharic groupings moved northwards, mixed with local Finnic peoples producing the Chuvash people.[47] The now increasingly Qïpchaq-speaking Volga Bulghars, intermixing with other peoples of the Golden Horde, gave rise to the Volga-Ural (Kazan, Astrakhan, Mishar) and Siberian Tatars of today. This process, involving internal displacements and the influx of Qïpchaq groupings, was probably not completed until the period of the Kazan Khanate in the fifteenth to mid-sixteenth centuries. The spread of Islam, long entrenched in Volga Bulgharia, following the conversion of Özbek (r. 1312–42), provided another source of identity, especially for the sedentary elements of the state.[48] Qïpchaq-speaking groups moved to the periphery of the Golden Horde zone, laying the foundations for the Crimean Tatar[49] and Siberian khanates[50] and the Noghay Horde.[51] The ruling house of the Noghay Horde, founded by a non-Chinggisid Manghït, Edigü (d. 1420), legitimized its position by claiming descent from the early leaders of Islam.[52]

Of similar origins were the Qïpchaq Uzbeks, who seized Transoxania from the Timurids and founded the Uzbek khanates in the beginning of the sixteenth century, the Qazaqs who split off from this same mass in the fifteenth century and the Qara Qalpaqs.[53] This last, unlike the Crimean,

46 The transition from Oghuric (surviving today only in Chuvash, spoken by 1,800,000 people in the Middle Volga region) to Qïpchaq is noticeable in grave inscriptions (from c. 1281 to 1361) combining Arabic, Volga Bulgharic and two types of Common Turkic, see Erdal, 1993, pp. 10–22.

47 Kuzeev, 1992, pp. 234–6; Kakhovskii, 2003, pp. 315 ff.

48 See DeWeese, 1994a. Rival claims for the 'Bulghar' legacy have been advanced by Tatar, Bashkir and Chuvash scholars, cf. Zakiev, 2003; Kakhovskii, 2003. On the uses of this legacy, see, in particular, Frank, 1998.

49 The Crimean Tatars are an amalgam of Turkicized Mongols, Qïpchaqs (themselves of complex origins) and the Turkicized population of the Crimea, reflected in a number of distinct dialects with Qïpchaq (eastern and western) and Oghuz roots, Kozlov and Chizhova, 2003, pp. 143–9; Golden, 1992a, pp. 388–9. For an overview of the Qïpchaq problem, see Stoianov, 2006.

50 Safargaliev, 1960 in Muslimov, 1996, pp. 468–77.

51 Kuzeev, 1992, pp. 67–85, 99–102, 238–47, 313–14; Golden, 1992a, pp. 301, 324–6, 392–6; Trepavlov, 2001b, pp. 51 ff.

52 Bartol'd, 'Otets Edigeia' in his *Sochineniia*, II/1, pp. 797–804; DeWeese, 1994a, pp. 382–92; Trepavlov, 2001b, p. 64.

53 On the Uzbeks and the later Jochid realms, see Grekov and Iakubovskii, 1998, pp. 297–312; Safargaliev, 1960 in Muslimov, 1996, pp. 453 ff.; Akhmedov, 1965a, pp. 11–16; Spuler,

Volga-Ural-Siberian Tatars, Uzbeks and Qazaqs did not have a khanal house of Chinggisid origin. A similar process of Qïpchaqization took place among the neighbouring Bashkir (Bashqort) people, a union of complex ethnic origins deriving from Oghuric, Common Turkic, Finno-Ugric and Iranian elements.[54]

Although some Cuman-Qïpchaq groupings fled to Hungary with the Mongol victory,[55] their numbers were replenished by other Turkic elements, apparently largely Qïpchaq, brought to the region either in flight from or as part of the Chinggisid forces.[56] Other Qïpchaqs fled to Romania, Moldavia and Balkan Bulgaria where their martial skills gained them entry into the local aristocracy. They played a key role in the foundation of the Second Bulgarian Empire and several subsequent Bulgarian royal houses.[57] Qïpchaqs were a major source of military slaves (*mamlūks*) in the Eastern Mediterranean Islamic lands.[58]

Ethnic processes in the *Ulus* of Chaghadai

By the 1340s, this troubled realm whose population had swelled with the influx of pagan Mongol and Turkic tribesmen, had divided into the *Ulus Chaghatay* (using the more common, Turkic form of the name) and Moghulistan. The former encompassed much of Western Turkestan which retained urban and rural sedentary Iranian populations along with its mix of Qïpchaqs, Turkī, Mongol and Turkicized Mongol tribesmen.[59] Moghulistan included Eastern Turkestan, which had substantial Turkī-speaking populations, parts of Kyrgyzstan and Kazakhstan. Mongol was still being used in official documents during the reign of Tughluq Temür (1359–63).[60] Islam, emanating out of long-established centres in urban Transoxania, continued to spread among neighbouring pagan steppe-dwellers. Aside from Kashgharia, the Islamization of Eastern Turkestan, retarded by weak Chaghadaid central authority,

1965, pp. 85–7; Golden, 1992a, pp. 297–302; DeWeese, 1994, pp. 336–48; Gökbel, 2000, pp. 87–97; Kliashtornyi and Sultanov, 1992, pp. 195 ff.

54 See Kuzeev, 1974, pp. 288, 376 ff., and Kuzeev, 1992, pp. 112–13, 236–8.

55 Berend, 2001; Murguliia and Shusharin, 1998, pp. 153 ff.

56 Dashkevich, 1988, pp. 63–4, suggests that the Cumano-Qïpchaqs were driven off or killed by the Mongols and were replaced by other Qïpchaq-speaking nomads. The data to substantiate such sweeping conclusions are lacking. On the ethno-linguistic complexity of the Qïpchaq union, see Golden, 1995–7. The Turkic of the *Codex Cumanicus* reflects a number of Qïpchaq dialects, see Golden, 1992b, pp. 41–3. See Drimba, 2000, for the most recent edition of the text and Schmieder and Schreiner, 2005, for the larger political, cultural and linguistic setting of this work.

57 Cf. the Terterids, Shishmanids, Rásonyi, 1981, pp. 141 ff.; Lăzărescu-Zobian, 1984; Fine, 1987, pp. 183–4, 198–9, 220–1, 224–8; and Vásáry, 2005.

58 Ayalon, 1963.

59 Manz, 1989, pp. 22–40, 154 ff.; Shāniyāzov, 2001, pp. 384–402.

60 Dūghlāt/Ross, pp. 55–6.

inter-Chinggisid strife, vassal statelets and resistance from the large numbers of pagan Turkic and Mongol nomads made slower progress.[61] Conversions, often by force, accelerated in the late fourteenth and early fifteenth centuries. The settled, commercially oriented, hitherto Manichaean, Buddhist and Nestorian Christian Uighurs were also Islamized, a process begun by the Qarakhanids. By the mid-sixteenth century, even the name *Uighur* had been forgotten and all the 'Moghuls' were Muslims.[62] In Transoxania, a further synthesis of Turkic and Irano-Islamic culture produced a new Turkic literary language, 'Chaghatay', based on Qarakhanid Turkī.[63]

In Moghulistan, they disdainfully termed the 'Chaghatays' *Qara'unas*, i.e. people of mixed ancestry.[64] The latter called the Moghulistani nomads *Jete* or *Chete* ('bandits').[65] Prominent among the *Jete/Chete* were the Dughlat, the local power-brokers, the Kereyit, the Qangli̇ and others.[66] *Qazaq* (Turkic 'free warrior, steppe marauder') was the equivalent of *Jete/Chete*.[67] Neither term is attested before the Mongol era.[68] This was an anarchic world of 'free' warrior bands and proto-unions of retribalizing Chinggisid military units.[69]

In lands further to the north, inter-Chinggisid turbulence began the movement of Qi̇rghi̇z out of their ancestral lands on the Yenisei.[70] Peoples bearing this ethnonym subsequently came to Moghulistan. It was here, on the territory of today's Kyrgyzstan, that the modern Qi̇rghi̇z, now Qi̇pchaqicized in language and incorporating other Turkic groups, took shape.[71]

61 Bartol'd, *Dvenadtsat' lektsii* in his *Sochineniia*, V, pp. 146–69; Kempiners, 1988, pp. 169–70.
62 Dūghlāt/Ross, pp. 12–15, 58, 148, 360; Kitapçı, 2004, pp. 202 ff., 233 ff.
63 On the complexities in defining this literary tongue, its origins and periodization, see Caferoğlu, 1964–9, II, pp. 102–49, 195–229, and the summation of views in Ercilasun, 2004, pp. 404 ff.
64 Bartol'd, *Istoriia kul'turnoi zhizni Turkestana* in his *Sochineniia*, II/1, p. 265, and his *Dvenadtsat' lektsii* in his *Sochineniia*, V, pp. 156, 169–70; Manz, 1989, pp. 32–4, 159–65; Abuseitova *et al.*, 2001, pp. 195–6; Morgan, 1986a, p. 95, terms them a 'synthetic tribe'.
65 Dūghlāt/Ross, pp. 75 (commentary), 148. The origin and etymology of *jete/chete* are obscure.
66 Kim, 1999, pp. 300–06.
67 Bartol'd, *Dvenadtsat' lektsii* in his *Sochineniia*, V, pp. 169–70; Mano, 1978; Pishchulina, 1977, pp. 15, 189; Iudin, 1983 reprinted in Iudin, Baranova and Abuseitova, 1992, pp. 52–3 and 157 n. 78.
68 The term *qazaq* is first noted in mid-fourteenth-century Mamlūk dictionaries, cf. the *Kitāb-i Majmūʿ-i Tarjumān-i Turkiyya wa ʿAjamī wa Mugalī*, most recently edited by Toparlı *et al.*, 2000, Arabic, p. 26b: *qazaq 'al-mujarrad'* ('freed, free'); Abu Ḥayyān (? or more likely his student of eastern Qi̇pchaq origin, Ṣalīḥ al-Dīn Khalīl b. Aybeg, see Halasi-Kun, 1985 [1987], pp. 169–73), *Al-Tuḥfat al-Zakiyya fī'l-Lughat al-Turkiyya*, ed. Atalay, 1945, facs. p. 24b: *qazaq bashli̇* (lit. 'with the head of a *qazaq*') *ʿʿāzib*' ('bachelor, single').
69 Cf. the '*qazaq*' activities of Toqtami̇sh as recorded by Ötemish Ḥājjī in the *Chingiz-name*, see Iudin, Baranova and Abuseitova, 1992, p. 142 (*qazaqlab yürüb*) or *Yasa'urī* 'Chaghadaid prince Yasa'ur, Bartol'd, *Dvenadtsat' lektsii* in his *Sochineniia*, V, p. 172.
70 Kyzlasov, 1984, pp. 92–9; Karypkulov *et al.*, 1984–5, I, pp. 381–90.
71 See Abramzon, 1971, pp. 10–70; Golden, 1992a, pp. 404–6; Baktygulov, 1996, pp. 164–79.

The new 'tribes' of the Chinggisid world

Prior to the fourteenth century, private warlord armies, if they existed, did not wield noticeable political power. Now, retribalized and sometimes bearing the names of their founders, these military conglomerations could expand into substantial unions. In this milieu, non-Chinggisids, such as Edigü and Tamerlane, achieved political prominence, legitimated to varying degrees by the presence of nominal Chinggisid overlords.[72] 'Uzbeks',[73] 'Noghays', 'Chaghatays' appear, as do 'Osmanlï' (Ottomans, 'servitors of Osman') and 'Qaramanlï' ('servitors of Qaraman') in Turkish Anatolia. Person-derived nomenclature marks a departure from earlier Turkic and Mongolic ethnonyms based on nomadism and martial might.[74] These new 'tribes' stemmed more from the *nökür*ized world of the Chinggisid armies and personal forces than from the traditional bonds of 'kinship'. In contemporary Turkic heroic epics, the personal bond between the chieftain and his *nökür*s was the bedrock of political loyalty. Thus, in the *Dede Qorqut* tales,[75] the separation of the *bey* from his *nöker*s is expressed in apocalyptic terms: *qïyamatuñ bir güni ol gün oldï, Big nökerinden nöker biginden ayrïldï*[76] ('that day was like Judgement Day, the *bey* separated from his *nöker* and the *nöker* from his *bey*'). Thus, one of the legacies of the Chinggisid conquests was the restructuring and reconceptualization of socio-political groupings.

A glance at the manpower deployment of the Mongol Empire shows that peoples from the Western Eurasian steppes, both Turks (Qïpchaqs) and Iranians (cf. the Alano-As, the Asud of the Mongols), held positions, high and low, in Yuan China, while Inner Asian, Eastern Turks (Uighurs) served in Western Eurasia and the Near East. When the Chinggisid realm split apart along the fault lines established by the different *ulus*es these divisions largely followed or reinforced the geography of the already established Turkic linguistic groupings: Oghuz-speakers were mainly under Ilkhanid rule; the Mongol conquests having caused a westward shift of many Oghuz–Türkmen tribes, adding to the already important Oghuz presence in Turkmenistan, Khurāsān, Azerbaijan

72 Bartol'd, *Dvenadtsat' lektsii* in his *Sochineniia*, V, pp. 148–51, 160–5, 171–2; Pishchulina, 1977, pp. 12–13, 39; Kempiners, 1988, pp. 171, 177–8; Manz, 1983, pp. 81–2; and Manz, 1989, p. 43.

73 Bartol'd, *Dvenadtsat' lektsii* in his *Sochineniia*, V, pp. 142–3, connects 'Özbek' (Uzbek) with the Jochid Özbek Khan, who was instrumental in the Islamization process, a conjecture not universally accepted.

74 Németh, 1991, pp. 56 ff.; Ratchnevsky, 1966, pp. 173–4. Sub-tribal units could bear names of anthroponymic origin.

75 The *Dede Qorqut* tales are part of a cycle of heroic epics deriving from the *Oghuz-nāmas* of the Oghuz–Türkmen peoples, see Tezcan, 2006, pp. 609–20. There are also Uighur *Oghuz-nāmas*, see Bayat, 2006, pp. 17, 19, 32 ff.

76 See Ergin, 1964, p. 25.

and Anatolia. The Mongol era undoubtedly was crucial to the Turkicization of Azerbaijan. Indeed, from the perspective of the Oghuz tribes, Anatolia and the Turkicizing parts of Iran represented one and the same continuum of tribal groupings. As elsewhere in the Chinggisid-dominated lands, Mongol (Jalayir, Suldus, etc.) and Turkic elements (Uighurs, Qïpchaqs, Qarluqs, etc.) were brought to the regions under their control as both administrators and soldiers. Mongol continued to be used, both for official and other purposes, for some time. But, by Ghāzān's era (he is reputed to have known, in addition to the expected Mongol and Turkic, some Arabic, Indic, Kashmiri, Tibetan, Chinese and 'Frankish'), Turkic was probably widespread among the elite. Islamization usually entailed Turkicization as well.[77] The rise of the Ottomans on the frontiers of the crumbling Ilkhanid realm should be seen within the context of this changing Chinggisid world. In keeping with the new Chinggisid practice, Osman's followers, his *nöküre*, as noted above, called themselves *Osmanlï*, the 'followers' or 'servitors of Osman'.

Turkī-speakers were concentrated in the *Ulus Chaghatay*. The Qïpchaq–Qanglï were fragmented among the *ulus*es of Jochi, Chaghadai and Ögödei. Mixing with other Turkic and Mongol groupings (e.g. the Naiman, Kereyit, Mergit and Jalayir), they formed new peoples, preserving *Qïpchaq* and *Qanglï* as clan names found today among Bashkirs, Uzbeks, Qara Qalpaqs, Türkmen, Qazaqs, Qïrghïz, Altay Turks, Noghays and Crimean Tatars.[78] Mongolic, unlike Turkic, did not spread significantly beyond its core territories.[79] The study of its linguistic impact on Turkic is presently undergoing a re-evaluation.[80] Turkic, however, continued its dynamic movement, consolidating its position in some parts of Central Asia, expanding in others and in important regions of the Middle East.

Finno-Ugric peoples, such as the Mari and Udmurts, lying on the periphery of the Jochid realm, felt the impact of the Mongols, largely through the filter of the Turks and Eastern Slavs. Some Finno-Ugric groupings were Turkicized, forming substrata within the Volga-Ural Turkic peoples. Their history is little reflected in the written records.[81]

77 Sümer, 1980, pp. 143–5; Spuler, 1985, 379–81.
78 Vostrov and Mukanov, 1968, pp. 32–6, 41–5; Kuzeev, 1974, pp. 356–9, 466–9; Sümer, 1980, pp. 142, 149, 634, 540; Togan, 1998, pp. 124–5; Gökbel, 2000, pp. 135–45.
79 Mogholī in Afghanistan is nearing extinction, see Weiers, 2003, pp. 248–9.
80 Previously, it was thought that the number of Mongolic loan-words in Turkic diminished the further away from the Mongolic centre these languages (e.g. the Volga-Ural Qïpchaq grouping) were located and that many of these words were transmitted by more easterly Turkic intermediaries. Recent scholarship indicates that the impact was more substantial and direct, see Csáki, 2006. On the complexities of this question, see Tuimebaev, 2005.
81 Kuzeev, 1992, pp. 85–8, 229–34; Kozlova, 1978, pp. 75–7; Ivanova, 1994, pp. 175–6.

7

Islamization in the Mongol Empire

DEVIN DEWEESE

Understanding the historical process of Islamization in the Mongol-ruled world, and amongst the Mongols themselves, is complicated by the nature of the sources, often themselves religious in their inspiration, through which we see the effects of that process, and even more so by the assumptions we bring to the issue of religious conversion and how it ought to be measured or detected. In both regards, it is important to ask questions of our sources that are more fruitful than those typically posed in the past, with regard to:

(1) the bearers or 'vectors' of Islamization, comprising not only representatives of Islam who went among the Mongols to do the work of conversion, but also the 'internal' representatives of Islam and of its institutional and communal infrastructure within the areas, and among the peoples, conquered by the Mongols;

(2) the targets of Islamization, both the elites, especially the rulers, and the ordinary nomads who formed the basis of the Mongols' military power;

(3) the factors facilitating religious change and its social accompaniments, including, for example, social and cultural prestige, enhanced economic access and participation, political legitimation (whether for the Mongols internally, as a counter to the Chinggisid principle, or for Mongol control over the conquered populations), social integration (involving both marital ties and broader issues of communal self-understanding and identification), and the specialized knowledge (e.g. in medicine, alchemy or sorcery) and/or charismatic impact of religious 'brokers';

(4) the diversity of modes of articulating conversion or religious change (i.e. in ritual contexts, in juridical spheres of law, inheritance and family relations, or lifeways, or in discursive venues ranging from genealogical identifications and appropriations, to 'doctrinal' or credal formulations, to integrative expressions of the mythological imagination); and

(5) the very nature of the change implicit in 'conversion' and Islamization.

Consideration of these issues in the context of our sources on Islamization in the Mongol era suggests the need to challenge or revise several standard elements of previous approaches. For example, the focus of our sources on royal converts should be recognized as a product of the royal historiography that predominates among our sources, rather than as an accurate reflection of the historical course of Islamization. Even if we have sparse data on the conversion of ordinary nomads, it is reasonable to assume – if we will relinquish the assumptions of the 'top-down' model of conversion that begins with the impact of the great ruler – that the conversion of a ruler, far from beginning the conversion of his subjects, may well have followed, and reflected, the conversion of a portion of his subjects large enough to induce the ruler to pay attention. This is particularly true for the Mongol successor states in periods of succession struggles, and in periods when the khans were politically weak and needed some other (i.e. non-Chinggisid) source of legitimacy.

More broadly, the alternatives we pose in our analysis of religious transformations are often unhelpful, beginning with the simple dichotomy assumed between 'religious' and 'worldly' motives in conversion (as if 'religion' is only to be found in the mosque or the cloister); such a dichotomy is wholly unsuitable for societies in which religion infused nearly all aspects of life, especially those most directly connected with such matters of health and prosperity that are regarded in secular society as decidedly 'worldly' concerns. Indeed, the focus of many historians on the 'sincerity' of a particular convert, and more broadly on conversion as the adoption of a set of ideas and as a 'change of heart', though often rooted in the ethic of the target religion itself, is nevertheless ultimately fruitless in terms of gauging the historical impact of conversion, entailing unproductive assumptions and explorations regarding motives, and turning scholarly attention away from the observable – i.e. the more substantial, and more visible, changes in communal affiliation, dress and foodways, self-designation and so forth – and towards the immeasurable. In the end, asking about the 'sincerity' of a particular ruler's conversion is much like asking about the 'sincerity' of the same ruler's feelings for a particular wife: neither is knowable, in the end, and neither would matter, as a historical subject, in the context of the externally visible social, familial and institutional consequences by which a conversion, or a marriage, can more readily be judged.

Such considerations could be multiplied, and must be, if we are to engage seriously with the historical problems posed by Islamization in the Mongol era; even if our sources were more abundant, or more accessible, or of a different type, we would still go astray in interpreting them without addressing these issues. Given the state of the field, the short survey that follows is inevitably selective and simplified, but attempts to take stock of some of the broader issues raised here. Islamization occurred, to various degrees of enduring effect, in all the Mongol successor states, but its significance was naturally greatest in those with a substantial Muslim presence in pre-Mongol times: Ilkhanid Iran, the Golden Horde, and the *ulus of* Chaghadai (Chaghatay in Turkic).

Ilkhanid Iran

The Ilkhanid state based in Iran ruled over an overwhelmingly Muslim population in territories where Islam had deep roots; at the same time, it had its origins in what was seen at the time as a devastating blow to the Islamic world – the destruction of the ʿAbbāsid Caliphate. These realities, together with the relative abundance of sources, lend a special appeal to the study of Islamization among the Ilkhans, with the familiar theme of the conquerors' cultural conquest by the conquered, and with a trajectory ranging from the initial 'penitential' responses prompted by Mongol destruction, to the celebration of the Mongol rulers as Muslim sultans.

The abundance of sources is worth stressing, not only in terms of their richness, but because of their variety as well; they often allow us to see clearly processes, of significance for the course of Islamization, that we can only surmise in the other Mongol successor states. The Ilkhanid realm is well known as the setting for some of the most essential historiographical production on the Mongols, such as the works of Juvaynī and Rashīd al-Dīn; the latter, in particular, is an invaluable source on the Islamization of the historical vision of the Ilkhans, as the Mongol rulers became patrons of their own memorialization within a Muslim historical framework (a process affecting even the genealogical place of the ancestors of Chinggis Khan). Beyond such pivotal works, however, and the broader late-Ilkhanid project of consciously integrating Mongol and Muslim traditions, the Ilkhanid realm and its successor states in the fourteenth century also produced a wealth of literary works of other sorts, which, while not typically classed as 'historical' sources, are nevertheless of direct relevance for the 'interface' of Mongol and Muslim society in Iran and the Middle East under Ilkhanid rule; much of this material still remains substantially unstudied. It includes, for instance, the administrative manual known as the *Dastūr al-kātib*;[1] the immensely rich biographical material

1 Nakhchivānī, *Dastūr*.

compiled by the remarkable Ibn al-Fuwaṭī (d. 1323);[2] and the abundant Sufi literature produced in the thirteenth and fourteenth centuries, which often provides an invaluable balance to the perspective of court histories.

The Sufi material is of particular importance for that Mongol–Muslim interface in the Ilkhanid realm. It includes hagiographical works such as the *Ṣafvat al-Ṣafā* (compiled in the mid-fourteenth century but edited in the sixteenth) on Shaykh Ṣafī al-Dīn (d. 1334) of Ardabīl, the ancestor of the Ṣafavid dynasty;[3] a virtually unknown hagiographical work from 1330, entitled *Dastūr al-jumhūr*, dealing with a hereditary Sufi community linked with the legacy of the ninth-century shaykh Abū Yazīd Bisṭāmī, and attesting to its patronage by Öljeitü;[4] and the intensely personal writings of the Sufi ʿAlāʾ al-Dawla Simnānī (d. 1336), who had abandoned his service to Arghūn following a spiritual crisis before the battle near Qazvīn, in 1284, in which Arghūn defeated the Muslim Aḥmad Tegüder. Simnānī's writings include long autobiographical passages recounting, for instance, his debates with Buddhist monks (Indians, Tibetans and Uighurs, he says), or his tense audience with Arghūn as the latter sought to induce Simnānī to return to royal service.[5]

The general course of the 'royal' Islamization of the Ilkhans is familiar, with the initial 'abortive' stage represented by Aḥmad Tegüder,[6] and the decisive phase begun under Ghāzān Maḥmūd. That these stages mask a gradual process of Islamization among the Mongol troops in the Ilkhanid realm is evident not only from the accounts highlighting the role of the Amīr Nawrūz in the conversion of Ghāzān, but from scattered reports of proselytization among the Mongols, the nobility and the commoners alike, during the thirteenth century; we have several such reports, for instance, regarding the famous Sufi figure of Saʿd al-Dīn Ḥammūyī (or Ḥamuwayī, d. 1252), from a prominent Khurāsāni family of scholars and shaykhs.[7] It is likely, in view of the family's prominence, that the role of these figures in the Islamization of the Mongols reflects the establishment of ties, on a local level, between Muslim elites and the Mongol officials and troops established in the region; such ties no doubt facilitated the integration of the Mongols into local society at the 'grassroots' level, but they also paved the way – and set up the mechanism – for the influence of Islamization among the troops to be felt at the level of the Mongol ruling house.

2 Ibn al-Fuwaṭī, *Majmaʿ*.
3 Tavakkulī, *Ṣafvat al-ṣafā*.
4 See the catalogue descriptions for the three known manuscripts, in *SVR*, III, pp. 223–4, nos. 2293–4, and in Munzavī, *Ganj-bakhsh*, IV, p. 2075, cat. no. 2464/MS no. 5753.
5 See Simnānī, *al-ʿUrwa*, pp. 314–25 (Persian text), 508–14 (Arabic version); cf. the parallel accounts in Simnānī, *Opera minora*, pp. 117–20, 186–8.
6 On Aḥmad Tegüder, see Amitai-Preiss, 2001, and Pfeiffer, 2003.
7 On the family, see Elias, 1994.

In the case of Ghāzān, however, accounts of his conversion and succession suggest more clearly the tension between the actual and paradigmatic sequence. The earliest reports imply that he too announced his adoption of Islam after his victory over his rival Baydu and his consolidation of power, and his success attests to a new alignment of forces in the decade after Aḥmad Tegüder's demise; later reports make his conversion, on the battlefield, essential to his victory, and these, fanciful as they may be, essentially agree with the gist of the earlier accounts in underscoring the interdependence of Ghāzān's willingness to 'come out' on the side of Islam, and the willingness of his troops, and their leaders, to support him. The role of the 'agent' of Ghāzān's conversion is of interest as well; though Nawrūz clearly played a central role in the young ruler's accession and conversion, most sources (Rashīd al-Dīn, for instance, in the first place, as well as Mamlūk historians of the early fourteenth century) assign credit for Ghāzān's adoption of Islam to Ṣadr al-Dīn Ibrāhīm Ḥammūyī (d. 1322), the son of the aforementioned Saʿd al-Dīn (and son-in-law of the historian Juvaynī). Here too we should no doubt understand Ṣadr al-Dīn's role to be genuine, but to be based above all on his social and familial prominence, rather than on his special skill as an expounder of doctrine in a fashion suitable to Mongol tastes.

With regard to Ṣadr al-Dīn's contribution, moreover, we are fortunate to have a rare combination of perspectives on his role: we have a wide range of independent sources linking him to Ghāzān's conversion; we have later elaborations of his role (in this case more literary than mythical); and we have what we lack in the case of other Mongol rulers: a historically contextualized eyewitness account of Ghāzān's formal, public declaration for Islam, in the words of the figure credited with engineering it, Ṣadr al-Dīn Ibrāhīm himself.[8] The account not only shows, with poignancy, the reticence of the young ruler placed in an unfamiliar ritual setting, and reminds us of the convert's firm focus on what he was supposed to do, rather than on what he was supposed to think; it also suggests the broader context of the event, as the spread of Islam among his troops is explicitly mentioned as an incentive to his conversion, and as the ceremonial announcement of his conversion is made the occasion for celebration, feasting and gift-giving.

It is also instructive, however, that our sources are not unanimous in crediting Ṣadr al-Dīn with Ghāzān's conversion, but ascribe the key role to other Sufi shaykhs; the lack of unanimity may tell us more about the prestige to be garnered by claiming a hand in such an event than about a real free-for-all

8 See the personal account of the shaykh as translated in Melville, 1990; see also Amitai-Preiss, 1996.

of religious influences, but it is quite likely that Ghāzān indeed associated with many figures who might have served as, and in any case might have been portrayed by later constituencies as, key figures in his 'acculturation' and adoption of Islam.

A different set of issues is brought to the fore by the multiple conversions of Ghāzān's brother and successor, Öljeitü, who appears to have dabbled in most of the faiths that had a presence in the religious marketplace of Ilkhanid Iran, before settling on Shīʿī Islam.[9] The chief Persian history of Öljeitü is an especially good source on the mutual cross-cultural interpretations of Mongol and Muslim traditions; while its depiction of Mongol disgust for the disputatious rancour of Ḥanafī and Shāfiʿī jurists may be a set piece, putting an internal critique of Muslim society into the mouths of outsiders, the implicit equation of Shīʿī Islam, with authority vested in natural descendants of the communal founder, and the Chinggisid principle of sovereign power, and its consequent dismissal of Sunnīs as the equivalent of those who think even amirs, without Chinggisid blood, were appropriate sovereigns, rings true as a point of contact eagerly highlighted by Shīʿites seeking favours from a ruler who appeared to be their champion.

A final legacy of the conversion of the Ilkhans may be noted here, in terms of the ongoing resonance of the issues it raised for its contemporaries; for as Rashīd al-Dīn and many others celebrated Ghāzān's adoption of Islam, some outside his realm found fault with the quality of his conversion. The critique of Ghāzān's Islam – and of those who regarded it as worthy – by Ibn Taymīya (d. 1328) continues even today to frame the debate about the duties required of the Muslim.[10]

The Golden Horde

In many respects it was the Islamization of the *ulus* of Jochi that had the greatest long-term consequences for the Muslim world, above all in terms of its ethno-religious ramifications; a remarkable range of modern Turkic 'national' and ethnic groups owe their origins, in communal terms, to the era of the Golden Horde, and to its ethno-political traditions. The heirs of the adoption of Islam in the Jochid *ulus* are thus found among the Turkic peoples today called Tatars, Bashkirs, Qaraqalpaqs, Qazaqs and Uzbeks, as well as less numerous national groups of the North Caucasus and the Crimea; these peoples traditionally framed their Islamization, within the polity of the Jochid *ulus*, as the key to their communal formation, in tales and legends that are circulated

9 See Pfeiffer, 1999.
10 See, for example, Jansen, 1986.

still today.[11] The Islamization of the Golden Horde also had short-term and long-term political ramifications, the former with regard to the alignment between the Jochid *ulus* and Mamlūk Egypt, the latter with regard to the foundations of the centuries-long struggle between the remnants of Mongol power and the emerging Russian state.

More so than the Ilkhanid realm, the Golden Horde was affected by multiple vectors of Islamization from outside, as well as indigenous traditions among the conquered peoples. Within the territory of the Jochid *ulus* lay not only the Muslim 'frontier' regions of the Caucasus and the Black Sea littoral, including the Crimea, but the realm of the Bulghars, for three centuries the northern-most outpost of Islamic civilization, and at least parts of the traditional Muslim centres of Central Asia, in Khwārazm (Khorezm) and the lower Syr Darya Basin. Outside these settled areas, in the steppe as well, Islam was clearly known among the nomads of the Dasht-i Qipchāq prior to the Mongol conquests, largely through their political and economic ties with the state of the Khwārazmshāhs; that there were Muslims already among the armies Batu led in conquering and organizing the heart of the Golden Horde, from 1236 to 1241, is suggested by Juvaynī's report that, just prior to launching the campaign, Batu asked the Muslims with him to gather and pray for victory, just as he himself went atop a hill to seclude himself in supplication for success in battle.[12]

In any case, the Golden Horde had a Muslim ruler earlier than any other Mongol successor state, with the accession of Berke in 1257.[13] The sources differ regarding when and how he became a Muslim; we find affirmations that he was raised as a Muslim, that he studied under a Muslim scholar in Khujand (an error for Jand?), that he converted in Bukhara on his way back from attending the enthronement of Möngke in 1251, and that he announced his adoption of Islam only after becoming khan (the latter, implied in the Egyptian accounts that note Berke's embassies to the Mamlūk court, is belied by Rubruck's reference to Berke's 'pretence' of being a Muslim already in 1253). There is considerable evidence, furthermore, linking Berke's conversion and/or religious training with Sayf al-Dīn Bākharzī of Bukhara; Berke's *de facto* rule over Mawarannahr under Möngke, after the dispossession of the Chaghatayids and Ögödeids, indeed coincides with the height of Bākharzī's prominence there. It is quite possible that there are elements of truth in all these accounts; what

11 See, for further references, DeWeese, 1994.
12 al-Juvaynī/Boyle, I, pp. 270–1.
13 On Berke, see the studies of Richard, 1967; Vásáry, 1990; and my comments in DeWeese, 1994a.

is clear in any case is the abundant and unambiguous contemporary evidence of Berke's adoption of Islam, of its considerable impact in political, diplomatic and military affairs, and of the large number of Mongol amirs who became Muslims at the same time.

Berke's Islam also lent a religious dimension to the struggle that developed as a result of Hülegü's conquests, shortly after Berke's accession, as the Ilkhanid state was established to the south of the Golden Horde. That the struggle, over the contested region of Azerbaijan, would have emerged without the added tension entailed by Hülegü's assault against the titular leader of Berke's religious community is beside the point; the adoption, or even the projection, of religious interpretations and justifications for certain policies is no less a part of the historical fact of Islamization than are more narrowly defined 'religious' motivations sometimes demanded as a measure of 'sincere' conversion. In any case Jūzjānī, already, writing around 1260, insists that Hülegü's destruction of the Caliphate was seen by contemporaries, if not by any means as the sole *casus belli*, at least as a genuine affront, and challenge, to Berke's standing that had to be answered.

The case of Berke's Islam is also instructive with regard to the 'instant' mythologization attendant upon an event whose profound significance was immediately recognized by its contemporaries; later tradition would surround his conversion with a host of themes rooted in a wide range of mythic and hagiographical conceptions, but Jūzjānī, again, confirms the circulation, still in Berke's lifetime, of the story that the infant Berke had been given to be nursed by a Muslim woman in order to make him a Muslim. The story was elaborated further, in later times, with regard to Berke, but it echoes a tale told already in the eleventh century with regard to the conversion of the Qarakhanid 'first Muslim', Satuq Bughrā Khan, and would be applied soon after Berke's time to the legendary Oghuz Khan.

Berke was succeeded by khans who were not Muslims, but his conversion – or simply the presence of substantial Muslim constituencies in the territories ruled by the descendants of Batu – seems clearly to have fostered the emergence of an Islamizing party with allies among the Mongol elite; among them was clearly the figure of Noghai, a supporter of Berke who later clashed with the khan Toqtogha, in a struggle that was also portrayed, by contemporaries, as shaped by religious antagonisms. Toqtogha's death in 1313 was followed by a coup, in effect, that brought to power his nephew, Özbek, with whose name and lineage the decisive Islamization of the Jochid *ulus* is typically associated, in a wide range of sources. The early accounts, again, depict Özbek as a Muslim already at the time of his struggle for power, and portray those defeated and killed following his victory as having opposed him, in part, because he sought to impose Islam upon them (or, we might suppose, because he was siding with the Islamizing party, the labels perhaps meaning more as slogans of loyalty and affiliation than as indicators of belief or practice); later stories dramatize Özbek's conversion by placing it well into his reign, and linking it to miraculous demonstrations by Sufi saints.

Aside from such later echoes of oral tradition with at least some roots in the Golden Horde, we have no indigenous sources from the Golden Horde on the history or Islamization of the Jochid *ulus*; we do, however, have evidence of the patronage of Islamic literature by khans of the Golden Horde, beginning already with Berke, including works produced in Arabic, Persian and Turkic. Much has not survived, but even the extant works have rarely been the focus of serious study with attention to religious and historical issues. This is particularly true of a few Turkic works, from the fourteenth century, that have drawn the attention of some Turkologists; their study has yet to advance beyond purely philological issues. Others, however, remain virtually ignored among the potential sources on the religious transformation underway in the Golden Horde during the thirteenth and fourteenth centuries. Of potentially enormous value, for example (though its neglect may stem from its language), is the Persian *Qalandar-nāma*, a large compendium of Sufi lore written in the Crimea by a certain Abū Bakr Rūmī during the reigns of Özbek Khan and his son Janïbek (it was begun in 1320).[14]

The realm of Chaghatay (Chaghadai)

The *ulus* of Chaghatay, finally, is typically described as a latecomer to Islamization, and as the Mongol successor state most resistant to the adoption of Islam – in short, as the 'least Muslim' of the three Chinggisid houses that eventually adopted Islam. There are many reasons for this characterization, some of which are historically and religiously justifiable, but there is as much justification, if not more, for recognizing the Chaghatay *ulus* as the *most* Muslim of the Mongol successor states. This should hardly be surprising, given the sheer strength of Islam in the urban and sedentary regions of the Chaghatay *ulus*, and given the prominence, in the Mongol administration of these regions, of native Muslims. The Mongol conquest of Central Asia, after all, was far from a religious 'clash of civilizations' as it is sometimes portrayed. Many local Muslim officials and religious figures cooperated with the Mongols, while the

14 The unique manuscript, copied in 1360, is preserved in Tashkent (MS IVRUz 11668, in 400 folios) and described in *SVR*, IX, pp. 471–4, no. 6705.

most obstinate opponents of the Mongols were often non-Muslim military forces garrisoned in Central Asian cities, and resented by the local Muslim population, through the imperial will of the Khwārazmshāh, whose own policies – both locally, through his dispossession of local Muslim rulers, and internationally, through his challenge to the ʿAbbāsid Caliph – were hardly those of a defender of Islam.

Islam had its defenders, however, in the long-standing centres of Islamic civilization and religious scholarship in the cities of Mawarannahr, parts of Khurāsān, and the western and southern parts of the Tarim Basin, all of which were incorporated into the *ulus* of Chaghatay; by the thirteenth century, moreover, Muslim scholarship had reached well beyond these prominent urban centres, and we hear of jurists of this era from the town of Īmil, 'at the furthest reaches of Turkistān', and from Qayalïq (Qayālïgh), a town of the Ili Valley in the heart of the Chaghatayid *ulus*.[15] All these regions provided a substantial Muslim constituency that could and did serve as a vector of Islamization among the nomads as well; this was particularly true in regions, such as Mawarannahr, where local geography favoured the close proximity of nomadic groups to towns and agricultural zones, fostering economic and social ties between the tribesmen and the settled Muslim population. While there were clearly regions of the *ulus* of Chaghatay that could support a 'purer' nomadism with disdain for the products and other appeals of sedentary culture, the notion of inveterate Chaghatayid hostility towards Islam, rooted in 'nomadic conservatism', is another of the common assumptions that ought to be abandoned.

Even among the descendants of Chaghatay, Islam and Muslims fared well quite early on. The engineer of renewed Chaghatayid independence in the 1260s, as Alghu was first installed by Qubilai's brother and rival Arigh Böke but then shifted his support to Qubilai and took advantage of their struggles to assert Chaghatayid prerogatives, was the powerful advisor Masʿūd Bek, son of Maḥmūd Yalavach and pupil of a Sufi shaykh linked through one intermediary to the celebrated Najm al-Dīn Kubrā (d. 1221). Masʿūd's sons maintained their influence in the Chaghatayid realm at least down to the late 1280s. Moreover, the descendants of Chaghatay included a royal convert to Islam only slightly later than in the case of Berke, as Alghu was succeeded as khan in the *ulus* by Mubārak Shāh, who the sources affirm was a Muslim (as is suggested by his name, though among the Mongol elite in this era, names assigned at birth are often a poor indicator of religious affiliation in maturity). Mubārak Shāh was

15 Ibn al-Fuwaṭī, *Majmaʿ*, II, pp. 284, 303–4.

then deposed by Baraq, sent by Qubilai; when Baraq, having broken with Qubilai and joined with the Ögödeid Qaidu, was defeated in a campaign against the Ilkhanid Abaqa in 1270, he reportedly converted to Islam in Bukhara shortly before his death, only to be buried according to Mongol rites on orders from Qaidu. These intrigues and struggles thus produced neither a single powerful ruler – until Qaidu, that is – nor a consistent or irreversible Islamization at court, but the examples of Mubārak Shāh and, especially, Baraq suggest that Islam was already a factor in political alignments within the *ulus*.

Islam did not again find a significant royal convert and patron in the Chaghatayid realm until the 1330s. Jamāl Qarshī praised Qaidu's justice and solicitude for Muslims without claiming him as a convert – a quite familiar pattern among Muslim writers in the Mongol era – and spoke of Qaidu's son Chapar in the same way (though insisting that his name reflected the mispronunciation of 'Jaʿfar'). In 1314, ʿAlāʾ al-Dawla Simnānī compared his own renunciation of royal service under Arghūn with the case of one of his disciples, a certain Muḥsin al-Dīn Muḥammad Turkistānī, who had previously been in the service of another son of Qaidu, Shāh Oghul,[16] suggesting that Qaidu's successors too remained impervious to Islam. We may see another case of abortive royal Islamization in the bid for power, early in the fourteenth century, by Nalighu, whose adoption of Islam may stem from his familial heritage (his mother came from the Muslim Qara Khitai dynasty of Kirmān), but this Chaghatayid was undone by the sons of Duwa, who consolidated their power around 1308. While most of them remained non-Muslim, the growing possibility of seeking support by announcing adherence to Islam is suggested by the case of Yasawur, a Chaghatayid prince who converted to Islam at the hand of Badr al-Dīn Maydānī (a Sufi and jurist known also, from Ibn Baṭṭūṭa, as an interlocutor of the Chaghatayid khan Kebek b. Duwa), and who was suspected of favouring the Muslim population to the detriment of Chaghatayid military success.[17] Yasawur was eventually forced to seek refuge with Öljeitü, and soon rebelled against him as well, suggesting again not the 'insincerity' of his Islam, but simply the complexities of Mongol politics.

The last of Duwa's sons to reign, Tarmashirin, adopted Islam and sought openly to rule as a Muslim monarch (in the early 1330s);[18] of the sources that affirm it, al-ʿUmarī's account of Tarmashirin's Islam, from the early 1340s, is particularly valuable for focusing less on the ruler's own role (though he affirms Tarmashirin's sincerity and praises his support for the *sharīʿa*) than on the

16 Simnānī, *Opera minora*, p. 8.
17 On Yasawur's career, see Kato, 1991.
18 For references to the sources on Tarmashirin's Islam, see Biran, 2002b.

context and consequences of his conversion. According to al-ʿUmarī, when Tarmashirin commanded his amirs and troops to adopt Islam as he had done, there were some among them who had preceded him in becoming Muslims, and some who responded to his summons and converted; Tarmashirin was assisted, the account adds, by the *imāms* and shaykhs of the country, who took advantage of 'the pliability of the Turk' in their proselytizing, and turned the people of Tarmashirin's realm into 'the most zealous of people in religion'. Though acknowledging that the rulers of the *ulus* of Chaghatay had been the most stubborn in clinging to the *yasa* of Chinggis Khan and to the customary rites of the Mongols, al-ʿUmarī affirms again that both the nomadic and sedentary population of this realm had preceded their rulers in adopting Islam early on, and suffered no harm for it 'despite the unbelief of their kings'.[19] While the first part of al-ʿUmarī's latter comment – despite its primarily rhetorical significance, in terms of the contrast al-ʿUmarī sought to make – has been influential in cementing the image of the Chaghatayid realm as hostile to Islam, the rest of this passage is remarkable for its express argument that Islam had spread at the 'grass-roots' level, both widely and deeply, before the 'royal conversion' of Tarmashirin.

That such Islamization was not as overwhelming as al-ʿUmarī hoped, especially in the eastern parts of the *ulus* of Chaghatay, is clear from the revolt that ousted Tarmashirin from power in 1334; he was followed by khans from the house of Chaghatay depicted as harshly hostile to Islam, and the tensions between political factions defined in part on the basis of religious affiliation – only in part, to be sure, but a significant part in terms of mobilizing particular constituencies – may in fact help explain why the political situation in the western part of the Chaghatayid realm collapsed at precisely this point into near chaos, with powerful tribal chieftains propping up Chaghatayid princes and warring among themselves. This situation lasted, in large measure, until the consolidation of power by one such warlord, Timur, during the later 1360s and early 1370s. During the middle part of the fourteenth century, indeed, we find a succession of Chaghatayid khans or would-be khans identified as devoted Muslims, but at a time when khans hardly mattered; as real power devolved into the hands of such powerful amirs as Qazghan and his son ʿAbdullāh (the father, in turn, of Timur's eventual rival Mīr Ḥusayn), the Muslim Chinggisid players range from an apparently serious contender such as Khalīl Sulṭān, a son of Yasawur who sought aid from the Kart rulers of Herat in his bid to seize power in Mawarannahr, to a succession of puppet khans such as Buyān Qulï,

19 al-ʿUmarī/Lech, pp. 38–41 (text), 117–19 (translation).

who to judge from his burial place in Bukhara was devoted to the Sufi tradition of Sayf al-Dīn Bākharzī, or Kābul-shāh, who is said to have been dragged from his Sufi retreat to be placed on the throne, only to be disposed of in short order. Given the dangers of being a Chaghatayid prince in such an environment, when princes of the blood were useful as potential front-men for ambitious amirs and were thus prime targets for other ambitious amirs, accounts of such dervish-princes are probably not mere rumours or exaggerations; retirement into a Sufi *khānaqāh* may well have seemed a potential way for a Chinggisid sultan to stay alive, whatever his spiritual aptitude.

In the eastern part of the former Chaghatayid realm, meanwhile, we find our latest example of a celebrated royal conversion in the Mongol world, with the case of Tughluq Timur Khan (d. *c.* 1363). This figure's status as a Muslim is evident from the fifteenth-century works of Timurid historiography, but much of his life and the entire extended narrative of his conversion were first recorded only in the middle of the sixteenth century, in the *Tārīkh-i Rashīdī* of Mīrzā Muḥammad Ḥaydar Dūghlāt.[20] From that work are evident several parallels, no doubt historical, with other royal converts, including a focus on the Islamization of the Mongol military forces and above all this khan's need for political legitimation; the contradictions, in early sources, about his Chinggisid lineage, as well as Mīrzā Muḥammad Ḥaydar's story making him in effect a 'foundling' child, discovered as a candidate for the throne by an amir of the Dūghlāt tribe, suggest that his right to be khan was insecure, and that the adoption of Islam may again have played a role in shoring up political alignments. At the same time, the account from the *Tārīkh-i Rashīdī* reveals stock themes in conversion narratives, both in the initial encounter between the khan and a Sufi shaykh, and in the dramatic 'contest' – in this case, the defeat of a Mongol wrestler by the frail shaykh – with which the story culminates. In this case too, the conversion narrative focused on Tughluq Timur Khan continued to resonate in some circles. Although not nearly as widespread as narratives rooted in the Golden Horde, expanded versions of the story were circulated among the putative descendants of the shaykhs responsible for his conversion at least as late as the nineteenth century.

As in the case of other parts of the Islamizing Mongol world, our information on the course of Islamization at the popular level in the Chaghatay *ulus* is quite sparse; in this case, however, we do have a wide range of still largely unexploited material, in the form of local hagiographical works and other religious literature, that illuminates the social and religious history of

20 Dūghlāt/Thackston, pp. 6–11.

Mawarannahr, at least, during the late thirteenth and fourteenth centuries. They suggest, on the one hand, the importance, for the process of Islamization, of communal affiliations between nomadic groups and local Sufi circles, often organized hereditarily, which provided an avenue for the nomadic population to become Muslim through religiously framed social bonds;[21] such affiliations are in some respects similar to patterns of affiliation and influence between shaykhs and rulers, which as a rule are more readily visible in our sources.[22] Such religious literature also suggests, on the other hand, the appeal of calls for stricter observance of Muslim juridical norms than could be expected of those newly brought into the fold of the Muslim community.[23] In this connection, the emergence of Timur out of the political environment of the *ulus* of Chaghatay, and the ongoing Islamization of the Timurid era, should remind us, finally, that Islamization must be understood as an incremental process whose parameters constantly shifted, rather than as a discrete step accomplished once and for all by an act of royal conversion or state support; in the Timurid era, after all, Islamization became less of a choice of affiliation and communal identification, and more a continuing internal dialogue within a nominally Islamic society about what Islam is and about what is required to be considered a Muslim in good standing. As such, that process continues today; but historians go astray when they privilege the most restrictive approaches to Muslim religious life and declare everything outside those rigorist views to be reflective of a substandard or 'incomplete' Islam.

Echoes

The process of Islamization in the areas ruled by the Mongols cannot, in the end, be separated from the broader currents of Islamization both before and after it; yet the Mongol era did bring distinctive new political, social and religious circumstances, as well as a unique paradox that was noted already, in somewhat cryptic terms, by the Egyptian writer Ibn al-Nafīs, around 1270:[24] in effect, the Mongols brought destruction to the Muslim world, but through their conversion they ultimately brought a significant expansion of the Dār al-Islām as well. The process of dealing with the Mongol legacy in the Muslim world was particularly problematical precisely in regions where Mongol traditions, in the form of the principle of Chinggisid rule, survived long after the

21 See DeWeese, 1996a and DeWeese, 1996b.
22 On such patterns, see Paul, 1990, and Potter, 1994.
23 See DeWeese, 1999a.
24 Ibn al-Nafīs, pp. 66–7 (trans.), 41–3 (text).

demise of the direct Mongol successor states; while writers in other parts of the Muslim world could stress the negative impact of Chinggis Khan and the Mongols, those whose patrons claimed the right to rule chiefly on the basis of their descent from Chinggis Khan found more creative ways of dealing with the seeming paradox of Mongols becoming Muslims.

Of particular subtlety in its religious symbolism is the explanation offered by an anonymous writer who compiled, around 1504, a Chaghatay Turkic history of the descendants of Chinggis Khan on behalf of the Chinggisid ruler of the Uzbeks, Muḥammad Shībānī Khan; using materials supplied by the khan himself, and portraying him as an upholder of Islam intent on rooting out elements of pagan traditions, this writer ascribed his understanding of the Islamization of the Mongols to a famous Sufi poet and contemporary of the Mongol conquests – none other than Jalāl al-Dīn Rūmī (d. 1273).[25] Rūmī, the account affirms, had 'predicted' to his disciples that the Mongols, despite the ravages they had inflicted on the Muslim world, would be transformed, in alchemical fashion, into Muslims, and that in this way, the 'Mongols' would indeed disappear (as his disciples hoped they would), not by being destroyed, but by 'becoming Muslim, and just', whereupon they would cease to bear the name 'Mongol' – 'just as when gold is produced through alchemy: when it becomes gold, what was copper in it no longer remains; all of it becomes gold'. The imagery used here may well be superior to many more modern ways of describing what remains a complex and mysterious process.

25 *Tavārīkh-i guzīda-yi nuṣrat-nāma*, London, British Library MS Or. 3222, ff. 4a–5a.

8

Mongols as vectors for cultural transmission

THOMAS T. ALLSEN

For more than a century, the place of the Mongolian Empire in world history has provoked intense debate, much of it heavily coloured by national sentiment and the dictates of official ideology. To some, the Mongolian onslaught was a regressive force in human history, one that 'retarded' the natural development of the numerous civilized societies that fell under their control. Others, in contrast, have celebrated the Mongols' religious tolerance and their political unification of large parts of the Eurasian landmass, thereby facilitating East–West communications. But whatever face of empire one chooses to emphasize, *Pax Mongolica* or 'Tartar Yoke', there can be no doubt that the Chinggisids did in fact greatly intensify cultural and commercial contact throughout the continent. While some of these contacts certainly came about as unintended consequences of their explosive expansion, many of the long-distance exchanges can be linked directly to imperial policies designed to further military conquest, enhance political prestige or satisfy native cultural tastes. In tracing this transcontinental cultural traffic, we start with particulars and then turn to general issues of explanation and interpretation.[1]

Transport of people

Culture, of course, can be transmitted by various means, through objects, texts or direct human agency. Normally all forms are present and in play but in the Mongolian era the movement of peoples, the frequent and forced resettlement of communities from one cultural zone of the empire to another, assumed a special importance. This practice was, in large part, a natural by-product of the Mongols' far-flung military campaigns, which, under Chinggis Khan's immediate successors, extended from Korea to Syria. Operations on

1 Unless otherwise noted, material for this chapter comes from my previous publications, listed in the bibliography.

this scale required the systematic mobilization of military manpower from both the sedentary and nomadic sectors of the empire.

The distances involved in these deployments are impressive and, under pre-modern conditions of transportation, quite unprecedented. The Alans, an Iranian-speaking people of North Caucasia, submitted to the Mongols in the late 1230s and thereafter 10,000 were transported to North China, about 4,700 air kilometres from their homeland. In the 1250s, an 'army' of Mongolian-speaking Oirat, a forest people (*hoi-yin irgen*) from the western shore of Lake Baikal, accompanied Hülegü to Iran, a distance of 4,000 kilometres. The 1,000 Chinese siege engineers posted to Western Iran at the same time travelled even further, some 5,200 kilometres. In most cases, these deployments were permanent; few units ever made the long trek home.

Also common were transfers of civilian populations. By early 1221, just months after its occupation, the Mongols had already established sizeable colonies of Chinese, Khitan and Tangut agriculturalists at Samarqand to help restore the local economy, which had suffered much during the conquest. Some time later, another contingent of North Chinese, called Khitāyān in the Persian sources, arrived in Marv. From there they were resettled in various locales in Azerbaijan; no figures are given but since the Chinese constituted the majority population in Khūi, a fair-sized town north of Lake Urmiya, they must have numbered in the thousands. The eastwards flow of civilian deportees was of similar proportions. The Mongols settled 3,000 households from Samarqand in Sīmālī / Xinmalin, north of Beijing, where they grew grapes and other fruits.[2] Another colony of Turkestani Muslims, relocated to Hongzhou, west of the capital, produced flour and cooking oil for the Yuan court.

The movement of artisans and other kinds of specialists was equally wide ranging. Thousands of Muslim artisans of various kinds were sent to 'the farthest countries of the East' in the immediate aftermath of the Turkestan campaign. For the most part, the many Chinese technicians in Iran, mainly metalsmiths and carpenters, came with the contingent of siege engineers, a unit originally conscripted from artisan families registered in the census of 1252 in North China.

While agriculturalists and artisans tended to be mobilized and transported as groups, the Mongols also impressed and attracted many highly skilled specialists as individuals, some of whom they sent on distant, one-way assignments. The occupational and ethnic backgrounds of those so assigned were extremely diverse: Russian goldsmiths, Nestorian sherbet-makers and Muslim

2 Pelliot, 1927, pp. 261–79.

musicians were dispatched to East Asia, while Chinese cooks, Mongolian wrestlers and Uighur scribes were posted to Iran. Of special importance in this transcontinental traffic in human talent were language specialists. Starting with Chinggis Khan, the Mongols eagerly sought out multilingual people to help them administer their vast, multi-ethnic state. Those recruited were often long-distance merchants or transplanted individuals reared in the cosmopolitan atmospheres of Mongolian courts, east and west. The career of Chaghan, a noted translator of Chinese classics into Mongolian in the fourteenth century, is representative of the type; he was the descendant of a family from Balkh in Afghanistan who submitted in 1220 and then relocated to China, where the young Chaghan grew up in Mongolian service, holding a number of responsible military and civil offices at the Yuan court.[3] Like other foreigners who took posts in China at this time, mastery of Chinese literary culture was much encouraged and well rewarded, but only so long as those who did so maintained their original ethnic identities and, of course, demonstrated continued loyalty to the Yuan regime.[4]

Transmission of texts

People with such skills were needed to tap into the cultural and literary resources of subject populations and some of this 'book' knowledge was transmitted over long distances and sometimes across linguistic divides. Under the auspices of Rashīd al-Dīn (1247–1318), the famed scholar-statesman at the Ilkhan court, Chinese works on statecraft and law were translated into Persian in the early fourteenth century, some of which are still extant.[5] East Asian texts were also involved in the remarkable collaboration between Rashīd al-Dīn and Bolad Aqa, a high-ranking Mongolian official from the Yuan court who arrived in Iran in 1285 with long experience in the governance of China and an intimate knowledge of the Chinese historiographical tradition. With his assistance, Rashīd incorporated much material extracted from Chinese and Mongolian sources into his *Collected Chronicles* (*Jāmiʿ al-tavārīkh*), a comprehensive history of Eurasia composed in the early fourteenth century with the active support of the Ilkhan court.

Another of their joint products, also encouraged by the court, was in the field of agronomy. As part of the package of reforms inaugurated under Ghāzān (r. 1295–1304) to reinvigorate the Ilkhan economy, Rashīd al-Dīn

3 Fuchs, 1946, pp. 62–4.
4 On these themes, see Brose, 2002.
5 Muginov, 1958, pp. 369 and 374.

compiled the *Book of Monuments and Living Things* (*Kitāb-i āthār va aḥyā*), an agricultural manual that contains an extensive section on Chinese crops and methods of cultivation.[6] Here again, the Persian minister drew upon his Mongolian colleague's prior experience at the Yuan court where he had for some years headed the Office of the Grand Supervisors of Agriculture (*Dasinong si*), a venerable institution in China dedicated to the dissemination of useful agronomical information in the countryside. More to the point, in 1273, this office, while under Bolad's direction, published its own manual, *Essentials of Agriculture and Sericulture* (*Nongsang jiyao*). Yuan precedent and praxis, as well as Chinese learning and textual traditions, especially when interpreted by a much-respected Mongolian intermediary, carried considerable weight at the Ilkhan court even after its official conversion to Islam.

The transmission of foreign texts was often associated with the transport of specialists; and, in the period from 1220 to 1320, the Chinggisids, for their own ends, instituted a lively exchange of scholars and scientists between China and the eastern Islamic world. The Bukharan astronomer, Jamāl al-Dīn, sent east during the reign of the qaghan Möngke (1251–9), later became the head of an observatory attached to the Imperial Library Directorate (*Mishu jian*), the archive of the Yuan court, that produced calendars, astronomical instruments and a terrestrial sphere for Qubilai (r. 1260–94) and his successors. According to an inventory compiled in 1273, the observatory had a substantial library of Islamic science, which included works on mathematics (Euclid in Arabic translation), astronomy, astrology, calendars, scientific instruments, technology, chronology and cartography.[7] This collection is perhaps best understood as the 'working' library for the Muslim scholars posted to the Directorate and, so far as is known, none of these works was translated into Chinese. Still, one of the major undertakings of Jamāl al-Dīn and his mixed Sino-Muslim staff, the *Comprehensive Gazetteer of the Great [Yuan] Dynasty* (*Da [Yuan] itong zhi*), an atlas of the Mongolian Empire with maps, issued in 1291, made available to Chinese scholars the riches of Muslim geography and cartography, particularly their detailed knowledge on Western Eurasia.

There was no exact equivalent of the Imperial Library Directorate in Iran, but the observatory founded by Hülegü at Marāghah in Azerbaijan had analogous features and functions. It was a major repository of scholarly books on many subjects and in many languages, and, like the Yuan Directorate, it, too, had a multi-national staff that undertook joint scientific projects.[8] Its first

6 Lambton, 1999.
7 Kōdō, 1957, pp. 103–18.
8 Sayili, 1988, pp. 187–223.

director, the noted polymath, Naṣīr al-Dīn Ṭūsī, working with a team that included at least one Chinese astronomer, produced in the early 1270s the famous *Astronomical Tables of the Il-Khāns* (*Zīj-i īl-khānī*), which contained a set of tables to convert dates between the major calendrical systems of Eurasia, those of the Greeks, Arabs, Persians, Jews, Christians, Chinese and Mongols. These were needed in the first place for administrative purposes but were also of great value to historians like Rashīd al-Dīn, who compiled his *Collected Chronicles* from extremely diverse sources using different methods of time reckoning.

Physicians, too, travelled with their professional literature. Practitioners trained in a wide variety of medical traditions – Chinese, Korean, Tibetan, Indian, Uighur, Muslim and Eastern Christian – were eagerly conscripted and accompanied Mongolian princes and commanders on their far-ranging campaigns.[9] The first wave of East Asian doctors arrived in the Muslim lands with Chinggis Khan and a fresh contingent came in the train of Hülegü. The latter remained permanently in Iran, where they practised their craft as court physicians throughout the thirteenth century. Rashīd al-Dīn, the son of an apothecary and himself a physician, took an avid interest in their literature and under his sponsorship a number of Chinese medical treatises were translated first into Persian and then into Arabic. Some have been lost but a work on sphygmology or pulse diagnosis as well as illustrations from a book on human anatomy have survived in the *Treasure Book of the Il-Khāns on the Sciences of China* (*Tanksūq nāmah-i īl-khān-i dar funūn-i ʿulūm-i khiṭāī*), whose preface, most certainly written by Rashīd al-Dīn, praises the many achievements of Chinese culture.[10]

In the opposite direction, Western medical practitioners, mainly Eastern Christians, first arrived in Mongolia during the reign of Güyük (r. 1246–8) and later took service with Qubilai in China. Chief among them was a language specialist, *ʿĪsā kelemechi*, 'Jesus the Interpreter', who founded around 1263 the Office of Western Medicine (*Xiyu iyao si*) that lasted, under different names, until the end of the dynasty. The Yuan court also took an interest in 'Western' *materia medica* and medical literature. A Muslim 'medical classic', quite possibly the *Qānūn* of Ibn Sina, was housed in the Imperial Library Directorate. Other medical literature must have circulated as well, for in the early Ming several works devoted to Muslim pharmacology were issued. The most notable is the *Huihui yaofang*, 'Muslim Medical Prescriptions', a composite work derived, apparently, from Persian sources, which supplies medicinal recipes

9 For a survey, see Olschki, 1960, pp. 414–32.
10 Rall, 1960, pp. 152–7, and Jahn, 1970, pp. 134–47.

and gives the names of the numerous plants and drugs in the Arabo-Persian script together with their Chinese transcriptions and translations.

Circulation of goods

By far the most common agents for the transmission of culture are objects. In the Mongolian era, vast amounts of goods circulated in the form of booty, trade items and princely presentations, the selection of which was strongly influenced by Mongolian tastes and needs. Their preferences are made abundantly clear in what they seized as spoils or demanded as tribute: horses, herd animals, pack animals, weaponry, gold, silver, gems, tableware, household furnishings, clothing and textiles, that is, military supplies and forms of movable wealth that could be accommodated to a nomadic lifestyle.

Of the goods demanded, one stands out – sumptuous textiles. For the Mongols, clothing, more especially gold brocade robes, was an essential element in their political culture. Called *jisün* in Mongolian, the lavish bestowal of these garments in elaborately staged investiture ceremonies established and publicized political hierarchies and, at the same time, created or reinforced the all-important personal bonds between ruler and servitor. Initially, the Mongols obtained their supplies through plunder and tribute, but their need was so great that they soon began impressing and transporting weavers to make gold brocade in government workshops and artisan colonies. In the 1220s, the Mongols sent 1,000 households of Muslim experts from Herat to Beshbalïq, the Uighur capital on the northern slopes of the Tianshan, and several thousand weavers from Turkestan to various locales around Beijing, where in later decades they taught their special craft to Chinese households. In this, as in other cases, what started out as the appropriation of desirable objects led directly to the appropriation and transportation of people, a noteworthy shift of attention from products to producers.

The movement of goods across cultural boundaries was further accelerated by the expansion of government and private trade in the Mongolian era, and this, too, had profound consequences for both consumers and producers. Among other things, it created in Iran a strong and enduring demand for Chinese goods, particularly blue and white porcelain. In response, the Chinese manufacturing centre at Jingdezhen, in northern Jiangsu, imported cobalt from as far away as Eastern Europe to achieve the colour tones most favoured by the Iranian market. So widespread was this attraction to East Asian goods and styles, that the common people of Yazd and Iṣfahān developed in the late thirteenth century a new cottage industry, making wine cups out of locally grown gourds which they decorated in the manner of chinaware (*ālāt-i khitā'ī*). Sensitivity to transcontinental currents in taste and fashion generated by the Mongols' imperial venture was by no means limited to elites or to court-sponsored workshops.

Distribution of cultural resources

In explaining the scale and range of this cultural traffic, one factor is immediately obvious: the immense size of the Mongolian Empire. It was the largest contiguous land-based empire ever created and in total territory the second largest in world history, surpassed only by the British Empire of the 1920s. Moreover, like the Achaemenids (559–330 BCE), who formed the first universal empire of ancient times, the Chinggisid state was approximately four or five times larger than any of its predecessors.[11] Thus, these two polities were not only the biggest of their own time, they were incomparably bigger than their closest rivals, something unprecedented, something contemporaries found difficult to comprehend except in terms of special cosmic or heavenly dispensations. More concretely, this quantum leap in the scale of political organization meant that within the frontiers of the unified empire, *c*. 1206–60, and its immediate successor states – the Yuan, Ilkhans, Golden Horde and Chaghadai Khanate – there was an extremely diverse array of natural environments and resources at their disposal. In their case, the notion of 'a lottery of natural resources', the random distribution of raw materials that normally precludes true autarky or even near self-sufficiency, hardly applies, since the Mongolian Empire had direct or ready access to materials and products from the Pacific to the Atlantic, from the subarctic to the subtropics.

Of greater consequence, there were also rich cultural resources within their frontiers. Certainly, no state before the Chinggisids commanded such a large portion of Eurasia's pool of human talent, everything from astronomers to animal trainers, weavers to wine-makers. This was all made possible by the fact that the Mongols united under their direct authority major components of three civilizations: the Sinitic, Islamic and Orthodox Christian. North China fell in 1234 and in the ensuing decades the Mongols conquered the rest of China as well as its cultural hinterlands, Korea and Vietnam; only Japan escaped their grasp. In the Islamic world, they first seized northern Iran and Asia Minor in the 1230s and 1240s and occupied the heartlands, Mesopotamia and western Iran, in the late 1250s. In the case of the Eastern Orthodox 'commonwealth',

11 For these comparisons, see the chart in Taagepera, 1978, p. 126.

the Mongols only subjugated the hinterlands, the Rus' principalities and Georgia during the 1230s and 1240s, while the core, the truncated Byzantine state, remained outside their control.

For our purposes it is important to recognize that each of the civilizations subdued by the Mongols participated in wider networks of exchange and that each therefore operated as an interactive, though not politically unified, cultural community. Such 'cultural empires' grow by borrowing and adapting institutions, ideologies and material culture from a centre which, because of its antiquity and reputation for success, is seen by surrounding peoples as a model, a source of legitimacy and prestige.[12] Thus, its expansion is accomplished, for the most part, by means of appropriation, not imposition, This, of course, is in contrast to the Chinggisids, whose state grew by military means and resulted in the imposition of a single political empire over three long-established cultural empires. And this imposition, in its turn, explains some basic features of exchange under the Mongols, notably its chronology and direction.

Direction of cultural traffic

While periodization schemes are usually rough approximations at best, the chronology of transcontinental exchange under the Mongols can be meaningfully linked to pivotal and datable moments in the rise and expansion of their empire. The initial stage and unquestionably the triggering event, was the campaign in Turkestan, 1219–21. For this large-scale assault westwards, the Mongols mobilized the resources of East Asia – troops, war *matériel* and various specialists, including Chinese physicians and engineers. Once active operations ended and garrisons were put in place, much of the Mongol leadership returned to the east with the prizes of victory, booty in the form of precious objects and human talent, thus inaugurating a massive exchange of cultural assets between China and the eastern Islamic world. The second stage came in 1255–60 with Hülegü's campaign against the ʿAbbāsids. Again the invading forces were composed of substantial numbers of East Asian troops and specialist personnel, most of which remained permanently in Iran. The third and final stage can be associated with the arrival of Bolad Aqa at the Ilkhan court in 1285. This period witnessed a definite shift in the nature of exchange; in the first two waves the emphasis was on objects and peoples transported as

12 On the concept of cultural empires, see Lohuizen-de Leeuw, 1970, pp. 41 ff.; Obolensky, 2000, pp. 272 ff.; and Holcombe, 2001, pp. 30 ff.

communities, whereas this latter phase saw mainly the movement of texts and individual specialists.

The major axis of this exchange clearly ran between two of the cultural empires dominated by the Mongols, the Sinitic and Islamic. This raises the question of why the third, the Orthodox Christian, was not an equal partner, or why Mongolian operations in East Europe did not produce equivalent exchange. There are several reasons for this, some rooted in Mongolian imperial policy and some in the differing character of the three cultural empires.

First of all, the Chinggisid civil war that broke into the open with the death of Möngke in 1259 led to a stable and long-term political–military alliance between the descendants of Hülegü and Qubilai. They were forced to join together to fend off the assaults of the lines of Jochi, Ögödei and Chaghadai, who resented the rise of the Toluids to the grand khanate and their effective seizure of North China and Iran, by far the richest, most productive sedentary sectors of the empire. Consequently, the Yuan and Ilkhan courts had compelling reasons to stay in contact, to coordinate their defence against common adversaries, and to continue to exchange information and personnel.

Secondly, both the Yuan and the Ilkhans to a large extent shared the same territory with their sedentary subjects and therefore shared similar problems of governance, providing yet another motive for sharing experience and personnel. Their situation contrasts sharply with that of rivals such as the Golden Horde, which remained in the steppe and ruled its most populous sedentary possessions, the Rus' principalities, by a kind of 'remote control'.[13]

Lastly, and on an even more fundamental level, this axis is a by-product of the simple fact that China and the Islamic world had equivalent cultural assets to exchange. The Mongols, to be sure, interested themselves in East Slavic military recruits and artisans – metalsmiths, bow-makers and the like – but there were no astronomers/astrologers, physicians, geographers, cartographers and mathematicians to be found in the Rus' principalities or Georgia, at least not of the stature and prestige of those produced in China or Iran. Similarly, there were no pools of administrative personnel in Russia that were potentially employable elsewhere in the empire. This, again, stands in stark contrast with the situation in North China and Iran, regions which for centuries had produced administrators skilled at assisting Inner Asian conquerors control and exploit their sedentary subjects. Thus, while Muslim officials and merchants served the Yuan bureaucracy in various capacities, the Russians, like the Alans, sent only contingents of troops to China.

13 Wittfogel, 1963, p. 635.

Communications

The geographical distribution of cultural resources has much to tell us about exchange, but the spread of such assets across space is also a matter of communications. Steppe nomads were in the business of moving goods, animals and people over extended distances, that is, they were very good at logistics. Still, the Mongolian elite, intent on enjoying the products of the sown while retaining their nomadic lifestyle, required a measure of state assistance in transporting and storing their newly acquired wealth.

These measures took various forms. In the course of its early expansion, the empire created much infrastructure for travel – roads, bridges and ferry services. Such improvements were particularly important since the Mongols, both khans and common herders, nomadized in large ox-drawn wagons and imperial policy required many to traverse difficult terrain on their way to postings in distant and unfamiliar climes. For the elite, support was also provided by the founding of small 'towns' across the steppe that functioned as winter camps and as political, craft and supply centres.[14]

Much better known, thanks to Marco Polo's vivid portrayal, is the Mongols' extensive postal relay system. Although their network of stations (*jam*, plural *jamud*) had ancient roots in Inner Asia, it was unique in one crucial respect – its vast scale. In the early empire, relay stations radiated out from Qara Qorum, the capital in central Mongolia, to China in the south and the lower Volga in the west. Sometimes compared to the American pony express, such a depiction is too limiting since the Mongolian system was responsible for much more than conveying messages by relay riders. The services provided were three: *morin* or 'horse' stations for moving people, couriers, officials and envoys; *narin* or 'careful [-handling]' stations for direct communication with the khan; and *tergen* or 'wagon' stations for hauling bulk goods. The latter were vital because the capital, Qara Qorum, the Mongols' 'sitting city' and their royal encampments or *ordos*, their 'moving cities', constituted unnatural and unsustainable concentrations of goods, people and animals in the steppe environment and wagon stations were needed to make up the deficit with supplies from the outside world.

This shortfall not only required the expansion of infrastructure but also special arrangements with long-distance merchants. To gain their cooperation, Mongolian courts underwrote merchants' transportation costs by allowing them access to the postal system, provided capital for joint commercial ventures and offered them artificially elevated prices for the delivery of desired

14 Cf. Egorov, 1969, pp. 39–49.

goods to their travelling camps. Merchants, in effect, served the Chinggisids as logistical officers specializing in the provision of foodstuffs and luxuries. Their basic function is well expressed in their Old Russian name, *ordobazarets*, 'camp merchant', while their background is accurately conveyed by the Chinese *wolotu shangfan huihuiren*, 'camp trading Muslim'. In acquiring their services, largely to meet daily needs, the Mongols became enmeshed in exchange networks formed long before their empire and operational far beyond its political frontiers. And, of course, it is just such interlocking networks that account for the extensive circulation of commodities, ideologies, technologies and pathologies that so characterizes the history of the Old World from ancient times.[15]

One of the earlier and most productive of these networks developed in consequence of the spread of Buddhism from India into adjoining regions. Though much atrophied by the thirteenth century, the Mongols' assertion of loose forms of suzerainty over Tibet and Kashmir in the 1240s and 1250s nonetheless temporarily reactivated the northern branch of this older network, producing visible, continental cultural consequences. In China, Tibetan monks successfully gained Qubilai's favour and exercised substantial influence on Yuan religious policy and ceremonial life, while Kashmiris served in civil posts and participated in Buddhist translation projects sponsored by the court. At the same time, Buddhists in some numbers settled in Iran where they established many religious communities and shrines with the support and patronage of the early Ilkhans. Although driven from the country shortly after Ghāzān's adoption of Islam, one of their number, a Kashmiri monk, assisted Rashīd al-Dīn prepare his *History of India* which includes a lengthy exposition of Buddhist doctrine.[16]

This revival, however, was but a pale reflection of the former influence and vigour of the aptly named 'Buddhist International' which at its height extended over much of Central, South and East Asia.[17] For centuries, Buddhist merchants and institutions had dominated interregional exchange throughout this vast territory but the decline of Buddhism on its home ground, India, gradually eroded their supremacy. In the course of the eleventh and twelfth centuries Arab and Persian merchants marginalized their Buddhist competitors along the Indian Ocean routes, and Muslim diasporas and institutions assumed the leading role in organizing and integrating the Chinese and Indian markets.[18] The Islamization of the long-time Buddhist system resulted in an

15 For one inventory of exchanges, see Kroeber, 1952, pp. 383–93.
16 Franke, 1981; Jahn, 1956b; and Jahn, 1956a.
17 This characterization is from Adshead, 1988, pp. 52–3 and 102.
18 On this transition, see Sen, 2000, pp. 165–8 and 236, and Clark, 1995, pp. 50–65.

interactive cultural–commercial community that now extended from China through India and westwards to Africa and the Mediterranean world.[19] And when the Song fell in 1279, the Mongols inherited direct access to a communications network fashioned by others, one that became increasingly important to the Yuan court as princely strife in Inner Asia inhibited overland travel.

To the north of the steppe, the Mongols revitalized and re-created a number of older tributary relationships that extended into the forest zone and beyond to the subarctic. Here the Mongols mimicked, and in some cases simply 'piggybacked' on, systems pioneered by their predecessors, the Rus', Volga Bulghars, Qïrghïz and the states of Manchuria, who specialized in the extraction of 'northern goods', notably, but not exclusively, furs. In this way, the Chinggisids came to have a significant, sometimes decisive, say in the 'trans-civilizational exchanges' between East and West and the 'trans-ecological exchanges' between North and South, which together formed a continental system of commercial–cultural transaction.[20]

This ready access to both axes of exchange, with their specific products, routes and market mechanisms, greatly increased the Chinggisids' effective range of action. The distances involved can be gauged by the kinds of products available to the Ilkhans at the turn of the fourteenth century. Through the Indian Ocean routes Iran was an active participant in the international traffic in South and East Asian medicines such as *shāh-ṣīnī*, a standard headache remedy in the Middle East 'brewed' by locals from a plant found along borderlands of south-western China and Tibet.[21] Even more remote was the source of the courts' raptor of choice, the gyrfalcon, a subarctic species which came to them from both the North Pacific and the North Atlantic, 5,000 to 6,000 kilometres from Iran.[22] This tells us that the Ilkhans' ability to attract goods from afar, their cultural reach, was coterminous with the outermost limits of the then known world.

Agency

In considering the Mongols' role in selecting cultural assets for wider dissemination and display, the first question to arise is how did nomads, from a distant corner of the steppe, become acquainted with the varied cultural resources of their diverse sedentary subjects? Part of the answer is that surrendering

19 Voll, 1992, especially 219.
20 Christian, 2000; especially 7–9.
21 Rashīd al-Dīn, 1980, folio 136r, plate 16, Persian text, and p. 39, German trans.
22 Polo, 1935–8, I, p. 178; al-Qāshānī, 1969, pp. 49, 53 and 205; and Paviot, 2000, pp. 315–16.

populations regularly offered the Mongols assorted 'gifts' they thought pleasing to the conquerors. From North China through the Islamic East, delegations seeking terms, accompanied by tribute goods and talented individuals – actors, musicians, animal trainers and weavers – emerged from surrendering cities, thereby providing the conquerors with a sampling of local wares and skills.

While these attractively packaged displays broadened the Mongols' horizons, native tastes and preferences also drove and guided the search. This is evident from Mongolian practice in North China, where they sent in commissioners (*shizhe*) to bring out scholars, physicians and technicians before cities were sacked.[23] Such quests, initially accomplished by sorting and sparing populations immediately upon their submission, were supplanted in later decades by systematic census-taking, a technique borrowed from the Chinese, as the primary means of identifying and mobilizing human and economic assets of every description.[24] From the Chinese sources, it is clear that the population registers contained separate categories for military, agricultural, merchant, artisan and physician households; thus, by the 1250s, Chinggisid rulers had extensive information on the talent pools available to them.

Once identified, cultural assets were widely shared among Mongolian elites and to some extent with common herders. Following their victories in North China, Mongolian commanders systematically apportioned shares of the accumulated booty to all participating soldiers, the emperor and to high-ranking officers residing 'in the northern desert'.[25] Indeed, such practices were deeply ingrained in nomadic society, which expected rulers, as well as those aspiring to positions of leadership, to be generous, to redistribute part of their wealth among their retainers and followers. The creation of clients and dependants, the basic building-blocks of steppe polities, was achieved through a variety of mechanisms: the organization of feasts and drinking parties, the bestowal of sumptuous garments and the sharing out of game following collective hunts. Since the early Chinggisids did not provide stipulated salaries for officials, their 'pay' came as irregular gifts of goods, grants of proceeds from agricultural lands, and participation in extended celebrations and ceremonies during which time those invited enjoyed a taste of the good life and lived off the resources of the court.

For the higher levels of military-political leadership, these shares in the profits of empire not only took the form of prestige goods but of skilled people, particularly artisans, appropriately termed 'sons of the yurt' (*ger-ün*

23 Haenisch, 1969, p. 11v, Chinese text, and p. 25, German trans.
24 Brosset, 1850, p. 551.
25 *Mengda beilu*/Wang, pp. 446–7. See also the comments of Haenisch, 1943, pp. 5–8.

köbegüd), who often travelled with their new masters. Competition for specialists of all types, like that for gold or fine horses, was sometimes intense and shares of any kind might be exchanged among elites; Ögödei, for example, once 'traded' five agricultural villages in Turkestan in return for Herati weavers resettled in Beshbalïq. All this was fully consistent with nomadic notions of society and politics, notions that were now applied on an imperial scale, resulting in the movement of quantities of goods and humans across many cultural divides.

The centrality of the Mongols in the selection and transmission of this transcontinental cultural traffic thus rests on strong and consistent evidence from both ends of Eurasia. For many of the products involved, robes, jewellery and other forms of art (or wealth) that can be worn or easily transported, their inclusion is quite understandable. So, too, is the Mongols' appropriation and dissemination of sedentary military technology and administrative method. But what of the more sophisticated achievements of urban-based civilization, especially scientific knowledge conveyed through learned textual traditions? At first glance, it may appear most unlikely that nomads were instrumental in identifying, valuing and transferring intellectual properties of this kind. Yet, even in this sphere, the imprint of the Mongols is unmistakable and readily demonstrable in the fields of medical theory and astronomy.

The Mongols' first exposure to sedentary medical tradition came in China and the experience left a lasting impression. By this time, of course, Chinese medicine had a long history, a rich literature and several identifiable schools, each with its own therapies and theories. One popular school of thought was based on the belief that physical and emotional well-being was determined by the interaction of *qi*, 'emanations' or 'influences' in the environment, with the human body, and that these interactions could be assessed and treated through pulse diagnosis. Such concepts were compatible with, if not identical to, long-held nomadic religious beliefs that the seat of human life force, the soul, was located in the blood and circulatory system. And in consequence of this convergence, the early Mongolian court enthusiastically embraced pulse diagnosis and later in the Yuan the classic texts of this school were made mandatory in the training and testing of physicians. Chief among them was the *Maijue*, the 'Secrets of the Pulse', the principal Chinese work selected for translation in Rashīd al-Dīn's *Tanksūq-nāmah*. In short, the Chinese medical theories explored in Iran were determined by Mongolian cultural filters, not by the preferences or interests of local Muslim practitioners.

For the Mongols, physicians from the sedentary world were the functional equivalents of healing shamans and, not unexpectedly, astronomers / astrologers were seen as the counterparts to their divining shamans. The ability of astronomers to predict, with considerable accuracy, eclipses and movements of the heavens had strong appeal for a people whose native religion centred on the cult of Heaven, Tengri, who granted the Chinggisids a mandate for universal rule on earth. Here again, astronomers were exchanged between China and Iran not because distant colleagues wanted to share scientific ideas or information but because Mongolian khans required their services for a variety of political reasons. In all pre-modern empires carefully managed prognostication was an essential political tool, one that enhanced majesty, validated policy, built morale and focused public attention and opinion. The Chinggisids were no exception; they recruited 'futurologists' of every type and put their most prized finds, the astronomers / astrologers of China and Iran, on display throughout the empire.

Consequences

Under the Mongols, cultural resources were moved around Eurasia by means of imperial postings, the sharing of spoils, the extension of trade and, of equal importance, by princely presentations that the Chinggisids regularly exchanged among themselves and with foreign courts.[26] In assessing the consequences of this traffic, it must be emphasized that because of the empire's enormous size and great prestige, some products closely identified with the Mongolian elite travelled under false colours; both the 'Tartar cloth' known from India to England and the 'Tatar armour' that so impressed East Europeans were products of Islamic workshops. The Mongols, in other words, were not engaged in exporting their own ethnic culture but in selecting, transporting, displaying and, in some cases, 'accrediting' the cultural assets of others.

One should not assume, however, that whatever was demonstrated was adopted. As a general proposition, it is fair to say that intellectual properties, medical theories and the like, did not travel well since they were typically linked to world views and their acceptance required the receiving society to question core values or even jettison portions of its inherited tradition. In contrast, foreign material culture, more specifically art, was often warmly accepted and creatively adapted to local conditions and tastes. The best documented instance in the Mongolian era is the deep and enduring Chinese influence on

26 For the Latin West, see Arnold, 1999, pp. 119–33.

Persian painting, which is manifest in the growing importance of landscape, in the treatment of clouds and horizons and in the use of colour.[27]

Technologies, too, are mobile and through Mongolian agency many diffused across the continent. According to Marco Polo, on Qubilai's orders, people from 'Babilonie', here meaning Egypt, established a manufactory at Yongzhun, north of Quanzhou (Zayton), and taught the locals the West Asian technique of clarification for making refined sugar, a product hitherto unknown in China.[28] Confirmation for his report is found in the Chinese sources, which affirm that in 1276 there was created a Sugar Office (*Shatang ju*), a branch of the Bureau of Household Provisions (*Xuanhui shi*), 'to manage the production of granulated sugar'.[29] In this specific instance, the introduction is probably related to the fact that the Yuan court had many servitors from West Asia for whom refined sugar was a welcome taste of home. In the next instance, the diffusion of distilled alcohol, the Mongols' own tastes are paramount.

The Mongols, whose native drink was *koumiss*, evinced a keen interest in the alcoholic beverages – grape wine, beer and mead – of neighbouring societies. Vast quantities of these beverages were consumed at the communal drinking sessions that marked and accompanied all important political and social events in the life of the empire.[30] While fermentation is an ancient technique, distilled alcohol was a relatively recent innovation discovered at least twice, once in Sicily in the twelfth century and earlier in China where 'burnt' or 'fired' wines are first mentioned as social drinks in the Tang era.[31] Somewhat unexpectedly, while the distilled version of *koumiss* is first attested in China, it was most likely produced by West Asians in Yuan service, more specifically by makers of sherbet, a refreshing drink of sugar, citrus juice and rosewater, a distillate widely used in Middle Eastern medicine and cuisine. This is indicated by the Mongolian term for spirituous liquor, *araki*, which derives from *ʿaraq*, the Arabic for 'sweat' and by extension for spirits distilled from date or raisin wine. In any event, the technique and the product, under its Arabo-Mongolian name, quickly spread from China throughout Central, North and South Asia. In this instance, we see the Mongolian Empire functioning as a huge sounding board that broadcast the technological achievements of one region of Eurasia to others. And this it did with another pre-existing and equally explosive technology – gunpowder.

27 Soucek, 1980, pp. 86–109, and Inal, 1976, pp. 108–43.
28 Polo, 1935–8, p. 347. On Muslim techniques, see Sato, 2004, pp. 94–7.
29 *YS*, 87, p. 2204.
30 Smith, 2000.
31 Huang, 2000, pp. 203–31.

The Chinese origin of gunpowder, which developed gradually between the ninth and twelfth centuries, is now firmly established; this technology, however, remained confined to East Asia until the rise of the Mongols. They first encountered explosives in the form of grenades and rockets during their operations against the Jin and soon adopted these devices, which they used in the Turkestan campaign of the early 1220s. And three decades later, the contingent of Chinese siege engineers who accompanied Hülegü to Iran had within their ranks gunpowder-makers (*huojiang*). Mongolian agency in the spread of this new technology, which reached most of the complex societies of Eurasia in the course of the thirteenth and fourteenth centuries, can hardly be doubted.

At this stage of its development, gunpowder weaponry was never decisive, and most certainly does not explain the Mongols' initial military success. Indeed, throughout this era, it remained marginal even in siege work since these first generation firearms were unreliable and often were used as much for their psychological as for their physical effect. Still, in the long term, the spread of gunpowder was a consequential step in the transformation of warfare. Further, the later history of gunpowder illustrates a crucial point concerning diffusion as a creative process. In the Latin West, this borrowed technology underwent considerable improvement, particularly corning, which increased its stability and explosive power, and was soon reintroduced into China by Jesuits aiding the Ming dynasty to fend off the Manchus. Here, as in other cases, the attempt to reproduce alien wares in new cultural settings often leads to variation and innovation and to a secondary round of diffusion for the new, improved product.

Besides moving technologies around, the Mongolian Empire stimulated the flow of geographical information within and beyond its own borders. It did this in several ways. First of all, the empire's size, communication system and fame of its courts attracted a multitude of merchants, missionaries, emissaries and adventurers from across the continent, some of whom prepared accounts of their travels on their return. The total number of journeys is unknowable but a recent study calculates that from Western and Eastern Christendom alone, over 126 individuals or embassies reached Central and East Asia between 1242 and 1448.[32]

Another reason for this flow is that the Mongols, for military, administrative and ideological purposes, systematically sought out and accumulated geographical data. Their own envoys collected topographical intelligence, while

32 Reichert, 1992, pp. 288–93.

Chinggisid courts queried all foreign envoys concerning strategic locations, demanded maps from surrendering states and sponsored major cartographical projects. While the Yuan courts' information on continental Asia was usually firsthand, their perception of maritime Asia and the lands of the Far West often drew upon the geographical knowledge of the Muslim world, which undoubtedly possessed the most sophisticated navigational and cartographical information of the age. Moreover, the open and active involvement of the court in overseas trade ventures encouraged some Chinese officials to travel the maritime routes and record their findings. With such sources available, it is arguable that Yuan familiarity with the Eastern Seas was at least on a par with, if not superior to, the early Ming, which is now so closely associated with the celebrated voyages of Zheng He.[33]

But this information flow was not just about routes, navigation instructions or the location of natural and cultural resources; it also served to advertise, extend and enhance technical and artistic reputations, which in turn encouraged the acceptance of, and the desire for, foreign wares. This can be seen in the heightened regard for Chinese achievements in Western Eurasia.

Muslim esteem for China, of course, long predated the Mongols. Some valuations extolling Chinese artists and artisans as the best in the world are quite generalized, but others' praise is expressed in a distinctive formula.[34] Thaʿālibī, writing in the tenth century, remarks that in the Arab lands any well-executed utensil is automatically attributed to the Chinese. He then records a saying he attributes to the Chinese themselves: 'Except for us, the people of the world are all blind – unless one takes into account the people of Babylon, who are merely one-eyed'.[35] The full meaning of this statement is elaborated upon by Marvazī, a near contemporary:

> The people of China [he relates] are the most skilful of men in handicrafts. No nation approaches them in this. The people of Rūm are highly proficient [in the crafts] but they do not reach the standards of the Chinese. The latter say that all men are blind in craftsmanship, except the people of Rūm who [however] are one-eyed, that is to say, they know only half the business.[36]

When we reach the Mongolian period, this high regard for Chinese artisanship, initially expressed in general terms, is now found among West Europeans.[37] But what is more interesting is that starting at the very end of

33 Ptak, 1995, and Deng, 1997, pp. 57–8 and 159.
34 al-Masʿūdī, 1861, I, pp. 322–4 and 357, and al-Andalusī, 1991, p. 7.
35 al-Thaʿālibī, 1968, p. 141.
36 Marvazī, 1942, p. 14.
37 For examples, see Dawson, 1980, p. 22, and Boccaccio, 1949, X.3 (p. 498).

the thirteenth century there are authors writing for European audiences who repeat and endorse the older Muslim formula on the superiority of Chinese arts and crafts. Hayton (Hetʿum), the prince of Lesser Armenia, who spent much time at the Ilkhan court, writes that 'the Cathayans say that they are the ones who see with two eyes, the Latins, they say, see with one eye, but other nations, they say, are blind'.[38] This is later repeated and accepted by European writers and travellers of the fourteenth and fifteenth centuries.[39] In the Latin West, as in the Muslim East, everything foreign and clever was now assumed to be Chinese.

Clearly, the reputation of the Chinese for excellence in the production of things that spread to Europe in the Mongolian period took over and embraced Muslim images and literary formulas of the Muslims' own Orient. This, of course, helped set the stage for growing European openness and appetite for 'china', the shorthand term for Chinese-style earthenware and porcelain tableware, a usage that has clear Arabic and Persian antecedents and analogues.[40]

Conclusion

The nomads of the Eurasian steppe were connectors linking distant cultures and peoples. Among them, the Mongols forged the greatest number of links. This was so because their empire and its own excellent communication system was superimposed on a variety of overlapping and interacting information circuits – cultural empires, commercial networks and systems of interstate relations, all of which circulated products, peoples and ideas long before the advent of the Chinggisids. The Mongols, therefore, benefited from and, at the same time, extended the range of, pre-existing circuits.[41]

The Mongols' undeniable role as mediators between sedentary civilizations requires adjustments in our notions about the cultural relations between the steppe and the sown. We are accustomed to thinking about Chinese, Tibetan or Muslim influence on the nomads. Such formulas have validity of course but leave a misleading impression; placed in such a framework the nomads appear as passive recipients, overcome by wily, culturally more sophisticated neighbours and rivals. Perhaps it is time to think in terms of the nomads' active and selective appropriation of sedentary culture. This, indeed, is what

38 Hayton, 1906, p. 121.
39 Mandeville, 1983, p. 143; González de Clavijo, 1928, p. 289; and Lord Stanley of Aldershot, 1873, pp. 58–9.
40 Yule and Burnell, 1903, pp. 198–9.
41 Cf. Kradin, 2002, pp. 380 and 383, and Adshead, 1993, p. 70.

the Mongolian Empire did on a continental scale: it appropriated, according to its own measures and predilections, the rich cultural resources of its highly diverse subject population. And in so doing, the Empire of the Great Mongols functioned as the cultural clearing house for Eurasia on the eve of European maritime expansion, which, in its time, fashioned a truly global network of interchange.

PART THREE

★

CHINGGISID DECLINE: 1368–*c.* 1700

9
The eastern steppe: Mongol regimes after the Yuan (1368–1636)

VERONIKA VEIT

In 1626 the Jurchen leader Nurhaci's eighth son, Hung Tayiji,[1] succeeded his father as Khan of the Aisin (= 'Gold') dynasty. Ten years later, in May 1636, he proclaimed himself emperor with the reign-title Chongde (1636–43) and changed the name of his dynasty to Da Qing.[2] Representatives of a number of Mongol tribes came to offer their felicitations as well as their formal allegiance to the new ruler. This act was to mark a turning point in the history of the Mongols, as shall be seen in the course of events.

The years after the fall of the Yuan dynasty, 1368, until 1636, mark a period in Mongol history which is often characterized as 'dark' – a term attributed to it by the nineteenth-century Russian scholar A. M. Pozdneev. 'Dark', because the Mongol confederations, eventually emerging after the end of the Chinggisid Empire and the disappearance of the successor states, no longer played a global role, but found themselves reduced to mere regional powers. Dark, because the events leading to it present a chaotic tableau of ruthless intertribal fighting for supremacy, of intrigues, political plots, betrayal and murder – not unlike the situation before the rise of Chinggis Khan. Dark, finally, because there are no contemporary autochthonous Mongol sources at our disposal to record the events. The earliest documents available date from the seventeenth century and are more notable for their literary qualities than for their historical accuracy. To bring some light into such 'darkness', historians have to rely on a critical correlation of Chinese records, Mongolian written traditions and later Manchu archive materials.

The accession of the Ming dynasty to power and the return of the Mongols to their homeland after 1368 immediately confronted both parties with the decisive question of their future political course. The experience

1 Erroneously also named Abahai. Cf. Stary, 1984.
2 Hauer, 1926, pp. 396–7.

of the Mongol conquest had so profoundly influenced the Ming approach to the steppe that its frontier policy differed completely from that of previous dynasties. Rather than coming to an accommodation with the nomads by gifts, trading and marriage-alliances, the Ming opted for other strategies. When their initial military actions failed to effectively counter the menace of Mongol incursions, they proceeded simply to lock the steppe nomads out. To begin with, the Ming built earthen bulwarks and walls along the open regions of the Ordos plateau, an area the Mongols had started to move to in the fifteenth century. These barriers were then gradually continued as far as Beijing. Not until the sixteenth century did the Ming start to build stone walls – walls we now admire as part of the Great Wall of China.

Such a short-sighted frontier policy proved a constant, not to say debilitating, strain on Ming military and economic resources, without bringing the hoped-for security. The realization that tribute and trade were, in the long run, the cheapest and most effective means for peace came rather too late, and a weakened Ming China had no strength left to oppose the incursions, and eventual conquest, by another Inner Asian power, the Jurchen, or Manchus, as they were to call themselves later.

The Mongols, for their part, had not forgotten the Yuan rule over China, either. Their claim to what they still regarded as theirs motivated the initial course of Mongol policy after their return to the steppe. The homeland of the Mongols, or the old Central Khanate (*ulus*), with the former imperial capital Karakorum, had lost its significance when Qubilai established the Yuan dynasty. The steppe became periphery and the centre of power shifted to the sedentary areas. In consequence, the Central Khanate, or Helin province as it was called in Yuan times, found itself reduced to a political backwater, its role at most that of a marshalling area, as, for instance, in operations against attacks of the traditionalist western Khanate of Chaghatai, later to become the domain of the Turkish conqueror Timur.

Nevertheless, the Mongol tribes still remaining in the Central Khanate, as well as those living to the south and east of it, had developed aspirations of their own. Therefore, with the return of the Yuan Mongols – some 60,000 according to the autochthonous tradition – intertribal rivalries for the position of power, the old bane of the steppe nomads, rarely ever broken in the course of their history, flared up once more. They eventually destroyed all chances for the Mongols to present a united front, not only with regard to China, but also with regard to their own political fate.

Initial claims by the descendants of Qubilai to rule over China

Toghan Temür,[3] the last Yuan emperor, died in Yingchang, north-west of Jehol, in 1370. His son Ayushiridara[4] succeeded to the Yuan imperial authority, and almost immediately found himself attacked by Ming troops at his temporary capital. Taken by surprise and overpowered, he escaped with a small force across the Gobi to Karakorum, where he took up residence until his death in 1378. Once again, Karakorum had become the seat of a Mongol Khan, for there is no doubt that Ayushiridara saw himself as the legitimate heir of the Yuan emperors. This claim was openly maintained by at least the first two Mongol rulers in the steppe, Ayushiridara and Toghus Temür,[5] who called their dynasty 'Northern Yuan'. Further evidence to prove this claim was Ayushiridara's assumption of a reign-title in the Chinese tradition, Xuanguang, and the issue of four Chinese language state-seals (two of them dated 1370, 1371 and 1375).[6] All four seals were supposedly issued, according to their Chinese inscription, by the Central Secretariat, Ministry of Rites (*zhongshu li bu zao*). Ayushiridara no longer had access to the offices of the Central Secretariat and the claim to have seals issued there must be seen as his attempt to uphold a Yuan dynasty still in power outside the Ming. Ayushiridara was posthumously canonized as Zhaozong as well as Biligtü Qaghan. Toghus Temür, Ayushiridara's younger brother, succeeded as Khan of the Northern Yuan. He, too, assumed a Chinese reign-title, Tianyuan, and was also posthumously canonized, though under a Mongol name only, Uskhal Qaghan. His aspirations to continue the line of the Yuan emperors was likewise documented by a state-seal, dated 1379, also supposedly issued by the Central Secretariat of the Li Bu.[7] These formal acts of claim were not, however, backed up by a matching military power. On the contrary, the Mongols had to accept a series of further weakening defeats by the Ming army. Nevertheless, military setbacks in no way discouraged the Mongol claimants in their attempts to regain what they had lost. Ayushiridara in particular completely ignored the Ming dynasty's repeated offers of peace, provided he surrendered and accepted the Hongwu Emperor's[8] authority. Not even the Ming court's courteous treatment of Ayushiridara's son Maidiribala,

3 Franke, 1976.
4 Dreyer and Chan, 1976.
5 Dreyer, 1976.
6 Weiers, 2002, pp. 2–6.
7 Weiers, 2002, p. 6.
8 Teng, 1976.

taken prisoner by the Chinese army during their pursuit of the Mongols to Karakorum, motivated the father to at least reply to the letters sent by the emperor. He simply continued with a policy of border-raids and the renewed rally of his forces.

The Ming response to such an unbroken Mongol spirit was initially remarkably restrained. Diplomatic missions, courtesy towards high-born prisoners, even a special messenger to attend the mourning ceremonies for Ayushiridara and a personal eulogy by the emperor, must certainly be seen as proof of the Ming's intention to win the goodwill of the Mongols. At the same time, of course, it was essential to their interest to keep the remaining Mongol military forces under control. Thus they successfully subdued a number of Ayushiridara's and Toghus Temür's principal supporters, and finally inflicted a crushing defeat on the Mongols in 1388. This battle put a temporary end to the Ming–Mongol armed conflict.

In the context of the post-Yuan claim to the Chinese throne, an interesting Mongol legend should be mentioned, first recorded in the seventeenth-century chronicle *Altan Tobci*.[9] It tells the story of how Ming Taizu, the Hongwu Emperor, after the fall of the Yuan capital, captured a Mongol princess, one of Toghan Temür's wives, who was then two or three months pregnant. The princess prayed for a prolongation of her pregnancy so as to preclude all suspicion regarding the identity of the father. When she finally gave birth, Ming Taizu indeed recognized the child as his son, who later succeeded him as the Yongle Emperor. The fact, of course, is that the first Ming Emperor was succeeded by a grandson, who, in his turn, was soon ousted by his uncle, Zhu Di, the Yongle Emperor. The legend is independently found in a number of Mongol chronicles of the seventeenth century, and also survived in an oral tradition in Ordos in the nineteenth century.[10] The Mongol claim to be emperor of China – impossible in reality–become true in a dream of legendary ancestry.

Internecine wars in the steppe for unified power

The defeat of the Mongol forces in 1388 had broken the power of the Yuan claimants for a number of years to come. Toghus Temür himself survived as a refugee until the winter of 1388/9, when he was murdered by one of his relatives. After his death, the Qubilaid rulers entered upon a period of short-lived reigns by weak khans, few of whom died of natural causes. Their line of succession, with but minor variations as to dates, is borne out by Mongol

9 Bawden, 1955, pp. 154–5.
10 Serruys, 1972, pp. 19–20.

and Chinese sources alike:[11] Engke Jorigtu (r. 1389–92), Elbeg (r. 1393–9), Güng Temür (r. 1400–08), Öljei Temür (r. 1408–10), Delbeg (r. 1411–15) – the latter mere puppets in the hands of the Oirats. Their control over the Mongol tribes was at best nominal, and none of them laid claims to a continuation of the Yuan dynasty. Rivalry was the order of the day, political fragmentation the outcome. Chinggis Khan's successful unification of all the people of the 'felt-wall tents', as they are called in the *Secret History* of the Mongols, had not led to the institutionalization of a centrally governed state other than the prerogative of his family to rule.[12] The inherent intransigence of clan-structured rule vs. centralized state-rule, originally having contributed to the dynamic rise of the steppe nomads, ultimately led to their undoing.

Mongol politics had not changed from the principle of the famous quotation of Lu Jia to the Han Emperor Gaozu (r. 202–195 BC), subsequently repeated by Yelü Chucai to Ögödei, and finally quoted by Liu Bingzhong in a memorial to Qubilai: 'Even though an empire may be conquered on horseback, it could not be administered on horseback'.[13] Besides, the Mongols of the thirteenth and fourteenth centuries had no concept of a nation in the modern sense, but solely of a people in relation to its ruler or rulers. Theirs was an aristocratic concept, not a popular one.[14]

The sequence of events in fifteenth-century Mongolia with its leading players was as complex as to be almost likened to a Shakespearean drama. In order to bring some clarity into this chaos of intrigues and fighting, it seems useful first to introduce the principal characters and groups with their respective interests:[15] Ming China with its well-established administration and its operationally capable army; the former Yuan Mongols, descendants of Qubilai, entitled to rule over the Mongol tribes according to Chinggis Khan's tradition – a mere loose confederation, however, without functioning administration and insufficient troops at their disposal; other descendants of Qubilai, not entitled to rule, i.e. individual tribal chieftains without administration or troops to speak of; Mongols other than descendants of Qubilai having remained in the old homeland of the Central Khanate, who simply formed loose tribal organizations; and finally the Oirats, or 'forest-dwellers' – the most complex and best-consolidated group of the Mongol tribes, based in their original homeland along the Upper Yenisei. The Oirats had been integrated into the

11 Pokotilov, 1949, p. 64.
12 *Secret History*/de Rachewiltz, I, p. 133.
13 Cf. de Rachewiltz *et al.*, 1993, pp. 248–9.
14 Cf. Bawden, 1968a, pp. 5–6.
15 Cf. also Weiers, 2004, pp. 159–61.

Mongol Empire by Chinggis Khan's elder son, Jochi, in 1218, and were obliged to render military service. Manifold ties bound them to Chinggis Khan's ruling house, and their chiefs held important posts in the time of the empire. Towards the end of the fourteenth century the Oirats had moved south and south-west of the old Central Khanate, as far west as the Qinghai Lake and the Tarim Basin.

The principal players in the evolving drama were doubtless Ming China, the former Yuan Mongols of Chinggisid origin and the Oirats. Rivalry for the leadership over the Mongol tribes between the latter two broke out at the beginning of the fifteenth century. According to Mongol tradition, the reason for it is said to have been an affair instigated by an Oirat, rife with cunning, betrayal and murder.[16] The true background, more likely, is that the Yuan Mongols were forced to realize that the Oirats had achieved a position of power that enabled them to challenge the Qubilaids' right to be Great Khans of all the Mongols. Elbeg died a violent death at the hand of an Oirat in 1399. The series of plots and counter-plots continued, when the Great Khan Güng Temür murdered a certain Engke Temür of Hami, who had been enfeoffed by the Yongle Emperor.[17] This led to considerable tension between China and the Chinggisids, but obviously also between the Chinggisids and their other Mongol rivals. Arughtai,[18] a chieftain who was not a Chinggisid, murdered Güng Temür and proclaimed another Chinggisid of his own choice, Öljei Temür, also named Bunyasiri, Great Khan instead. Arughtai and Öljei Temür then killed the envoy sent by the Yongle Emperor to bring about a reconciliation. The murder was a clear act of challenge to the Chinese. The Yongle Emperor's strategy followed the old established Chinese practice of 'subduing the barbarians by using the barbarians', supporting in turn the weaker of the Mongol chieftains and letting them settle their rivalries among themselves. To this effect, he induced the Oirat leader Maḥmūd, also called Batula Cingsang,[19] to attack Arughtai and Öljei Temür, who were defeated and forced to retreat to the Kerulen River. When a second expedition, aimed finally to subdue them, failed, the Ming Emperor himself went to war against Arughtai and Öljei Temür. As a result, the Mongols were routed at the Onon River and fled in different directions. Öljei Temür fell into the hands of Maḥmūd and was murdered. Maḥmūd then proclaimed the latter's son Delbeg Great Khan by his grace. The plot thickened further. Arughtai, having escaped the Chinese punitive expedition, again sought good relations with the Ming and reported that Maḥmūd was

16 Bawden, 1955, pp. 157–9.
17 Mote and Goodrich, 1976a.
18 Rossabi, 1976a.
19 Rossabi, 1976b.

planning incursions into Chinese territory. Maḥmūd, suspicious of Arughtai, who had regained the favour of the Ming, then moved to attack him, backed up by Delbeg Khan's troops. This initiated the Yongle Emperor's third expedition against the Mongols – Maḥmūd and Delbeg – in 1414. The battle, on the upper runs of the Tula and Kerulen, ended in a great victory for the Chinese side. Arughtai, mindful of Maḥmūd's betrayal, took advantage of the latter's defeat and killed him, together with his protégé Delbeg Khan, in 1415.

Maḥmūd's son Toghan then succeeded as leader of the Oirats. Arughtai now had the upper hand in the camps of the Chinggisids, as well as their other Mongol rivals. Nevertheless, he pursued his own political goals, which mostly consisted in amassing booty in order to supply and reward his followers. He raided Chinese border settlements, pillaged caravans on their way to and from Beijing, harassed and robbed Chinese envoys to Mongolia and Central Asia. Arughtai's continued provocations finally induced the Yongle Emperor to mount his fourth campaign against the Mongols in the autumn of 1423. During his last military action against Arughtai in 1424, however, the emperor fell ill and died, and Arughtai eluded him without being defeated. Arughtai then ceased to harass the Chinese, as he was confronted with a new menace himself: the Oirats, having regained strength under their leader Toghan, forced him to move eastwards. They also proposed Toghto-bukha, a great-grandson of Toghus Temür of the Qubilai line, to be the new Great Khan of the Mongols, in competition with Arughtai's nominee Adai, supposedly a descendant of Chinggis Khan's younger brother Otcigin. Toghan married his daughter to Toghto-bukha, thus securing his ties to the house of Qubilai. Toghan's own mother, too, the Princess Samur, had been a descendant of the Borjigit (Borjigid) clan, daughter of the Great Khan Elbeg. Arughtai, meanwhile, had continued his profitable tribute relations with China, but in the end was killed in battle during one of the numerous Mongol–Oirat armed clashes in 1434, near the city of Baotou in present-day Inner Mongolia.

Toghan killed Arughtai's protégé Adai in 1438 and installed Toghto-bukha as Great Khan of the Mongols, under the title of Dayisung Khan. Toghan himself died in 1439. He was succeeded by his able son Esen, who was to lead the Oirats to the peak of their power.[20] Through his successful military campaigns, he soon controlled an area stretching from Hami in the Tarim Basin to the borders of Korea. It is interesting to note, though, that neither Esen himself nor his father Toghan had aspired to be Great Khan of the Mongols, but rather were satisfied to have a descendant of Qubilai under their control. It

20 Rossabi, 1976c.

seems reasonable to assume that the Oirats were afraid to forfeit the allegiance of the remaining Mongol tribes unnecessarily and thereby to provoke endless further conflicts.

Nevertheless, Esen appears to have fallen prey to a certain hubris. The Ming court not only became apprehensive about Esen's territorial gains, but was also concerned over the question of the Oirats' tribute practices. For the Mongols, these tribute embassies had proved to be a most lucrative enterprise. Even small numbers of horses, the most common of Mongol tribute offerings, were usually rewarded by rich return-gifts and the payment of the envoys' expenditure. They also provided the chance to trade. Esen increasingly began to take advantage of the system, and between the years 1442 and 1449 he dispatched more than 2,000 envoys with a comparatively insignificant number of horses. The Ming retaliated with paltry gifts, insufficient payments and even mistreatment of the envoys. The final aggravating incident – the alleged rejection of Esen's son's proposal to marry a Ming princess – eventually turned the Ming–Oirat dispute into an armed conflict. Esen prepared for war, supported by his protégé the Chinggisid Dayisung Khan. The Oirats were victorious and even succeeded in capturing the Zhengtong Emperor [21] at Tumu, north of Beijing, in September 1449. Instead of using their advantage by pressing on to Beijing, the Oirats withdrew with their prize. Meanwhile, the Ming not only had time to recover, but also installed the captured emperor's younger brother in his place. Esen, realizing the now-reduced value of his hostage, moved against Beijing, demanding ransom. When this was rejected, he laid siege to Beijing, but withdrew in the face of an unexpectedly determined resistance. Chinese–Oirat relations remained hostile until the end of 1450, when Esen, after a series of successful negotiations, conciliatory on both sides, finally released the Zhengtong Emperor. The sources are in agreement that an obvious bond of sympathy had sprung between Esen and his captive, a touching detail which might well have contributed towards the satisfactory outcome of the affair.

After the release of the emperor and his renewed enthronement, tension again arose between Esen and Dayisung Khan, who wished to pursue his own interests rather than be content with the status of Esen's 'puppet'. Betrayed, however, by his own brother Aghbarji Jinong, who sided with the Oirat, Dayisung Khan was defeated in 1452 and murdered as he fled from the scene of battle. Esen now proclaimed himself Great Khan of the Mongols. This act proved to be his undoing, though, and soon led to his downfall. Esen was not descended from the Borjigit clan through the agnatic line and therefore had

21 Tu Fang and Fang, 1976.

no valid claim to the title according to Chinggisid tradition. Opposition also arose, it is said, as a result of the Khan's arbitrary treatment of his retainers, his increasingly debauched ways and his excessive drinking. Esen, undoubtedly one of the ablest leaders of the fifteenth century, met his death in 1455 at the hand of a man whose father he had once murdered.

The next twenty years were characterized once more by intertribal fighting and the complete lack of political order. Chinese as well as Mongol sources, though in some confusion as to dates,[22] note the names of the succeeding Great Khans: Mar-körgis (also known as Mergüs or Ükegtü Khan, d. *c.* 1465);[23] Molon (also known as Tögüs, d. *c.* 1466);[24] and Mandughul (also known as Mandulu, d. *c.* 1479; perhaps the most powerful of the three).[25] Nothing much seems to be known about them, except the story of Mongol chieftains trying to display independence and to launch bold raids on the Chinese border.

The return of the Chinggisids

With Batu Möngke Dayan Khan,[26] the Chinggisid rulers re-entered the stage. To reconstruct his career poses a number of problems. 'All in all', writes Serruys, 'the historical material concerning him is extremely confused, and it seems well-nigh impossible to clarify all aspects, and reconcile satisfactorily the Mongol sources with the Chinese records'.[27] Nevertheless, enough facts emerge to shed some light on the course of events and the history of Dayan Khan himself.

Batu Möngke, such was his personal name, was probably born around 1466, according to Mongol tradition, as the great-grandson of Aghbarji Jinong, the Great Khan Dayisung's younger brother, who had betrayed the Khan and defected to the Oirats. Batu Möngke's father Bayan Möngke had been killed young, and his mother had been taken captive by the Oirats around 1470.[28] According to the *Altan Tobci*, the boy Batu Möngke was then given into the care of the widow of Mandughul Khan, Mandukhai Sechen Khatun, an intelligent, capable, and beautiful woman.[29] In Mongol tradition she has always

22 The most careful correlation for the period in question yet is still to be found in the work of Pokotilov and Franke, 1949.
23 Serruys, 1976a.
24 Pokotilov and Franke, 1949, pp. 45–9, 64.
25 Pokotilov and Franke, 1949, pp. 48–50, 64, 75–9.
26 Miller, 1976.
27 Quoted according to Miller, 1976. p. 17.
28 For a correlation of the facts according to the Mongol sources cf. Serruys, 1958, pp. 12–15.
29 Bawden, 1955, pp. 182–4.

been a heroic figure, much admired down to the present day. Mandughul Khan himself had died without male offspring in 1479. The Princess Mandukhai acted as regent until Batu Möngke came of age and later married him – the age-gap being about sixteen years.[30] The marriage appears to have worked well; eight children are recorded: the twins Törü Bolud and Ulus Bolud (b. 1482); the twins, princess Töröltü and prince Barsu Bolud Sayin Alagh (b. 1484); Arsu Bolud; the twins Alcu Bolud and Ocir Bolud (b. 1490); and finally the son Ara Bolud.[31] Four more sons were born to a second and third wife, among them Geresenje (b. 1489), the ancestor of the ruling princes of the Khalkha of the Seven Tribal Camps (Mong. *otogh*) in the north. Through his sons, Batu Möngke established the future lines of Mongol leadership, ultimately going back to Chinggis Khan by virtue of the genealogical connection with Qubilai of the Yuan imperial house.

Batu Möngke's royal style, Dayan Khan, is alleged to have been an attempt to link him to the Yuan dynasty, Dayan being a loanword version of Chinese Dayuan.[32] As new Great Khan of the Mongols, Dayan came close to fulfilling the dream of uniting the Mongol tribes and of reviving the Mongol imperial confederation. His principal aim, to begin with, was to gain the upper hand over the Oirats and to strengthen the allegiance of his followers by holding out the prospect of success in material goods and power. After the defeat of the Oirat chieftain Ismāʿīl in the 1480s, Dayan seemed to have been quickly accepted as leader of the Mongol tribes. Successful raids on Chinese territory gained him further recognition. He also began to enlarge his own area of control by taking possession of the plateau within the confines of the Huang-ho bend. Until Dayan's annexation, neither the Chinese nor the steppe nomads had lived there for any length of time. The area was thereafter to be called 'Ordos', meaning 'palace-tent', because the Eight White Tents of Chinggis Khan, cenotaph and site of his cult were supposed to have been installed there during the reign of Qubilai.[33]

Around the year 1500, Dayan Khan disposed of several secure bases in Liaodong and in Ordos, whence his unified forces were now able to mount well-organized attacks against China. China's military leadership during that period proved sadly incompetent, not least because of the bane of late Ming times: eunuch intrigues. Dayan Khan's military power would no doubt have carried him right into China itself, had it not been for an albeit

30 Bawden, 1955, p. 184 n. 3.
31 Serruys, 1958, pp. 16–17.
32 Serruys, 1958, p. 12.
33 Sagaster, 1976, pp. 193–202.

temporary breakdown of Mongol unity. The reason, not surprisingly, was another instance of the fatal 'querelles mongoles', thereby further revealing the precariousness of Mongol unity. In accordance with an originally military tradition of the Mongols, Dayan Khan had divided his domain into an Eastern or Right Wing (Mong. *ghar*) – comprising the Chakhar, the Khalkha of the Five Tribal Camps and the Uriyangkhad – directly subordinate to the Great Khan Dayan; the Western or Left Wing – comprising Ordos, Tümet (Tümed) and Yüngsiyebü – was to be subordinate to a Jinong or viceregent. When Dayan attempted to appoint his son Ulus Bolud to this post, he met with opposition from the powerful Ordos chieftain Mandulai Aghulkhu. Mandulai found an ally in Ibrahim[34] of the Oirats, who had been displeased by Dayan's territorial expansion and growing power. In 1510, Ibrahim murdered Ulus Bolud and as war erupted Ibrahim, accompanied by his ally Mandulai Aghulkhu, fled to the south-west, where he remained the target of repeated campaigns by Dayan Khan. Hostile actions did not cease until 1533, when Gün Bilig Mergen, one of Dayan's grandsons, finally routed Ibrahim's forces. Soon afterwards Ibrahim was murdered.

Although intertribal conflicts of this sort weakened Mongol military power, Dayan nevertheless was able, from about 1513, to construct fortified camps and bases from which to launch attacks against China. The sources speak of his army as a highly mobile cavalry force of about 15,000 men. In the years 1517, 1523 and 1532, Dayan's troops pressed dangerously close to Beijing, but were defeated by the Ming army for the first time, after fifty years of military failures against the Mongols. Not long afterwards, Dayan Khan appears to have begun to lose control over the Mongol tribes he initially had so impressively managed to unify. The date and circumstances of Dayan Khan's death are uncertain, but 1532 or 1543 seem to be most likely.[35] Dayan Khan had five successors as Great Khan of the Mongols, each of whom acceded to the position as eldest living son of the previous Khan: Bodi Alagh (d. 1547), Darayisun (d. 1557), Tümen Jasaghtu (d. 1592), Buyan Tayiji Sechen Khan (d. 1604) and Ligdan (d. 1634). None of them, however, was able to gain any support beyond the confines of their territory, with the exception, perhaps, of Ligdan, the last of the Mongol Great Khans.

In the estimation of traditional Mongol historiography, Dayan Khan was a hero of true Mongol mould, satisfying the ideals of successful military ventures and heroic personal achievements. He accomplished the unification of the Mongol tribes and brought the Oirats under his control. His frequent

34 Rossabi, 1976d.
35 Okada, 1966.

incursions into China supplied his followers with much-desired material goods. In spite of his considerable success, though, Batu Möngke Dayan Khan failed to consolidate a central authority over all, or most, Mongol tribes. His weakness became obvious as soon as he tried to impose his will on local tribal leaders in matters other than gainful raids, for example the political move to install a Jinong. A nomadic empire that could be built by his heirs was to remain a dream.

Altan Khan and the role of northern Buddhism

Dayan Khan had numerous male descendants – eleven sons and twenty-seven grandsons, not all of whom survived him – who, upon his death, divided among themselves the territory and tribes he had controlled.

The political map of the Mongol tribes according to the post-Dayanic division subsequently presented itself as six myriads (Mong. *tümen*) divided into a Left Wing and a Right Wing.[36] The Left Wing was ruled by the Great Khan, lineage of Dayan Khan's grandson and successor Bodi Alagh (1504–47). The tribal composition of these myriads was as follows. The first myriad comprised the Chakhar, Abagha, Abaghanar, Aokhan, Dörben Keüked, Kesigten, Muuminghan, Naiman, Ongniut (Ongnighud), Khaucit (Khaghucid), Sünit (Sünid), Üjümücin and Urat (Urad) tribes. The second myriad comprised the Khalkha of the Seven Tribal Camps and the Khalkha of the Five Tribal Camps (Bagharin, Jarut, Khunggirat, Bayighut, Ucirat). The third myriad comprised the Uriyangkhad, Aru Khorchin, Dörbet (Dörbed), Ghorlos, Jalayit (Jalayid) and Khorchin tribes. The Right Wing was ruled by the Jinong, or viceregent, lineage of Dayan Khan's third son, Barsu Bolud Sayin Alagh (1484–1532). The first myriad comprised the Ordos. The second myriad comprised the Tümet tribe. The third myriad comprised the Asud, Kharachin and Yüngsiyebü tribes.

This fragmentation into patrimonial territories (Mong. *ulus*) was to form the basis of the final division of the Mongol tribes, valid, with but minor variations, throughout the Qing period and into the twentieth century. Such a fragmentation, in addition to further weakening the precarious position of a Mongol Great Khan, nourished individual aspirations and encouraged the rise of powerful regional rulers. Notable among these were the three Khans of Geresenje's *ulus*, the Seven Tribal Camps of Khalkha: the Tüsiyetü Khan Gömbodorji (d. 1655), the Jasaghtu Khan Subadi (d. 1650) and the Sechen Khan Sholoi (d. 1655).[37] Their fate, however, falls outside the scope of this chapter.

36 Serruys, 1958, pp. 16–18, 40, 151–4; Veit, 1986a, p. 390.
37 Veit, 1986b, pp. 435–7.

By far the most notable and most powerful of the regional rulers of his time was Altan Khan (1507–82).[38] A grandson of Dayan Khan and the second of Barsu Bolud's seven sons, he commanded the Twelve Tümet as his *ulus*, with their pastures north of the Shanxi border, in today's Inner Mongolia. Altan Khan's father's position of Jinong had gone to the first son Gün Bilig Mergen (1506–1542/3), along with the Ordos as his *ulus*. By virtue of talent, political acumen and fortune in war, Altan Khan ruled for over forty years, and became the unofficial head of the Left Wing after his brother's death.

The nominal Great Khan of the time was Tümen Jasaghtu, leading the Chakhar, whose pastures were situated on the western slopes of the Hsingan Mountains in Liaodong. Altan Khan and his brother continued their grandfather Dayan's policy of putting pressure on China by frequently raiding the border. This course of action lasted for about forty years, reaching a climax in 1550, when Altan arrived at the gates of Beijing. The Mongols' traditional aims were to hold out prospects for goods and power in order to rally their followers. A favourite means to achieve this had been to induce China to grant tribute privileges and to open horse markets. This policy served to provide the Mongol leadership with supplies of food, clothes and luxury goods. We have evidence that Altan Khan would have preferred to obtain such commodities by peaceful means – but all his overtures, prior to 1570, were repeatedly treated with suspicion by the Ming Court and rejected. He therefore resorted to the old steppe tactics of border-raids. A change of policy did not seem possible until October 1570. At that time, Dayicing Tayiji (*c.* 1552–83), one of Altan Khan's grandsons, defected to the Chinese because of a personal grudge against his grandfather. Upon the advice of the able governor-general of Datong, Wang Chonggu, who understood the Mongol situation, Dayicing Tayiji was given shelter, and a peace was effected by taking advantage of Altan Khan's concern for his grandson.[39] The subsequently concluded treaty made arrangements for the presentation of an annual tribute and the opening of horse fairs in several places along the border. In addition, Altan Khan was granted the title of *Shun-i wang* ('Rightful and Obedient Prince').[40] After decades of insecurity, the northern frontier finally enjoyed a period of peace, until the early seventeenth century, when the Jurchen, newly risen to power, formed an alliance with Mongol tribes and once more threatened China.

Altan Khan not only proved his political talent in his dealings with China, he also turned out to be fortunate in his military enterprises. He subdued the

38 Serruys, 1976b, pp. 6–9.
39 Serruys, 1976b, p. 7.
40 Serruys, 1960.

Oirats and chased them from the area of the former Mongol capital, Karakorum. The domain was then taken over by Geresenje and the Khalkha, their new territory roughly corresponding to today's Mongolian Republic. Altan Khan also undertook successful campaigns in areas as far west as Qinghai on the border of Tibet and northern Sinkiang. Around 1560 he founded the city of Köke Khota[41] as his new capital.

Altan Khan's name is associated with the revival of Tibetan Buddhism (or Lamaism) among the Mongols. Throughout the Ming period, we find evidence, albeit sporadic and fragmentary, that Lamaism had not altogether disappeared from Mongolia since Yuan times. Members of the Mongol nobility seemed to be more or less familiar with it and to have some knowledge of the role it had played during that period.[42] Altan Khan's own first contacts with Buddhism probably occurred in 1573 during one of his campaigns to the west. Among his prisoners were said to have been two lamas who preached the doctrines of Buddha to him and converted him.[43] The turning point in the religious history of Mongolia came three years later, when Altan Khan's great-nephew, his brother Gün Bilig Mergen's grandson, Khutukhtai Sechen Khung Tayiji (1540–86),[44] persuaded him to invite to Mongolia the abbot of the 'Bras-spuns monastery in Lhasa, bSod-nams rgya-mts'o (1543–88),[45] a man of great spiritual prestige and integrity. The Khung Tayiji said to Altan Khan, as recorded in the Erdeni-yin Tobci of 1662:

> You have taken your revenge on the Chinese who once conquered our city [i.e. Beijing] and have established relations with them. You have avenged yourself on the Oirats, who seized Karakorum, and have overcome them and brought them into subjection. But now your years have increased, and you are approaching old age. The wise say that what is necessary for this and the future destiny is the Faith. Now it appears that in the western land of snows [i.e. Tibet] there dwells, in corporeal form, the Mighty Seer and Pitiful One, the Bodhisattva Avalokiteshvara. Would it not be wonderful if we were to invite him, and re-establish the relations between Church and State as they once existed between the Emperor Khubilai and the lama Pagspa?[46]

From this pious interpretation of the course of events, no doubt added retrospectively, emerges an important point. Altan Khan obviously intended to appeal to the old alliance of Buddhist religion and state. This alliance was

41 Hyer, 1982.
42 Serruys, 1963.
43 Bawden, 1968b, p. 28.
44 Serruys, 1976c.
45 Petech, 1976a.
46 Schmidt, 1961, p. 225. Trans. Bawden, 1968b, p. 29.

based on the political theory of the Two Principles (Mong. *khoyar yosun*). Its most important exponent, though not its originator, is said to have been hP'ags-pa Lama (1239–80) at the court of Qubilai.[47]

The principle of the *khoyar yosun*[48] implied that the dual order of religion – presided over by the lama – and state – presided over by the king – were dependent upon each other. The lama had to teach religion, and the king to guarantee a rule that enabled everybody to live in peace. The lama corresponded to Buddha, the king to the Cakravartin, the universal Buddhist monarch. In the present context, the most interesting feature of this political theory is the question of the cakravartin kingship. Buddhism, with its supranational character of a world-religion, provided the conceptual model of a universal emperor which transcended the sinocentric, monocultural idea of the emperor. The model of the cakravartin-raja – the universal emperor who turned the wheel of the law – was therefore most attractive to rulers in India, Tibet and Central Asia. It also legitimized Qubilai's rule over China upon his ascension to – or usurpation of – the Yuan throne. Furthermore, the ideology of the cakravartin kingship was used, in retrospect, to sanctify the lineage of the Chinggisids, from the thirteenth century onwards, by providing it with the succession of ancestors of the Buddhist holy rulers, beginning with the mythical Mahasamadi and the Sakya kings, Ašoka and the Buddhist kings of Tibet down to Chinggis Khan himself. The Mongol emperors, therefore, do not appear as the factual successors of a Chinese dynasty only, but of the Buddhist universal emperors, the cakravartin-rajas. This sacralization of Mongol rule through Lamaist Buddhism had lasting effects in particular on the Mongolian historiography from the beginning of the seventeenth century onwards.[49]

To what extent Altan Khan himself was conscious of all these implications cannot be ascertained. What is evident, though, is that it was certainly political considerations which motivated him to invite the Tibetan dignitary and, by appealing to the ideology of the Two Principles, strengthened his claim to rule over the Mongol tribes. In 1578, therefore, bSod-nams rgya-mts'o and Altan Khan met in a temple on the banks of the Qinghai Lake. On this occasion, Altan Khan conferred the title of Vajra-dhara Dalai Lama on the Tibetan dignitary, who in turn named Altan Khan Cakravartin Sechen Khan and declared him to be the incarnation of Qubilai. bSod-nams rgya-mts'o thus became known as the Third Dalai Lama, his two predecessors being the first and second successors of the great reformer Tsong kha pa (1357–1419). Altan Khan

47 Franke, 1978, p. 61.
48 The description of the 'Two Orders' follows Franke, 1978, pp. 52–61 (interim).
49 Schuh, 1977, pp. 58–69.

died not long afterwards, in 1582. The strength of the Mongol-Buddhist connection first became evident after the death of the Dalai Lama in Mongolia in 1588, on his way to Beijing. The Tümet nobles seized the opportunity to have a member of Altan Khan's family, his great-grandson, hence also a descendant of Chinggis Khan, declared to be the next reincarnation. Yon-tan rgya-mts'o, the Fourth Dalai Lama (1589–1617),[50] was to be the only non-Tibetan, though, in the long line of incarnations, which later was to go through an independent development in Tibet itself.

Buddhism in its Tibetan form from then on quickly spread and firmly established itself among the Mongols. Missionary lamas became active in Mongol society, mindful too of their own position, which was to be of equal rank to that of the Mongol nobility. Their missionary work was mainly addressed towards the latter and the rulers, so that, as Bawden states, 'something like the principle of "cuius regio eius religio" was in operation'.[51] Most notable among the missionaries was the Torghut Neyici Toyin (1557–1653),[52] the St Boniface of the Mongols, whose superior theology, art of healing and magic powers were used to defeat the old shamans. Such a missionary effort over time also led to mass conversions among the ordinary Mongol people.

Altan Khan's example was soon followed by another regional ruler, Abadai Khan of the Northern Khalkha (1554–87). He is said to have built the great temple of Erdeni Juu alongside the site of the old capital Karakorum, in 1586.[53] The decisive step towards the shaping of the political role of Buddhism, also among the Khalkha, was taken in 1639, when the politically astute Tüsiyetü Khan Gömbodorji had his younger son, born in 1635, accepted by the assembly of the Khalkha nobles as head of the faith in the land. Educated in Tibet, he received from the Dalai Lama the title of Jebtsundamba, under which he and his seven successors were subsequently known. Gömbodorji's far-sighted decision in creating a centrally attractive force in alliance with the Buddhist religion not only served its purpose at the time, but also continued to be a decisive political factor in 1911, when the Khalkha declared their independence from China ruled by the Qing dynasty. After its fall, it was the Jebtsundamba Khutukhtu who became the natural rallying-point for the sympathies of the Mongols almost everywhere.[54]

Apart from its political aspect, Buddhism also proved to have a profound influence on the cultural and economic development of Mongol society. Buddhist

50 Petech, 1976b.
51 Bawden, 1968b, p. 32.
52 Heissig, 1953, pp. 1–44; 1954, pp. 21–38.
53 Bawden, 1968b, p. 31.
54 Bawden, 1968b, pp. 53, 195.

canonical texts from the Kanjur and Tanjur, as well as other texts, were translated and circulated. A native liturgy arose through the translations. A wealth of new literature was made available, at least to the upper classes, simultaneously enriching and stimulating autochthonous literary genres. A knowledge of reading and writing in the native Mongol, as well as in Tibetan, spread, encouraged by the educational activities in the monasteries. Lastly, through its close relations with the nobility, its successful missionarizing and its educational work, Tibetan Buddhism quickly achieved a position of power in Mongolia. The monasteries began also to amass considerable wealth in land, stock, books, artifacts and other treasures, which was to make them a formidable economic power until the 1930s, when they were dispossessed and destroyed.[55]

Mongol relations with Ming China: war, tribute and trade

For most of the Ming dynasty's history, the steppe nomads constituted a threat. For the Mongols, on the other hand, Ming China meant a challenge to obtain what they felt entitled to – the right to send tribute-missions and to trade. It is this conceptually different approach towards each other we therefore have to be mindful of when we assess Mongol–Ming relations.

According to Serruys, China regarded its superiority in material and cultural wealth as sufficient to fascinate the barbarians and to draw them into its orbit.[56] Relations with foreign nations generally took the form of 'tribute' or homage paid to the emperor, an act that implied the recognition of Chinese suzerainty. Granting tributary status was a question of favour to be either accorded or withdrawn, at the Chinese court's discretion. The tribute system, as it was practised in Ming times, could therefore quite rightly be called the material manifestation of a political relationship.

The views of the steppe nomads, on the other hand, could not have been more fundamentally opposed. To them, Chinese culture, while surely not without a certain appeal, was never the decisive factor for their interest in their neighbour. What they were really after was profit. If they paid homage to the emperor by sending tribute, thus formally recognizing Chinese suzerainty in the eyes of the court, this was understood by the Mongols as an act of allegiance in accordance with Central Asian traditions.

According to these, the recognition of a khan and the declaration of allegiance to him was a voluntary act, on the whole between equals, and it

55 Bawden, 1968b, pp. 157–70.
56 Serruys, 1967, p. 19.

implied loyalty and services to be rendered in exchange for power and suitable rewards. The Mongols therefore considered the rich return gifts, the subsidies and the trade concessions granted by the Ming Court as their due for the respectful recognition of the Chinese 'Khan' and a well-merited reward for services given to him, as some Mongol chronicles maintain.[57] The Ming Court no doubt was aware of the Mongols' attempt to benefit as much as possible from the system of tribute and trade – at times even taking advantage of it quite shamelessly, as we have seen. It is understandable, therefore, that the Ming were not always prepared to pay the price for the tribute coming from the Mongols, even though it could mean war, or at least border-raids – a continuous dilemma the court had to face, and one that was never quite satisfactorily resolved. As the governor-general of the three Shensi military districts put it in 1532: '[The Mongols'] desires will be difficult to satisfy; if we do not give in, border violations will come swiftly; and if we do yield, we cannot trust them'.[58]

The problem was more complex than the mere greed of the Mongols, though, because it had political as well as economic implications. In order to provide an incentive for tribes to declare their allegiance to a steppe nomadic Khan, to recognize him as their leader and also to join among themselves in solidarity, he had to hold out the prospect of success in material goods and power, among other prerequisites. Many examples in the history of the steppe-nomadic empires illustrate this point. Besides, the steppe nomads had a genuine need in their daily lives for Chinese commodities, such as grain, flour, cotton cloth, metal pots or tools, in addition to the coveted silks, silk garments or other luxury goods. Their own economy rested on mobile, extensive pastoralism and was therefore easily affected by drought and famine – not to mention the often long periods of destructive intertribal conflicts.

When we go back to the beginning of Mongol–Ming relations, we notice that the collapse of the Yuan dynasty, according to Barfield, had not so much been the result of an anti-foreign uprising by Chinese nationalists, but rather a traditional rebellion against a dynasty which had lost the 'Mandate of Heaven'.[59] The first Ming Emperor, Zhu Yuanzhang, therefore encouraged the surrender of Mongol military units left in China by the complete confusion of the Yuan retreat and incorporated them into his army. He also permitted the settlement in China of remaining Mongol families and other Central

57 Examples given in Serruys, 1967, pp. 22–5.
58 Serruys, 1967, p. 34.
59 Barfield, 1992, p. 231.

Asian foreigners formerly in the service of the Mongols, as well as retaining a number of Yuan institutions and policies.[60]

Nevertheless, the Yuan pretenders and their Mongol followers in the steppe posed a potential menace to the newly established Ming dynasty. Potential to the extent that the Mongol army did not have the power to reconquer China; real because the Mongols could still threaten Ming control of the north-western border. To begin with, the Hongwu Emperor's strategy was therefore basically defensive. His several successful expeditions into Mongolian territory were primarily sent to destroy the military power of the Yuan Khans Ayushiridara and Toghus Temür rather than to attempt a conquest. At the same time, the emperor garrisoned the border to defend against Mongol incursions. To this end, he enfeoffed nine of his elder sons in 1370, giving them strategic territories on the northern and western frontiers. The fourth son, Zhu Di, the later Yongle Emperor, perhaps the most ambitious and able of the sons, received the title Prince of Yan with his seat at Beijing.[61] A further measure was the creation of the Three Uriyangkhad Commanderies in the northern part of modern Jehol province and north-western Manchuria. In 1389, the Mongol princes of three groups of tribes – known as Douyan, Taining and Fuyu – had submitted to China while continuing to rule their own territories independently. The princes received Ming military ranks, were granted the status of tribute-bringers, and served to garrison the border.[62] Later Ming emperors followed this example and created many more commanderies, mostly Jurchen, in present-day Manchuria.[63] The more defensive character of the Hongwu Emperor's strategy towards the Mongols is shown, furthermore, in several initiatives taken to induce Ayushiridara to submit to China voluntarily. They were all ignored, together with all peace-offers and courtesies, as we have seen earlier.

The only Ming emperor who made war his preferred means of policy and ambitiously campaigned in Mongolia, was the third, Zhu Di, the Yongle Emperor.[64] He moved the Ming capital from Nanjing in the south to Beijing in the north, the princely fief originally granted to him by his father. Although the new site was strategically in a far more advantageous position for controlling the steppe, it was also more vulnerable, as later events were to prove. When Yongle acceded to power in 1403, the menace from Yuan pretenders was over,

60 Serruys, 1980, pp. 19–21.
61 Mote and Goodrich, 1976b.
62 Serruys, 1980, pp. 282–6.
63 Serruys, 1967, pp. 6–7; Serruys, 1955, pp. 73–92.
64 Franke, 1945.

but the threat of new Mongol confederations was growing, notable among these the Oirat one and the one led by Arughtai. The Yongle Emperor began by skilfully playing tribal politics, shifting alliances between leaders, and attacking those who appeared most likely to unite the steppe. Nevertheless, the emperor saw himself forced to mount the six famous large-scale expeditions into Mongolia that we have already referred to. His death on the way home from the last campaign in 1424 marked the end of wide-ranging Ming military enterprises in Mongolia, but not the end of steppe ambitions, as the examples of Esen, Dayan and Altan Khan proved.

The Khan of the Oirat confederation, Esen, had developed a particularly skilful way to manipulate the tribute missions in order to gain maximum profit. When these tactics were thwarted by the court, and military action, including the bold capture of the Zhengtong Emperor, did not produce the expected positive result, Esen finally adopted a more conciliatory approach. The Ming Court chose to yield to the lesser evil, and the tribute embassies, reduced to acceptable numbers, were resumed along with their lucrative trade facilities, thus restoring good relations between China and the Oirats. Thereafter, Ming military actions against the renewed Mongol incursions under Batu Möngke Dayan Khan and Altan Khan grew increasingly defensive, despite the fact that both Mongol leaders had changed their *modus operandi* from scattered border-raids to well-organized attacks. By the end of the sixteenth century, a kind of impasse was reached. It can be said to have been the result of incompetent Ming military resistance on the one hand and, on the other, of an increasingly weakened Mongol unity through intertribal conflicts. In the end, skilful diplomatic negotiations on both sides made possible the peace agreement between the Ming Court and Altan Khan of 1571. In this context it is interesting to note that, after Altan Khan's death in 1582, it was one of his wives, the so-called Sanniangzi or Third Lady, named Erketü Khatun or Noyanci Jünggin (*c.* 1551–1612), who wielded great power in Mongolia, and used her influence in favour of cooperation and peaceful relations with China. She was so competent that, as Serruys states, 'Chinese border officials considered her the best if not the only guarantee that the Mongol princes would remain faithful tributaries without reverting to the border-raids so prevalent before 1570'.[65]

In the early years of the Ming dynasty, war with the Mongols had been a necessary strategy to secure its power. Later it became the question of a policy to stabilize the frontier. The tribute system and trade concessions were the

65 Serruys, 1975, p. 191.

price the Ming had to pay for peace with the steppe. The realization that this, in the end, proved a far more effective, and much cheaper, way than warfare and frontier garrisons, did not dawn until the end of the dynasty, when it was almost too late. The border remained peaceful for about fifty years after the agreement of 1571. The period came to an end when Ming China and the Mongol tribes were confronted by a third power, the Jurchen.

The stage was reset: enter Nurhaci, who paved the way for the most successful and long-lasting of all foreign dynasties in China – the Manchurian Qing.

The incorporation of Mongol tribes in the Aisin state under Nurhaci and Hung Tayiji

In the course of its history, Ming China not only had to accommodate the steppe nomads along its western and northern borders, it also had to contend with the Jurchen tribes on its north-eastern frontier. The Jurchen were the descendants of the people who had established the Jin dynasty, ruling over the northern part of China until they were destroyed by the Mongols in 1231. They had returned to their homeland, where they mainly engaged in hunting, fishing, farming and stock-raising. In Ming times they lived in scattered tribal groups, west of the Yalu, along the Korean border, in south Manchuria and in the far north-east on the Upper Amur. Generally, they maintained friendly relations with China. Those tribes in direct contact were organized in small units called *wei-suo*,[66] which were part of the Ming military auxiliary, not unlike the Uriyangkhad commanderies mentioned before. They also enjoyed tribute and trade privileges. Towards the end of the sixteenth century, the leader of one of the Jurchen tribal groups, Nurhaci (1559–1626), rose to a position of power, under conditions similar to those of the young Temüjin, the later Chinggis Khan.[67] To consolidate his authority over his relatives and Jurchen tribesmen, Nurhaci employed the traditional tactics of war, marriage alliances and the Chinese tribute system. One of his most effective measures was the introduction of a new military organization. He created company units known as 'arrows' (Ma. *niru*) that were the building-blocks of a supratribal army, consisting of 'Banners' (Ma. *gūsa*). The Eight Banners eventually to be established formed the core of the political and military organization of the Jianzhou Jurchen (later Manchus). Nurhaci's success soon attracted the attention of the neighbouring Mongol tribes. The first to take notice and to seek contact,

66 Serruys, 1955, pp. 2–8; see also n. 63 and n. 64.
67 Fang, 1964a.

as early as the end of the sixteenth century, were the Khorchin Mongols and the Khalkha of the Five Tribal Camps. A regular exchange of messengers followed, but these should be seen as acts of diplomacy rather than acts of political submission. Both tribal groups were close neighbours of Nurhaci, with pastures situated along the Upper Liao River. In 1607, Enggeder Tayiji of the Five Tribal Camps of Khalkha led a party of emissaries from the leaders of the said tribal groups to offer a gift of horses and camels, respectfully addressing Nurhaci by giving him a new title: 'Kündülen Khan'.[68]

Apart from reorganizing the army, Nurhaci took steps to install a civil administration. In 1599 he ordered the Mongol script to be adapted to the Jurchen language. Prior to 1599, Mongolian appears to have been the only written language the Jurchen used in communication with the Mongol tribes as well as among themselves.[69] At some stage between 1616 and the 1620s, Nurhaci established the records office (Ma. *bithei jurgan*), in order to keep written documentations of his dealings with the Mongols as well as all other events and decisions.[70]

Nurhaci went beyond the stage of being a mere tribal leader when, in 1616, he declared himself Khan and founded an independent Jurchen State. He called it 'Aisin' (Manchu for 'gold'), in a deliberate continuation of the old Jin (Chinese for 'gold') dynasty. For the Ming, the proclamation of a new 'Golden State' was an act of rebellion and implied the repudiation of Chinese sovereignty.

For the three contending nations – Ming China, the Aisin State and the Mongol confederation – the years 1618/19 constituted a turning point. What set off the chain of events, as the final spark on a political powder-keg, was an open conflict over economic problems. Nurhaci's expanding state needed supplies beyond its native resources, all the more so since the Ming had stopped granting tribute and trade privileges. They also had successfully attracted the Yehe people away from Nurhaci in order to cause discord among the Jurchen confederation. The Yehe, a half-Tungus/half-Mongol tribe, whose ancestors were said to be of Tümet descent, had under their command thirteen Chinese cities which they used as profitable sources of income, so-called 'subsidiary cities' (Mong. *idekü khota*).[71] Nurhaci successfully subjugated the Yehe and then proceeded to raid the Chinese border.

At this point, the Mongols re-enter the scene. In 1604, Ligdan (1592–1634) established himself as Great Khan of the Mongol confederation. His power

68 Farquhar, 1968, pp. 198–9.
69 Farquhar, 1968, p. 203.
70 Weiers, 2001.
71 Heissig, 1979, p. 19.

was only nominal, as the feudal fragmentation after Dayan Khan's death had long since favoured the rise of regional leaders, as we have seen. Ligdan, however, harboured different dreams. He wanted to reunite the tribes in a new, powerful Mongol state, setting his aims as high as the example of his ancestor Chinggis Khan. Some of the titles he gave himself serve well to prove the point: 'Holy Cakravartin Ligdan Khutukhtu Daiming Chinggis Khan', 'Baturu Chinggis Khan', 'Daiming Sechen Chinggis Khan'.[72] As it was, the tribes Ligdan actually had under his command at the time of his accession were the Chakhar, the Kesigten and the Khaucit. Besides, the power of Altan Khan had forced the Chakhar to leave their old pastures north of Datong and to move to the east, along the Liao River in Liaodong. If Ligdan wanted to win the allegiance of the Mongol tribes and to consolidate his position as Great Khan, he had to prove his worth. His activities were therefore manifold: first and foremost was the question of organizing enough material goods to satisfy his followers; making a profit trading horses with the Ming was a useful sideline in this respect; last but not least, on the ideological level, he aimed at surpassing Altan Khan in the propagation of Buddhism, thus securing an additional legitimation bonus for himself.

In order to obtain supplementary provisions, Ligdan, like many local Mongol rulers of his time, had taken to rely on agriculture and the support of so-called 'subsidiary cities'. The conflict between Ligdan and Nurhaci, hitherto on reasonably peaceful terms, broke out over one of these 'subsidiary cities' – the notorious Guangning affair. In 1619, Nurhaci threatened the Chinese city of Guangning, situated west of the Liao River and close to the Great Wall, which Ligdan regarded as his own source of income. A fascinating, as well as revealing, exchange of letters ensued, dated 27 November 1619 and 20 February 1620.[73] Ligdan insulted Nurhaci by minimizing his power as 'merely in command of thirty thousand Water-Jürcit (Jürcid)', and Nurhaci retaliated by calling Ligdan's claim to rule over the united Mongol tribes 'tall talk about facts of ancient times'. Although this did not lead to immediate military action, the conflict between the Mongol Khan and the ruler of the Aisin dynasty from then on was open, and forced the other Mongol tribes to decide what side they were to join. Consequently, the years between 1620 and 1632 presented a tableau of alliances and counter-alliances, ever changing in the rivalry for power.[74] If the relations of the Mongol tribes with Nurhaci prior to 1619 had mainly been acts of diplomacy, they now took on a decidedly political

72 Heissig, 1979, pp. 30–1.
73 Weiers, 1979a, pp. 74–7.
74 Veit, 1986a, pp. 398–9.

character. The first in the series of alliances was the treaty with the Khalkha of the Five Tribal Camps.[75] Such agreements strengthened the power of Nurhaci and later Hung Tayiji in their challenge to the Ming and made valuable allies of the Mongols in their conquest of Chinese territory. They were sanctioned by a ritual of oath-taking, which is described in Manchu documents as follows: 'Swearing an oath to Heaven and Earth, they killed a white horse and a black ox; they burnt incense and filled bowls with meat, blood, bones, spirits and earth. Beise and Amban all donned their harness and kotowed nine times, whereupon the documents were read and subsequently burnt.'[76] Beforehand, a copy of the oath was made in the records office, or '*bithei jurgan*', so that the text is still extant. In similar fashion, alliances were made with the Khorchin, in 1626,[77] and with the Kharachin, in 1628.[78] While the early Aisin–Mongol treaties were concluded between more or less equal partners, the balance of power shifted in favour of the Aisin within a few years.

Nurhaci died in 1626, and his eighth son Hung Tayiji (1592–1643)[79] succeeded as ruler of the Aisin State, assuming the title of Sure Khan (Chin. Tianzong, this was also the name of the first reign-period, 1627–35). Hung Tayiji considered the allied Mongol tribes to be part of his domain, whose loyalty and military support he therefore had the right to demand. His claim to sovereignty was further documented in a series of laws laid down in meetings with the noblemen of several Mongol tribes, dated 1631 and 1632, though these laws were still the result of bilateral negotiations.[80] Last but not least, Nurhaci and Hung Tayiji also made good use of a practice of long historical standing between powers in China and Central Asia – the contracting of marriage alliances. Manchu–Mongol intermarriage was to create strong and manifold family ties, one of the most famous later examples, perhaps, the Kangxi Emperor's grandmother, a Khorchin princess, the Empress Xiaozhuang Wen Huanghou, 1613–88,[81] who had great influence on her grandson's education. Even after the Manchus had become emperors of China, this practice of intermarriage was continued until well into the nineteenth century.

Returning to the fate of Ligdan Khan, it was not so much his ambition to bring about a new Mongol imperial confederation which the Mongol tribes

75 Weiers, 1987.
76 Weiers, 1979b, p. 150.
77 Weiers, 1983.
78 Weiers, 1996.
79 Fang, 1964b.
80 Weiers, 1979b, pp. 137–90; Weiers, 1986.
81 Gates and Fang, 1964.

opposed, but the ruthlessness of his methods including his despotism, his arrogance and his constant harassment of the other tribal leaders.[82] Not even his considerable meritorious efforts for the propagation of Buddhism were able to turn the tide, such as the invitation of Tibetan dignitaries, learned lamas, the building of temples or the establishment of the editorial committee for the translation of the Kanjur canonical texts.[83] Hung Tayiji was particularly irked by Ligdan's continuous successful horse-trade with China, apart from the rivalry over the 'subsidiary cities'. As it was, the end came rapidly. In May 1632, Hung Tayiji ordered the allied Mongol tribes to join him in a campaign against Ligdan. Upon hearing this, Ligdan rallied all his remaining forces and escaped to the Qinghai region, where he died two years later, presumably of smallpox. His vision of being Great Khan must have been alive to the last, as he took away with him the Chinggis Khan memorial of the Eight White Tents.[84]

Hung Tayiji showed mercy to the defeated Chakhar people and to Ligdan's wives and children. Two of his sons, one after the other, were married to Princess Makata (1625–63), one of Hung Tayiji's daughters by a Khorchin princess. Ligdan's grandson Burni later was killed in the course of his attempted rebellion against the Qing.[85] With his death, the elder male line of the Tolui-Borjigit, Chinggis Khan's youngest son and father of Qubilai, had become extinct. A claim to the title of Great Khan of all the Mongols was never again put forward.

In the spring of 1636, forty-nine princes from sixteen Mongol tribes – the Chakhar, Khorchin, Jalayit, Dörbed, Ghorlos, Aokhan, Naiman, Tümet, Jarut, Dörben Keüked, Aru Khorchin, Ongnig, Kharachin, Urat and Khara Cherik – declared their formal allegiance to the victorious Hung Tayiji and from then on were to become but a part of his new state, the later Chinese Empire of the Manchurian Qing dynasty.[86] In the previous year Hung Tayiji had forbidden to refer to his people as Jurchen (*jušen*), decreeing that the name Manchu should be used henceforth.

In 1368, the Mongols had left China, no longer its sovereigns; in 1636, they prepared to re-enter China, if not as its sovereigns, at least as the allies of its new conquerors, the Manchus.

82 Heissig, 1979, pp. 31–3.
83 Heissig, 1979, pp. 20–2.
84 They were later returned to the Ordos, cf. Heissig, 1979, pp. 38–40.
85 Fang, 1964c.
86 *Huang-tsing k'ai-kuo fang-lüeh*, pp. 395–6.

10

Temür and the early Timurids to *c.* 1450

BEATRICE FORBES MANZ

Temür, or Tamerlane, rose to power in Transoxania, on the border between the sedentary and nomadic worlds. He was at once Muslim, Turk and Mongol and his grandiose career of conquest covered all the central Islamic lands along with much of the Western Mongol Empire. At his time the descendants of Chinggis Khan had lost effective power over Iran, China and the western part of the Chaghadayid Khanate. Nonetheless, the idea of the Mongol Empire remained important and Chinggisid descent was a requirement for legitimate sovereign power in most regions of the former empire. Of the Turko-Mongolian tribal leaders who had taken control in Iran, Transoxania and Western Mongolia, almost all bolstered their position through formal ties with the Chinggisid house.[1]

Transoxania lay within the western section of the Chaghadayid Khanate, which also contained the region stretching from Balkh to Ghazna and Qandahar – the territory of the Qara'unas, a group that developed from the Mongol garrison (*tamma*) troops centred in Qunduz and Baghlan. After the rule of Tarmashirin Khan (1331–4) the khanate had fallen into confusion and had begun to separate into eastern and western sections. In 1347 the Qara'unas chief Qazghan[2] killed the Chaghadayid Qazan Khan and took power over the western regions, legitimating his rule through a Chinggisid puppet khan. In the same year, Tughluq Temür Khan gained power over the eastern khanate with the help of the powerful Dughlat tribe. The Dughlat controlled the oasis region centred in Kashghar, and its chiefs apparently monopolized the position of *beglerbegi*. From this time on, the western region was known as the *Ulus Chaghatay*, and its Turko-Mongolian population as Chaghatay. The eastern section was called either Moghulistan or the eastern Chaghadayid Khanate, and its people Moghuls or sometimes *Chete* (alternately *Jete*).[3]

1 Aubin, 1991, pp. 175–84.
2 Often rendered as Qazaghan.
3 Aubin, 1969; Kim, 1999, pp. 300–02; Michal Biran's chapter in this volume.

The *Ulus Chaghatay* can best be characterized as a tribal confederation. Politics were fluid; the rulership was often contested and tribes were frequently split in their loyalties, with rivals for power backing different candidates for central rule. Losers in the struggle for tribal or supra-tribal power often sought help outside the *ulus*, with the Iranian powers of Khorasan or the eastern Chaghadayids. Several tribes – the Jalayir, the Suldus and Temür's own tribe, the Barlas – claimed descent from the leaders attached to Chaghadai by Chinggis Khan.[4] Tribes apparently collected the taxes of their own regions and their members had close relations with the settled elite. Some local rulers and religious figures, most notably the Shahs of Badakhshan and the Khāndzāda sayyids of Termez, played an active role in political contests and both notables and Sufi shaykhs participated in city defence.

Temür's rise to power

Although the *ulus* had separated from the eastern Chaghadayid Khanate, it is not certain that either side considered the split as permanent, and their politics remained connected. In 1361, when the *ulus* tribes unseated ʿAbd Allāh, the over-ambitious son of Qazghan Qara'unas, Tughluq Temür Khan took over the region. His conquest was probably connected to his policy of centralization and Islamization; the addition of the cities of Transoxania would have been a significant advantage.[5] Some tribal leaders of the *Ulus Chaghatay* joined Tughluq Temür but others fled, including Ḥājjī Beg Barlas, the chief of Temür's tribe. It is at this time that we first hear of Temür, then probably about thirty years old.[6] In Ḥājjī Beg's absence Temür persuaded Tughluq Temür to grant him leadership of his tribe even though he was not part of the ruling lineage. He quickly formed a web of alliances with chiefs unfriendly to Ḥājjī Beg, most notably Qazghan's grandson, Amīr Ḥusayn, now leader of the Qara'unas.

Over the next years Amīr Ḥusayn continued to fight for power over Transoxania – with Temür among his followers – sometimes taking refuge in Khorasan, where both men spent several years serving local rulers. In 1365 Amīr Ḥusayn took power over the *ulus*, and the threat from the Moghuls receded; however he now had to face increasing resistance from Temür and other tribal chiefs. The Timurid dynastic histories present Temür as Amīr Ḥusayn's main rival, but it is likely that he began as one of several dissidents, and rose

4 For the Barlas tribe and inheritance of command, see Grupper, 1992–4, pp. 11–97.
5 Kim, 1999, pp. 302–3.
6 See note 9.

gradually to greater power. He spent most of two years – 1366–8 – in Khorasan and Moghulistan but when Amīr Ḥusayn decided to make his capital in Balkh, outside his own region, Temür staged a successful rebellion and Amīr Ḥusayn was killed soon thereafter.

Temür arranged a convocation (*quriltai*) and had his Chinggisid khan Soyurghatmïsh acknowledged by the power holders of the *Ulus Chaghatay* on 9 April 1370. Soyurghatmïsh was a descendant of Ögödei, not Chaghadai, but the Timurid histories do not comment on this fact. Temür chose Samarqand, close to the western centre of Chaghadayid power, as his capital and gained the right to use the title *güregen* (royal son-in-law) by marrying Saray Malik, the Chinggisid wife of Amīr Ḥusayn. For the first twelve years of his rule he faced numerous challenges from the tribal chiefs, sometimes aided by the Moghuls and the ruler of Khorezm (Khwārazm). His most reliable force was his personal following, from which he recruited his most important commanders and with whom he replaced the leadership of rebellious tribes. The first such appointment was the assignment of his closest Barlas associate, Amīr Chekü, over Amīr Ḥusayn's Qara'unas troops. He further cemented the loyalty of his new elite through numerous marriage alliances.

Temür's early campaigns show his concern with the legacy of the Mongol Empire. Between 1370 and 1372, he went against the Dughlat emir Qamar al-Dīn, who had rebelled against the Chaghadayid khans.[7] Qamar al-Dīn had taken the chieftainship of the Dughlat from his nephew Khudāydād, appointed *beglerbegi* by Tughluq Temür. He had also seized central power and claimed the title of khan. Despite dissent within the khanate, Qamar al-Dīn was not an easy enemy to destroy, and Temür's army suffered from Moghulistan's difficult climate and terrain.[8] In 1372 or 1373, Temür undertook the first of several campaigns against the Qunqirat Sufi dynasty of Khorezm, on the dubious claim that Chinggis Khan had bequeathed the revenues of its cities Kat and Khiva to Chaghadai.[9]

As his reign progressed, Temür increased his claims to power. Between 1375 and 1378, after another successful campaign against Qamar al-Dīn, he appointed his eldest son ʿUmar Shaykh governor of Andijan, thus laying claim to the Ferghana Valley. This action elicited a swift reaction from Qamar al-Dīn, helped by dissident emirs of the *Ulus Chaghatay*, and Temür had to campaign against him several times, finally pushing him into exile. In 1375–7, Temür

7 The dates of Temür's earliest campaigns are uncertain, because Persian historians differed in their conversion from the animal cycle.

8 Kim, 1999, pp. 299–307.

9 Woods, 1990a, p. 104.

further enhanced his prestige when Toqtamïsh, a pretender to the throne of the Blue Horde on his northern border, took refuge with him. Temür helped Toqtamïsh win his throne in the winter of 1379 and, having acquired a khan of the Jochid house as protégé, began to present himself as a conqueror in the mould of Chinggis Khan. In 1379–80 he undertook a successful campaign against Khorezm and this time he razed the city of Urgench and divided up its population, saving artisans and scholars to grace his new capital city. This action marked a radical departure from his earlier campaigns, and was probably designed to evoke the Mongol conquests. The next year he appointed his third son, Amīrānshāh, as governor of Khorasan and began a series of campaigns to subjugate its rulers, notably the Kartid kings of Herat, who were defeated in 1381 and removed after a rebellion in 1383.

Temür soon began to expand westwards. In 1384 he took Mazandaran and bestowed it on a local Chinggisid, Luqmān b. Taghay Temür, son of an earlier pretender to the Ilkhanid throne. He allowed Luqmān to retain the Ilkhanid title *pādshāh*, but clearly considered him a vassal. Next he took Sulṭāniyya, the site of Öljeitü's mausoleum, where the later Ilkhanids had been enthroned. From this time on, Temür implicitly laid claim to the Ilkhanid inheritance; it is notable that the birth date of 1336 later invented for him coincides with the death of the last Ilkhan, Abū Saʿīd.[10]

The great conquests

Temür's claims to the Ilkhanid territories did not go uncontested. In 1382 his former protégé Toqtamïsh had succeeded in taking over the Golden Horde, and promptly formed an alliance against Temür with the Mamlūk sultans. In the winter of 1385–6, Toqtamïsh attacked Tabrīz, thus reasserting the Golden Horde's claim to Transcaucasia and initiating a duel between the two rulers which occupied both for a decade.[11] In the spring, Temür set out on his 'three-year campaign' in Iran and that summer defeated the Turko-Mongolian leader Aḥmad Jalayir in Azerbaijan. In 1387 Toqtamïsh again attacked. Now Temür confronted him, and according to the Timurid sources he defeated him; numismatic evidence however suggests that Toqtamïsh held Baku, Darband and other cities for several years after this.[12]

At the end of 1387, Temür learned that Toqtamïsh had attacked Transoxania with the help of Qamar al-Dīn. Toqtamïsh had several local allies, and the

10 Manz, 1988, pp. 113–14; Nagel, 1993, p. 175.
11 Manz, 2001, pp. 137–41.
12 Yazdī / ʿAbbāsī, I, pp. 298–302; Safargaliev, 1960, pp. 146–7.

disturbance encouraged insubordination among Temür's subjects. Returning east, Temür attacked Khorezm, which appears to have been subordinate to Toqtamïsh, and again destroyed Urgench. Since the new eastern Chaghadayid khan Khiḍr Khwāja had welcomed Toqtamïsh, in the spring of 1389 Temür undertook two expeditions against him, campaigning up to Lake Zayzan and Chalish. After this he pursued Toqtamïsh up to the Volga, where he defeated him on 18 June 1391.

Temür's first major campaign in the northern steppes seems to mark a shift in his territorial goals, towards greater interest in settled regions. His army suffered hardships on the campaigns in steppe and mountain areas, and local Iranian rulers took advantage of his absence. He did not attempt to annex the Jochid regions but from this time he began to create provincial governments over settled territories, installing his offspring as governors. In 1391–2 he appointed his grandson Pīr Muḥammad b. Jahāngīr to Kabul. On 5 August 1392 he began his 'five-year campaign' in Iran, destroyed the Muzaffarid dynasty and placed southern Iran under his eldest son ʿUmar Shaykh. Near the end of 1394 Temür learned that Toqtamïsh had again attacked the Caucasus, and headed against him. He defeated him decisively at the Terek River on 15 April 1395, then campaigned nearly to Moscow and looted Hajji Tarkhan and Saray, permanently weakening the Golden Horde. He made no attempt to install a permanent administration.

On his return Temür appointed Amīrānshāh to Azerbaijan and replaced him in Khorasan with his fourth son, Shāhrukh. At about this time he designated as heir apparent his grandson Muḥammad Sulṭān b. Jahāngīr, distinguished for his maternal ancestry. Jahāngīr had been Temür's only son born of a free woman, and Muḥammad Sulṭān's mother Khanzāda was descended from Chinggis Khan. This appointment probably lay behind attempted rebellions by two princes who may have considered themselves in line for succession: Amīrānshāh and Pīr Muḥammad b. ʿUmar Shaykh, who had inherited the governorship of Fars on his father's death.[13] Temür's next campaigns were designed to destroy his rivals within Islamic lands. In December 1398 he took Delhi, which his army sacked and burned, then, in autumn of 1399, after a brief sojourn in Samarqand, he left for his 'seven-year campaign' in the Near East. His main targets were the Mamlūk sultan Faraj and the Ottoman sultan Bayezit. He invaded Syria in the autumn of 1400, defeated the Mamlūks and sacked several cities. In the spring of 1402 he headed into Anatolia and in July 1402 defeated Bayezit near Ankara. As in the steppe, he created no permanent administration.

13 Woods, 1984, pp. 333–4; Ḥāfiẓ-i Abrū, 1997–9, II, pp. 317–20.

Having established his primacy within the Islamic world, Temür turned back to a long-standing ambition – the conquest of China. In 1397 he had detained the Chinese ambassadors, and later had welcomed a pretender to the throne of the northern Yuan, known as Taishi Oghlan or Ilchi Temür, who remained in his suite until his death.[14] In the autumn of 1404 he staged a *quriltai* in Samarqand to prepare for the campaign. The Spanish ambassadors led by Ruy Gonzáles de Clavijo noted Temür's contemptuous treatment of the Chinese.[15] On 27 November 1404 Temür set out with a huge army to winter in Otrar, but died there on 17 or 18 February 1405.

The organization of Temür's realm

Temür's strength lay in his ability to exploit both nomad and settled resources. His army contained a central corps of Chaghatay cavalry augmented by foot soldiers and cavalry from the settled territories. Subordinate leaders had to contribute troops to his campaigns and local nomads were also conscripted. The regional Iranian armies created by the Mongols (*cherig*) made up part of the provincial armies led by his governors. Temür rarely delegated significant military authority and usually began his campaigns with a unified army, but paused periodically to send contingents in several directions. Thus he combined overwhelming force with the advantage of unpredictability, which confused his foes. He had exceptional control over his army and his famous massacres were reserved for selected cities; although his army pillaged and occasionally wreaked deliberate destruction, he often took measures to restore agriculture after the army's departure.

We have few details on Temür's formal administration. He had a central chancellery, the *dīvān-i aʿlā'*, staffed with Persian bureaucrats, which travelled with him, and also a *dīvān* staffed by Turkic scribes writing in the Uighur script, whose function remains obscure. The histories mention a *dīvān-i buzurg*, which seems to have functioned as a tribunal for Turko-Mongolian commanders, probably equivalent to the Mongol *yarghu* court. In the court and army, most offices bore Mongolian or Turkic names and the position of *amīr al-umarā'* (*beglerbegi*) is well attested, but the office does not appear to have had the importance it held in the Golden Horde. The two branches of government were not entirely separate. In particular the Turko-Mongolian commanders were often closely involved in the affairs of the

14 Togan, 1958, pp. 284–5. This person is to be identified with Öljeitü Bunyashiri, who became ruler of the northern Yuan in 1408, see Honda, 1958, p. 239.

15 Clavijo, 1928, pp. 222–3.

Persian chancellery, most notably in tax-collection and the investigation of provincial *dīvāns*.[16]

Temür controlled his subordinates largely through manipulation and balance. Like Chinggis Khan he organized his army in decimal units with his offspring and personal followers as the primary commanders. He did not destroy the tribes of the *Ulus Chaghatay* but he did undermine their political authority, and was careful also not to allow the families of his followers to create new centres of power; their families were divided up among different provincial armies.[17] In his settled territories Temür destroyed the most powerful dynasties like the Karts and the Muzaffarids, but left the most smaller dynasties intact.

Temür installed a permanent administration only over the primarily settled, Persian-speaking territories previously under Mongol rule, and he promoted both agriculture and commerce. Historians mention his concern with security and economic infrastructure, and his foreign contacts show a desire to further long-distance trade.[18] The dynasty controlling the rich port of Hormuz remained largely independent but compliant and their bazaars were frequented by Timurid merchants. Thus, the sea route was connected to the land routes crossing northern Iran and Transoxania.[19] Trade with China was promoted by Temür and his successors, even during periods when diplomatic relations were suspended.[20]

The struggle for succession

Temür's heir apparent, Muḥammad Sulṭān b. Jahāngīr, died in 1403 and Temür did not immediately name another successor. At about this time he undertook a major reorganization which echoed the disposition of Chinggis Khan's lands into *ulus*es. Dividing his realm into four regions, he put each under the family of one of his sons: Azerbaijan and Iraq under the line of Amīrānshāh (*c.* 1367–1408), southern and central Iran under the children of ʿUmar Shaykh (*c.* 1354–94), the south-eastern regions under Pīr Muḥammad b. Jahāngīr (1376–1407), and the north-eastern lands under Shāhrukh (1377–1447) and his sons. At the end of his life Temür appointed Muḥammad Sulṭān's half-brother Pīr Muḥammad to succeed him. This was not a workable choice, since

16 *Muʿizz al-ansāb fī shajarat al-ansāb*, Paris, Bibliothèque Nationale, MS no. 67, ff. 97b–98b; Manz, 1989, pp. 115–16, 167–75.
17 Manz, 1989, pp. 84–8, 118–27.
18 Aka, 1996, pp. 15–21.
19 Kauz, 2001, pp. 37, 55–6; Samarqandī, 1941–9, pp. 767–8; Clavijo, 1928, pp. 152–3, 159–63.
20 Kauz, 2005, pp. 6–8, 26–8.

Pīr Muḥammad was not a forceful commander and governed the peripheral province of Kabul. At Temür's death a struggle broke out at two levels – within each family line for regional pre-eminence, and around Samarqand for sovereign leadership. Azerbaijan had never been securely under Temür's control, and Amīrānshāh's line was soon displaced; in 1408 the Turkmen Qaraqoyunlu killed him in battle and took over Azerbaijan. In central and southern Iran the descendants of ʿUmar Shaykh fought among themselves. At Temür's death the senior prince was Pīr Muḥammad b. ʿUmar Shaykh, governor at Shiraz, who made peace with Shāhrukh. However, after his murder by a follower on 18 May 1409, his younger and more ambitious brother Iskandar gained pre-eminence.

The struggle for central power also began immediately after Temür's death. Amīrānshāh's son Khalīl Sulṭān had his emirs raise him to the throne. His mother was Jahāngīr's widow, Khanzāda, who was married to Amīrānshāh after Jahāngīr's death. Despite disapproval from Temür's chief emirs, Khalīl Sulṭān entered Samarqand on 18 March and was proclaimed ruler. As a figurehead khan he installed his nephew Muḥammad Jahāngīr b. Muḥammad Sulṭān. Since Khalīl Sulṭān also had Chinggisid blood, this appointment was probably intended to attract the emirs who had served Muḥammad Sulṭān and had remained faithful to his descendants.[21] Khalīl Sulṭān emphasized the dynasty's connection to Mongol traditions by honouring Chinggisid princes at his court and commissioning a genealogy connecting the Timurids to the line of Chinggis Khan.[22] Cordial relations with China were quickly restored.[23]

Khalīl Sulṭān and Shāhrukh agreed that Khalīl Sulṭān would rule in Transoxania and Shāhrukh would control Khorasan, where he began minting his own coins.[24] Shāhrukh nonetheless provided support to Temür's designated heir, Pīr Muḥammad b. Jahāngīr, who continued attacks on Transoxania until his murder in February 1407. The greater threat to Khalīl Sulṭān came from Sulṭān Muḥammad's emirs, led by Khudāydād Ḥusaynī and Shaykh Nūr al-Dīn, aiming to install one of Muḥammad Sulṭān's young sons. They received help from the eastern Chaghadayid khans who apparently still hoped to reunite the Chaghadayid Khanate with Chinese help.[25] Khalīl Sulṭān depended heavily on the foreign troops settled in Transoxania, who began to desert him as his treasury became depleted.

21 Komaroff, 1986, p. 216.
22 Ando, 1996, pp. 17–22.
23 Kauz, 2005, pp. 82 ff.
24 Komaroff, 1986, p. 216.
25 Kim, 1999, pp. 314–18.

Of all the Timurid princes, Shāhrukh was the least involved in the early succession struggle. Thus, he had not exhausted his treasury and was in a good position to profit from the defeat of his relatives. In 1409 Amīr Khudāydād captured Khalīl Sulṭān and handed him over to Shāhrukh, whom he had invited into Transoxania. Shāhrukh came to Samarqand on 13 May 1409, installed his son Ulugh Beg as governor, and then returned to Herat, which remained his capital.

Shāhrukh's early reign

Shāhrukh's claim to supreme power and his incorporation of Transoxania apparently surprised Khudāydād and Shaykh Nūr al-Dīn, who had probably expected Shāhrukh to remain in Khorasan.[26] Khudāydād was soon killed, but in April 1410 Shaykh Nūr al-Dīn attacked and defeated the army of Transoxania. When he tried to take Samarqand, however, the notables refused to admit him. It required two campaigns by Shāhrukh to pacify the province and Ulugh Beg's governorship was secure only after Shaykh Nūr al-Dīn's murder in 1411.[27] In 1412–13 Shāhrukh's army took Khorezm from the Jochids.

Shāhrukh's first duty as ruler was to avenge the death of his brother Amīrānshāh and retake Azerbaijan – 'the kingdom of the Ilkhans'. However he was delayed by his nephew Iskandar b. ʿUmar Shaykh in central Iran, who had adopted the title 'Sulṭān' and written to local rulers seeking an alliance against Shāhrukh. In the course of two campaigns, in 1414 and 1415, Shāhrukh defeated Iskandar and his brothers and installed his own son, Ibrāhīm Sulṭān, as governor in Shiraz. Another son, Baysunghur, became governor of Mazandaran and Western Khorasan but continued to spend most of his time in Herat. On 21 August 1420 Shāhrukh set out for Azerbaijan against Qara Yūsuf Qaraqoyunlu. Qara Yūsuf was a formidable foe and it was fortunate for Shāhrukh that the Qaraqoyunlu ruler died of natural causes on 13 November 1420. Shāhrukh was able to take the region and defeat Qara Yūsuf's sons, but left without appointing a Chaghatay governor. He had now completed his takeover of Temür's realm, in almost its full extent.

Many of the emirs appointed to serve with Shāhrukh during Temür's lifetime later proved unfaithful to him, but he was well served by emirs who owed their power to him personally. Two men stand out: ʿAlīka Kükeltash and Amīr Fīrūzshāh, both active in the central government and in local affairs. In addition, the sons of Temür's follower Ghiyāth al-Dīn Tarkhan, related to

26 Ḥāfiẓ-i Abrū, 1993, I pp. 278–81.
27 Manz, 2007, pp. 24–8.

Shāhrukh through his powerful wife Gawharshād, played a prominent role especially in the early years. Like Temür, Shāhrukh kept firm control over his princely governors, who joined him on his campaigns and were held answerable for problems in their own regions. In his *dīvān* Shāhrukh allowed greater autonomy to his Persian bureaucrats than Temür had done, but controlled them through periodic accusations and investigation of accounts. For most of Shāhrukh's reign, the *ṣāḥib dīvān* was Ghiyāth al-Dīn Pīr Aḥmad Khwāfī, wealthy, well connected, and almost universally praised by historians. However, he had to work with a partner, often not of his own choosing, and several princes and emirs, notably Baysunghur and Amīr Fīrūzshāh, were intimately involved in *dīvān* affairs.[28]

On 22 January 1427, a member of the Ḥurūfī sect made an attempt on Shāhrukh's life as he left the Friday mosque in Herat. The incident resulted in a spate of executions of Ḥurūfīs, and harassment of religious figures suspected of connections to them. The strong reaction indicates concern over contemporary religious movements with political goals, including that of the aspiring *mahdī* Muḥammad Nūrbakhsh, who began his career as a disciple of the Kubravī shaykh Khwāja Isḥaq in Khuttalan and later became active in Luristan.[29] In 1428–9 Iskandar Qaraqoyunlu began to plunder the western Timurid regions, including Sulṭāniyya, and Shāhrukh again headed west. On 18 September 1429 he defeated Iskandar at Salmas, and installed Qara Yūsuf's youngest son Abū Saʿīd.

Shāhrukh's later reign

In 1429–30, the Jochid Abū'l-Khayr Khan, whose followers were termed 'Uzbeks' (Özbeks) rose to power in the Aral Sea region; his army soon began to attack Khorezm, and in 1434–6 he annexed its northern region. From 1431 onwards, Shāhrukh stationed an army in Mazandaran through the winter to protect his frontier, but by the end of his reign the Uzbeks were regularly raiding Transoxania. In 1434–5, pressure from the Qaraqoyunlu, now again under Iskandar, resulted in Shāhrukh's third Azerbaijan campaign. Once more he succeeded, and he now installed Jahānshāh b. Qara Yūsuf as ruler. Although Shāhrukh's western border remained secure, his internal control gradually weakened. One problem was the death of many senior emirs and most of his adult sons. His son Soyurghatmïsh, governor of Kabul, died in 1426, Baysunghur, who was important in the *dīvān*, on 20 December 1433, and Ibrāhīm

28 Manz, 2007, pp. 88–99.
29 Bashir, 2003, pp. 44–65.

Sulṭān, governor of Fars, on 3 May 1435. In the late 1430s, several major emirs died and after the death of Amīr ʿAlīka in 1440 Fīrūzshāh became the pre-eminent emir. He began to abuse his power, particularly in the *dīvān*, where he clashed with the *ṣāḥib dīvān*, Pīr Aḥmad Khwāfī.[30]

In the spring of 1444, Shāhrukh became seriously ill and troubles broke out throughout the provinces. Since he had not appointed a successor, Gawharshād pushed Fīrūzshāh to swear allegiance to her personal favourite, ʿAlāʾ al-Dawla b. Baysunghur, an act which angered the other princes. Fīrūzshāh furthermore was implicated in a major *dīvān* scandal, and when Shāhrukh recovered and investigated, he was disgraced and died.[31] Shāhrukh's son Muḥammad Jūkī [Chökey?] died the same year, leaving Ulugh Beg as Shāhrukh's sole surviving son. In 1442, Shāhrukh had given the governorship of northern Iran to Baysunghur's son Sulṭān Muḥammad. While Shāhrukh was ill, many local rulers in central and northern Iran looked towards Sulṭān Muḥammad b. Baysunghur as a protector, and on 2 May 1446, Sulṭān Muḥammad entered Isfahan at the invitation of its notables, thus issuing a direct challenge to Shāhrukh.[32] When, despite ill-health, Shāhrukh headed against him, Sulṭān Muḥammad fled west. Shāhrukh wintered near Rayy and planned to proceed against Sulṭān Muḥammad in the spring, but on 13 March 1447, he died.

Transoxania

Throughout his career Temür imported captured artisans to develop Samarqand into a capital city consonant with his ambition. According to Ibn ʿArabshāh, Temür founded new towns around Samarqand named after the capitals of conquered regions; the fortified town of Shiraz is mentioned by later historians.[33] In 1373–4, Temür began the construction of a second capital at his birthplace of Kish, where he erected a magnificent palace and a number of religious buildings.[34] Since many of the Chaghatay – both personal followers and tribesmen – were assigned to provincial armies outside the original *ulus*, Temür imported personnel into Transoxania to develop the province and replace tribal armies. Although Chaghatay tribes remained in Transoxania, by the end of Temür's life the region's major armies seem to have been made up of outside soldiers. The urban population apparently changed less; we find the same local rulers and notable families active throughout the early Timurid

30 Manz, 2007, pp. 96–7.
31 Samarqandī, 1941–9, pp. 793–5, 837–40.
32 Manz, 2007, pp. 252–7.
33 Ibn ʿArabshāh, 1936, p. 310; Babur/Thackston, 1993, I, pp. 76–9.
34 Golombek and Wilber, 1988, pp. 271–81.

period.[35] Temür expanded the borders of the region in the north from the Jaxartes south of Sighnaq, to include Yasï and Otrar, stretching east to the Issyk Kul and beyond Kashghar. Soldiers and rulers – both settled and nomad – from all conquered territories were stationed in frontier forts. In Yasï he commissioned a magnificent shrine to the Sufi shaykh Aḥmad Yasavī, and to the east built a major fort, Ashpara, furnished with a new agricultural settlement.[36]

During Shāhrukh's reign Transoxania gradually lost its importance. V. V. Bartol'd's depiction of Ulugh Beg as almost a co-ruler with Shāhrukh has been questioned by more recent scholars.[37] Shāhrukh restricted Ulugh Beg's power as governor of Transoxania by appointing other princes to many of its southern regions. Ḥiṣār-i Shādmān was entrusted to Muḥammad Jahāngīr b. Muḥammad Sulṭān, perhaps to appease the party loyal to his family. Balkh, Khuttalan, Badakhshan and Andijan were all assigned to other princes; Andijan later came under Ulugh Beg's jurisdiction, but the other regions remained separate. The region of Kashghar at first reverted to eastern Chaghadayid rule. During the first part of his reign, Shāhrukh encouraged Ulugh Beg to campaign in the eastern Chaghadayid territories. Few campaigns penetrated deeply into Moghul territories, but Ulugh Beg did succeed in regaining Kashghar about 1414. Over the next years, both Shāhrukh and Ulugh Beg showed reluctance to interfere in the complicated politics of the eastern Chaghadayids, in which both the central throne and the leadership of the Dughlat were often contested. Various dynastic candidates and the families of both Khudāydād Dughlat and Temür's former enemy Qamar al-Dīn came to solicit aid, but received little encouragement.[38] Despite disorders in Moghulistan, commercial and diplomatic ties with China remained strong, especially up to the death of the Yongle Emperor in 1424.

During the reign of Shīr Muḥammad Khan (1421–5), the eastern Chaghadayids began to encroach on Ulugh Beg's territories in the Ashpara region and in Kashghar. In 1425, despite objections from Shāhrukh, Ulugh Beg undertook an ambitious and successful campaign against them.[39] In dealing with the powers to the north he was less fortunate. Baraq Khan of the Blue Horde, whom he had formerly favoured, arrived in Sighnaq in 1426 and laid claim to the region. Shāhrukh forbade Ulugh Beg to campaign against him and sent his

35 See for example, Ando, 1994, pp. 255–60.

36 Ibn ʿArabshāh, 1936, pp. 193–4, 212; Yazdī/ʿAbbāsī, I, p. 341, II, pp. 182, 450.

37 Bartol'd, *Ulugbek i ego vremia*, in his *Sochineniia*, II/2, pp. 25–177; Akhmedov, 1965b; Manz, 'Ulugh Beg,' *EI*², x, p. 812b.

38 Ḥāfiẓ-i Abrū, 1993, II, pp. 713, 744, 747–8, 753, 884–5; Dūghlāt/Thackston, II, pp. 34, 39.

39 Ḥāfiẓ-i Abrū, 1993, I, pp. 877–93, Bartol'd, *Ulugbek i ego vremia*, in his *Sochineniia*, II/2, pp. 105, 180–1 ('Prilozheniia').

son Muḥammad Jūkī [Chökey?] with an army in 1427. Defying Shāhrukh's orders, the two princes attacked and were badly defeated. On their return to Samarqand, part of the population proposed shutting the gates against them. Shāhrukh punished Ulugh Beg by briefly suspending him from his governorship.[40]

Until 1433–4, Ulugh Beg made some attempt to protect his borders, but he remained aloof from Moghul affairs and did not apparently campaign in person. Sometime between 1426 and 1435, the pretender to the Chaghadayid throne, Yūnus Oghlan, sought refuge with him; Ulugh Beg promised asylum but treacherously murdered many of his followers. Shāhrukh scolded him and dispatched Yūnus to Iran, where he remained until the reign of Abū Saʿīd.[41] In about 1434–5, the Dughlat re-established their hold over Kashghar, built a fort on the border of the Ferghana Valley and began to raid the Andijan region, apparently without eliciting a reaction from Ulugh Beg.[42] By the end of Shāhrukh's reign the followers of Abū'l-Khayr Khan were regularly raiding northern Transoxania, reaching almost to Samarqand and Bukhara.

Ulugh Beg has been portrayed as a prince particularly attached to the Turko-Mongolian tradition, who continued to maintain a puppet khan in Samarqand. The evidence for this characterization, however, comes mainly from the much later *Tārīkh-i Rashīdī* of Muḥammad Ḥaydar Dughlat. No contemporary source mentions Ulugh Beg's khan and when Ulugh Beg claimed sovereignty after Shāhrukh's death, it was Temür's name he added to his own on his coins.[43] Many of the stories concerning his attachment to Mongol lore are likewise questionable, and the historical work on the Mongol khans attributed to him – the *Tārīkh-i arbaʿulus* – was derivative from earlier Timurid histories.[44]

Religious and cultural patronage

The Timurids and their followers – known as Chaghatay – considered themselves superior to Persians as inheritors of Turko-Mongolian traditions, but likewise above the Moghuls and the 'Uzbek' inhabitants of the Dasht-i Qipchāq in their understanding of high culture.[45] There is evidence that many were still nomadic at the time of Temür's death and the belief in the superiority

40 Ḥāfiẓ-i Abrū, 1993, p. 907; Samarqandī, 1941–9, pp. 311–12.
41 Dūghlāt/Thackston, II, pp. 39, 45; Babur/Thackston 1993, I, pp. 18–20.
42 Dūghlāt/Thackston, II, pp. 40–2, 46; Samarqandī, 1941–9, p. 671.
43 Woods, 1990a, pp. 115–16; Komaroff, 1986, p. 220.
44 Manz, 2008.
45 Manz, 1992, pp. 36–8.

of nomad armies remained strong. The elite, however, was bilingual and competent in both the Islamic and Turko-Mongolian heritage; they retained a dual cultural loyalty, while deliberately maintaining a separation between the two cultures. Throughout his career Temür invoked both the Mongolian *yasa* and the Islamic *sharīʿa*, and the education he arranged for his grandchildren fitted them for rule within both traditions. The etiquette of his court was primarily Mongolian, with the open consumption of alcohol and the women of the court as central participants, although they apparently wore at least light veils.[46] At the same time Temür presented himself as an Islamic monarch. Although illiterate, he was highly intelligent – indeed intellectual – well versed in history and religious studies. Shāhrukh did not disavow his father's heritage. He was a man of great piety, and near the beginning of his reign he proclaimed the restoration of the *sharīʿa* and the abrogation of the Mongolian *yasa*. Nonetheless he claimed publicly to uphold the *yasa*, continued the *yarghu* court, and sponsored literature in the Uighur script.[47]

Temür allowed little independent cultural activity, but under Shāhrukh princely courts became active centres of patronage which mirrored the cultural tastes of individual princes, while showing shared concerns. Fars under both Iskandar Sulṭān and Ibrāhīm Sulṭān was a centre for historical writing, where Mongolian and Central Asian traditions appear to have been particularly well preserved. Baysunghur was noted for his expert patronage of the arts of the book. Ulugh Beg remains famous primarily for his promotion of astronomy and mathematics, centred around the observatory he built in Samarqand. The star tables produced there were used throughout the Middle East and Renaissance Europe.

Temür commissioned several histories of his reign, in Turkic and in Persian, only one or two of which have survived. Shāhrukh also showed a strong interest in history, and under his patronage Ḥāfiẓ-i Abrū undertook an ambitious project of world history based on the *Jāmiʿal-tavārīkh* of Rashīd al-Dīn, illustrated in the style of the early Mongol manuscripts. Shāhrukh also commissioned a continuation of Rashīd al-Dīn's Mongol genealogy, adding a genealogy of the Barlas. In the last decade of his life Temür had begun to develop a new foundation myth centred on a common ancestry with Chinggis Khan and the claim that the Barlas ancestor Qarachar, assigned to Chaghadai, had held a pre-eminent position within the Chaghadayid Khanate which he had passed on to his descendants. After the death of his second puppet khan,

46 Clavijo, 1928, pp. 244–8, 257–63.
47 Khalidov and Subtelny, 1995, pp. 211–12, Manz, 2001, p. 146.

Maḥmūd, in 1402, Temür did not replace him and in the last years of his reign issued some coins in his own name.[48] Shāhrukh never installed a Chinggisid khan, and some histories written during his reign omit mention of earlier ones.[49] Instead he openly claimed sovereignty and adopted the title 'Pādshāh-i Islām', earlier used by the Ilkhanids and applied to Temür's puppet khans. Some contemporary histories and correspondence refer to him as *qaghan*, though the title did not appear on coins.[50] Shāhrukh further elaborated the Barlas myth and the histories written in Herat and provincial courts during his reign include the four branches of the Chinggisid line, highlighting the history of Qarachar Barlas and his descendants.

In religious policy there were significant continuities between Temür and Shāhrukh. Temür gathered a brilliant array of scholars, particularly in the religious sciences, including Saʿd al-Dīn al-Taftazānī, Muḥammad al-Jazarī and Sayyid ʿAlī Jurjānī. The same scholars, or their students, remained dominant under Shāhrukh. Unlike Temür, Shāhrukh rarely favoured individual scholars, preferring institutional patronage. He completed a *madrasa* and *khānaqāh* in Herat in 1410–11 and his wife Gawharshād constructed a magnificent complex on the outskirts of Herat, completed in 1437–8. Shāhrukh also erected a new shrine to Shaykh ʿAbd Allāh Anṣārī, considered the protector of Herat, while both he and Gawharshād contributed to building at the shrine of the eighth *imām* in Mashhad.

In their relations with Sufi movements, the two rulers were not far apart: both showed honour to the shaykhs of Jām and other local shaykhs, while both had difficult relations with the incipient Niʿmatullāhī order, Sayyid ʿAlī Hamadānī and his disciples, and the Ḥurūfī movement.[51] At this period Transoxania and Khorasan were the locus of much religious activity, led largely by individuals. Sufi shaykhs were numerous and active, and many communities are mentioned, most importantly the Yasaviyya, Kubraviyya and Khwājagān. However, with the possible exception of the Niʿmatullāhī, most *ṭuruq* were loosely organized and many shaykhs had multiple affiliations.[52] Bahāʾ al-Dīn Naqshband was active during Temür's career and several of his disciples were well known under Shāhrukh, but the powerful Naqshbandiyya led by Khwāja Aḥrār was a later phenomenon.[53]

48 Haider, 1976, p. 70; Woods, 1990a, p. 121 n. 75.
49 Woods, 1987, pp. 104–5.
50 For example: Faṣīḥ Khwāfī, 1960–1, III, pp. 200, 205 and *passim*; Navāʾī, 1977, pp. 151, 171.
51 Manz, 2007a, pp. 243–4.
52 DeWeese, 1993, pp. 33–6.
53 Paul, 1998.

The succession struggle after Shāhrukh

By the time that Shāhrukh died, battle lines over succession had been drawn, and order quickly broke down. Ulugh Beg claimed supreme power and began to mint coins in his own name. The other major contenders were Baysunghur's three sons. ʿAlāʾ al-Dawla, based in Herat, soon also claimed the sultanate. Sulṭān Muḥammad returned to Isfahan to consolidate his control over Iran, while Abū'l-Qāsim Bābur took his father's province of Mazandaran. In the spring of 1448 Ulugh Beg and his elder son ʿAbd al-Laṭīf seized Herat, but the city quickly changed hands, going first to the Turkmen prince Yār ʿAlī, and then to Abū'l-Qāsim Bābur b. Baysunghur in February 1449. Over the next months Abū'l-Qāsim gained power in the eastern regions at the expense of ʿAlāʾ al-Dawla and Ulugh Beg.

Ulugh Beg was not a gifted commander and proved inept in personal relations. He alienated ʿAbd al-Laṭīf by denying him recognition for his role in conquering Herat. By early summer 1449, ʿAbd al-Laṭīf was in open opposition and had gathered support from Chaghatay emirs around Balkh. Ulugh Beg had no choice but to go against him; he was defeated, and when he tried to retreat into Samarqand, he found the gates closed against him. He fled to Shāhrukhiyya, and was again denied admittance. At this point he surrendered to ʿAbd al-Laṭīf, who appointed a puppet Chinggisid khan to try him 'according to the *sharīʿa*'. Not surprisingly, the verdict went against Ulugh Beg, who was allowed to leave for the pilgrimage but murdered along the way, on 25 or 27 October 1449. This was a shocking act, condemned in the Timurid histories.

ʿAbd al-Laṭīf soon stopped the Uzbek raids but he was harsh towards Ulugh Beg's emirs, and, on 16 May 1450, these men killed him. In his place they installed the youthful son of Ibrāhīm Sulṭān, ʿAbd Allāh, previously governor of Shiraz. ʿAbd Allāh had brought many of his followers with him and these men now came into conflict with local emirs. This dissension opened the way to a candidate from a different Timurid line: the prince Abū Saʿīd, a descendant of Amīrānshāh who had served in Ulugh Beg's army and seems to have based his strength on the Arghun tribe of the northern border. He enlisted the aid of Abū'l-Khayr Khan whose daughter he married, and seized power on 21 or 22 June 1451.

Abū'l-Qāsim Bābur and Sulṭān Muḥammad continued to compete for the lands below the Oxus. Sulṭān Muḥammad attempted to take Khorasan, but was defeated on 9 January 1452; following the example of his relatives, Abū'l-Qāsim had him killed. In central and southern Iran however Abū'l-Qāsim had to retreat before the Qaraqoyunlu, who held most of Iran by the summer of 1452. The long succession struggle on Shāhrukh's death did much to discredit his line, and it was at this time that Temür's realm began to shrink significantly.

Conclusion

Temür's dramatic career left a strong stamp on the regions he conquered and also consolidated changes that had begun earlier. The legitimation he formulated was a combination of the systems he found in his dominions, based on both *yasa* and *sharīʿa*. In abandoning his western Islamic conquests and the steppe regions he had taken, he formalized existing distinctions between the steppe and settled, Mongol and non-Mongol. By combining a persona which deliberately echoed Chinggis Khan with religious and cultural patronage based largely on Perso-Islamic norms, he provided a new founding father for the mixed society which had come into existence.

With Shāhrukh's rise to power we see another shift, but here again the transformation had begun earlier. During Temür's reign, Transoxania marked a midpoint from which his expeditions branched out north, south, east and west, but by the end of his career the economic centre lay in the primarily settled regions of Iran where many of his Chaghatay following were stationed. The territories to the east and north were buffer regions, manned by troops from the conquered population. When Shāhrukh moved the capital to Herat, therefore, he was recognizing the fact that Transoxania was no longer the centre of the Timurid dominions. Khorasan offered a stronger agricultural base and a more central location from which to manage the realm.

Temür had left a realm which had reached its logical boundaries; there was no reason for further conquest. With a ruler not constantly on campaign, regional courts developed more fully and the central administration became a fixed one, centred in Herat. It was the succession struggle after Shāhrukh's death that brought major change, and the Timurid realm both shrank and divided. By the end of the contest most of Iran was in the hands of the Turkmens Khorasan and Transoxania were under different princes, and the confederation of Abū'l-Khayr Khan had begun to influence the politics of Transoxania.

11

The later Timurids *c.* 1450–1526

STEPHEN DALE

While lacking the ferocity and seemingly tireless aggression of Temür himself, Shah Rukh and Ulugh Beg had maintained a degree of Timurid authority in Iran, Mawarannahr and Afghanistan for four decades. However, Timurid power quickly atrophied after Shah Rukh's death in 1447 and Ulugh Beg's assassination in 1449. During this second half of the Timurid century that concluded with the Uzbek occupation of Samarqand in 1501 and Herat in 1507, Temür's heirs not only dissipated their collective power in internecine struggles, but by that time also groups whom Temür had terrorized and cowed, recovered and reasserted themselves. The outer boundaries of the Timurid Empire began to shrink as Uzbeks (Özbeks), Turkmen and Mongols moved on the principal centres of Timurid wealth and power in Mawarannahr, Fars, Iraq-i ʿAjam and Khurāsān. Meanwhile these weakened rulers of territories, whose kingdoms by the late fifteenth century had shrunk to little more than a congeries of Timurid city-states, competed for cultural precedence, creating a *fin-de-siècle* era of literary and artistic florescence. Among these states Herat particularly resembled a dying star that flashed out briefly but spectacularly in the Islamic world before its extinction. Still, despite the disintegration of the late Timurid world, the idea of a Timurid revival survived in the minds of its protagonists, one of whom, Ẓahīr al-Dīn Muḥammad Bābur, laid the foundation in 1526 for a Timurid renaissance that became known later as the Mughal Empire of India.

Dynastic history

Shah Rukh and his son, Ulugh Beg, had left the Timurid political structure essentially unchanged from what it had been at the time of Temür's death in 1405. It consisted of competing lineages and family members who never demonstrated even the slightest sign that they thought of themselves as members of a cooperative Timurid dynastic enterprise. By the evidence of their actions, each Timurid *mīrzā*, or prince, shared but one goal, a desire to destroy his kinsmen and rule in their stead. Therefore, there was no such thing as a Timurid Empire after 1405, but merely an ever-increasing number of Timurid offspring, each of whom possessed comparable legitimacy and ambition. This fundamental underlying reality of the Timurid world explains the accelerated fragmentation of the Timurid realm during the second half of the fifteenth century and partly also the cultural florescence that accompanied it.[1]

The one innovation that Shah Rukh and his son bequeathed to the Timurid world was its *de facto* division into two principal territorial entities, Khurāsān and Iran, with the capital at Herat, and Mawarannahr, centred on Temür's own capital, Samarqand. This separation was not formally recognized or institutionalized, but resulted initially from Shah Rukh's *de facto* administrative division of the Timurid lands into his hegemonic sphere in Khurāsān and Iran, with his son, Ulugh Beg, functioning as an autonomous governor in Samarqand. Temür had ruled both these regions as part of his larger empire. Still this division was in a sense a natural one that reflected historic geographic and cultural realities of the Timurid world. Herat was located in one of the wealthy agrarian centres of ancient Iranian civilization, separated by desert and steppe from the oasis cities of Turan, set amidst a large Turko-Mongol population, which further east in Moghulistan, still retained most of its nomadic traditions. The territorial division continued immediately after Shah Rukh's death when Ulugh Beg decided to return to Samarqand in late 1448 after his son, ʿAbd al-Laṭīf, had occupied the city for him earlier in the year.

The possibility that the two cities might be united again under one Timurid prince lessened when ʿAbd al-Laṭīf first defeated and then assassinated his father in 1449, only to be killed himself in 1450 by men who, if questionable stories are to be believed, were offended by his patricide. Simultaneously two former Timurid governors of Iranian territories fought each other for control of Iraq-i ʿAjam, Fars and Khurāsān. These men were Sulṭān Muḥammad b. Baysunghur, now the nominal ruler of Iraq-i ʿAjam and Fars, and Abūʾl Qāsim Bābur, who controlled territories around Mashhad. Abūʾl Qāsim Bābur defeated and executed his kinsman in 1450, seized most of Khurāsān, including Herat, and marched on Shiraz to seize control of Baysunghur's former territories. In 1454 he also led his forces into Mawarannahr, but found a rival already entrenched there. Three years earlier another Timurid, Abū Saʿīd b. Muḥammad Mīrānshāhī, had survived the tumult that ensued after ʿAbd al-Laṭīf's death, occupied Samarqand, executed a Timurid rival, a

1 This political narrative is abstracted from Roemer, 'Timur in Iran' and 'The Successors of Timur', in *CHIran*, VI, pp. 42–146, and Savory, 1964.

grandson of Shah Rukh, and subsequently consolidated his control throughout the surrounding region. After their conflict stalemated in 1454, Abū'l Qāsim Bābur and Abū Sa'īd explicitly recognized the Amu Darya or Oxus as the boundary between their respective states or spheres of influence. With the exception of a nine-year period between 1459 and 1468, when Abū Sa'īd was able to occupy Herat as part of his broader and ultimately unsuccessful campaign to reconquer the former Timurid territories in Iran, the Amu Darya continued to delimit these two principal centres of Timurid power until the Uzbek conquest of both regions.

The fratricide, patricide and regicide that marked Timurid politics in mid-century further fragmented the resources of individual rulers and encouraged three non-Timurid groups to exploit their divisions. These were the Uzbeks, Turkmen and Mongols who threatened Timurid possessions from the north, west and east. Uzbeks, settled or camped on the Timurids' northern Mawarannahr boundaries, posed the greatest threat. Already in 1448 Uzbek forces attacked Ulugh Beg as he returned to Samarqand from Herat. Abū'l-Khayr Khan, the Chinggsid leader of this predominantly Turkic tribal confederation, demonstrated his interest in exploiting chaotic Timurid politics when he intervened to help Abū Sa'īd defeat his rivals for the control of Samarqand in 1451, receiving in apparent gratitude a daughter of Shah Rukh in marriage. Uzbek aid, however, was less an alliance than, typically for the times, a cynical exploitation of Timurid divisions, and just three years later the Uzbek chief intrigued against Abū Sa'īd with a competing Timurid prince. In fact the Uzbeks made repeated incursions into Mawarannahr during Abū Sa'īd's lifetime, and continued these raids throughout the rest of the century, finally conquering the last Timurid territories in Mawarannahr and Khurāsān.

In Iranian territories to the west of Herat two Turkmen tribal confederations, the Qara Qoyunlu and Aq Qoyunlu, threatened Timurid lands. Thus, in the same year that Abū'l-Khayr Khan intervened in Mawarannahr, the Qara Qoyunlu, formerly vassals of Shah Rukh, stripped most Iranian territories from Timurid control when they forced Abū'l Qāsim Bābur to abandon his campaign to occupy Fars and Iraq-i 'Ajam. In 1458 the Qara Qoyunlu even briefly occupied Herat itself, although their own internal dissensions made it impossible for them to retain the city. Indeed, it was this assault that allowed Abū Sa'īd to occupy Herat and Mazandaran in the following year. During the same decade, Mongols (Moghuls) of the eastern Chaghatay Khanate led by Esen Bugha Khan twice attacked Abū Sa'īd and, while repulsed at the time, these Mongols later sent raiding parties into the Ferghana Valley, especially during the periods when Timurid princes were actively at each other's throats.

The next phase of Timurid political disintegration began with Abū Saʿīd's ultimately disastrous campaign against the Turkmen in Iran in 1468–9, climaxed by his capture by Aq Qoyunlu forces, the successors of the Qara Qoyunlu in western and central Iran and the precursors, in dynastic respects at least, of the Ṣafavids. Uzun Hasan, the Aq Qoyunlu chief, gave Abū Saʿīd over for execution to the young Timurid, Yadgar Muḥammad, a great-grandson of Shah Rukh, who, ostensibly at least, now took revenge for Abū Saʿīd's murder of Gauhar Shād, Shah Rukh's prominent and politically influential wife. This typical Timurid event represented another transitional phase in the Timurid century. It precipitated a return to the division of Timurid lands between Herat and Samarqand and also made way for a new generation of Timurid rulers, who presided over the final, relatively stable phase of their now shrunken territorial legacy, distinguished by the political inertia and cultural aspirations of its principal rulers. In retrospect Abū Saʿīd was himself a transitional figure, a representative in certain respects of a disappearing Timurid past but linked in important respects with what remained of the lineage's future.

Abū Saʿīd was one of two notable late Timurid rulers, the other being Sulṭān Ḥusayn Bayqara of Herat. Abū Saʿīd was, first of all, the last Timurid to make a serious attempt to unite the dynasty's central territories of Mawarannahr and Iran. After 1469, no Timurid prince demonstrated such ambition. He was also the last Timurid whose military power rested to a considerable degree on pastoral nomadic tribal foundations, in his case the Arghuns, who had chosen him as their chief. Unlike the Uzbeks, whose predominantly Turkic tribes possessed a significant degree of social and military cohesion, the Timurids after Abū Saʿīd did not control large coherent tribal fighting forces but instead relied upon ad hoc, habitually unstable coalitions for their military support. In two significant respects, however, Abū Saʿīd's policies established precedents for his Timurid successors. First, he formed a kind of alliance with the Naqshbandī Sufi shaykh, Khwāja ʿUbaydullah Ahrār (d. 1490), a shaykh who exercised remarkable political and religious influence in Samarqand during and after his reign, as well as accumulating enormous land holdings in Mawarannahr and Afghanistan during his lifetime. While helping Abū Saʿīd to maintain his authority in Mawarannahr, Khwāja Ahrār also convinced him to administer his territories as a Muslim sultan much like Shah Rukh in Herat, and to purge his administration of some identifiable Turko-Mongol traditions, such as the notorious Mongol commercial or trade tax, the *tamgha*. By the end of Abū Saʿīd's life Khwāja Ahrār had attained the status of a Timurid patron saint, and was revered as such even after his death by rulers who often invoked his spiritual power to aid their military adventures. Second, Abū Saʿīd also tried to bolster his legitimacy by minting coins with Shīʿī as well as Sunnī formulas, an appeal for sectarian support that some of his successors made as well.[2]

Following Abū Saʿīd's death his sons took control of Mawarannahr, with Sulṭān Aḥmad (r. 1469–94) ruling over Samarqand and Bukhara and exercising nominal authority over the remainder of the region that was in reality, however, parcelled out in appanages to his kin, who functioned as *de facto* independent rulers. These men included ʿUmar Shaykh Mīrzā, ruling the Ferghana Valley, and Maḥmūd Mīrzā, governing Balkh in northern Afghanistan. While constantly threatened both by Uzbeks and Mongols, Sulṭān Aḥmad and his relatives sporadically fought with one another while enjoying the modest resources of their respective territories and exhibiting a distinct lack of their ancestor's will to power. The same absence of imperial ambition seems to have been true of the Timurid ruler of the distant Kabul appanage, Ulugh Beg Kābulī and equally true also of Sulṭān Ḥusayn Bayqara (r. 1469–1506), who took advantage of Abū Saʿīd's death to seize Herat, which had been controlled for a brief, drunken two-month period by Yadgar Muḥammad, the puppet of Uzun Hasan Aq Qoyunlu. Ḥusayn Bayqara himself, while presiding over a magnificent Perso-Islamic and Turkic cultural florescence, was singularly cautious, not to say indolent when it came to reconstituting a Timurid empire. He conceded the Turkmen domination of central and Western Iran, implicitly at least recognized the Amu Darya boundary and spent much of his restrained military career fighting with his adult sons, who treated their own modest appanages as independent city-states.

The deaths of Sulṭān Aḥmad in 1494 and Ḥusayn Bayqara in 1506 precipitated the climax of the Timurid century, as their relatives and descendants fought over the scraps of their ancestor's once great empire. They proved themselves manifestly incapable of uniting to resist the Uzbek threat to their existence, whose new leader, Shaybaq (Shaybānī) Khan, first snuffed out, in his own language, the candle of Timurid rule in Samarqand in 1501, and then followed with the occupation of Herat in 1507. Refugees of this debacle fled west to Iran or the Ottoman dominions or east to the minor Timurid outpost of Kabul. It was there that Ẓahīr al-Dīn Muḥammad Bābur, the hitherto unknown Timurid prince from a bucolic appanage in the Ferghana Valley, far east of Samarqand, took refuge in 1504, first attempting to reclaim Samarqand before abandoning the dynasty's homelands for the far richer fields of the Punjab and the Gangetic valley.

2 Illustrated by Timurid coins. See Darley-Doran, *EI*², X, fasc. 177–8, p. 525.

Society and government in the late Timurid era

The later Timurid period lacks documentary evidence that could reveal the details of the social hierarchy, government structure, administrative apparatus and economy for even the principal Timurid successor states in Herat and Samarqand. While voluminous information is available about the military and political history and literary and artistic activities of the period, especially during its final three decades in Herat, there is no source for the later Timurid era comparable to Ḥāfiẓ-i Abrū's survey of the *buluks* (*bölüks*) or districts around Herat in the early fifteenth century.[3] Indeed, Ḥāfiẓ-i Abrū (1361–1430) was the single most important historian/scholar of the Timurid era, whose geographic and ethnographic interests were not matched by any of his successors. He is a source for, among other important topics, the Ming Dynasty embassies to the Timurid courts in the early fifteenth century. Well-informed historians such as Khwāndamīr offer detailed military and political synopses of the entire period, but their histories are of sharply limited use when it comes to understanding the underlying economic, political and social realities of the era. And even Khwāndamīr concentrates on Herat and Samarqand while providing little if any information about the outlying Timurid lands. The single best source for understanding the late Timurid political and socio-economic scene is Bābur's massive autobiographical memoir, the first two parts of which deal with the last dozen years of the Timurid century, from 1494 to 1506.[4]

Members of the Turko-Mongol military aristocracy still dominated most of Mawarannahr and Khurāsān during the second half of the Timurid century. Timurids comprised the majority of this ruling class, with Chaghatay Mongols controlling the Tashkent region and some towns in the western Ferghana Valley. These Timurid *mīrzās* and Chinggisid khans continued to rule with a firm, unshaken and unselfconscious belief in their own legitimacy, which Bābur with his habitual frankness described as his 'ambition for rule and desire for conquest'.[5] Dispatched at a relatively young age to govern their father's territories with the aid of military-political tutors known as *beg atekes*, the predominantly Timurid princes in these miniature courts quickly developed individual, independent political ambitions, separated from their natal families and their own brothers or half-brothers. These *mīrzās* seem to have held their territories or appanages as *soyurghals*, semi-autonomous assignments that involved military service but were largely free of financial obligations.[6]

3 Ḥāfiẓ-i Abrū, 1970.
4 Bābur, 1995. For translations see the bibliography.
5 Bābur, 1995, f. 55b.
6 Petrushevskii, 1949.

Each prince relied on a small core of *begs* or senior commanders, initially at least dominated by their father's loyalists. This inner circle rarely exceeded two or three hundred individuals, each one of whom usually led a retinue of his own. If the nominal Timurid head of these small constellations survived long enough, his immediate entourage might evolve into a relatively cohesive band of loyalists, some of whom would be linked through marriage ties with each other or even with the Timurids themselves. Many of these senior loyalists also held land assignments, possibly those known as *tiyul*, which, if the few known examples are a reliable guide, conferred less military and financial autonomy than *soyurghals*.[7]

Taxes on agricultural lands, domesticated and/or nomadic animals and commerce constituted the principal sources of wealth of the Turko-Mongol military aristocracy, although the relative percentages of agrarian and commercial revenues are not known. However, it can be assumed from the *al-Hidaya* text of the twelfth-century Ferghana Valley scholar, Burhān al-Dīn ʿAlī Qïlïch al-Marghīnānī, that Mongols and their Timurid successors were familiar with a wide range of taxation techniques, including taxes in kind as well as a percentage of agricultural produce, levies on sheep and goat herds and a full range of imposts on both long-distance trade and business conducted within the bazaar.[8] Muslim rulers stricken with pious reflection might sometimes abolish the *tamgha* commercial tax, infamous for its association with Mongol rule, but these men still could levy many canonical taxes to make up the difference.

Herat and the surrounding Khurāsān region represented by far the more productive of the two Timurid regions, a wealth reflected in the scale of patronage that Ḥusayn Bayqara and his boon companion, ʿAlī Shīr Navāʾī, dispensed during the last three decades of the fifteenth century. Mawarannahr was distinctly less wealthy, with a far smaller agricultural base than Khurāsān. Still, this region, like Khurāsān, derived substantial income from the commerce that passed through the region. While the level of that commerce is unknown a story that Bābur tells about his father, ʿUmar Shaykh (d. 1494), suggests that in the late Timurid decades substantial trade continued to flow along the Silk Road tracts that connected Mawarannahr with China. Thus Bābur mentions, without unfortunately supplying the date, that his father, exemplifying his sense of *ʿadālat* or justice, carefully guarded the goods of 2,000 caravan merchants who had died in the mountain snows bordering the eastern Ferghana Valley, and contacted the relatives of those who had perished so that

7 Lambton, 'Tiyūl', *EI*[2], X, fasc. 171–2, pp. 550–1.
8 Dale, 2004, pp. 172–3.

they could claim their families' merchandise. ʿUmar Shaykh was undoubtedly aware that by securing these deceased merchants' goods he would guarantee that taxable caravans would traverse his territories in the Ferghana Valley in the future.[9] Bābur also describes the high volume of trade he observed when he ruled Kabul from 1504 to 1525, reporting that 20,000 households travelled from India through Kabul to Iran and Central Asia each year. In these decades just prior to and immediately following the eruption of Europeans into the Indian Ocean, it seems reasonable to suppose that the commerce flowing through Central Asia to and from China, the Middle East and India still generated substantial incomes for Timurid rulers. Indeed, taxes on this trade probably comprised a principal source of silver for the Timurid silver coin, the *tanga*, whose gradual decline in weight during the Timurid century may possibly reflect the fragmentation and atrophying of Timurid power.[10]

Timurid Samarqand and Herat in particular were home to substantial numbers of prosperous merchants, whose mercantile and landed income was often the target of new conquerors, who, when they entered these cities, usually imposed pernicious indemnities, such as the infamous protection money, the *māl-i amān*, on the *arbāblar*, its substantial inhabitants. Individual merchants' names are almost never mentioned in the narrative sources, including Bābur's otherwise idiosyncratic memoir, but some urban property holders are identified in catalogues of *waqf* deeds. Thus in the extant *waqf* deeds of Khwāja ʿUbaydullah Ahrār, the Naqshbandī shaykh who was so influential in Abū Saʿīd's reign, the names of property owners in Bukhara, Tashkent, Samarqand and Kabul are normally specified in cases where their land, shops or water-powered grain mills abutted the shaykh's *waqf* property.[11] The number of these individuals offers just a faint indication of the size of the property-owning class, who would have included some of the otherwise anonymous *arbāblar*. Khwāja Ahrār himself was one of the largest agrarian and urban property owners in Mawarannahr in the late Timurid period. He converted many if not most of his properties into *waqf* holdings to ensure his descendants' continued control of them. He had acquired these properties through donations, some undoubtedly from Timurid *mīrzās*, many others from small holders who preferred to place themselves under his protection and probably also by purchase, using funds from his own commercial activities. It was quite common for *ʿulamāʾ*, whether Sufis or others, to trade, and as was the case in contemporary Europe, many clerics became

9 Dale, 2004, p. 179.
10 Davidovich, 2001, p. 135.
11 Chekhovich, 1974.

wealthy men. Bābur's own spiritual mentor, a descendant of the scholar al-Marghīnānī and a Naqshbandī disciple himself, was a relatively wealthy individual, although the source of his wealth, which in his case was partly manifested by his herds of sheep, is not known.

The *ʿulamāʾ*, of course, represented a distinct professional class, even if in economic terms they were spread out along a spectrum from impoverished *mullas* to wealthy men such as Khwāja Ahrār. In pre-Mongol times the Timurid territories constituted a region that nurtured important Muslim religious scholars. Balkh and Bukhara in particular had been major centres of scholarly activity, and while Mongols virtually destroyed Balkh, Bukhara continued to be a centre of religious learning in Timurid times. The small town of Marghinan in the Ferghana Valley was itself the birthplace of important scholars of Ḥanafī Sunnī Islam both before and after Mongol times. Indeed, it is still a conservative religious centre even in twenty-first-century Uzbekistan. In the Timurid century both Samarqand and Herat also attracted internationally known Ḥanafī scholars, then as now the dominant legal school in Mawarannahr. The author of the famous collection of *ḥadīth*, the ninth-century scholar, Imām Bukhārī, came from this region and a splendid late twentieth-century shrine outside the city commemorates his achievement. In the late fifteenth century Herat was home to Sayf al-Dīn Aḥmad, a descendant of the famous Khurāsānī Ḥanafī Sunnī *ʿālim*, Saʿd al-Dīn Masʿūd b. ʿUmar b. ʿAbd Allah al-Taftazānī (1332–90), whom Temür brought to Samarqand in 1382. Sayf al-Dīn was killed by the Shīʿī ideologue, Shah Ismāʿīl Ṣafavī, when the Iranian monarch occupied Herat in 1510. Another significant figure was Ikhtiyār al-Dīn b. Ghiyāth al-Dīn al Ḥusaynī, the *qāḍī* of Herat and the author of Persian-language works on jurisprudence and *akhlāq*. The Naqshbandī shaykh, Khwājah Ahrār, himself personified the relatively conservative Ḥanafī Sunnī ethos of Mawarannahr. Both his own and subsequent Naqshbandī disciples, whether Timurid *mīrzās* or others, practised a restrained form of Sufi spiritualism, distinguished by the absence of music or dance and the performance of a silent *dhikr* instead of the vocal chanting of God's name.[12]

Ḥusayn Bayqara and the Timurid florescence

The Timurid century – and the late Timurid period in particular – was characterized by an ever-increasing degree of political fragmentation. Yet, as was the case with competitive Italian Renaissance cities, Timurid rulers also

12 Paul, 1998, pp. 18–30.

distinguished themselves by the intensity and breadth of their religious and cultural interests. Ulugh Beg's personal commitment to and patronage of astronomical and mathematical scholarship constituted the most significant intellectual achievement of the century. Yet, his father, Shah Rukh, also illumined his rule in Herat and Khurāsān by financing notable religious architecture and illustrated historical and literary manuscripts marked by what became the signature Timurid traits of geometric balance and harmonious, brilliantly coloured miniatures. Nonetheless, despite these notable achievements, many contemporary and subsequent Muslim rulers and scholars regarded the artistic and literary activities of Ḥusayn Bayqara's Herat as the golden cultural moment of the post-Mongol era in the eastern Islamic world. Muṣṭafā ʿÂli (1541–1600), the Ottoman historian and official, was one such individual who looked back to Ḥusayn Bayqara as the paradigmatic Perso-Islamic ruler and patron.[13] Indeed, Muṣṭafā ʿÂli portrayed himself as the Ottoman counterpart of the two outstanding literary luminaries of Ḥusayn Bayqara's court, ʿAbd al-Raḥmān Jāmī (d. 1492) and ʿAlī Shīr Navāʿī (d. 1501). Muṣṭafā ʿÂli's enthusiasm for Ḥusayn Bayqara's Herat may have been fuelled in substantial measure by his own frustrated ambition and sense of Ottoman decline, but even contemporaries such as Ẓahīr al-Dīn Muḥammad Bābur saw Ḥusayn Bayqara as the last great Timurid ruler of the century and felt that his reign in Herat was a unique cultural moment. Bābur, who visited the city in December 1506, just after Ḥusayn Bayqara's death, reported that the city had no equal in the 'inhabited quarter of the world', and substantiated his comment by observing that it was 'full of learned and matchless people' who 'sought to complete . . . [their] work to perfection'.[14]

When Ḥusayn Bayqara seized Herat in 1469 he returned to his native city after a long stateless period characteristic of many aspiring Timurid rulers, one that Bābur in describing his own early years, characterized as *qazaqlïq*, the status of a throne-less, wandering political vagabond. Based on Bābur's candid analysis of Ḥusayn Bayqara's temperament and political ambitions – an analysis largely ratified by the political history of the era – once Ḥusayn Bayqara seized Herat from his drunken younger cousin, Yadgar Muḥammad, he settled down to enjoy himself. Despite his considerable military experience – or because of it – he did not seriously attempt to expand his political base beyond Herat and Khurāsān. Bābur's portrait of his relative is marked by respect for his lineage, praise for his cultural achievements and dismay at his military

13 Fleischer, 1986, pp. 70, 141, 169 and 186.
14 Bābur, 1995, f. 177b.

indolence. He was particularly critical of Ḥusayn Bayqara's failure to come to Bābur's aid as the Uzbeks of Shaybaq Khan (Muḥammad Shibānī Khan) eradicated the last vestiges of Timurid rule in Mawarannahr. After taking Herat he did nothing, writes Bābur, except to engage in *fesq u fujūr*, 'immorality and debauchery', prompting many of his followers to drift away to seek employment with other rulers. Yet as part of this Buddenbrooks-like shift in Timurid energies from conquest to culture, Ḥusayn Bayqara presided over the florescence of the Perso-Islamic arts and the foundation of Turkic literature. Much of the credit for this explosion of superbly realized art and literature goes to his amanuensis and long-time companion, Mīr ʿAlī Shīr Navāʾī.

Navāʾī (1441–1501) was a Herat native who came from a Turkic (Uighur) family of professional *bakhshīs*, that is, accountants and administrators. He spent his early life in the city where he was educated, and, according to Bābur, he attended the same *madrasa* as Ḥusayn Bayqara. Following the death of Shah Rukh, Navāʾī's family experienced the vicissitudes of the period, moving about in Iran and Khurāsān and, in 1453, settling for a time in Sabzawar, the former Sarbadar capital. Navāʾī continued his education there and later in Mashhad before returning for a time to Herat and then in the 1460s, accompanying the amir and sometime poet, Aḥmad Ḥājjī Beg Duldai, the son of Sulṭān Malik Kāshgharī, to Samarqand, where Aḥmad Ḥājjī Beg became the *eshik ikhtiyarī* or principal minister to the Timurid, Sulṭān Aḥmad Mīrzā. Very little is known about Navāʾī's life during this period, other than the fact that he was already an accomplished poet. Indeed, his first *diwan,* or book of collected verse, was evidently completed sometime in 1465–6, and was compiled not by Navāʾī himself, but by the renowned calligrapher Sulṭān ʿAlī Mashhadī. However, typically for pre-modern Muslim writers, his verse offers few reliable autobiographical insights into the man himself at this period. Mīr ʿAli Shīr Navāʾī returned to Herat in 1469, invited there by Ḥusayn Bayqara to take up the post of Keeper of the Seal, a position that gave him direct and continuous access to the sultan.[15]

Thus began more than thirty years of service for this *adīb*, who, never marrying, devoted himself to Ḥusayn Bayqara's court and the development of Turkī literature. By 1472 Ḥusayn Bayqara recognized Navāʾī as an amir or *beg* and gave him the prestigious right to imprint his seal on documents above and therefore superior to other Herat aristocrats. However, in matters of status and social precedence Navāʾī has, and not just in Soviet literature, a reputation for modesty and social egalitarianism, a reputation seemingly ratified by his

15 Sultan, 1985.

verse, in which he wrote in one poem that it was more important to consider what was said, rather than dwelling on the status of the author. In fact Navāʿī's contemporary and posthumous fame is due primarily to his importance as a writer of Turkī verse and as a patron of the arts in Herat, and already by the mid-1470s he had become famous well beyond the bounds of Khurāsān. His greatest legacies were the elevation of Turkī verse to the level of an authentic and recognized literary tradition and the spread of his image throughout the eastern Islamic world as the epitome of the ideal courtier, more than a courtier, the personification of civilized Turko-Mongol, Perso-Islamic culture.

In Herat, Navāʿī's name is inextricably connected with ʿAbd al-Raḥmān Jāmī, the man who is regarded by many, although not by E. G. Browne, as the last great classical Persian poet.[16] However, his standing in the Persian poetical world has never been as great as Ḥāfiẓ, Saʿdī or even Amīr Khusrau Dihlavī. Indeed, Jāmī has been relatively neglected by scholars both in Iran and Afghanistan, not to speak of the European world, where only small portions of his work have been translated, mainly by German scholars. His contemporaries said that he was so well known it was not necessary to describe him, so only a few biographical accounts date from that period. It seems most reasonable to approach Jāmī first as a religious scholar and committed Naqshbandī Sufi, who wrote much of his poetry in service of his faith and his devotion to that particular order. Thus his poetry is praised for its clarity and accessibility, some of it was explicitly didactic, but also criticized for its lack of subtlety and inventive imagery.

Jāmī was born in 1414 in Jām, near Nīshāpūr, of a clerical family that originated in Isfahan, but he lived in Herat virtually his entire life, with the exception of a brief period of study in Samarqand. While the recipient of an outstanding education, he was by all accounts a non-conformist and eventually turned from a possible bureaucratic career to join the Naqshbandī order. In terms of Jāmī and Navāʿī's friendship, one of the most important aspects of Naqshbandī Sufism was the belief of its founder and later shaykhs that their disciples ought to participate actively in everyday life. Rather than being required to retire from society as Sufis of some orders were expected to do, Naqshbandīs were actively encouraged to participate in society and politics. They were required only to show absolute loyalty to their shaykh. So when, in 1476/7, Navāʿī recognized Jāmī as his shaykh or *pīr* he was not required to withdraw from his political or literary work. And the relationship between the two men ripened into a remarkable sympathetic and long-lasting friendship,

16 Browne, 1964, III, pp. 507–48.

in fact one of the great and mutually influential literary friendships that is recorded for period. It is occasionally reflected in explicit verse, as when Jāmī wrote in his long poem, 'Laila and Majnun', that 'friendship is the key to the treasury of hope'.[17] The two constantly corresponded, often, as is the custom even today in Iran and Afghanistan, doing so by exchanging mutually appreciative poems. When they died within nine years of each other in 1492 and 1501 even contemporaries must have felt that it was the end of an age.

It was indeed the end of an era in many respects, not merely because its two most famous citizens were dead. That is from 1469 until 1501 Mīr ʿAlī Shīr personally presided over the economic, architectural and artistic development of Herat to the extent that the city became the cultural capital of the Perso-Islamic world. In the account of the premier late Timurid historian, Khwāndamīr, Mīr ʿAlī Shīr was responsible for the construction of at least 135 structures. The majority of these buildings were caravanserais and bridges, structures that would have helped to stimulate the commercial economy of the region. Otherwise Mīr ʿAlī Shīr's projects included a major mosque, *madrasa*, *khānagāh*, *ḥammām* and hospital complex north of the city. He probably located it there because it was the site of Ḥusayn Bayqara's Bāgh-i Jahān-Arā or 'World Adorning Garden', built on a site near the ruler's birthplace. Such gardens had been since Temür's day the political and cultural centres of Timurid cities, the residential and administrative residences of the ruler and the sites of the literary *majlis*es or *symposia* for which Herat during this period became especially famous. It was at these formal *symposia* where Mīr ʿAlī Shīr exercised his authority as the demanding literary arbiter of late Timurid Herat. And apart from Jāmī's didactic verse, it was a literature by and for the court aristocracy that became increasingly technical and complex, a rhetorical preference perhaps seen most clearly in the interest in and practice of compiling *muʿammās* or enigmas, an allusive and illusive form of verse of interest only to the professional literati.

Apart from the literary activities of Navāʾī and Jāmī and the dozens of poets who were attracted to Herat during their lifetimes, Ḥusayn Bayqara's era witnessed the revival and elaboration of the art of the book, distinguished by brilliantly illuminated manuscript editions of many historical and literary classics.[18] Some of these were explicitly Timurid works, such as Yazdī's *Ẓafar Nāma* or Book of Victory that celebrated Timur's conquests. Others were traditional Persian literary works, such as Saʿdī's *Gulistān* or Amīr Khusrau Dihlavī's *Hasht Bihisht* or *Eight Paradises*, and the popularity of such texts reflected the

17 Bertel's, 1965, p. 119.
18 Lentz and Lowrey, 1989, pp. 239–302.

continued dominance of Perso-Islamic culture at a Turko-Mongol court where Navāʿī and others also composed Turkī poetry. The miniature paintings that illustrated these manuscripts were sometimes as allusive as Heratī poetry, but some of them, in particular those demonstrably by or attributed to the painter Bihzād, depicted everyday activities and did so, in some instances, with a kind of naturalism that represented figures in three-dimensional space. Scenes depicting Sufis were especially popular subjects of miniature painters, reflecting, evidently, the pervasive influence of devotional or mystical Islam among the Timurids and, of course, Jāmī in particular. One of the intriguing artistic aspects of the period is the sudden appearance of signed paintings that make it possible to identify individual artists, such as Bihzād, who in later times was regarded as the miniaturist par excellence, although his contemporaries were less enamoured of his work, with Bābur, for example, who was always free with his artistic opinions, pointedly criticizing his painting of beards.

Bābur and the Timurid Renaissance

One aspiring poet who had sought Navāʿī's approval or recognition in 1500 was Ẓahīr al-Dīn Muḥammad Bābur. At the time he had just occupied Samarqand, or, more accurately, he had surreptitiously entered the city and turned out a small Uzbek force while Shaybaq Khan was otherwise occupied. Within two years Bābur would be a hunted man within his Ferghana Valley appanage, and after another two years in virtual hiding, he fled as a refugee from Mawarannahr, harassed by Uzbek raiding parties as his rag-tag contingent of less than 300 men and women marched through central Afghanistan towards Kabul. In late 1504 he entered Kabul, the eastern-most Timurid appanage, which he initially hoped to use as a base to recapture the Timurid homelands. However, by 1507 Shaybaq Khan had expelled or killed most Timurids and their matrilineal relatives, the Chaghatay Chinggsids, from Mawarannahr and taken Herat itself. He then turned his armies east towards Qandahar, where he briefly occupied the city, but not the citadel, before turning back west to deal with internal dissension and, ultimately, the threat from the Ṣafavids, who were then consolidating their power over the Iranian plateau. Bābur, in his memoirs, conveys something of the desperation he felt in 1507, knowing that he could not survive a direct Uzbek attack. He reports that he and his *begs* held a council in which they debated whether they should escape to north-eastern Afghanistan or to India. Finally they decided that they would flee towards Peshawer and hastily abandoned Kabul with little more than the shirts on their backs. While Shaybaq Khan's withdrawal a short time later allowed them to return to Kabul, 1507 marks the first recorded instance when Bābur began considering India as the site of a new Timurid state, legitimized in his mind by Temür's invasion and brief but typically brutal occupation of Delhi in 1398. However, it was not until he took and lost Samarqand for a third time in 1511–12 that Bābur finally abandoned his revanchist hope for Mawarannahr and gradually turned his full attention to India. He decided on an invasion of the subcontinent no later than 1519, when he named his newly born son Hind-al, the 'taking' or 'the conquest of Hind'.

Bābur's Turkī or Chaghatay Turkish autobiographical memoir of events, the *Vaqāʿiʿ*, is the single most original and important Timurid prose composition and, considering literature in both Europe and Asia, the richest autobiographical work of the period sometimes known as the 'early modern era'. Ulugh Beg made the greatest Timurid scientific contributions, Navāʿī elevated Turkī to the status of an established literary tongue, Jāmī produced the last corpus of classical Persian prose, Ḥusayn Bayqara presided from his exquisite gardens over the final, brilliant florescence of Timurid culture and Bābur composed the outstanding Turkī prose work. Now made available in a definitive text for the first time by the Japanese Turkologist, Eiji Mano, Bābur's autobiography offers the single best insight into the realities and quixotic personalities of late Timurid politics. Unlike the formulaic poetry of the Herat court and the baroque prose of many contemporary historians like Yazdī, the *Vaqāʾiʿ* is direct, dynamic and remarkably fresh. Its vitality can perhaps be explained by the fact that while Bābur was intimately familiar with contemporary Perso-Islamic historical and literary works, he experienced a tumultuous life lived outside the confines of fastidious court circles, and his concern for lucid explanation trumped his interest in high literary style. As he told his son Humāyūn in a tart letter criticizing the latter's elaborate and opaque Persian prose, a letter's meaning should be clear; it should not be written as a *muʿammā*, an enigma.

Apart from providing uniquely valuable socio-economic and political information about the late Timurid world, Bābur offers the single most detailed account of warfare available for Central Asia and the Perso-Islamic world of the late fifteenth and early sixteenth centuries. First of all he shows that however disciplined Chinggis Khan's and Temür's troops may have been, the armies of the late Timurid era were more often than not coalitions of wilful subordinates or temporary and unreliable allies.[19] His descriptions also illustrate that battles were fought in orthodox, traditional *yasal* formations with

19 Dale, 2004, pp. 67–133.

units in decimals of tens or hundreds assigned definite positions in the centre, vanguard and the wings, which were subdivided into smaller units. Usually a Timurid *mīrzā*'s immediate family members commanded the most important and / or prestigious positions, assignments that were often reflected in the precedence shown them in court ceremonials, where proximity to the ruler and height of position at a reception indicated dynastic status or military rank. However, in the 1490s no Timurid or Chaghatay Chinggisid army proved capable of winning battles against the Shaybaq Khan's forces, whose disciplined cavalry manoeuvres Bābur enviously records.

It is difficult to estimate accurately the numbers involved in late fifteenth-century battles among the Timurids or between particular Timurids and Shaybaq Khan. Suffice it to say that contemporary or later chroniclers' accounts of these conflicts should never be taken at face value, especially when they estimate troop strength. While this general caveat should be observed for military history in general, it is particularly apparent from the evidence of Bābur's autobiography and from the autobiographical memoir of his Moghul cousin, Ḥaydar Mīrzā Dughlat. Both men reveal that they or other commanders often did not know themselves how many troops they commanded in any particular battle, partly because many contingents were brought to conflicts by temporary allies. Unless either of these men names the units under his nominal command and shows that the troops were actually counted by *bakhshīs* or other officials, even their own estimates cannot be accepted. And when it comes to accounts of their enemies' forces, scepticism should always be the rule. Bābur, for example, says that 12,000 men crossed the Indus with him in 1526 during his climactic campaign to conquer north India. Yet he also mentions that merchants and *ṭālibān* or religious students were included in this number, and his daughter, Gulbadan Begim, writing at the end of the century, says that her father had no more than 6,000–7,000 'serviceable troops' when he won the decisive Battle of Panipat north of Delhi in April 1526.[20] Bābur's own estimate of 100,000 Afghan enemy troops facing him at Panipat is, in all likelihood, both improbable and self-serving.

Late Timurid battles, including those Bābur fought in India, were primarily won with lightly armoured cavalry using bows and arrows and swords. By the late fifteenth century, Timurids had begun using firearms; Ḥusayn Bayqara supposedly had one or more *qazans*, some kind of mortar, as early as 1495. By this time guns were spreading eastwards from the Ottoman lands and north-eastern Iran, where Italians had begun supplying Aq Qoyunlu troops with

20 Gulbadan, 1972, f. 9b.

arms in their attempt to counter their Ottoman opponents in the west. By 1519 Bābur was using some kind of matchlocks and at Panipat his troops evidently fired both these and perhaps two kinds of cannon, one the *zarb-zanan* initially at least fired by Ottoman advisors. Nonetheless, unlike the Ottoman use of cannon in their siege of Constantinople, there is no convincing evidence to show that firearms decided late Timurid battles. In fact, the evidence of Bābur's text strongly suggests that the decisive factor in his major victories at Panipat in 1526 and the following year at Kanwah, was the critical flanking role of Mongol contingents who occupied the prestigious positions on the extreme right and left wings of the army in both confrontations. Thus, even though Bābur repeatedly denounces the Mongols as treacherous in battle and destructive and rapacious in both defeat and victory, he describes their classic *tulghama* or flanking manoeuvre as critical to his major victories in Afghanistan and India.

Bābur's victories in India laid the basis for a new Timurid state, and his brief, four-year period of rule in India before he died in December 1530 represents the denouement of the late Timurid era and an introduction to its syncretistic descendant, the Timurid-Mughal Empire of Agra and Delhi. First of all, from Bābur's own point of view it is obvious from repeated references in the *Vaqāʾiʿ* that he never intended to remain in India, but planned to return to Kabul and govern his Indian territories from there as a kind of latter-day Ḥusayn Bayqara. He was certainly aware of Maḥmūd of Ghazna's empire and perhaps had it in mind when he told his governor of Kabul that he planned to return there when he pacified Hindustan, the region of India that included the Punjab, the Ganges-Jumna *dūāb* and the Gangetic Valley. Residence in India was, as he expresses it most vividly in his poetry, a *ghurbat* or exile – both from his friends and his favourite cities of Kabul and Samarqand. As he writes, alluding to the Ramaḍān month of fasting in 1527 or 1528

> In exile this month of fasting ages me.
> Separated from friends exile has affected me.
> . . .
> I deeply desired the profits of this Indian land.
> What is the profit since this land enslaves me?[21]

His descendants, who were unfamiliar with Mawarannahr, themselves retained this sense of exile in an attenuated, revanchist and nostalgic form. Bābur's points of political and cultural reference were, to the end of his life, Samarqand and, for religious questions, Bukhara. By writing his autobiography

21 Yücel, 1995, no. 24, p. 190.

in Turkī he defined his principal audience, the Timurid and Chaghatay elite and the broader Central Asian population who were literate in this tongue common to Turks and Turko-Mongols of the Central Asian region.

Bābur's transitional status is reflected in the modern historiography of both the original Timurid homelands and India. He occupies little more than a footnote in historians' accounts of Temür's fifteenth-century descendants in Mawarannahr and Khurāsān. He was, after all, the heir to a very minor appanage and, like his kin, personified the impotence of the Timurid lineage in the face of Uzbek expansion. Historians of Mughal India scarcely give him any more attention, and often ignore him altogether. In their minds he was a foreign adventurer whose son, Humāyūn, was expelled from India in 1540, to return only a year before his death in 1555. Thus in the eyes of these scholars, Bābur was certainly not the founder of the Mughal Empire: that honour belongs to Bābur's grandson, Akbar (r. 1556–1605). This historiography reflects, more than anything else, the artificial division between scholarship on the Middle East, which usually includes Muslim Central Asia but not Muslim India, the site of what many regard as a *soi-disant* Islamic culture, and the scholarship on Muslim India, which takes remarkably little account of Central Asia, other than seeing it as a reservoir of barbarian conquerors. Yet Bābur's incipient state in India was, in every respect, including most of all his own assumptions, a geographic extension of the late Timurid world, whose characteristics are marked in the attitudes and policies of his descendants. The Mughal Empire, better known as the Timurid-Mughal Empire represented the Timurid Renaissance, a renaissance like its Italian contemporary in that it was simultaneously a renewal but dramatically different from the society it revered.

The character of Bābur's South Asian state can be inferred to a limited degree by the respect that Bābur showed to certain groups of individuals. These comprised principally: Turko-Mongol aristocrats, Aḥrārī Naqshbandīs and representatives of late Timurid Perso-Islamic high literary and artistic culture. In political and social terms, therefore, the Timurid-Mughal Empire in its initial phase was just that, a Turko-Mongol state, commanded by Bābur, a patrilineal Timurid and matrilineal Chaghatay Mongol, who offered his relatives a refuge from the Uzbek debacle and, in the last days of his life, married two of his daughters to descendants of one of his Chaghatay uncles. In religious terms this empire retained the moderate Sunnī Muslim character of its predecessors, and its rulers continued to express preference for Sufi devotionalism over formal worship throughout the history of the dynasty, showing special preference for two Central Asian orders, the Naqshbandīs and the Chishtīs. Part of this Sunnī inheritance was Bābur's and his descendants' knowledge of al-Marghinānī's *Hidāya* text, a work that became a canonical guide to administrative policy in India. Bābur manifested his intensely felt admiration for Heratī high culture by welcoming refugees from Herat itself. These men began arriving in India shortly after Bābur's major victories in 1526 and 1527 and included among them the outstanding court historian of the day, Khwāndamīr. Thus the Timurid-Mughal Empire was, both in its origins and later under Bābur's descendants, a Turko-Mongol conquest state of moderate and, indeed, often unreflective Sunnī Muslims, who revered Sufi shaykhs and patronized Perso-Islamic literary and artistic culture – Persian verse, miniature painting and music. The lineage absorbed novel traits under the influence of its predominantly Hindu environment but in most respects retained its original characteristics even in decline. It was in fact a late Timurid dynastic artefact with indigenous South Asian overtones that the British discovered when they entered Delhi in the eighteenth century.

PART FOUR

★

NOMADS AND SETTLED PEOPLES IN INNER ASIA AFTER THE TIMURIDS

12
Uzbeks, Qazaqs and Turkmens

YURI BREGEL

At the time of Temür's death (1405) the nomadic population of the Dasht-i Qipchāq was in a state of turmoil. After the defeat of Toqtamïsh Khan and the devastation caused to the *Ulus* of Jochi by the campaigns of Temür, this *ulus* began to disintegrate. The eastern part of it, the Kök Orda (or the former *Ulus* of Orda), broke up into several independent groups, the most powerful of which was the tribal confederation of the Manghïts. This confederation, which became known west of the Volga under the name of the Noghay[1] and was ruled until 1419 by the famous amir (or *beglerbegi*) Edigü, in the first quarter of the fifteenth century occupied the territory between the Volga and the Yayïq. East of the Manghïts, the nomadic population of the *Ulus* of Shiban became known under the collective name Uzbek (actually, Özbek) apparently already in the second half of the fourteenth century. It is usually assumed (following the explanation given by the seventeenth-century khan-historian Abu'l-Ghāzī of Khiva)[2] that this name was given due to the conversion to Islam of the entire *Ulus* of Jochi carried out by Uzbek Khan in the first quarter of the fourteenth century.[3] In the early fifteenth century the

1 See below, Chapter 13.

2 See Abu'l-Ghāzī Bahādur Khan, 1871–4, I, 175; II, 184. Abu'l-Ghāzī says that the entire people (of the *ulus*) of Jochi assumed the name of Uzbek.

3 Such an explanation is consistent with the well-known ideas of the conversion to Islam as the basis of communal identity and of Islamizer as communal founder (see DeWeese, 1994a, esp. pp. 363–5 and 492–3). A Russian Orientalist A. A. Semenov tried to disprove the connection between the name of Uzbek Khan and the name of the people Uzbek, claiming that during the lifetime of Uzbek Khan and shortly after his death this name was not used as an ethnic marker (see Semenov, 1954a, pp. 9–13), but his arguments were unconvincing. In the most recent general history of Uzbekistan (*Istoriia narodov Uzbekistana*, III, Tashkent, 1993, p. 39; the respective section written by R. G. Mukminova) additional arguments are provided against connecting the ethnic name Uzbek with the name of Uzbek Khan: Sharaf al-Dīn Yazdī mentions a raid of Uzbek troops in the region of Tabriz in an account of the events of 1289, long before the time of Uzbek Khan, and the *Tārīkh-i arbaʿulūs* (i.e. *Shajarat al-atrāk* by Ulugh Bek) mentions that 'the rule over the ulus of the Uzbeks' was transferred to Uzbek Khan. However, these are not contemporary evidence: both Yazdī and Ulugh Bek wrote in the fifteenth century and could have applied the ethnic name (or, rather, political term, cf. below) Uzbek anachronistically. Irrespective of

authority over the Uzbeks was contested by several descendants of Shiban. One of them, Jumaduq, son of Ṣūfī Oghlan, was proclaimed khan in 1425/6, but his authority seems to have been limited to the southern regions of the *Ulus* of Shiban. Competing with him were Maḥmūd Khoja Khan, Muṣṭafā Khan, and Dawlat Shaykh Oghlan, the last of whom ruled in the northernmost region of the *ulus*, in Western Siberia. For a brief period, yet another Chinggisid gained some prominence in the competition for power in the *Ulus* of Shiban: in 1423 or 1424 Barāq Oghlan, a grandson of Urus Khan of the Kök Orda (who had briefly ruled the Golden Horde before Toqtamïsh), became khan in the southern regions of the *ulus*; but around 1428 he was killed in a battle with the Manghïts under the sons of Edigü, Ghāzī and Nawrūz. About the same time Jumaduq Khan was also killed in a battle with rebels, mostly also the Manghïts. Shortly after this, in 1429, a son of Dawlat Shaykh Oghlan, named Abu'l-Khayr, was elected as khan in Chimgi-Tura (later Tümen) by the nobility of the *ulus* and with the support of the Manghïts under Vaqqāṣ Biy, grandson of Edigü. This town remained his capital (or, rather, the place of his summer encampment) until 1446.

During the next four years Abu'l-Khayr, in relentless military campaigns, established his authority over almost the entire *Ulus* of Shiban.[4] Abu'l-Ghāzī[5] says that there were none of his relations who had not been hit by the khan's arrow or who had not felt the weight of his hand. In these campaigns crucial military support was provided to Abu'l-Khayr by the head of the Manghïts, Vaqqāṣ Biy, grandson of Edigü, who served as a chief amir (*beglerbegi*) of Abu'l-Khayr.[6] In winter 1430/1 Abu'l-Khayr invaded Khorezm (Khwārazm) and occupied the northern part of the country with its capital, Urgench. However, in summer the Uzbeks had to retreat from Khorezm because of great heat and a plague that began there. Another reason may have been a threat from two Jochid rulers of Astrakhan, Aḥmad Khan and Maḥmūd Khan; Abu'l-Khayr defeated them in a battle somewhere in the western part of the Dasht-i Qipchāq and captured their chief encampment (*ordu-bāzār*). In 1435–6 Abu'l-Khayr invaded and plundered Khorezm for the second time, but only briefly. Muṣṭafā Khan (who ruled the eastern part of the *ulus*) did not recognize the authority of Abu'l-Khayr longer than other Chinggisids: he was defeated by

the question of Islamization, numerous cases are known of small and large ethnic groups adopting the name of their (real or legendary) founders; the closest example, in terms of time, is the ethnic name Chaghatay.

4 On Abu'l-Khayr, see Barthold, 'Abu'l-Khair', *EI*[1], pp. 95–6; Bregel, 1983b; Akhmedov, 1965a (and review in Iudin, 2001b).

5 Abu'l-Ghāzī Bahādur Khan, 1871–4, I, p. 190; cf. II, p. 203.

6 On the relations between Abu'l-Khayr and Vaqqāṣ see Trepavlov, 2001b, pp. 97–100.

Abu'l-Khayr around 1446 and fled to the Mangïshlaq peninsula. From there he came to Khorezm in the 1450s and ruled its northern part (where he built the city of Vazir) until 1460/1, when he was removed by a chieftain of the Uzbek tribe Qongrat, whose *yurt* was, apparently, to the north-west of Khorezm. In 1440/1 the Uzbeks raided Astarabad – the north-western province of the Timurid Iran; this raid must have been conducted from the area of Khorezm. ʿAbd al-Razzāq Samarqandī[7] describes these Uzbeks as 'a group of the Uzbek army who became Qazaqs', which makes one think that it was a splinter group that did not recognize the authority of the Shibanid khan (like the Qazaqs who emerged in the 1460s, see below). The following years Sultan Shāhrukh Mīrzā, the Timurid, had to keep considerable troops to defend Gorgan and Astarabad from the raids of these Uzbeks.

In 1446, after his victory over Muṣṭafā Khan, Abu'l-Khayr captured the regions in the lower and middle course of the Syr Darya, with the towns of Sïghnaq, Suzak, Arquq, Uzgend and Aq-Qurghan, which were important centres of trade between Mawarannahr and the Dasht-i Qipchāq. Sïghnaq became his winter capital, and the border between the Uzbeks and the empire of the Timurids passed to the north of Yasi (later Turkestan). This made it possible for Abu'l-Khayr to interfere in the affairs of the Timurids when he would find it advantageous. When Ulugh Beg, the Timurid ruler of Mawarannahr, was engaged in the struggle for Herat after the death of Shāhrukh (1447), Abu'l-Khayr raided Mawarannahr; the Uzbek troops reached Samarqand, but they were unable to capture the city and retreated, having plundered the region.[8] In the summer of 1451 the Timurid prince Abū Saʿīd, who rose against ʿAbdallāh Mīrzā, the son of Ulugh Beg, and captured Yasï, came to the encampment of Abu'l-Khayr asking for help. The Uzbek troops marched on Samarqand, and in a battle about fifteen miles north of Samarqand the Uzbeks and Abū Saʿīd defeated the more numerous army of ʿAbdallāh, who was killed.[9] Abū Saʿīd deceived the Uzbeks, having entered Samarqand without them and closed the city gates before his allies. Abu'l-Khayr and his troops were compensated with rich presents; Rabīʿa Sulṭān Begum, a daughter of Ulugh Beg, was given in marriage to Abu'l-Khayr, and the Uzbeks returned to the Dasht-i Qipchāq.[10]

7 See Tizengauzen, 1941, text, p. 258; trans., p. 199.

8 See Bartol'd, *Ulugbek i ego vremia*, in his *Sochineniia*, II/2, pp. 154–5.

9 See Bartol'd, *Ulugbek*, p. 164. While crossing a steppe on their way to Samarqand, the Uzbek sorcerers are said to have used the 'rain stone' (*yada*) to cause rain; so ʿAbd al-Razzāq Samarqandī, see Tizengauzen, 1941, text, p. 259; trans., pp. 199–200.

10 See ʿAbd al-Razzāq Samarqandī in Tizengauzen, 1941, pp. 259–60; Khwāndamīr, 1954, p. 50; *Tārīkh-i Abu'l-Khayr Khānī*, St Petersburg, Institute of Oriental Studies, MS C-480, ff. 328b–336a; Bartol'd, *Ulugbek*, in his *Sochineniia*, II/2, pp. 163–6.

About 1457, a severe blow to Abu'l-Khayr and his Uzbeks was inflicted by the Kalmyks, or Oirats (Western Mongols), under Uz (or Az?) Temür Tayshi, who invaded the Dasht-i Qipchāq from the Chu Valley. Abu'l-Khayr's forces suffered a crushing defeat near Kök Kashane (south of Sïghnaq), and Abu'l-Khayr retreated to Sïghnaq, under the protection of its walls, while the Qalmaqs were plundering the region. Later Abu'l-Khayr was still able to interfere in the Timurid affairs: in 1460 he sent some Uzbek troops to help Muḥammad Jūkī Mīrzā (Ulugh Beg's grandson) to fight Abū Saʿīd. This expedition ended in failure: the Uzbeks, having plundered Mawarannahr, abandoned Muḥammad Jūkī, who had to submit to Abū Saʿīd. But Abu'l-Khayr himself was already unable to do anything about it: his *ulus* was greatly weakened by the internal dissent. First, his relations with the Manghïts, whose support had been instrumental for his rise to power, apparently soured. The powerful ruler of the Manghïts, Mūsā Biy (son of Vaqqāṣ), switched his support from the family of Abu'l-Khayr to that of Yādigār Sultan b. Tīmūr Shaykh, who belonged to another line of the descendants of Shïban, going back to ʿArabshāh (a brother of Abu'l-Khayr's grandfather), and Yādigār was proclaimed as khan. According to the Khivan historian of the nineteenth century, Munis, this happened in 1457/8.[11] It is not known what was the source of Munis for this date and it is not clear whether it can be trusted; but if such a proclamation of a rival khan indeed took place while Abu'l-Khayr was still ruling his *ulus*, it could be a sign of the weakening of his authority in the immediate aftermath of the Qalmaq invasion. The Uzbek tribes ruled by the ʿArabshahids occupied, apparently, the part of the Dasht-i Qipchāq north of the Aral Sea, being the eastern neighbours of the Manghïts.

Another, even heavier, blow to Abu'l-Khayr's authority was a split in his *ulus* and the migration of a group of Uzbeks, under the sultans Kirāy and Janïbek (Jānībek), to the Semirech'e. Kirāy and Janïbek belonged to another line of the Jochids, whose ancestor was the thirteenth son of Jochi, Togha-Tīmūr (they were grandsons of two different sons of Urus Khan, himself a great-great-grandson of Togha-Tīmūr);[12] the members of the Togha-Timurid family were

11 See Abu'l-Ghāzī Bahādur Khan, 1871–4, I, p. 189; II, p. 201. Cf. Munis, 1999, p. 26. Abu'l-Ghāzī does not give the date, which is provided only by Munis. Munis describes Mūsā Biy, son of Vaqqāṣ, not as a Manghït, but as a Qongrat (obviously, wrongly, out of his 'anti-Manghït' bias; see Bregel, 1982, pp. 391–2).

12 See their genealogies in Ibragimov *et al.*, 1969, pp. 39–42. In modern historical literature there is also a different opinion, according to which Urus Khan belonged to the descendants of Orda, the elder son of Jochi and the first ruler of the Kök Orda; see Sultanov, 2001, pp. 140–4 (in his earlier work Sultanov mentions two versions of the genealogy of Urus Khan found in different sources without giving preference to either of them; see Kliashtornyi and Sultanov, 1992, p. 198).

long-time rivals of the Shībanids in the Dasht-i Qipchāq. Kirāy and Janībek, with their people, established themselves in the Chu Valley region, in the western border area of Moghulistan, which was given to them by the khan of Moghulistan Esen Bugha;[13] the latter wanted to use this group as a buffer between his possessions and those of his brother Yūnus Khan, who claimed Moghulistan for himself and was supported by the Timurid Abū Saʿīd. The exact date of this migration is not given, but, since Esen Bugha died in 1461/2, the migration of Kirāy and Janībek must have taken place sometime between 1458 (the Qalmaq invasion) and 1461.[14]

The group that split off from the *Ulus* of Abu'l-Khayr became known as *Uzbek-Qazaq*. The etymology of the word *qazaq* is unknown, and numerous attempts at establishing it have been unsuccessful.[15] However, the historical meaning of the word *qazaq* is well known and attested in various sources: it was applied to both individuals and groups who would abandon their clan, tribe or ruler, and live the life of a vagabond, adventurer or freebooter;[16] this explanation is given also by Muḥammad Ḥaydar, whose work is our main source for the early history of the Qazaqs: 'Since they had first of all separated from the mass of their people, and for some time had been in an indigent and wandering state, they got the name of Kazak'.[17] Probably, the Uzbek-Qazaqs who migrated with Kirāy and Janībek to the Semirech'e were originally not

13 See: Dūghlāt/Ross, pp. 82, 272–3; Dūghlāt/Thackston text, pp. 50–1; trans., p. 43.

14 Iudin, 2001c, p. 195.

15 For the most recent discussion of these attempts, see Iudin, 2001d,. The word *qazmaq* (from which *qazaq* was supposedly derived) was registered by Vambery and Pavet de Courteille (and, with reference to them, by V. V. Radlov, *Opyt slovaria tiurkskikh narechii*, II, St Petersburg, 1899, pp. 361–2), but this meaning is not supported by other sources; see *Etimologicheskii slovar' tiurkskikh iazykov: Obshchetiurkskie i mezhtiurkskie leksicheskie osnovy na bukvy 'K', 'Ḳ'* (Moscow, 1997), p. 185. The expression *Uzbek-Qazaq* seems to be found only in the *Tārīkh-i Rāshidī* and another contemporary source, *Mihmān-nāma-i Bukhārā* by Rūzbihān Iṣfahānī, who accompanied Shībānī Khan in his campaign against the Qazaqs in 1509 (see below).

16 Cf. Bartol'd, *Sochineniia*, vol. II/2, p. 36. The historical meaning of the term *qazaq* was repeatedly discussed in historical and linguistic literature; for an overview, see W. Barthold and G. Hazai, 'Ḳazaḳ', *EI²*, IV, pp. 848–9; Doerfer, 1967, pp. 462–8; Blagova, 1970 – all these works with further references. The word *qazaq*, apparently, retained this meaning also later (when the Qazaqs had already been long established as an ethnic group): Abu'l-Ghāzī, in his work written in 1663, clearly uses this word in the meaning 'pretender to the throne' or 'adventurer' (see Abu'l-Ghāzī Bahādur Khan, 1871–4, I, pp. 275–6; cf. Munis, 1999, p. 557 n. 223, where the erroneous translation of Desmaisons is emended). The reading *Uzbek-i Qazaq* (as a Persian construction) in the text of the *Tārīkh-i Rāshidī* proposed by some is hardly felicitous, and the reading *Uzbek va Qazaq* with the translation 'Uzbek and Kazakh' in Thackston's edition of the *Tārīkh-i Rāshidī* (see Dūghlāt/Thackston, text, p. 51; trans., pp. 43–4) is erroneous. Inexplicably, Thackston 'emends' the text several times to *Uzbek va Qazaq* leaving 'Uzbek-Kazakh' in the translation.

17 Dūghlāt/Ross, pp. 272–3; Dūghlāt/Thackston, p. 176 and p. 227.

very numerous, but their number increased when major disturbances began in the Dasht-i Qipchāq upon the death of Abu'l-Khayr. There is a disagreement among Central Asian and Persian historians concerning the circumstances of his death. According to the Timurid historians Mīrkhwānd and Khwāndamīr, in 1468 Abu'l-Khayr received in his camp the Timurid prince Sulṭān Ḥusayn Bayqara, who asked his help against Abū Saʿīd; Abu'l-Khayr assembled troops to send with Sulṭān Ḥusayn, but the khan was already seriously ill, and before the army set out he had died.[18] According to the historian Maḥmūd b. Valī (first half of the seventeenth century), Abu'l-Khayr, shortly before his death, moved with numerous troops against the Moghuls, but in the locality Aq-Qïshlaq (probably in the region of modern Almatï) he died.[19] Yet another version of the khan's death is given by Abu'l-Ghāzī (second half of the seventeenth century), according to whom Abu'l-Khayr was killed by his rebellious relatives.[20] The date of his death is given in the *Tārīkh-i Abu'l-Khayr-khānī* (which does not mention in this connection any military campaign or rebellion) as 1469–70, but the Year of the Mouse is given as the year of the animal cycle, which should correspond to 1468.[21]

The death of Abu'l-Khayr was followed by a long period of wars between the members of the Shïbanid family supported by different Uzbek tribes. As Abu'l-Ghāzī writes, 'at that time there was a proverb: "If enemies attack your father's house, join them in this attack"'.[22] Most of the Chinggisids of the Dasht-i Qipchāq united against Abu'l-Khayr's successor, his second son Shaykh Ḥaydar, and he was killed when his encampment was attacked by Ībāq (or Aybāq) Khan, a Shïbanid, who around this time (or, probably, a little later) began to rule a separate khanate of Tümen, in Western Siberia.[23] The disturbances in the Dasht-i Qipchāq after the death of Abu'l-Khayr caused a large number of nomads of his *ulus* to flee eastwards, in search of a safe haven, and to join the Uzbek-Qazaqs in the Semirech'e. According to Muḥammad Ḥaydar, it was actually since this time that this group began to be called 'Uzbek-Qazaq'.[24] This term was used, besides Muḥammad Ḥaydar in his *Tārīkh-i*

18 Mīrkhwānd, Muḥammad b. Khandshāh, 1959–61, pp. 32–4; Khwāndamīr, 1955, IV, pp. 131–3 (his illness is described as *maraḍ-i fālij* 'paralysis').

19 See Ibragimov *et al.*, 1969, pp. 358–61.

20 See Abu'l-Ghāzī Bahādur Khan, 1871–4, I, p. 190; II, p. 203.

21 See Ibragimov *et al.*, 1969, p. 171.

22 Abu'l-Ghāzī Bahādur Khan, 1871–4, I, p. 191; II, p. 203.

23 On Ībāq see Frank, 1994, pp. 12–13; Golden, 'Sibīr', *EI²*, IX, p. 532; and Chapter 13 below. In the text accompanying a map in my historical atlas of Central Asia (see Bregel, 2003, p. 48) it is erroneously mentioned that it was Shah Budaq (the elder son of Abu'l-Khayr) who was killed by Ībāq.

24 See Dūghlāt/Thackston, text, p. 51; trans., pp. 43–4; Dūghlāt/Ross, p. 82 (cf. note 16 above).

Rashīdī,[25] by another contemporary author, Faḍlallāh b. Rūzbihān Iṣfahānī, who accompanied Shïbānī Khan in his campaign against the Qazaqs in 1509, in his account of this campaign entitled *Mihmān-nāma-yi Bukhārā*.[26] Muḥammad Ḥaydar claims that the new arrivals from the former *ulus* of Abu'l-Khayr greatly increased the number of the Uzbek-Qazaqs, which now reached 200,000. Probably, this figure should not be taken at its face value (cf. below, the fantastic figure of 'more than one million' when the same author writes about the army of Qāsim Khan). Some of these Uzbek-Qazaqs must have remained in the Semïrech'e, but the majority, most probably, returned to the Dasht-i Qipchāq with Kirāy and Janïbek when they took part in the fight for supremacy with the Shïbanids. Apparently, sometime in the 1470s, after the killing of Shaykh Ḥaydar Khan, Kirāy became khan, while Janïbek was a co-ruler, also with the title of khan;[27] thus, Shïbanids were replaced by Togha-Timurids in the Dasht-i Qipchāq. It is not clear how long their *ulus* retained the name of Uzbek-Qazaq (if it ever had it); in any case, in the early sixteenth century the descendants of Kirāy and Janïbek (and their subjects) were already called simply 'Qazaqs'.

The Shïbanids did not yield to the Togha-Timurids without a fight. A grandson of Abu'l-Khayr, Muḥammad Shāh-Bakht (the future Shïbānī Khan; see Chapter 15 below), having eliminated his Shïbanid rival, Bürge Sultan, son of Yādigār Khan (whom he attacked and killed in his winter encampment on the lower Syr Darya), tried to carve out for himself a part of his grandfather's *ulus*, but was only able to capture a region along the northern bank of the Syr Darya in its middle course. By the end of the fifteenth century the successors of Kirāy and Janïbek already dominated the central and eastern Dasht-i Qipchāq. Between their territory and that of the Manghïts there was the *ulus* of the two surviving sons of Yādigār Khan, first Abūlak and then Amīnak,[28] who were controlled by Mūsā Biy (on whom see above). The Qazaqs were ruled for a long time (according to some information, more than thirty years, at least to 1511) by Burunduq Khan, son of Kirāy; he was succeeded by Janïbek's son Qāsim. During this period Shïbānī Khan apparently abandoned his hopes of restoring the authority of his family in the Dasht-i Qipchāq and, instead, embarked upon the conquest of the Timurid states in Mawarannahr and

25 See Dūghlāt/Thackston, text, pp. 65, 67, 70, 75, 83, 232, 275; trans., pp. 80, 82, 87, 93, 104, 309, 385; Dūghlāt/Ross, pp. 119, 122, 127, 134–5, 146, 336, 373 (which has 'Qazaq-Uzbek'), 453. However, Muḥammad Ḥaydar uses more often simply the term 'Qazaq'.

26 See Iṣfahāni, 1976, facs., p. 83b; trans., p. 103. In another place (facs., p. 95b; trans., p. 123) the author calls the Qazaqs *ūzbekān-i qazāq-nizhād* ('Uzbeks of Qazaq descent'), as distinct from the *ūzbekān-i shībānī* ('the Shïbānī Uzbeks'). But on several other occasions he uses just the term Qazaq (cf. the previous note).

27 See Trepavlov, 2001b, p. 104.

28 See Munis, 1999, pp. 26–7; Trepavlov, 2001b, pp. 116–17.

Khorasan, which was accomplished in the first decade of the sixteenth century. At least two dozen tribes of the Uzbek *ulus* participated initially in these campaigns under Shïbānī and the princes (sultans) of the Shïbanid family. Some of these tribes seem to have abandoned the Dasht-i Qipchāq completely, but many of them were split between the *ulus* of the Shïbanids and the *ulus* of the Togha-Timurids, to judge from the identical tribal names later found among the Qazaqs and the Uzbeks; among the latter were such major tribes as Qïpchaq, Qarluq, Qongrat, Nayman, Qanglï, Jalair, Uysun, Nukuz and Manghït.[29] Some Uzbek groups who belonged to the *ulus* of the Yadigarids (ʿArabshahids) also joined the Uzbeks of Shïbānī Khan. There were some attempts in scholarly literature to calculate the total number of the Uzbeks who came from the Dasht-i Qipchāq with Shïbānī Khan, based on occasional figures for the Uzbek troops engaged in various campaigns of Shïbānī in Mawarannahr. According to such calculations made by T. I. Sultanov for the first decade of the sixteenth century,[30] this number was around 40,000–60,000; assuming that each soldier was supplied by one family and a nomadic family had six members on the average, the total number of nomads who came from the Dasht-i Qipchāq with Shïbānī would be 240,000–360,000. This number, however, is impossible to verify, and the ratio of soldiers to the total population could be less than one to six. The only safe conclusion would be that the conquests of Shïbānī Khan were accompanied by a substantial migration of nomads from the Dasht-i Qipchāq to the southern regions of Central Asia with mostly sedentary population. As to the number of the Qazaqs, Muḥammad Ḥaydar gives different figures on different occasions: in winter 1509/10 the army of Qāsim Khan (son of Janïbek), who succeeded Burunduq Khan in 1511, was more than 200,000; in 1513, the army of the same khan was 300,000; and, in another place, the same author claims that Qāsim Khan had an army of more than one million.[31] None of these figures is reliable, but the last one is especially often quoted by modern (primarily Qazaq) historians, despite its obvious fantastic character; but we can probably surmise, at least, that the number of the Uzbeks who left the Dasht-i Qipchāq was smaller than the number of the Uzbek-Qazaqs who remained there.

The words 'Uzbek' and 'Qazaq' were still collective *political* terms used for the population of two rival *ulus*es, the Shïbanids and the Togha-Timurids, but gradually they acquired an ethnic meaning; the structure of the Qazaq and

29 These were, most probably, some Manghït groups that did not come from the Manghït *ulus*, but had belonged to the Shïbanid *ulus* even before.

30 See Sultanov, 1982, pp. 19–21.

31 See Dūghlāt/Thackston, text, pp. 197, 92, 51; trans., pp. 154, 74, 44; Dūghlāt/Ross, pp. 230 (where the number is erroneously given as 20,000), 133, 273.

Uzbek polities became quite different, and cultural differences also developed between them by the seventeenth century. By the early seventeenth century (or already at the end of the sixteenth) the Qazaqs were divided into three major groupings called *zhüz*; each *zhüz* included a certain number of tribes, and neither of them was found in the other two *zhüz*es. Both the origin and the etymology of this term (corresponding to *yüz* in other Turkic languages), as well as the circumstances of its emergence are unknown, and various explanations have been offered, none of which is convincing.[32] It is possible (but cannot be proven) that it was connected with the incorporation into the Qazaq polity, in the west, of some Noghay (Manghït) tribal groups and the migration and incorporation, in the east, of some tribal groups of the Moghuls of Eastern Turkestan. The Qazaqs continued to be ruled by the descendants of Janïbek down to the first half of the nineteenth century until the final annexation of the Qazaq *zhüz*es by Russia, when the position of the khans was abolished by the Russian administration (see Chapter 18 below). The Qazaqs remained predominantly nomadic until the twentieth century. As distinct from them, the Uzbeks, after their migration to the areas with predominantly sedentary population, began to sedentarize or, at least, were becoming semi-nomadic; but this process lasted far into the eighteenth (and in some areas – nineteenth) century. Living mostly interspersed with the sedentary they experienced their strong influence in various aspects of life, from language to economy to political culture. However, they did not merge with this sedentary population into a new ethnic entity transferring to it their name 'Uzbek' (as Soviet and modern Uzbek historians would have it):[33] until the revolution of 1917 in Russia, the name 'Uzbek' was applied only to the tribal Uzbeks, who clearly distinguished themselves from the rest of the population, while the old sedentary population which lived in the same areas was referred to (and would call itself) as Tajiks, Sarts and even Chaghatays, or just by the names of their localities (Urgenji, Tashkendi, Khojendi, etc.; cf. Chapter 20 below). A similar situation existed in Afghan Turkestan, where Uzbek tribes were interspersed with the old Tajik population.

Turkmens in the fourteenth to early eighteenth centuries

The Turkmens are mentioned in Islamic historical sources as early as the tenth century, but this term did not yet have a clear ethnic meaning: it was rather

32 See Iudin, 1983.
33 See a review of such theories in Bregel, 1996, pp. 13–14, 45–6.

used as a collective name for various Turkic groups in some steppe areas of Central Asia bordering the Islamic world who had converted to Islam, irrespective of their tribal affiliation. Due to the conversion to Islam of a part of the Oghuz and the beginning of the Seljuk movement at the end of the tenth and early eleventh centuries, this name (whose etymology is not clear)[34] became associated with the Islamized Oghuz, the majority of whom were the supporters of the Seljuk dynasty. Turkmen tribal genealogies, reflected in the historical sources of the eleventh and thirteenth centuries, traced their origin to the mythical Oghuz Khan, the progenitor of all the Oghuz; according to these genealogies, there were twenty-four original Oghuz tribes; many of their names are still the names of the modern-day Turkmen tribes or clans. As a result of the Seljuk conquests and the rise of the Seljuk Empire in the eleventh century, the Turkmens increased in number and migrated from their original home in the lower reaches of the Syr Darya as far west as the Fertile Crescent and North Africa.[35] However, from the beginning of the Seljuk movement a part of the Turkmens did not migrate west with their fellow tribesmen, but remained in the steppes and deserts between the Aral Sea and Khorasan, where groups belonging to almost all Oghuz tribes could later be found. Some Turkmen groups that moved westwards returned east later on, probably in the thirteenth and fourteenth centuries, and joined those who had remained in Central Asia.

During the Mongol conquest, battles and skirmishes between the Mongols and the Turkmens in Khorezm and northern Khorasan are mentioned in historical sources, but historians of the Mongol and Timurid periods are silent about these Turkmens. Only a few events of Turkmen history during these periods can be tentatively reconstructed on the basis of the Turkmen historical tradition (as recorded by Abu'l-Ghāzī in the seventeenth century)[36] and some circumstantial evidence. It seems that in the course of the Mongol conquest of Central Asia the Turkmens were driven away from the vicinity of the oases of Khorezm and northern Khorasan, and during the next three centuries they mainly nomadized along the eastern coast of the Caspian Sea, from the Mangïshlaq peninsula in the north to the Balkhan Mountains and the

34 See on it Golden, 1992a, pp. 212–13.

35 The early history of the Turkmens, their political role and migrations have been repeatedly discussed in modern literature, beginning with the groundbreaking work by V. V. Bartol'd, *Ocherk istorii turkmenskogo naroda* (1929; reprinted in his *Sochineniia*, II/2, pp. 547–623; English trans. V. and T. Minorsky in Barthold, 1962, pp. 73–170). The most recent summaries (with further references): Golden, 1992a, pp. 216–23; Sevim, 1998, pp. 145–55.

36 Abu'l-Ghāzī's *Shajara-yi tarākima* ('Genealogical tree of the Turkmens'), written in 1660-1, is actually a somewhat edited collection of Turkmen tribal traditions, as the author himself admits; see Abu'l Ghāzī, 1958, text, p. 5; trans., p. 36.

borders of Iran in the south.[37] The Mongols were obviously little interested in this area, which was unfit for the Mongol type of horse-breeding economy, so that the Turkmens were left to their own devices, practising relatively short-range nomadism based on camels (dromedaries) and sheep, and divided into independent tribes. As distinct from the nomads of the Dasht-i Qipchāq, they were not incorporated into the Mongol tribal and imperial structure, and, as a result, they remained outside the Mongol imperial tradition: they did not have any Chinggisid rulers, they did not have a 'noble estate' comparable to the Qazaq 'white bone', and they were not directly subjected to the Chinggisid khans. A possible exception to this last is indicated in a Turkmen tradition recorded by Abu'l-Ghāzī, according to which the Turkmens who lived on the Mangïshlaq and the Balkhan Mountains were once subjected to Janïbek Khan of the Golden Horde (1342–57); but then they killed Janïbek's governor (and, presumably, regained their independence).[38] Even if the Golden Horde had indeed, temporarily, some authority over a part of the Turkmens,[39] it must have lost it with the beginning of major internal feuds after the death of Janïbek Khan.

The first data about the location of individual Turkmen tribes in Central Asia[40] point to the events and personalities of the mid-fourteenth century. A Turkmen tradition, as given by Abu'l-Ghāzī, mentions the eponymous ancestor of the tribe Ersarï (see below), Ersarï Baba, as the contemporary of Shaykh Sharaf, who wrote for him a religious and didactic treatise *Muʿīn al-murīd*. Since this work, which has come down to us, was written in 1313–14, it places Ersarï Baba in the early fourteenth century; at that time, according to the same tradition, the tribe Ersarï lived in the region of the Balkhan Mountains.[41] The information about the small Turkmen tribes which settled along the old bed of the Amu Darya, the Uzboy, should also refer to the fourteenth century, because it was at that time that some water from the Amu Darya was reaching the Caspian Sea through the Uzboy.

37 One known exception was the tribe (or tribal union) Yazïr (the original Oghuz name Yazghïr), which had occupied before the Mongols the western part of the northern rim of Khorasan; the remnants of this tribe found refuge in the foothills of the Kopet Dāgh mountains and later became known as Qaradashlï.

38 Abu'l Ghāzī, 1958, text, p. 72; trans., pp. 74–5.

39 The name of Janïbek Khan appears also in the story of the tribe Tiveji (in modern Turkmen Düyachi), which originated allegedly from herdsmen sent by Janïbek with his herd of camels to the Balkhan Mountains as the best place for rearing camels (Turkm. *düya*).

40 They are all found in the two historical works of Abu'l-Ghāzī Khan, *Shajara-yi tarākima* and *Shajara-yi Turk*.

41 See Abu'l-Ghāzī, 1958, text, pp. 73–4; trans., p. 75; cf. Bartol'd, *Ocherk istorii turkmenskogo naroda*, in his Sochineniia, II/2, p. 594; Bregel, 'Ersari', *EI²*, Suppl., p. 281.

Much more detailed information about the location of various Turkmen tribes is available for the time after the Uzbek conquest of Khorezm in the early sixteenth century, both from the works of Abu'l-Ghāzī and from some Persian sources. At that time several major groups of Turkmen tribes, as well as their location, are mentioned. The northernmost group, called Esen-eli, or Esen-khani, included the tribes Chowdur, Ighdïr, Bozachi, Arabachi and Abdal; they were located in the north of the Mangïshlaq peninsula and on the Üst-Yurt plateau. To the south of them were the Salors, which was the name both of a particular tribe (going back to one of the 'original' Oghuz tribes, Salghur) and of a larger group of tribes, in which the Salors had some seniority. This larger group was divided into the 'Inner (*Ichki*) Salors' and 'Outer (*Tashqï*) Salors'. The 'Inner' Salors consisted only of the Salor proper and lived on the Mangïshlaq, while the 'Outer' Salors, who included 'Khorasanian Salors', Ersarï, Teke, Sarïqs and Yomuts,[42] nomadized on a large area between Mangïshlaq and Khorasan. To the south-west of them, along the south-eastern shore of the Caspian Sea, was another group of tribes, which consisted of the tribes Yemreli, or Imreli, Göklen and Oqlu, or Okhlu; they are mentioned at that time only in the Persian (Ṣafavid) sources, where they are called 'Yaqa Turkmens' or 'Ṣāʾin Khanī Turkmens'.[43] The first name means 'Coastal Turkmens', while the second is usually interpreted as 'Ṣāʾin Khan's Turkmens', where Ṣāʾin Khan is the well-known nickname of the Mongol khan Batu of the Golden Horde.[44] This latter interpretation, however, seems to be dubious. There is no indication in the known sources that the authority of Batu extended beyond the Caspian Sea and that his *ulus* included any Turkmens. Moreover, the spelling Ṣāʾin, found in the Persian works of the Ṣafavid period, does not reflect correctly the original Turkmen name, which is Söyin, or Seyin; it is the Turkmen pronunciation of the name Ḥusayn – a counterpart to the name Esen (in the name Esen-eli, or Esen-khani), which is the Turkmen pronunciation of the name Ḥasan. It is not clear why and how the names of Ḥasan and Ḥusayn began to be used for these two groups of Turkmen tribes, but, in any case, it has apparently nothing to do with Batu Khan and the Golden Horde.[45]

42 The text of Abu'l-Ghāzī is not quite clear on this; according to Bartol'd's interpretation, only Teke, Sarïqs and Yomuts belonged to the 'Outer Salors' (see Bartol'd, *Ocherk istorii turkmenskogo naroda*, in his Sochineniia, II/2, p. 597).

43 According to the Ṣafavid sources, they also included some Salors. It could be that by the end of the sixteenth century this group also included the tribes of Teke, Sarïq and Yomut, which had belonged before to the 'Khorasanian Salors'.

44 The first to offer this interpretation was Bartol'd (see his *Sochineniia*, II/1, p. 598).

45 On the names Seyin (or Söyin)-khani and Esen-khani (otherwise Seyin/Söyin-eli and Esen-eli) see Dzhikiev, 1991, pp. 124–9. Dzhikiev does not refer to the names Ḥasan and Ḥusayn. The composition of these two groups is given differently in different sources.

Yet another group of Turkmen tribes seems to have emerged in the fourteenth and fifteenth centuries along the Uzboy, the old dry bed of the Amu Darya, when part of the Amu Darya's water was flowing through it (especially after the devastation of Khorezm by Temür at the end of the fourteenth century). It included originally the 'Üch El', i.e. 'Three Tribes': from west to east, the Qara-Öyli, Ali-eli and Khïzïr-eli. The Qara-Öyli were joined by another newly formed tribe, Tiveji (cf. n. 39), and they lived between the Balkhan Mountains and the Caspian Sea, while the part of the Khïzïr-eli closest to Khorezm became known as the Adaqlï (from Adaq, the region of Khorezm east of Lake Sarïqamïsh). The *Shajara-yi Tarākima* by Abu'l-Ghāzī gives detailed accounts of the emergence of these new tribes out of various disparate groups, both Turkmen and non-Turkmen, who were attracted to this area due to its new favourable ecological conditions.

These conditions, however, began to change in the fifteenth century. The Amu Darya changed its course again, and the Uzboy gradually dried up. Moreover, the water-table under the Qaraqum Desert and the Üst-Yurt plateau lowered, so that many wells in these areas, which were essential for the Turkmen pastoral economy, also began to dry up or to salinize. It was a slow process, but eventually it caused some Turkmen tribes to migrate east and south, closer to the irrigated areas of the agricultural oases of Khorezm and northern Khorasan. In addition, the tribes located on the Mangïshlaq and the Üst-Yurt were subjected to attacks from the north by stronger nomads: the Manghïts (Noghays) and later the Qalmïqs and the Qazaqs. The drying up of the Uzboy was, apparently, the immediate cause of the migration of the Üch El. Among them, the tribe Adaqlï (or Adaqlï-Khïzïr) was already found in the north-west of Khorezm by the beginning of the sixteenth century: it played a prominent role in the defence of Khorezm from Shïbānī Khan. The rest of the Üch El still lived along the Uzboy at the time of the Uzbek conquest: they are mentioned there by Abu'l-Ghāzī as practising agriculture at the time of the ʿArabshahid khan Ṣufyān (1529–35). The Uzbeks who conquered Khorezm quickly subjugated most Turkmen tribes to the west and south-west of Khorezm, from Mangïshlaq to the borders of Khorasan. These tribes were divided between the appanages of the ʿArabshahid princes (sultans), so that each prince would receive a town in Khorezm (which they called *Su boyu* 'The side of the water'), a town at the northern rim of Khorasan (which they called *Tagh boyu* 'The side of the mountain') and a particular Turkmen tribe. The Turkmens had to pay to their Uzbek rulers a tribute in sheep, the amount of which was originally not fixed. In the reign of Ṣufyān Khan there was a Turkmen rebellion, in which the Khorezmian tax-collectors were killed. As a result of a punitive expedition of Ṣufyān Khan, the Turkmens were brought to submission, after which the amount of the tribute to be paid annually by each tribe was established. Abu'l-Ghāzī (our only source for these events)[46] does not mention how long these tributary relations continued. But soon the relations between the Turkmens and the ʿArabshahids acquired another aspect too: the Uzbek rulers of Khorezm began to resort to the Turkmens as auxiliaries in their military campaigns. The first such case was in 1539, when Dīn Muḥammad Sulṭān set out from Khorasan to reconquer Khorezm from ʿUbaydallāh Khan of Bukhara; on his way he recruited 1,000 horsemen from the tribe Adaqlï-Ḥïzïr, to whom he promised equal rights with the Uzbeks and tax-free status.[47]

It seems that ʿAli-eli was the first among the Üch El group to completely abandon the Uzboy Basin: by the end of the sixteenth century they are mentioned in various places in northern Khorasan, from Nesa and Durun in the west to Merv in the east. Then the Ersarï and a part of the Salors (most probably, the 'Inner' ones) migrated to Khorezm: in the first half of the seventeenth century they participated in the feuds between the different members of the ʿArabshahid dynasty that resulted first in the victory of two brothers, Isfandiyār Sulṭān and Abu'l-Ghāzī Sultan, over their two half-brothers, Ḥabash and Ilbārs. Abu'l-Ghāzī drew his support from the Uzbeks, while Isfandiyār was supported by the Turkmens.[48] Under Isfandiyār the Turkmens played a prominent role in Khorezm; his Uzbek opponents began to concentrate mainly in the region of the Amu Darya Delta, Aral. After Abu'l-Ghāzī came to power in 1643 or 1644, he started a series of military campaigns against various Turkmen tribes, as a result of which they dispersed from Khorezm in several directions. The Ersarï and some Salors migrated from Khorezm up the Amu Darya, to its middle course; they were joined by the Ersarï who began to move gradually eastwards from the Balkhan Mountains. But already under Abu'l-Ghāzī there was some reconciliation between him and the Turkmens, and under his son Anūsha Khan (1663–85), who had a Turkmen wife, Turkmens recovered (at least partially) their position in Khorezm. Their numbers grew due to the migration of Turkmen groups to Khorezm from the Mangïshlaq peninsula and from south-western Turkmenia. In the second

46 Abu'l-Ghāzī Bahādur Khan, 1871–4, text, pp. 207–11; trans., pp. 221–5.

47 Abu'l-Ghāzī Bahādur Khan, 1871–4, I, 225; II, 241. Cf. Munis, 1999, pp. 32 and 554 n. 174.

48 For a detailed discussion of the relations between the Turkmens and the ʿArabshahids and the role of Turkmens in Khorezm in the first half of the seventeenth century see: Karryev *et al.*, 1954, pp. 216–27.

half of the seventeenth and the early eighteenth century the Turkmens on Mangïshlaq were subjected to growing pressure, first by the Qalmïqs and later by the Qazaqs; during this period the Salors still remaining on Mangïshlaq left for Khorezm. The Salor chieftains still had some political importance in Khorezm in the first half of the eighteenth century,[49] but they were eclipsed by the new Turkmen arrivals from Mangïshlaq and Khorasan. A group of the Esen-eli tribes left Mangïshlaq at the end of the seventeenth century, and in the early eighteenth century migrated to the lower reaches of the Volga and became Russian subjects (later they migrated to the northern Caucasus). But another, probably more numerous, group, in which the Chowdurs were predominant, during the same period came to Khorezm and established themselves in the south-western part of Aral. Other migrations of Turkmen tribes originated in south-western Turkmenia and affected both northern Khorasan and Khorezm. In the first quarter of the seventeenth century the group of the Yaqa Turkmens, as a result of its defeats in the wars with the Ṣafavid governor of the Astarabad province, disintegrated: the tribe Oqlu seized to exist,[50] the tribe Göklen moved east, to the upper course of the Gürgen (Gorgan) River, and the tribe Yemreli moved further north-east, to the foothills of the Kopet Dāgh. From the middle of the seventeenth century the Yomuts, who moved south from the Balkhan Mountains, replaced the Göklen and the Yemreli and occupied the entire region between the lower course of the Atrek and the Caspian Sea. In the early eighteenth century one branch of the Yomuts named Bayram-Shalï was invited to Khorezm in order to fight the enemies of Shīr Ghāzī Khan (1714–27);[51] until the early nineteenth century these Yomuts were several times banished from Khorezm, but each time they would soon come back, and they became the most numerous Turkmen tribe there. During the first half of the eighteenth century the tribe Teke also migrated from the Balkhan region in two directions, partly to Khorezm (where they did not play an important role, probably because of their small number), but mostly towards the oases in the foothills of the Kopet Dāgh. The Turkmens gradually replaced the old (Iranian) sedentary

49 See Munis, 1999, p. 582 n. 375 (according to Muḥammad Kāẓīm).

50 The Persian work *Futūḥāt-i Farīdūnīya,* written in 1614 and describing the exploits of Farīdūn Khan, the governor of Astarabad (since 1603), boasts of his numerous victories in the fights with the tribes Göklen, Salor, Tiveji and especially Okhlu, many of whom were allegedly annihilated; see a short summary in M. T. Dānish-Pazhūh, *Fihrist-i Kitābkhāna-yi markazīyi Dānishgāh-i Tihrān*, XI (Tehran, 1961), p. 2297; Storey–Bregel, II, pp. 872–3. Whether these claims were exaggerated or not, Oqlu (or Oqlï) does not appear in later sources, including ethnographic descriptions of Turkmens.

51 Munis, 1999, p. 186.

population of these oases, which became possible only after the death of Nādir Shāh (1747) and the collapse of Persian authority in Khorasan. In their movement to these oases the Teke were preceded by the Yemreli; as a result of the pressure by the more numerous Teke, most of the Yemreli had to leave this area and to migrate to Khorezm in 1803 or 1804,[52] leaving the Teke in possession of the northern rim of Khorasan.[53]

52 See Bregel, 1961, p. 31.
53 See the maps of the Turkmen migrations and the location of Turkmen tribes in the early twentieth century: Bregel, 2003, pp. 72–5, maps 36A–B, 37.

13
The western steppe: Volga-Ural region, Siberia and the Crimea

ALLEN J. FRANK

Edigü and the final disintegration of the Golden Horde

Challenges from Chinggisid rivals to the Manghït amir Edigü following the death of Toqtamïsh around 1406, led to the final disintegration of Chinggisid political unity in the western steppe. Henceforth political power would be centred in specific regions (*yurts*) that would become the foundations of Chinggisid successor states of the Golden Horde. These states emerged primarily in the first half of the fifteenth century. While their dates of existence varied, ultimately most met similar fates of either disintegration or annexation to powerful neighbours such as Muscovy and the Qazaq Khanate. These successor states include the Noghay, or Manghït, Horde, the Great Horde, the Crimean and Siberian khanates, and the khanates of Kazan, Astrakhan and Kasimov.

Following a period of political chaos and confusion in the first decades of the fifteenth century, Temür's defeat of Toqtamïsh in 1395 resulted in several decades of turmoil in the *Ulus* of Jochi that ended in the final disintegration of the Golden Horde and the establishment of a number of successor states in the western Dasht-i Qipchāq. The first two decades of the fifteenth century were characterized above all by the ongoing conflict between Toqtamïsh and his son Jalāl ad-Dīn on the one hand, and the Manghït amir Edigü and his Chinggisid allies and puppets on the other.[1] Following the death of Edigü in 1419 independent successor states emerged, most notably the so-called Uzbek

1 On Edigü's career cf. DeWeese, 1994a, pp. 336–52; Trepavlov, 2001b, pp. 72–89; cf. also Izmailov, 1992. Edigü's career, and especially his conflict with Toqtamïsh, figure as the subject of an oral-epic cycle recorded among numerous Turkic peoples of the western Dasht-i Qipchāq; cf. DeWeese, 1994a, pp. 411–20.

(or Özbek) Khanate of the Shibanid Abū'l-Khayr Khan in the eastern *Ulus* of Jochi (see Chapter 12), the Noghay (or Manghït) Horde, led by the descendants of the amir Edigü, and the khanates of Sibir, the Crimea, Kazan and Astrakhan, led variously by Toqay-Timurid and Shibanid dynasties.

At the beginning of the fifteenth century the Manghït amir Edigü, who had figured prominently in the struggles between Temür and Toqtamïsh, now faced his main challenge from Toqtamïsh. Following the death of Temür Qutlugh Khan b. Tīmūr-Malik in 1399 Edigü effectively ruled independently as *beglerbegi* through a Chinggisid named Shādī-Bek b. Küchik, the nephew of Temür Qutlugh Khan. Based on numismatic evidence, at that time, around 1400, Edigü and Shādī-Bek had established their authority in several important centres of the Golden Horde, including the Crimea, Astrakhan (Hajji Tarkhan), Derbent, Baku and even Khorezm (Khwārazm). For his part, Toqtamïsh had established himself in Western Siberia, in the vicinity of the modern-day city of Tiumen', where he died in 1406.[2]

Despite his elimination of Toqtamïsh, Edigü's position remained unstable. While he was in Siberia, Shādī-Bek attempted to rule independently of the Manghït amir, but the following year Edigü overthrew him and established Shādī-Bek's son Pūlāt on the throne, who appears to have ruled from the city of Bulghar, in the Middle Volga region. Jalāl ad-Dīn b. Toqtamïsh then installed himself as khan, overthrowing Pūlāt, but within a short period Edigü succeeded in expelling Jalāl ad-Dīn. Following the death of Toqtamïsh, his sons became the main rivals to Edigü, and regularly clashed with the khans through whom Edigü ruled. Following Jalāl ad-Dīn's expulsion from Bulghar, two of Toqtamïsh's sons, Jalāl ad-Dīn and Karīm-Bīrdī, found refuge in Lithuania with Grand Duke Vitovt, while another son, Kubak, found refuge in Sïghnaq, along the Syr Darya River, within the territory of the Blue Horde.[3]

It was in 1408 that Edigü led a campaign against the Russian principalities. Following the defeat of Toqtamïsh at the hands of Temür they had ceased paying tribute to khans of the Golden Horde. In that year he was besieging Moscow when news arrived that Pūlāt Khan was under attack from a rival khan, probably Jalāl ad-Dīn, who at that time was receiving support from Vitovt, and who was able to retake control of the Crimea. Pūlāt was succeeded as khan around 1411 by Temür Khan b. Temür Qutlugh Khan, who managed to defeat Jalāl ad-Dīn and expel him from the Crimea. The Nikonian Chronicle indicates that Temür Khan then turned against Edigü, defeated him, and forced him to flee to Khorezm. The scene of these dynastic struggles then shifts to

2 Safargaliev, 1960, pp. 180–1.
3 Safargaliev, 1960, pp. 184–6.

the east, to Khorezm, where Edigü succeeded in marrying one of his daughters to the son of the Timurid ruler of Samarqand, Shah Rukh. At the head of a Khorezmian force, Edigü marched westwards to his own *ulus*, evidently located along the lower Yayïq River, and there met defeat at the hands of Temür Khan. Temür Khan pursued Edigü and the defeated Khorezmian forces and laid siege to the Khorezmian capital, Urgench. A new threat from Jalāl ad-Dīn, who had come out of Lithuanian exile and rallied the support of a portion of the nomadic population in western Dasht-i Qipchāq, forced Temür Khan to lift the siege of Urgench and face Jalāl ad-Dīn, who had managed to establish a measure of control over Bulghar and Astrakhan. Evidently Jalāl ad-Dīn prevailed, because by the end of 1411 Jalāl ad-Dīn had regained control over most of the western *Ulus* of Jochi, with the exception of Khorezm, whither Jalāl ad-Dīn had marched to face Edigü and his supporters. Both sides were forced to quit Urgench, however, when Shah Rukh took control of the city. Consequently, Edigü returned to his own Manghït *Ulus*, and Jalāl ad-Dīn returned to the western *Ulus* of Jochi. Internecine conflicts among his brothers cut short Jalāl ad-Dīn's tenure as khan, when in 1412 or 1413 one of Jalāl ad-Dīn's brothers murdered him. The sources place responsibility for this act on different individuals, but Russian sources name Karīm-Bīrdī b. Toqtamïsh as the culprit. Karīm-Bīrdī evidently had a degree of support among the Russian princes and he installed himself as ruler by 1413. Numismatic evidence indicates he ruled in the cities of Qïrïm, Saray and Astrakhan. He ruled for perhaps five months before he was succeeded by his brother Kebek, in whose name coins were struck in Bulghar and Astrakhan between 1414 and 1418. Other sources indicate that Kebek was himself murdered by one of his brothers in 1416.[4]

By 1414 Edigü, based in Saraychïq at the mouth of the Yayïq River, was able to mount another challenge to the sons of Toqtamïsh. In that year he installed on the throne of the Golden Horde a puppet Chinggisid from the Togha-Timurid branch, known alternatively as Chakrī and Chingīz Oghlān. However, Edigü's puppet was himself overthrown by Jabbār-Bīrdī b. Toqtamïsh. From 1416 until 1418 Edigü continued to rule from his base in Saraychïq through puppet Chinggisids. Based on numismatic evidence, Edigü was able to exert some control of the cities of Saray, Astrakhan and Derbent. In any case Toqtamïsh's sons continued to find refuge, when needed, in Lithuania, and at this time, one son, Qādir-Bīrdī, established himself in the Crimea with the support of amirs of the Shirin tribe. In 1419 he led an army against Edigü and they fought a battle near the mouth of the Yayïq River, where Edigü's

4 Safargaliev, 1960, pp. 187–9.

army was defeated and Edigü himself killed, while Qādir-Bīrdī soon died from wounds sustained in the battle.

By the time of the death of Edigü it appears to have become customary for the tribal elite of nomadic communities throughout the western *Ulus* of Jochi to install and support Chinggisid rulers at the regional level. Thus, by 1421 there were as many as six separate figures claiming to rule as khan of the Golden Horde. One particularly prominent figure at this time who would eventually play an important role as the founder of the independent Kazan Khanate, was Ulugh Muḥammad, a Togha-Timurid, and possibly a cousin to the sons of Toqtamïsh.[5] Nevertheless, we also see in this period the emergence of several Chinggisid dynasts who emerged as regionally prominent figures and eventually became the founders of autonomous successor states in their own right. Initially supported by Vitovt and declared khan in the Crimea with the support of a portion of the Crimean tribal elite, Ulugh Muḥammad was declared khan in the Crimea in 1421. In 1423 Baraq Khan b. Quyurchaq b. Urus Khan,[6] subordinated much of the Uzbek (Özbek) *Ulus* in the eastern Dasht-i Qipchāq and conquered most of the western regions claimed by Ulugh Muḥammad. Nevertheless, Baraq returned to his own territories, allowing Ulugh Muḥammad to reclaim his original territories, at this time presumably limited primarily to the Crimea. However, numismatic evidence indicates that by 1427 Ulugh Muḥammad also controlled the cities of Bulghar and Astrakhan.

A major rival to Ulugh Muḥammad was Kichī-Muḥammad b. Temür Khan b. Temür Qutlugh Khan.[7] Kichī-Muḥammad's base had been the eastern *Ulus* of Jochi, and he had in fact briefly succeeded Baraq Khan b. Quyurchaq as khan in 1430 or 1431. By 1433 he re-emerged as ruler in Astrakhan, having wrested control of that region from Ulugh Muḥammad and was later to emerge as the founder of the nomadic Great Horde.

Another important figure, who was to play a role in the creation of the Siberian Khanate was Ḥājji-Muḥammad Khan, a Shibanid and rival to Baraq Khan.[8]

5 While Ulugh Muḥammad's status as a Togha-Timurid is beyond doubt, several differing versions of his genealogy appear in both Islamic and Russian sources. cf. Iskhakov, 2002, pp. 63–74.

6 This Baraq Khan was the father of Kirāy Khan and Janïbek Khan, who founded the independent Qazaq Khanate later in the fifteenth century; on the political role of these figures cf. Pishchulina, 1977, pp. 246 ff. For his genealogy cf. Abū'l Ghāzī Bahādur Khan, 1871–4, p. 188.

7 He also appears in the sources as Kichik-Muḥammad. The two are occasionally confused. Safargaliev, 1960, pp. 205–7; cf. also Berezin, 1854, pp. 154–5.

8 Safargaliev, 1960, pp. 205–7; cf. also Berezin, 1854, pp. 154–5; in some sources Ḥājji-Muḥammad's name appears as Maḥmūd-Ḥājjī; cf. also Abū'l Ghāzī Bahādur Khan, 1871–4, p. 186.

After conquering a portion of the middle Syr Darya Valley, Baraq turned his attention to the Shibanid realms in Western Siberia around 1427. However, with the support of the Noghay amirs Hājji-Muḥammad succeeded in killing Baraq Khan and thereby the eastern *Ulus* of Jochi fell under the control of the Shibanids, with Siberia under the control of Hājji-Muḥammad and the regions to the south-east under Abū'l-Khayr Khan.[9]

Thus, by 1430 the unification of the Golden Horde had become a military and political impossibility for the Chinggisid dynasts in the *Ulus* of Jochi. As a result, we see the competing khans beginning to concentrate their power in separate *yurts* of the Golden Horde, thereby preparing the way for future dynasties and states in those regions. These include Ulugh Muḥammad in the Middle Volga region, who was to later establish the Kazan Khanate, Hājji-Muḥammad, whose descendants were to rule the Siberian Khanate, and Kichī-Muḥammad, whose descendants were to rule the Great Horde. A crucial factor in this period was the role of the non-Chinggisid tribal elite, who appear most prominent in the Crimea, and especially in the Noghay Horde. In fact, during the fifteenth and sixteenth centuries the descendants of Edigü, and the Noghay Horde, would play an increasingly important role as a *de facto* autonomous state within the Chinggisid realms of the *Ulus* of Jochi, and as power-brokers among the contending Chinggisid rulers.

The Noghay Horde

The Noghay Horde was centred in the *yurt* of the Manghït tribe.[10] This territory was based roughly between the Ural (Yayïq) and Emba (Jim) rivers, in what is today Western Kazakhstan. While the political and cultural history of the Noghay Horde is a major chapter in the history of the western steppe, and of Inner Asia as a whole, it has only come under focused scholarly attention relatively recently, in the past ten to fifteen years.[11] The founder of the Noghay Horde was Edigü, who held the position of *beglerbegi* under several khans in the late fourteenth and early fifteenth centuries, although a fully independent Noghay Horde, formally ruled by descendants of Edigü, only emerged in the

9 Safargaliev, 1960, p. 203.

10 In fact, already in the sixteenth century the terms 'Manghït' and 'Noghay' were being used interchangeably in references to the Noghay Horde; Trepavlov, 2001b, p. 112.

11 The main study of the political history of the Noghay Horde is Trepavlov, 2001b; for an examination of the religious and cultural history of the Noghay Horde and its dynasts cf. DeWeese, 1994a. The use and interpretation of the oral traditions of the steppe nomads distinguishes much of the recent scholarship on the Noghay Horde. For a study of the political history of the Noghays focusing on the later sixteenth and seventeenth centuries cf. Kochekaev, 1988.

second half of the fifteenth century, under Edigü's great-grandson Musa b. Waqqāṣ b. Nūr ad-Dīn.[12]

The descendants of Edigü were not Chinggisids, but rather were Bakrids, that is, they claimed descent from the righteous Caliph Abu Bakr, through a Muslim saint named Baba Tükles whom the oral traditions of the steppe nomads identify as having convinced Uzbek Khan, the ruler of the Golden Horde in the first half of the fourteenth century, to accept Islam. In this regard, we see already in the fifteenth century Islamic legitimacy emerging as a counterweight to Chinggisid legitimacy, and well into the eighteenth century we can witness throughout the Dasht-i Qipchāq the gradual displacement of Chinggisid legitimacy by Islamic legitimacy.

At the time of Edigü's death in 1419 it would be still premature to speak of an independent Noghay Horde. Nevertheless Edigü's descendants were able to remain actively engaged as power-brokers among the feuding Chinggisids. It appears that soon after Edigü's death in 1419 his son Manṣūr provided support to the Shibanid Hājji-Muḥammad, and declared him khan, becoming his *biy*. Similarly, during the fifteenth century a regional dynasty with close ties to the Noghays, located in Western Siberia, and known as the Taybughids, seems to have experienced unremittingly hostile relations with the Shibanids following the death of Hājji-Muḥammad Khan; during the fifteenth and sixteenth centuries the descendants of Hājji-Muḥammad repeatedly sought to re-establish their authority of the '*yurt* of Sibir'.[13] By the second half of the fifteenth century it is evident that the Noghay amir Mūsā b. Waqqāṣ functioned as an independent ruler, with his capital in the city of Saraychïq, at the mouth of the Ural (Yayïq) River.[14] The territory that comprised the Noghay Horde at this point certainly included the traditional Manghït *yurt*, and possibly extended as far west as the Volga River, including perhaps the important commercial centre of Astrakhan.

In the middle of the fifteenth century it is also clear that Noghay influence extended into some of the Chinggisid successor states of the Golden Horde. For example, Ībāq Khan, a grandson of Hājji-Muḥammad Khan who briefly re-established Shibanid authority in Western Siberia appears to have been largely dependent on Noghay support.[15] Similarly, there is little doubt that Noghays played an important political role in the Great Horde as well,

12 Trepavlov, 2001b, pp. 100, 107.
13 Frank, 1994, pp. 20–3.
14 Trepavlov, 2001b, pp. 100–1. For a discussion of the significance of this city for the Noghay Horde cf. Trepavlov, 2001a.
15 Safargaliev, 1960, p. 203; cf. also Berezin, 1854, 154–5; Trepavlov, 2001b, p. 95.

which was founded by Kichī-Muḥammad and centred along the lower Volga River. However, even under Mūsā Biy, the communities in the eastern part of the Manghït *yurt* remained under the control of the Qazaq Khanate under the rule of Janïbek and Kirāy, the sons of Baraq Khan.[16] Noghay figures also held a prominent political role in the Kazan Khanate, particularly in the latter half of the fifteenth century.

The first major challenge to the continued existence of the Noghay Horde came from a unified and aggressive Qazaq Khanate, whose rulers, the descendants of Baraq Khan, were eager to gain control over the lower Syr Darya Valley and the steppes north of the Aral Sea. The first of these attacks took place in 1472 under Burunduq Khan b. Kirāy Khan. But a more serious situation developed in 1519 when the Qazaq ruler Qāsim Khan b. Janïbek Khan carried out the complete conquest of the Noghay lands east of the Volga River, including the city of Saraychïq, forcing many Noghay *mīrzās* to flee to the Crimea.[17] Qāsim Khan even made Saraychïq his headquarters, where he died in 1521. Following Qāsim's death, the Noghays were able to reconquer all of this lost territory, and in fact expanded their control as far east as the Irtysh River.[18] During the first half of the sixteenth century the Noghays also succeeded in expanding their authority to the north-west as well, into the Bashkir lands of the southern Ural Mountains as far as the Kama River.[19]

During the 1530s and 1540s the descendants of Mūsā b. Waqqāṣ and Nūr ad-Dīn b. Edigü brought the Noghay Horde to the peak of its power, controlling a vast region from the Irtysh River to the Volga and as far as the Kama River in the north-west. The Noghay *biys* also exerted substantial influence in the Chinggisid successor states of the Golden Horde, particularly the khanates of Astrakhan and Kazan. In the middle of the sixteenth century, during the reign of Yūsuf Biy b. Mūsā, the Noghay Horde proved unable either to retain its influence in the successor states, or contend with the rising power of Russia or the Ottoman Empire, which was expanding its control over its own client state, the Crimean Khanate. In the decade previous to the Russian conquest of the khanates of Kazan and Astrakhan in 1552 and 1556 respectively, the Noghay *biys* had no longer been able effectively to influence the internal politics in the khanates, and in fact did not even supply military assistance to their supporters resisting the Russians. In the 1550s struggles also broke out within the Noghay ruling elite itself. Ismāʿīl Biy emerged as the victor in these struggles,

16 Isin, 2004, pp. 46–7.
17 Trepavlov, 2001b, pp. 158–9.
18 Trepavlov, 2001b, p. 159; Berezin, 1854, p. 163.
19 Trepavlov, 2001b, p. 205.

but by this time the political unity of the Noghay Horde was in permanent decline. A substantial portion of Noghay nomads refused to recognize the authority of Ismāʿīl Biy b. Mūsā and his successors. One such group, known as the Lesser Noghays, pastured their flocks in the steppes of the North Caucasus. The communities that remained under the authority of the Noghay *biys* in Saraychïq became known as the Great Noghay Horde.[20] Another of these groups was the so-called Jemboyluq Horde that was also known as the Altïulï Horde. They resided on the steppes between the Emba and Syr Darya rivers. These Noghays were nominally subjects of Moscow and into the seventeenth century retained their independence from both the Great Noghay Horde and the Qazaqs.[21]

Ismāʿīl Biy's successor was his son Dīn-Aḥmad, who ruled as *biy* from 1563 until 1578.[22] Following Dīn-Aḥmad's rule we see the territorial and political cohesion of the Great Noghay Horde permanently fragment. Part of this disintegration was caused by external factors. Following the Russian conquest of Astrakhan in 1556, and especially the conquest of Siberia in 1581, Russian Cossacks, often acting outside of the control of the Russian authorities in Moscow, were increasingly encroaching on Noghay territory along the Volga and Ural rivers. In 1581 Cossack forces succeeded in sacking Saraychïq itself. It was also in the latter half of the sixteenth century that the Bashkir tribes in the southern Ural Mountains submitted to Russia. Perhaps even more consequential to the integrity of the Great Noghay Horde was the loss of its lands between the Irtysh and Emba rivers to the Qazaq ruler Ḥaqq-Nażar Khan by 1570. Qazaq raids west of the Emba River continued through most of the 1570s.[23]

Toward the end of the sixteenth century the constant raiding and warfare, and the inability of the Noghay *biys* to protect the communities constituting the Great Noghay Horde, including the capital of Saraychïq, compelled many Noghays to migrate to calmer and more stable areas, either under Qazaq, Russian or Crimean control. These migrations further weakened the Noghay *biys*, and during the first decades of the seventeenth century the final collapse of the Great Noghay Horde occurred. This collapse was accelerated by internecine fighting within the Noghay elite, and resulted in a substantial portion of the Noghays migrating into the Black Sea steppe and coming under Crimean rule, or moving into the Terek steppe north of the Caucasus and the Caspian Sea.[24] However,

20 Trepavlov, 2001b, p. 205; Kochekaev, 1988, p. 104.
21 Kochekaev, 1988, p. 104.
22 Trepavlov, 2001b, p. 368.
23 Trepavlov, 2001b, pp. 368–9; on Ḥaqq-Naẓar's campaign, see especially Isin, 2004, pp. 82–9.
24 Kochekaev, 1988, pp. 115–18; Trepavlov, 2001b, p. 381.

the death blow to the Noghay Horde was the arrival of the Qalmaqs during the first third of the seventeenth century. The period from 1607 until the 1630s was a period of constant warfare between the Noghays and Qalmaqs. The Qalmaqs prevailed in these conflicts and occupied the pasturelands across the entire northern Dasht-i Qipchāq, including the heart of the Manghït *yurt* east of the Volga River, effectively cutting the Noghays off from the Qazaqs and the Central Asian khanates.[25]

The remaining Noghays coalesced into four separate *uluses*. These were the Yedisan Horde, which by the eighteenth century was located primarily along the Black Sea coast in Bessarabia, and the Yedishkul Horde, which was scattered from the Kuban region to Bessarabia. In the eighteenth century those groups were under the authority of the Ottoman Empire.[26] The third group was the Jemboyluq (or Altïulï) Horde, which, as we have seen, was centred along the Emba River, and in the first half of the seventeenth century came under complete Qalmaq control, but eventually become assimilated into the Qazaq Junior Zhüz.[27] The fourth group was the Bujaq Horde, which was located primarily north of the Black Sea along the lower Don River and near Aq Kerman. This group came under the authority of the Ottoman Empire as well.[28] During the late seventeenth and eighteenth centuries these Noghay nomads found themselves increasingly constrained between the Ottoman Empire, which controlled the Black Sea coast, and Russia. By the end of the eighteenth century these nomads had virtually all come under Russian control, except for communities in Bessarabia and Dobruja, who remained in the Ottoman Empire. Despite the collapse of the Noghay Horde in the seventeenth century, some Noghays managed to retain a separate identity, and have continued to exist as separate communities in northern Daghestan and in the Astrakhan region to the present day.

The Kazan Khanate

The Kazan Khanate emerged as a powerful successor state of the Golden Horde in 1437 or 1438. Its founder was Ulugh Muḥammad, a Togha-Timurid who is mentioned above.[29] Ulugh Muḥammad had been ruling in Saray, before

25 Kochekaev, 1988, pp. 120–5; Trepavlov, 2001b, pp. 411–15.
26 Trepavlov, 2001b, pp. 434–44.
27 Trepavlov, 2001b, pp. 446–7.
28 Trepavlov, 2001b, pp. 451–2.
29 Some scholars, beginning with V. Vel'iaminov-Zernov, argue that the Kazan Khanate was only founded as an independent state in 1445, and they identify Ulugh Muḥammad's son Maḥmūd as the actual founder. However, most Muslim and Russian historians identify Ulugh Muḥammad as the founder; cf. Khudiakov, 1991; Marjānī, 1885–1900, I, pp. 123–5.

his archrival Kichī-Muḥammad b. Temür Khan expelled him from that city. Ulugh Muḥammad fled to the Crimea, and then to the Russian town of Belev, where he hoped to enlist the support of the erstwhile Russian vassal Vasilii II, the Grand Prince of Muscovy. Perhaps fearing the actual khan in Saray more than the former one, Vasilii turned on Ulugh Muḥammad, attacking him with a much larger military force. Ulugh Muḥammad nevertheless prevailed, and soundly defeated the Muscovite forces. Following this battle, which took place in December 1437, Ulugh Muḥammad moved his troops and followers to the Middle Volga region. After displacing some local dynasts, probably non-Chinggisids, he established his capital in the city of Kazan.[30] Kazan remained the capital of the Kazan Khanate until the Russian forces of Ivan the Terrible conquered it and annexed its entire territory in 1552.

The territory of the Kazan Khanate fluctuated, but had at its centre the city of Kazan, located at the confluence of the Volga and Kazanka rivers. It must be emphasized that neither the Kazan Khanate nor any of the other successor states of the Golden Horde were nation-states in the modern sense of that term, and any discussion of the territorial extent of these states must suppose a degree of fluctuation.[31] Historically the political and commercial centre of the Middle Volga region had been the city of Bulghar, located to the south of Kazan, at the confluence of the Volga and Kama rivers. This city had been a regional economic and administrative centre both before the Mongol conquest, and during the era of a politically unified Golden Horde. However, it had fallen into decline in the second half of the fourteenth century, and was largely abandoned after the Russians sacked the city in 1432. In fact, by 1408 there is numismatic evidence that Kazan had become the region's new administrative centre, and was then known as 'Bulghār al-Jadīd', or 'New Bulghar'.[32] From its founding until its destruction by the Russians in 1552 the core territory Kazan Khanate included Muslim farming villages on both banks of the Volga River, and east of the Volga primarily on the north bank of the Kama River. The rulers in Kazan continued existing tributary relationships with non-Muslim communities to the north and west. These included Chuvash, Udmurts and Maris (or Cheremis). The degree of influence the khans in Kazan exercised

30 Khudiakov, 1991, pp. 23–5; Marjānī, 1885–1900, I, p. 24; Iskhakov, 1994, pp. 9–10; the dynastic affiliation of the local rulers that Ulugh Muḥammad displaced in Kazan is unclear, although some Muslim historians in Kazan linked them to a dynasty of semi-legendary Bulghar rulers who appear in the conversion narratives of the Bulghar khans; cf. Ḥusayn b. Amīrkhān, 1883.

31 Several modern scholars, including both Russians and Tatars, have tended to interpret the history of the Kazan Khanate as the history of a Tatar nation- state; cf. especially Khudiakov, 1991; Atlasi, 1993, pp. 185–428; Iskhakov, 1994.

32 Abdullin *et al.*, 1988, p. 24.

over these groups varied as they also competed with Russian influence, but it is evident that they maintained a rather close association with the Maris, who consistently provided military support to the Kazan Khanate.

In geopolitical terms the Kazan Khanate found itself between Russia to the west, where political and military power was increasingly centred in Muscovy, and the Noghay Horde, whose vassals in closest proximity to the Kazan Khanate were the Bashkir tribes located in the southern Ural Mountains and south of the Kama River. The north-eastern outposts of the Kazan Khanate may have also been in contact with the Khanate of Tiumen' in Western Siberia. The Kazan Khanate's geographic connections with the Crimean or Astrakhan khanates were probably more tenuous, since there is little evidence that the khans of Kazan extended their authority any substantial distance along the Volga south of the city of Bulghar.[33]

Early on, Ulugh Muḥammad's main political goal as khan of Kazan appears to have been to bring Muscovy back into submission. In 1439 he occupied the Russian frontier outpost of Nizhnii Novgorod and for a time even besieged Moscow itself.[34] In 1444 and 1445 he again invaded Russian territory, this time capturing Vasilii II following a battle near the city of Suzdal', forcing the Muscovite Grand Prince to pay a heavy tribute. The two decades following Ulugh Muḥammad's death in 1445 were marked by rather peaceful relations between Moscow and Kazan. Maḥmūd b. Ulugh Muḥammad succeeded his father as khan, and the Muscovites granted his brother Qāsim b. Ulugh Muḥammad lands near the town of Meshcherskii Gorodets.[35] This town became known as Kasimov, and was the capital of the Russian-supported Khanate of Kasimov, whose rulers came to play an important role in Chinggisid dynastic politics, and which will be discussed in more detail below.

During the reign of Ibrāhīm b. Maḥmūd (r. 1467–79) there were protracted dynastic struggles among the Chinggisids in Kazan. These dynastic conflicts persisted until the end of the khanate in 1552, and neighbouring powers increasingly exploited the conflicts by trying to place their own candidates on the throne. In broad terms, within Kazan these conflicts pitted a 'Russian party', closely associated with Russian political interests, and an 'Eastern

33 Khudiakov places the authority of the Kazan Khanate as far south as the city of Saratov, or Sarï Taw in Muslim sources; however, he bases this on information contained in a nineteenth-century Muslim shrine catalogue purporting to date from the sixteenth century, and in fact it is unlikely that the authority of the khanate extended far below the mouth of the Kama River.

34 Khudiakov, 1991, p. 26.

35 Maḥmūd b. Ulugh Muḥammad appears in some sources as Maḥmūtek; Khudiakov, 1991, pp. 26–7, 32–3.

party', supporting the interests of the Noghay Horde, and especially in the sixteenth century, the interests of the Crimean Khanate. These 'parties' included not only Chinggisid dynasts, but also local elites, whose interests likely transcended purely dynastic concerns, and rather included internal political and economic interests.

Beginning in the 1480s the dynast most closely associated with the 'Russian party' was Muḥammad-Amīn b. Ibrāhīm Khan, and his chief rival was his brother ʿAlī b. Ibrāhīm, who enjoyed Noghay support.[36] This period also coincided with the reign of the Grand Prince of Muscovy Ivan III (r. 1462–1505), who is best known in Russia for throwing off the 'Mongol-Tatar Yoke', but who also conducted a very effective policy that minimized potential military and political threats from Kazan. In support of Muḥammad-Amīn, Ivan III waged major military campaigns against Kazan in 1482 and 1487. In the latter year Ivan captured ʿAlī Khan and imprisoned him and his family in Russia.[37] Following the overthrow of ʿAlī Khan, Ivan III first placed Muḥammad-Amīn on the throne. In 1496 Māmuq Khan, a Shibanid from Siberia, evidently with local support in Kazan, overthrew Muḥammad-Amīn and established himself as khan. The following year Māmuq's erstwhile allies in the khanate turned against him, and Ivan succeeded in placing Muḥammad-Amīn's brother ʿAbd al-Laṭīf on the throne. It was Muscovite military force that kept further threats from the Siberian Shibanids at bay, and by 1502 Ivan was able to simply replace ʿAbd al-Laṭīf with the former khan, Muḥammad-Amīn.[38] The deaths of ʿAbd al-Laṭīf Khan in 1517 and of Muḥammad-Amīn Khan in 1519 ended the political fortunes of the descendants of Ulugh Muḥammad. Vasilii III, the Grand Prince of Muscovy, placed one of the khans of Kasimov on the throne of Kazan, Shāh ʿAlī b. Allāh-Yār, who was a descendant of Kichī-Muḥammad b. Temür Khan.[39]

Ṣāḥib-Girāy Khan b. Menglī-Girāy Khan replaced Shāh ʿAlī on the throne in 1521. His father had been the Crimean khan and was also the half-brother of Muḥammad-Amīn and ʿAbd al-Laṭīf. Although his rule was relatively brief (1521–4) the political balance in the khanate shifted decisively after 1521 and the rulers in Moscow found it increasingly difficult to keep their candidates on the throne. The period from 1524 until the final Russian conquest saw a succession of rulers installed and deposed by the local political elites in Kazan.

36 Muḥammad-Amīn is known in some Muslim sources as Ījem Khan; cf. Marjānī, 1885–1900, I, p. 127.
37 Khudiakov, 1991, p. 26; cf. also Fennell, 1961, pp. 19–28.
38 Khudiakov, 1991, pp. 54–5; Atlasi, 1993, p. 253; Fennell, 1961, pp. 182–4.
39 Shāh ʿAlī held the throne of Kazan three times: 1519–21, 1546 and 1551–2. He was closely allied with Russian interests.

These included Ṣāḥib-Girāy's nephew, Ṣafā-Girāy b. Fātiḥ-Girāy, who occupied the throne three separate times (1524–31, 1535–46, 1546–9), Jān-ʿAlī Khan b. Allāh-Yār (r. 1532–6), Shāh ʿAlī Khan, Ötemish-Girāy Khan (1549–51) and Yādigār Khan b. Qāsim Khan (1552) (for details on relations between Muscovy and the Kazan Khanate, see Chapter 16).

Our sources only allow the reconstruction of the Kazan Khanate's internal political and social structures in the broadest terms. As noted above, the social and political core of the khanate was the Turkic-speaking Muslim communities inhabiting both banks of the Volga River, and the north bank of the Kama River. These were sedentary agricultural communities with a feudal elite identified in Muslim sources as '*beks*' and '*mīrzās*'. Ethnically and socially these Muslim communities appear to have been in rather close contact with the Noghays.[40] The non-Muslim Finno-Ugrian and Chuvash communities between the central Kazan Khanate and Russian territory appear to have been connected with the Kazan Khanate exclusively by means of tribute relationships that at times included the provision of military support. Kazan, like Bulghar before it, remained an important commercial centre throughout this period. The khanate's location on the Volga River, the major trade thoroughfare between Russia and the Caspian Sea, certainly contributed to its wealth, but at the same time contributed to its strategic importance to Russia. Similarly, there is little reason to doubt that the existence of local trade relationships and interests with Russia to the west, or Muslim centres to the south, exacerbated tensions and rivalries among local commercial elites in Kazan, thereby eroding political unity among urban and even rural elites.

The Chinggisid khan occupied the summit of the political constitution of the khanate; however, the sources make it abundantly clear that other estates could exert their influence by means of established political institutions. The authority or effectiveness of these institutions is difficult to determine. It is evident that under the khans stood the tribal aristocracy, 'amirs'. The evidence from the later Golden Horde, and particularly from the Noghay Horde, indicates that the tribal aristocracy, particularly with an effective leader, could rule through a Chinggisid puppet. There is evidence for such a development in the Kazan Khanate at the beginning of the sixteenth century, when a *bek* named Kel-Aḥmad effectively employed executive authority to steer the khanate towards a more pro-Russian policy.[41] There is also evidence that the political structure at its highest levels was fundamentally similar to that of the Crimean

40 On the place of Noghays in the genealogies of Muslims in the Volga-Ural region cf. Äkhmätjanov, 2002.

41 Khudiakov, 1991, pp. 54–5.

Khanate.[42] Another political institution was the *qurultay*, which is reflected in primarily Russian sources as a sort of Estates-General that was usually convened to enthrone a khan, but that also exerted some executive authority during an interregnum. One such *qurultay* was convened in August of 1551, and included members of the religious elite (*sayyids*), and the tribal elite, including '*qarachi beks*, *amirs*, and *mīrzās*'.[43]

Islamic institutions in the Kazan Khanate were dominated by *sayyids*, that is, families claiming descent from the family of the prophet Muḥammad. In the case of the Kazan Khanate, there is evidence that local *sayyids* traced their descent to the Central Asian Yasavian saint Ḥakīm Ātā.[44] First appearing in Russian sources in 1489, their activity as diplomats drew the attention of Russian chroniclers. Most prominent among these during the final years of the khanate's existence was Qul-Sharīf, who figured in the final defence of the city.[45] Beyond indications in the sources that mosques existed, there is also evidence that a system of pious endowments was in place in the sixteenth century, if not earlier, for local shrines. This was the case for the shrine of Maʿlūm-Khwāja on the south bank of the Kama River, where such a pious endowment survived into the Russian era.[46]

The Siberian Khanate

The Siberian Khanate, or the Khanate of Sibir, was associated with a Shibanid named Küchüm Khan, who founded the khanate in 1563, and who was its ruler until its conquest in 1581 by the Russian Cossack adventurer Yermak.[47] The Western Siberian lands, comprising the northern extremes of the Dasht-i Qipchāq, had formed part of the *Ulus* of Jochi. The political history of Western Siberia in the fifteenth century is rather obscure, but what emerges from the sources is that the local Shibanids, who sought to dominate the region, encountered substantial resistance from a local non-Chinggisid dynasty known as the Taybughids, after their semi-legendary founder Taybugha Biy. The political centre of Western Siberia during the fifteenth century was Tura, or Chimgi-Tura, located at the mouth of the Tura River near the site

42 Khudiakov, 1991, pp. 188–9.
43 Khudiakov, 1991, pp. 191–2. For an overview of the Kazan Khanate's economic and political structure cf. Iskhakov, 2004, pp. 48–53.
44 Togan, 1959–60; Iskhakov, 1997, p. 32.
45 Iskhakov, 1997, p. 35.
46 Mel'nikov, 1859, pp. 179–81.
47 Monographs on the Siberian Khanate include Atlasi, 1993; Atlasi's history of Siberia first appeared in Kazan in 1914 under the title *Sībīr Tārīkhī*; and Abdirov, 1996.

of the modern Russian city of Tiumen'. This was the capital established by Hājji-Muḥammad Khan in 1427, when he founded the Siberian Khanate, before being killed by Abū'l-Khayr Khan the following year.[48] After his death, the Taybughids established themselves in Tura, and their semi-legendary genealogy indicates that their founder, Taybugha, was the first to rule in Tura.[49] This dynasty shared certain political characteristics with the Noghay Horde, including an emphasis on Islamic legitimacy over Chinggisid charisma, and a broadly similar political structure, including a degree of shared political terminology. Nevertheless the relationship between the Taybughids and the Noghay Horde was evidently complex, since, as we shall see, in the late fifteenth century the Noghay Horde sought to install Shibanid dynasts in Tura. In any case, the genealogical evidence leaves little doubt that the Taybughid dynasty was above all a locally rooted dynasty. The Shibanids succeeded in re-establishing their control over Siberia by 1481, when Ībāq (Ibrāhīm) Khan, the grandson of Hājji-Muḥammad, expelled the Taybughids from Tura with substantial support from the Noghay Horde.[50] In that year Ībāq helped the Noghays eliminate the Great Horde and kill its ruler Aḥmad Khan. The Russian chronicles containing the history of the Taybughids indicate that a descendant of Taybugha, a certain Mamat, who had also married Ībāq's sister, nevertheless destroyed the city of Tura and killed Ībāq Khan. After killing Ībāq, at some point after 1493, Mamat established a new capital at Sibir (also referred to as Isker), on the Irtysh River, near the modern city of Tobol'sk. Ībāq's death appears to have encouraged the Shibanids in Siberia to seek to establish themselves elsewhere. In 1496 Ībāq's brother Māmuq briefly ruled as khan of Kazan. Three years later Māmuq's brother, Agalak, also sought the throne of Kazan, but had even less success than his brother, and it appears that by 1499 the Shibanids in Siberia were largely dependent on Noghay support. The Taybughids were able to maintain control over Western Siberia for most of the sixteenth century. In 1555, their ruler Yādigār Biy offered his submission to Russia, presumably as a means of ensuring Russian support against the descendants of Ībāq Khan. The Taybughids were unsuccessful in resisting the Shibanids, however, and in 1563 Ībāq's grandson Küchüm Khan established himself in Siberia as khan.[51] The genealogical sources are clear that Küchüm Khan b. Murtaẓā was a descendant of Hājji-Muḥammad, but while some sources, such as Qādir-ʿAlī Bek Jālāyirī, indicate he was the grandson of Ībāq Khan, others say he was the

48 Safargaliev, 1960, p. 222.
49 Frank, 1994, p. 12.
50 Trepavlov, 2001b, pp. 108–10; Frank, 1994, p. 12.
51 Frank, 1994, pp. 14–15.

grandson of Ībāq's brother Maḥmūtak.[52] Whatever his precise genealogy it is evident that Küchüm enjoyed a degree of support from the Noghays, and probably from the Qazaqs as well.[53]

The structure of the Siberian Khanate under Küchüm evidently differed little from what had existed under the Taybughids. Economically and geographically the Siberian Khanate shared certain peculiarities with the Kazan Khanate. Both states were located at the geographic and economic margins of the Dasht-i Qipchāq. As a result pastoral nomadism had less effect on their social structures. In addition to a core population of Turkic-speaking Muslims, the rulers in both Kazan and Sibir sought to extend their influence into non-Muslim populations to the north and west. In Siberia these communities consisted of Ob Ugrians (Mansi and Khanty, referred to sometimes as Voguls and Ostiaks) who were sources of tribute and military support to both Küchüm and his Russian rivals. The Muslims inhabiting the Siberian Khanate were at the northern margins of agriculture, and they supplemented their livelihoods with stock-breeding, and particularly fishing and hunting. Agriculture was even more marginal, or non-existent, among the Ob-Ugrians. The main commercial activity was the fur trade. Pelts were the main article of tribute, and in 1555 Yādigār's submission to Muscovy required an annual tribute of fur.[54]

Between 1563 and 1581 Küchüm Khan was able to expand significantly the influence of his khanate. He succeeded in exacting tribute from the Ob-Ugrians on a larger scale than the Taybughids had been able to. He organized a series of raids into the Russian territories west of the Ural Mountains, and he extended his rule over Muslim and non-Muslim communities far to the east, including the Baraba steppe and the Tom' River. His raids into Russia evidently encouraged the Stroganov family, who controlled the fur trade in that region, to mount a Cossack expedition against Küchüm. In 1581 the Cossack leader Yermak defeated Küchüm in a series of battles and claimed the territory of the khanate for Russia.[55] Without success Küchüm continued to resist the Russians until his death in 1598.

Siberian Muslims also retained traditions of Küchüm Khan as Islamizer well into the twentieth century. As we have seen, the Shibanids' rival dynasty in Siberia, the Taybughids, was clearly a Muslim dynasty, and indeed appears to have invoked Islamic legitimacy to bolster its authority, perhaps in the same

52 This is Abū'l-Ghāzī's version; Abū'l Ghāzī Bahādur Khan, 1871–4, p. 186; Berezin, 1854, p. 156; cf. Atlasi, 1993, pp. 63–5.

53 Miller, 1937–40, I, p. 196.

54 Frank, 1994, pp. 24–5; Iskhakov, 2006, pp. 142–52.

55 For translations of the Russian chronicle accounts of Yermak's conquests cf. Armstrong, 1974.

manner as the Noghays invoked Islamic legitimacy in their struggles with their Chinggisid rivals. However, on the basis of Siberian legends and genealogies, it appears likely that Küchüm Khan did bring *sayyids* with him from Central Asia, and the framework of as Islamic establishment.[56]

The Great Horde and the Astrakhan Khanate

The lower Volga region, which included the site of the Golden Horde's original capital, Saray, as well as the city of Astrakhan (or Hajji Tarkhan, as it is known in Muslim sources), located in the Volga Delta, during the fifteenth century was associated with the descendants of Temür Qutlugh. In the 1430s this region came under the rule of Kichī-Muḥammad b. Temür, the grandson of Temür Qutlugh, and became known as the Great Horde, led by the sons of Kichī-Muḥammad, Maḥmūd Khan and Aḥmad Khan, and later by Aḥmad's son Sayyid-Aḥmad.[57] The territorial extent of the Great Horde is difficult to determine with any precision, but it was centred west of the Volga River, perhaps extending as far west as the Dnepr River, and comprising the Kuban region and the Caspian steppe. The first ruler, Maḥmūd, was khan already by 1465, and by 1469 his brother Aḥmad was conducting numerous military campaigns. In 1469 Aḥmad attacked and killed Shaykh-Ḥaydār b. Abū'l-Khayr Khan, the ruler of the nomadic Uzbeks, and forced his son to flee to Astrakhan. He attacked Muscovite territory in 1468 and 1471, and sought to force Ivan III to reconfirm Russia's dependency to him, as nominal ruler of the Golden Horde. However, by 1480 Aḥmad was unable to force Ivan to submit to him, and the following year his forces were crushed in an attack led by the Siberian Shibanid Ībāq Khan and the Noghay *biys* Mūsā and Yamghurchï.[58] The sons of Aḥmad Khan proved unable to maintain the Great Horde. In 1502 a combined Crimean and Muscovite force destroyed the Great Horde once and for all.[59]

It is clear that the Great Horde ceased to exist after 1502, but the date for the emergence of a separate Khanate of Astrakhan is less clear. The descendants of Kichī-Muḥammad retained control over Astrakhan after his death. In 1466 Maḥmūd b. Kichī-Muḥammad had identified the area as his patrimony in a letter to the Ottoman sultan, Muḥammad II. Numismatic evidence further

56 Iskhakov, 1997, pp. 53–64.
57 Safargaliev, 1960, pp. 265, 267.
58 Safargaliev, 1960, p. 267.
59 Zaitsev, 2004, p. 58.

confirms Maḥmūd's position as khan at that time.[60] Later travellers' accounts identify the sons of Maḥmūd as khans in the city.

However, more recent scholarship maintains that the Khanate of Astrakhan did not exist as a separate khanate until after the destruction of the Great Horde in 1502, and that it is only identified in the sources as a separate khanate in 1505. I. V. Zaitsev suggests that until the 1480s Astrakhan was a constituent part of the Great Horde, evidently ruled by Maḥmūd Khan, and he argues that from the 1480s until 1502 it was in fact the capital of the Great Horde. After its destruction, the Khanate of Astrakhan emerged rather as a successor state of the Great Horde.[61] In characterizing the history of the 'independent' Khanate of Astrakhan in the sixteenth century, it is clear that its main political importance was as a dynastic seat and bone of contention between the Crimean Khanate, the Noghay Horde and, finally, Russia. This political and military weakness of the khans of Astrakhan is undoubtedly one reason that the dates and activities of these rulers are so faintly represented in the sources, when they are represented at all.

The first khan of Astrakhan after the collapse of the Great Horde was ʿAbd al-Karīm Khan b. Maḥmūd Khan, who ruled from 1502 until 1514. It is likely that he was in fact a nominal khan, with the real authority devolving to the Noghay ruler Yaghmurchï Biy, who had married one of Maḥmūd Khan's daughters. The main threat to ʿAbd al-Karīm Khan was the Crimean khan Menglī-Girāy, who evidently perceived the Astrakhan Khanate as simply a continuation of the Great Horde, and who launched an unsuccessful invasion of Astrakhan in 1509.[62] ʿAbd al-Karīm was succeeded by his brother Janïbek Khan b. Maḥmūd Khan (r. 1514–21), who also was dependent upon Noghay support. In 1523 the new Crimean khan, Muḥammad-Girāy b. Menglī-Girāy, launched an invasion of the Astrakhan Khanate in alliance with a Noghay chieftain named Mamāy. Muḥammad-Girāy managed to take the city, and as his forces were returning to the Crimea, the Noghay forces attacked them, pursuing them back to the Crimea, and killing Muḥammad-Girāy Khan. There is no reliable indication as to who was khan in Astrakhan at this time, but it may have been Janïbek's son Ḥusayn.[63] During the following three decades our information on the reigns, and even names, of the khans of Astrakhan is particularly sparse and contradictory. Nevertheless, this was also a period that witnessed an increase in the influence of the Crimean Khanate, and a gradual decline in the authority of

60 Marjānī, 1885–1900, I, p. 134; Safargaliev, 1960, p. 265.
61 Zaitsev, 2004, p. 61.
62 Zaitsev, 2004, pp. 69–70.
63 Zaitsev, 2004, pp. 92–3.

the Noghay Horde. It was characterized by a rapid succession of dynasts, both descendants of Aḥmad Khan and Maḥmūd Khan, as well as Islām-Girāy, the son of the former Crimean khan Muḥammad-Girāy.

During the 1530s and 1540s the main contending powers were still the Noghays, who were able to exert power to the degree that their internal affairs were stable, the Crimean Khanate, and 'Circassians' (Cherkes), inhabitants of the North Caucasus who were able to exert military pressure as far as Astrakhan.[64] Indeed, the Astrakhan Khanate was dependent on Noghay support to the very end, and in 1556, with the acquiescence of the Noghay *biy* Ismāʿīl, the Russians occupied and annexed Astrakhan without any serious opposition.

The Crimean Khanate

The Crimean Khanate was the most enduring of the Chinggisid successor states, forming in the first half of the fifteenth century, and remaining in the hands of the Giray dynasty until its annexation by the Russian Empire in 1783. After 1475 the khanate was a vassal of Ottoman Turkey, and over the nearly three centuries of its existence, the southern coast of the Crimean peninsula was gradually integrated as a province of the Ottoman Empire. Unlike the other Golden Horde successor states in western Inner Asia, the history of the Crimean Khanate is particularly well documented. In the seventeenth and eighteenth centuries Crimean and Ottoman historians compiled several narrative histories of the Giray dynasty that emphasize the Chinggisid credentials of the Girays.[65] In addition throughout much of this period the Crimea retained close cultural ties with Istanbul and the Mediterranean world. In dynastic terms the Crimean Khanate can also be considered the most internally stable of the Chinggisid successor states. While subordinate to the Ottoman Empire for much of its history, its rulers nevertheless maintained a semi-independent foreign policy, especially in the fifteenth and sixteenth centuries.

The political structure of the Crimean Khanate was dominated by an aristocracy consisting of the royal family and its dependants, and the tribal aristocracy. The Crimean Khanate maintained a political structure characteristic of the Mongol Empire as a whole and of its successor states, but that is particularly

64 Trepavlov, 2001b, p. 220.

65 The most extensive of these histories is the eighteenth-century *As-sab' as-sayyār* of Sayyid-Muḥammad Riżā, printed in Kazan, in 1832. We can also list among these the anonymous *Tawarikh-i dasht-i qipchaq* compiled in the seventeenth century, and published in 1966, as Zajączkowski, 1966.

well documented in the historiography of the Crimean Khanate. In this system, together with the ruling house, there were four royal tribes, known as *qarachï*, that were each headed by a figure known as a *qarachï bek*. It was this council of four *qarachï beks*, headed by the *bash-qarachï*, who commonly maintained the power to elevate the khan to the throne. In the Crimea these four tribes, in order of seniority, were the Shirin, Barïn, Arghïn and Qïpchaq. Later sources identify a fifth tribe, the Manghït. The bulk of the khanate's military forces came from these tribes. The internal politics of the Crimean Khanate throughout its existence was dominated by a three-way struggle between the dynasts of the ruling family, the tribal aristocracy and the Ottomans.[66]

The Girays were a Togha-Timurid family descended from Tāsh-Tīmūr Khan, who had ruled briefly as khan of the Golden Horde in 1395. The first member of this family to rule in the Crimea was Dawlat-Berdī b. Tāsh-Tīmūr, who was proclaimed khan of the Golden Horde in 1426, but whose actual realm was the Crimean peninsula and some adjacent areas. By 1428 he had been able to conquer Astrakhan, but soon lost all of his territories, including the Crimea, to Ulugh Muḥammad and probably died in the same year.[67] Ulugh Muḥammad remained in the Crimea, contending with his rival Kichī-Muḥammad, until 1437, when he left, and ultimately founded the Kazan Khanate. During the 1430s several other Chinggisids were contending for the throne in the Crimea. They included Dawlat-Berdī's nephew, Ḥājji-Giray Khan b. Ghiyās ad-Din b. Tāsh-Tīmūr, who had been in exile in Lithuania, and was evidently proclaimed khan by the tribal aristocracy in the Crimea.[68] Ḥājji-Giray's reign lasted until about 1460, during which time the Ottoman sultan Muḥammad II conquered Constantinople, shifting the balance of power along the Black Sea coast. Ḥājji-Giray, and later his fifteenth- and sixteenth-century successors, were certainly involved in the military and political struggles of the Black Sea littoral that involved the Ottomans and Genoese, among others. But at the same time dynastic imperatives resulted in a strong desire to gain control of the throne of the Golden Horde in the Lower Volga region, called *takht il* in some Crimean sources, signifying 'the territory of the throne'.

The era of Ottoman hegemony over the Crimean Khanate is commonly established as beginning in 1478, the year when Menglī-Girāy established himself as khan with the help of an Ottoman fleet. Seventeenth- and eighteenth-century Crimean sources, written at a time when the Crimea

66 Inalcik, 1979–80; Manz, 1978.
67 Safargaliev, 1960, pp. 233–4.
68 Safargaliev, 1960, pp. 242–3.

had become much more firmly integrated into the Ottoman Empire, described a 'treaty' between Menglī-Girāy and Muḥammad II. Whatever the formal agreement he reached with Muḥammad it is clear that over the following century the Crimean khans, while offering military support to Ottoman campaigns along the Black Sea coast, staked substantial resources, and occasionally their lives, in military campaigns and adventures involving the Astrakhan Khanate, the Noghay Horde and the Kazan Khanate. In addition, while the sedentary southern coastal regions were administratively and economically more integrated into the Ottoman Empire, in the northern steppe regions pastoral nomads and their political elites remained integrated in steppe politics. Thus, we have seen how in 1509 Menglī-Girāy led an attack against ʿAbd al-Karīm, the khan of Astrakhan, resulting in a disastrous defeat for the Crimeans.[69] In 1523 during another campaign against Astrakhan his successor Muḥammad-Girāy Khan b. Menglī-Girāy was killed and his army dispersed by his erstwhile Noghay allies.[70] Similarly, Crimean dynasts occupied the throne in the Khanate of Kazan. Ṣāḥib-Girāy Khan b. Menglī-Girāy first reigned as khan there, before returning to assume the Crimean throne (r. 1532–51) and waging campaigns both against the Noghays, and in support of the Ottomans in Moldavia. He was also credited with the establishment of a genuine Muslim city in the Crimean capital Bakhchisarai, including the building of mosques, baths and a palace. One eighteenth-century Crimean historian also credits him with sedentarizing the nomads, and dividing agricultural lands amongst them.[71]

Following the Russian conquest of Kazan and Astrakhan, and the weakening and later disintegration of the Noghay Horde, the Crimean Khanate's primary political concerns became its relations with the Ottoman Empire and, increasingly, with Russia. Ṣāḥib-Girāy's successor, Dawlat-Girāy Khan b. Mubārak-Girāy (r. 1551–77), remained active in steppe politics, supported Sultan Selim II's campaign against Astrakhan, and tried in vain to sustain the existence of the Kazan Khanate. During the late sixteenth and seventeenth centuries Crimean military forces regularly took part in Ottoman campaigns, not only along the Black Sea coast, but in the Balkans, Hungary and Persia. At the same time, Slavic settlement of the steppe increasingly brought the Crimeans into conflict with the Zaporozhian and Don Cossacks, although even here the relationship was complex. For instance in 1648 Crimean forces offered a degree of support to Bogdan Khmel'nitskii's Cossack rebellion

69 Jaubert, 1833, pp. 353–4.
70 Jaubert, 1833, pp. 360–1.
71 Jaubert, 1833, pp. 366–7.

against Poland. During the seventeenth century there was a rapid succession of dynasts, largely installed and deposed by the Ottomans. By the beginning of the eighteenth century the Ottoman Empire was rapidly losing territory around the Black Sea to Russia, and in the 1730s Russian forces repeatedly invaded the Crimea. By 1770 the Russians had isolated the Crimean khans from the political remnants of the Noghay Horde which remained on the Black Sea steppe. The khanate remained nominally independent until 1783, when the Empress Catherine II annexed the Crimea to Russia.

The Kasimov Khanate

Unlike the other successor states that emerged on the basis of regional power centres that had constituted the territory of the Golden Horde, the Kasimov Khanate was entirely a Muscovite creation designed to host friendly Chinggisid dynasts and their military supporters, and provide legitimate dynasts who could be placed on the thrones of rival Chinggisid states.[72] To be sure, some Golden Horde successor states did emerge as, or evolve into, puppet states of more powerful Chinggisid states. The Astrakhan Khanate was clearly subordinate to Noghay power, and the Crimean Khanate became an Ottoman vassal state in 1478. However, while the independence of dynasts in those states *vis-à-vis* their suzerains is subject to debate, the same cannot be said under any circumstances regarding the khans of Kasimov, who remained under tight Russian control from the khanate's founding in 1467 until its final dissolution in 1694. The founder of the khanate was Qāsim b. Ulugh Muḥammad, to whom the Grand Prince of Muscovy, Vasilii III, granted the town of Gorodets, on the Oka River after Qāsim's brother, Maḥmūd, was enthroned as sovereign of the Kazan Khanate. The city then became known in Russian sources as Kasimov, and in Muslim sources as Khan Kirmān, or simply Kirmān. Qāsim's son, Dāniyār, succeeded his father, probably in 1469. By 1486 the throne had passed to a member of the Crimean Giray dynasty, first Nūr-Dawlat b. Ḥajjī-Giray, whose brother, Menglī-Girāy, occupied the Crimean throne, and then to two of Nūr-Dawlat's sons. By 1512 the throne had passed to another dynasty, this time from Astrakhan, beginning with Allāh-Yār Khan, a descendant of Temür Khan b. Kichī-Muḥammad. Allāh-Yār's sons, Shāh ʿAlī and Jān-ʿAlī, alternated the throne several times after 1516, and Shāh ʿAlī and his troops played an important role in the Kazan Khanate, ruling as khan in Kazan on

72 Our main source remains Vel'iaminov-Zernov 1864–8; cf. also Howorth, 1880, pp. 429–47. The main Muslim sources on this dynasty are: Marjānī, 1885–1900, I, pp. 139–48; Fäyezkhanov, 2006, pp. 242–52.

three separate occasions. After the fall of Kazan, Kasimov's dynasts figure only marginally in Russia's relations with the surviving Chinggisid states. The significance of the Kasimov Khanate for our understanding of the successor states of the Golden Horde is indeed quite disproportionate to its political power. During the seventeenth century it was precisely in Kasimov that the tradition of Chinggisid court historiography survived, leaving important works such as the *Jāmiʿat-tavārīkh* of Qādir-ʿAlī-Bek Jālāyirī (1602) and the *Daftar-i Chingīz Nāma* (c. 1680).

14

Eastern Central Asia (Xinjiang): 1300–1800

JAMES MILLWARD

The history of eastern Central Asia – a region also known as Moghulistan, Eastern Turkestan, Chinese Turkestan, Xinjiang and by a variety of other historical names – is more than usually influenced by geography and environment. Generally speaking, the northern half (the slopes of the Tianshan and plains and desert of the Zungharian Basin) suits horse breeding and nomadism; to the south, oases of the Tarim and Turfan basins provide fertile farmland, urban religious centres and a chain of commercial entrepots. As a result of this geography, southern Xinjiang was, since long before the Chinggisid age, a prime target for nomadic conquerors who coveted the grain, tax and tribute revenue available from the oases and who on the strength of their cavalry were easily able to dominate the peoples settled in the oasis towns.

In this regard, the pattern of nomadic-settled relations in eastern Central Eurasia resembles that of western Central Eurasia (Transoxania), with which its politics and ruling families were often linked. From the fourteenth to the sixteenth centuries, the frontiers of Moghulistan (land of the Moghuls, or the Islamized Turko-Mongol tribes of the east) ranged across what is now northern Xinjiang, Eastern Kazakhstan and Kyrgyzstan, depending on the fortunes of the khans and those of the Uzbeks, Qazaqs, Qïrghïz and Oirats ('Qalmaqs') moving into those same pastures. From these pastures, and especially the Issyk Kul area, Ferghana and Kashgharia (Altisharh, the Tarim Basin) could be raided and ruled, as could Uyghuristan (the Turfan Basin). However, despite some episodes when one power held cities and agrarian centres on both sides of the Pamirs, it proved difficult to maintain trans-Pamir political unity for long.

The region that is now Xinjiang differed from Transoxania in that it often faced a great power to the east. Moreover, relations between China and eastern Central Eurasia followed a recurring pattern: regimes based in North China, when engaged in struggles with nomadic states in Mongolia or Zungharia, attempted to control the Gansu Corridor, Hami and Turfan and if possible to extend power further into the Tarim Basin in order to block their rivals' access to the grain and wealth of the oases. This had been the case during the Han (206 BCE – 220 CE) and Tang (618–907) dynasties. The Mongol Empire at first transcended the pattern by unifying North China, Mongolia and Central Eurasia; after the seizure of the Great Khanship by the Toluids (1251), however, eastern Central Eurasia again became a locus of competition and struggle between China-based and steppe-based powers: from China, Qubilai cut off grain shipments and tried but failed to conquer the Tarim Basin in an effort to undermine his steppe-based rival, Arigh Böke. Despite its relatively weak military capacity, the Chinese Ming dynasty (1368–1644) opened channels to Central Eurasian princes and fought remaining Chaghatayids over Turfan and Hami. The far stronger Qing dynasty (1644–1911) expanded deep into Central Eurasia in the course of its rivalry with the Zunghars. In the Qing case, the combination of Inner Asian nomad cavalry and post-Chinggisid political ideology with Chinese agrarian wealth and bureaucratic capacity helped the Manchu rulers overcome, to an extent, geographic constraints and lay the groundwork for Chinese rule over eastern Central Eurasia that has lasted, with interruptions, for the past 250 years.

The Moghul Khanate (1300s–1680)

The long decline of the Chinggisids was especially fraught in eastern Central Eurasia, where even at the height of the Chinggisid Empire Chaghatayid rule had been ambiguous and unstable. The drawn-out unravelling of Mongol rule across Eurasia led to centuries of complex internecine conflict, a story made more challenging to tell for this region by the limited sources available from before the Qing period. Perhaps out of despair, many historians have treated the period of Central Eurasian history between the Mongol and the modern empires as one long slough of despond. Beyond all the military vicissitudes, however, these centuries saw great social, political and economic changes. These may be characterized as a set of dynamics: between Islam and 'infidel'; steppe pastoralism and urban agrarian society; high Islamo-Persian culture of western Central Eurasia and the Turko-Mongolian culture of the nomads in the eastern steppes; Chinggisid khans and non-Chinggisid amirs; old tribal confederations and new groups; and nomad-type empires and empires based in the agrarian states of the Eurasian rimlands. Against the background of geographic and environmental influences, these cross-cutting and interacting dynamics led to changes of great moment for later times, and even for the present day.

Several events in the fourteenth century mark the onset of the major cultural and political shifts of the period we consider in this chapter: the division of the Chaghatayids, the Islamization of eastern Central Eurasia, and the rise of new peoples and powers.

The khan Tarmashirin's (r. *c.* 1331–4)[1] conversion to Islam precipitated a split in the Chaghatayids: while his own successors carried on in the west, the Buddhist, Christian and shamanist tribes to the east established a new khanal line in what came to be known as Moghulistan (*ulus-i Moghul*)[2] and Kashgharia.[3] The religious division did not hold, however, as one of the first of the Moghul khans, Tughluq Temür (1347/8–1362/3), famously converted under the influence of the shaykh Jamā ad-Dīn and his son Arshad ad-Dīn, reportedly bringing 160,000 followers with him. Kim Ho-dong has argued that Tughluq Temür adopted Islam as a centralizing ideology to help him consolidate power. This was necessary because, increasingly, in both eastern and western Central Eurasia, the Chaghatayids competed for power in an environment crowded not only with their own relatives but also with powerful non-Chinggisid amirs. While Temür (Tamerlane; r. 1370–1405) of the Barlas clan rose in the west, it was the Dughlat family, with a power base in the Tarim Basin cities, who served as king-makers in Moghulistan. They had raised Tughluq to the khanship, but could also take power in their own right. In 1365 Qamar al-Dīn murdered Tughluq's successor and seventeen other Chaghatayid princes, attempting to assume the title of khan for himself. Though never legitimate in Moghul eyes, he remained in power in the east for over twenty years, until Temür's invasions of Moghulistan in the 1370s and 1380s broke Qamar and set the other Dughlat families looking for new Chaghatayid candidates to unify them in resistance to Temür. The candidate who succeeded, Khiḍr Khwāja, also conquered Qarashahr and Turfan to the east, thus furthering the process of Islamization of 'Uyghuristan'. Khiḍr also married a daughter to Temür, allowing the latter to take the prestigious title of 'son-in-law' (i.e. of a Chinggisid khan). Despite suffering another destructive raid in 1399–1400, when Temür's grandson attacked Kashghar, Yarkand

1 Tarmashirin's dates are not precisely known. For a discussion of his career and the reasons for his relative obscurity, see Biran, 2002b.

2 The variant spelling 'Mughal' is used for the dynastic line established by Babur Padishah (1483–1530) in India. Babur's mother, Qutlugh Nigar Khanim, was the daughter of Yunus Khan of Moghulistan, but Babur and his successors stressed his paternal descent and thus considered themselves Timurids. Nevertheless, the northern Indian population referred to their rulers as Moghuls (i.e. 'Mongols') and Europeans began applying the term in the sixteenth century, hence our 'Mughal'. See W. M. Thackston, 'Editor's Preface', in Dūghlāt/Thackston, ix.

3 Ho-dong Kim distinguishes between Moghulistan, a geographical term, and *ulus-i Moghul*, which indicated the polity. The *Tarikh-i-Rashidi* uses the Mongolian term 'Mangalay Sübe' ('strategic point to the front') for the cities of the western Tarim Basin, which are also known as Kashgharia and, somewhat later, Altishahr. Kim, 1999, p. 290 n. 1, p. 300 n. 42.

and Aqsu, Khiḍr Khwāja's reign imposed a measure of stability, and the affairs of the Dughlat amirs prospered.[4]

Then in the spring of 1405, with the mares foaling in Moghulistan, an ambassador arrived from the west. The Dughlat amir Khudāydād had just offered a ceremonial first cup of kumis to Khiḍr Khwāja, the Chaghatayid khan who owed both his life and his khanship to Khudāydād. But the ambassador's news was dire: Tamerlane had mounted a massive invasion, bound for Khitay, and would require the Moghuls to pay tribute and supply his army as it crossed their lands. Khiḍr Khwāja spilled his kumis. Yet before the khan had time to reflect further, another rider, clad all in white, spurred a black horse past the guards straight through the camp to where the khan was sitting and shouted, 'Amir Timur is dead!' Having delivered this second momentous message of the day, the mysterious rider galloped off.[5]

One may speculate as to the likelihood of Tamerlane's success against the Ming dynasty in China, but the impact of his armies' passage through Moghulistan would certainly have been weighty and immediate. His death and the curtailment of his campaign meant that the eastern and western Chaghatayid lands would not be reunited, and eastern Central Eurasia would remain until the mid-eighteenth century an intermediate political space, an arena for internecine struggles and an opportunity for new powers. Mīrzā Muḥammad Ḥaydar (1499–1551), the scion of the Dughlat clan who relates the anecdote of Khiḍr's spilled kumis, understood this marginality: 'The Moghuls have become a most isolated and paltry people. No one but a Moghul could be interested in this history.'[6]

So he wrote in 1547, as he finished the narrative that provides our best source for the fourteenth to mid-sixteenth centuries. Nor is his modesty entirely misplaced: the endless battles and betrayals which comprise the bulk of his narrative hold little interest for today's reader. However, his *Tārīkh-i Rashīdī* also illuminates the urgent cultural concerns of his milieu during a transitional era. Despite a history of close relations with Transoxania, and even a century after Tughluq Temür's conversion, the Moghuls, Dughlats and other families to the east were still seen by western Chaghatayids and Timurids as boorish

4 Barthold, 1956–62, 1, p. 144; Dūghlāt/Ross, pp. 51–2. There is another English translation of the *Tarikh-i Rashidi*: Mirza Haydar Dughlat, *Tarikh-i-Rashidi: A History of the Khans of Moghulistan*, Persian text edited by W. M. Thackston, English trans. and annotation by W. M. Thackston. Sources of Oriental Languages and Literatures 37 and 38 (Cambridge, Mass: Harvard University, Department of Near Eastern Languages and Civilizations, 1996). Hereafter I will cite these translations as Ross, *TR* and Thackston, *TR*. All direct quotations from Ross, *TR* unless otherwise noted.

5 The anecdote appears in Ross, *TR*, pp. 53–4; Thackston, *TR*, p. 29.

6 Ross, *TR*, p. 148; Thackston, *TR*, p. 85.

country cousins. For example, Ulugh Beg (*c.* 1393/4–1449), Timurid patron of arts and sciences and ruler of Samarqand, once asked a supplicant from the east if there were donkeys in Kashghar. 'Since the Chaghatai [i.e. Moghuls] have come', the man replied, 'there are a great number of donkeys'. Though intimately related with those very 'donkeys', many of the Dughlats and some Moghuls sought to distinguish themselves from the nomads. When Ulugh Beg asked the Dughlat Amir Khudāydād to teach him the law code of Chinggis Khan, Khudāydād agreed to do so if Ulugh Beg insisted, but hastened to point out that he had himself embraced *Sharīʿa* and no longer observed the *jasaq* (*törä*, Chinggisid legal code).[7]

Some years later, the Mughal khan Muḥammad Dost (r. 1461/2–1468/9) caused a scandal when he sought to marry one of his deceased father's wives (his own step-mother). One by one the khan requested seven ʿulamāʾ to condone the marriage, and when each refused, he had them executed. The eighth, a learned Sufi, finally replied that 'for such a one as you it is lawful', and the marriage went ahead; however, the dervish had merely meant that since Muḥammad Dost was obviously an infidel, he could lawfully 'marry his mother'. After his father berated him in a dream for this act, Muḥammad Dost, we are told, died an early and painful death as a result of his apostasy. But of course, Muḥammad Dost was simply following the old Mongol custom.[8]

Even in the early sixteenth century, when the pious Manṣūr Khan supposedly spent four-fifths of his time reciting the Koran and only one-fifth governing, the best Koran teacher he could find was a known reprobate whom the khan's advisers openly accused of bestiality. '"I'm learning the Koran from him", Mansur could only reply, "not how to fuck cows"'.[9]

These examples reveal the culture clash, or at least transition, playing out among the Moghuls: Eastern Turkestan lay across a fluid frontier between a settled, urbane, Persianate and self-consciously Islamized society of urban Central Asia on the one hand, and the camps of the nomadic khans and their followers on the other. The latter, while quite rapidly absorbing the Islam brought to them by Sufi shaykhs and miracle-workers, also still hearkened back to the days of Chinggis Khan for cultural as well as political legitimacy. The Chaghatayid and Dughlat lineages in Moghulistan and Kashgharia, Mīrzā Ḥaydar's relatives, included people on both sides of that physical and cultural frontier.

The khan Yunus (r. 1416–87) is particularly interesting as a bridging figure. A prince who lost out in a struggle for succession in Moghulistan to his brother

7 Ross, *TR*, pp. 69–70, 76; Thackston, *TR*, pp. 37–8, 41.
8 Ross, *TR*, pp. 89–90; Thackston, *TR*, pp. 47–8.
9 Thackston, *TR*, p. 71 (Ross, *TR*, p. 129 elects not to translate the passage).

Isen Bugha (r. 1432–1461/2), Yunus spent his youth under the protection of the Timurid Shahrukh and the tutelage of Sharaf al-Dīn Alī Yazdī, author of the famous *Ẓafar nāmah*, a panegyric of Temür. Yunus's years of study in Yazd, in central Iran, followed by travels through Persia and Iraq, gave Yunus the courtly graces that later surprised a cleric who had expected him to be a 'beardless… Turk of the desert'. So impressed was the cleric by this meeting that he is said to have enjoined neighbouring sultans no longer to enslave Moghuls, since 'they are people of Islam'. Yet when Yunus later returned to Moghulistan, he faced the opposite form of discrimination: as he struggled against rivals for the khanship, the Moghul amirs first joined him and then betrayed him. This, they explained, was because 'he had always tried to make them settle in towns and cultivated countries… places… hateful to them'. By forswearing urban life henceforth himself, Yunus restored his amirs' loyalty and went on to consolidate control over Moghulistan and add Turfan to the Moghul lands. Nevertheless, he achieved this only with continued support from the Timurids in Transoxania, and he would spend the end of his days in Tashkent.[10] He thus led his life partly in elegant cities, partly in felt tents on the steppe – as one might expect of Babur's maternal grandfather.

Cultural tensions alone do not account for the turmoil in the region under the Moghuls. Rather, the primary explanation was structural and environmental, as identified by Mīrzā Ḥaydar himself, who observed that 'agriculture is laborious and bears little produce. In Kashghar it is impossible to maintain an army on one harvest.'[11] In the fragmented and competitive political environment of the Tarim Basin in the fourteenth to eighteenth centuries, personal armies were necessary. But since the revenue from these cities and their farms could not keep followers happy and loyal, ambitious khans, sultans and amirs[12] repeatedly raided each other's cities as well as neighbouring states in the Pamirs, Kashmir, Ferghana and the western frontiers of China in order to secure loot with which to reward their chiefs.[13] Hence the successive battles between brothers, uncles and cousins that dominate this era.

There were, however, a few exceptional periods of longer, relatively stable reigns. Yunus's was one such; another occurred after 1514, when Yunus's grandson Sultan-Saʿīd, despite having claimed khanship in his own right in the

10 Ross, *TR*, pp. 74, 85, 95, 97–8, 115; Thackston, *TR*, pp. 40, 45, 50–2. Yunus was the maternal grandfather of Babur Padishah (1483–1530), founder of the Mughal Empire in South Asia (see the genealogical tables in Thackston, 'Editor's Preface', pp. xii, xiv).

11 Quotation from Thackston, *TR*, p. 192 (Ross, *TR*, p. 303).

12 In *TR* and other Islamic sources, 'khan' and 'sultan' refer to Chinggisids, 'amir' to eminent members of other clans.

13 Wei Liangtao makes this point in Wei, 1996, p. 388.

western Tarim Basin,[14] concluded a treaty with his elder brother Manṣūr Khan (r. 1501/2–1543) who ruled Moghulistan and Turfan. Thanks to their arrangement, which lasted until Saʿīd's death in 1533, 'there was such security and prosperity among the people that it was possible to travel from Qamul [Hami] in China to the province of Ferghana without provisions or escort and without any fear or difficulty'.[15] Likewise, though involved in frequent skirmishes with Qazaqs and Qïrghïz, from the 1570s until 1610, the khans ʿAbd al-Karīm Khān (r. 1559/60–1591/2) and Muḥammad Khān (1591/2–1609/10) unified the area south of the Tianshan, the latter ruling Yarkand, Kashghar, Aqsu, Ush, Kuche, Qarashahr (Jalish), Turfan and Hami – that is, the entire Tarim and Turfan basins.[16]

During such relatively tranquil periods – and indeed, even at other times – trade caravans passed with some frequency to and from China.[17] Even skirmishes over Hami did not always prevent the Ming from trading with the Moghuls and other Central Asians. However, our understanding of this trade and of the Xinjiang region's east–west linkages have been distorted by two historiographical paradigms: the practice of calling Ming trade 'tribute' and the notion that post-Mongol Central Eurasia suffered near total economic collapse due to anarchy and the sixteenth-century rise of direct maritime connections between Europe and Asia. From the early fifteenth century through the dynasty's fall in 1644, the Ming received foreign missions from Central Asia and the Islamic world, emissaries who came to '*jingong*' – 'present *gong*'. The term *gong* has been translated into English as 'tribute', though the actual ceremony involved an exchange of gifts between a Chinese court and an independent state (or merchants masquerading as official representatives of a foreign monarch), rather than a rendering up of forced payments by a vassal to

14 For modern Chinese scholars, Sultan-Saʿīd's accession to the throne in Kashghar in August or September 1514 inaugurates the 'Yarkand Khanate', which they distinguish as a distinct polity from the line of the Moghuls. In Uyghur language materials from the PRC, this polity is called *Sä'idiyä Khandanliq*, the Saʿīdiyya Khanate. On the other hand, *TR*, our main source on these events, treats both Saʿīd Khan and his son and successor Abdul-Rashid Khan, as well as Manṣūr Khan and his son and successor Shah Khan, as all as legitimate continuations of the Moghul line, with one branch ruling in Kashgharia and another in Turfan and Jalish (Qarashahr).

15 Quotation from Thackston, *TR*, p. 75 (Ross, *TR*, p. 134).

16 Wei, 1996, p. 393, citing Shah Maḥmūd Churās, *Khronika* (Russian trans. of the Persian text *Shāh Maḥmūd ibn Mirza Fazil Churas-i tarikh*), trans. O. F. Akimushkina. Pamiatniki Pis'mennosti Vostoka, 45 (Moscow: Izdatel'stvo Nauka, Glavnaia Redaktsiia Vostochnoi Literatury, 1976), p. 177.

17 A chronological table listing envoys from Central Asia to the Ming may be found in Watanabe, 'Index', pp. 285–347. Note that in the title 1466 should read 1644. Wei Liangtao discusses trade and diplomatic relations between eastern Chaghatayids and the Ming in Wei, 1996, pp. 381–6.

a Chinese Caesar. In fact, the gifts from the Chinese side were often the more lavish. Most important, the diplomatic missions were generally accompanied by trade caravans with entourages of merchants who traded for Chinese goods either in frontier markets or in Beijing. The term *jingong* thus implies both a foreign embassy and an associated trade-fair. China specialists, for unknown reasons, continue to call these 'tribute missions' or 'tributary trade', knowing full well that they were anything but; scholars in other fields should not be fooled. The Ming *Veritable Records* (*Shilu*) logs 766 embassies arriving overland from Central Asia during the Ming period (1368–1644); the fifteenth century was busier than later, but for 1536 we learn of 150 'princes' reaching Beijing from Mecca, Samarqand, Turfan and elsewhere, and even in the century following Mansur's death (1544), the twilight of the Ming, there were seventy-seven missions.[18] Most of these, such as the one licensed by Muḥammad Khan in Yarkand in 1604 which the Jesuit lay-brother Bento de Goes joined and described, passed through the Tarim Basin cities, and many were channelled through Hami.[19]

Though the question of overall economic 'decline' in Central Asia involves more than simply commerce across southern Xinjiang,[20] the evidence suggests on-going, albeit fluctuating, caravan trade along these routes, from the fifteenth to the seventeenth centuries. As will be seen below, moreover, both trade linking the oases with the steppes and that between China and Central Eurasia would increase in the seventeenth to nineteenth centuries with the coming of the Zunghar, Russian and Qing empires.

The Makhdūmzādas and the Zunghars

During the sixteenth and seventeenth centuries new tribal confederations and other powerful groups arose, resulting eventually in the total eclipse of the Chaghatayids. The Qazaq confederation formed in the steppes north of the Syr Darya, in Semirech'e, and Zungharia. The Qïrghïz, mountain nomads, occupied the valleys of the Pamirs, the Tianshan and the Issyk Kul area. The Oirats (known in Islamic sources as Qalmaqs) gathered power on the steppe further east, occasionally warring with Moghul rulers. From these Oirat tribes the Zunghar confederation and empire would emerge by the early seventeenth century. Thus other peoples occupied the steppelands that had

18 Based on tables in Watanabe, 'Index', pp. 289–326. See also Rossabi, 1972.
19 On Goes's journey, see Wessels, 1924, p. 25.
20 For a history of and challenge to the early modern Silk Road 'decline' thesis, see Levi, 1999.

comprised the core of Moghulistan, and the Moghuls, despite Yunus's promise never to do so, gradually sedentarized, turning into local landed nobility in the Tarim Basin.

Meanwhile, the Dughlats lost their prominence. Their role of associate, king-maker and occasional rival to the remaining Chaghatayids was ultimately taken up by members of the Naqshbandī Sufi order. Followers of the activist reform movement launched by Baha᾽ ad-Dīn Naqshband (1318–89) from Bukhara, these Sufi masters, known as *khwājas* (*khojas*), threw themselves into political affairs, advising khans and sultans, marrying into ruling clans, acquiring large land holdings and promoting Islamic rule. One, Khwāja Tajuddin (Taj ad-Dīn), died (*c.* 1533) fighting the Ming for Mansur Khan.[21]

It was the descendants and disciples of the Naqshbandī master Makhdūm-i A᾽ẓam ('Great Master', also known as Ahmad Kasani; 1461–1542) who had the most impact on the history of eastern Central Eurasia. Makhdūmzāda miracle-workers and spiritual advisers entered the Tarim Basin at the start of the seventeenth century, and soon established themselves in the south-west under Muḥammad Khan (r. 1592–1609). Ultimately two competing lines of Makhdūmzāda saints emerged, the Isḥāqiyya (also called *Qara taghliq* 'Black Mountain') and Āfāqiyya (*Aq taghliq* 'White Mountain') and engaged in a bloody rivalry. Soon after assuming power in 1670, Ismāʿīl, the last Chaghadayid khan, drove Khwāja Āfāq out of Kashghar at the urging of the Isḥāqiyya. Āfāq fled south, where he paid a call on the 'Shaykh of the Brahmans' (that is, the fifth Dalai Lama, 1617–82): whether or not the Sufi bested the lama in a magic contest (as Āfāq's hagiography claims), he did gain the latter's support against the Isḥāqiyya. The Dalai Lama wrote to Galdan, whom around this time he would designate '*boshoqtu khan*' of the Zunghar confederation of Oirat Mongols, and invited him to help Khwāja Āfāq return to Kashgharia. This the Zunghars did in 1678–80 by seizing the Tarim and Turfan basins, installing the Khwājas and remnant Moghul aristocracy (the latter known as *begs*)[22] as local authorities, and requiring of them an annual payment: this was a 'tribute' worthy of the name, with the city of Kashghar alone liable for over 40,000 silver ounces, labour *corvées* and large quantities of grain, cotton and saffron annually.[23] Thus the Zunghars became overlords of the Tarim Basin, in the old pattern of rule from the north. Following Galdan's death in the early eighteenth century, Āfāqī *khwājas* together with members of the old Moghul clans rebelled and

21 Ross, *TR*, p. 127; Thackston, *TR*, p. 70.
22 Kim, 2004, pp. 11–12 n. 50.
23 Figure from the *Tazkira-i Khwājagan*, cited in Shaw, 1897. Qing sources give a similar figure. See Millward, 2007, p. 92 and n. 22 for a discussion of the issue.

temporarily ousted the Zunghars, but Tsewang Rabdan (d. 1727) later restored Zunghar rule. The Zunghars had displaced the Chaghatayids as khans in eastern Central Eurasia.[24]

The rise of the Zunghars is a noteworthy watershed. On the one hand, with its clan politics, herds of livestock and cavalry-based warfare the Zunghar state resembled the long line of steppe-based empires that preceded it in Eurasian history, many of which had ruled over the Tarim Basin from pastures north of the Tianshan. On the other hand, as the early chiefs of the Zunghar tribe, especially Batur Hongtayiji (r. 1635–53), worked to forge a broader confederation in the middle decades of the seventeenth century, they did several things that on the surface do not fit the stereotype of a Central Eurasian state, although we can find precedents for most of them in former early nomad and Turko-Mongol political formations. They invested in agriculture, resettling farmers from the Tarim Basin to river valleys north of the Tianshan; they opened and worked mines; they brought in artisans from their urban-agrarian neighbours to cast weapons, draw maps, and work metal, stone and wood; they even built towns, mainly trading centres but also a fortress with stone walls six metres high. They acquired religious legitimacy and clerical expertise from the Tibetan Buddhist church; the itinerant monk Zaya Pandita (1599–1662), an adoptive son of an Oirat khan, developed the script used for the western Mongolian dialect. They fostered diplomatic and trade relationships with Tibet, Russia and the Qing. In short, their bid for power in Central Eurasia was based on more than military might and a noble Chinggisid lineage – the latter of which they lacked in any case (Galdan received his 'khan' title from the Dalai Lama).[25]

The Zunghar bid for a Central Eurasian empire came at a significant moment. For the first time since Tamerlane, large powerful empires were extending power across Central Eurasia: the Muscovites were coming east, the Manchus were moving across Mongolia and conquering China. Wielding a different form of power, the Gelugpa church under the Dalai Lamas was consolidating control over Tibetan areas and proselytizing and forging military alliances among Mongol tribes. It was a time when the various Oirat and Khalkha Mongol tribes saw potential advantages in unification. At a grand

24 On the *khwājas* in Xinjiang, see Shaw, 1897; Fletcher, 1995; Schwarz, 1976; and Papas, 2005. On Khwāja Āfāq's meeting with the fifth Dalai Lama, the source is Muḥammad Sadiq's *Tazkira-i Khwājagan*; see Shaw, 1897, and Zarcone, 1996.

25 Principal accounts of the Zunghars are Zlatkin, 1983; Bergholz, 1993; and Miyawaki, 1995. Most recently, Perdue, 2005, a detailed military and economic history of the Qing Zunghar campaigns in Mongolia, Xinjiang, Qinghai and Tibet, casts the Zunghar story as parallel to the empire-building efforts of Russia and the Qing.

quriltai in 1640 they agreed to adopt Tibetan Buddhism and to systematize measures to avoid conflict and provide mutual protection. But neither then nor over the next fifty years would the Zunghars succeed in attaching the Eastern Mongols, by persuasion or force, to their confederation. Moreover, Zunghar control over the western Mongols always remained tenuous. Already as the Zunghars rose in the early seventeenth century, the Khoshuud tribe had fled the intra-Oirat struggles north of the Tianshan for Kokonor (Qinghai). The Torghut tribe had likewise decamped west to the banks of the Volga River (some Torghuts would return east again in 1771). The 1640 *quriltai* did not result in a unified Mongol resistance to rising Qing or Russia.

After his conquest of the Tarim Basin, Galdan's attempts in the late 1680s and 1690s to expand eastwards succeeded merely in driving the Khalkhas into Qing protection and goading the Kangxi emperor into launching a personal vendetta against the Zunghar khan. Thanks to a combination of logistical ability and luck, the Qing just managed to catch up with and destroy Galdan and his much diminished force in 1696.[26] Over the next six decades, the Qing–Zunghar rivalry played out over a broad front extending from Tibet through Kokonor to Mongolia. As had frequently been the case in previous conflicts between powers based in North China and those in Inner Asia, the Urumchi–Turfan–Hami area was a particular hot-spot. Meanwhile, from their base north of the Tianshan range, the Zunghars fought off and on with Russians and Qazaqs and in 1723 raided Tashkent and other Transoxania cities.

The Zunghars also capitalized on their geographic position between China and Transoxania to promote the east–west caravan trade and trade with Tibet. As usual for Central Eurasian powers in their position, when not engaged in outright hostilities (especially after reaching a truce with the Qing in 1739), the Zunghars appealed to the Qing to permit ever larger delegations and more frequent visits, while the Qing ministers and contract merchants complained about the administrative and financial burdens the Zunghar trade placed on them. The Qing archives contain the first quantifiably detailed record we have of what goods in what quantities China exchanged with Central Asian merchants in the context of diplomatic missions and regulated border markets. The Muslims conducting the trade on the Zunghar side (called 'Bukharans' in the Chinese-language sources but likely including merchants from the Tarim Basin and Ferghana) purchased vast quantities of tea, silks and rhubarb in exchange for livestock, hides, raisins, sal ammoniac and antelope horn. Thus, the Zunghar merchant contractors brokered commodities available on the

26 Perdue, 2005, pp. 193–208.

steppe and in Turfan Basin vineyards for Chinese luxuries bound for markets much further away in Central Asia and Russia. Though we do not know exactly where these goods (or those sold to the Qazaqs in the latter half of the eighteenth century) ended up, judging from the quantities and the merchants involved, it seems clear that this was the early modern expression of 'Silk Road' commerce. Both east–west and north–south trade flowed when political and military circumstances permitted; the Eurasian maritime trade was of no evident consequence to eastern Central Eurasia.[27]

A Zunghar state on the Qing–Central Asian border, with imperial ambitions and cultural ties both to the Mongols and to Tibet, posed a threat to the Qing both strategically and – because the Qing trumpeted its own special status *vis-à-vis* Mongols and Tibetans – ideologically. The Qianlong emperor thus took advantage of the succession struggles following the 1745 death of Galdan Tsering to dispatch Qing forces through Mongolia and Zungharia as far as the Ili Valley. With the help of many Zunghar defectors, this first attack succeeded in 1755, and the Qing court attempted to divide Zungharia under four Qing-appointed Oirat 'khans'. It also put two Āfāqī *khwājas*, former Zunghar hostages, in charge in Altishahr. The attempt to control eastern Central Eurasia by proxy failed, however, when the proxies rebelled. Resistance to the Qing coalesced around Amursana in the north and the Āfāqī *khwāja* brothers Khwāja Jihān and Burhān ad-Dīn south of the Tianshan. The massive Qing retaliation in 1756–9 employed near-genocidal tactics against the Zunghars[28] and battled oasis-by-oasis through the Tarim Basin, eventually chasing the Makhdūmzāda brothers beyond the mountains to Badakhshan, whose ruler Sulṭān Shāh executed them. Qing columns penetrated as far as Talas (Taraz), Khoqand and Tashkent – the first trans-Pamir extension of a Chinese-based power for a millennium, and a great shock to local rulers, though in the event the danger was short-lived.[29]

Qing rule in Xinjiang to *c.* 1800[30]

Open dissent was impossible in eighteenth-century China, but the Qianlong court faced persistent murmurings and back-handed proposals regarding the

27 Lin and Wang, 1991, pp. 82–130, provide a detailed overview based on archival data. Other studies of this Zunghar trade include Cai Jiayi, 1982; Zhang Yuxin, 1986, 1987; and Ye Zhiru, 1986.

28 Perdue, 2005, pp. 282–7.

29 Newby, 2005, pp. 22–6.

30 Monographic studies of Qing-era Xinjiang include Zeng Wenwu, 1986; Saguchi, 1963 and 1986; Fletcher, 1978a, 1978b; Luo Yunzhi, 1983; Lin Enxian, 1988; Wang Xilong, 1990; Kataoka Kazutada, 1991; Hua Li, 1994; Millward, 1998; Kim, 2004; and Newby, 2005.

Central Asian campaigns, which some literati and officials considered reckless adventurism. The emperor thundered in his edicts about the strategic and fiscal benefits to be derived from control of the far north-west, but it was nonetheless clear to Qing officialdom that in only a few years, unintended, the dynasty had extended its ambit over vast, distant lands of dubious economic value and, in the eyes of Chinese chauvinists at least, over peoples of questionable loyalty and alarming barbarity.[31]

But the empire's reach had not, initially at least, exceeded its grasp. Qing *imperium* was indeed established in Zungharia and the Tarim Basin – territories collectively known in Chinese both as the 'western regions' (*xiyu*) and, by the late eighteenth century, as 'Xinjiang', or 'new frontier' or 'new dominion'.[32] Historians of modern Central Eurasia have been slow to apprehend the significance of this Qing expansion into the heart of the continent. The tendency to refer to eastern Central Eurasia after the mid-eighteenth century simply as 'China' is just one example of how the point is missed. In fact, the Qing expansion into the region was simultaneously a continuation of old patterns and a completely new phenomenon; its methods were both 'Chinese' and 'Inner Asian', and the imperial endeavour in many ways paralleled that of Russia and other European powers in Asia and elsewhere.

The Qing invasion of Xinjiang arose, as described above, from a rivalry between a North China based power and a power based in the steppes to the north, a geopolitical rivalry not unlike that between the Han and Xiongnu, Tang and Turks, or Toluid Yuan and Ögödeids and Chaghatayids in Mongolia and Zungharia. But Qing conquest and rule of Xinjiang drew on a new amalgam of centralized, agrarian-based, bureaucratic empire with steppe-based cavalry power, and was informed by a facility with Central Asian tribal politics and religious ideology few China-based states could boast. Superficially, especially in its first decades, the Qing approach to controlling Xinjiang did not appear to differ greatly from that of the Zunghars, Moghuls, Qarakhanids or any other northern nomadic power that had once controlled the Tarim and Turfan basins. For all its logistical and bureaucratic competence, the Qing could not escape the environmental constraint noted by Mīrzā Muḥammad Ḥaydar long before: the Tarim Basin oases could

31 Millward, 1998, pp. 38–43.

32 It is often asserted that the name 'Xinjiang' was applied to this region only after it became a province in 1884. In fact, the name may be found in use a century earlier, side by side with *Xiyu*, *Huibu*, *Zhunbu* and so on. A simple demonstration of this occurs in the titles of Qing works: see, for example, Su-er-de *et al.*, 1968, a Qianlong era (1736–95) manuscript; more famously, though a bit later, is Song-yun, Wang Tingkai, Qi Yunshi and Xu Song, 1821.

not support armies. Thus the Qing stationed its 40,000–50,000 bannermen (Manchu and Mongol) troops in the Ili Valley and Urumchi area, with only token forces in the southern cities. Yet unlike its predecessors, the Qing did not simply send horsemen around the oases at harvest time to collect taxes and then leave again. Rather, it built a permanent ruling structure that penetrated local society, appointing local authorities of different types and ethnicities depending on the local people to be governed (*begs* in settled Turkic areas, *jasaghs* in Mongol areas and the hereditary princedoms of Turfan and Hami, Chinese magistrates in areas colonized by Chinese), all under an overlay of military government. The higher-level Turko-Mongolian officials and princes in Xinjiang were symbolically enrolled in the Qing conquest elite through a rankings system based on nominal familial relationship with the imperial clan; they gave ritual thanks for imperial grace and favour as vassals to a liege lord.[33] These were not the forms of Chinese provincial administration: the particularistic, feudal rhetoric was familiar from Chinggis's day; in mapping its administrative and legal structures to the ethno-cultural patchwork of the region, Qing practice is reminiscent of the Ottoman Empire; in the density of its paper communications and its ideologically coloured project to collect, categorize and archive knowledge about new subject peoples and territories, the Qing resembled British and Russian contemporaries, though without, initially, the civilizing mission of European imperialists.

Qing economic policies in its first decades in Xinjiang were largely driven by the need to support an outflung arm of empire far from its agrarian heart. On a network of state farms, mostly in the Urumchi area and the Zungharian plains, Chinese immigrants, soldiers, convicts and Turkic Muslims from the south grew grain and paid taxes to support the military garrisons and growing capital city of Urumchi. Through tax policy and standardization, the Xinjiang government encouraged Turkic Muslims in the oases to grow cotton and manufacture cloth, which officially contracted merchants then traded along with Chinese silk to the Qazaqs in the north for livestock – again, to provide for the Qing military. Though until 1831 the Qing prohibited permanent settlement by Chinese in the Muslim south, it encouraged Chinese merchants to do business there, renting them retail space and taxing them. The state ran a jade monopoly (often evaded by smugglers) to mine and collect this valuable stone and export it to Beijing and eastern provinces. It manipulated copper–silver exchange rates in Xinjiang to garner arbitrage profits. And authorities in Xinjiang garrisons and cities tried their hand at a variety of enterprises,

33 See Millward and Newby, 2006, pp. 119–20.

from tea-sales to timber-yards to pawn shops, as a way to offset operational expenses.[34]

Xinjiang's agricultural and infrastructural development required large initial outlays; moreover, despite successes in land reclamation and commercial ventures, the cost of Qing administration in Xinjiang, mainly salaries and upkeep of officials, soldiers and their families, still outstripped local revenues. To make ends meet, the dynasty shipped silver specie overland from provinces to the east by the hundreds of thousands of silver *taels* (ounces) annually. In 1795, for example, Xinjiang's silver stipend totalled 895,000 *taels* (the stipends spiked at times of military emergency, and the baseline increased to over one million *taels* after 1828, when the Qing upgraded its military presence in southern Xinjiang).[35] This was certainly something new: although the Tarim Basin had for at least two millennia usually been dominated from the north, never before had the conquering power paid for the privilege of ruling it.

While the Qing presence was visible, in the form of walled citadels, government yamens and the occasional official hastening through the narrow streets in a sedan chair, in the eighteenth century the Qing did not attempt to impose itself ideologically upon the Muslim population of southern Xinjiang. Unlike Chinese subjects, no Turkic subject was required to wear the queue (after 1828 loyal *beg* officials were 'permitted' to do so). There was no effort to promote Chinese language or education among the local population until near the end of the nineteenth century. Few legal cases made it into central government records, an indication that the vast majority of crimes, including capital cases, were locally adjudicated. The Qianlong emperor extended modest patronage to Islam, primarily to build the Sulayman mosque in Turfan, but for the most part the Qing authorities left the clerics and the faithful alone while allowing mosques, *madrasas* and shrines supported by *waqf* lands to retain tax-free status (relatively few source materials on the official relationship with Islam in the Qing period have been found or studied).[36]

Some scholars have suggested that from the start the Qing ruled over a resentful and restless Turkic Muslim population; that the conflicts in southwestern Xinjiang starting in 1820 and, indeed, the region-wide rebellion of 1864, had been brewing for decades either because the Muslim population spontaneously sought *jihad* against infidel rulers or due to egregiously rapacious

34 Millward, 1998, chs. 2 and 3.

35 Millward, 1998, ch. 2; on silver stipends, see pp. 58–61.

36 Fletcher, 1978a, p. 75. In at least one much later case, the *hākim* and other *begs* in Kucha borrowed state funds to repair a Sufi tomb complex. It is unclear whether this was common policy earlier. Qing-ying, Palace memorial (*zhupi zouzhe*) *minzu shiwu* category, 0639–11, Xianfeng 8.4.15 (1858), in the Number One Historical Archives, Beijing.

practices of local officials backed by the Qing military.[37] In part this impression arises from the viewpoint of later Islamic sources, in part from assumption.

One must be careful not to view eighteenth- and early nineteenth-century Xinjiang through the lens of the latter nineteenth and, indeed, twentieth centuries. There are good reasons to distinguish the first six decades of Qing rule in Xinjiang from what followed 1820. First of all, except for a rebellion in Ush in 1765, which was indeed sparked by misrule (including sexual exploitation) on the part of Qing officials and which was promptly, if brutally, contained and repressed, there were no sizeable disturbances before the onset of invasions by Āfāqī *khwājas* and Khoqand in the 1820s.[38] On the contrary, during these decades cultivated land area increased and trade flourished. Not only did merchants benefit from this trade, and the khanate of Khoqand rise to power off its profits, but the fact that inflation in Xinjiang during this period remained modest despite large annual inflows of silver and the introduction of new copper coinage indicates that the economy was expanding sufficiently to absorb the increased money supply.[39] Moreover, the population of Turkic Muslims in the oases (today's Uyghurs) was probably rising. Qing censuses from the late eighteenth and early nineteenth centuries tallied 300,000 to 400,000 Turkic Muslim inhabitants (undercounting successful tax-evaders); by 1947, the Uyghur population would be over three million.[40] It seems likely that a good part of this approximately eight-fold increase in Uyghur population over these two centuries occurred during the sixty years of *pax Manjurica* before 1820, just as in the provinces of China, particularly since later periods in Xinjiang were more troubled.

There were certainly abuses of power by Qing officials in Xinjiang,[41] and taxes must have weighed heavily despite official Qing claims to the contrary (the tax burden in Xinjiang would increase dramatically after around 1853,

37 This is the implication of Fletcher's writings (see, for example, Fletcher, 1978a, p. 90) as well as of passages in Newby, 2005, for example pp. 251–2, and Kim, 2004, for example p. 10.

38 The Ush rebellion may have had wider linkages: see Kim, 2004, p. 20.

39 See Millward, 1998, ch. 2 and p. 248.

40 My own estimate is 320,000, based on a Qing census of households published in 1818 but conducted somewhat earlier (see Millward, 1998, p. 33n. and p. 271 n. 21); Kim, 2004 (p. 10), cites two Japanese scholars who arrive at a figure of 370,000 for the combined population of Kashghar, Yarkand, Khotan, Ush, Aqsu and Kucha in the mid-eighteenth century (Saguchi, 1963, pp. 197–9; Hori, 1997, pp. 264–88). None of these estimates includes Turkic Muslims in Turfan or Hami which Qing sources did not include with western Tarim cities. The figure of over three million Uyghur population for 1947 includes both Uyghurs and Taranchis in Xinjiang and was compiled by Su-bei-hai while working with the research department of the Xinjiang *jingbei silingbu*; cited in Liu Weixin *et al.*, 1995, p. 880, '1947 nian Xinjiang gezu renkou tongji biao'.

41 Fletcher, 1978a, p. 86; Newby, 2005, ch. 3.

when rebellions in the eastern provinces of China led to a curtailment of the silver shipments to Xinjiang).[42] The fact that local *beg* officials, though Turkic Muslims, were selected from lineages loyal to the Qing based in oases far from their postings, may have irritated some; that the region's overlords were infidels likely disturbed others. But in a system that relied on popular uprisings to alert central authorities to the extent of abuses by field officials, there were no risings between 1765 and 1820, except for small-scale local events. Indeed, one can find no similarly tranquil half-century period in this region at any point during the preceding 500 years.

42 Millward, 1998, pp. 235–8.

15

The Chinggisid restoration in Central Asia: 1500–1785

R.D. McCHESNEY

During the first decade and a half of the sixteenth century, the last Timurids to hold power in Central Asia[1] were ousted from all the cities and towns north of the Amu Darya by the Abu'l-Khayrid/Shibanids, a clan of the descendants of Chinggis Khan through his eldest son Jochi. At the end of the first decade, a collateral Shibanid clan, the ʿArabshahid, which would be continually at odds with the Abu'l-Khayrids, seized control of the Amu Darya Delta region and then consolidated its hold over the towns and cities of the lower Amu Darya, the historic Khwārazm (Khorezm).

The contested territory

The landscape on which this restoration of Chinggisid sovereignty was re-established is an irregular rectangle some 2,400 kilometres from east to west and 1,600 from north to south, an area about the size of India. Its northern region was known at the time as the Qïpchaq steppe (Dasht-i Qipchāq, today the Qazaq steppe), a grassland stretching from the Volga Basin to the Jungarian Gate, the narrow corridor separating the Altai and Tarbagatai mountain ranges. To the west it is bounded by the Caspian Sea and the lower Volga. To the east, the eastern slopes of the Tien Shan range and the oasal centres at the foot of those slopes (Kucha, Āqsu, Kashghar, Yārkand and Khotan) served to mark its furthest extent. To the south-east where the Tien Shan and Himalayas joined in the so-called 'Pamīr Knot', the mountains proved an effective barrier to the movement of armies and hence a *de facto* limit to political ambitions. The southern boundary was formed by the more penetrable mountain

1 For the purposes of this chapter, the term 'Central Asia' denotes Transoxania (Māʾ Warāʾ al-Nahr), Cisoxiana (Balkh) and Khwārazm. This region is also known as 'Western Turkistān'. Today Transoxiana includes southern Kazakhstan, Uzbekistan, Tajikistan and Kyrgyzstan. Cisoxania is Afghanistan north of the Hindu Kush Mountains, and Khwārazm is Turkmenistan.

ranges of the Hindu Kush and the other ranges fanning out from the Pamīrs to the west and south-west. The south-western limits of the region were the Murghab and Harī Rūd basins. Despite the apparent sweep of the territory, about three-quarters of the land is desert. Most human activity was, and still is, concentrated in and around the main oases (Balkh, Samarqand, Bukhara, Khiva, Tashkent, the Ferghana Valley, the Amu Darya alluvial fan and the eastern slopes of the Tien Shan), flatlands along the main rivers (Amu, Syr, Zarafshān or Kūhak, Murgh, Balkh, Harī and their tributaries) and on the routes connecting those oases.

Culturally, Central Asia has served as a nodal point linking the distant civilizations of South and East Asia and the Mediterranean. More locally it has also served as a zone of transition between the steppe and *taiga* to the north and east and the agrarian Perso-Islamicate oasal world to the south and west. Steppe political customs and values first meet those of the Perso-Islamicate world in Central Asia and are translated, acculturated, modified and to some degree codified here. It is in Central Asia that promoters and purveyors of Islamicate civilization encountered and worked out an accommodation with the cultural values brought by steppe peoples. One of the most intense infusions of steppe culture came with Chinggis Khan and the Mongols in the early thirteenth century. The impact on politics of that period was profound and its reverberations were still felt centuries later.

Chinggisids and non-Chinggisids: the Shibanid claimants

The Shibanids were a descent line from Jochi (d. 1227), the eldest son of Chinggis Khan, whose historic territory was the lower Volga Basin (the Golden Horde). From the thirteenth to the sixteenth centuries, Central Asia was considered the patrimony not of the line of Jochi but of Chaghatay (d. 1241?), Chinggis Khan's second son. This right was upheld, at least in theory, throughout the Timurid era. After 1500 Central Asia became Jochid territory and the Chaghatayid line was confined to what is now Xinjiang Province in China.

Until the second half of the eighteenth century, sovereignty over Central Asia was recognized as residing in three distinct Jochid lines. In Transoxania and Cisoxania, this was first the Abu'l-Khayrid Shibanid line which controlled Central Asia from 1501 with the final capture of the Timurid capital, Samarqand, until 1598 and the death of the last significant Abu'l-Khayrid Shibanid khan, ʿAbd Allāh b. Iskandar. The Abu'l-Khayrids were then supplanted by the

Togha-Timurid (or Toqay-Timurid) Jochid line (commonly but misleadingly known as the Ashtarkhanid or Jānid).[2] Their rule, first effective and then nominal, lasted until about 1785. In Khwārazm, sovereignty was held by the ʿArabshahid Shibanid line from 1510, when its members captured the city of Ūrganj, until sometime in the first quarter of the eighteenth century when the last nominal khan was enthroned.

The principal political significance of the ouster of the Timurids by the Abu'l-Khayrid and ʿArabshahid Shibanids at the beginning of the sixteenth century was the restoration of the Chinggisid mandate. In most areas of life – language, upbringing, general mode of living, economic policy, and sport and entertainment – there is nothing to distinguish the Timurid and Jochid ruling groups. In terms of political administration the differences are more philosophical than practical. First, the change revived and reinstituted what had generally been thought to be legitimate sovereignty, that is the actual supremacy of the Chinggisid khanate, as distinct from the lip-service paid to the institution by the Timurids. Ever since the Mongol conquests of the early thirteenth century, the political classes agreed, as a kind of constitutional principle, that legitimate sovereignty resided only in the agnatic descendants of Chinggis Khan and no non-Chinggisid could claim the khanate and take the title *qān/qaghan* (Arabized as *khāqān/khān*). The rise of the non-Chinggisid Temür, a leader of the Barlās people, and his capturing political power in the late fourteenth century put strains on the khanate and reduced it to a nominal status but did not change its fundamental constitutionality in the eyes of its chief constituents. Temür himself used the title 'amir', and recognized the temporal authority of a Chaghatay khan as a way of legitimizing his position among the other warrior bands. His lineal successors, while further marginalizing Chaghatayids in the Timurid realms, still avoided using the appended title khan (or usually '*bahādur* (hero)-*khan*') and instead took as a royal title *mīrzā* (short for *amīrzādah* 'born of the amir', i.e. descended from Temür). Generically, the terms *sulṭān*[3] and *pādshāh* were employed to refer to rulers. The Chinggisid principle remained sacrosanct in political thought, if dormant in political life, and thus allowed for the re-emergence of genuine Chinggisids once they were able to muster the necessary military force and show they were worthy heirs to the khanate.

2 See discussion of their early history in chapter 12.

3 Many of the Timurids had 'sulṭān' as part of their given names, not as a title (thus Sulṭān-Ḥusayn Bayqara and Sulṭān Abu Saʿid). Generally speaking, the title of office appears at the end of the name as in ʿUbayd Allāh Khan or Sulṭān-Abu Saʿīd Mīrzā. For the Chinggisids, the title 'sulṭān' meant 'prince' and was also an appendix to the name, for example ʿAbd al-ʿAzīz Sulṭān, the son of ʿUbayd Allāh Khan.

However, by the beginning of the sixteenth century, the khanate was far differently constructed in the minds of its proponents than at the time of Chinggis Khan himself. In the first place, the khanate had become thoroughly infused with Islamic values and recognized the authority (in most areas of life) of the *Sharīʿa*. Chinggisid norms (expressed in terms like *yasa* – the laws attributed to Chinggis Khan – or *yosun* embracing the concept of a Chinggisid 'Way') prevailed in the military and political realms so that the claimants and holders of the khanate saw themselves both as defenders of Islam and proponents of the Chinggisid way.

Besides conflating Islamic and Mongol tenets as 'two rings on one finger', the Abu'l-Khayrid Shibanids reintroduced the appanage system of territorial administration and the institution of the *quriltai* or royal clan conclave. The appanage system was the practical application of the policy that every male member of the ruling Chinggisid clan had a right to a portion of the territory under Chinggisid suzerainty and the *quriltai* was the instrument for distributing that territory. The khan himself presided at *quriltai*s but was little more than a first among equals. Although Islamicate historians felt bound by a traditional outlook to focus on the khan as 'king', in fact every member of the royal clan was king in his own appanage. On occasion, when these appanaged sultans were young children, the khan was often able to extend his authority through an *atalïq* (father-surrogate) to the appanage as well. As a sovereign in the Muslim tradition, the khan was accorded the prerogative of *sikkah* and *khuṭba* but in line with Chinggisid traditions of corporate rule that prerogative was also freely exercised by other appanage-holders as well.[4]

The Abu'l-Khayrid Shibanids also revived seniority as a qualification for office, making succession to the khanate unpredictable and giving rise to the more or less formal institution, if the sources are to be trusted, of the *qaʿalkhān* (*qaʿalghah*, *qonalghah*) or heir-apparent, a compromise with the Perso-Islamicate system of lineal succession. Of the few cases we know where such an appointment was made, only one led to the *qaʿalkhān*'s actually succeeding to the khanate throne. More common was the emergence of a militarily talented and often charismatic figure who could fulfil the main role expected of a khan (expansion of the khanate territory through military campaigns) and yet who did not have seniority and could not assume the title of *khan*. Sixteenth- and seventeenth-century historical sources adumbrate this situation first by focusing on the activities of the most powerful of the Chinggisids and secondly by the use of contrasting terms such as 'nominal khan' (*khān-i ṣūrī*)

4 See Davidovich, 1992, especially ch. 5, where coins of appanage heads who were not the titular ruling khans bear the title *bahādur-khān*.

and 'real khan' (*khān-i maʿnawī*) or, in other words, regnant khan and puissant khan. ʿUbayd Allāh (regnant khan only from 1533 to 1540) played the role of puissant khan through the regnant khanates of his great-uncle Küchkünji Khan (r. 1512–30) and then of Küchkünji's eldest son Abū Saʿīd (r. 1530–3). Later in the century the Janïbekid ʿAbd Allāh (regnant khan 1583–98) played that same role under his uncle Pīr Muḥammad (r. 1556–61) and then his father Iskandar (r. 1561–83). For the entire period 1556–98, ʿAbd Allāh was for all intents and purposes the supreme leader.

In the appanage system there were certain constraining factors which necessarily limited membership in the royal clan. The most important was the direct relationship between territorial expansion and appanage availability. Although the area of Central Asia is vast, its habitable regions are quite restricted and the possibility of expanding their productivity is severely limited by the availability of water. In theory, the development of industries (paper manufacture, for example, in which Samarqand long retained a leading role) and services (mercantile and banking) offered potential that was never realized, in part because the capital needed for investment in these areas, when available, seems to have been used instead on monumental architecture in support of the cult. With a limited territorial base for appanage creation, the passage of time and the maturing of new generations naturally increased the pressure for appanage territory. This would have two consequences: first, a preferred policy of the royal clan was outward expansion and this policy was followed whenever there was opportunity. Second, when such opportunities did not exist, as was usually the case, the pressure for territorial expansion had to be satisfied at the expense of another appanage holder. The first policy was implemented in the campaigns waged against Ṣafavid Khurāsān (1508, 1510, 1526–40 and 1587–98); in the campaigns into the Qazaq steppe (1509–10, 1582, 1613, 1635); in the early and late sixteenth centuries, campaigns against the ʿArabshahid Shibanids in Khwārazm (1576, 1593, 1595); the Timurid (Mughal) provinces of Badakhshān (1584); and Kabul in the late sixteenth and in the second quarter of the seventeenth centuries. But the nature of the appanage system made it difficult to consolidate gains made in the south and south-west. In addition, the Abu'l-Khayrid Shibanids and their seventeenth-century successors the Toqay-Timurids confronted powerful empires in the Indian Timurids or Mughals and the Iranian Ṣafavids.

The second consequence of the appanage system, turning inwards in order to expand, led to the elimination of sections of the appanaged clan and the creation of new royal eponymous clans. Thus the Abu'l-Khayrid

Shibanid clan was made up of the lines of Abu'l-Khayr, especially his sons Shah Budaq (the father of Muḥammad Shibani), Küchkünji and Suyunjuq (Süyünch, Süyünchük) and grandson Janïbek b. Khwajah Muḥammad. By 1526, the Shah Budaqids had the Bukharan oasis; the Küchkünjids, Samarqand; the Suyunjuqids, Tashkent; and the Janïbekids, Balkh and Miyānkāl-Karmīnah, a district between Samarqand and Bukhara. By the end of the century, as will be seen below, the Janïbekids had emerged as holders of all the Abu'l-Khayrid territory by violently eliminating the representatives of the other three lineages. At the beginning of the seventeenth century, when the Toqay-Timurid line from Jochi b. Chinggis Khan seized control of the main oasal centres from the last of the Janïbekids, two major sub-clans emerged, the lines of the brothers Dīn Muḥammad (d. 1598) and Walī Muḥammad (d. 1612). The sons of the former, Imām Qulī and Nadhr Muḥammad, with the help of their amirs, eventually eliminated the line of Walī Muḥammad (although his descendants would live under Ṣafavid protection and be restored to nominal authority in Balkh in the early eighteenth century) and created a double khanate made up of Transoxania and Cisoxania (Mawarannahr and Balkh) that would survive more or less without modification for three-quarters of a century.

A similar process was taking place among the ʿArabshahid Shibanids of Khwārazm. Limited by the power of the Abu'l-Khayrids to their south-east and the Ṣafavid state to the south-west, internal pressures were only temporarily relieved by the elimination of cousin clans. As each new generation came of age, the same pressures arose and could only be released by internal contest. The campaigns directed outwards against the Ṣafavids (1524–5, and repeatedly between 1543 and 1565) and against the Toqay-Timurids (1657, 1681 and 1694) produced booty and slaves but no long-term expansion of territory. Instead, the ʿArabshahids whose territory divided more or less on ecological grounds between the 'riverside' (Amu Darya alluvial fan oasis) and the 'mountainside' (the northern watershed of the Kopet Dagh range) engaged in the same kind of internal political campaigning to eliminate rivals that their cousins in Transoxania and Cisoxania conducted.

A further pressure for territorial expansion, besides that created by a new generation coming of age, came from the amirs whose loyalty was bought with sub-infeudations. As their offspring reached maturity more resources had to be found to satisfy them. Ultimately the appanage system was best suited to an environment where there were few constraints on territorial expansion or where the population of eligibles did not significantly expand from generation to generation.

The Chinggisid legacy

Writing at Balkh in the mid-1630s, Maḥmūd b. Amīr Walī was acutely conscious of the Mongol practices that were still noticeable among the heirs to the Chinggisid traditions and his work offers much evidence of the survival of these traditions. His own perspective on them seems unequivocal. They were remnants of an infidel culture and a good ruler would make every effort to stamp them out. In a polemical discourse about these survivals he makes the following points: the customary law of the Mongols (which he says is known to them as *yasa* and to the Uzbeks as *töre*) stands in opposition to the 'commands and prohibitions' of Islamic law. Up until the time of his own patron (Nadhr Muḥammad Khan, d. 1651) this 'evil innovation' had been promoted by provincial governors, police (*dārūghagān*), and other keepers of the peace (*mustaḥfiẓān*), in other words the amirs. But his patron had worked hard to undermine their efforts to use *yasa* and *yarghu* (the Mongol tribunal) 'to achieve their ends'. He then proceeds to demonstrate how rich and embedded many aspects of Chinggisid Mongol culture were and how strong was the sense that these things should be attributed to the Mongols.[5] Maḥmūd b. Amīr Walī's list includes the enthronement ceremony,[6] court protocol,[7] the symbolic use of *koumiss*, the *qoruq*s or royal hunting preserves, the *yurt* as the khan's capital, and the reception of envoys.[8]

Enthronement

At the centre of the enthronement ceremony was the white-felt carpet on which a new khan was elevated, to signify the attainment of sovereignty. The honour of holding the four corners of the carpet was granted at first to amirid figures. As time passed, the privilege passed to religious figures, part of the Islamization process that was always at work. When the Janïbekid ʿAbd Allāh Khan was enthroned in late June 1582, the felt carpet was sprinkled with water brought from the well of Zamzam at the Kaʿbah, a way of Islamizing what was universally believed to be a Chinggisid ceremony. The elevation ceremony using a white-felt carpet continued well into the nineteenth century under the non-Chinggisid successors to the Chinggisid lines, the Mangghïts in Bukhara

5 Maḥmūd b. Amīr Walī, *Baḥr al-asrār*, VI/4, ff. 387b–389a
6 See Sela, 2003, and McChesney, 2000.
7 Bartol'd, 'Tserimonial pri dvore', in his *Sochineniia*, II/2, pp. 388–99, and McChesney, 1983.
8 On the drinking of *koumiss* (*qumīz*) and the reception of envoys, see Maḥmūd b. Amīr Walī, *Baḥr al-asrār*, VI/4, ff. 388b–389a.

and the Qunghrāts in Khiva. But the passage of time had made such an icon of the carpet that at Amīr Ḥaydar's elevation in 1800 people scrambled to touch the carpet and participate in the elevation. One source lists thirty-one individuals who were said to have held the carpet at the amir's enthronement. The old tradition of four Uzbek amirs holding the corners was still remembered, though no longer practised.[9]

Court protocol and rank

Another enduring practice ascribed to Chinggis Khan was the hierarchical disposition of individuals around the khan at a public assembly. In the early seventeenth century, Maḥmūd b. Amīr Walī described in detail the seating arrangements and rules (*asālīb*) at his patron's court. He introduces his text with a discourse on the indissoluble link between kingship and religion, that there could be no religion without kingship and one of the roles of the king is to create ranks and hierarchies so there would be gradations of respect and nobility, a particularly Persianate idea. He then gives a description of the levels or ranks (*ūrūnāt* [*orunat*]) at a session of court. The main places were allotted by virtue of membership in specific Uzbek groupings, the Naiman, Durmān, Qushchï, Qunghrāt and Mangghït taking precedence. Their pre-eminence is ascribed to the privileges and rights they were granted by Chinggis Khan for services these military groups had performed for him.

Koumiss and its use

Maḥmūd b. Mir Walī provides a very detailed description of the court use of *koumiss*, fermented mare's milk, as a ceremonial drink. Most of the depictions we have of it from the time of Chinggis Khan himself describe it in libations[10] but here, although 'the rules concerning its use are numerous and the ordinances regarding it are limitless', still the author feels obliged to describe the performance of *koumiss*-quaffing in a royal assembly. At such a gathering (called here both by the Turkic term *körünüsh* and the Arabic *majlis*) the *koumiss* 'bowl and cup' (*ayagh wa qadaḥ*) are passed and drunk from in a set choreography supervised by an official called the *ūydāchī* (*idēchi*). Maintaining the protocol throughout the performance is considered sufficiently serious that any break in it made the violator liable to a tribunal (*yarghu*) the usual outcome of which was execution of the defendant.

9 Sela, 2003, pp. 46–50.
10 See *Secret History*/de Rachewiltz, paras 85, 213.

The *yurt* as 'capital city'

The interplay between the traditions of the Chinggisid steppe and those of the Perso-Islamicate oases of Central Asia also emerges over the issue of capital city. A highly mobile and expanding appanage state has its centre wherever the khan's *yurt* (or in the Persianized form, *yūrtgāh*) is located. The term *yurt* in this period refers both to the residence of the khan and by extension to its location. By the sixteenth century, the Perso-Islamicate idea of the *dār al-salṭanah* ('abode of authority or sovereignty') or fixed capital city (in Persianized form *takhtgāh* the 'throne place') had supplanted the idea of a moveable centre. The bureaucratic needs of an agrarian state more or less require a fixed permanent geographic centre. For Central Asia, that centre had become Samarqand, thanks to the efforts of Temür in making it the centre of the entire Islamicate world and to his successors' continuing use of it as the Transoxanian political centre. Control of Samarqand then conferred some degree of credibility and legitimacy on its holder, hence the struggles for it by the Timurid Ẓāhir al-Din Babur and Muḥammad Shibani and the latter's making it his capital from 1501 until his death in 1510. But of the cities of Mawarannahr, Bukhara also had a long-standing tradition as Islamic capital dating back to the Sāmānids in the tenth century.

For the first half of the sixteenth century, the Chinggisid *yurt* tradition prevailed in Transoxania, with the centre of the Abu'l-Khayrid state being Samarqand the *yurt* of Shibani Khan (1501–10) and his successors as titulature khans, Küchkünji (r. 1512–30) and Abū Saʿīd b. Küchkünji (r. 1530–3). When the seniority principle shifted the khanate to the Shah Budaqid, ʿUbayd Allāh (the nephew of Muḥammad Shibani, r. 1533–40), the capital became his *yurt*, Bukhara. In 1540, again thanks to seniority, the khanate and the capital returned to Samarqand where it remained until 1552 under ʿAbd Allāh b. Küchkünji (r. 1540) and ʿAbd al-Laṭīf b. Küchkünji (r. 1540–52). It then shifted to Tashkent under the Suyunjuqid, Barāq Khan (aka Nawruz Ahmad, r. 1552–6). By the end of his khanate, inter-appanage struggles were well underway and while the khanate capital moved briefly to Balkh under the Janībekid, Pīr Muḥammad b. Janībek (r. 1552–61), the capture of Bukhara and the elimination of the Shah Budaqid clan by the Janībekids made Bukhara the political centre and thus the capital of Transoxania and Cisoxania from then on. By the middle of the sixteenth century, the Perso-Islamicate tradition of the fixed 'throne place' and 'abode of sovereignty' had completely eclipsed the Chinggisid idea of the moveable *yurt* as royal centre and Bukhara had taken the mantle of 'capital' from Samarqand.

The Mongol tradition of receiving envoys

Another surviving custom that Maḥmūd b. Amīr Walī attributed to a Chinggisid origin was the protocol for receiving ambassadors. When an ambassador arrived at court, an official called the *shighāwul,* or chamberlain, met him at a suitable distance from the khan then brought to the khan whatever oral or written message and gifts the envoy came with. After presenting these things, the *shighāwul* would step back a few paces. If the ambassador was 'one of the great amirs, or a person of high rank, like a *toqsanbay* or a *parwānachī*', two courtiers of similar dignity would escort him up to the throne and then withdraw. Thereupon the khan would signal to the ambassador where he was to sit, either to his right or left. There he was to remain in silence unless addressed by the khan.[11]

The Chinggisid origins of these urban-acclimated traditions or their ascription presumably helped cement the necessary loyalty of the amirid class, generation after generation. But this public display of Chinggisid sentiment was clearly a continuing irritation for the intellectuals whose worldview was framed by Islamic loyalties and who saw *yasa* or *töre* (*türe*) as a challenge to the hegemony of the *Sharīʿa*. Even such late Chinggisid loyalists as Mīrzā Ḥaydar, whose status in life was determined by his birth into the Turko-Mongol clan of the Dughlat, found the survival of some Chinggisid norms and customs at the very least incompatible with the universal claims of *Sharīʿa*.[12] But for most amirs, the *yasa* of Chinggis Khan and the *Sharīʿa* of the Prophet Muḥammad worked well together and were mutually reinforcing, or so the long survival of Mongol ways in public life would seem to suggest.

The non-Chinggisid military: the amirs

The principal upholders and promoters of the Chinggisid legacy were the amirs, a warrior caste whose identity was shaped in large part by the collective memory of the Mongol conquests of the early thirteenth century and the roles played by the amirs' ancestors during that time. The extensive nomenclature that has survived, identifying the separate elements of this social grouping, which non-indigenous sources subsume together under the name 'Uzbek', shows durable separate identities for Chinggisids and non-Chinggisids.

The ethnogenesis, if such it can be called, of the Uzbeks began with the formation of a short-lived steppe empire of nomadic tribes in what is now

11 Maḥmūd b. Amīr Walī, *Baḥr al-asrār*, VI/4, fol. 389a.

12 See, for example, his didactic story about Ulugh Beg's interests in the *töra* of Chinggis Khan, Haydar, 1898, pp. 69–70.

Western Siberia and northern Kazakhstan under a descendant of Chinggis Khan, the Jochid Abu'l-Khayr Khan (r. 1428–68). The Turko-Mongol tribes which he succeeded in conquering and subordinating in the forty years of his rule came to be known generally as 'Uzbeks'. Where that name originated still remains uncertain. To their sixteenth- and seventeenth-century Central Asian memorialists they were known by scores of distinct names that linked them to the military and political legacy of Chinggis Khan.[13] The most frequently encountered of these names were (in no particular order and in a variety of spellings): Durmān (Dörben), Arlāt, Ūyrāt (Oirat), Bahrīn, Qïpchaq, Qïrghïz, Mangghït, Mīng, Yüz, Qaṭaghān, Naiman, Barlās, Kanīkas (Keneges), Markīt (Merkit), Alchïn, Tarkhan, Qonggirāt (Qunghrāt, Kungrad), Kirāyit (Kereyit), Uyghur, Qushchï, Qānqlī (Qanglï), Qalīmāq and Jalāyir. According to the lore, a full listing of these 'Uzbek' bands would contain either thirty-two or ninety-two names.[14] The leaders of these groupings are rarely referred to by their domestic contemporaries as Uzbeks. When writers of the period from within Central Asia use the term 'Uzbek' it is often a sign of disparagement or condescension. It might be applied to rustic and presumed unlettered individuals, often nomads and peasants, but occasionally members of the urban lumpen as well. But there are exceptions to this limited use of the term. Sulṭān Muḥammad 'Muṭribī' Samarqandī (1559–*c.* 1630), poet, anthologist and long-time resident of Bukhara consistently refers to his contemporary the Janïbekid, ʿAbd Allāh Khan, as 'ʿAbd Allāh Khan Özbek'. Muṭribī was a loyal native son of Samarqand and when he wrote about the Küchkünjids, the Abu'l-Khayrids who held Samarqand as their appanage for most of the first half of the sixteenth century, he writes, 'although these sulṭāns are of the Ūzbekiyyah (*az ṭabaqa-i ūzbakīya*) with lineage back to Chinggis Khan, still they possess the son-in-law relationship of Abu'l-Khayr Khan to the martyred sultan Ulugh Beg Guragān'. He cites this as a reason for the close friendship of one of Küchkünji Khan's sons with the Mughal ruler, Akbar.[15] As a man who admired the Mughals, especially Akbar and his son Jahāngīr, Muṭribī respected but apparently had no great liking for ʿAbd Allāh Khan, the man who eliminated the Küchkünjids and was most responsible for ending Samarqand's long tradition as political and intellectual centre. In writing of the Küchkünjid sultans, on the other hand, he emphasizes their cultural achievements and draws an unmistakable

13 There is a wide range of Mongol, Turkish, Persian and Arabic terms found in the texts of this period and used more or less synonymously for these groups: *il*, *ulus*, *oymaq*, *tümen*, *qoshun*, *ṭāʾifa*, *qabīla* and *qawm* are the most commonly encountered.

14 Sultanov, 1982.

15 Muṭribī, 1998, p. 69.

parallel between the time of Samarqand under the Küchkünjids with what he describes as its glory days under Ulugh Beg (1409–49). His emphatic and atypical use of 'Özbek' after ʿAbd Allāh Khan's name perhaps hints at those civic loyalties. With this telling exception, the term 'Uzbek' was not used as a dynastic label except by outsiders – Iranian and Indian writers in particular.

Although the distinctive names of the Turko-Mongol organizations encompassed by the name Uzbek remain well preserved for centuries (some even into the 1924 Soviet census), we know little about what those names stood for in terms of numbers or group solidarity. There is a general belief that the early sixteenth century saw a major influx of Uzbeks into the oases of Central Asia with the rise of the Abu'l-Khayrid and ʿArabshahid Shibanids. Early on, Bannāʾī (d. 1513) lists fifty-six amirs supporting Muḥammad Shibani at the beginning of his career. They represented sixteen different Uzbek groups, the largest number being from the Naiman and Durmān with seven each.[16] But does this represent the total manpower Shībānī Khan could rally or should it be assumed that each named amir stands at the head of a contingent of many more warriors? Muḥammad Shibani's own brother and companion in his *qazāqī*, Maḥmūd Sulṭān, also had a similar contingent of personal amirs as did Muḥammad Shibani's uncles, Küchkünji and Suyunjuq. Once the oasal centres were conquered and appanages were distributed, each had his own military force and it seems more than likely that the core in each force was made up of men with long-standing ties to the Chinggisid figure. What is striking is that the numbers in the case of Muḥammad Shibani are very small and beg the question: where did the 250,000 Uzbeks come from who have been identified as forming a mass migration into Transoxania and Balkh at the beginning of the sixteenth century?[17]

There is little evidence among Uzbek groups of the kind of solidarity or internecine conflict that marked contemporary inter-Qïzïlbash relations in Iran, where the relationship between royal clan and amirid supporters was similar. While sixteenth-century Ṣafavid history is punctuated by fierce struggles between the Turkic Qïzïlbash *ūymāq*s (*oymaqs*), the Ustajlu, Tekellü, Dhū'l-Qadr and Shamlu, for example, there is no such record of conflict between the various Uzbek groupings in Mawarannahr and Greater Balkh. In fact loyalties and ambitions seem to have centred on one's own Chinggisid lord even if it brought one into conflict with individuals from one's eponymous group supporting another Chinggisid. At the height of the inter-appanage

16 Bannāʾī, 1997.
17 Bregel, 2003, p. 50.

struggles that would mark the second half of the century, we find Naiman amirs fighting alongside all three major contenders from the Küchkünjid, Janïbekid and Suyunjuqid clans of the Abu'l-Khayrids. And among those three, no single tribal grouping seems to have predominated. As long as they were appropriately rewarded, amirs were faithful to their Chinggisid lords. However, when slighted in some fashion, they had no compunction about seeking another patron and when they did it occasionally had profound consequences for the spurned Chinggisid. According to the principal narrator of Abu'l-Khayrid history, Ḥāfiẓ-i Tanish, when the Janïbekid, ʿAbd Allāh b. Iskandar, set out from Bukhara against his Janïbekid cousin at Balkh in 1572, his campaign was prompted by complaints from Naiman amirs in Balkh of persecution.[18] A similar complaint in 1599 from Durmān amirs at Bukhara allowed the Toqay-Timurid Bāqī Muḥammad b. Jānī Muḥammad to put an end to Abu'l-Khayrid Shibanid authority in Transoxania.[19]

The absence of inter-amirid struggle may have been due to the long-maintained practice of changing amirid assignments thus keeping them from becoming too closely attached to a place while still rewarding them adequately for their services. It was only later in the seventeenth century, when amirs and their bands began to be more permanently attached to their assigned territories (for example, the Mīng in the Maymanah area of present-day northwest Afghanistan, the Qaṭaghān in the region east of Balkh, the Mangghït in Bukhara, the Yüz in Khoqand and the Keneges [Kanīkas] in the Kulab region) that struggles began to arise between them.

To be considered an amir in the sixteenth and seventeenth centuries did not necessarily mean membership in one of the eponymous Uzbek groups. In general, amir just meant a non-Chinggisid performing primarily military and administrative duties. In several cases of prominent amirs, the written record omits an affiliation with one of the Uzbek groupings, suggesting either that the affiliation was unknown to the writer or that the amir was perhaps of non-Uzbek origin. Two of the most prominent amirs of the sixteenth century, Jan Wafa Biy, one of Shïbānī Khan's stalwarts, and Qul Baba Kökeltash, ʿAbd Allāh Khan's right-hand man, are never associated with one of the named Uzbek groups. Qul Baba's father, Amīr Yār Muḥammad, likewise has no such identifier.

The amirs performed duties that today might be considered distinctly both 'civilian' and 'military'. Qul Baba Kökeltash is a good, perhaps unique, example

18 Ḥāfiẓ-i Tanīsh, 1983, fol. 179b.
19 Maḥmūd b. Amīr Walī, *Baḥr al-asrār*, VI/4, fol. 59a-b.

of how the military and civil functions of the state were not clearly differentiated. He was ʿAbd Allāh Khan's commander-in-chief and led a brilliant siege to take Herat in 1588, among many other campaigns. He also became Herat's governor for a decade. In addition, he held the post of overseer of the fisc (*musharrif-i dīwān*) and supervised the auditing of financial records. He held the title *ṣadr-i khānī* as well, or chief administrative judge, responsible for the workings of the *Sharīʿa* courts. In that capacity he supervised the probate of ʿAbd Allāh Khan's father's estate. In his own *waqf-nāmah* Qul Baba refers to himself as 'possessor of sword and pen' (*ṣāḥib al-sayf wa'l-qalam*).[20] In addition to all the official functions, he was also famed as a patron of literature, art and architecture.[21] A comparable figure in the seventeenth century in terms of military prowess, administrative and fiscal experience, and public patronage was Yalangtush Bi Alchïn, most remembered as builder of the *madrasas* standing on the north and east sides of the Rīgistān in Samarqand today but in his own day probably more famous as governor, military leader and patron of the Dahbīdī Naqshbandī order.

The religious classes

Individuals who were noted for their intellectual and spiritual authority formed a kind of counterweight to the political influence of the amirs. Figures from this large and amorphous group were most outspoken in defence of the *Sharīʿa* (the 'Muslim Way') and vocal in criticizing the continuing force of *yasa* and *yosun* (the 'Chinggisid Way'). The group included individuals (*ʿālim* pl. *ʿulamāʾ*) known for their formal learning and authority as teachers. Those with recognized descent from the Prophet Muḥammad, the *sayyids*, also possessed an intrinsic authority and many of the *ʿulamāʾ* were also *sayyids*. A third forceful element in this group were those who were connected to Sufi organizations – the Naqshbandī, the Kubravī and the Atāʾī being three of the most important – especially those with large well-endowed shrine centres, for example the Jūybārī Naqshbandīs in Bukhara, the Parsāʾī Naqshbandīs in Balkh, the Aḥrārī Naqshbandīs in Samarqand and Tashkent, and the Atāʾīis at the Yasavī shrine in Turkestan. Another component of this grouping were 'holy men', those individuals who attracted attention, regard and influence for leading lives of uncompromising spirituality. These were men remembered for denying themselves the pleasures, and even sometimes the bare necessities,

20 Central State Archive of the Republic of Uzbekistan, Fond 1–323, no. 55/9.
21 See especially, Muṭribī, *Tadhkirat al-shuʿarā* (Tehran, 2003), pp. 459–62 and Muṭribī, 1998.

of life. Terms like *qalandar, darwīsh* and *malāmatī* often appear as descriptors following their names.

The importance of this segment of society in the political life of Central Asia lies in the roles its leading members were expected to play mediating conflict, interceding between sovereign and subject, and intervening against policies seen as detrimental to their own constituents, the general populace. These were the *de facto* representatives of the people and the medium through which rulers remained bound to their subjects. They were thus the primary beneficiaries of state patronage; they formed the pool from which clerical, judicial and educational positions controlled by the state were filled; and the more prominent of them were given large endowments to administer on behalf of cult and educational facilities.

Events and personalities

The events that make up the bulk of Central Asian history as it is generally known involve the activities of the political classes – the khans, sultans, and amirs.[22] The revival of Chinggisid fortunes in Transoxania, Cisoxania and Khwārazm begins with the rise of the Shibanid line of Abu'l-Khayr b. Dawlat Shaykh Oghlan, who is named khan on the banks of the Irtysh River in 1428 and soon captures most of the steppe region held by his eponymous ancestor, Shībān, a grandson of Chinggis Khan.

Abu'l-Khayr also extended his influence into Khwārazm and as far as Astarabad in north-eastern Iran through raids, battles and occasional conquests of towns and cities. Although there was never much expectation of gaining territory at the expense of the Timurids in Transoxania and Khurāsān, their internal rivalries offered him opportunities for the sale of his military services. One of those resulted in an ideologically important marriage, that to Rabiʿa Sulṭān Begum, a daughter of Ulugh Beg in 1451. Out of this marital alliance came Küchkünji (or Küchüm) and served later to tie the fortunes of the Küchkünjid clan to the former Timurid centre of Samarqand.

After Abu'l-Khayr's death, the empire he had built up collapsed, but was revived on the territory of the Timurid state by his grandson, Shībaq. Shībaq or Shaybaq was also known to writers of his time as Shāhī Beg and Shah Bakht but became best known by the *takhalluṣ* or *nom de plume* of Shibani, or Muḥammad Shibani. His grandfather's death forced him as a young man to take refuge in Bukhara where he enjoyed the protection of the Arghun amir,

22 An excellent synopsis is the narrative text accompanying the maps in Bregel, 2003, pp. 50, 52, 54, 56, 58, 60.

Sulṭān ʿAlī Tarkhan and no doubt gave military service in return. Bannāʾī says he spent two years studying Qurʾānic readings (*qirāʾāt*) but this was not incompatible with military service. From Bukhara, he drifted back towards his grandfather's former territory, along the way attracted other freelancers and by the mid-1480s had developed sufficient force to raid and briefly take towns in Khwārazm. This brought him to the attention of the Timurid ruler of Samarqand, Sulṭān Ahmad Mīrzā, who bought his allegiance for a campaign in 1488 against the Chaghatayid Chinggisid, Sulṭān Maḥmūd Khan, who held Tashkent and threatened Timurid holdings in the Ferghana Valley. But Muḥammad Shibani deserted the Timurid army at Tashkent and joined the Chaghatayid side. When it defeated the Timurid army, he was rewarded with the town of Arqūq on the Syr Darya, at the time a flourishing commercial entrepôt. From 1488 until 1500 the sources are silent about Muḥammad Shibani. He re-emerges in the latter year in a campaign to take Samarqand, ostensibly for his patron, Sulṭān Maḥmūd Khan, but if so, he soon discarded that obligation. Samarqand fell in 1500 to his forces and Bukhara in the same year and it is from that moment that the Abu'l-Khayrid / Shibanid empire was revived. Though the Timurid Babur briefly retook Samarqand, Shibani recaptured it in 1501 and held it until his death in 1510. The capture of Samarqand and Bukhara was soon followed by successful campaigns in 1502 into the Ferghana Valley and Tashkent (taken that same year), Urganj and Khiva in 1504–5, Balkh (1505), Herat and Qandahar (1507), then westwards to Astarabad through Mashhad, Nīshāpūr, Sabzawar and Bastam (1508). After a brief respite in Samarqand he returned to Khurāsān in 1510 to confront a new threat, the forces behind the rise of the Ṣafavīs, a family of Sufi origins whose legitimacy rested in their role as *murshids* or religious guides of their Turkic followers. Near Merv in late November 1510, Shībānī Khan was killed in battle and most of the territory he had conquered was quickly lost to his kinsmen and supporters.

In late winter and early spring of 1512, his uncle Suyunjuq and his nephew ʿUbayd Allāh, the son of his brother Maḥmūd who had died in 1504, separately led attacks against Tashkent and Bukhara respectively and put an end to the brief Timurid and Chaghatayid resurgence in those two places. In addition, though the Ṣafavid-Qïzïlbash forces took Herat and were to hold it with only a few interruptions until 1588, Iranian ambitions for Transoxania were permanently thwarted in 1512.

There is no evidence of an enthronement ceremony or of a *quriltai* being convened at the moment Shibani first took Samarqand and Bukhara. Certainly he had no need for such ceremony, being the unarguably pre-eminent figure in the Abu'l-Khayrid family at the time. His assertion of sovereignty in the Islamic mode can be dated to 1501–2, the second and decisive taking of Samarqand and the issuing of coins bearing his name.[23] After his death however, the seniority principle came into play. Küchkünji's khanate may be considered to begin with the defeat of the Ṣafavid-Timurid alliance in 1512 and the ouster of Babur for a third time from Samarqand and of amirs loyal to him from Tashkent and Bukhara. According to the late sixteenth-century historian, 'by ancient (Chinggisid) law, the sultans consulted together on the issue of the khanate. Since Küchkünji Sulṭān was the eldest they gave him the title of khan. The title of *qaʿalghah* which means heir-apparent, they conferred on Suyunjuq Sulṭān.'[24] At the same time a distribution of appanages took place, the outcome of which would establish the main political units of Transoxania for more than four decades. Küchkünji, the son of Abu'l-Khayr and the grandson of Ulugh Beg through his mother, received the ancient Timurid capital of Samarqand. For two years or so, Küchkünji and his family shared the appanage with Shībānī Khan's son, Muḥammad Temür, but he was killed fighting in what is now southern Tajikistan in March of 1514 and left no eligible claimants. From then on, Samarqand became exclusively Küchkünjid and would remain so until 1578. In 1512, the Janībekid clan was given Miyānkāl and Karmīnah and then in 1526 received Balkh after its capture from the last Timurid governor there. Bukhara went to the clan descended from Muḥammad Shibani's father, Shah Budaq b. Abu'l-Khayr. Its head was his nephew ʿUbayd Allāh Sulṭān who would be the most militarily active of the Abu'l-Khayrids until his death in 1540. Tashkent was claimed by Suyunjuq b. Abi'l-Khayr and his clan and they would hold it until 1582.

All of the appanages during this period had external rivals to contend with. In Tashkent, Suyunjuq (d. 1525) and his son and successor, Nawruz Ahmad (aka Baraq Khan), were faced with pressure from the north from the 'Qazaq' or renegade Shibanids, a group that had split with Abu'l-Khayr Khan in the preceding century to maintain a nomadic empire in the Qïpchaq steppe between Lake Balkhash and the middle reaches of the Syr Darya. To Tashkent's east and south-east along the commercial routes linking Transoxania with western China were the still-powerful Chaghatayid Chinggisids. At first the Suyunjuqids had to fight the Chaghatayids to keep them out of the Ferghana Valley as well as Tashkent and later, allied with them, attempted to expand against the Qazaqs. In Samarqand, the Küchkünjids looked south to the river valleys of present-day Tajikistan and to Badakhshan for territory into which to expand. In Bukhara, ʿUbayd Allāh led numerous campaigns against Eastern

23 Davidovich, 1992, pp. 77, 268.
24 Ḥāfiẓ-i Tanīsh, 1983, fol. 33b.

Khurāsān, in particular the important commercial centre of Herat.[25] The Janībekids in their bifurcated appanage, part along the Zarafshan River, part centred on the city of Balkh, were somewhat constrained from doing much more than consolidating their hold over the territory south of Balkh up to the passes through the Hindu Kush, beyond which the Timurid Babur had re-established his authority.

After the death of Küchkünji Khan in 1533, the khanate duly passed to the next senior member, by now the Shah Budaqid, ʿUbayd Allāh. (Suyunjuq, though designated heir-apparent, had predeceased Küchkünji.) But one should understand the khanate to have been a nominal and ceremonial honour with no real power to control, or moral authority to persuade, the cousins to act in common. On occasion, the nominal supreme khan was also the most powerful political figure but for the most part power and title did not coincide in the same individual. By the time Küchkünji died there seems to have been a general expectation that the appanages as distributed in 1512 were the exclusive right of their respective recipients and would not be distributed again. Demands from sultans coming of age in the appanages had to be satisfied from that patrimony. Consequently, sub-appanages and sub-infeudations (for the amirs) were created within each appanage to respond to each cousin clan's particular needs.

Civil war: 1550–82

The logical next step for the appanage holders, once expansion beyond the khanate-area was no longer possible, was internal conflict, both between the cousin-clans and within each cousin-clan itself. For thirty years beginning at mid-century, there was more or less continual alignment and realignment of the cousin-clans against each other, often to seize on an opportunity created by dissension and strife within one of the clans. By the end of the period three had been eliminated: the Shah Budaqids, purged from Bukhara in 1557; the Küchkünjids driven into oblivion from Samarqand in 1577; and the Suyunjuqids who lost Tashkent and disappear from the historical record in 1582. The elimination of clans narrowed the pool of khan candidates. Though seniority remained an essential qualification, the view of what constituted the royal clan became more and more restricted. By the end of the period, only the Janībekid, which had itself undergone an internal purge with the elimination of its branch at Balkh, survived to claim the Chinggisid mantle of khan.

25 See Dickson, 1958, for a detailed account of the seven major campaigns conducted between 1526 and 1540.

In 1568 Iskandar the son of Janībek was recognized as khan on the basis of seniority and in 1582, when the Suyunjuqids were eliminated, he held nominal though brief sway over the entire region once subject to Shībānī Khan. Iskandar Khan was a man in his late sixties or early seventies by the time he came to the throne. He himself was not militarily active but is instead remembered for his great religiosity and moral authority. His three sons, ʿAbd Allāh, ʿIbād Allāh and ʿAbd al-Quddus, were all stalwart warriors on his and the Janībekid clan's behalf and led the forces that eliminated the other Abū'l-Khayrid clans from Transoxania. Of the three, ʿAbd Allāh was clearly dominant, not only in the eyes of his own chronicler, Ḥāfiẓ-i Tanish, but also in the view of writers who were actively hostile or of mixed opinion about him. One of these latter was the above-mentioned Samarqand native, Muṭribī. In his anthology, *Nuskhah-i zībā-yi Jahāngīrī*, Muṭribī has much to say about ʿAbd Allāh but makes it clear that, in his view anyway, ʿAbd Allāh was very much subject to the moral authority of his father, Iskandar Khan.[26]

It is during this transitional time that members of the religious establishment appear in the sources to play significant mediating roles. The Aḥrārī family in Samarqand and the Jūybārī family in Bukhara, both nominally Naqshbandī in allegiance but with often competing political interests, emerge as major social, economic and political forces in their respective regions.[27]

The unified khanate

With the death of Iskandar Khan in June 1582, the title of khan passed to his son, ʿAbd Allāh. It is unlikely that he was senior member of the Janībekid clan at the time but there is no doubt that he was widely recognized as the most powerful. In an enthronement ceremony held at Nafrandi, near Ura Tapah (modern Ura Tiube) some 130 miles east of Samarqand, ʿAbd Allāh was seated on the white-felt carpet, sacralized with water from the Zamzam well, and was ceremoniously elevated to the Chinggisid khanate.

A new age of expansion: 1584–98

The momentum of internal consolidation was directed outwards after ʿAbd Allāh became khan. Janībekid / Uzbek forces made major gains in Badakhshan, Khurāsān and Khwārazm before the death of ʿAbd Allāh caused the newly reformed Chinggisid Empire to collapse in mid-1598. His new military power

26 Muṭribī, 1998, pp. 120–1.
27 See McChesney, 1996a, esp. pp. 109–14.

is not difficult to explain. The elimination of the other Abū'l-Khayrid clans had forced large numbers of Uzbek amirs to find new patrons. Many chose to make their peace and ally themselves with the Janïbekids and ʿAbd Allāh, both to keep their existing sub-infeudations and for the promise of new territorial expansion and campaign booty. In order to meet those expectations, ʿAbd Allāh Khan in turn was compelled to turn his gaze outward, where there were many new opportunities.

Badakhshan, for example, had remained a centre of Timurid power, but was often at odds with the Timurids of Kabul and Hindustan and suffered from internal factional fighting as well. For the most part, the Badakhshani Timurids had been able to resist inroads from either the Suyunjuqids in Samarqand to the north or the Janïbekids in Balkh to the west until now. In a ten-month campaign launched in January 1584, ʿAbd Allāh Khan's forces seized Kulab in what is now southern Tajikistan along with Ṭaluqān, Ghūrī and Qunduz in present-day northern Afghanistan.[28] An attempt two years later to restore Timurid control failed and, from that point on, Badakhshan remained in Chinggisid / Uzbek hands.

In 1587, ʿAbd Allāh turned his attention to Khurāsān, an area he had once before raided. At this time the Ṣafavid state was in the midst of a major succession crisis involving large-scale inter-Qïzïlbash fighting. The Shamlu Qïzïlbash governor at Herat, ʿAlī Quli Khan, appealed to ʿAbd Allāh Khan for support against the Ustājlū Qïzïlbash governor of Mashhad, but when ʿAbd Allāh took this as an invitation to invade the Herat oasis in the spring of 1587, ʿAlī Quli Khan changed his mind and barred the gates of the city against the Shibanid / Uzbek forces.

Two types of warfare dominated the tactical thinking of military leaders of the time. The choreography of battles in the field involved the division of the fighting forces into a left-wing, right-wing and centre. Mongol and Turkic terms for these formations survived alongside the Arabo-Persian indicating the venerability of the battle formation.[29] Assignment in one or the other sections carried with it a prestige reflected in court seating arrangements as well. Skirmishers (*qarāwulān*) would provide the intelligence for the decision whether to fight, withdraw or surrender. Withdrawal, which was usually to a walled town, often led to the second tactic, that of the adopting of siege

28 Ḥāfiẓ-i Tanīsh, 1983, ff. 410b–31a.

29 The centre was known as *qalb* ('heart') in the Arabo-Persian and *qol* in the Turko-Mongol; the left wing was called *maysarah* (Arabo-Persian), *sol* (Turki) and *jawānghār* or *jawānqār* (Mong. *jeün ghar*); and the right wing *maymanah* (Arabo-Persian), *ong* (Turki), and *barānghār / barānqār* (Mongol).

positions by both parties. The besieging force needed tunnellers and explosives experts to undermine the walls and artillerymen to bombard the town's interior. In the attack on Herat the Shibanid/Uzbek army was assigned to siege stations called *mūrchal*s outside the gates of the city. The besieged force in turn defended itself with the city walls, a moat (generally dry and serving mainly to make the work of the tunnellers more difficult) and barricades or breastworks called *shīr ḥājjī*s (apparently a variant of *shīrāzī*) set up outside the city walls. These were temporary outposts from which the defenders could harass the besiegers and keep them, if possible, out of artillery range. The ability to effectively blockade the city and starve it or seriously damage its commerce, or to suborn a defender into opening a gate, was often the proximate cause of victory for the besiegers. But if foragers were unable to provide the besieging force with adequate food and fodder, the siege would have to be lifted and victory would go to the besieged. Hence the original attractiveness of the offer from ʿAlī Quli Khan Shamlu to ʿAbd Allāh Khan came from the prospect of capturing a major centre of commerce and a large agricultural region at little cost. When the governor reneged, the siege proved difficult and long.[30] Herat was not taken until February 1588 after a nine-month investment but its fall opened the way for further campaigns into Ṣafavid Khurāsān: Mashhad, Nīshāpūr, Sabzawar and Isfarāʾin all fell to the Shibanid/Uzbeks over the next few years and Simnān was raided as late as 1597.

The capture of Herat had two important consequences for the history of Central Asia. In the first place it introduced a new tension into the Janībekid house. ʿAbd al-Muʾmin Sulṭān, the only son of ʿAbd Allāh Khan to reach maturity, had been given Balkh in November 1582 on his father's succession to the khanate. He played a major role in the siege of Herat and led the army successfully against Mashhad in 1589. His father's decision to award Herat to the Uzbek amir Qul Baba Kökeltash and not to him was a source of considerable resentment. For the next decade, his feelings towards both his father and Qul Baba were cool, if not openly hostile.[31] He had a reputation for incorrigible anti-social behaviour and had few amirid allies when he succeeded his father. Muṭribī relates that as an adolescent ʿAbd al-Muʾmin terrorized Bukhara with nocturnal intrusions into private homes accompanied by his Qalmaq bodyguards. His father reportedly ordered him to stop his marauding and even issued an order for his arrest and execution when he refused to comply. But

30 A detailed discussion of this siege and the sources for it is found in McChesney, 1993.
31 See Burton, 1997, pp. 91–2. Muṭribī, 1998, p. 122, even tells of a failed attempt engineered by ʿAbd al-Muʾmin to poison his father.

the khan was persuaded to be lenient by Qul Baba Kökeltash.[32] When ʿAbd Allāh Khan died, ʿAbd al-Muʾmin's reign was short and brutal. He tortured and killed Qul Baba Kökeltash along with Qul Baba's son and had many of his own relatives executed if he thought they might prove to be rivals for the khanate. Ever suspicious of his father's amirs, ʿAbd al-Muʾmin ordered 'every *qaṣaba* and *sarāy* between Bukhara and Samarqand be destroyed lest amirs use them as fortifications against him'.[33] Four months after he took the throne in February 1598, he had embarked on a purge of amirs when a group of them assassinated him.

The second major consequence of the ten-year Chinggisid/Uzbek rule over Khurāsān was the emergence of a new Chinggisid clan, the Toqay-Timurid. This was a family either from the Astrakhan region (hence the designation Ashtarkhānī sometimes given them) or from the Mangïshlaq peninsula to the north-east of the Caspian Sea. Their actual origins are obscure as is the date of their arrival in Central Asia[34] but their bona fides as descendants of Jochid through his thirteenth son Toqay-Tīmūr seem to have been readily accepted by the Janïbekids who forged marital ties with the newcomers. Their head, Yār Muḥammad (who died sometime between 1605 and 1611 at the age of ninety-six), was given Maʿṣūma Sulṭān Khānum, a daughter of Iskandar Khan and full sister of ʿAbd Allāh and Yar Muḥammad's sister, Mihrjān Khānum, was given to ʿAbd Allāh in return. Maʿṣūmah Sulṭān Khānum produced four children (two sons and two daughters) for Yār Muḥammad the eldest of whom, Jānī Muḥammad, was serving the Janïbekids as a governor when ʿAbd Allāh Khan died in 1598 and was arrested by ʿAbd al-Muʾmin.[35] Jānī Muḥammad's eldest son, Dīn Muḥammad (d. 1598) with his brothers Bāqī Muḥammad and Walī Muḥammad, led a contingent of the Shibanid/Uzbek army into the Qūhistān region of Khurāsān and took Khargird and Bakharz on behalf of ʿAbd

32 Muṭribī, 1998, pp. 126–7.
33 Muṭribī, 1998, p. 127.
34 According to Maḥmūd b. Amīr Walī, the main source for the arrival of the Toqay-Timurids in Transoxania and probably fairly partisan, Küchkünji Khan had given Merkit Khan, the first Toqay-Timurid to enter Transoxania, 12,000 cavalry to help him reclaim his territory from the 'Rūs'. When he was unsuccessful he then gave him refuge. Meanwhile, we are told, the Abu'l-Khayrid Janïbek had 'adopted' Mangïshlaq as one of his sons because of the favour the latter's father had shown to Janïbek's father. (*Baḥr al-asrār*, ff. 4a ff.) A member of the third Toqay-Timurid generation in Transoxania, Dīn Muḥammad is said to have been born in 1564–5. His paternal grandmother is called Mahd-i ʿUlyā by Maḥmūd b. Amīr Walī (a common Persianate title for a queen and probably the same as Maʿṣūmah Sulṭān Khānum) and was the daughter of Iskandar Khan (*Baḥr al-asrār*, fol. 42a) so it is quite possible that the family was firmly established in Transoxania as early as the 1520s. Iskandar Khan (b. *c.* 1495) might have had a marriageable daughter as early as *c.* 1530–5 whose son could have fathered Dīn Muḥammad in 1564–5.
35 Muṭribī, 1998, 127.

Allāh Khan. While in Khurāsān he married the daughter of a Riẓavī shaykh at Mashhad and she bore him two sons, Imām Qulī and Nadhr Muḥammad, in 1589 or 1590 and 1591 or 1592, respectively.

At the death of ʿAbd Allāh Khan, the Toqay-Timurid family chronicler, Maḥmūd b. Amīr Walī, says that Dīn Muḥammad who was in Sistan proclaimed his grandfather khan as senior Jūchid Chinggisid. Yār Muḥammad reportedly refused and passed the mantle to his son Jānī Muḥammad, presumably next eldest.[36] The most militarily active member of the Toqay-Timurid house, Dīn Muḥammad, died in August 1598, fighting the Ṣafavid / Qïzïlbash in an unsuccessful attempt to retain control of Herat at which point his brothers returned to Transoxania. Within a year, the rest of the Toqay-Timurid family was firmly established at Samarqand, which Jānī Muḥammad made his capital and by the end of 1599 the last of the Janïbekid / Shibanid claimants to the khanate was eliminated from Bukhara.

To some degree, the Toqay-Timurids followed the Abu'l-Khayrid pattern of appanage distribution, internal consolidation, efforts to expand externally, and then internecine struggles and the elimination of cousin claimants to the khanate. The territory they laid claim to was comparable to the territory held by the Abu'l-Khayrid / Shibanids in 1512 but there were far fewer Toqay-Timurids than Abu'l-Khayrids and hence there was a lower level of inter-appanage conflict.[37] The main division occurred after Bāqī Muḥammad, who succeeded his father, Jānī Muḥammad, in 1603, himself died in 1605. His brother Walī Muḥammad was eldest and claimed the khanate but his nephews, Imām Qulī and Nadhr Muḥammad, now in their teens and backed by a group of ambitious amirs, soon challenged him. In subsequent fighting, in which the Ṣafavid Shah ʿAbbās lent support to Walī Muḥammad, the latter was killed and by 1611 Imām Qulī had been recognized, on the basis of age, as khan. His younger brother, Nadhr Muḥammad, already established at Balkh, remained there as appanage khan. For the next thirty years, the two units – greater Balkh stretching west to the Murghab Basin, south to the Hindu Kush and east into Badakhshan, and greater Bukhara including Samarqand and the lands between the Zarafshan and the Amu – lived in relative harmony. Each had its own external problems to contend with. Imām Qulī was confronted by the challenge of the 'Qazaqs' of the Tashkent area. In 1612, to reward the Qazaqs who had supported his fight against his uncle, he conferred Tashkent

36 Maḥmūd b. Amīr Walī, *Baḥr al-asrār*, fol. 61b.

37 Ibid. 62a. The *quriltai* of 1599 and the distribution of territory showed the Toqay-Timurids in control of Bukhara, Samarqand, Sagharj, Ura Tapah, Shahr-i Sabz and Khuzar. Tashkent, Balkh and parts of the Ferghana region would be taken shortly thereafter.

and the middle reaches of the Syr River to the Qazaq leadership as his lieges. But apparently the Qazāqs had their own Chinggisid aspirations and Imām Qulī was forced to send periodic expeditions to Tashkent and to Andijan at the eastern end of the Ferghana Valley to assert his claims.

Nadhr Muḥammad had two fronts that he was concerned with his southern marches with the Mughals in Kabul and the Murghab Basin to the west, the marchland with the Ṣafavids. In 1627, perhaps responding to an opportunity created by the succession crisis following the death of the Mughal emperor Jahāngīr, he sent his eldest son, ʿAbd al-ʿAzīz, with a large army to take Kabul. The force penetrated as far as Laghmān to the east of Kabul but was unable to take the city itself and retreated back through the Hindu Kush. In the west, Nadhr Muḥammad had reached a *modus vivendi* with Shah ʿAbbās but ʿAbd al-ʿAzīz his son threatened that peace with several prolonged raids into Khurāsān following Shah ʿAbbās's death in 1629.

In general, however, the Bukharan and Balkh khanates enjoyed a relatively uneventful and prosperous three decades of coexistence. In 1641, Imām Qulī, suffering from progressive blindness, abdicated and left Central Asia for the Hijāz where he lived out the two years remaining in his life. As senior clan member, Nadhr Muḥammad succeeded him, moving from Balkh to Bukhara. But like the Janībekid ʿAbd Allāh Khan, Nadhr Muḥammad Khan had an ambitious son in ʿAbd al-ʿAzīz, who was backed by a powerful group of amirs. Moreover, the amirs of Bukhara found themselves at odds with the Balkh amirs who accompanied the khan. A succession crisis ensued and Nadhr Muḥammad was deposed by his son in Bukhara in 1645 and returned to Balkh. In the meantime, the Mughal emperor, Shah Jahan, now firmly in control in Delhi, sent his son Awrangzib (ʿAlamgir) to regain the Timurid's patrimony lost nearly a century and a half earlier. The Mughal army managed to capture and hold Balkh for a year (1646–7) and forced Nadhr Muḥammad out. But the Mughal force encountered increasing resistance and withdrew without gaining their true goal, the reconquest of Samarqand. Nadhr Muḥammad Khan then returned to Balkh from Ṣafavid domains where he had taken refuge but as a result of growing strife between ʿAbd al-ʿAzīz and another son, Subḥān Qulī, he followed his brother's example and in 1651 departed on the *ḥajj*.[38]

In the aftermath, the greater Balkh khanate was assumed by Subḥān Qulī and, from mid-century, there ensued another thirty-year period of a Chinggisid khanate divided between two brothers. It was a time marked by

38 For a detailed account of the decade 1641–51, see Burton, 1997, pp. 212–64.

increasing pressure from the ʿArabshahid Shibanids in Khwārazm, by the growing autonomy of certain Uzbek groups, notably the Mīng, Qaṭaghān, Mangghït, Yüz and Kanīkas, and by very cool relations between ʿAbd al-ʿAzīz and Subḥān Qulī. In Bukhara, ʿAbd al-ʿAzīz, remembered as particularly devoted to Islamic learning, found himself repeatedly facing invasions of the Khwārazmian Shibanids. For the first half of the seventeenth century, during most of which the Toqay-Timurid double khanate remained relatively free of internal factionalism, it had been able to exploit divisions within Khwārazm to maintain occasionally direct control and at other times received tribute from its governors. But the situation was reversed in the middle of the century. A strong and charismatic figure, Abu'l-Ghāzī b. ʿArab Muḥammad (r. 1644–63), returned from exile in Iran to claim the khanate and by uniting or eliminating the rival amirid and princely factions developed sufficient military strength to conduct as many as four major expeditions against Bukhara. None succeeded in taking the oasis but defending against them drained the resources of ʿAbd al-ʿAzīz and he received no assistance from his brother in Balkh. On one occasion Subḥān Qulī even acted in alliance with the Khwārazmians. Anūsha Khan (r. 1663–85), Abu'l-Ghāzī's son and successor, continued the campaigns against Bukhara with considerably more success than his father. Although the chronology is disputed, he conducted at least four campaigns, three during ʿAbd al-ʿAzīz Khan's reign (in 1666–7, 1675 and 1679) and one particularly devastating one during Subḥān Qulī's (r. 1681–1702) khanate in Bukhara in 1684.[39] The Khwārazmian campaigns against Bukhara are considered a major cause of ʿAbd al-ʿAzīz Khan's abdication in 1681 and, following his father's and uncle's examples, his departure for the Holy Cities on *ḥajj*.

More significant for the later political history of Central Asia was the increasing independence of the Uzbek groups. In part because of the fighting between ʿAbd al-ʿAzīz and Subḥān Qulī and in part because of the failure of the Toqay-Timurid state to add new territory during the seventeenth century, the Uzbek groups over the course of the century became firmly attached to the territories initially given them. By century's end, the Qaṭaghān, Ming, Yuz and Kanikas most notably had turned their sub-infeudations into more or less autonomous petty states with only nominal allegiance to the khanly centres of Balkh and Bukhara. The Qunghrat and Mangghït on the other hand had their power concentrated around their respective khanly centres, Khiva and Bukhara, and were dominant forces in those two regions.

39 For a detailed chronology of this period, see Burton, 1997, pp. 265–328.

Although the Toqay-Timurid khanate in Transoxania and Cisoxania continued to be recognized by the amirs until the middle of the eighteenth century, real power had passed to amirid leaders like Maḥmūd Bi Qaṭaghān who ruled Badakhshan from Qunduz and founded a local dynasty there, Danyal Bi the Mangghït who founded a dynasty in Bukhara, and Uraz Bi Ming who accomplished the same in Maymanah in present-day Afghanistan.

The Chinggisid appanage system as it had evolved through the seventeenth century slowly succumbed to the emergence of the small Uzbek amirates. Although the prestige of Chinggisid descent remained, the power traditionally associated with that prestige disappeared with the easy conquest of Central Asia by the forces of the Iranian warlord, Nadir Khan Afshar, in 1737. Nevertheless, Chinggisid influences remained strong in Central Asia during the coming years in military and administrative terminology, in court ceremonial and in the remembrance of the political power that the region had once possessed.

16

The western steppe: the Volga-Ural region, Siberia and the Crimea under Russian rule

CHRISTIAN NOACK

Conquest

> With the aid of our Almighty Lord Jesus Christ and the prayers of the Mother of God... our pious Tsar and Grand Prince Ivan Vasilievich, crowned by God, Autocrat of all Rus', fought against the infidels, defeated them finally and captured the Tsar of Kazan' Edigai-Mahmet. And the pious Tsar and Grand Prince ordered his regiment to sing an anthem under his banner, to give thanks to God for the victory; and at the same time ordered a life-giving cross to be placed and a church to be built, with the uncreated image of our Lord Jesus Christ, where the Tatar colours had stood during the battle.[1]

On 2 (15) October 1552, Russian and allied Tatar troops stormed what was left of the Kazan Kremlin after a short siege. As the chronicle reported, the tsar ordered the surviving male defenders of the city except for the Khan to be put to death as traitors, and the remaining buildings were symbolically consecrated and Christianized. Already the contemporary Russian chroniclers[2] understood the conquest of Kazan and the subsequent incorporation of the Khanate into Muscovite body politic as an unprecedented incident and a turning point in history: for the first time Moscow's Grand Prince conquered and annexed a sovereign, military power and economically developed neighbouring Muslim state.

Muscovy's relations to its southern neighbours had always been sensitive and periods of intensive collaboration alternated with mutual warfare from the very moment Moscow rose to importance among the Russian principalities in the thirteenth century.[3] During the fifteenth century the Muscovite Grand Princes emerged as contestants for superiority among the other rulers

1 *PSRL*, XXIX, p. 108. Trans. Hosking, 1997, p. 3.
2 Cf. Kämpfer, 1969, pp. 8–29.
3 Crummey, 1987.

in the Golden Horde's successor states – the only Christian sovereign among Muslims and, except for the Kazan Khan, the only one ruling over a predominantly sedentary peasant population. By the end of the fifteenth century, after the conquest of Novgorod at the latest, Moscow's natural and human resources surpassed those of neighbouring Kazan, and the increasingly centralized state apparatus allowed the Grand Princes to exploit them rather efficiently. The Khanate on the contrary suffered from inconsistencies between the social and political orders: the Khan's rule was patterned on the model of nomadic steppe confederations like the Golden Horde, and it could not but control loose conglomerations of various people and principalities rather superficially.

Beginning with Ivan III in the 1480s the Grand Princes began to pursue their interests in Kazan actively. These interests were firstly the pacification of the common frontier that suffered from repeated incursions of Tatars and other steppe nomads, secondly military assistance in campaigns against Poland-Lithuania and the Great Horde and, finally, a share in the important fur trade down the Volga. Later Moscow felt increasingly pressed to look for new territories to colonize and distribute among its quickly augmenting military service estate. Indeed, with Moscow's increasing supremacy a growing number of Tatar princes and nobles offered their service to the Grand Princes and weakened the Khanate further.[4]

In the course of the sixteenth century Muscovy improved her military technology with the use of modern infantry (the *strel'tsy*) and artillery inasmuch as she could ultimately defeat the Khanate. For the time being, however, the geopolitical situation did not allow the Grand Princes to concentrate their efforts on Kazan: each of the competing Christian powers in Eastern Europe, Muscovy and Poland-Lithuania, was allied with a strong successor of the Golden Horde, the Crimean Khanate and Great Horde, respectively. This balance of powers granted the status quo. Only after the break-up of the long-standing political alliance between Muscovy and the Crimea in 1519 did both sides begin to compete actively for political influence in Kazan. For most of the second quarter of the sixteenth century the Crimeans proved to be more successful and khans from the Gireay dynasty provided the rulers of Kazan between 1521–31 and 1533–46.[5]

Already before he was crowned 'Tsar of all Russia', young Ivan IV had tried to exploit a crisis of succession in the Kazan Khanate in 1546 to install one of

4 Khudiakov, 1991, pp. 50–82; Pelensky, 1974, pp. 23–61; Kappeler, 1982, pp. 39–66; Martin, 1986, pp. 86–109.

5 Kusber, 1998; Khodarkovsky, 2002, pp. 91–103.

his Tatar vassals on the throne. The geopolitical setting seemed favourable. Moscow at that time faced no challenges on the Lithuanian border, and the most powerful neighbours in the south, the Crimean Tatars and the Noghays, were engaged in mutual warfare. On the request of a pro-Russian party in Kazan, Ivan invested Shāh ʿAlī, then ruler of the Russian puppet Khanate of Kasimov on the Oka. Shāh ʿAlī's second reign – he had briefly governed Kazan between 1518 and 1521 – proved to be rather short-lived. After only one month the Kazan Tatars replaced him with his predecessor Ṣafā-Girāy.

With the appointment of a pro-Russian candidate on the throne failing, Ivan resolved for methods that violated the established rule of steppe diplomacy and traditional clientele policy pursued by his ancestors from the 1480s onwards. After two large, but largely unsuccessful, military expeditions under his personal command in 1547/8 and 1549/50, the tsar carefully prepared the third and final blow. Moscow renewed alliance with the Noghays and set out to exploit social and ethnic tensions among the multinational population of the Khanate. The Russians won over significant parts of the non-Muslim elite on the right bank of the Volga by granting them their status quo and temporary exemption from tributes. Gradually wresting the so-called *gornaia storona* out of the Khanate, Moscow dared to erect a strong fortress on the estuary of the Sviiaga River, some 150 kilometres east of the former frontiers 'on the shoulders of Kazan', as the chronicle put it.[6] This stronghold allowed Moscow to maintain troops and artillery in the Khanate's heartland during military retreats and established firm control over the right bank. Sviiazhsk, governed by a *voevoda*, became the temporary residence of the Muscovite contender Shāh ʿAlī and other Tatar nobles. The factual division of the Khanate's territory and the establishment of a counter-capital did not fail to impress the Tatars, and in August 1551 Kazan reopened his gates for Shāh ʿAlī. The severe conditions Moscow imposed on the Khanate – the virtual partition of the Khanate, the imposition of a permanent garrison of Russian gunners and Kasimov Tatars in the city of Kazan and, finally, the handing over of all Russian prisoners – frustrated the indigenous elite and the new ruler likewise: in March 1552 Shāh ʿAlī abdicated again, Muscovite occupying forces were slaughtered and a new Khan of Noghay origin enthroned.[7]

Preparing his final military campaign against Kazan in 1552, Ivan essentially had to overcome the reluctance of his own service nobility. Ignoring the advice of some war-weary Boyars, Ivan raised another huge army and

6 Kämpfer, 1969, p. 34.
7 Khudiakov, 1991, pp. 124–49; Kämpfer, 1969, pp. 29–47; Kappeler, 1982, pp. 68–76; Khodarkovsky, 2002, pp. 103–7.

renewed his alliance with the Noghays. After the repulsion of a minor attack of Crimean troops against the Oka line, Ivan marched his troops to Kazan without encountering much resistance. The Russians laid siege to the town and blocked the crossings on the Volga, Kama and Viatka rivers. Cut off from possible relief, the weak Tatar forces in and around the city set up fierce resistance but could not match the numerical and technical superiority of the Muscovite forces.[8]

The Noghays, although uneasy about Moscow's advance, were determined to profit from the alliance in order to get rid of the Khanate of Astrakhan on the Lower Volga, too. The much smaller Khanate of Astrakhan controlled the river crossings between Noghay pastures and occasionally sided with their rivals, the Crimean Tatars. The Noghay *biy* Ismāʿīl repeatedly invited Ivan to send his troops for a common assault down the Volga. With Noghay support Moscow installed a puppet rule in Astrakhan in 1554, but when the latter tried to side with the Crimean Tatars, Ivan resolved to conquest again. Without reinforcements from outside, the city easily fell victim in 1556.[9] After the fall of Astrakhan, Moscow completely controlled the Volga way and was in a position to block the passage of nomad herds, Oriental goods and Muslim pilgrims across the river. The Ottoman Empire, engaged in enduring wars against Ṣafavid Persia, could no longer ignore Moscow's advance towards the Caucasus which it regarded as its own sphere of interest. Yet the most serious attempt to repel Moscow, a large-scale Ottoman-Crimean campaign in 1569, ended in a military fiasco, not least because of Crimean stalling tactics. The Girāys obviously feared Ottoman supremacy in the area no less than Muscovy's advance. Moscow complied with some Ottoman demands, dismantled a forepost on the River Terek and reopened the Astrakhan route for Muslim merchants and pilgrims.[10]

Orthodoxy, autocracy and imperial ideology

Ivan's campaigns against Kazan had been conducted with missionary zeal, and the Orthodox Church was instrumental in providing additional spiritual and political justification for the transgression of traditional rules of steppe policies. After all, with the recurrent technique of indirect rule failing, Ivan had betrayed Muscovite political customs already with the annexation of the

8 Khudiakov, 1991, pp. 149–55; Kämpfer, 1969, pp. 47–91; Kappeler, 1982, pp. 76–7.
9 Khodarkovsky, 2002, pp. 109–14.
10 Khodarkovsky, 2002, pp. 116–17. On the historiography of Ottoman–Muscovite relations cf. Zaitsev, 2002, pp. 269–313.

right bank in 1551 – foreign territory that never had belonged to Eastern Slavic principalities. The Chronicles, though, suggested the opposite and depicted the Middle Volga as a constituent part of Kievan Rus' allegedly settled by Orthodox Slavs.[11] Finally, in 1552 Ivan's symbolic policies left no doubt about the fact that Muscovy had swallowed an entirely different and hitherto independent body politic. However, against all historical evidence Ivan claimed the 'Kazan *yurt*' as his patrimony, and referred to the fact that already his grandfather Ivan III had invested rulers there. Against this backdrop the tsar and contemporary Russian historiography interpreted the continued Tatar resistance against the tsar's candidates and envoys as treason.[12]

The tsar's symbolic procedures throughout the campaign referred to historical analogies, above all Dmitrii Donskoi's victorious campaign against Māmāy, in order to entrench his policy in Muscovite tradition: Dmitrii, like Ivan, had deliberately crossed a river and marched deep into the hostile steppe to defeat the Tatar khan.[13] Ivan, drawing on the example of Donskoi, demonstratively strove to embody the ideal of a pious ruler, and most of the chronicles aligned their narratives of the campaign around miracles and omens denoting divine support. But even ecclesiastical sources felt compelled to explain why the tsar ignored the biblical ban on annexation.[14] The main religious motives legitimizing the conquest were the defence of the fatherland and the liberation of enslaved Christian prisoners of war. While the first argument hardly veiled the aggressive character of Ivan's policy, the second was more plausible – the Kazan Khanate like the Crimean had engaged in slave trade. Nonetheless the frequent repetition of the reasoning in the sources underlines that the motive for conquest was perceived as being far from self-evident.[15]

In fact, the conquest of Kazan, the development of imperial doctrine and the elaboration of autocracy were intrinsically linked: in Ivan the leading ideologues of the Josephite Orthodoxy saw the reincarnation of the lost *basileos* and strove actively to remodel the Muscovite body politic on the Byzantine model of symphony between Church and State. Clerics had developed the idea of the 'Third Rome' in the late fifteenth century and incessantly strove for acknowledgement of the title of 'tsars'. Since Ivan III, the Grand Princes themselves were using it reluctantly in diplomatic exchanges. In the domestic realm, the Church's upgrading of the tsar's rank helped Ivan to undermine

11 Kämpfer, 1969, pp. 120–3; Pelensky, 1974, pp. 104–35.
12 Pelensky, 1974, pp. 76–87.
13 Kämpfer, 1969, pp. 62–3, 128–31.
14 Kämpfer, 1969, pp. 38–43, 45–53.
15 Kämpfer, 1969, pp. 114–18.

the customary limits of his self-rule: the binding laws of tradition and the institutions that went with it, like the Boyars' consultative share in power.

In external relations the rise of Muscovy to pre-eminence among the Eastern Slavic principalities owed as much to the intensive interrelations with the Chinggisid steppe empires, as to the Grand Prince's increasingly autocratic rule backed by the Orthodox clergy. While Muscovite diplomacy continued to pay lip-service to the superiority of the Chinggisid dynasties throughout the sixteenth century, power-relations and treaties that steppe rulers negotiated with Moscow were interpreted as a permanent and binding acknowledgement of the tsar's sovereignty. After the fall of Kazan the increasingly self-confident Ivan IV referred to the incorporation of the former Chinggisid realm to upgrade his own rank among the Christian rulers.[16]

Incorporation

After 1552, Tsar Ivan's incorporation of Kazan into the Muscovite state remained symbolic for some time, since it took another five years to quell armed resistance. The main repository of the insurgence proved to be the *lugovaia storona*, the large forests stretching out on the Volga's left banks north of the Kazanka River. They provided refuge for the local Mari elite that sided with Tatar nobles from the Arsk region in their efforts to regain independence. From there resistance carried away almost all of the former Khanate's territories on the left bank. Representatives of all social and ethnic groups participated in the insurrection. The insurgents erected a fortress on the River Mesha in 1553 and defeated several Muscovite armies on both sides of the Volga. Moscow faced severe problems during the uprising since its Tatar and other non-Russian auxiliary troops several times defected and reinforced the insurgents led by the Tatar *mīrzā* Mamich-Berdei. The insurgents left no doubt about their political objectives when they established contact with the Noghays and brought a Chinggisid princeling to the Volga. Moscow gained the upper hand only after several devastating punitive campaigns on the left bank. Finally, in 1556 loyal non-Russians on the right bank captured Mamich-Berdei and delivered him to Moscow. A year later the last Tatar princes from the Arsk region, some Bashkir chiefs and the *lugovye liudi* swore the oath of allegiance.[17]

The scale and intensity of resistance, however, left no doubt that Moscow was well advised adopt a more cautious policy. In fact, the destructive wars

16 Cherniavsky, 1959, esp. pp. 473–6; Keenan, 1967; Khodarkovsky, 2002, pp. 51, 103–4, 106, 114.

17 Kappeler, 1982, pp. 83–92.

following the 1552 conquest had decimated the non-loyalist elements significantly, and the Tatars and their Islamic culture had been driven out of the few larger towns like Kazan and Arsk. Russian merchants and foreign *gosti* came to replace the Tatars in the important Volga trade. As for the administration of the rural areas, Muscovy reverted to the proven method of collaboration with the Tatar nobles and the non-Russian elite (*sotniki* and *tarkhany*). The tsar granted them status and privileges and used them to collect tribute (*yasak*) or levy armed men to reinforce his army. The local elite was controlled by three military governors, the *voevody*, residing in the fortresses of Kazan, Sviiazhsk and, after 1555, Cheboksary. With the erection of new fortresses the number of territorial divisions rose, and by the end of the seventeenth century the formerly non-Russian territories in the Volga-Urals still known as the 'Tsardom of Kazan' comprised twenty-six provinces. The Russian administration largely refrained from interfering in local matters, particularly where native customs or religion were concerned. Direct rule remained limited to the military apparatus of the *voevody* and the city and district administrations in larger settlements and military outposts.[18]

The exceptional status of the newly conquered territories found its expression in the establishment of an administrative body in Moscow, the *Kazanskii dvoretskii* or *Prikaz Kazanskogo dvortsa*. Initially created as one bureau of the Boyar Duma, the *prikaz* was charged with the general administration in the territories of the former Khanates from 1553 until its dissolution in 1720. All matters were divided among several bureaus: justice (*sudnyi*); finances and taxation (*denezhnyi*); public order (*streletskii*); and military administration (*razriadnyi*). The *prikaz* sent its agents (*prikaznye liudi*) to the provinces to oversee the management of crown estates, the collection of taxes (*obrok*) from Russian colonists and *yasak* from non-Russians. Another important task was the deportation of exiled subjects and hostages to the Kazan lands that had already begun in 1563. In short, the *prikaz* assured the economic exploitation of the area, controlled the administration and provided law, order and basic protection for both Russian and non-Russian subjects of the tsar.[19]

For the time being Moscow refrained from large-scale colonization in the conquered territories. Deserted land-holdings that had belonged to the Khan or the killed noblemen were distributed among Russian and non-Russian service-men or bestowed upon the archdiocese and monasteries. Although no more than 10,000 colonists settled around the fortresses and along the main

18 Kappeler, 1982, pp. 96–103.
19 Rywkin, 1988. From 1599 to 1637 the newly conquered Siberian territories were under its jurisdiction, too.

rivers in the first decade after the conquest, the number of Russian farmsteads was sufficient to make the military outposts independent of supply from Muscovy's heartlands.[20]

As we have seen, Orthodoxy had played an important role in the justification of Ivan's policy, and a strong sense of missionary zeal runs through contemporary sources. Ivan and his advisers from the clergy initially intended to convert the population of the Khanate swiftly and entirely, with the result that mosques were destroyed and natives converted by threat of force.[21] Tatar Muslim high culture was ruralized, but Islam survived and probably took roots even more deeply. Not least because of the intense native resistance, Moscow resolved on a more pragmatic approach to Islam after 1555. Ivan exhorted Archbishop Gurii to win over the natives with 'tenderness and love'. Conversion was no longer to be enforced but materially encouraged. Nevertheless, there had obviously been no systematic tax-exemption for newly converted Christians in the region, and during the 1590s Moscow renewed its concern about the slow pace of conversion in the Kazan lands. Tsar Fedor threatened Christian apostasy with severe punishment and ordered the destruction of mosques and the isolation of new converts from their former co-religionists – clearly a sign of the strong influence Islam exerted, probably also among converted former animists.[22] Beyond missionary activities, the Church became an important repository of Muscovite rule in the former Khanates. Among the beneficiaries of the land distributions were the newly founded seat of the Archbishop of Kazan, important Russian spiritual centres like the Troitskii-Sergievskii Monastery, or newly founded monasteries in or near Kazan, Sviiazhsk and Cheboksary. The monasteries not only played a privileged role in the economic development of the conquered territories, but carried out important military and administrative functions.[23]

Resistance

Although Moscow adopted a more cautious policy towards the indigenous population and refrained from large-scale conversions, rebellions continued to surface whenever Muscovy showed signs of weakness. This was the case during the first half of the 1570s, in the aftermath of the Livonian Wars,

20 Kappeler, 1982, pp. 108–14. A significantly larger number of Russian peasant households migrated to the pacified frontier regions east of Murom and Nizhnii Novgorod.

21 Kämpfer, 1969, pp. 101, 123–5.

22 Kämpfer, 1969, pp. 103–4; Kappeler, 1982, pp. 115–21; Gilyazov, 1996.

23 Romaniello, 2000.

Crimean and Noghay raids and the disastrous consequences of the *oprichina*. The insurgency started in 1571 and had its strongholds on the left bank of the Volga. Muslims and non-Muslims besieged Russian towns and fortresses, plundered monasteries and villages and even raided the vicinity of Nizhnii Novgorod. While some of the insurgents rose in protest against the continued levies of troops and taxes, others proclaimed the restoration of an independent Khanate. Moscow exploited these disagreements successfully and offered concessions to those who would change sides. By 1573 Moscow had regained control, only to see the whole region rise up again in the first half of the 1580s, when the continued war in the west and Ivan's death destabilized Muscovy. Unrest spread from the left bank again and, as during the early 1570s, insurgents tried to storm Russian towns and strongholds, pillaged monasteries and looted villages. Although the Commonwealth had agreed to an armistice in 1582 and gave Moscow a free hand on the Volga, the Russians had to at least seven military campaigns until 1585, when they finally quelled the insurrection.[24]

In order to reinforce her control over the former Khanate, Moscow had erected new fortresses on both banks of the Volga in 1570/4. This policy was intensified in the mid-1580s. The military colonization concentrated on the rebellious *lugovaia storona*. With Ufa a first stronghold was put up beyond the natural barrier of the Kama in 1586, and in the same decade Samara, Saratov and Tsaritsyn were founded as fortified settlements down the Volga. These fortresses increased the administrative penetration of the conquered territories, and their surroundings were settled with Russian servicemen.[25]

Although the insurrections of the second half of the sixteenth century did not affect all social and ethnic groups of the former Khanate synchronously – a fact exploited by Muscovy in her pacification policies – a clear anti-Muscovite orientation had been predominant and no Russians backed the insurgents. When the Middle Volga rebelled again against Moscow during the 'Time of Troubles' (1606–16), this picture changed substantially. Except for the epilogue of 1615–16, when non-Russians rose for independence for the last time, Russians and non-Russians revolted together against the local agents of Muscovite rule, that is the military administration, the tax-collectors and the monasteries. A restoration of the Khanate had finally become less important than improvement in the economic, social and political situation within the Russian state.[26]

24 Kappeler, 1982, pp. 138–40.
25 Kappeler, 1982, pp. 140–2; Khodarkovsky, 2002, pp. 122–3.
26 Kappeler, 2002, pp. 148–58.

MUSCOVITE AND RUSSIAN EXPANSION AND RULE TO 1762

Expansion

The succession crises of 1598 and the ensuing 'Time of Troubles' halted Muscovy's drive eastwards only briefly. With the Romanov dynasty firmly established, Moscow's military and political potential continued to grow at the expense of her western and eastern neighbours, and during the seventeenth century Russia's eastwards expansion and steppe policies displayed remarkable continuity with those developed under the last Riurikids. They were not completely abandoned during the first half of the following century, although the Westernization of Russia's elite began to influence her outlook on her Asian neighbours. The empire's eastern conquests were increasingly legitimized in terms of European colonial thinking. When Catherine II ascended the throne in 1762 Russia not only firmly controlled the southern Urals and Siberia, but was in a strong position in the adjacent steppes among Qazaqs and Qalmaqs. And the Crimean Khanate, her long-time rival in the steppe, was on the verge of independent existence.

Siberia

The initial stage of the conquest of Siberia deviated from the patterns developed on the Volga. It was characterized by a close interplay between private and governmental initiative. From the end of the fifteenth century the Stroganovs, a merchant dynasty, had built up an enormous economic enterprise based on the extraction of salt and furs in the Russian north. On the tracks of Novgorodian fur-hunters, their agents collected valuable pelts east of the Urals, on the lower Ob' and the Arctic coast. The tsars, highly valuing the substantial payments the Stroganovs contributed to their treasury, commissioned them to build strongholds and levy armed detachments against native resistance and Tatar raids.[27]

Direct diplomatic exchange with the Taybughid principality of Sibir' intensified after its ruler, Khan Yādigār, impressed by Moscow's victory over Kazan, swore submission in 1555. In the wake of Moscow's expansion, Russian fur-hunters no longer felt confined to the difficult passages in the north, and a Cossack detachment under Yermak Timofeev, who was on the Stroganovs' payroll, crossed the Ural through Bashkir territory in 1581/2. Their intention

27 Martin, 1988; Huttenbach, 1988, pp. 77–80.

was to extract furs from Vogul and Ostiak tribes on the Middle Ob'. In doing so, they clashed with armed forces of Yādigār's successor, the Shibanid Khan Küchüm. Küchüm had ceased payments to Moscow in 1572 and regarded the tribes on the Middle Ob' as his own *yasak*-paying subjects. The Cossacks, numbering some 500 men only, were joined by Tatar dissenters and defeated Küchüm on the Lower Irtysh in 1582. Küchüm escaped to the steppe and rallied Noghay support to win back his dominion. He might have succeeded if Muscovite policies had not reoriented east after the humiliating defeats suffered during the Livonian Wars. In the 1580s, Moscow erected new fortresses along its steppe frontier and one of them, Ufa, controlled an old passage across the Ural to the headwaters of the Tura and on to Tiumen', where the Cossacks had restored the former Tatar stronghold the same year.[28]

Under Ivan IV's successor Fedor, the state followed up the Cossacks, sent regular troops and erected fortresses on the Ob' beyond Tiumen', such as Tobol'sk in 1587 and Tomsk in 1604. These strongholds were designed to deter Noghay and Bashkir raids and enabled the Russians to collect *yasak* from the Voguls and the Ostiaks regularly. In the following decades, Western Siberia served as a springboard for further advance along the Siberian rivers. In doing so, the Russians still preferred to avoid the open steppe, for even after Küchüm's death in 1598 the number of Cossacks, *streltsy* and Tatar cavalry was too small to deter continuous Bashkir, Noghay, Qalmaq or Qazaq attacks. To be sure, the numerically small indigenous population in the forests of the north offered fierce resistance, too, but this could be relatively easily overcome by firearms, vodka and disease. The first Russian strongholds were built on the Yenisei by 1607 and on the Lena by 1630. Cossack detachments attained the Sea of Okhotsk in 1639. Lake Baikal was reached in 1643 before Mongol and Manchu resistance prevented further penetration to the south.[29]

Since private initiative and fur greed had propelled the first stage of Russian advance, the 'Time of Troubles' did not halt the eastwards rush. On the contrary, Muscovy continued to rely heavily on the economic exploitation of Siberian furs. This was acknowledged with the institution of a separate administrative body, the Siberian *prikaz*, in 1637. During the second half of the seventeenth century, the extraction of natural resources other than fur, above all minerals such as silver and iron, began to play an increasing role in the Siberian economy. Muscovy adopted familiar strategies to profit as much as possible at minimal expense: relying on collaboration with native elders, the Russian administrative apparatus was modest. Under the military

28 Nolde, 1952–3, I, pp. 1, 144–50, 155–62.
29 Nolde, 1952–3, pp. 163–6; Nolte, 1969, pp. 78–9; Kappeler, 1992, pp. 36–42.

administration of the four *voevody*, a small bureaucracy of *diaki* worked in the provincial centres or in the *prikaznye izby* of the smaller towns. With the *iamskoi prikaz* and its outposts scattered over the vast Siberian lands, Muscovy installed an effective system to move goods and people back and forth. However, distances and insufficient manpower restrained control. The permanent rotation of the *voevody* and a rather elaborate Siberian customs bureaucracy indicates how seriously Moscow was concered about corruption.[30]

Facilitated by the spatial separation of Russian and non-Russian settlements, Russian administration pursued a policy of non-interference: it guaranteed status and privileges for the indigenous elite in return for submission and tribute, mainly furs. But unlike the Tatars, other indigenous elites had no chance to be co-opted into the Russian service class, and Moscow made no effort to integrate larger groups into its estate system. Nonetheless Moscow faced serious revolts after a relatively easy conquest. The autochthonous people rose against maladministration and economic exploitation. As happened on the Volga, the Siberian *voevody* were instructed to encourage and reward loyal behaviour or, if necessary, use native forces against insurgents.[31]

Religious justification played a minor role in the acquisition of Siberia. Yet the Church followed the fur-hunters and Cossacks closely. Larger convents were founded in Tiumen', Tobol'sk and Verkhotur'e shortly after the establishment of Russian administration. In 1621 Tobol'sk was elevated to the seat of the Archbishopric of Siberia. But before the eighteenth century the state clearly did not regard Orthodox mission among natives as a priority and backed it only as long as it did not interfere with economic and security interests.[32] The fact that Moscow displayed religious tolerance wherever it suited her interests is illustrated by its encouragement of Muslim immigration from Central Asia. Above all, merchants were encouraged to settle in the major Western Siberian towns and trade at the important fairs. As time went on these Bukharans came to supplement, or even replace, the small indigenous Muslim elite of Tatar servicemen.[33]

Bashkiria

After the conquest of Kazan some Bashkir tribes had recognized Muscovite suzerainty. But Moscow initially exercised little influence south of the Kama, and even the fortification of Ufa in 1574 brought little in the way of change.

30 Dmytryshyn, 1991; Huttenbach, 1988, pp. 86–8, 92–3, 96.
31 Nolde, 1952–3, I, pp. 178–89; Collins, 1991.
32 Huttenbach, 1988, pp. 94–5; Kappeler, 1992, p. 40.
33 Noack, 2000.

The semi-nomadic or nomadic Bashkirs, living between the Kama in the north, the Tobol' and Yayïq (Ural) rivers in the east, the Samara in the south and the Volga in the west, continued to raid Russian settlements occasionally, sometimes in alliance with Noghay Tatars or, later, Qalmaqs. However, since they were subdivided in numerous clans without central authority, the Bashkirs were no priority in Muscovy's steppe policy.

After the construction of a new chain of fortresses between the Volga and Menzelinsk in the 1650s, the northern and western Bashkirs found themselves exposed to closer Russian military-administrative supervision, and more Bashkir clans swore allegiance and agreed to paid *yasak*. The new strongholds of the Trans-Kama line were manned by the *Meshcheriaki* – servicemen mostly of Tatar origin – and reinforced by Cossack units. Other Cossacks had settled on the Yayïq River before, though beyond the area of Muscovite control and at their own will. These Cossacks occasionally contributed troops to the tsars, but, in general acted independently. Cossack raids against Bashkirs, Noghays and Qalmaqs were a permanent issue in the diplomatic exchanges between Muscovy and the rulers of the steppe. Beyond the encroachments of the Cossacks, the ruthless extraction of tributes by local officials marred relations with the indigenous population.[34]

Revolts broke out in 1662 and quickly developed into a full-fledged war that involved Tatars, Bashkirs and even some Qalmaq princes. Heirs of Khan Küchüm tried to seize the opportunity and restore the Siberian Khanate, thereby elucidating the close interrelation between Bashkiria and Western Siberia. It took two years of intensive diplomatic negotiations with the Qalmaqs and substantive military endeavour to pacify the region. To prevent further insubordination, Moscow demonstratively rewarded loyal Bashkir leaders, relieved Bashkir obligations and limited land seizure at the expense of the indigenous population. This policy initially seemed to pay off, as the Bashkir participation in the Stepan Razin uprising (1667–71) was marginal. However, from 1675 onwards, new unrest spread. Since Noghays and Qalmaqs initially sided with insurgent Bashkirs, Russian rule over Bashkiria was seriously endangered until the Qalmaqs changed sides and fought against their former allies. Bashkir resistance collapsed in 1683.[35]

A century of nominal Russian sovereignty over Bashkiria had thus brought little evident change: Moscow continued to exercise a rather loose tributary dominion, and fortified strongholds could not have been advanced

34 Nolde, 1952–3, I, pp. 166–8, 191–3; Donnelly, 1968, pp. 21–3, 29–31; Kappeler, 1982, pp. 173–4.

35 Donnelly, 1968, pp. 23–6.

significantly southwards. In contrast to the Kazan lands and Siberia, the authorities did not encourage peasant colonization and even tried to halt it after 1660. But repeated waves of spontaneous immigration of Russian and non-Russian peasants brought about substantial changes in the demographic and economic composition of the area. The so-called Teptiars settled in agreement with Bashkir elders on their pastures and paid *quitrent*. Others, the *bobyli*, initially came as condoned squatters and gradually became serfs on Bashkir land-holdings. During the eighteenth century, increasing social and economic tensions between Bashkirs and non-Bashkir immigrants constituted a potential lever for Russian policy, since the immigrants frequently supported Russian military expeditions and were rewarded in return for their loyalty.[36]

Under Peter the Great, Bashkiria remained a sensitive issue for several reasons: firstly Peter, having opened 'the window to the West', wished to establish Russia as the main intermediary for European trade with the East. Secondly, the extraction of furs and natural resources from Siberia remained a cornerstone of the empire's economy. Beyond it the southern Urals turned into Russia's most important centre of mining and iron processing during the early eighteenth century.[37] But trade or industry in many respects depended on the natives' good will, and mines and foundries were repeatedly attacked. Renewed Bashkir uprisings between 1705 and 1711 seriously endangered Russia's hold on the steppe fringe, the more so as the Northern War and, after 1710, Ottoman and Crimean hostility did not allow it to dislocate larger forces. Alliance with the larger steppe federations again became the decisive question for insurgents and Russians. The Bashkirs dispatched envoys as far as the Crimea and the Porte – to no result – but successfully invited some Qalmaq tribes to join their attacks on Russian forts and settlements. In 1708, they broke through the Trans-Kama defence line and were repelled in the vicinity of Kazan. Finally, the Russians persuaded Khan Ayuki to intervene and a considerable Qalmaq detachment broke Bashkir resistance in 1710.[38]

Under Peter's successors, the Oriental direction remained vital. The most ambitious project, the Orenburg Expedition, entirely reflected the Westernization of Russia's elite: it combined military and scientific explorations of the steppes south of Russia's possessions in the Urals and Western Siberia with great designs for the extraction of natural resources and the stimulation of Oriental trade. A fortified town was erected on the confluence of the rivers Or' and Yayïq: Orenburg. This became the main trading

36 Nolde, 1952–3, I, pp. 204–7; Donnelly, 1968, pp. 32–3; Kuzeev, 1992, pp. 121–7, 143–56.
37 Nolde, 1952–3, I, pp. 236–73.
38 Donnelly, 1968, pp. 45–9.

centre between the empire, the Qazaqs and Central Asia. Similar projects had been designed earlier, but it was only in 1734 that the state financed and equipped a large-scale expedition.[39] Bashkir rebellions threatened to turn the whole endeavour into a disaster, since Russia was simultaneously waging war against Ottoman Turkey. To subdue the Bashkirs, the leaders of the expedition resorted to traditional methods like the construction of forts, the commissioning of loyal groups among the Bashkirs or immigrants and, last but not least, the deployment of Qalmaq warriors. Finally, a policy of scorched earth broke Bashkir resistance morally and economically after five years of warfare.[40]

The remaining Bashkirs found themselves cut off from the steppe by a new line of forts built between the Lower Volga and the Yayïq River. Modelled after the Cossacks, loyal Bashkirs and Mishars (*meshcheriaki*) were reorganized into the irregular troops of the Bashkir military Host, and the Russian administration began to regulate the complex economic, social and legal interplay between Russian or non-Russian colonists and the indigenous population, to the disadvantage of Bashkir land-holders. The Bashkir rebellion of 1734–40 proved to be the last anti-colonial war waged by the indigenous populations against Russian dominion. Bashkirs participated in the later revolts of Batïr Shah (1755) and Yemelian Pugachev (1773–4), yet these revolts expressed social or religious grievances and involved other ethnic groups.[41]

Steppe policies

Well into the seventeenth century, the pacification of the great nomadic federations, the Noghays and the Qalmaqs, remained beyond Muscovy's military ability. Even during the first half of the eighteenth century Russia could not prevent nomad raids into her territories resulting in substantial losses of peasants sold on Crimean or Central Asian slave markets. Against the backdrop of a chronic shortage of manpower in Russian agriculture, the steppe frontier stimulated the enserfment of the peasantry and, at the same time, prevented the appropriation of the fertile southern lands by the Russian service class. To secure her borderlands Muscovy had to rely on payments and unruly vassals like the Cossacks. On the other hand, Moscow's technological superiority, above all the possession of firearms and artillery, prevented the nomads from overrunning fortified Russian settlements. And with the conquest of

39 Donnelly, 1968, pp. 54–63; Khodarkovsky, 2002, pp. 156–61.
40 Donnelly, 1968, pp. 64–138. Cf. Kuzeev, 1992, p. 137.
41 Kuzeev and Ovchinnikov, 1975; Gilyazov, 1996; Kappeler, 1992, pp. 42–5.

Astrakhan Muscovy had driven an important wedge into the steppe belt and controlled the movement of nomads between the pastures on both sides of the Volga.

Steppe policies continued to depend on the political relationship between the East European great powers, the Ottoman Empire, Poland-Lithuania and Muscovy. Changes inevitably provoked shifting coalitions between Moscow and the rulers of the steppe, with later bargaining for substantial payments for either military assistance or non-interference. Still using traditional symbols and means of interaction – like contracts (*shert*), the mutual provision of hostages (*amanat*), the collection of tribute (*yasak*) and the exchange of presents (*pominki*) – the tsars came to perceive these relationships increasingly in terms of statehood and sovereignty. Muscovy supposed unmistakable and stable hierarchies – with the Muscovite ruler at the head – and clear-cut boundaries between Russian territories and those of her nomadic neighbours. In fact, however, Russia's steppe diplomacy frequently continued to bargain with the nomads about the terms of alliances, non-aggression treaties or simply forms of trade.[42]

That Muscovy's claims of suzerainty in the steppes did not remain pure rhetoric over the course of the seventeenth and the first half of the eighteenth centuries can be related to two important factors: firstly, the ever-increasing power of Muscovy and imperial Russia, as well as the concurrent decline of Poland-Lithuania and the Ottoman Empire, enhanced her desirability, or even inevitability, as an ally. Secondly, Russian diplomacy developed remarkable skills in exploiting the internal differences within the loose nomadic federations: the authority of the steppe rulers depended largely on their ability to furnish the clan leaders with a share of booty or payments. Negotiations with, and payments to, certain of these clan leaders would allow the Russians to antagonize the clan or turn the nobility against the Khan. This strategy, though, could backfire when no central authority would protect Russian territory from aggression by dissident groups.

Moscow's instruments of expansion into the steppe were similar to those of the preceding centuries: mainly the advance of fortified lines and the settlement of armed frontier people in these lands. Moscow resumed this policy in the mid-seventeenth century, pushing the old *Zasechnaia cherta* from the Oka about 100 miles down to the south. New lines of fortresses, watchtowers or moats were built first from Akhtyrka (west of Belgorod) to Tambov (1635–46); then further to Simbirsk on the right bank of the Volga (1648–54) and on the

42 Khodarkovsky, 2002, pp. 46–69.

left bank to Menzelinsk south of the Kama (1652–6). In 1685, the *Isetskaia cherta* advanced the frontier between Tambov and the Volga, including the new towns of Penza and Syzran'. Muscovy encouraged small land-holdings and temporarily refrained from a return of fugitive peasants to reinforce her troops along the fortification lines.[43]

Beyond the defence lines, Moscow employed the Cossacks against the nomad federations and the Crimean Khanate. The diplomatic exchanges with the steppe rulers betray the fact that Cossack raids affected the nomadic economy substantially, and Muscovy unleashed her allies whenever felt necessary. To be sure, the Cossacks displayed a high degree of obstinacy and, in times of Muscovite weakness, they regularly turned against the tsars and participated, for example, in the rebellions of Stepan Razin (1667–71) or Kondratii Bulavin (1707–8). Only in the second half of the eighteenth century, with Russian military dominance in Eastern Europe firmly established, the Cossacks increasingly lost their *raison d'être* and, subsequently, their freedom of action.[44]

The Great Noghay Horde and the Qalmaqs

The first group to fall victim to the continued contest between the Ottomans, the Crimean Khanate and Muscovy were the Noghay Tatars. During the sixteenth century they had emerged as the most powerful successors of the Great Horde in the steppes between the Volga and the Yayïq River. Military alliance with Moscow in the conquests of Kazan and Astrakhan had not paid off since the nomads lost the tribute that the Khanates had formerly delivered. Moreover, the Russian advance to the Lower Volga curtailed Noghay pastures. A substantial group, the Kazy Noghays, moved to the North Caucasus lowlands and accepted Crimean suzerainty. Other clans remained on the Lower Volga and grew increasingly dependent on trade with or payments from Moscow.

In the second decade of the seventeenth century, the latter groups were pressed from the east by the intrusion of Qalmaq (Oirat) clans. Russian diplomacy faced the difficult task of protecting her Noghay allies in order to prevent their defection to the Crimea and, at the same time, to disengage with the Qalmaqs, whose military power was clearly superior to that of other groups in her southern approaches. After the death of Ishterek Biy in 1618 the Moscow-friendly Great Noghay Horde plunged into internal fighting, and when in the early 1630s larger Qalmaq *uluses* crossed the Yayïq and moved into the pastures of the Noghays on the Lower Volga, neither the Tatars nor the Russians were

43 Kappeler, 1982, pp. 173–7, 191–2; Keep, 1985, pp. 16–17, 20, 36, 77–9.
44 Keep, 1985, pp. 73–5; Kappeler, 1992, pp. 50–1; Khodarkovsky, 2002, pp. 131, 137–8, 224.

prepared to halt them. The defeated Noghays fled to the Crimea and joined raids on Russian territory during the 1630s before they were finally scattered among the neighbouring people.[45]

The arrival of the Qalmaqs, a strong and belligerent Western Mongolian tribal confederation, required political and military rearrangements on Muscovy's southern frontier. Initially Moscow, waging another war with Poland-Lithuania, had to rely on the Cossacks to protect her southern flank, which was already experiencing intensive Crimean assaults. This time, the Cossacks proved to be too successful as they waywardly conquered and defended the Ottoman fortress of Azov between 1637 and 1641, bringing Moscow to the brink of war with the Porte. Moscow's position would probably have become even more precarious had not the Central Asian rulers, the Northern Caucasus federations and the Crimeans shared the perception of the Qalmaqs as a common threat. The latter's military force as well as their ethnic (Mongolian) and confessional (Buddhist) dissimilarity united the former opponents for a short period. The concentration of forces resulted in a decisive victory in 1644 that temporarily halted the Qalmaq advance. But the truce did not last long, as the Qalmaqs were continuously pressed in the east by the Qazaqs. As a result, Bakhchesaray and Moscow competed for a Qalmaq alliance, and in 1655 Moscow signed a treaty that contained serious Russian concessions: the Qalmaqs were entitled to graze their herds on both sides of the Lower Volga and trade freely in Russian towns. Moscow, in well-entrenched tradition, interpreted the treaty as an oath of allegiance, but for the time being lacked the means to enforce her claims. However, under Khan Ayuki the Qalmaqs repeatedly ignored Russian requests to join military campaigns against the Crimeans, and continued to raid Russian and Bashkir territories as late as the 1680s.[46]

Finally, the Russian seizure of Azov in 1696 and the construction of new fortresses between the Volga and Don near Tsaritsyn during the 1720s strengthened Russia's position, allowing tighter control over Qalmaq movements. At the same time, the Qalmaqs' continuing wars against Karakalpaks and Qazaqs made them increasingly reluctant to cross the Volga eastwards with their herds. Russia exploited their growing dependence and repeatedly sent them against Bashkir insurgents. Moreover, Qalmaqs served as irregular troops in the Northern War and during Peter the Great's Persian campaign. However, the empire still lacked the political and military means to subdue the nomads. This became apparent when in 1724, after the death of Khan Ayuki,

45 Khodarkovsky, 2002, pp. 126–30.
46 Khodarkovsky, 1992.

Russian diplomacy switched from appeasement to open interference and tried to replace the Khan with a 'viceroy'. As a result of the refusal of Qalmaq candidates to participate and the risk of an anti-Russian coalition of the Qalmaqs with the Crimea, St Petersburg partly retreated and opted for a compromise candidate. After 1732, when the Qalmaqs had elected a leader of their own, St Petersburg resorted to the proven strategy of supporting loyal elements among the Qalmaq elders that drove deep wedges between the elite. The Russian administration continued to interfere in Qalmaq matters, but it did little to halt the influx of peasant colonists that curtailed the former's pastures and resulted in an overall decline in the nomad economy. The increasing Russian encroachment exacerbated discontent among the Qalmaq elite, with the latter becoming susceptible to Chinese offers to resettle in Zungharia. Finally, in 1771, 150,000 Qalmaqs or three-quarters of the population under the guidance of 'viceroy' Ubashi left the Caucasian steppes for the long journey eastwards. Exposed to extraordinarily hard climatic conditions and continuous Qazaq raids, just one-third of the migrants reached Chinese territories. The 50,000 Qalmaqs who remained on the Volga were placed under the supervision of the 'Qalmaq expedition' attached to the governor of Astrakhan.[47]

The Crimean Khanate

The Crimean Khanate was the most enduring attempt in early modern state-building after the decline of the Golden Horde. The first khans successfully integrated powerful clans from the Great Horde into their realm and thus based their rule on the sedentary, non-Muslim and Muslim population as well as on the nomadic clans roaming the adjacent steppe. The Crimean Tatar state disposed of a viable government with a strong, centralized and sufficiently effective administration, a well-developed Muslim legal and educational system and a highly differentiated social system with a substantial percentage of urban population. The Khanate's economy was largely based on trade, particularly in slaves. Politically, Crimea closely depended on the Ottoman Empire since the late fifteenth century. The Crimeans were obliged to take part in Ottoman military campaigns and could expect guns and ammunition in exchange. These factors allowed the Crimean khans to compete with Moscow for the heritage of the Golden Horde. As long as this competition did not concern Ottoman interests directly, the Crimean Khans were relatively free.[48]

47 Khodarkovsky, 2002, pp. 139–46.

48 Fisher, 1978, pp. 15–28, 39–41. The Porte ruled some Crimean territories directly as the *velayat* of Kefe, Fisher, 1978, p. 34.

Even after the Girāys had abandoned their plans to wrest the conquered Khanates of Kazan and Astrakhan from Muscovy in the late sixteenth century, the Crimean Khanate continued to struggle for dominion over the steppe. Throughout the seventeenth century, Moscow lacked the means to prevent Crimean raids and slave-hunting along its steppe frontier. Funds for the ransom of prisoners were both a serious financial burden for Muscovy and a major source of revenue for the Khans, while the productive land in the Khanate remained under the control of the great Tatar clans or Muslim institutions. At the turn of the eighteenth century, however, both the dependence upon Ottoman protection and on slave trade turned out to be of doubtful value: with the decline of the Ottomans and the military reforms in Russia, the Crimeans were forced onto the defensive – a fact illustrated both by the fortification of Perekop against Cossack raids in the second half of the seventeenth century and expiration of Russian tribute payments in 1699. The decline of the slave trade and the non-payment of tribute and ransom by Russia seriously destabilized the Khanate, since the khan's influence on the land-holding Tatar clans and their military force loosened. The peninsula plunged into inner feuds.[49]

For Russia, the seizure of Azov in 1696 opened a passage to the Black Sea. New prospects for agriculture in, and grain export from, the fertile southern steppe emerged if Russia could prevent Crimean raids against permanent settlements. However, the empire's preoccupation in the west delayed further initiative, and it was not until between 1736 and 1739 that the Russians invaded the Khanate and destroyed its capital, Bakhchesaray. Without substantial support from the Porte, the Crimean khans redressed their policy towards St Petersburg and sought to strengthen their political and economic ties with Russia. In the following decades, Russia intervened in the Khanate through her consulate in Bakhchesaray. Under Catherine the Great, during the Ottoman War of 1768–74, Russian troops invaded the peninsula again and installed a protectorate in 1771. In 1783 the last khan was deposed and the Crimea finally incorporated into the empire. The road for the Russian colonization of the steppes and northern shores of the Black Sea – *Novaia Rossiia* – was open.[50]

Incorporation and Russian rule, 1600–1760

Moscow's policies towards the eastern people under her dominion and those conquered in the course of the seventeenth and eighteenth centuries

49 Fisher, 1978, pp. 46–51.
50 Nolde, 1952–3, II, pp. 6–12, 115–32, 152–67; Fisher, 1970.

displayed a high degree of continuity. The imminent interest in the conquered territories was to safeguard Russian rule. Numerically small but well-equipped Muscovite armed forces were garrisoned in fortified towns and forts all over the territory to allow for a quick and merciless suppression of resistance, frequently aided by participation of loyal native forces. The ban on weapons and metal goods, introduced first in Siberia and then extended to the Volga-Urals during the 1620s, as well as the obligation to deliver hostages were designed to deter the indigenous population from rebellion. On the other hand, Muscovy continuously co-opted Tatar *mīrzā* into its own nobility and rewarded elite loyalty among the other non-Russian people on the Middle Volga and Siberia. Hence, the local administration was repeatedly encouraged to refrain from direct interference in the non-Russians' everyday life, particularly when it concerned customs and religious traditions.[51]

Aside from external and internal security, Russia's interests in the Volga region and Siberia were economic: in order to secure the levy of obligations, taxes and soldiers, instructions repeatedly reflected concern for preserving the economic basis of the non-Russian population. Consequently, the protection of the non-Russian's individual status quo, and above all guarantees for the land-holdings or the use of productive lands, characterized state policy.[52] The *ulozhenie* of 1649 and most later decrees clearly distinguished between Russian and non-Russian, or rather non-Orthodox, lands, and banned exchange, selling or purchase across these lines. This policy implied not only a unilateral guarantee for non-Russian land-holdings, but also a protection for non-Russian peasants against enserfment. Precisely because in Muscovy, as in most early modern societies, estate and confession were the most important categories that determined the social and legal status of the subjects, the problem of conversion complicated matters. Except for the nobility, the conversion to Orthodoxy meant a necessary precondition for the incorporation of non-Russians into the Muscovite estate system. Since the Orthodox serf-peasants constituted the lowest stratum of the population this potentially meant social degradation. Land-holdings of converts were therefore temporarily treated as a specific category that enjoyed protection.[53]

51 Nolte, 1969, pp. 64–5; Kappeler, 1982, pp. 163–4, 189–90.

52 Although the relative importance of non-Russians in the army decreased after the military reforms of the mid-seventeenth century, service and *yasak* people continued to replenish the ranks of the commoners and remained an important element along the steppe frontier. Kappeler, 1982, p. 172.

53 Kappeler, 1982, p. 168. For example, the *ulozhenie* included a ban on non-orthodox landlords employing orthodox slaves (*chlopy*). For exceptions and the legislation of 1651, cf. Kappeler, 1982, pp. 176, 189–90, and Nogmanov, 2002, pp. 36–48.

Muscovite conceptions of pragmatic co-operation with native elites or of specific privileges for indigenous groups, however, found little resonance in the European philosophies that had dominated Russian political thought since Peter I. Under the guidelines of mercantilism, the centralized fiscal and military state aspired to an optimal exploitation of the human and natural resources and hence pursued the aims of systematization and unification with little regard for traditional rights, social structures or value-systems. For the former Khanates and Siberia this meant, first of all, a reorganization of the conquered lands as ordinary Russian provinces and the dissolution of the *prikaz* administration. The *prikaz* of Kazan disappeared around 1720 with the implementation of the Petrine reforms; its functions were distributed among the new departments (*kollegia*) of the government. The Siberian *prikaz* was closed five years later, only to reopen between 1730 and 1755 – a clear indication that entrenched traditions endured during the eighteenth century.[54]

On the Volga, the restructuring of administration was accompanied by the final assaults on the privileges of the non-Orthodox land-holding Tatar nobility. In 1681, an *ukaz* by Tsar Fedor had threatened the Muslim gentry with the removal of their Orthodox serfs. Although the decree was significantly watered down a year later, it resulted in mass conversions of nobles in the territories belonging to the simultaneously dissolved Khanate of Kasimov. Peter renewed the *ukaz* in 1713 and demanded its strict application, with the result that even estates with Muslim peasants were expropriated. Finally, a decree issued in 1718 obliged the remaining 50,000 non-Orthodox service people to cut, treat and float timber for the shipyards that Peter's admiralty was building along the main rivers. The Tatar *mīrzā* and the non-Muslim elite of the former Khanate were confronted with the alternative: convert and assimilate, or be socially downgraded. Those who preferred the latter constituted the new social category of the tax-paying *lashmany*. The severe obligations they had to shoulder forced many to sell and abandon their inherited estates.[55] At the same time the former tribute-paying communities (*yasachnye liudi*) were legally equated with the Russian state peasantry. For the non-Russians the new system of poll-taxes brought about a significant increase in payments and obligations.[56]

In Siberia, where the native population already constituted a minority settling away from the economically important territories and communication lines, the state refrained from integrating the indigenous population into the

54 Rywkin, 1988, p. 15.
55 Nolte, 1969, pp. 70–2; Kappeler, 1982, pp. 245–59; Nogmanov, 2002, pp. 137–87.
56 Kappeler, 1982, pp. 259–67.

Russian estate system. Except for the Siberian Tatars, they retained their previous status and formed the estate of *inorodtsy* ('from a different kin'). In Bashkiria, where the continued resistance of the native elite prevented a full-scale integration, the state again refrained from unification for the time being.[57]

In the end, living conditions of the non-Russian subjects were largely determined by the local administration's implementation of these policies. The state was represented in the provinces only by the heads of the military or civil administration, the *voevody* or *namestniki* (governors) from the higher nobility. Their number remained fairly small; for example, there were just four in the whole of Siberia. An equally small bureaucracy at the city (*prikaznye izby*) or district level (*uezdy*) was manned by minor officials from the lower nobility or service classes, the *d'iaki*. Their exchange with the autochthonous population depended on the local elite or indigenous translators, and this, in turn, opened the way to abuses, as a result of the unawareness and subordination of the natives. In fact, before and after Peter, the aims and intentions of the government continued to be seriously distorted by individual authorities and native elders.[58]

Even the realignment of the Middle Volga and Siberia to the level of 'ordinary' provinces left these territories under-administered. Russian rule continued to depend on collaboration with the indigenous elites. Throughout the period under consideration, petitions and revolts under the participation of natives testify to the amount of maladministration in the conquered lands. This was particularly true for Siberia, regular revisions notwithstanding. The most contested issues were the amount of taxes and obligations, military conscription, access to commonly used woods or pastures, and land surveys. And although native land-ownership or the use of land by indigenous peasants and hunters was protected by law, local authorities tended to cover the appropriation of land by privileged estates or Russian colonists.[59]

This could only result in periodic unrest, most prominently during the Stepan Razin uprising of 1667–71, when the non-Russian servicemen from the frontier regions and the peasantry on the Volga's right bank joined the insurgents *en masse*.[60] Non-Russians, however, played an insignificant role during the revolts of the early eighteenth century, such as the rebellions of Astrakhan 1705–6 or of Kondratii Bulavin 1707–8. More importantly, Tatars

57 Kappeler, 1982, p. 291.
58 Nolde, 1952–3, I, pp. 178–81; Collins, 1991, pp. 37–8, 49–52.
59 Kappeler, 1982, pp. 159–65, 187–9, 194–8, 237.
60 Khodarkovsky, 1997.

joined the Bashkirs in their 1705–11 uprising, but generally non-Russian resistance remained localized and passive until mid-century, when the assault on Islam (below) provoked combined Tatar and Bashkir protest.[61] Thus, in the course of the seventeenth and early eighteenth centuries a trend increased during the 'Time of Troubles': non-Russian insurgence lost its ethnic colouring and instead became socially induced.

Peasant colonization, economic and demographic changes

Even during times of pragmatic or affirmative nationality policy, Russian authorities periodically ignored specific privileges or sanctions in order to reinforce new fortification lines or to stimulate the colonization of strategically important lands. For example, the state refrained from returning fugitive peasants from the frontier zone or forcibly settled Russian and non-Russian peasants there as long as this seemed necessary to maintain external or internal security. But, in the long run, both measures could only undermine the state's own economic interests as well as those of the landed gentry, on whose service the Russian state continued to depend. Consequently the state preferred a strictly controlled migration of peasants.[62]

Nonetheless, voluntary and forced peasant colonization increasingly changed the demographics of the Volga region and Siberia. During the seventeenth century, Russian peasants were either moved by their noble or monastic landlords, or they came as fugitive peasants of their own will. During the first half of this century, the percentage of Russian peasantry was increased disproportionate on the right bank of the Volga and around the administrative centres of Kazan and Sviiazhsk. After 1650, both Russian and non-Russian peasants poured into the frontier belt along the new fortification lines. Until the end of the eighteenth century, an estimated two million peasants migrated or were moved south in European Russia, while about 400,000 went east to the Urals and Siberia. The non-Russian population of territories experiencing the large influx of Russian peasants, particularly on the right bank of the Volga and in the former Khanate of Kasimov, migrated into Bashkir lands across the Kama. These trends resulted in the emergence of new non-Russian diaspora groups along the old steppe frontier. In most of the central parts of the former Khanate of Kazan, especially along the rivers and around the administrative

61 Kappeler, 1982, pp. 178–87, 292–8.
62 Nolde, 1952–3, I, pp. 181–5; Huttenbach, 1988, p. 91; Dmytryshyn, 1991, pp. 22–3; Collins, 1991, pp. 39–40.

centres, the Russian population already constituted a majority. By 1760, only the recently integrated Bashkir lands and most of the north-eastern territories of the former Khanate, due to their inaccessibility and poor soil quality, retained a dominant non-Russian population.[63]

Demographic changes were even more dramatic in sparsely settled Siberia. Whereas in 1650 some 60,000 Russians lived among 250,000 Siberian natives, this changed to more than 800,000 Russians and 360,000 non-Russians, mainly Yakuts and Buriats settling east of the Yenisei, in 1795. Already by the turn of the eighteenth century, Russian settlements in Siberia were agriculturally self-sufficient.[64]

The state's limited willingness to protect non-Russian legal titles also became evident with the growing interest in natural resources in Siberia and the Urals. The ruthless extraction of pelts decimated the number of fur-bearing animals so quickly that the hunters were forced to move ahead continuously in search of new hunting grounds. After 1660, when silver was discovered on the eastern slopes of the Ural and on the Yenisei, the state monopolized its extraction and sent in miners, engineers and other specialists, while the growing demand for iron stimulated the development of hundreds of registered and unregistered foundries in Siberia in the seventeenth century and in the Urals in the early eighteenth century. Bashkir lands, otherwise legally exempted from purchase, were sequestrated for mining and the building of factories. Additionally, the government assigned state peasants as workers to the industrial enterprises. This proto-industrialization resulted in a large-scale deforestation, to the disadvantage of the native economy.[65]

Mission

During much of the seventeenth century Moscow adhered to earlier confessional policies. While conversion, in particular of the native elite, was welcomed, it remained unsystematically encouraged. Large numbers of baptisms occurred mainly along the old north-western border of the former Khanate of Kazan, particularly after the 1681 decree restricting the rights of non-Orthodox land-holders. But whenever the State saw its own interests of security and economic profit endangered, it sacrificed mission on the altar of pragmatism.[66]

63 Kappeler, 1982, pp. 228–34, 323–31. For more data, see Kuzeev, 1992.
64 Data from Huttenbach, 1988, p. 91; Kappeler, 1992, pp. 104–5; Bell-Fialkoff, 2000, p. 1.
65 Huttenbach, 1988, pp. 88, 98; Khodarkovsky, 2002, pp. 161–2; Kappeler, 1982, pp. 268, 344.
66 Nogmanov, 2002, pp. 51–63; Kappeler, 1982, pp. 176–7, 195, 236; Kappeler, 1992, p. 122; Zahidullin, 1997, pp. 54–5.

Under Peter the Great the situation changed substantially. Peter had subordinated the Orthodox Church to the state, and while proclaiming religious tolerance for foreign specialists he perceived the conversion of non-Orthodox subjects of the East as a necessary precondition for their integration into the *Untertanenverband*. Therefore the state, from 1720 onwards, systematically offered converts exemption from taxes and recruitment. These promises, though, were frequently dodged by the local administration, and the campaign remained largely unsuccessful among the Animist or Muslim population on the Middle Volga. In Western Siberia the state simultaneously enforced large-scale conversions of Voguls (Mansi) and Ostiaks (Khanty). After Peter's death, large waves of apostasy demonstrated the superficial character of these conversions: Orthodox mission had hardly ever been accompanied by pastoral care or systematic consolidation, for example through Orthodox schools.[67]

The obvious failure of state-sponsored mission resulted in its reorganization. In 1731 a 'Commission for the Matters of the Newly Converted' was founded in Sviiazhsk. This board was designed to take care of the converts and to co-ordinate mission among non-Christians. Finally, the appointment of resolute clerics from the famous Kiev academy and significant funding in the early 1740s marked a turning point in the history of Orthodox mission. An *ukaz* from 1740 confirmed the Petrine privileges for converts and additionally burdened their former co-religionists with payments to compensate for the treasury's potential losses. Beyond that, the converts were promised money, valuable gifts and, temporarily, even amnesty in case of capital crimes. Several decrees called for a spatial separation of converts from their former co-religionists and threatened non-converts with resettlement. Violence – the destruction of sanctuaries and the prohibition of rites – and persuasion – temporary relief from growing fiscal pressures – resulted in a wave of conversions that swept through the former Khanates. By 1760 almost all Mordvins, and most of the Chuvash, Mari or Udmurts, were legally Orthodox Christian. However, later developments illustrated that baptism for the majority of the former Animists was a superficial act. Their social and economic integration into the empire remained marginal, and under the cover of Orthodoxy they continued to profess their traditional faith or synthetic forms of Christianity.[68]

Most obviously, Russian authorities in the 1740s abandoned their former restraint towards Islam. Missionary activities among the Tatars on the Middle Volga had shown little in the way of success, and the few baptized 'new converts' (*novokriashennye*) after one or two generations professed Islam again.

67 Nolte, 1969, pp. 23–5, 34–6, 83, 87–9; Kappeler, 1982, pp. 270–3.
68 Kappeler, 1982, pp. 274–9.

Measures designed to prevent apostasy among the converted turned out to be a serious challenge for the Muslim establishment. According to a forged late sixteenth-century document, a 1742 decree demanded the demolition of all mosques erected after the Russian conquest of Kazan and forbade the construction of new ones in the vicinity of Christian communities. Given the dispersed nature of settlements in the Middle Volga, this came close to a total ban. In fact, by 1744 in the Kazan province 418 of 536 mosques had been destroyed, and the same was true for 127 of 170 mosques in the adjacent territories down the Volga. However, this short-sighted suppressive policy did not annihilate but rather drove Islamic institutions underground. Religious oppression added to social grievances and resulted in strong Tatar and Bashkir support for the Batïr Shah and the Pugachev rebellions.[69] Catherine the Great's manifesto of toleration finally marked a break in missionary activities, and Russian authorities resolved on a policy of registration, protection and active support for Islam and its institutions.[70]

Conclusion

In the two centuries following the conquest of Kazan, Russian expansion and rule displayed a remarkable stability in aims, instruments and styles. Combined interests of external security and economic exploitation motivated military conquest and the ensuing gradual incorporation of adjacent southern and eastern territories. The former had been of greater importance in the relations with the nomadic peoples of the steppe and the Crimean Khanate, the latter dominated in Siberia. Both motives were important for the conquest of the Volga Khanates, and the perspectives of eastern trade occupied Russia's rulers and officials well after Peter's opening of the window to the West. While Muscovy had justified its eastwards expansion with a specific imperial ideology comprising elements of dynastic legitimacy, great power policy and religious zeal, the Russian drive to the East was influenced by Western ideas of a civilizing mission during the Petrine period. Asian neighbours, particularly the steppe nomads, were no longer regarded as more or less equal partners or opponents. This had serious consequences for those Asian peoples who fell victim to Russian conquest after the eighteenth century: they, like the Siberian natives, were denied integration into the Russian estate system.[71]

69 Kappeler, 1982, pp. 276–7; Gilyazov, 1996, pp. 78–84; Azamatov, 1996, pp. 96–9.
70 Azamatov, 1996, pp. 100–11; Fisher, 1967, pp. 542–53; Frank, 1998, pp. 34–9; Kemper, 1998, pp. 18–50.
71 See Khodarkovsky, 1997, pp. 8–32; Slezkine, 1994.

Throughout the period under consideration, Russian dominance was characterized by the coexistence of two strategies that can be labelled as 'pragmatic' and 'ideological', respectively. Ideology had its strongest repercussions on politics shortly after the conquest of Kazan in the sixteenth century; it flared up occasionally during the seventeenth century and forcefully re-emerged with Russia's Westernization in the first half of the eighteenth. It was characterized by repeated assaults on the religious autonomy of the native population, and by efforts to replace or at least to diminish the role of the indigenous elite as agents of Russian rule. Continued resistance and repeated rebellions of the autochthonous population marked the limits of this strategy. As soon as the primary aims, security and economic profit were endangered, the state usually resorted to a pragmatic policy. The 'pragmatic' strategy encompassed both the pitiless subjugation of armed resistance and a policy of large-scale non-interference in the everyday life of non-Russian subjects, as long as the latter remained peaceful and fulfilled their obligations and financial duties.[72]

Chronologically, Russian conquest and incorporation followed a three-stage model: in the first stage, Moscow concluded treaties of alliance and, although it proclaimed formal suzerainty, continued to deal with the respective rulers through the *posol'skii prikaz*, a forerunner of the Ministry of Foreign Affairs. In the second stage, territorial boards accountable to the monarch and the *boiars*, the *prikazy* of Kazan and Siberia, would administer the conquered territories while preserving particular privileges for the non-Russian population. A special status was conferred on frontier regions governed by a military administration. Finally, the formerly separate territories would lose their specific status and be treated as ordinary provinces, with the non-Russian or non-Orthodox population enjoying the general rights and duties of minorities within the multi-ethnic empire.[73] Only the Middle and the Lower Volga and Siberia went through all three stages. In these territories administrative integration coincided with forced modernization. The non-Russian people of the Volga Khanates and Western Siberia experienced Westernization as an assault on former status and privileges, resulting in the social degradation of the elite and an often disadvantageous equation with the Russian (state) peasantry. Some European territories like Bashkiria do not follow the model, since they retained a peculiar status even after the institution of the Orenburg *guberniia* in 1740. Most of the steppe territories remained within the jurisdiction of the *posol'skii prikaz* and, later, the Senate; they were not incorporated and colonized before the reign of Catherine II (*Novaia Rossia* and Crimea).

72 Cf. Raeff, 1971, pp. 22–42; Kappeler, 1982, pp. 287–92; Kappeler, 1992, pp. 53–5.
73 Cf. Rywkin, 1988, pp. 9–11; Keep, 1985, pp. 36–7.

PART FIVE

★

NEW IMPERIAL MANDATES AND THE END OF THE CHINGGISID ERA (18TH–19TH) CENTURIES

17

The Qing and Inner Asia: 1636–1800

NICOLA DI COSMO

The proclamation of the Qing dynasty in 1636 signalled the beginning of a new phase in both Chinese and Inner Asian history. The dynasty established by the Manchurian Aisin Gioro royal clan was going in a few years to conquer China and rule it down to the year 1911. During this period of time the political and territorial configuration of the eastern part of Inner Asia, and in particular Mongolia, Xinjiang and Tibet, would be transformed as the Qing extended their rule over these regions. The year 1636 marked not only a new dynastic beginning, but also the end of a period of consolidation during which the Jin dynasty founded by Nurhaci in 1616 and continued by his son Hong Taiji (r. 1627–43) led to the completion of several military and political projects. These projects were milestones on the road to the self-strengthening of the Manchu regime *vis-à-vis* the Ming, while at the same time anticipated the transformations in the political and social fabric of the Inner Asian borderlands under Qing rule.

Early achievements included the unification of the Manchurian aristocratic kingdoms, the military defeat of the Ming and conquest of the Liaodong peninsula, and successful expeditions against Korea. Above all, however, it was arguably the success of the Manchus' multisided policy with regard to the south Mongol tribes that contributed the most to stabilizing the Inner Asian front and allowing the Manchus to reorganize the Mongols as a component of the newly minted Qing dynasty. It is in the context of the inter-Mongol wars fought to defeat the Chakhar Ligdan Khan (1592–1634), a Chinggiskhanid noble with imperial aspirations of his own, that Manchu rule was established over the Mongols and that the Qing began what was arguably going to be one of their most important political legacies: the creation of a Sino-Inner Asian empire that, notwithstanding some similarities with the Han and Tang, was not modelled after Chinese precedents. By the 1760s, the Inner Asian regions ruled from Beijing included the north-eastern provinces (Manchuria), Inner and Outer Mongolia, Kokonor (Qinghai), Tibet and Zungharia, the Tianshan region and the Tarim Basin in the northwest. The Qing view of, and policy towards, Inner Asia and the systems of government of the frontier regions were shaped from the beginning first by the special circumstances of the Manchu dynasty's identity as a frontier regime, and second by the significance of the Mongol factor in the state-building process. The result was an entirely new configuration of imperial expansion and government of the Inner Asian and especially Mongolian dependencies. The purpose of this chapter is to trace the main lines of the changes taking place in Mongolia in the seventeenth and eighteenth centuries, whose role was central to the system of 'imperial tutelage' set into place by the Manchus to rule the 'outer regions' (Ma. *tulergi golo*) of the empire.

Manchuria before the rise of the Manchus

At the end of the sixteenth century the Jurchens who inhabited Manchuria were politically divided into three main groupings: the Haixi were located in the valley of the Sunggari rivers; the Jianzhou to the south of the Haixi, in the basin of the Liao and Yalu River; closer to the Liaodong border with China; and the Yeren (savage) Jurchen, to the north of the Haixi, in the forest zone of the Amur River. Both Haixi and Jianzhou Jurchen entertained tribute relations with the Ming, with annual visits to court in which they typically offered horses. Breeding horses was, together with hunting, gathering and agriculture, an important part of Jurchen economy, which has traditionally been regarded as 'mixed' or – less properly – as 'semi-nomadic'. Environment and tradition dictated the form of subsistence that prevailed in one or another area.

After the fall of the Yuan dynasty (1368) the Ming began to intervene militarily in Manchuria to curb residual Mongol resistance and sever Mongol-Jurchen political ties. The Ming offensive, which relied also on diplomatic means, resulted in the establishment of a series of garrisons or 'guards' (*wei*) and 'posts' (*suo*) during the reign of the Yongle Emperor (1403–24). In practice, these corresponded to pre-existing Jurchen political groupings, organized on tribal and territorial bases.[1] Their leaders were turned into Chinese 'commanders' (*zhihuishi*) of various ranks and acquired, together with the titles, certain privileges and obligations *vis-à-vis* the Ming Emperor. The first important *wei*, the Jianzhouwei, was created in 1403, headed by its chief Ahacu. This was to become the ancestral home of the Manchu royal family, the Aisin Gioro clan. The Wuzhe and Nuergan *wei* were established in 1404, and Maolian in 1406.

1 For a full analysis of the distribution of the Jurchen people and list of Jurchen Guards in the Ming period, see Wang, 1956a.

Over the next 200 years in total the Ming established 368 *wei*, in addition to twenty *suo*.[2] The Jianzhou Jurchen obtained two additional *wei*, the Jianzhou zuowei (1405) and the Jianzhou youwei (1438). While the Ming court did not exercise any direct control over these subdivisions, prominent Jurchen chiefs could be promoted to high positions within the Ming military-administrative system of the region. One of the ancestors of Nurhaci, Möngke Temür (r. 1405–33) was first commander (*zhihuishi*) of the Jianzhou zuowei, then rose to Assistant Governor (*duduqianshi*) and finally attained the post of Vice-Governor (*duduqianzhi*).[3]

One of the key advantages of high rank consisted of the permits the chiefs received from the Ming government. In total the Ming issued permits for 1,500 Jurchen people, 1,000 from the Haixi and 500 from the Jianzhou. These allowed Jurchen aristocrats in positions of leadership to carry out commercial activities in trading towns along the border. They were also required for the annual presentation of tribute to the court in the capital. 'Tribute bearing' missions were lucrative ventures, as the members of the 'delegation' were able to trade and sometimes plunder along the way. The 'gifts' received in exchange from the emperor, moreover, surpassed the value of the tribute presented. Hence, competition among Jurchen tribes developed over access to border markets (the so-called horse markets, *mashi*) and over the permits that allowed presentation of tribute. Nurhaci himself, in the late fifteenth and early sixteenth centuries, fought consistently to appropriate the licences and trading rights held by other Jurchen chiefs.

Historians concur in finding that the Jurchen society of southern Manchuria underwent a massive economic development in the period from the Yongle (1403–24) to the Wanli era (1573–1620). Both internal and external factors are responsible for this development. Among the factors of internal development we see a large increase in agricultural production, which was especially significant in southern Manchuria. Demographic growth and the chronic need for iron agricultural implements such as ploughs and hoes, or farming animals such as oxen, are already noticeable from the second half of the fifteenth century. Only from 1600 onwards did autochthonous production of iron tools increase with the development of mining and the establishment of local workshops in Manchurian territories. Jurchen, Chinese and Korean artisans (some migrants, some war prisoners) were employed as blacksmiths but local production still remained insufficient to replace imports.

2 The best study in English on the establishment of *wei* and *suo* garrisons in Manchuria remains that by Serruys, 1955.

3 Cf. Serruys, 1967, p. 613.

The development of agriculture had an important side-effect, as hunting and foraging, which were formerly subsistence activities, could be harnessed to provide luxury products sought by Chinese merchants. Among the most precious Jurchen exports we find pearls, furs – from fox, sable, marten, leopard, lynx, Siberian squirrel and other animals – and ginseng. They also traded horses, honey, and forest products such as wild mushrooms and nuts. Economic data from the late sixteenth century show a significant difference in value between Manchurian imports and exports, with substantial quantities of silver flowing into Manchuria to make up for the difference.[4]

One of the effects of the prosperity of southern Manchuria, irrespective of the pendulum swings of the political relations with the Ming, is the migratory movement and relocation of northern peoples to more southern places, closer to the Liaodong frontier. The most common causes of attrition between Jurchen and Ming were the breaches or abuses of trading rights, which often led to disruption of peace and to violent raids carried out by the Jurchen against Ming cities. Intense bouts of military confrontation occurred in the mid-fifteenth and in the mid-sixteenth centuries. In the first case the support given by the Jurchen to the Oirat ruler Esen Khan (r. 1438–54) led to economic sanctions and to the further fortification of the north-eastern frontier. In the 1570s military clashes along the Sino–Jurchen border resulted from the Ming policy, already started with regulations issued in 1536, to curb the size of tribute missions and to subject border trade to more rigorous controls and taxation.[5] However, this is a period in which tensions develop especially among the various Jurchen 'tribes' and aristocratic groups, fuelled by rampant military and economic competition.

Jurchen society at the time can be said to comprise three main classes of people: the aristocracy, the commoners and the slaves. The aristocracy was primarily engaged in the exercise of political power and military activities. Its members were called *beile* and *beise*, and belonged to families traditionally powerful, and often connected to the Ming court. To this class belonged also the companions-in-arms, or *gucu*, of high-ranking political figures. Access to aristocratic rank could therefore come from the association, usually at a young age, with a successful leader. Slaves (*aha*, *booi aha*, *booi niyalma*) were initially mostly household slaves, and typically consisted of people captured in battle or in the course of pillaging raids in Chinese and Korean borderlands. During the sixteenth century the spectrum of their activities expanded together with their number and social function, as they began to be employed

4 Zhou, 1979, p. 160.
5 Rossabi, 1982.

in agriculture and handicraft production. The expanding Jurchen economy required manpower that came from south of the border, often as war prisoners. The commoners were called *jušen*, a Manchu term that designated both the Jurchen people as a whole and the non-aristocratic members of society. They tilled the land, hunted, bred animals and followed their clan leaders in war. Their social position gradually became less free and more subordinated to the aristocracy, which implied an increase in compulsory taxation, corvées and military service. In Nurhaci's time they made up the bulk of the Eight Banner system, a military and administrative institution that produced an even steeper verticalization of social relations.[6]

The rise of Nurhaci, from the 1580s to the early years of the seventeenth century, took place at a time that is described in the Manchu annals as a period of turmoil and great political instability. This was also, however, a period of overall economic development, of demographic expansion and of intense militarization of Jurchen society. The aristocracy became especially powerful. The accumulation of riches in the hands of a few political leaders is nowhere exemplified better than by Nurhaci's own strategy, as he made effective use of his growing political influence with the Ming to carry out, by war and diplomacy, a monopolistic concentration of the tribute and commercial privileges granted to the Manchurian leaders.[7] The consolidation of power in the hands of Nurhaci was, at least in part, due to a process of monopolistic control of economic resources, of militarization of the commoners and of astute diplomacy.

Nurhaci's strategy was not limited to intra-Jurchen politics and border relations with China and Korea. It was increasingly clear after the establishment in 1616 of the independent regime known as the Latter Jin dynasty (Ma. *amaga aisin gurun*) that the very survival of Nurhaci's political creation depended on his ability to accompany the military expansion into Ming territory (the Liaodong Peninsula) with efficient ways to organize the newly conquered population and territory and to defend these gains against a growing number of current or potential enemies. It also appeared in 1619 that Nurhaci's ambition to establish an independent regime was not going to go unchallenged, as Ligdan Khan of the Chakhar Mongols rose to political prominence. If the defection of Chinese advisors who joined Nurhaci following the conquest of Liaodong is held responsible for 'teaching' the Manchus how to rule China, it is in the context of the developing relationship with the Mongols that the Aisin

6 For a list of the economic and military obligations to which the *jušen* were subject in the early reign of Hong Taiji (1627–43) see Wang, 1956b.
7 Liu, 1978.

Gioro rulers, Nurhaci and his son Hong Taiji, expanded the range of tools at their disposal to control nomadic peoples and incorporate territories that, for their intrinsic qualities, could not be easily incorporated within the still young and evolving Jurchen state. Thus the seed was planted for a frontier strategy that differed deeply from that of any previous Chinese dynasty.

The Qing expansion in Inner Asia

A useful concept in examining the relationship between the Qing and Inner Asia has been put forward by James Millward, as he speaks of 'imperializing' projects that developed on the northern frontier among the Mongols and the Manchus. According to Millward, regarding the relations between Manchus and Mongols, the 'Qing looks almost like a project to restore an empire along Mongol lines by gathering clans and eliminating rivals'.[8] Several attempts had been made by various Mongol leaders during the Ming dynasty to 'imperialize' and unify the Mongols into large power centers, whether or not they attempted to re-create Chinggis Khan's empire. Among them the political projects of Esen Khan (r. 1438–54), Dayan Khan (r. 1480?–1517?), Altan Khan (1508–82) and Ligdan Khan were especially bold and far reaching. As the Manchus began their rise, and even long after the conquest of China had been completed, such attempts to unify the Mongols constituted an explicit or implicit threat to the realization of the Manchus' own political ambitions. In this regard, we must note that, while the Mongol imperial tradition in theory regarded a descendant of Chinggis Khan to be the only legitimate authority to launch and realize 'imperializing' campaigns and to adopt an imperial rhetoric, the Western Mongols, or Zunghars, proved equally capable of expressing imperial aspirations even though, with the exception of the Khoshut, they could not claim a Chinggisid ancestry (see below). The Chinggiskhanid legacy did not lose its political importance, and continued to play a role at some rhetorical level, but the most influential Zunghar khans relied primarily on the legitimation obtained through the support of the Dge-lugs-pa sect and the Dalai Lama.[9] The Manchus countered such projects by extending their rule into the borderlands and making them part of their empire. At the same time, these regions remained ethnically and culturally distinct and administratively separate from the rest of China nearly to the end of the dynasty. How this was achieved is one of the fundamental questions in the history of early modern Inner Asia.

8 Millward, 2004, p. 110.
9 Miyawaki, 1999, pp. 319–31.

The Qing expansion into Mongolian territories cannot be conceived as a 'manifest destiny'. Rather, it progressed as a response to a series of challenges spanning a century and a half. Schematically, we can identify four phases which, however, should not be seen as disconnected, but as part of a continuous and evolving frontier strategy. The first phase includes the relations between the early Manchu rulers, Nurhaci and Hong Taiji, and Mongol leaders before and after the foundation of the Jin (or Later Jin) regime (1616–35), leading to the organization of southern Mongols into 'Banners' (Mong. *sumu*, Ma. *niru*). This phase also includes the early development of the Lifan Yuan as the main government branch in charge of frontier administration. The wars by the Kangxi Emperor against the Zunghar leader Galdan constitute the second phase of this process, as they led to the submission of the Khalkha khans to the Qing at the Dolon Nor Conference, and to the subdivision of Mongolia into administrative units. The third phase is one of continued conflict with the Zunghars, which brought the Qing to occupy some towns in Eastern Turkestan and especially to establish political rule in Tibet through the system of imperial residents (Ma. *amban*). The fourth and last phase can be identified in the Qing military conquest of what later became Xinjiang, the 'New Frontier', as a result of which new territories and diverse populations, including Muslim oasis settlers and Qazaq and Qïrghïz nomads, came under Qing rule.

*

When Nurhaci began to assert himself as regional strongman and leader of the Jianzhou Jurchen the political relationship between him and the southern Mongols worsened. In 1593 a group of Mongol aristocrats, later to become staunch allies and even close relatives of Nurhaci himself, joined Jurchen tribes in an anti-Nurhaci coalition. The military successes of the Jianzhou Jurchen – the Manchurian political union headed by Nurhaci – led to territorial and economic expansion, and with the growth of Nurhaci's regional power Khalkha Mongol tribes reached a diplomatic agreement with him in 1606/7.[10] On that occasion they 'bestowed' upon him the honorific title of Kündülen Khan, meaning 'Most Respected Ruler', a title higher than he enjoyed even among his own people.

From 1620 the Manchus were drawn more deeply into Mongol politics as a consequence of the rise of the Chakhar leader Ligdan Khan, who began a series of bloody raids against other Mongol groups meant to terrorize them into submission.[11] The Manchu leadership chose to intervene, both to curtail

10 *QTZWHSL*, II, p. 28.
11 On Ligdan the best work remains Heissig, 1979.

Ligdan's ambition to re-create a unified Mongol Empire and to stop the flow of refugees from Mongolia to Manchu-controlled territory. Nurhaci and his son and successor Hong Taiji proved in the end able to attract Mongol aristocrats to their side by offering them protection and by actively fighting Ligdan. At this time we can already detect in the Manchu diplomatic exchanges with various Mongol leaders the essential aspect of tutelage that characterized the Qing attitude towards the Mongols and was later extended to the other dependencies on the frontiers. The act of granting protection was sanctioned ritually by swearing oaths, and involved a series of obligations by both parties, among which the integration of Mongol troops in the Manchu army was paramount. The Mongols who joined the Manchus and moved into Manchu territory were then organized into companies (*niru*, *zuoling*), and in this way were incorporated within the Eight Banner system created by Nurhaci in the early seventeenth century. With a larger population of southern Mongols accepting Manchu sovereignty, the number of Mongols incorporated into Banner companies grew steadily throughout the 1620s and early 1630s. As more and more Mongol aristocratic families and subjects were brought into the fabric of the Manchu state, they became actively involved in the Manchu military.

The culmination of this phase can be dated to 1635, when Hong Taiji extracted the Mongol companies from the Manchu Banners to which they had been assigned and reconstituted them into a separate and autonomous formation as Mongol Eight Banners (*Menggu Baqi*). While the Mongol Banners were still subordinated to the Manchu Banners of the same colour, they retained a separate ethnic profile.

The Eight Banner Mongols came from the oldest and closest allies of the Manchus, and as such enjoyed the privileges of the Qing ruling elite, continued to intermarry with the Manchu aristocracy and were promoted to high-ranking positions in the military as well as civilian hierarchies. Yet these represented only about a fifth of the total of the Mongol population under Qing rule. The remainder of the southern Mongol 'nations' were organized into new territorial units that were also called Banners but had no connections, as a political and administrative system, with the Eight Banners.[12] It was rather a system of rationalization of the political

12 Often called 'tribes', Mongol political and territorial groups are however not based on common ancestry, but on ties that are territorial, political and sanctioned by common traditions. They are closer, in actual historical meaning, to Native American 'nations' than to generic 'tribes', while collectively as a people they recognized themselves as 'Mongol'. The word 'nation' in that sense may therefore be better than 'tribe' to refer to socio-political units such as Chakhar, Khalkha, Khorchin and others.

boundaries among southern Mongol groupings that was imposed onto them along lines of pre-existing as well as newly emerged geopolitical configurations resulting from the upheaval caused by the Chakhar wars and subsequent population shifts.

The reorganization of southern Mongolia after its pacification proceeded through the early period of the Qing dynasty. In 1635 southern Mongolia was organized into forty-nine Banners, whose names are still visible on current maps of Inner Mongolia. To facilitate communication between the Banners and the court, and to allow for consultation among Banners on a series of issues such as serious criminal offences, the ruling officials of the Banners met on a regular basis. The groups of Banners that held these meetings together were referred to as 'Leagues' and were altogether six in number. The Banners were designated by the names of the main Mongol sub-ethnic groups (tribes or 'nations') that constituted them. One such nation could have more than one Banner, with multiple Banners of a single group differentiated by a positional indicator (usually 'right' or 'left'). These were as follows:[13]

1. Ten Banners, respectively belonging to the four nations of the Khorchin (6), Jalayit (Jalayid) (1), Dörbet (Dörbed) (1) and Ghorlos (2), forming the Jerim League.
2. Eleven Banners comprising the Mongol nations of the Aokhan (1), Naiman (1), Ongniut (2), Barin (2), Jarut (2), Khalkha of the Left Wing (1), Aru Khorchin (1) and Kesigten (1) in the territory of Juu Uda League.
3. Five Banners of the Karachin (3) and Tümet (Tümed) (2) nations, both of them staunch allies of the Manchus, in the Josutu League.
4. Ten Banners of the Silinghol League, comprising the Üjümchin (2), Abagha (2), Abaghanar (2), Khauchit (2) and Sünit (Sünid) (2) nations.
5. Six Banners of the Dörben Keüked (1), Khalkha of the Right Wing (1), Urat (Urad) (3) and Maominggan (1), which formed the Ulanjab League.
6. The seven Ordos Banners, which formed the Yeke Juu League.

In addition to these there were the Chakhar Banners. These were units of a mixed nature that straddled the military-administrative organization of the Eight Banners and the territorial structure of the *jasagh*-ruled *sumu*. They were first created in 1634 after the defeat and death of Ligdan Khan, when the Chakhar who submitted to Hong Taiji were organized as Eight Banner Chakhars. The following year Ligdan Khan's son Erke Khonggor Eje (1622–41)

13 Brunnert and Hagelstrom, 1911, pp. 455–63 (nos. 884–901). See also Veit, 1986a, p. 402. An excellent map of the Inner Mongolian Banners and Leagues can be found in Lattimore, 1934.

submitted to the Qing with the remainder of the Chakhar people. At this point the Chakhars regained considerable independence, Hong Taiji raised Eje to the highest nobility honours and settled the Chakhars in the nomadic pastureland in today's south-eastern Inner Mongolia, forming there a Chakhar Banner. The actual status of these Chakhars has been in question until recently, when newly discovered Mongolian documents show that they were organized not as part of the Eight Banner system but as a *jasagh* Banner, thus enjoying the privilege of territorial autonomy and relative political independence. In 1669 the arrest of the Chakhar leader Abunai precipitated a situation of tension leading to the revolt by his son Burni, in coincidence with the Rebellion of the Three Feudatories in southwest China (1673–81). The rebellion was quashed by Kangxi in 1675 and ended with the death in battle of Burni, and the execution of Abunai and many other members of his family and officials of the Chakhar forces. The Kangxi Emperor then dissolved the Chakhar people as an autonomous *jasagh* Banner and reorganized them into Eight Banner units directly under the supervision of the same-colour Qing banners. Some of them were given land and organized into 'pastures' as a service agency of the court charged with providing pastoral products to the capital. All twelve Chakhar units were under the supervision of the Manchu resident *amban* (*dutong*) at Kalgan (Zhangjiakou).[14]

The most critical element of the political remaking of the southern Mongol nations lies in the figure of the *jasagh*, a Mongol term derived from the words 'to rule' that indicates the local ruling authority, the 'puissant' lord, and was instituted as a Qing administrative position in 1635, with the formation of the Inner Mongol Banners. Each Banner was headed by a *jasagh* who acted as the highest political and judicial authority. The *jasagh* were all local aristocrats and virtually all Chinggisids, whose position was hereditary, although it needed to be confirmed by the Qing Emperor, who might also rescind or alter the succession line. While the *jasagh* had to abide by the laws and regulations of the Lifan Yuan, the position retained ample powers. Among its prerogatives were the supervision of the census, the collection of taxes, the adjudication of the lower crimes, and military assistance as needed. The *jasagh* was also responsible for regulating trade and providing support to Qing officials and other government representatives travelling through his Banner's territory, a task that, however, was made less onerous during the Kangxi period by the creation of a postal station system under the direct control of the Lifan Yuan. The *jasagh* communicated with the Lifan Yuan

14 Dalizhabu, 2005a; see also Serruys, 1978.

on any number of issues related to civil, administrative, legal, military and political matters. The system of 'indirect rule' devised by the Qing based on the cooptation of local elites combined with local imperial presence with supervisory powers that we have defined above as a system of 'tutelage' was later adopted in Outer Mongolia, and contributed one of the chief principles for the establishment of Qing rule in Tibet and Xinjiang. It is hard to gauge, however, the degree to which the authority of the *jasagh* was accepted by the common people. A 1651 regulation of the *Menggu lüshu* (Mongol statute book) forbidding the people from turning directly to the local Qing government officers, thus bypassing the authority of the *jasagh*, indicates that the central government and its chief agency in Mongolia, the Lifan Yuan, at least initially needed to prop up the authority of the *jasaghs*.[15] (This statute disappears in later editions of the code.)

The other crucial achievement of this phase, which will be discussed in greater detail below, is the formation of the Lifan Yuan, the administrative lynchpin of the Qing policy for the rule of Mongolia and other Inner Asian dependencies and the political transmission belt between the Manchu court and the local Mongol, Turkestani, Tibetan and other elites. This term has received several English translations in addition to the traditional, and now less favoured, 'Court of Colonial Affairs',[16] such as 'Department of Tributary Territories',[17] and others based on the Manchu or Mongol names of the same, for instance 'Ministry Ruling the Outer Provinces' (*tulergi golo be dasara jurgan*),[18] and 'Court of Administration of the Autonomous Mongolian States' (*ghadaghadu Mongghol törö-yi jasakhu yabudal-un yamun*).[19] The Mongol translation in particular indicates that in 1638 the terms *fan* and *tulergi golo* in the Chinese and Manchu versions referred specifically to Mongolia. *Fan* is a term that was applied in ancient Chinese texts to liminal regions, beyond the control of a central authority, but possibly within its sphere of action, as in the sentence in the Zhouli, 'jiu zhou zhi wai wei zhi fan guo',[20] that is, 'what is outside the nine divisions [the Hua-Xia states] is called the "fan" [foreign or outer] countries'. Taking that as the central allusion of *fan* in Lifan Yuan, a translation such as 'Board of Government of the Outer Regions' is probably the most fitting, but for clarity's sake the term Lifan Yuan will be used in this chapter.

15 Heuschert, 1998, p. 322.
16 This translation has been deemed unsatisfactory by Chinese scholars in view of the anachronistic use of the term 'colonial'. See Wang Zhonghan, 1984, p. 167.
17 Wang, 2000, p. 130 n. 11.
18 Chia, 1993, p. 61.
19 Atwood, 2004, p. 333.
20 *Zhouli*, 1991, I, p. 491.

*

The second phase of expansion brought the Kangxi Emperor to assert his rule over the Khalkha Mongols of Outer Mongolia, a fateful development resulting from the long-brewing rivalry between Khalkhas and Zunghars, finally erupting into open conflict in 1686. The Qing relationship with the Western (Oirat) and Eastern (Khalkha) Mongols had been settled as a tributary relationship in the early years of the dynasty, when the dust of conquest had yet to settle and the Manchus were busy 'pacifying' Chinese provinces loyal to the Southern Ming. In 1655 eight Khalkha chiefs were accepted as tributary *jasaghs* and presented the tribute of the 'nine whites' (eight white horses and a white camel) to the Qing Emperor, thus establishing trade and tribute relations and accepting the Qing as the superior power. The Qing, on the other hand, used the tribute system hoping to maintain peaceful control over an especially troublesome frontier.

In the meantime, the Oirats, a confederation that included several separate nations, had undergone a process of expansion under Batur Hongtayiji (r. 1635–53), whose project to 'imperialize' the Western Mongols by establishing a Zunghar 'khanate' had been essential to the strengthening of the Zunghars in relation to the Eastern Mongols. While Batur Hongtayiji never assumed the title of Khan and therefore it is not possible to speak of a khanate until Galdan received the title of Boshoghtu Khan in 1678, the political intention and trajectory was doubtless that of creating an imperial entity that may eventually unify all Mongols.[21] In this phase a shift took place from a purely Chinggisid legitimation, which allowed only Chinggisids to aspire to both the title of Khan and the political project to form a true 'khanate'. [22] This principle held true among the Mongols up to Ligdan Khan, but it gradually lost consistency in the following decades.

This development has been partly attributed to the acceptance by southern Mongols that the political authority deriving from being associated with the Mongol imperial legacy had been appropriated by the Manchus. Already in the *Precious Summary* (*Erdeni-yin Tobči*) compiled in 1662 by the Ordos nobleman Sagang Sechen, there are passages that suggest a Manchu succession to the Mongol imperial legacy, for instance by stating that Hong Taiji (Mong. *Sechen Khan*; Ma. *Sure Han*) 'took the state' of the Mongol khans and by establishing a connection between Chinggis Khan and Nurhaci that posited the latter

21 Perdue, 2005, p. 105.

22 On the issue of legitimate access to khanship among the Khalkha and Oirat Mongols, see Miyawaki, 1984.

as the political descendant of the former.[23] In eighteenth-century texts such as Rashipungsug's *Crystal Rosary* of 1774 it is stated explicitly that the Qing emperors enjoyed the blessing of the Holy Chinggis Khan.[24]

Hong Taiji's support for Tibetan Buddhism, culminating in the construction of the Māhākala temple complex in Mukden (now Shenyang) in 1636, together with the ceremonies that accompanied the victory against Ligdan and the public ceremony that announced recovery of the 'seal' of the Yuan dynasty in 1635, are unmistakable signs that the Manchus' political propaganda aimed to establish an image and reputation for themselves as the successors of the Mongol imperial khans without recourse to the legitimation principle of Chinggisid ancestry.[25]

Indeed, not all Mongols who attempted to grow into an imperial entity could boast membership of the Chinggisid lineage. As mentioned above, the Zunghars were able to make an 'imperializing' claim upon other Mongols without blood ties to Chinggis Khan. This goes to show that among seventeenth-century Mongols the principle of being a descendant from the Chinggisid agnatic line was an important but not unique path to imperial rulership. Absence of a royal genealogy was most effectively compensated for, as in the case of Galdan, by the investiture from the Tibetan Buddhist chief hierarch, the Dalai Lama. It is possible that the erosion of the principle of Chinggisid legitimacy among the Mongols, and its at least partial replacement by that of religious investiture, facilitated the transfer of a notion of universal *imperium* (as conceived in the Mongol and Tibetan political language) to the Manchus.

In 1640 the Khalkha Mongols under the Jasaghtu Khan and the Oirats under Batur Hongtayiji met at a great assembly that gathered also the Volga Kalmyks (Qalmaqs) and the Kokonor Mongols, but excluded the Inner Mongols that had submitted to the Qing. On this occasion Oirats and Khalkha signed a peace treaty and issued a legal code. The code was meant to buttress Mongol unity, punish those who violated the peace, establish ways to resolve dispute between tribes and increase the power of the aristocracy. On this occasion Tibetan Buddhism was formally proclaimed the official religion of the Mongols.[26] In the 1640s Batur also managed to establish and formalize

23 Elverskog, 2006, pp. 44, 81.

24 Elverskog, 2006, p. 80.

25 On early Manchu relations with Tibetan Buddhism, see Grupper, 1984. On the recovery of the jade seal of the Yuan dynasty, see the account of ceremony in which Hong Taiji thanks Heaven see *CMCT*, II, pp. 258–61.

26 Perdue, 2005, p. 107.

trade relations with Russia, and a treaty signed in 1647 allowed commercial exchanges between Oirats and Russians to expand.[27] The prosperity and peace created by Batur was short lived as his death in 1653 was followed by a series of succession disputes that eventually led, in 1670, to the assassination of Batur's son and successor Sengge. It was after 1670, with the rise of Galdan, that the Western Mongols again found a unifying leader.

On the eastern front the 1660s witnessed increasing tensions. The Khalkha were divided into four 'khanates': two on the right flank or wing (western side) and two on the left flank (eastern side), each named after the titles of their khans, all of them of Chinggisid descent. The two right-flank ones were named after the Jasaghtu Khan and the Altyn Khan, the left-flank ones were the Tüsiyetü Khan and the Sechen (Setsen, Chechen) Khan. A civil war broke out in 1662 among the right-flank Khalkha Mongols when one of their two rulers, the Jasaghtu Khan, was killed by the other ruler Lobzang Tayiji (r. 1652–67), who was honoured as the Altyn Khan. The Altyn Khan's territory was located in north-western Mongolia, and his subjects were mainly Oirats who had been subjugated by Khalkha princes in the late sixteenth and early seventeenth centuries. One of the two left-flank Khalkha rulers, the Tüsiyetü khan Chakhundorji (r. 1655–99), intervened in defence of the Jasaghtu Khan's rights, defeating Lobzang Tayiji, who was subsequently captured by the Oirat ruler Sengge. This war caused widespread destruction and the displacement of many of the Jasaghtu Khan's Mongols, who ended up as subjects of the Tüsiyetü Khan, either because seized by his troops or because they moved to his territory to escape the war and seek protection. The new Jasaghtu Khan, after being installed in 1670 with the support of the Tüsiyetü Khan, requested that the former subjects of his domain be returned by the Tüsiyetü Khan. Because of lack of progress on the return of these people the dispute dragged on, leading to a worsening of the relations between the two wings of the Khalkha Mongols.

The Oirat camp was at the same time troubled by internal wars as Galdan (1644–97) rose to avenge the death of his brother and ruler of the Zunghars Sengge, assassinated in 1670 by a half-brother. Galdan had previously been sent to Tibet to become a disciple of the Panchen Lama and of the Dalai Lama. He then broke his vows, defeated his enemies, and subsequently overthrew the Ochirtu Khan, the highest Oirat authority, thus unifying all Oirats under Zunghar leadership. In 1678 the Dalai Lama bestowed upon him the title of Boshoghtu Khan (the 'legitimate' or 'mandate-holding' khan) and by doing so

27 Bergholz, 1993, pp. 58–9.

made Galdan his champion in the Mongol political world. Galdan soon began a political expansion into Eastern Turkestan and launched raids against the Qazaqs, while keeping good relations with Russia.

In 1686 Galdan entered the broader theatre of Mongol politics as he tried to mediate between the Jasaghtu and the Tüsiyetü khans at a conference held at Küriyen Belčiger.[28] At this meeting Galdan took offence at a supposed affront suffered by the representative of the Dalai Lama, who was given a post of honour equal to that of the Jebtsundamba Khutukhtu, the highest Buddhist authority among the Khalkhas, a position held by the brother of the Tüsiyetü Khan. The meeting ended with a general oath of peace and the promise to return all displaced people to their respective domains. Soon after, however, Galdan accused the Jebtsundamba of having challenged the authority of the Dalai Lama. He then prepared to attack the Tüsiyetü Khan by moving closer to the Jasaghtu Khan's territory and holding talks with the right-flank Khalkhas. The Qing emperor Kangxi tried to resolve this dispute diplomatically, but matters precipitated when the Tüsiyetü Khan, possibly fearing a coalition against him, launched an attack in 1687 against the Jasaghtu Khan, in the course of which Galdan's brother, who was assisting the Jasaghtu Khan, was killed. Galdan retaliated with an all-out war invading the eastern Khalkha with 30,000 troops and inflicting heavy losses on the Tüsiyetü Khan. Galdan's march through Khalkha territory was marked by much violence, and by the wholesale destruction of temples and religious establishments. It caused tremendous upheaval among the Khalkha population and as the Khan and the Khutukhtu fled to seek protection in the territory of the Sechen Khan (the second ruler of the left-wing Khalkhas), the common people could only save themselves by running away and moving closer to the Qing border. The masses of refugees made the Qing look at Galdan's advance with increasing apprehension, and persuaded the Kangxi Emperor to send troops to the border to keep the situation under control.

Both the conduct of Galdan in war, who showed no mercy for religious places, and his rage at the treatment of the Dalai Lama's representative show that Galdan's attack, while allegedly meant to avenge his brother's death, had as its main objective the destruction of the power of the Khutukhtu, which he feared might grow independent of that of the Dalai Lama. It was not possible for him to tolerate the existence of two foci of spiritual leadership, especially in consideration of the inextricable ties that the heads of the Tibetan Buddhist clergy had with Mongol leaders, and the critical role they played in Mongol

28 Hevia, 1993.

politics. Galdan therefore would not budge on his request that the Khutukhtu be surrendered to him and sent to the Dalai Lama to make amends.

In 1690 Galdan's position as leader of the Oirats was challenged by Sengge's son Tsewang Rabdan (r. 1697–1727). After some fighting the latter gained the upper hand and proclaimed himself the ruler of the Zungharia. Galdan survived the civil war, and continued to lead the troops still loyal to him against the Khutukhtu, the Tüsiyetü Khan and the Sechen Khan. In the course of this campaign he wished to negotiate with the Qing and came into Inner Mongolia, which was of course under Qing rule. At this point the Kangxi Emperor, outraged by Galdan's continuous disruption of the peace, launched a military campaign that he led in person. The expedition was by no means a triumphal march for the Qing, who suffered many casualties and had severe supply problems.[29] A decisive battle was fought at Ulan Budung on 3 September 1690, celebrated as a major Qing victory even though, while the Qing certainly inflicted heavy losses on Galdan, they were unable to crush him.[30] Galdan was allowed to withdraw and present an oath of submission in which he promised to refrain from further military activity. At this time Galdan also found that the Russians were not willing to help him as the Tsar had, the year before (1689), signed the Treaty of Nerchinsk with the Qing Emperor that strictly regulated international relations between China and Russia and prevented any intervention in internal affairs.[31]

The most important outcome of these events from the point of view of the Qing rule in Mongolia lies in the decision by the Khalkha rulers to submit to the Qing, a historical determination made at the Dolon Nor Convention (1691). The Kangxi Emperor organized the gathering with great pomp and an impressive display of power and grandeur, securing the submission of the Khalkha khans, the Jebtsundamba Khutukhtu, and 550 noblemen. This fateful event led to the complete restructuring of the political and administrative order of northern Mongolia, modelled after the reorganization of Inner Mongolia. The Khutukhtu was enshrined as the nominal head of all Khalkhas and the Khalkha population was divided into thirty-four Banners (*khoshuu*) that were included in three *ayimagh* named after the Tüsiyetü, Jasaghtu and Sechen khans. A fourth was added in 1725, named after the Sayin Noyan Khan. The *khoshuu* was in effect an aristocratic appanage while the term *ayimagh* originally meant 'tribe' or 'clan'. After 1691 they were given clear administrative meaning, and

29 On the logistical difficulties met by Qing armies, see Perdue, 1996.
30 Perdue, 2005, pp. 155–8.
31 On the treaty of Nerchinsk, see Sebes, 1962; for the Latin, Russian and Manchu texts of the treaty, see Stary, 1974, respectively pp. 308–11, 311–14, 317–19.

their evolution responded to the administrative logic of the Qing Empire. The number of *khoshuu* increased throughout the eighteenth century from thirty-four in 1691 to fifty-three in 1725 and eighty-six in 1765. After 1778 the *ayimaghs* were given the same status as the Inner Mongol leagues (*meng*). The heads of the *khoshuu* were the *jasaghs*, who met every three years to discuss major political or legal issues. Most of the Qing civil and military posts in Mongolia were created after 1725, when the Khalkha nobility was directly subordinated to imperial residents, the highest of whom was the military governor of Uliasutai.[32] The whole of northern (or Outer) Mongolia was thereafter ruled through the same mechanism of tutelage that applied to Inner Mongolia, with resident *ambans*, military commanders, and especially the representatives and personnel of the Lifan Yuan that actively supervised the Mongol aristocracy while allowing ample latitude of internal government.

The concluding episode of this phase consists of the second expedition of Kangxi against Galdan. Galdan's attempts to gain support in Western Mongolia and Xinjiang, and his intention to reach Tibet, possibly to establish his own rule there with the support of the Dalai Lama or the regent (who had ruled Tibet by keeping secret the demise of the Dalai Lama until 1693), persuaded Kangxi that it was necessary to eliminate him once and for all by launching a second campaign, also led by the emperor in person. The Qing expeditionary troops under the command of the Manchu general Fiyanggū engaged Galdan on the battlefield of Jao Modo, on the Kerulen River close to today's Ulan Bator. Here Galdan and his Zunghar troops were severely defeated on 3 July 1696. Galdan fled and was pursued by the Kangxi emperor for nearly a year, finding his death on 4 April 1697 in Western Mongolia from causes unknown.

*

The third phase of the consolidation of Qing control of the frontiers and definition of the system of frontier administration begins in the late seventeenth century and lasts until the Qing conquest of Xinjiang and complete destruction of the Zunghar khanate. In the process, Qing armies acquired control over Kokonor (Qinghai) and Tibet, setting up civil and military resident officers that led to critical changes in the role, structure and size of the Lifan Yuan.

With the death of Galdan the new ruler of the Zunghars, Tsewang Rabdan, tried to keep good relations with China and Russia while fighting against the Qazaq 'hordes' (as their main divisions were called, namely the Senior, Junior

32 Barkmann, 1988.

and Middle Horde), who suffered for several years from the punishing raids of the Zunghars. Relations with the Kangxi Emperor, however, had already soured in the early years of the eighteenth century over territorial disputes as well as over the Zunghars' recalcitrance to be reduced to the dependent status of the other Mongols, as the Kangxi Emperor had explicitly requested. Moreover, developments in Tibet increasingly drew attention from both sides for the inherent political sensitivity of the religious issue, stemming from the power games that the Regent in Lhasa had engaged in for decades, and because of the weak and ineffective role played by the Sixth Dalai Lama. The latter apparently behaved in a manner unbefitting his religious vows and, perhaps more worryingly from the viewpoint of the Qing, was a political puppet of the traditionally pro-Zunghar Regent. Therefore the Qing supported a takeover by the Lazhang Khan (r. 1703–17), a Khoshut (Khoshuud) descendant of Güüshi Khan (r. 1636–56), and traditionally both the main Mongol power in Kokonor and Tibet, and a staunch ally of the Manchus. The removal of the Sixth Dalai Lama and installation of a new Sixth Dalai Lama by Lazhang Khan caused great displeasure among the Tibetans, and offered the Zunghars, who had seen themselves since Galdan's time as the secular defenders of the Dalai Lama's dignity, the opportunity to intervene militarily.

In 1715, as the Qing and the Zunghars came to blows in Western Mongolia over territorial disputes and Zunghar incursions into Khalkha territory, and as Kangxi was preparing for a new campaign against such a crafty rival, Tsewang Rabdan launched a devastating campaign against the Khoshut Mongols in Tibet. The Zunghars overcame Khoshut resistance, occupied Lhasa and, in the process, killed Lazhang Khan. This turn of events brought the Kangxi Emperor into direct military confrontation in Tibet. The first Qing expeditionary army was soundly defeated by the Zunghars in 1718 but subsequent military operations were successful, and in 1724 Tibet was freed of the Zunghars.

Tibet was now fully under the control of the Qing, and a series of institutional changes was introduced under Kangxi and especially under Yongzheng, in 1727. The spirit of the system was to allow the government of Tibet to remain in the hands of the Dalai Lama and the Council of Ministers, the *bka-shags*, which included secular and religious members. Yet it was to remain under a regime of supervision and arbitration operated by two Qing resident officials, one senior and one junior, and by the designated offices of the Lifan Yuan. The Qing officials, or *amban*, had at their disposal also a standing military force of 2,000. The tasks and duties of the Lifan Yuan in Tibet were similar to those they carried out in the Mongolian Banners, namely to supervise the payment of taxes; to arrange for the appointments, promotions, demotions and stipends of local officials and noblemen; to make appropriate arrangements, supervise and regulate the journeys to Beijing and visits to court of the Tibetan nobility and Buddhist hierarchs. This system allowed a greater degree of autonomy than the *jasagh* system of Inner and Outer Mongolia, but in 1750, following an anti-Qing revolt, the powers of the resident *amban* were strengthened, and they began to take a more active role in the government of Tibet. The *amban* became directly involved in the nomination of civil and religious officials and their appointment by the government. In practice, all major economic, legal and political government activities of the Dalai Lama and Panchen Lama, as well as those of the local ministers (*bka'-blon*), were now to be carried out jointly with the Qing residents.[33]

*

The fourth and final phase of the Qing 'march' to establish primacy over Inner Asian territories refers to the last act of the Zunghar conflict and to the conquest of Xinjiang. Going back to the late Kangxi relations with Tsewang Rabdan, at the time of the expedition to expel the Zunghars from Tibet, Qing forces had also attacked and captured the Turkestani cities of Barkul, Hami and Turfan, the latter being especially critical as it allowed the Qing to open anti-Zunghar negotiations with the Qazaqs.[34] At the end of the Kangxi period Qing troops were poised to launch yet another campaign against the Zunghars, but this required time and considerable resources considering the remoteness of the Zunghar homeland, near the Altai Mountains in today's northern Xinjiang.

The death of the Kangxi Emperor in 1723 temporarily removed the threat of an imminent Qing assault on the Zunghars. In 1727 Tsewang Rabdan also died, and was succeeded by his son Galdantsering (r. 1727–45). In the 1720s, relations between the Yongzheng Emperor and the Zunghars, while remaining hostile, were less heated. In the 1730s, however, Galdantsering, who had spent his first years in power reorganizing the Zunghar state, resumed attacks on the Khalkha Mongols, who had been for so long the target of Zunghar expansionism. The Qing intervened militarily in order to protect their Eastern Mongol subjects, and especially to preserve their hegemony in the region, defeating the Zunghars on several occasions. Eventually a peace treaty was signed in 1739 that settled the border between the two states, by which the Zunghar

33 Kolmaš, 1994; Xiao, 1977.
34 Bergholz, 1993, p. 313.

suffered extensive territorial losses, including Tuva. Official trade, however, was resumed, and the Zunghars were allowed to send triennially commercial delegations to China. This treaty held until the 1750s.

At the death of Galdantsering a succession struggle broke out that eventually saw a Zunghar nobleman, Dawachi (r. 1753–5), accede to the throne in 1753 with the assistance of the Khoyd chief Amursana. Within a few months the newly unified Oirat state was again troubled by massive defections to the Qing and internal dissent. Amursana himself revolted against Dawachi, siding with China. The Qianlong Emperor (r. 1736–95) took advantage of the Zunghar weakness to settle the situation once and for all, and a force of 25,000 Manchu and Mongol troops moved into Zungharia practically unopposed. Having gained an easy victory, Qianlong planned to reconfigure the Oirats politically, and divided them into four units according to their original tribal affiliation, namely the Dörbet, Khoshut, Khoyd and Choroos (as the Zunghars were renamed). These tribes were to be headed by Mongol-style khans with equal standing, and to replicate the organization that obtained in Outer Mongolia. Amursana, however, aspired to something grander than being confirmed chief of the Khoyd, and proclaimed himself the Hongtayiji (the supreme Oirat title of old, formerly held by Batur Hongtayiji) of all Oirats in 1756.[35] This rebellion was followed by the so-called Chingünjav rebellion (1756–7), that is, an attempt by some Khalkha princes to rise against the Qing.[36] However, support for either rebellion melted quickly as the Khalkha khans and princes fell in line with the diktats of the Qing, and initial supporters defected. Chingünjav himself was captured and executed in 1757. Amursana fled to Russia after having been hunted down by the Qing forces sent to 'pacify' Zungharia, and died there of smallpox in the same year.

The campaign led to the final incorporation of Zungharia and Eastern Turkestan into the Qing Empire, to the destruction of the Zunghar khanate – that is, the Oirat tribal confederation headed by the Zunghar khans – and to the disappearance of the Oirats, who were almost completely wiped out in the course of an extremely bloody campaign, as protagonists of steppe politics. The colonization of the northwest followed, to a certain degree, principles already in place in the Mongolian dependencies, while at the same time being more complex and articulated across different ecological, economic and ethnic regions. Xinjiang (the 'New Frontier') was divided into three regions under the general authority of a military governor (the Ili Jiangjun) based in the

35 Miyawaki, 1997.
36 Bawden, 1968a.

northern region (Zungharia, the Ili Valley) at Ningyuan with deputy military commanders in major centres in the east and the south. The army brought to Xinjiang included a number of Mongol and Manchu troops relocated from the east, such as Chakhar, Solon, Daghur, Sibe, regular Bannermen, Green Standard soldiers from the nearby provinces of Ningxia and Shaanxi, and local Western Mongols. These military units were largely expected to be self-sustaining through the system of military farms.[37]

Civilian administration included different territorial divisions. In eastern Xinjiang, which included Urumqi, Turfan and Hami, some areas were turned into prefectures and counties under the supervision of the Gansu provincial government, but these were relatively few. The Mongols in the region and even some Muslim towns were organized along the model of the *jasagh*-Banners. The overall regional authority rested with the Lieutenant Governor (*dutong*) based in Urumqi. In southern Xinjiang, which included the oasis cities of the Tarim Basin, known as Kashgharia or Altishahr, several resident officials (*canzan dachen* and the subordinate offices of *banshi dachen* and *xieban dachen*) and a military commander (*lingtui dachen*) represented Qing authority, while the actual civil administration was entrusted to local Muslim officials, known as *beg*. The whole Qing administration of Xinjiang was brought under the jurisdiction of the Lifan Yuan, in collaboration with other ministries, and the '*beg* system' in force in southern Xinjiang was in effect the result of the fusion of the pre-existing Turco-Muslim administrative structure within the framework provided by the Lifan Yuan. These officials were appointed by imperial decree, through a complex system of nomination and confirmation that was managed by the Lifan Yuan. They wore Qing official robes and imperial insignia, while retaining their Turkic and Muslim titles. The Lifan Yuan remained critical to Qing rule in Xinjiang in many areas of government, from carrying out land surveys and censuses for fiscal purposes, to keeping accurate accounts, to selecting candidates to fill political positions, and by managing the international relations with bordering states and independent nomadic groups, in particular Russia, Khoqand, and Qïrghïz and Qazaqs tribesmen. Matters of international trade, tribute relations and all diplomatic correspondence were dealt with through the Lifan Yuan representatives. The Qing system of 'indirect rule' granted nonetheless considerable autonomy to the local elites, especially in judicial matters where the Muslim law was applied by local judges (*qādi*).[38]

37 For a fuller account of Xinjiang under Qing rule refer to James Millward's essay in this volume.

38 On the relationship between the *begs* of Altishahr and the Qing, see Newby, 1998.

The Lifan Yuan: structure and function

As mentioned above, the keystone of the whole border administration from Mongolia to Tibet was the Lifan Yuan. This critical office was established in the late 1630s in the context of the incorporation of Mongols within the ruling elite, social fabric, and military and administrative infrastructure of the Manchu state. Early relations between Manchus and Mongols were based on the Inner Asian system of tribal alliances. These were sealed in two ways, by sworn oaths and by diplomatic marriage. While there are differences between the two, both entailed a series of mutual obligations. The policy of intermarriage between Manchu and Mongol aristocracies over several decades created bonds of fealty that allowed the most trusted among the Mongol allies of the Manchu imperial household to integrate within the elite military caste and higher political echelons of the state. With the growth of the Mongol population and territory under Manchu rule, and with the replacement of a relationship of diplomatic equality with one of political subordination, a new type of territorial control over the Mongol aristocracy and management of local governments was needed. The Lifan Yuan was the branch of government intended to provide structural coherence to the administration of non-Han borderlands and organic connectivity between the court and the local elites coopted within the system of rule of these regions.[39]

Created in 1636 as the Bureau of Mongol Affairs (see above, Ch. *menggu yamen*), in 1638 the office changed its name to Lifan Yuan, and began in the early years after the conquest of China to define its role and prerogatives in the government of the Mongols south of the Gobi. At this time the Lifan Yuan was restructured, and several new positions were created. The most important were the president (Ch. *shangshu*, Ma. *aliha amban*), of ministerial rank, and two vice-presidents (Ma. *ashan-i amban*), of whom the left-side one was the senior and the right-side one the junior. In addition, there were altogether eight assistant directors in charge of the four departments (Ma. *aisilakū hafan*). Finally, a supervisor (Ma. *mujilen bahabukū*) was appointed.[40] The higher officers were all Manchus and Mongols, with Han employees being hired in lower clerical positions, typically as scribes and secretaries.

From its inception and through the initial phase of its existence, in the Shunzhi period (1644–61), the Lifan Yuan was headed by a minister with two vice-ministers (Ch. *shilang*). Its administrative structure was formalized in 1661 into four main bureaus: the Bureau of Rewards for Meritorious Service (Luxun),

39 Di Cosmo, 1998.
40 Li, 1997, pt 2, p. 22.

the Guest Reception (Bingke) Bureau, the Bureau for Cherishing the Distant (Rouyuan) and the Bureau of Punishments (Lixing).[41] Through the Kangxi and especially the Qianlong periods the Board underwent several reforms. After 1764 the number of bureaus was expanded to six, as new responsibilities were added in consequence of the conquest of the north-west (Xinjiang).[42]

The Luxun Bureau handled rewards, rank assignments and appointments to local political and military posts. It also was in charge of supervising postal stations, frontier posts and commercial traffic. It carried out investigations into criminal cases, such as mishandling and theft of government animals and other property allocated to the postal stations, and pursued fugitives. During the Kangxi period all the ranking aristocrats of the outer regions (*waifan*) began to be meticulously registered together with family affiliation. This office compiled short biographies with details of their meritorious service, promotions and other relevant personal information. In this way, it was possible to keep updated records and résumés of aristocrats who came periodically to visit the court to pay homage by performing the *chaojin* ritual, or who were proposed for appointments and rewards.

The Bingke Bureau handled all the preparations and matters relative to the *chaojin* annual visits, the royal hunt and the presentation of tribute by the Mongol *jasaghs* and later by other *waifan* dignitaries, including Tibetans and Turkestanis.[43] It fixed the dates and itinerary of each delegation every year according to a rotation principle (*nianban*), established the names and number of the participants, the rank order and the sequence according to which they would be received. There were specific rules also about the tribute that each Mongol Banner was allowed to present and about the banquets prepared for the visiting delegation. The tribute was established and received by the personnel of the Lifan Yuan before being handed over to the Ministry of Rites. These regulations changed over time and remained an important aspect in fixing the delicate balance of power between the Qing court and the regional centres of power represented by the Mongol aristocracies and, later, by the Muslim *begs* and Tibetan lamas in their respective territories.

The Rouyuan Bureau was above all in charge of monitoring the presence of Tibetan Buddhist lamas among the Mongols. Every aspect of their activity was subject to supervision, from their number in each Mongol Banner to their movements in and out of Mongolian territories, and from the management of religious property, down to the colour of the robes and rank insignia they

41 Li, 2007, pp. 130–1.
42 Yuan, 1996, pp. 43–8.
43 On the *chaojin*, see Chia, 1993.

were allowed to wear when they visited the court, to the books kept in each monastery. If lamas were given overnight accommodation by Mongols while travelling, they had to be reported to the Lifan Yuan, and duly recorded under penalty of legal sanctions. These regulations were the same across all the territories under the jurisdiction of the Lifan Yuan, and applied to all Mongols. The close attention paid to lamaist activities throughout Mongol lands speaks to the great importance attached to the supervision of the relations between Mongol aristocracies and Tibetan hierarchies, and of the political control exerted by the Qing, through the Lifan Yuan, upon this relationship.

A central function of the Lifan Yuan in the Inner Asian territories was the exercise of legal powers, whose spectrum was ample and ranged across military, criminal and civil law. The personnel of the Punishment Bureau of the Lifan Yuan intervened in all Mongol Banners as investigators, consultants to the local *jasagh*, supervisors of the legal proceedings and members of the judicial process, usually in collaboration with the local authorities. Until the nineteenth century several codes and regulations were issued by the Qing government for the administration of the law in these territories that were periodically revised or updated (see below).

The Punishment Bureau was in charge of keeping the Mongols and other nationalities informed of any new regulations or modifications of the legal codes and statutes, and of transmitting copies of the code to the Banners. In practice, the Lifan Yuan was to be involved in every legal case, a report of which was to be made and recorded. The role of legal supervision and judicial powers were entrusted to the Lifan Yuan early on and there are records of legal proceedings among the Mongols handled by the Lifan Yuan dating from the Chongde period (1636–43), as in the case of three Bannermen sent to investigate a criminal case among the Khorchin in 1638.[44] Manchu envoys of the Lifan Yuan could investigate, indict Mongol *jasagh* and propose their removal from office, as in the case of the *jasagh* of a Jarut Banner, thus intervening directly in the administration of justice within the Mongol territories.[45]

It is important to underscore the relevance of the legal codes and statutes for Mongolia and the other Inner Asian dependencies issued by the Qing dynasty, whose development can be traced back to before the conquest. It is in the military regulations that were issued to Mongol troops during the military operations in Chinese territory in the late 1620s and 1630s that one can locate the earliest instances of legal regimentation that the Manchus imposed on

44 Li, 1997, pt 2, p. 12
45 Li, 1997, pt 2, p. 9.

their Mongol subjects and allies.[46] Legal and administrative procedures, in addition to requirements of tribute, visits to court, and regulations regarding appointments to political positions (either by inheritance or by merit) formed the basis of the regime of tutelage that the Manchus gradually devised for their rule of Mongol tribes and later extended to other frontier regions, though with differences dictated by local circumstances.

The vast literature on the legal aspects of the Qing rule in Mongolia has stressed the statements by Manchu emperors on their intention that laws for the Inner Asian regions had to suit existing customary laws and local conditions.[47] At the same time, this declaration of principle was countermanded by the Qing promulgation of written codes to imbricate the administration of justice in a bureaucratic net that clearly delineated the powers of the central government *vis-à-vis* the local ones. If the Lifan Yuan was the bureaucratic structure through which the legal authority of the Qing was preserved and reinforced, the legal codes (*Menggu lüshu*, *Menggu lüli*, *Lifan Yuan zeli*), repeatedly revised, were a critical tool in the exercise of their power. It has been argued that over time the whole legal system of Mongolia was transformed by the introduction of Chinese laws, and contributed to the gradual assimilation of Mongolia within the Qing imperial system.[48]

In 1643, Manchu armies crossed the Shanhai Pass, and the Lifan Yuan began to collate the legal edicts issued to the Mongols during Hong Taiji's period into a single code, called *Menggu lüshu* ('Mongol statutes'). This is the earliest version of what we know as the *Menggu lüli* ('Mongol statutes and regulations') and the predecessor, therefore, of the *Lifan Yuan zeli*, issued in 1811.[49] Periodic editions of the *Menggu lüli* in the Kangxi and Qianlong reign periods reflect changes in the administration of Mongolia, which required new edicts and modifications to existing laws.

Extant Mongol traditions regarding trials and punishments were not based on a judicial apparatus separate from the ruling aristocracy. Under the new regime, the noblemen's legal powers were limited by the establishment of a multi-tier process based on which the decisions on controversial or especially serious crimes were to be deferred to higher administrative levels and subject to supervision and examination by Lifan Yuan officials. Hence, minor offences and civil disputes were handled by the local *jasagh*; more difficult cases were reported to the league head who, in consultation with other *jasaghs*, issued

46 Di Cosmo, 2002, pp. 343–47.
47 Yang and Shi, 2005, p. 35.
48 Yang, 2006, p. 101
49 Dalizhabu, 2003.

a verdict. Then the sentence was transmitted to the regional Qing administrative or military officers (*dutong*, *ambans* and so on) for review, after which the case was reported to the Lifan Yuan. In areas in which there were no ruling *jasaghs* the competent authorities were by default the Qing officers and Bannermen stationed in that area. If a case involved a Mongol and a Han person then it was to be handled jointly by the Mongol and Qing authorities. The laws prescribed harsh penalties for serious crimes such as theft, plunder and murder. Members of the aristocracy, however, normally received only a monetary fine or a demotion. Cases in which a particularly harsh sentence was contemplated, such as exile but excluding the death penalty, had to be reported directly to the Bureau of Punishments, which had the power to adjudicate and impose the penalty. In cases that involved the death penalty the verdict by the same Bureau required consultation with the three judicial organs of the Qing administration, namely, the Board of Punishments, the Censorate and the Supreme Court, and in some special cases the final decision was only made by the emperor at the autumn assizes. Therefore, the Qing legal system and the role played by the Bureau of Punishment of the Lifan Yuan, with its broad range of competence, overrode in the most important cases the authority of local native rulers.

One key principle of the borderlands' legal system was that the applicable laws had to conform to the code of the place where the crime was committed. Therefore a Mongol committing a crime in Mongol lands was to be judged according to the Mongol statute laws, but if the crime was committed in China (*neidi*) then the Qing code would apply.[50] A precedent for this principle can be found in the pre-Qing period, when regulations issued as early as 1631 stipulated that a Manchu who committed a crime in Mongol territory (Khorchin or Abagha) had to be judged according to Mongol laws; conversely, a Mongol in Manchu territory was subject to Manchu laws.[51] Only in those cases for which there were no clear regulations in the Lifan Yuan statute books, nor customary laws to rely upon, could one resort to the 'metropolitan' Qing code.

A special legislation applied to the Khalkha tribes of Outer Mongolia after their submission to the Qing. A legal code, known as *Khalkha Jirum*, was issued in 1709 and remained effective, albeit with some overlap with the *Menggu lüli*, until 1790. This has led to the impression that the Khalkha princes enjoyed a greater degree of independence. Recently found Mongol documents, however, show that these statutes applied essentially only to the appanages subject to Tüsiyetü Khan and to the Jebtsundamda Khutukhtu. In fact, from 1694 to

50 Uljitokto, 2004, p. 69.
51 *MWLD*, V, pp. 506–7.

1709 the statutes of the *Menggu lüli* were transmitted to Outer Mongolia and used through the various *aimaghs*.[52]

The *Khalkha Jirum* issued in 1709 contained eighteen sections on administrative and legal matters, from the management of temples and postal stations to military matters, marriage and inheritance laws, commerce regulations, hunting rights, handling of fugitives and penalties for criminals. The relationship between the Khalkha aristocracy of Outer Mongolia and the court continued to be regulated by the Lifan Yuan according to the rules of the *Menggu lüli*, and Qing military posts were established in northern Mongolia. Communication between *aimaghs* was likewise subject to governmental supervision, and the legal proceedings within each territory were monitored by the Lifan Yuan. If the *Khalkha Jirum* can be interpreted as a sign of greater autonomy conceded to a portion of Khalkha aristocracy, its existence does not necessarily imply a weaker Qing political presence in the region.

Another area in which the Lifan Yuan had an important role was the management of marriage relations between the Manchu imperial household and the Mongol aristocracy. Already in Nurhaci's time alliances with Mongol tribes were initiated or sealed by marriage agreements.[53] The strategic goal to expand the Manchu political role among the Mongol aristocracy by seeking marriage alliances was pursued even more extensively by Hong Taiji, who was himself related by marriage to the Khorchin. After the establishment of the Lifan Yuan the marriages between Mongol and Manchu royalties were handled by its officials. When a Mongol *efu* (imperial son-in-law) was sought for marriage to a Manchu princess the Lifan Yuan sent letters to the *jasaghs* of the Khorchin and the other thirteen Inner Mongol Banners with which the Aisin Gioro entertained marriage relations for the names of suitable candidates. When these were received, their birthdates and backgrounds were checked for up to three generations. Then the Lifan Yuan selected a few and submitted the 'shortlist' to the Imperial Household Department for additional screening, while the final decision had to be signed off by the emperor.

The Lifan Yuan was also in charge of relief to the local people in case of a natural calamity. The Qing imposed light taxes and few corvées upon the Mongols, but in areas hit by natural disasters it required that the *jasaghs*, wealthy families and monasteries provided aid to the local population. In case this was not sufficient, the entire league had to pool its resources to help the affected population. The families receiving aid were to be registered and reported to the Lifan Yuan. In particularly dire circumstances the league chief

52 Dalizhabu, 2005b.
53 Di Cosmo, 2007.

and *jasaghs* asked the Lifan Yuan to send inspectors to assess the gravity of the emergency and deliver assistance as needed. While statistics are incomplete, it has been calculated that the Lifan Yuan took direct responsibility for relief operations forty times during the Kangxi reign, and eighteen and fourteen respectively for the Yongzheng and Qianlong periods.[54]

The Lifan Yuan was also directly involved in the organization of the collective gatherings of the six Inner Mongolian leagues, held typically every three years, and made sure that protocol was observed. These were solemn occasions meant to affirm political allegiance, but especially to review the most serious criminal cases. After 1751 the presence of government officials at these meetings was discontinued, but the *jasaghs* had to report to the Lifan Yuan whenever special issues arose, in which case the Qing government would dispatch its representatives.

The Lifan Yuan personnel also took charge of the logistic network established by the Qing in Mongolia. A network of postal stations and military routes reminiscent of the Mongol *jam* system allowed government agents, military personnel and anyone else with official licence to use these logistic facilities. Prior to 1692 horses and victuals needed by government officials, both civil and military, travelling in the border regions were in effect requisitioned or borrowed from local Mongols, causing considerable hardship to the population. The Kangxi Emperor changed the system entrusting the Lifan Yuan with the task of establishing government-operated postal stations along several routes. Altogether fifty-one stations were set up in Inner Mongolia to connect the various Banners, and over 120 in northern Mongolia on routes to the most remote regions, including Altai, Uliasutai, Kobdo and Khiakhta. Military posts (Ma. *karun*) were also established at various locations between those outer regions (*fan*) and the 'inner' domains as well as along the frontiers of the Qing Empire to check the credentials and identity of travellers. Typically a postal station had to take care of twenty horses, in addition to camels, sheep and food. The personnel included, for every two adjacent stations, one Mongol officer with ten soldiers, two *bošokū* (corporals) and one secretary. They all depended on the Lifan Yuan. Among their tasks were the reception and distribution of dispatches from the court and imperial edicts through the areas under their jurisdiction. The relay stations network was also used to send military supplies, salaries, agricultural tools and provide logistic support wherever needed, such as to escort criminals or couriers. Only people with permits issued by the Lifan Yuan were allowed to use these facilities, and

54 Zhao, 1994, p. 176.

horses, lodging and food were allocated to them according to specific regulations. Moreover, these stations functioned in peacetime as market places for those living in the area.

In conclusion, the Manchu and Mongol officials of the Lifan Yuan became, even before the conquest of China, the physical expression of the Qing imperial government among the Mongols and the other Inner Asian dependencies. They were charged with sensitive tasks related to keeping peace and order after the 'pacification' of politically unstable frontier regions.

The most salient aspect of the remaking of Inner Asia by the Qing is to be recognized in the forms of political tutelage that the empire established over indigenous communities. Political tutelage took chiefly two forms. The first consisted of norms that defined the relationship between the local aristocracies and the center of the empire, namely the emperor, the imperial clan and the court. The second consisted of the creation of a bureaucracy that allowed the central government to regulate through administrative and legal means the social and political life in the 'outer borderlands'.

The former policy grew out of the incorporation of Mongol aristocrats within the Manchu elite, through alliances, marriage, cooptation, voluntary submission, military conquest or other means based on the historical contexts. These circumstances determined the political conditions upon which the allegiance and participation of the Mongols in the Qing imperial project was predicated. The latter policy is embodied in the development of the outer regions' government structure, of which the Lifan Yuan was the lynchpin. The political, ritual, judicial, logistic and administrative tasks entrusted to its bureaucracy, and the normative codification of statutes and laws that underpinned its activity, testify to the comprehensive, and yet not burdensome and relatively fluid, control the Qing retained over Mongolia. These regulations provided a key element of the supporting structure of the Qing colonization of Inner Asia.

How to attract to their side the masses of internally divided and politically capricious Mongols became one of the critical questions confronting the Manchu leadership even before the conquest of China. Peaceful cooptation and legal control of the local elites, joined with military intervention, continued to inform the frontier strategy after the conquest of China. During the first half of the Qing dynasty (1644–1795) the dynasty honed the tools developed in the 1630s to produce an expert and efficient bureaucratic apparatus able to consolidate the political gains made on the battlefield. As a conclusive thought we should remind ourselves, however, that the Qing conquest of Inner Asia occurred at a time during which these frontier regions and their societies were undergoing intense transformations. The emergence of strong ties between the Mongol aristocracy and the Tibetan Buddhist religious elites, the progressive erosion of the political values inherent in the notion of Chinggisid legitimation, and an international scene profoundly modified by the Russian expansion were some of the most critical intervening changes that contributed in some measure to the establishment of Qing rule in Inner Asia.

18
The Qazaqs and Russia

ALLEN J. FRANK

The Qazaq Khanate in the sixteenth and seventeenth centuries

The formation of the Qazaq Khanate and the emergence of a Qazaq ethnic and political identity at the beginning of the sixteenth century were centred in the Semirech'e (or Zhetisu) region in what is today Eastern Kazakhstan (see Chapter 13 above). During the following two centuries a politically unified Qazaq Khanate ruled by the descendants of Baraq Khan and his sons Kirāy and Janïbek gradually expanded. In the sixteenth century the Qazaq khans contended with Shibanid rulers in Central Asia for the cities of the Syr Darya Valley, eventually making this region the political, economic and religious centre of their khanate. In defeating the Chaghatayid Moghuls in the Semirech'e, and soon after in the middle of the sixteenth century incorporating the Altïulï Manghïts out of the disintegrating Noghay Horde, the Qazaq rulers created a nomadic confederation that extended from the Yayïq (Ural) River in the west to the Irtysh River in the north, and the Syr Darya Valley and the Semirech'e in the south and east.

The Syr Darya Valley was the major bone of contention between the Shibanids in Central Asia and the Qazaq khans in the sixteenth century and suffered frequent raids during the first decade of the sixteenth century led by the Qazaq khan Qāsim Khan b. Janïbek Khan. Early in his career Qāsim Khan's main rival was his cousin Burunduq b. Kirāy Khan, but by 1511 Qāsim had forced Burunduq into exile among the Shibanids. Following the death of Muḥammad Shïbānī in 1510, Qāsim made a series of aggressive raids in the Syr Darya Valley, seeking to gain control of the region, and reaching as far as Tashkent and Sayram, effectively establishing Qazaq control over the region by 1517. In the east, by 1514 he had expelled the Chaghatayid Moghuls from the Semirech'e into Eastern Turkestan.[1]

1 Kliashtornyi and Sultanov, 1992, pp. 261–76; on the position of the Syr Darya Valley in the history of the Qazaq Khanate cf. Pishchulina, 1969.

Under Qāsim's successors, particularly Ṭāhir Khan (d. 1526), a grandson of Janïbek Khan, the military and political fortunes of the khanate declined considerably. Qāsim Khan's cooperative relationship with the Noghays became hostile, and the Qazaqs suffered a series of military defeats along with defections of part of the nomadic population to the Moghuls who in the 1520s were seeking to re-establish themselves in the Semirech'e.[2] The fortunes of the Qazaq khanate changed again under Ḥaqq-Naẓar Khan b. Qāsim Khan, who became khan probably around 1538.[3] Among his accomplishments was making peace with the Shibanids and launching a decisive campaign against the Noghays in 1568, resulting in the incorporation of a significant proportion of erstwhile Noghay nomads into the Qazaq Khanate. Ḥaqq-Naẓar's victory extended the grazing lands of the khanate as far as the Yayïq (Ural) and Irtysh rivers.[4]

Towards the end of the sixteenth century Tawakkul b. Shïghāy became khan.[5] He is particularly prominent as a heroic figure in Qazaq folklore. During his rule he was engaged in campaigns against his former suzerain, the Shibanid ʿAbdullāh Khan, for the city of Tashkent. In 1598 Tawakkul led a devastating attack against the Shibanid realms, and again brought the cities of the Syr Darya Valley under Qazaq control.[6] Following Tawakkul's death in 1598, Ishim (Esim) (r. 1598–1628) ascended the throne, and made the city of Turkestan (formerly known as Yasï) his capital; it remained the residence and burial place of the Qazaq khans throughout the seventeenth century.[7] Following the death of Ishim Khan, Jahāngīr Khan (d. 1652) was elected khan. He was succeeded by Tawke Khan, who ruled until 1718 and can be considered the last ruler of a unified Qazaq Khanate.[8]

The tribal composition of the Qazaq Khanate appears to have evolved from its formation at the beginning of the sixteenth century through to the beginning of the eighteenth century. The formation of the three Qazaq hordes (*zhüz*), the Senior Zhüz (Ulu Zhüz), Middle Zhüz (Orta Zhüz) and Junior Zhüz (Kishi Zhüz) may have been in effect already in the early seventeenth

2 Isin, 2004, pp. 61–2; Kliashtornyi and Sultanov, 1992, pp. 280–1.
3 On the conflicting accounts of when Ḥaqq-Naẓar assumed the throne cf. Kliashtornyi and Sultanov, 1992, p. 290.
4 Isin, 2004, pp. 82–3; Trepavlov, 2001b, pp. 366–7.
5 The dates of his rule are uncertain, but it appears he became khan at some point between 1583, when he returned to the Qazaq steppe after his service to the Shibanid Khan ʿAbdullāh, and 1594, when he sent an ambassador to Moscow; cf. Kliashtornyi and Sultanov, 1992, p. 293.
6 Kliashtornyi and Sultanov, pp. 293–5.
7 Pishchulina, 1969, pp. 20–1.
8 The date of Jahāngīr's investiture is not precisely known; cf. Kliashtornyi and Sultanov, 1992, p. 304.

century, as the first mention of the existence of separate *zhüzes* appears in a Russian source from 1616.[9] However, the first mention of the three *zhüzes* by name appears in the sources rather late, only in 1731.[10] The origin of these three entities is unclear, but it is likely that this tripartite division emerged after the incorporation of the Noghay Altïulï Horde in the late sixteenth century.[11] In all likelihood the formation of the Senior Zhüz was connected with the incorporation of former Moghul tribes, and several of the tribes of the Senior Zhüz, including the Dulat, Jalayir, Alban and Qanglï had been constituent elements in the tribal make-up of Chaghatayid Moghulistan.[12] The origin of the Junior Zhüz is more obscure, and it is unclear whether its name refers to a genealogical relationship to the Senior Zhüz. However, there is little doubt that the Noghay Altïulï tribes were a constituent element in the formation of the Junior Zhüz.[13] The unique tribal structure of the Junior Zhüz suggests additional evidence of the integration of these Noghay elements. Unlike the Senior and Middle Zhüzes, which were made up of separate tribes, the Junior Zhüz was made up of three clan confederations, the Bayulï, Alïmulï and Zhetiru. The Zhetiru is made up of genealogically unrelated clans, and the ancestors of these clans are identified in some Qazaq traditions as 'newcomers' (*kilümsäk*).[14] The Middle Zhüz was probably the last to form, and may have received its name in relation to the Junior Zhüz.[15] It included three major tribes, the Arghun, Qïpchaq and Nayman, and a number of smaller tribes, including the Qongrat, Kiräy and Waq. The largest of its tribes was the Arghun, and the name of this tribe was often used interchangeably with the Middle Zhüz as a whole.[16]

By the middle of the seventeenth century, Qazaq society, while basically ethnically and linguistically homogenous, consisted of various groups defined above all by ancestry, which was documented by oral or written genealogical charters. The communities forming the three *zhüzes* were considered Qazaqs. Reflecting the Islamic heritage that dominated Qazaq society, all complete genealogies that have come down to us ultimately begin with the prophet Adam; however, the Qazaq tribes and clans in the three *zhüzes* generally traced their ancestry to a figure named Alash, and in the earliest recorded genealogies,

9 Sultanov, 1982, p. 8.
10 Vostrov and Mukanov, 1968, p. 10.
11 Iudin, 1983, p. 143.
12 Pishchulina, 1977, pp. 238, 265; Iudin, 1965, p. 65.
13 *Istoriia Kazakhskoi SSR*, I (Alma-Ata, 1957), p. 150.
14 Qurbān-ʿAlī Khālidī, 2005, pp. 9–10.
15 Iudin, 1983, p. 145.
16 Mukanov, 1974, p. 47; Sultanov, 1982, p. 35.

dating from the nineteenth century, the three *zhüzes*, and the various tribes and clans descend from this Alash.[17] These Qazaq nomads formed the so-called 'black bone' (*qara söyek*) or 'black people' (*qara khaliq*), who were so-named in contrast to the 'white bone' (*aq söyek*) or aristocratic communities. There were at times other non-Qazaq nomads, such as some Qaraqalpaq and Kazan Tatar communities in the eighteenth and nineteenth centuries who lived as communities among the Qazaqs, but strictly speaking were not part of the Qazaq tribal system. The elite among the tribal Qazaqs were the *biys*, who served as military leaders, but who also administered customary law (*ʿadat*). These positions were not hereditary, but rather *biys* were selected on the basis of a combination of personal character, influence, wealth, military prowess and legal skill.[18]

The 'white bone' communities retained genealogical lineages different from those of the Qazaq nomads. These included first of all the Chinggisid nobility, primarily claiming descent from Baraq Khan and his sons Janïbek and Kirāy. These Chinggisids included the khans, who by the beginning of the eighteenth century were claiming to rule over the individual *zhüzes*, rather than over a united Qazaq Khanate, which by that time had become politically unsustainable. The sons of khans were called sultans, and by the nineteenth century often ruled over individual tribes. The descendants of these sultans were called *töräs*, and often ruled individual clans. During the eighteenth and especially the nineteenth century, diplomatic and legal duties often were the responsibilities of these sultans and *töräs*.[19]

Another group bearing aristocratic status were the *khwājas* (*qozhas* in Qazaq), that is, sacred descent groups whose ancestry derived ultimately from the family of the prophet Muḥammad, but whose own genealogies emphasized connections to figures prominent in local Yasavian Islamization legends, and to local Muslim saints. Such descent groups were, and continue to be, found elsewhere in Central Asia, particularly among the Turkmens, Qaraqalpaqs, Siberian Tatars, and the sedentary Turkic- and Persian-speaking communities of Central Asia. *Khwājas* figured prominently in the Golden Horde successor states in the western Dasht-i Qipchāq. In nomadic Qazaq society literacy and a reputation for Islamic knowledge distinguished them from tribal

17 There is a vast literature on Qazaq genealogy, and many genealogical works have been, and are being, published in independent Kazakhstan. For the most comprehensive accounts of Qazaq oral genealogical traditions cf. Qurbān-ʿAlī Khālidī, 1910, pp. 146–9, 220–9 and *passim*, and Köpeev, 2003–7, VIII and IX.

18 On Qazaq social structure, with an emphasis on the tribal community cf. Tolybekov, 1971.

19 On the *töräs* and their role in Qazaq society cf. Qurbān-ʿAlī Khālidī, 1910, pp. 453–79.

Qazaqs and Chinggisids alike, and their activities included Islamic education and conducting Islamic rituals.[20]

The centre of religious life in the Qazaq khanates was the shrines and cities of the Syr Darya Valley, particularly the city of Turkestan. Most prominent were the shrines of Aḥmad Yasavī in Turkestan, the tomb of Arslan-Bab (Arïstanbab) near Otrar, as well as the multitude of tombs in and around the city of Sayram.[21] The city of Turkestan was certainly the most prominent and sacred site for the Qazaqs. It was the residence and burial place of the Qazaq khans and was also a pilgrimage site that attracted Qazaqs from throughout the steppe.[22]

Russian relations and annexation

The expansion of the Qalmaq Empire in the seventeenth and eighteenth centuries into the Dasht-i Qipchāq, Central Asia and the Volga-Ural region created a crisis for the nomadic and sedentary Muslim communities alike and their rulers. The Qazaqs and their rulers bore the brunt of this last Mongol invasion and suffered enormous human, material and territorial losses as a result, particularly during the first half of the eighteenth century. The Qalmaq assaults compelled the khans of the Junior Zhüz to seek Russian protection by submitting to St Petersburg, and this formal act of submission, along with the political collapse of Chinggisid authority, gradually led to the incorporation and effective integration of the Qazaq tribes into the Russian Empire in the nineteenth century.

Qazaq conflicts with the Qalmaqs dated back at least as far as the middle of the sixteenth century, when Tawakkul Khan conducted raids against them. In the early seventeenth century Qalmaqs had occupied the steppe lands in Western Siberia, in the Tiumen' and Tara regions, and by 1630 were occupying territory along the Lower Volga River. During the seventeenth century all of the Qazaq khans, including Ishim Khan, Jahāngīr Khan, and particularly Tawke Khan were leading campaigns against them.[23] The conflict with the Qalmaqs turned calamitous for the Qazaqs in 1723, when the Qalmaqs, having recently signed a treaty with the Qing Empire in China, were able to

20 In recent years there have been several substantial studies on the *qozhas*; cf. DeWeese, 1999b; Muminov, 1998; cf. also Safi ad-Din Orïn Qoylaqï, 1992, Muminov and Zhandarbekov, 1992, and Zhandarbek, 2002.

21 For an overview of the major shrines in the Syr Darya Valley cf. Castagné, 1951, pp. 57–65; cf. also Privratsky, 2001, pp. 163–7.

22 Qozha, 2000, pp. 34–5; cf. also Zhandarbek, 2000, and Sapabekulï, 1996, pp. 123–32.

23 Tynyshpaev, 1998, p. 184.

concentrate forces against their Muslim rivals in Central Asia and the Dasht-i Qipchāq. In that year the Qalmaqs overran virtually all of the Qazaq pasture-lands in the Semirech'e and along the Irtysh, and also sacked and occupied the cities of the Syr Darya Valley. The Qazaqs of the Senior and Middle Zhüzes had to flee into Central Asia, specifically to the environs of Khojend, Tashkent and Samarqand, and those in the Tashkent area submitted to the Qalmaqs. The Qazaqs of the Junior Zhüz moved primarily to Khiva and Bukhara.[24]

Despite their disastrous losses the Qazaqs evidently recovered relatively quickly. Between 1723 and 1730 they were able to retake a substantial portion of their lost territory. The most aggressive and effective Qazaq leader at this time was Abū'l-Khayr Khan b. Hājjī Sultan (d. 1748), a descendant of Janïbek Khan b. Baraq, and khan of the Junior Zhüz. Around 1726 he was selected leader of the unified Qazaq forces against the Qalmaqs, but the internal fighting among the Qazaq sultans in the face of the continuing Qalmaq threat compelled Abū'l-Khayr to appeal to Russia for submission.[25] Nevertheless, during these events conflicts between the Chinggisid dynasts for the position of the largely nominal position of khan of the three *zhüzes* vitiated the military unity of the Qazaqs.[26] Relations between the Qazaq khans, particularly Abū'l-Khayr Khan in the Junior Zhüz and Abū'l-Mambat Khan in the Middle Zhüz, a grandson of Tawke Khan, became particularly difficult after they had neutralized the Qalmaq threat.[27] However, one result of the wars with the Qalmaqs between 1723 and 1730 was that a unified Qazaq Khanate ceased to exist after 1723, and essentially from that point we see by the second half of the eighteenth century that the Qazaq khans were functioning as the rulers of politically separate *zhüzes*.

When Abū'l-Khayr Khan requested Russian protection and submitted to Russia in 1730 he did so, in fact, in a position of relative military strength regarding the Qalmaq threat, but in a position of weakness with respect to dynastic conflict among the Qazaq khans, due to the junior position of his family line within the House of Janïbek Khan.[28] The Russian empress Anna Ivanovna accepted Abū'l-Khayr's submission proposal, and the immediate effect over the next several years was to increase diplomatic contacts between Abū'l-Khayr and the imperial court. While Abū'l-Khayr's submission was a legal step that in time led to the integration of the Junior Zhüz into the Russian

24 Tynyshpaev, 1998, pp. 184–5; Levshin, 1996, p. 167.
25 Viatkin, 1948, p. 422.
26 Tynyshpaev, 1998, pp. 189–95. Tynyshpaev provides a good summary of Qazaq oral traditions regarding these events.
27 Tynyshpaev, 1998, pp. 195–6.
28 Levshin, 1996, p. 178.

Empire, in the 1730s neither Abū'l-Khayr nor the Russian authorities possessed the means to fully control the Qazaq nomads either politically or otherwise. The first concrete result was the Orenburg expedition in 1734, which led to the founding of a Russian fortress at the confluence of the Or' and Yayïq rivers (in 1741 the site was moved down river, to the confluence of the Saqmar and Yayïq rivers; the original site became known as Orsk, or Yaman Qalgha in Muslim sources). The Russians named the fortress Orenburg; it was built as an administrative, commercial and religious centre for the Qazaq Junior Zhüz. The fortress, naturally, was also a military centre, and one of its roles was also to exert control over the Bashkir tribes in the southern Ural Mountains and along the Yayïq River.[29] Of particular interest to the authorities in St Petersburg was redirection of the lucrative Central Asian caravan trade through Orenburg.[30]

Abū'l-Khayr Khan's murder in 1748 by one of his rivals, Baraq Sultan, resulted in a dynastic division in the Junior Zhüz. The Russian authorities supported Abū'l-Khayr's son, Nūr-ʿAlī (r. 1748–60), and in 1748 a number of Qazaq notables proclaimed him khan in Orenburg. Several other tribes supported Barāq Sultan b. Tūrsūn, who ruled as khan over half of the Junior Zhüz until Nūr-ʿAlī and his supporters were able to murder him in 1750.[31] By 1785 the chronic instability that characterized Chinggisid politics under Abū'l-Khayr and Nūr-ʿAlī was beginning to encourage the Russian authorities to implement changes in the political structure of the Junior Zhüz. In that year they sought unsuccessfully to reorganize the Junior Zhüz by dividing it into its three constituent clan confederations, and appointing a non-Chinggisid *biy* to each of the confederations. The Russians would provide at government expense a staff to each of these *biys*, however by 1790 they instead appointed a new khan, Er-ʿAlī b. Abū'l-Khayr (r. 1790–4), and after him, Ishim (Esim) Sultan (r. 1795–7).[32] Following the death of Ishim Sultan the Russians installed Āy-Chuvāq b. Abū'l-Khayr Khan (r. 1796–1805), and initially placed him at the head of a 'royal council' (*khanskii sovet*), but by 1798 allowed him to rule alone. Āy-Chuvāq's successors were his sons Jān-Törä (r. 1805–9) and Shīr-Ghāzī (r. 1812–24), after whose death the Russians abolished the position of khan in the Junior Zhüz.[33]

In 1733 Abū'l-Mambat Khan b. Būlāt (r. 1733–71) became khan of the Middle Zhüz, but the situation there was rather different than in the Junior Zhüz.

29 Levshin, 1996, p. 178; cf. also Dobrosmyslov, 1900.
30 Bukanova, 1997, pp. 88–9.
31 Levshin, 1996, pp. 216–17; Tulibaeva, 2001, pp. 75–6.
32 Tulibaeva, 2001, pp. 76–7.
33 Levshin, 1996, pp. 216–17; Tulibaeva, 2001, p. 77.

The khans of the Middle Zhüz, Abū'l-Mambat Khan, and especially his successor, Ablay Khan b. Walī Sultan (r. 1771–81), were able to conduct a more independent policy regarding their neighbours. In 1740 Abū'l-Mambat Khan and Ablay formally swore fealty to Russia in a ceremony in Orsk, but the ability of the Russians to control the Middle Zhüz was even more limited than for the Junior Zhüz.[34] In the eighteenth century the Russians were establishing a series of fortresses and commercial centres in Siberia along the northern Dasht-i Qipchāq, which would soon after become commercial, administrative and religious centres for the Qazaqs of the Middle Zhüz. The main centres along this line were Troitsk, Petropavlovsk and Semipalatinsk. These were connected by a string of outposts manned by Cossack colonists, mainly of the Siberian and Orenburg Cossack Hosts.[35] In 1756, when Qing forces annihilated the Qalmaq Khanate in Western Mongolia, the Qazaqs reoccupied the grazing lands that the Qalmaqs had abandoned, bringing them into contact with the Russian settlements. The Senior Zhüz managed to reoccupy much of the Semirech'e, but the Qazaqs of the Middle Zhüz expanded beyond their original grazing lands along the Irtysh. They expanded far to the east, occupying grazing lands over much of Zungharia, and as far as the Altai Mountains and Western Mongolia. These migrations brought the Middle Zhüz into contact with the Qing Empire. Ablay showed particular skill in diplomatic manoeuvring between the Chinese, the Russians and the emerging Khanate of Khoqand. In addition to swearing fealty to Russia in 1740, in 1756 he swore fealty to the Qing Emperor and in 1758 to Nārbūta Biy, the ruler of Khoqand. But in practical terms Ablay Khan was the last Qazaq khan to operate as an independent sovereign.[36] Significantly Ablay chose as his residence, and place of burial, the city of Turkestan, the former capital of the Qazaq khans, and refused Russian directives to make the cities of Troitsk or Orenburg his home.[37] In 1782, shortly after Ablay Khan's death, the Russians persuaded Ablay's son and successor, Walī Khan, to hold his accession ceremony in the city of Petropavlovsk, where the Russians had built him a stone palace that was to become the residence of the khans of the Middle Zhüz until 1822.[38]

Although already in the 1730s Qazaq khans and other notables were agreeing to similar conditions of submission to Russia as those of the Junior

34 Suleimenov and Moiseev, 1988, p. 29.
35 Bukanova, 1997, pp. 128–36; Kasymbaev, 1990, pp. 17–18.
36 Valikhanov, 1985, IV, p. 114; Viatkin, 1948, p. 423.
37 Suleimenov and Moiseev, 1988, p. 123.
38 Tumanshin, 1961, p. 49.

and Senior Zhüzes, the Senior Zhüz did not come under direct Russian control until the middle of the nineteenth century. During the second half of the eighteenth century they reoccupied much of the Semirech'e. At that time the Tashkent and Chimkent regions, and the Qazaqs in the vicinity, were under the authority of Ablay Khan. However, beginning in 1792 or 1794 Tashkent proper came under the control of a local *khwāja* dynasty headed by Yūnus Khwāja, and subsequently during the first half of the nineteenth century the Syr Darya Valley, and even a portion of the Semirech'e, came under the control of the Khoqand Khanate (see Chapter 20 below).[39]

Russian administration and the integration of the Qazaqs into the Russian Empire

If in the 1730s and 1740s submission to Russia was primarily a formal matter for the Qazaq khans, over the course of the eighteenth century the Russian authorities in Orenburg and Tobol'sk, and later in Omsk, acquired greater control over the khans themselves, and gradually over the nomadic communities of the Junior and Middle Zhüzes. During the eighteenth century the border settlements, and commerce, were the primary Russian interests in the Dasht-i Qipchāq, and to these ends Russian officials were willing to support the political fortunes of khans amenable to Russian aims. By the beginning of the nineteenth century fighting on the steppe among the Qazaqs, and the growing influence of the khanates of Khoqand and Khiva, as well as the Qing Empire, was compelling the Russian authorities to establish a more direct form of rule over the Qazaqs.

Already in 1801 the Russian authorities permitted a large body of Junior Zhüz Qazaqs to migrate across the Russian border along the Ural River (Catherine II had ordered that the Yayïq River be renamed the Ural River following the suppression of the Pugachev Rebellion in 1775) and occupy pasturelands between the Volga and Ural rivers that had been vacated by the Qalmaqs in the 1770s. They detached this group from the authority of the khan of the Junior Zhüz, made Bükäy Khan b. Nūr-ʿAlī Khan its ruler, and named it the Inner Horde.[40]

39 *Istoriia Kazakhstana*, III (2000), pp. 279–80.

40 The Inner Horde is also known as the Bükäy Horde. In some sources the Inner Horde is mistakenly identified as a 'fourth' Qazaq *zhüz*, together with the Junior, Middle and Senior Zhüzes. In fact, genealogically all of the Qazaqs of the Inner Horde were part of the Junior Zhüz, but were part of a different political organization; cf. Khanykov, 1847, pp. 34–7.

In 1822 the Senate in St Petersburg approved far-reaching legislation entitled 'The Statute on the Siberian Kirgiz' (Qazaqs).[41] This statute was intended to reorganize the administration of the Middle Zhüz. The statute established the city of Omsk as the administrative centre for the Siberian Qazaqs, moving it from Tobol'sk, and formalized the position of Qazaq nomads as Russian subjects, ascribing to them the estate status (*soslovie*) of *inorodtsy*, a type of tribal status. For the Qazaqs such a status distinguished them from 'peasants' (*krestiane*). Whereas peasants were liable for military conscription and the poll tax, *inorodtsy* were generally immune from either of these onerous duties, and instead had to pay tribute. In addition to abolishing the position of khans, the legislation divided Qazaqs into fixed administrative units. The basic unit was the nomadic encampment (*aul* in Russian or *awïl* in Qazaq), consisting of fifty to seventy *yurts*. Ten to twelve *auls* constituted a sub-district (*volost'* in Russian, *bolus* in Qazaq). The statute defined the *bolus* as consisting of genealogically related clans, and Qazaq genealogical sources sometimes indicate the number of *bolus* descending from a particular ancestor.[42] Ten to twelve *bolus* constituted a district (*okrug* in Russian). Typically the administrative centre of an *okrug* was a Russian fort or Cossack settlement within the steppe. The Qazaq *bolus* was administered by a Chinggisid *törä*, and a 'Senior Sultan' (*starshii sultan* in Russian, *agha sultan* in Qazaq) would be elected as the head of an *okrug*. The Senior Sultan was responsible to the Russian authorities, and was vested with full police powers to maintain order, with the proviso that he act in conjunction with the Russian *okrug* administration. 'Elders' (*starshina* in Russian and Qazaq) would administer an *awïl*. The administration of customary law was left in the hands of local *biys*.

The statute regulated the Qazaqs' movement and pasturelands by categorizing communities based on their geographical proximity to the Russian lines of settlement. The statute distinguished districts (*okrug*) according to their proximity to the Russian fortified line. Those located between the fortified lines and the military frontier outposts deeper in the steppe were termed 'inner line districts' (*blizlineinye okrugi*), while those near the frontier outposts were termed 'border districts' (*pogranichnye okrugi*). The former districts restricted Qazaq movement by limiting their migrations across the line of settlement. Similarly, the statute banned Qazaqs living in border districts from moving

41 During the imperial period Russians commonly referred to Qazaqs as 'Kirgiz', or 'Kirgiz-kaisak'. As for the Qïrghïz proper, Russian sources in the imperial period commonly refer to them as 'dikokamennye kirgizy'. In Russian sources after the 1920s these two groups came to be called 'Kazakh' and 'Kirgiz' respectively.

42 Qurbān-ʿAlī Khālidī, 2005, pp. 8–9.

across the border into territory not claimed by Russia. On the whole, limitations on the movement of Qazaqs proved more difficult to enforce than to legislate, and generally increased pressure on Qazaq access to pasturelands.[43]

The Qazaqs east of the Ural River were administered from Orenburg. After the death of Shīr-Ghāzī Khan in 1824 no new khan was appointed for the Junior Zhüz, and instead the newly formed Orenburg Border Commission implemented a series of administrative reforms that reflected the Siberian statute to the extent that it enlisted Chinggisids to administer specific regions in conjunction with the Russian authorities, and formally divided Qazaq communities into fixed administrative units. In 1844 the Russian administration promulgated the 'Regulation for the Administration of the Orenburg Qazaqs'. The 'Regulation' formally declared the territory of the Junior Zhüz to be part of the Russian Empire, and decreed that it be administered by the Ministry of Foreign Affairs. The statute allowed for the continued use of Chinggisids as administrators of the steppe, and also devoted additional resources to expanding police powers of local administrators.[44]

During the first half of the nineteenth century substantial numbers of Qazaqs living within the Russian fortified line found themselves under the direct rule of Russian administrators. Generally these Qazaqs retained the status of *inorodtsy*, but also found themselves in frequent conflict with peasants, Cossacks and tribal communities, especially the Bashkirs, over pasturelands. The largest group of Qazaqs living within the Russian lines, and hence on Russian territory proper, were the Qazaqs of the Inner Horde. This rather large group of Qazaqs was administered directly by their khan Jahāngīr b. Bükäy Khan (r. 1824–45). Jahāngīr Khan was successful in keeping an acceptable degree of order, with Russian administrative and military support.[45] Smaller Qazaq communities lived within the Russian lines in Cheliabinsk province and across Western Siberia.

Three interrelated processes introduced cultural changes among the Qazaqs that accelerated their integration into the Russian Empire in the later decades of the eighteenth century and the first half of the nineteenth century. To varying degrees these processes were accelerated by the Qazaqs themselves as much as they were promoted by the tsarist authorities. These three processes were: (1) the expansion of commercial activity on the Qazaq steppe; (2) the settlement of the Qazaq steppe by Russian subjects; and (3) the transformation of Qazaq Islamic life under Russian rule.

43 The complete text of the statute appears in Levshin, 1996, pp. 399–426.
44 *Istoriia Kazakhstana*, III (2000), pp. 314–16.
45 On the Inner Horde under Jahāngīr Khan cf. Ivanov, 1895; cf. also Zhanaev *et al.*, 2002.

Until the development of railroads in Russia in the second half of the nineteenth century, commercial activity involving Russia and the Qazaqs was of two main varieties. The first type of trade was the caravan trade between Russia and Central Asia, which passed through the Qazaq steppe. The caravan trade used routes connecting the cities of Central Asia with Russian commercial centres along the Volga River and, in addition, with the cities of Western Siberia. These routes predated the Russian conquest of the latter areas, and in the seventeenth and early eighteenth centuries among the important destinations for Central Asian caravans were the cities of Kazan, Astrakhan and Tobol'sk. The newly established Russian administrative centres along the Qazaq steppe, especially Astrakhan, Orenburg, Petropavlovsk and Semipalatinsk became major trade centres, and customs posts for the Russian authorities, and keeping the caravans safe from raids became a significant priority for the Russian authorities. For Russia the significance of this caravan trade transcended issues of customs income. Until the construction of railroads Western Siberia's major trade routes were more linked to Central Asia than to central Russia, and the caravan trade supplied the region with goods more effectively than suppliers in Central Russia were able. Astrakhan was connected by river to central Russia markets, and increasingly the Qazaq steppe and Central Asia became markets for Russian manufactured goods. After its establishment in 1718 Semipalatinsk became a major port-of-entry for Russian trade with Mongolia, Zungharia and Western China.[46]

The second type of trade on the Qazaq Steppe was the so-called steppe trade, which involved Qazaq nomads directly and grew in importance over the course of the nineteenth century. Generally it involved the Qazaq sale of live animals (especially horses and sheep) and animal products, such as hides, butter and wool. This trade was conducted in settlements all along the edges of the Qazaq steppe, and in the Russian forts and nomadic encampments deep in the steppe. The main commodity the Qazaqs purchased was grain, which peasants could easily grow on the northern and western margins of steppe, but which was often difficult for growers to transport to markets within Russia. The Qazaqs also sought Russian manufactured goods, which tended to be cheaper than similar articles from Central Asia.[47] During the first half of the nineteenth century this trade grew slowly, but steadily, and seems to have expanded in proportion to Russian industrialization during the second half of the nineteenth century.[48] It took different forms, and from the Russian

46 Cf. Ziiaev, 1983; Mikhaleva, 1982.
47 Cf. Apollova, 1960.
48 For a Qazaq view of this early period of trade cf. Daulbaev, 1881, pp. 100–1.

side was dominated by Muslim merchants from the Volga-Ural region. There existed regular trade fairs at the larger settlements along the steppe, such as the towns of Aleksandrov Gai and Chertanla (renamed Novouzensk in 1835) bordering the territory of the Inner Horde, where the main articles of trade were wheat and livestock, as well as in the vicinity of Uralsk.[49] There were large-scale wealthy merchants, mainly Muslims, in the cities of Orenburg, Uralsk, Troitsk, Petropavlovsk and Semipalatinsk.[50] Muslim merchants from Russia often settled in the Qazaq steppe well before the arrival of Russian military outposts. In the Semirech'e, which Russian forces began penetrating from Semipalatinsk in the 1820s, numerous Muslim itinerant merchants from Kazan province in Russia had already begun establishing themselves among the Qazaqs around 1800.[51]

It was also in the late eighteenth and first half of the nineteenth century that a large influx of settlers began to make itself felt on the steppe. These included peasant and Cossack settlers, many of whom were neither Slavic nor Christian, but Muslim. In addition, the fast-growing urban settlements also included many Muslim merchants and craftsmen from both Russia and Central Asia.[52] Where settlers and Qazaq nomads were forced to compete for the same pasturelands there was often tension between the groups, often, but not always, to the disadvantage of the Qazaqs.[53] However, the influx of settlers, as well as the gradual economic integration of Qazaqs and the Qazaq steppe into the Russian economy, were factors that were beginning to change Qazaq nomadic society by creating wealthy urban Qazaq merchants, by beginning the sedentarization or semi-sedentarization of the Qazaq nomads, and by creating a partially integrated multi-ethnic Muslim society on the steppe that included Qazaqs, Volga-Ural Muslims and Central Asians.

The third process that accelerated the integration of Qazaqs into imperial Russia was the transformation of Islamic culture and Islamic life on the Qazaq steppe. The transformation of Islamic life for the Qazaq nomads was closely connected to the simultaneous economic and demographic changes under way. As previously mentioned, the early imperial Russian period was characterized by a gradual intensification of commercial activity on the steppe, and the integration of the Qazaqs into the larger Russian economy. Volga-Ural

49 Frank, 2001, pp. 47–55, 70–7.
50 For descriptions of the Muslim merchants in Semipalatinsk cf. Frank and Usmanov, 2001, pp. 14–15.
51 Qurbān-ʿAlī Khālidī, 1910, pp. 385–91.
52 Central Asians, particularly from the Ferghana Valley, appear to have been particularly prominent in the eastern steppe; cf. Frank and Usmanov, 2001, pp. 31–2.
53 For discussions of ethnic relations among Muslims cf. Vasil'ev, 1898.

Muslims were prominent in both of these processes, and played an even greater role in bringing about an Islamic revival among the Qazaqs, integrating Qazaq Muslims into Sufi and educational networks centred in Russia. In fact, at precisely the same time as Russian demographic and economic expansion was underway on the steppe, beginning in the late eighteenth century, Russia's Volga-Ural Muslims were experiencing an intense revival of Islamic institutions, literature, Sufism and scholarship, much of which was funded by commercial fortunes earned on the Qazaq steppe (for more on this revival in the Volga-Ural region see Chapter 19). Some of the major centres of Sufi and scholarly activity in this revival were the cities of Orenburg (and its Muslim suburb of Qarghalï), Troitsk, Petropavlovsk and Semipalatinsk. Increasingly these centres attracted Qazaq students, and many local mosques and *madrasas* were increasingly being funded by Qazaq merchants. Just as itinerant merchants brought commerce to the Qazaqs' encampments, itinerant teachers were often hired by wealthy Qazaqs to provide local children with an Islamic education.[54]

Some scholars have mistakenly interpreted this Islamic revival among the Qazaqs as a result of a Russian policy to 'Islamize' the Qazaqs. The Russian administrators in St Petersburg, in drafting the 1822 'Statute on the Siberian Kirgiz' (Qazaqs) were clearly unfamiliar with the religious situation on the Qazaq steppe. When they expressed the belief that the Qazaq nomads were 'barely Muslim, and rather pagan', and appealed for the Christianization of the Qazaqs, they not only misunderstood the essential role of Islamic institutions in furthering Russian policy aims on the steppe, but also the nature of religious life among the Qazaqs. However, it appears that Russian administrators on the steppe ignored the provisions calling for the Qazaqs' Christianization.[55]

To be sure, beginning in the first half of the eighteenth century Russian authorities were actively promoting Muslim institutions and relying on Muslim clerics in their relations with the Qazaq khans. As early as the 1740s Russian officials were encouraging the establishment of mosques in the frontier settlements bordering the Junior Zhüz, especially in the city of Orenburg and in the Cheliabinsk region, and investing local clerics with varying degrees of authority in administering both Volga-Ural Muslims and Qazaqs. Among these figures we find the first *imām* in Orenburg, Ibrāhīm b. Muḥammad-Tulāk, whom the Russian officials in Orenburg appointed *mufti* of that city in 1744, and a later figure, ʿAbdullāh b. Muslīm (d. 1794 or 1795), whom the authorities

54 For examples of such teachers in Semirech'e cf. Qurbān-ʿAlī Khālidī, 2005, p. 27; Qurbān-ʿAlī Khālidī, 1910, pp. 407, 411.

55 Levshin, 1996, pp. 419–20; cf. also Crews, 2006, pp. 192–240.

appointed as *akhund* in Cheliabinsk district in the 1770s.[56] In addition to their religious duties, the Russian authorities entrusted these figures with important diplomatic tasks on the steppe. In the 1740s Ibrāhīm b. Muḥammad-Tulāk (Ibraim Tliakov in Russian sources) was directly involved in the submission negotiations concerning Qazaq dynasts in the Junior and Middle Zhüzes.[57] ʿAbdullāh b. Muslīm received awards from the Russian authorities for carrying out a diplomatic mission to Bukhara.[58] Later figures, particularly the *muftis* of the Orenburg Muslim Spiritual Assembly, Muḥammad-Jān al-Ḥusayn (d. 1824) and ʿAbd as-Salām b. ʿAbd ar-Raḥīm (d. 1840), were active in several important diplomatic missions among the Qazaqs in the eighteenth and nineteenth centuries.[59] Catherine II had begun a policy in 1782 of building mosques in frontier administrative centres such as Orenburg, Petropavlovsk and Verkhneural'sk, but the construction of such institutions also furthered Russia's economic and diplomatic aims, since the presence of mosques, bazaars and Russian-guaranteed security attracted merchants, Qazaq khans and Muslim scholars alike. In many cases the Russian authorities built these mosques at the request of the Qazaq khans themselves.[60] It was common before and after the reforms of the 1820s for Russian administrators to appoint reliable Muslim clerics to serve Qazaq rulers. Before the reforms, these typically served Qazaq khans and sultans. Following the reforms the Russian authorities would appoint Muslim clerics to a specific *okrug* or *bolus*. Often these figures were selected by the Qazaq themselves, and at other times the authorities appointed them.[61] Unlike among the 'Orenburg and Siberian Kirgiz' (Qazaqs) in the Inner Horde Jahāngīr Khan administered his Muslim institutions directly, creating a religious administration modelled after the Orenburg Muslim Spiritual Assembly, but particularly emphasizing the Islamic education of the Qazaq nomads, and the training of Qazaq clerics.[62]

The gradual spread of imperial Russian Islamic institutions was to reveal its greatest effects on Qazaq society during the second half of the nineteenth century, when the integration of Russia and the Qazaq steppe was to intensify.[63] However these effects were already evident well before 1868. This spread of new types of institutions on the steppe was powered by a highly dynamic

56 Marjānī, 1885–1900, II, p. 209; Riḍā ad-Dīn b. Fakhr ad-Dīn, 1900–08, I12, pp. 40–1, 71.
57 Sazonov *et al.*, 1992, pp. 375–80.
58 Riḍā ad-Dīn b. Fakhr ad-Dīn, 1900–08, I12, p. 71.
59 Viatkin, 1939; Frank, 2003, p. 270.
60 Frank, 2003, p. 269.
61 Qurbān-ʿAlī Khālidī, 1910, p. 407; Kasymbaev and Agubaev, 1998, p. 141.
62 Frank, 2001, pp. 278–92.
63 On these later effects see Frank, 2003.

Islamic revival underway among the Volga-Ural Muslims of Russia, and this revival encouraged many Qazaqs to reform, or abandon, their own older Islamic institutions, which had developed during the era of the Qazaq Khanate. These included the reform of 'un-Islamic' practices, which were deemed improper, such as certain types of prayers and offerings that did not exist in the Islamic practices of Volga-Ural Muslims.[64] The political role of the *qozhas* declined significantly as the authority of the khans declined, and then disappeared altogether. While they retained much of their authority in the Syr Darya Valley, which would not come under Russian control until the 1860s, in the regions under Russian control their political importance declined as Russians relied on their own Volga-Ural clerics for diplomatic and other political tasks, and as the Qazaq khans themselves often relied on the same Volga-Ural Muslims as teachers and diplomats, partially because of their access to the Russian authorities. In the Inner Horde, while the *qozhas* retained their noble social status, tribal Qazaqs increasingly were trained as mullahs in Russia or by Volga-Ural clerics.

By the 1860s some members of the former elite, such as the *qozha* Muḥammad-Ṣāliḥ Babadzhanov, and the Chinggisid Chokan Valikhanov, both of whom had received Russian and Islamic educations, were calling for the russification of the Qazaq nomads. These russified members of the former elite had become alienated from Qazaq society, and in their Russian writings minimized or ignored the Islamic traditions of their people. They argued that the Qazaqs were not 'really' Muslim, but that manifestations of Islamic behaviour and culture among them were the results of an imported 'fanaticism' introduced by Volga-Ural clerics supported by an unwitting government policy. These writings appealed to a growing Islamophobia that was becoming fashionable in Russian ruling circles at the time.[65]

The Islamic revival, which was closely linked to economic and social integration into the Russian Empire, was enthusiastically received among many Qazaqs, but did not so much displace traditional Qazaq religious practices as complement them. If the *qozhas* lost much of their political influence, they nevertheless remained a significant and authoritative community in Qazaq society as a whole. During this period oral tradition evidently remained the chief manner of disseminating Islamic knowledge among the Qazaq nomads.

64 To be sure, not all Volga-Ural clerics challenged traditional Qazaq practices either, but such practices were topics of debate; cf. Qurbān-ʿAlī Khālidī, 2005, pp. 59–60.

65 The writings of Babadzhanov, and especially of Valikhanov, have become rather influential in establishing perceptions (or misperceptions) of Islam among the Qazaq in the nineteenth century; cf. Valikhanov, 1985, IV, pp. 71–5, and Babadzhanov, 1861.

In the first half of the nineteenth century Islamic publishing houses in the cities of Kazan and Orenburg began producing books in vernacular Qazaq based on Qazaq oral tradition. Here again publishing and oral tradition clearly complemented one another. Similarly, the cities of the Syr Darya Valley, particularly Turkestan, already the spiritual centres of Qazaq religious life in the eighteenth century,[66] remained so throughout the nineteenth century and arguably remain so to the present.

66 Andreev, 1998, p. 40; Köpeev, 2003–7, IV, pp. 150–7.

19

Russia and the peoples of the Volga-Ural region: 1600–1850

ALLEN J. FRANK

With the annexation of the khanates of Kazan and Astrakhan in the 1550s, and the formal submission of the Bashkir tribes in the second half of the sixteenth century, large populations of non-Slavic and non-Christian populations found themselves under Russian rule. Already before the annexations of the Kazan and Astrakhan khanates there were substantial Finno-Ugric and Muslim populations residing in Muscovy. As early as the eleventh century the Russian principalities of Vladimir and Suzdal' were established on territories that several Finno-Ugric peoples inhabited, the Merya, Muroma and Meshchera.[1] By the sixteenth century the latter groups had become russified, but as Russia gained control of territories in the Oka and Middle Volga regions other Finno-Ugric and Turkic groups became Russian subjects, but were not russified, retaining separate cultural and linguistic identities. As early as the end of the fourteenth century Turkic Muslims also formed part of the Muscovite state, and Muslims were among the troops of Ivan IV in the conquest of Kazan. These were so-called 'service Tatars', who included the khans of Kasimov and Muslim communities inhabiting the Oka Valley. Similarly, even before the 1550s, the Muscovite nobility and especially servitor class reflected a similar multi-ethnic character.[2] In general terms cooperation and mutual accommodation characterized the relations between the Russian authorities and the native inhabitants, and particularly the elites, of the Volga-Ural region between 1600 and 1850. Native peoples, both Muslim and non-Muslim, generally belonged to more privileged estates than did their Russian counterparts, and most native communities accommodated to Russian rule. In fact, most cases of violent rebellion in the region were linked not to the mere fact that 'Russians' ruled 'non-Russians', but rather were linked to attempts by Russian authorities to

1 Kluchevski, 1960, pp. 203–10.
2 Khafizov, 1998, p. 13; Alishev, 1984, pp. 56–7; Sharifullina, 1991, pp. 15–18.

alter the conditions of a community's estate status, or to change the status outright to a less privileged one.[3]

This period also revealed considerable dynamism among the region's native populations. Most non-Muslim groups subjected to official Christianization campaigns (see Chapter 16) in the eighteenth century did eventually accept Christian status, but at the same time successfully resisted russification. For the Finno-Ugric and Turkic non-Muslims of the Volga-Ural region the period from 1600 to 1850 was generally characterized by violent Christianization campaigns and the erosion of collective estate status from tribute-(*yasak*) paying tribal communities to serfs or state peasants. As a result, large numbers of both Muslims and non-Muslim native peoples fled to the Bashkir lands in the Urals in the seventeenth and eighteenth centuries where they succeeded in escaping Christianization and obtaining more favourable estate relationships.[4]

Not just in the Urals, but also in the Middle Volga region, many of the older religious foundations of social and economic organization remained in force well into the early twentieth century, preventing these communities' russification. The Finno-Ugric and Turkic non-Muslims during this period remained almost entirely agrarian and illiterate. Before 1850, the Church had enjoyed some success in creating native monastic institutions among some Mari and Chuvash communities, but for the most part forced conversions and later fruitless struggles against apostasy, or even conversion to Old Believer and other non-conformist sects, were evident in this period, particularly among the Mordvins. It was not until the latter half of the nineteenth century that the Russian Orthodox missionaries began implementing religious and educational policies that led to the creation of native clergy and a Christian revival within some of these communities.[5]

Among Muslims this era saw much more dramatic changes in economic and religious life. By means of expanded religious and economic privileges the Muslim community experienced remarkable revitalization in Islamic life and commercial integration into the Russian economy. Such economic and religious dynamism also encouraged an indigenous self-redefinition into a unified community that accommodated estate and tribal divisions. The Islamic revival, the Christianization of non-Muslims, and the distribution of communal privileges by the Russian state also resulted in widespread transformation of

3 See for example, Werth, 1999; similarly, cf. Chuloshnikov, 1940, pp. 10–11.
4 On the eastwards migration of the native peoples of the Volga-Ural region under Russian rule cf. for example, Geraklitov, 1926; Rakhmatullin, 1988.
5 Werth, 2002, pp. 200–22.

communal, and later even ethnic, identities among the native peoples of the Volga-Ural region.

Ethnicity, religion and estate

In the sixteenth century neither Muscovy, nor the successor states of the Golden Horde were ethnic nation-states in the modern sense of the term. Both in Muscovy and in the Kazan Khanate the population was organized into separate communities having an established relationship with the central authority. This was true of the nobility, the peasantry, nomads and tribal communities. With considerable success, the Russian authorities retained and expanded such a system for governing the peoples of the Volga-Ural region and Siberia in the seventeenth, eighteenth and most of the nineteenth centuries. During this period identities were complex and entwined. They included, of course, ethnic identity, religious identity and also corporate identity, that is, affiliation with a specific legally recognized estate (*soslovie* in Russian usage). Estate determined a community's relationship with the Russian state, its privileges and liabilities, and distinguished it from other communities.[6] While estate was a concrete legal relationship, it also became for many communities a crucial factor in communal and even religious identity during this period, particularly among Russia's Inner Asian subjects in the Volga-Ural region, Siberia and the Qazaq steppe.

During the period in question the non-Russian peoples of the Volga-Ural region comprised several different ethnic groups. These included Finno-Ugrians, the Udmurts (Votiaks), Maris (Cheremis) and Mordvins. The latter two groups were each further divided into two groups speaking mutually unintelligible, albeit related, languages. Another major ethnic group in the region was the Turkic-speaking Chuvash. The Finno-Ugric peoples and the Chuvash were generally non-Muslims. After their Christianization in the middle of the eighteenth century they retained for the most part nativized Christian religious practices, and some communities of Udmurts, Maris and Chuvash retained a legal status as 'pagans' (*iazychniki*) down to 1905. However, ethnic affiliation could cross linguistic lines. During this period there emerged communities of Tatar-speaking Mordvins, Maris and Chuvash, and communities of Mari- and Udmurt-speaking Muslims.

The Muslim population was the largest single group in the Volga-Ural region. In ethno-linguistic terms it was fairly unified. Muslims for the most

6 Freeze, 1986.

part spoke a number of mutually intelligible Turkic dialects. Already long before the Russian conquest they possessed a written Turkic literary language, as well as access to the Arabic and Persian literary languages through Islamic education. Russian nomenclature in this period primarily identified two Muslim groups, 'Tatars' and 'Bashkirs'. While the term 'Tatar' did exist among some estate communities as an ethnonym during this period, it did not come into common usage among Muslims until the twentieth century. During the seventeenth and eighteenth centuries it appears to have been one among many manifestations of corporate identity. Among Muslims, 'Tatar' as a self-appellation was mainly restricted to *mīrzās* claiming nobility based on ancestral status dating to the successor states of the Golden Horde. In fact, in Russian sources the term 'Tatar' is used much more broadly than for Volga-Ural Muslims. It was also used to refer to a wide range of Inner Asian people in the Volga-Ural region, Siberia, the Caucasus and Central Asia.[7] The other major Muslim group was the Bashkirs. These were primarily nomadic or semi-nomadic communities inhabiting the Ural Mountains south-east of the Kama River, and north and west of the Ural River. The Bashkir tribes had formerly been subjects of the Noghay Horde. Beginning in the second half of the sixteenth century they began coming under Russian suzerainty as tribute-paying tribal communities. These communities, who enjoyed hereditary privileges as communal landowners (*votchinniki*) distinguished themselves from other estates as *athaba*, derived from an Islamic legal term signifying 'agnates'.[8] Finally, in the Astrakhan region there were small pastoral nomadic Noghay communities, who retained separate ethnic and corporate identities throughout this period.[9]

During most of this period a community's estate was often understood as being part of its religious and ethnic affiliations. Bashkir genealogies, for example, were often layered narratives retelling a sacred history of the tribe or clan, the genealogical relationships of its constituent elements, and the precise historical and contractual nature of its relationship to Russia.[10] Other Muslim communities included narratives of their ancestors' submission to the Russians, often in obvious sacred terms. In some Muslim villages the members of separate estates maintained separate mosques and even cemeteries, indicating the existence of essentially separate communities.[11] Other genealogies

7 Frank, 1998, p. 43.
8 For a general overview cf. Usmanov, 1960, and Donnelly, 1968.
9 Arslanov and Viktorin, 1995.
10 For examples see Kuzeev, 1960.
11 Frank, 1998, p. 40; Frank, 2001, pp. 66–7.

recorded estate status while claiming ancestry from *sayyids* or other sacred figures from Islamic history.[12] At the same time, estate status was elastic, particularly in frontier areas, where an individual, or even a group, could join a more privileged estate, or form an entirely new one. For example, Muslim peasants who came to the eastern Qazaq steppe in the first half of the nineteenth century as itinerant merchants formed their own estate known as 'Chala-Qazaqs'. This was a community in principle descended from non-Qazaq fathers and Qazaq mothers, and was excluded from the patrilineal Qazaq tribal system. However, as a tribute-paying community exempt from the poll tax and military conscription, Chala-Qazaq status offered obvious benefits to Volga-Ural peasants, many of whom gained admittance to the estate without marriage to, or descent from, Qazaq women.[13] The presence in Siberia of Bukharan merchants and their descendants, who in the eighteenth century were one of the most privileged communities in the Russian Empire, influenced local Muslim tribal communities to feature legends of their communities' Central Asian origins in their Islamization narratives.[14]

Economic expansion and Islamic revival

Many Muslims in this era understood the economic expansion and Islamic revival that their community experienced in this period as two aspects of the same phenomenon.[15] Official material support of Islamic institutions was largely symbolic and the expansion of Islamic education and other Islamic institutions relied for the most part solely upon the economic resources of the Muslim community. At the same time, stimulus for these processes also originated from rather consequential state policies that accorded religious and economic privileges that had until then been restricted or denied. Ultimately the economic interests of a significant portion of the Muslim community became closely tied to Russia, and these interests were expressed in Islamic terms. This identification only increased with the formation of new Volga-Ural Muslim communities on the commercial centres of the Qazaq steppe and the penetration of merchants into Central Asia.

Russian state privileges for Muslim merchants existed rather early on. In the late sixteenth century, almost immediately after the Russian conquest,

12 Äkhmätjanov, 1995, pp. 48–9.
13 Cf. Qurbān-ʿAlī Khālidī, 1910, pp. 384–91
14 Tomilov, 1981, pp. 161–2.
15 On Islamic ethics and 'the Spirit of Capitalism' in the Volga-Ural region, see Kemper, 1998, pp. 147–72.

Central Asian merchants in Siberia were accorded a series of privileges to re-establish caravan routes with Central Asia that had been disrupted by the Russian conquest of Siberia.[16] For the Volga-Ural region there is an official document from 1685 reaffirming the trade privileges of Tatar merchants in Kazan's Old Tatar Quarter.[17] Trade privileges for some Muslim communities expanded during the Petrine era and as Russian military and economic power penetrated Bashkiria and the Qazaq steppe Russian officials sought to encourage Muslim merchants from both the Volga-Ural region and Central Asia. The establishment of a large Tatar merchant community in 1745 near Orenburg in the settlement of Seitovskii Posad (Qarghalï) was emblematic of this policy. Not only did Seitovskii Posad become a major commercial centre, but it evolved into one of the most influential centres of Islamic scholarship and education in Russia.[18] During the reign of Catherine the Great (r. 1762–96) restrictions on Tatar commercial activity in Russia were effectively loosened, and Tatar merchant colonies developed with particular intensity on the Qazaq steppe (see Chapter 20). Tatar merchants were also increasingly active in Central Asia, either independently or as agents for Russian merchants. Of course Muslim merchants were active in the Volga-Ural region as well, not only in the major fairs in Nizhnii Novgorod and Irbit, but also in cities, especially Kazan, but also in Astrakhan, Saratov and many smaller towns. The expansion of Muslim commercial activity in this period, and particularly at the beginning of the nineteenth century, is closely tied to Russia's overall economic expansion, and in the Qazaq steppe and Central Asia, with its political and military expansion as well.[19]

For the period before 1762 we can only speak of religious policies towards Muslims, rather than a religious policy (see Chapter 16). These sometimes contradictory policies included: (1) gradual conversions of communities and individuals; (2) militant and forceful Christianization campaigns leading to the official conversion of large communities of non-Muslims and small groups of Muslims, resulting in conflicts within the native communities during the nineteenth century and causing the authorities to have to deal with problems of apostasy; and (3) the protection and active support of the *ʿulamāʾ* and Islamic administrative institutions on the part of frontier governors, particularly those in Bashkiria and in proximity to the Qazaq steppe. Against the

16 Ziiaev, 1983, p. 23.
17 Nogmanov, 2005, pp. 78–9; Nogmanov suggests these privileges may have been established by Ivan IV.
18 Mikhaleva, 1982.
19 See Deviatykh, 2002; Apollova, 1960.

background of these policies it should be emphasized that Muslim soldiers, diplomats, spies and merchants were an essential element in Russia's political, military and economic enterprise at that time, and throughout the imperial period.

The accession of Empress Catherine the Great soon led to a unified policy towards the non-Orthodox religious communities, including the unChristianized 'pagans' and Muslims of the Volga-Ural region. During the 1770s and 1780s, under the influence of European Enlightenment thought and the realities of administering an empire along the steppe frontier, Catherine afforded official recognition of religious status to the communities of the Volga-Ural region (as well as of Western Siberia and of the Qazaq steppe).[20] During Catherine's reign Muslims were granted the privilege to establish and staff their own Islamic institutions, primarily mosques and *madrasas*. Muslim communities were also granted the privilege of using *sharīʿah* law in family and inheritance matters. Members of Muslim communities were also formally off-limits as targets of Christian missionaries and, similarly, Muslims were forbidden to proselytize among non-Muslims. The Russian authorities conferred the same privileges to 'unbaptized' Chuvash, Mari and Udmurts who had successfully resisted Christianization and now enjoyed formal recognition of their 'pagan' status.

In 1788 Catherine created the Orenburg Muslim Spiritual Assembly, which was to play a major role in the religious and political life of Volga-Ural and Siberian Muslims throughout the period in question. The Spiritual Assembly was a government-funded organization that had as its basic tasks the supervision of Islamic law in Russia. In fact, Catherine founded two Spiritual Assemblies. The Orenburg Muslim Spiritual Assembly was soon moved to the city of Ufa, had jurisdiction over the Volga-Ural region, Siberia and the Qazaq steppe. The Tauride Muslim Spiritual Assembly, based in the Crimea, had jurisdiction over the Crimea, the Black Sea steppe and Russia's Polish provinces. The precedent for such organizations was already established by territorial authorities in Bashkiria and Orenburg in the 1730s.[21] However these new organizations had authority over a much larger area, and were established by imperial-level legislation. The new organizations were headed by a *mufti*. The *mufti* presided over a council of *qazis*, who made rulings on questions of Islamic law, and who issued *fatwas*. Catherine's reforms also established a unified legal framework for the activities of the *ʿulamāʾ* and for religious institutions at the

20 Fisher, 1967.
21 Frank, 1998, pp. 30–2; Azamatov, 1996.

village level. Russian law permitted villages meeting certain criteria to build and finance mosques, to appoint and support *imāms* and muezzins, and to create and support educational establishments in the villages and cities where Muslims resided. These included primary schools (*maktabs*), and the more advanced centres of Islamic learning, the *madrasas*. One important task of the Spiritual Assembly was to conduct examinations to test the qualifications of prospective *imāms*, but in keeping with Russian administrative practice, it was the provincial-level civil authorities who actually issued permits for mosque construction and licences for *imāms*.

The Islamic revival and Islamic discourse in the Volga-Ural region

During the late eighteenth century Muslim society in the Volga-Ural region began experiencing a dynamic and far-reaching Islamic revival, although the roots of this revival reach back to the end of the seventeenth century. Russia's economic expansion in the late eighteenth, and especially nineteenth centuries powered this revival by funding the establishment and maintenance of Islamic institutions on a vast scale. The main urban centres of Islamic learning, where there was a large concentration of scholars and permanently staffed *madrasas*, were also the major commercial centres. These were the cities of Kazan, Orenburg (and its Muslim suburb Seitovskii Posad) and Astrakhan, as well as Troitsk, Petropavlovsk and Semipalatinsk on the Qazaq steppe. However, there also existed famous and influential *madrasas* in smaller communities, such as those in the villages of Sterlibashevo in Bashkiria and Machkara in the Middle Volga region. Volga-Ural Muslims were establishing Islamic institutions and especially spreading Islamic education not only in the Volga-Ural region proper, but also in Siberia, and the Lower Volga and Qazaq steppes, bringing their Islamic revival to the Noghays, Qazaqs and Siberian Muslims, and altering the traditional Islamic practices of these regions. Particularly on the Qazaq steppe the Volga-Ural *'ulamā'*, supported by Muslim merchants and by Russian officials, were at the forefront of Russian imperial administration and expansion in this period. Beyond its relationship to Russian economic and political expansion, the Islamic revival in the Volga-Ural region was above all an internal movement that comprised several differing, and occasionally competing, strands. This type of debate has been called 'Islamic Discourse', that is, the debates and discussions of social, political and religious issues expressed through traditional Islamic literary genres and institutions, such as Sufism and Sufi treatises, theology, law and historiography.[22]

Among the issues debated in this Islamic Discourse were the relationship Muslims can or should have as subjects of a non-Muslim sovereign, and the nature of a common Muslim identity in the face of existing tribal and corporate or estate identities. In the Volga-Ural region the Islamic revival and its discourse did not occur in isolation, but contact with Islamic scholars outside of Russia further stimulated Islamic thought in the region. Initially, beginning in the first half of the eighteenth century, the main destination for study among Volga-Ural Muslims was Daghestan. That region remained an important destination for scholars from the Volga-Ural region well into the nineteenth century and, conversely, many Daghestani scholars came to the Volga-Ural region. However by the late eighteenth century Bukhara had become the most prestigious destination to study, and remained so well into the twentieth century. *Imāms*hips in the major scholarly centres of Kazan, Petropavlovsk and Semipalatinsk were dominated by scholars who had studied there, and were known as 'Bukharis'.[23] To be sure, these religious connections were strengthened by commercial ties between merchants in these cities and Central Asia. The most popular forms of Islamic literature, especially Sufi literature, were based on Central Asian originals. For example, one of the most widespread *madrasa* textbooks, Tāj ad-Dīn b. Yālchīghul's *Risāla-yi ʿAzīza*, was written at the end of the eighteenth century, as a commentary of Ṣūfī Allāh-Yār's work *Thūbat al-ʿAjīzin*.

The significance of Bukhara, however, went well beyond its reputation as a centre of Islamic learning. It appeared in some of the Islamization narratives of Bashkirs and other communities. Other genealogies identified sacred ancestors, often *sayyids*, as having come from Bukhara or its environs. In Siberia, where privileged Bukharan communities intermixed with native Siberian Muslims, the religious bonds with Bukhara and its *sayyids* were even more explicit in local genealogies and histories. In this respect many Muslims in Russia viewed Bukhara as a holy city and source of Islamic status. The prestige associated with Bukhara came to be felt even in the fashion and material culture of the Volga-Ural and Siberian Muslims. The wealthiest and most authoritative citizens in both cities and villages wore clothes either imported from

22 Kemper, 1998, pp. 1–4; Frank, 2001, pp. 1–2.

23 For an overview cf. Kemper, 1998, pp. 89–90. The case of Semipalatinsk provides a good sampling of the locations where Volga-Ural Muslim scholars chose to study; cf. Frank and Usmanov, 2001; for the foreign study destinations of the ʿ*ulamā* in a rural district cf. Frank, 2001, pp. 116–20.

Bukhara or made from Central Asian fabric. Similarly jewellery and cosmetics were either imported from Central Asia or made from Bukharan originals. Even Central Asian dishes became commonplace at religious assemblies or for other festive occasions.[24]

Islamic scholarship was one of the main arenas in which the discussion of political issues coincided with the technical details of scholarly debates. The debates between the early reformist scholar Abū'n-Nāṣir al-Qūrṣawī (1776–1812) and his opponent ʿAbd ar-Raḥman al-Ūtiz-Īmānī (1754–1834) were emblematic of the theological disputes that characterized this discourse. In this conflict Qūrṣawī, who in his theological writings on the topic of divine attributes challenged the works of established theology, and emphasized *ijtihād*, that is, the authority of direct appeal to the Qur'an and the *sunna* in theological matters. Such a position while he was in Bukhara directly challenged the authority of established theological thought there, and elicited a violent reaction among some of the Bukharan scholars, forcing him to flee the city in 1808 or 1809 to escape a death sentence. In the Volga-Ural region such a position brought him into conflict with local scholars, such as ʿAbd ar-Raḥman al-Ūtiz-Īmānī, not only regarding this particular theological issue, but on other issues, such as the requirement or non-requirement for the obligatory night prayer in northern areas where the sun does not set.[25]

In broad terms we can identify three major currents among scholars at this time. The first was the reformist current, represented by Qūrṣawī and popularized in the latter half of the century by Shihāb ad-Dīn Marjānī (1818–89), who himself became a major influence on the modernist (*jadīd*) movement in the early twentieth century. Second were pietists, such as Tāj ad-Dīn b. Yālchīghul al-Bāshqordī (d. 1838). These were primarily Sufis who accepted the theological and political status quo in Russia. They were closely tied to Sufi traditions and established norms of corporate and sacred Islamic identity, as well as the legitimacy of the Spiritual Assembly. Finally, there were the traditionalist scholars who were also vocal opponents of the authority of the Orenburg Muftiate. Characteristic of this group was al-Ūtiz-Īmānī, whose intellectual heirs, such as Bahā' ad-Dīn Vaisov, were strong opponents of both the Spiritual Assembly and the later modernists.[26]

The Islamic revival also reinvigorated Sufism in the Volga-Ural region. From the late eighteenth century Sufism in the Volga-Ural region was dominated by the Naqshbandī-Mujaddidiya tradition, which had emerged in India in the

24 Vorob'ev and Khismatullin, 1967, pp. 118, 151, 161, 167–8.
25 Kemper, 1998, pp. 272–307.
26 Kemper, 1998, ch. 5.

seventeenth century, and itself came to dominate in Central Asia, effectively displacing the Yasaviya. Its existence in the Volga-Ural region is documented already during the Kazan Khanate and as late as the 1750s there are reports of Yasavi shaykhs still active in the Astrakhan region.[27] The first Naqshbandī shaykh known to have been active in the region was ʿAbd al-Karīm b. Bālṭāy, who had trained in Central Asia and in the 1750s was serving as an *imām* in Seitovskii Posad.[28] By the turn of the eighteenth and nineteenth centuries two major Naqshbandī-Mujaddidiya shaykhs were attracting adepts from the Volga-Ural region, Fayẓ-Khan al-Kābulī (d. 1802) in Kabul, and Niyāz-Qul at-Turkmānī in Bukhara (d. 1820/1). The students of these shaykhs and their disciples were to dominate Sufism in the region down to the twentieth century.[29]

A key element in the evolution of collective identities among Volga-Ural Muslims was the development of local Islamic historiography in the late eighteenth century, replacing the older tradition of Chinggisid court historiography. These Chinggisid works are important sources for the dynastic history of the later Golden Horde, the most prominent of which is the *Jamīʿat-Tawārīkh* of Qādir-ʿAlī Bek Jālāyirī, compiled in 1602, and the *Daftar-i Chingīz Nāma* by an anonymous author, compiled in the late seventeenth century.[30] Towards the end of the eighteenth century we see a new type of historiography emerge, emphasizing the sacred history of the local Muslim community. The focus of these sacred histories was the miraculous conversion to Islam of a legendary khan in the city of Bulghar by Companions (*aṣḥāb*) of the prophet Muḥammad in the year 630–1 CE (9 AH). The earliest work of this type appeared in the late eighteenth century, and its author was a prominent Sufi and scholar in Orenburg, Wālid b. Muḥammad-Amīn al-Qārghālī, also known as Walī-Muḥammad Īshān. This work, entitled *Tawārīkh*, contains a conversion narrative, as well as a shrine catalogue of prominent saints and tombs in the Volga-Ural region. Numerous other similar works featuring the conversion narrative and shrine catalogue appeared in the following decade, but the most influential of these works appears at some point after 1825, the *Tawārīkh-i Būlghārīya*, attributed to a certain Ḥusām ad-Dīn b. Sharaf ad-Dīn al-Bulghārī. All of these works emphasized the mythical sacred Islamic origins of the community, but also by means of their shrine catalogues, defined very sacred clear boundaries identifying a unified regional Muslim community, essentially conforming to the jurisdiction of the Orenburg Muftiate. These

27 Riẓā ad-Dīn b. Fakhr ad-Dīn, 1900–08, I/2, p. 44.
28 Kemper, 1998, pp. 82–8.
29 Kemper, 1998, pp. 90–8.
30 On these works cf. Usmanov, 1972, pp. 33–133; Ivanics and Usmanov, 2002.

works emphasized a regional Bulghar identity that both incorporated and bridged the estate-based identities that existed among Volga-Ural Muslims at that time, and indeed in this period the ruins of Bulghar at the confluence of the Volga River became the area's object of pilgrimage for Muslims. Just as in the discussions of Islamic jurisprudence and dogma, historiography, particularly the *Tawārīkh-i Būlghārīya*, alluded to current political concerns facing Muslim scholars, such as discouraging Muslims from attempting to convert Russians.[31]

The emergence and widespread acceptance of Bulghar identity that was adduced in sacred terms in this historiography was in some respects the beginning of a common political identity for Volga-Ural Muslims, in that it indicated the existence of a conscious regional Muslim community within Russia, existing beyond the traditional tribal and corporate identities. It also revealed an awareness of being a discrete Muslim community within the Islamic *umma* as a whole. At the same time, it did not replace local identities so much as complement them, as versions of the conversion narrative were also included in the sacred traditions of local groups, such as Volga-Ural Muslims in Semipalatinsk, among Muslims in the Kama region, who incorporated the conversion narrative into their sacred legends of their ancestors' submission to Ivan IV, and among the Bashkirs, who incorporated the conversion narrative into their own tribal genealogies.[32]

The Islamic revival of this period, and the Islamic discourse and traditions it created, became targets for reformist and modernist critiques in the late nineteenth century, although even at that time the traditional forms of identity and scholarship largely succeeded in holding their own against modernist and reformist critics. But the appreciation of this Islamic revival should not be limited to its role in bringing later Muslim intellectuals to accepting 'modern' ideas. Unlike the later modernists, whose own works were generally derivative and often amateurish imitations of European literary genres, the *ʿulamāʾ* during the Islamic revival can be said to have contributed to and developed an indigenous style of literary and scholarly discourse specific to the Volga-Ural region, and at the same time made significant contributions to the vast body of Islamic scholarship in a number of fields.

31 Frank, 1998.
32 Qurbān-ʿAlī Khālidī, 1910, pp. 176–9; Frank, 1998, pp. 90, 113–15.

20

The new Uzbek states: Bukhara, Khiva and Khoqand: *c.* 1750–1886

YURI BREGEL

In the first half of the eighteenth century the sedentary regions of Central Asia experienced, to various degrees, a political and economic crisis, which manifested itself in the decline of the ruling dynasties in the two Uzbek khanates, Bukhara and Khiva, the weakening or even the total collapse of the central governments, the resurgence of tribal forces, increasing interference by the steppe nomads in the affairs of the sedentary states, and the disruption of economic life.

An important factor in the history of Central Asia since the late seventeenth century was the gradual movement of Turkmen tribes, most of whom until then had inhabited the arid regions of the Qaqa-Qum desert and the Mangïshlaq peninsula, to the oases of northern Khorasan and Khorezm. Among the major tribes, the Chowdur came to Khorezm from Mangïshlaq partly at the end of the seventeenth and partly in the early eighteenth centuries; one branch of the tribe Yomut came to Khorezm in the early eighteenth century (the other one remained in south-western Turkmenia); and the tribe Teke began to infiltrate the oases of northern Khorasan.

The first of the two khanates to be affected by the crisis mentioned above was that of Khorezm. The seemingly successful reign of Anūsha Khan, son of Abu'l-Ghāzī, who repeatedly invaded Mawarannahr and was on the verge of annexing a part of it, came to an abrupt end in 1685, when his amirs, probably tired of the incessant and inconclusive military campaigns, deposed and blinded the khan at the very beginning of the last such campaign. Within the following thirty years (1685–1715) eleven or thirteen khans succeeded one another; two or three of them were the sons of Anūsha, two or three others traced their origin to other ʿArabshahid khans, while the rest were of obscure origin and even outright impostors.[1] During this period tribal chieftains were usually instrumental in enthroning new khans. From this time

1 For detailed information on the succession of khans in Khorezm during these thirty years, see Munis, 1999, pp. 565–9 (n. 285).

on an especially prominent role was played by the nomadic Uzbeks of Aral (the region of the delta of the Amu Darya), who mostly only nominally recognized the authority of the khan of Khiva; sometimes they acted in alliance with some groups of the Qazaqs who nomadized between the lower Amu Darya and the Syr Darya and increased their interference in the affairs of Khorezm. During the same period there was a marked increase in the number of Turkmens in Khorezm; they migrated to this region from the areas along the borders of Khorasan and along the Caspian shores, and they participated in internal feuds, often allying themselves with various Uzbek factions. Turkmens also began to play an important part in the raids on Khorasan conducted by the khans of Khiva. Shīr Ghāzī Khan (1714–27) captured and sacked Mashhad twice, in 1716 and 1719.[2] He was killed in Khiva by Persian and Russian slaves, and he was the last khan of ʿArabshahid origin; almost all those who ruled after him, mostly nominally, until the end of the eighteenth century, were from among the Qazaq Chinggisids.

An internal crisis in the khanate of Bukhara began a quarter of a century later than in Khiva, but was no less severe. Under the last Ashtarkhanid (Togha-Timurid (Toqay-Timurid)) khan, Abu'l-Fayẓ, who succeeded his brother ʿUbaydallāh, killed in 1711 as a result of conspiracy of his amirs, the country practically disintegrated into a number of tribal principalities. Balkh separated from the khanate and was ruled by the chieftains of the Uzbek tribe Ming, who invited from Khorasan as a puppet khan a member of another branch of the Ashtarkhanids. The tribes of Keneges in the region of Shahrisabz and Yüz in the region of Hisar hardly recognized the authority of Bukhara, while Ferghana Valley was under several independent rulers from the end of the seventeenth century. In 1722 Ibrāhīm Biy, chieftain of the Keneges tribe, together with several other tribal leaders, started rebellion in Samarqand, where they enthroned Rajab Sultan, a cousin of Shīr Ghāzī Khan of Khiva. He sought help from the Qazaqs, who at that time suffered from the devastating raid of the Qalmaqs and, having fled from them and crossed the Syr Darya, began to ravage Mawarannahr, destroying fields and orchards and pillaging cities and villages. The sedentary population began to flee from the central regions of the khanate, so that Samarqand was reportedly entirely abandoned, and in Bukhara only two city quarters remained inhabited. People fled mostly to the south-eastern regions of the khanate and to the Ferghana Valley (which contributed to the growth of cities in these areas). By 1730 the Qazaqs returned to Dasht-i Qipchāq, but the central government in Bukhara

2 Munis, 1999, pp. 56–8.

was irredeemably weakened, and in the 1730s its authority remained limited to the districts closest to the capital.[3] In the capital itself power was concentrated in the hands of the khan's *ataliq*, Muḥammad Ḥakīm Biy Manghït.

While both Bukhara and Khiva were suffering from such a steep political decline, they became an easy prey to a foreign conqueror – Nādir Shah of Iran.[4] In 1737, when Nādir Shah was campaigning in India, his eldest son Riḍā-Quli Mīrzā occupied Balkh and Andkhuy and then crossed the Amu Darya, defeated Abu'l-Fayẓ Khan and besieged him in Qarshī. Having learned about this, the khan of Khiva Ilbārs set out to Mawarannahr – according to one version, to come to help Abu'l-Fayẓ, according to another, in order to capture Bukhara while the khan was not there.[5] But Riḍā-Quli was recalled from Mawarannahr by Nādir Shah, Abu'l-Fayẓ Khan returned to his capital and Ilbārs Khan hurried back to Khiva. In 1740 Nādir Shah invaded Mawarannahr himself. The khan did not try to resist and offered his submission at Nādir Shah's camp set out in a suburb of Bukhara. The city was spared a Persian occupation, but the khanate had to supply to the Persian army a large quantity of grain and fodder as well as 10,000 horsemen, under Muḥammad Raḥīm Biy, the son of Muḥammad Ḥakīm Ataliq. After that Nādir Shah marched against Khiva, defeated the Khorezmian army in two battles and besieged Ilbārs Khan in the city of Khanqah. After a short siege Ilbārs surrendered and was executed along with twenty of his amirs; Khiva surrendered several days later, after an intense bombardment. The khanate of Khiva had to pay a much heavier price, for its belligerence, than Bukhara: the greatest punishment imposed on it (besides the requisition of grain and from 4,000 to 18,000 horsemen for the Persian army, according to different accounts) was the freeing of all slaves, mostly Persians, who had been kept in the khanate and employed in agriculture and as domestic servants; by order of Nādir Shah they were sent to Khorasan. Nādir Shah installed in Khiva as khan a certain Ṭāhir Khan, allegedly an Ashtarkhanid, but after six months he was killed as a result of an uprising in the city, and Nādir Shah had him replaced by Abu'l-Ghāzī Khan (II), a son of Ilbārs Khan. For several years following his conquest of Bukhara and Khiva, Nādir Shah did not try to administer these countries directly but, instead, relied upon the local Uzbek chieftains, who happened to be, in both cases, the leaders of the Manghït tribe: Muḥammad Ḥakīm Ataliq and his son Muḥammad Raḥīm Biy in Bukhara, and Artuq Inaq and Khurāz Bek in Khiva.

3 See Vel'iaminov-Zernov, 1855, II, Appendix, p. 22.
4 See on him *CHIran*, VII (1991) (with further references).
5 Munis, 1999, p. 575 n. 353.

Muḥammad Ḥakīm Atalïq died in 1743, and in Mawarannahr tribal feuds followed, in the course of which the city of Bukhara itself was sacked by rebellious Uzbek tribes. Nādir Shāh sent Muḥammad Raḥīm Biy to restore order, having given him the Uzbek troops who had served in the shah's army since 1740, together with Qïzïlbash and Ghilzai (Afghan) troops, equipped with artillery. With this force Muḥammad Raḥīm was able to suppress the tribal rebellions, and he appointed his men to the key positions in the administration. When Nādir Shah was assassinated in Iran in 1747, Muḥammad Raḥīm Biy had Abu'l-Fayẓ Khan killed, and the khan's twelve-year-old son, ʿAbd al-Mūʾmin, was proclaimed khan, while Muḥammad Raḥīm became his *atalïq*. Within a year or two Muḥammad Raḥīm ʿAbd al-Mūʾmin had also killed, upon which an obscure Chinggisid prince (possibly of Khorezmian origin) named ʿUbaydallāh was proclaimed khan; he was also killed in 1756, and at the end of 1756 Muḥammad Raḥīm was himself enthroned as a new khan, having married before that a daughter of Abu'l-Fayẓ Khan. Thus, he founded a new, non-Chinggisid, dynasty, which became known under its tribal name Manghït. Muḥammad Raḥīm's marriage did not provide sufficient legitimacy to his usurpation and, in a speech at the assembly convened for his inauguration (as put in his mouth by his historian), Muḥammad Raḥīm stressed that his right to the throne was based on the fact that he was a strong leader, who restored the order in the country, eliminated corruption and suppressed rebellions.[6] The elevation of Muḥammad Raḥīm to the royal rank was preceded and followed by almost uninterrupted wars with several Uzbek tribes who refused to recognize the new ruler: the Burqut in the middle Zarafshan region, the Keneges in Shahrisabz and, especially, the Yüz in Hisar. Soon after the suppression of these rebellions Muḥammad Raḥīm Khan died (in 1758);[7] he had no male offspring, and an under-age son of his daughter (and great-grandson of Abu'l-Fayẓ Khan) named Fāẓil Töre was enthroned as khan, while Muḥammad Rahīm's uncle Dāniyāl Biy became the actual ruler with the title of *atalïq*. Most Uzbek tribes and provincial rulers refused to recognize the new khan and rebelled; the rebels even besieged the city of Bukhara and were repelled with great difficulty. After that Dāniyāl Atalïq deposed Fāẓil Töre, had another puppet khan enthroned named Abu'l-Ghāzī (probably of Ashtarkhanid lineage), and continued to rule himself, assisted by his son Shāh Murād, who was his chief military commander and the governor of Karmina and later Qarshi.

6 See Muḥammad Vafāʾ Karmīnagī, *Tuḥfat al-khānī*, f. 255b.
7 So in most sources; von Kügelgen gives 1759 (see von Kügelgen, 2002, p. 73).

Together, they defeated the rebels and recovered most of Mawarannahr. After a rebellion in Bukhara in 1784 Dāniyāl Ataliq transferred most of the business of governing to his son, and in 1785 Dāniyāl Ataliq died and was succeeded by Shāh Murād.

Shāh Murād did not assume the titles of 'khan' or 'ataliq', but retained only the title of 'amir'.[8] He was distinguished by his great piety, which earned him the nickname *Amīr-i Maʿṣūm* ('Sinless amir') and the reputation of a 'dervish on the throne'. He took important measures for the improvement of the economy: a monetary reform, the restoration and reconfirmation of numerous pious endowments (*vaqf*), the restoration of various public buildings in Bukhara and Samarqand, etc.[9] But he also fought numerous wars with his neighbours in the south. At the beginning of his reign he started military campaigns against Merv which, since the death of Nādir Shāh, had been an independent principality inhabited by the Qajars, one of the Qïzïlbash tribes. Merv was captured after the second campaign, in 1788 or 1789, most of its population was deported to Bukhara (where they have lived ever since, becoming known as 'Ironi') and a Bukharan garrison was installed. After that Merv served as a staging ground for plundering raids into Khorasan which continued until the end of Shāh Murād's reign. Shāh Murād also confronted the Afghan ruler Timūr Shāh in the province of Balkh and seems to have retained the western part of this region (Maymana and Aqcha) under Bukharan jurisdiction. After the death of Shāh Murād at the very end of 1799, he was succeeded by his son (from the daughter of Abu'l-Fayẓ Khan) Ḥaydar.[10] It was Ḥaydar who adopted the honorific *Amīr al-muʾminīn*, which was not used by his successors. At the same time his claim to legitimacy was based also on his Chinggisid lineage. The later rulers of Bukhara (until the revolution of 1917) had always put the title 'khan' after their name (which was its usual place) and the title 'amir' preceding the name. Therefore it is equally possible to call Bukhara under the Manghïts, since Amir Ḥaydar, a 'khanate' or an 'amirate' (a term that began to be used only recently in modern literature).[11] Neither was the native usage: the country itself was called in the

8 Vel'iaminov-Zernov (1859, p. 412) claimed that the title 'amir' adopted by Shāh Murād stood for *amīr al-muʾminīn* 'commander of the faithful', the title of the caliphs; the same repeated by V. V. Bartol'd (*Istoriia kul'turnoi zhizni Turkestana*, in his *Sochineniia*, II/1, p. 279) and in my article 'Bukhara. III' in *Encyclopaedia Iranica*, IV, p. 518. According to von Kügelgen (2002, p. 281), this is unsubstantiated.

9 Cf. on his (probably putative) reforms: Bregel, 2000, pp. 17–18 n. 65.

10 On the date of death of Shāh Murād and the accession of Ḥaydar cf. von Kügelgen, 2002, pp. 80–1; Bregel, 2000, p. 2 n. 6.

11 The most recent collective work *Istoriia Uzbekistana*, III (*XVI–pervaia polovina XIX veka*) (Tashkent, 1993) has ridiculous statements that 'the khanate of Bukhara began to be

nineteenth century, both by its inhabitants and neighbours, Mawarannahr, '(Vilāyat-i) Tūrān' or '(Vilāyat-i) Bukhara'.

Amir Ḥaydar (1800–26) followed the example of his father as patron of Islamic institutions and scholars. He also had claims on being an Islamic scholar himself and used to lecture in a Bukharan *madrasa*; but, as distinct from Shāh Murād, he used to surround himself with splendour and all external signs of authority. As a military commander he was not always successful. His main achievement was the annexation of the territories south of the Amu Darya (Balkh, Maymana, Badakhshan and Qunduz) in 1817; however, these regions remained largely semi-autonomous. He had to fight various rebellious Uzbek tribes within Mawarannahr. A rebellion of two major Uzbek tribes, Khitay and Qïpchaq, in the middle Zarafshan Valley, lasted from 1821 to 1825. The most stubborn enemies of the Manghïts were the Keneges of Shahrisabz and Kitab, whose final subjugation was achieved only by the end of the rule of Ḥaydar's successor, Naṣrallāh. The relations of Bukhara during his rule with two neighbouring Uzbek states, Khorezm and Khoqand, were mostly hostile. In 1806 the Bukharan army routed the army of Eltüzer Khan of Khiva in a battle on the banks of the Amu Darya in Khorezm, but later Bukhara, in its confrontations with Khiva, was usually on the defensive. Merv was lost to Khiva in 1822. In 1821–4 Khivan troops, taking advantage of the rebellion of Khitay and Qïpchaq, were raiding and plundering Bukharan territory along the Amu Darya almost with impunity. In the east, Ḥaydar had often to fight the attacks from the rulers of Khoqand. The city of Ura-Tübe was the main bone of contention. Ḥaydar was able to retain it, but he lost the city of Turkestan and the entire region north of the Syr Darya captured by Khoqand in 1815.

Ḥaydar's son and successor Naṣrallāh (1826–60) began his reign with a brutal suppression of his (real and imagined) opponents, executing hundreds during the first month of his rule and gaining a nickname *Amīr-i Qaṣṣāb* 'Amir the Butcher'. His main efforts were towards the suppression of the tribal separatism. To this end he appointed persons of mean origin as provincial governors, completely dependent on him, and he established a standing army, mostly infantry, recruited from the sedentary population and partly equipped with firearms, including artillery.[12] This helped him to consolidate his rule within the khanate, but did not always have a noticeable effect in his confrontations

called amirate from the time of rule of Muḥammad Raḥīm Biy' (p. 150) and 'the first khan of the Manghït dynasty, Muḥammad Raḥīm Biy, having become an amir, ruled the Bukharan amirate autocratically' (p. 151).

12 Cf. on the firearms and artillery in Khiva: Munis, 1999, pp. 384–6 n. 383 and pp. 617–18 n. 679.

with the neighbours. He conquered Shahrisabz only in 1856, after numerous military campaigns. He lost all territories south of the Amu Darya to Dost Muḥammad Khan of Afghanistan in 1849–50. In 1842 he defeated the khanate of Khoqand and even captured its capital, but soon lost it as a result of a popular uprising in the city; the next year he invaded Khorezm, but his troops were defeated at Hazarasp, and he had to retreat. By the end of Naṣrallāh's rule his authority in the country was strengthened, but it was exercised over a much-reduced territory. His son and successor, Muẓaffar al-Dīn, often referred to as Amir Muẓaffar, tried to expand the khanate at the expense of its eastern neighbours, but he succeeded only with Russian help, after the khanate of Bukhara itself was defeated by Russia (see below).

In Khorezm[13] the situation after the death of Nādir Shah remained very unstable for the next three decades. There were sharp conflicts between some major ethnic groups in the country: the Sarts (old sedentary Turkic-speaking inhabitants of the southern part of Khorezm called *Besh Qalʿa* lit. 'Five Towns'), the Uzbek tribes, especially those in Aral (the Amu Darya Delta region), several Turkmen tribes, whose role in Khorezm (especially that of the Yomut) was steadily growing, and the Qazaqs of the Junior Zhüz who nomadized next to Aral. As distinct from the Manghït leaders in Bukhara, the Manghït chieftains in Khorezm, facing a strong opposition from their rivals, especially the Qongrat tribe, were unable to secure their predominant position. They stayed in power only for four years after Nādir Shah's death and in 1753 they were killed by Ghāyib Khan, a Qazaq Chinggisid, who had before accompanied Nādir Shah and whom the Manghït chieftains themselves had brought to Khiva. Ghāyib Khan, however, caused a general rebellion by imposing heavy taxes and had to flee the country in 1758. Upon the request of the representatives of all groups of the population of Khorezm, Muḥammad Raḥīm Khan of Bukhara sent to Khiva as a khan Tīmūr Ghāzī Sulṭān, a brother of the last nominal Ashtarkhanid khan of Bukhara. He was killed in 1764, after which for forty years all the power in the country was in the hands of Uzbek amirs (primarily of the tribe of Qongrat), who used to invite khans from among the Qazaq Chinggisids and depose them at will.[14] In 1770, after the Yomut

13 The name of the country in local usage has always been 'Khorezm'. The name 'Khanate of Khiva' ('Khivinskoe khanstvo' in Russian) was adopted in Russian and West European literature from the eighteenth century. Until then it was usually referred to as 'Urgench' (or 'Iurgench' in Russian documents); this was also sometimes the name under which it was mentioned in Iran and Bukhara, and 'Urganji' was often the collective name given to its people.

14 See detailed accounts on the events of the second half of the eighteenth century in Khorezm in Munis, 1999, pp. 66–79 and 587–90 nn. 388–401.

Turkmens captured the capital, Khiva, and began to raid towns and villages, the country was plunged into a state of anarchy, and famine spread. Muḥammad Amīn Ināq, the leader of the Qongrats, defeated the Yomuts later the same year and banished them from the country (several years later he brought them back). He became the actual ruler, but continued to invite Chinggisids from the steppe as puppet khans. Only his second successor, Eltüzer Ināq, was strong enough to have himself proclaimed as khan (in 1804), thus founding the new dynasty known under its tribal name, the Qongrats. Like the Manghïts in Bukhara, the Qongrats tried to prove their connection with the Chinggisids in order to legitimize their rule, but they did it differently: by tracing back their origin to the Mongol clan Qongrat, which was connected to the clan of Chinggis by marital ties.[15]

Very soon after his accession Eltüzer Khan began a war with Bukhara, which ended for him disastrously: in 1806, in a battle on the banks of the Amu Darya, in Khorezm, his army was routed and he himself drowned in the river. His younger brother, Muḥammad Raḥīm, who succeeded him and ruled until 1825, was much more successful. He unified the country, conquering the region of the Amu Darya Delta, Aral, in 1811 and bringing to submission the nomadic Uzbeks of this area, who had remained independent throughout the eighteenth century. Muḥammad Raḥīm Khan brutally suppressed rebellions of several Uzbek tribes, so that towards the end of his rule there was no one to question his authority. He was aggressive in the relations with Khorezm's neighbours: almost annually the Khivan troops would raid either the Turkmens and Persians in Khorasan, the Bukharans in Mawarannahr, or the Qazaqs north of the Syr Darya. The aim of these campaigns was plunder and the exaction of tribute, but he would also resettle some groups of population to Khorezm. He especially took care of bringing to Khorezm numerous Turkmens from northern Khorasan (cf. below); some of them were encouraged to migrate voluntarily, others were brought by force. Turkmens formed a substantial part of the Khivan army and, for their military service, they were given land for cultivation and enjoyed a partially tax-exempt status. The first successors of Muḥammad Raḥīm Khan – his son, Allāh-Quli (1825–42), and two grandsons, Raḥīm-Quli (1843–6) and Muḥammad Amīn (1846–55) – pursued a similar policy. The only territorial acquisition of the khanate was Merv, which was abandoned by Bukhara in 1822 and then was intermittently under indirect or direct Khivan control until 1843, when the Turkmen tribe Sarïq inhabiting the oasis became completely independent.

15 See Bregel, 1982, pp. 357–98.

The Qongrat rulers paid great attention to the development of an irrigation system in the khanate, which was based entirely on a single source, the Amu Darya. New canals were built, especially in the western parts of the country, and substantial areas were irrigated and cultivated. These lands were settled partly by the Turkmens and partly by other groups that were deported to Khorezm during the military campaigns in Mawarannahr and northern Khorasan, like Tajiks and Jamshidis. Relations with the Turkmens, both outside and inside Khorezm, became of crucial importance for the Qongrat khans. The tribe Teke, which in the second half of the eighteenth century occupied the entire area along the northern rim of Khorasan (having pushed out the tribe Yemreli, which had to migrate to Khorezm), had to recognize their authority, but it was limited to occasional payment of *zakāt* and participation in some Khivan campaigns against Iran. After the Sarïqs of Merv asserted their independence, Muḥammad Amīn Khan began annual campaigns against Merv, which continued until 1854, when the Sarïqs were finally subdued and Merv captured. The next year Muḥammad Amīn Khan turned against the Teke who lived on the Tejen River, south-west of Merv; but in a battle near Sarakhs with the Teke, assisted also by a detachment of Persian troops, the Khivan army was routed and Muḥammad Amīn Khan killed.

This was a major setback for Khiva, since not only was Merv lost for good, but it also triggered rebellions of Turkmen tribes in Khorezm itself, initially joined also by the Qaraqalpaqs. Two new khans of Khiva were killed by the Turkmens within two years (in 1855 and 1856). Rebellions continued, with ups and downs, till 1867, and they seriously weakened the khanate, which also lost all its positions in southern Turkmenia.[16] However, it still tried to assert its authority over the Qazaqs of the Junior Zhüz who nomadized on the Mangïshlaq peninsula and in the Qïzïl-Qum Desert, which was causing increasing tensions with Russia.

In the eighteenth century a third Uzbek khanate emerged in the Ferghana region. From the end of the seventeenth century most of this region had been under the authority of the Naqshbandī shaykhs (*khojas*) residing in the village of Chadak in the northern part of the valley, while the area of Khojend at its western end was dominated by the Uzbek tribe of Yüz. The chieftains of another Uzbek tribe, the Ming, in the western part of the Ferghana Valley east of Khojend, gradually gathered strength and extended their influence to the entire valley. Shāhrukh Biy Ming eliminated the khojas of Chadak in 1709. Another Ming ruler, ʿAbd al-Karīm Biy, founded the city of Khoqand (or Qoqand,

16 Detailed discussion of all these events in Bregel, 1961, pp. 197–227.

in popular pronunciation Quqon) in the western part of Ferghana in 1740, and it became the capital of the Mings. At the end of the 1750s, according to Chinese accounts, Ferghana was still divided between four principalities: Andijan, Namangan, Margelan and Khoqand, of which this last was the strongest. After the destruction of the Qalmaqs by China in 1758–9, Īrdāna Biy, the ruler of Khoqand, sent an embassy to Beijing expressing submission, but it was a pure formality and did not signify the extension of Chinese rule over Ferghana. By the end of the rule of Īrdāna Biy's successor, Nārbūta Biy (1770–98; according to other data, from 1763), the entire Ferghana Valley was united under the Mings of Khoqand. During this period the region enjoyed a relative stability, which contributed to the influx of population from other areas, especially Mawarannahr and Kashghar.

Nārbūta's son and successor, ʿĀlim (1798–1810), assumed the title of khan and can be considered the founder of the dynasty. For the legitimization of the new dynasty a genealogical legend was fabricated tracing the origin of the Ming rulers to Bābur and, through him, to Chinggis Khan. ʿĀlim Khan tried to exterminate his opponents and gained the nickname *ʿĀlim-ẓālim* (ʿĀlim the tyrant'). He formed a strong army, the core of which consisted of mercenaries – Tajik mountaineers mainly from Qarategin, and some Afghans – and began conquests beyond Ferghana. In 1805 he conquered Khojend and in 1809 Tashkent, which soon became a base for the further expansion into the Qazaq steppes. After the death of ʿĀlim Khan (killed as a result of a conspiracy), the expansion of the khanate was continued even more vigorously by his first two successors, ʿUmar Khan (1810–22) and Muḥammad ʿAlī Khan (1823–42). By the end of the rule of the latter the territory of the khanate beyond Ferghana included the southern part of the Qazaq steppe, stretching from the lower course of the Syr Darya in the west to Lake Issyk-Köl in the east (and thus including a large part of the Senior Horde and a part of the Middle Horde), as well as mountainous areas south of Issyk-Köl inhabited by the Qïrghïz. In 1834 Muḥammad ʿAlī conquered Qarategin, and his authority was nominally recognized by Kulab, Darvaz and Badakhshan. But in 1842 civil strife broke out in Ferghana. Amir Naṣrallāh of Bukhara used this opportunity to attack the khanate; he captured Khoqand and several other cities and put to death Muḥammad ʿAlī and some of his relatives. Less than three months later the Bukharans were driven out as a result of a popular revolt, but for the following three decades the country suffered greatly from political instability and frequent bitter fighting between various ethnic groups.[17] After the retreat of

17 For detailed description of events in the khanate of Khoqand during the last three decades of its existence, see Nalivkin, 1886, pp. 145–215.

the Bukharans from Khoqand a nephew of Nārbūta Biy, Shīr ʿAlī, was enthroned as khan, with the support of the Qïrghïz and the Qïpchaqs; but in 1844 the Qïpchaqs under Musulmān-Qul rebelled and captured Khoqand. Shīr ʿAlī Khan was killed the same year and replaced with Khudāyār, an under-age son of Shīr ʿAlī, but the actual authority was with the Qïpchaqs, who oppressed the sedentary population in Ferghana and established a regime of tyranny and violence. There was no unity among the Qïpchaqs themselves, and when in 1852 a rebellion against them began in the khanate, they were defeated in a major battle, and Musulmān-Qul executed. In 1858, while the amir of Bukhara Muẓaffar al-Dīn besieged Khojend, the elder brother of Khudāyār, Malla Bek, the governor of Tashkent, rebelled and, with the support of the nomads of Ferghana, mainly the Qïrghïz, captured Khoqand and was proclaimed khan. During his rule (1858–62) a prominent role belonged to the Qïrghïz. Muẓaffar al-Dīn continued to interfere in the affairs of Khoqand, supporting Khudāyār Khan who briefly (1862–3) became khan again. In 1863 the Qïrghïz and the Qïpchaqs seized power again, and an energetic military commander, ʿĀlim-Qul, a Qïrghïz, became the actual ruler. After the fall of Tashkent to the Russians in 1865 (see below) Khudāyār became khan for the third time, with the support of Muẓaffar al-Dīn; eleven years later his state ceased to exist.

The three Uzbek khanates which emerged at the end of the eighteenth and the early nineteenth centuries had both similarities and differences in the composition of their population, administration, economy and culture. Ethnically, all three states were highly heterogeneous. In all three khanates the term 'Uzbek' was used to denote only the tribal population, descendants of the Uzbeks of Dasht-i Qipchāq origin, whether nomadic or sedentary. Bukhara had the greatest percentage of Tajiks (Iranians), especially in Bukhara and Samarqand and in the eastern, mountainous parts of the country (where the population speaking Iranian dialects was called 'Galcha'). In the central part of Mawarannahr, Tajiks often lived intermingled with Uzbeks and other Turkic-speaking groups who had lived there already before the Uzbeks. By the middle of the nineteenth century these Tajiks became largely bilingual and, curiously, were called 'Chaghatay' (pronounced *Chigatoy*).[18] Besides these major ethnic groups, in the khanate of Bukhara there was a large group of Turkmens, mostly of the Ersarï tribe, who lived along the middle course of the Amu Darya; they were also interspersed with Tajiks and Uzbeks. In the khanate of Khiva the Turkicized descendants of the old indigenous Iranian

18 See Karmysheva, 1976, pp. 146–7. The term *Sart*, which was used for similar (but completely Turkicized) groups of population in Khorezm, Tashkent and Ferghana (see below), was not known in Mawarannahr.

population, who were called Sarts, were concentrated mainly in the southern part of the country, both in the cities and the countryside, while the Uzbeks, intermingling freely with them, retained their tribal affiliation and separate identity, and the majority of them lived in the northern half of the country, especially in Aral. The Turkmens, who formed compact tribal groups along the southern and western fringes of the oasis of Khorezm, made up almost a quarter of its entire population; the Qaraqalpaqs, another compact group, occupied a large part of Aral. Similar distinct ethnic divisions existed in the khanate of Khoqand. There the sedentary Turkic-speaking population consisted of tribal Uzbeks and non-tribal Sarts, living interspersed in Ferghana and Tashkent, Qaraqalpaqs in the centre of Ferghana along the Syr Darya, and Tajiks; the latter name was used in Khoqand for the mountaineers from Qarategin, Matcha and other regions south of Ferghana, otherwise known as Kūhistānī or Galcha. Nomads were represented by the Qïpchaqs, a numerous group concentrated mostly in the north and east of Ferghana, the Qïrghïz in the east of Ferghana and the Tien-Shan, and the Qazaqs in the southern steppe.

Of the three states the khanate of Khiva was the most Turkic, with Chaghatay (or 'late Chaghatay') as the language of literature and chancery and Persian only known by the learned and probably still surviving among some Sarts as the second language. The culture of the khanate of Khoqand was bilingual, though Tajik was used more than Turkic in literature and was almost the sole language used in the chancery. In the khanate of Bukhara, Tajik was practically the only language of literature and chancery, and Mawarannahr was looked upon as a Tajik country by the Uzbeks of Khorezm, who used to refer even to the troops of Bukhara, somewhat contemptuously, as the Tajik army, although it had mainly Uzbek soldiers.

All three Uzbek khanates were despotic monarchies, in which the Uzbek tribal aristocracy had somewhat higher social status, but persons of low (or non-Uzbek) origin tied to the ruler by personal loyalty often held key positions in administration. The khanate of Bukhara, by far the most populous and richest of the three, was also the most autocratic, and the tribal nobility there retained very little of its former influence, although the Manghïts held a disproportionately great number of administrative posts. The country was divided into provinces (*vilāyāt*), whose governors (*ḥākims*) collected taxes and had a great deal of autonomy. There was a similar situation in the khanate of Khoqand, where, however, the members of nomadic groups, such as the Qïpchaq and the Qïrghïz, played a much greater role, not only in the army, but also in the central administration. The khanate of Khiva, the smallest of the three, was the most centralized: very little authority was delegated to provincial governors, and taxes were collected by specially appointed officials of the central government once or twice a year. The tribal population in Khorezm was not under the jurisdiction of provincial governors, but was ruled by its own autonomous chiefs. In the khanate of Khoqand, in the course of the conquest and occupation of Qazaq and Qïrghïz lands, a number of fortresses were built from the lower Syr Darya in the west to the Chinese border in the east, with permanent garrisons, whose commanders collected taxes from the nomads; next to some fortresses permanent settlements sprang up populated by Sarts and Uzbeks who migrated from the Ferghana Valley, and some of them grew to become small towns, like Chimkent and Awliya-Ata. But in the mountainous regions south and east of Ferghana, access to which could be difficult, the Khoqandian control over the Qïrghïz was often only nominal.

In the economy of all three khanates the main role belonged to agriculture based on artificial irrigation. The khans of Khoqand were especially successful in building new canals and thus increasing the area of irrigated lands in the Ferghana Valley; these works continued even during the political upheavals in the khanate in the second half of the nineteenth century. In Khorezm new canals were also built, especially in the 1840s, and cultivated lands were expanded; however, as a result of the Turkmen rebellions in the late 1850s and 1860s, some of these lands were abandoned. In the khanate of Bukhara there was no comparable expansion of irrigation. The city of Bukhara was the most important centre of crafts and commerce in the whole of Central Asia, but Tashkent became the second in importance due to its role in the growing trade with Russia. From the early 1860s cotton became the most important item of Central Asian export to Russia, and Ferghana became the main cotton-growing region.

The trend towards centralization and unification in the political life of Central Asia in the nineteenth century was inconclusive. Large areas were not incorporated into any of the three khanates. In the south-east, the mountain principalities of Kulab, Qarategin and Darvaz remained independent (the last two under Tajik rulers with the title *sho* [i.e. *shāh*]), except for a very brief period in the 1830s, when they were subjected to Khoqand. The province of Hisar most of the time was semi- or completely independent. But the largest region of Central Asia that remained outside of the Uzbek khanates was the desert to the south-west, which by the end of the eighteenth century was inhabited entirely by the Turkmens. By the early nineteenth century the tribe Teke occupied the oases of northern Khorasan, along the foothills of the Kopet-Dagh Mountains, and spread eastwards, up to the Tejen River, pushing out the tribe

Yemreli, which migrated to Khorezm. After the Teke defeated the army of Khiva at Sarakhs in 1855 (see above), the Persians installed their governor in Merv. After that the Teke successfully fought the Sarïqs for the possession of Merv, and the Sarïqs had to migrate to the south, up the Murghab River; in 1861 a Persian army was sent against Merv, but it was totally defeated by the Teke under Qowshīt (or Qowshūt) Khan. Already earlier, in 1858, another Persian army sent against the Turkmens in south-western Turkmenia was defeated in a battle with a coalition of three Turkmen tribes, Teke, Yomut and Göklen, under the Teke Nūr-Verdi Khan. Since then, for more than two decades, the land along the northern rim of Khorasan, from the Caspian Sea in the west to Merv in the east, with the adjoining Qaraqum Desert to the north, was the territory of independent Turkmen tribes; they did not have any central authority or paramount chief, and each clan or group of clans formed an autonomous community. The Turkmens built fairly sophisticated irrigation systems in the oases that they settled and practised both agriculture and stock-breeding. They were also frequently raiding Persian territory, plundering villages and taking prisoners, who were mostly sold in the slave markets of Khiva; the Persian authorities in Khorasan were unable to prevent this raiding, and it ceased only after the Russian conquest of Turkmenia.

The Russian conquest of Central Asia

Direct contacts between the sedentary states of Central Asia and Russia became possible after the conquest of the khanates of Kazan (1552) and Astrakhan (1556) by Ivan the Terrible. Diplomatic exchanges between Russia and the Central Asian khanates began in 1558 with the travel of Anthony Jenkinson, a representative of the English Muscovy Company, who went from Moscow to Khiva and Bukhara in order to find land routes to China. He carried an official message from the tsar to the local rulers, and when he returned the next year, he was accompanied by envoys from Khiva, Bukhara and Balkh. This event is usually regarded as the beginning of regular diplomatic exchanges between Russia and the Central Asian khanates. These exchanges were concerned primarily with the questions of trade, as well as with the release of Russian subjects captured by Qazaqs and Qalmaqs along the Russian borders, and by Turkmens on the Caspian shores, and sold as slaves to the Central Asian khanates. The Russian government constantly tried to obtain their release, but without much success. Peter the Great, who had strong imperial ambitions and was prompted by the rumours about gold deposits found in Central Asia and information about the internal feuds in the khanates and who hoped to find river routes from Central Asia to India, dispatched two military expeditions, one from Astrakhan to Khiva, under Prince Bekovich-Cherkasskii, and another one from Tobol'sk up the Irtysh River, under Lieutenant-Colonel Buchholtz. The force under Bekovich-Cherkasskii was totally annihilated in Khiva in 1717, and the one under Buchholtz was repulsed, with heavy losses, by the Qalmaqs in 1716. These two debacles compelled the Russian government to delay all attempts at active penetration into the Central Asian khanates as long as they were separated from the Russian territory by hundreds of miles of the Qazaq steppes. This situation changed by the early nineteenth century: the nominal allegiance to Russia pledged by the Qazaq *zhüzes* in the eighteenth century (see Chapter 18) became an actual submission, so that the khanates were more accessible; at the same time, caravan trade between Russia and Central Asia was rapidly growing, with Russia becoming the main trade partner of the khanates and the development and protection of this trade becoming a major issue in Russian foreign policy. Of a special concern to the Russian government were the relations with the khanate of Khiva: its expansion into the territory of the Junior *Zhüz*, its support to the groups of Qazaqs of this *zhüz* who did not recognize Russian authority, and plundering of Russian trade caravans by Khivan troops or by the Qazaqs under the Khivan patronage. The accounts about the Russian slaves in Khiva also increasingly irritated the Russian government. After several years of growing tension, a military expedition against Khiva from Orenburg, under the governor of Orenburg, Perovskii, set out in winter 1839/40; but the Russian troops, having suffered heavy losses of men and pack animals because of the severe winter, had to turn back half-way.

After the failure of this expedition the Russian government changed its strategy and decided first to strengthen the Russian positions in the Qazaq steppes and move them closer to the sedentary areas of Central Asia. This allowed it to bring finally the Qazaqs to submission and created a springboard for the conquest of the khanates. Most of the Qazaq steppes bordered in the south the khanate of Khoqand, and it became the main adversary of Russia. The Russians began to advance gradually into the southern parts of the Qazaq steppes simultaneously from the west, along the Syr Darya, and the east, in Semirech'e. In 1847 the Raimskoe fortress was built near the Syr Darya Delta and a fortress named Kopal was built in Semirech'e. In 1852 Russian and Khoqandian troops clashed twice on the Syr Darya, and in 1853 Russian troops under Perovskii stormed and captured the Khoqandian fortress Aq-Masjid in the lower course of the Syr Darya. This was the beginning of a direct military confrontation between Russia and the Central Asian khanates.

The systematic conquest of the khanates lasted for three decades. It seems that the Russian motives in this conquest were of both a political and an economic nature. Rapid development of Russian industry in the second quarter of the nineteenth century had no parallel in the growth of the purchasing capacity of the population, a great majority of which, until 1861, were serfs. Therefore Russia needed foreign markets for her industrial goods, and a natural direction for the Russian trade expansion was to the east, especially to Central Asia, a region with strong traditional commercial ties with Russia. In the middle of the nineteenth century the prevailing opinion in Russian commercial circles was that under the political conditions of Central Asia and given the threat of British competition (usually exaggerated in the Russian press) the only way to ensure Russian trade interests in that region was to establish Russian rule there or, at least, firm political control. However, for determining Russian policy in Central Asia Russian global political interests, especially related to Anglo-Russian rivalry, sometimes played an equally, or even more, important role. As to the Central Asian khanates themselves, their military means to resist the Russian expansion were inadequate against the overwhelming military superiority of Russia; their rulers did not appreciate the imminent danger and made no attempts to join their forces in resistance.

The Russian government had already decided on the military offensive against the Central Asian khanates in 1854, but it was delayed by the Crimean War. The offensive was preceded by a number of reconnaissance raids between 1858 and 1863, mainly to the south of the Ili, and in 1863 a large part of the mountainous country to the south of Lake Issyk-Köl inhabited by the Qïrghïz was annexed to Russia. In December 1863 the tsar signed a decree, according to which the new border with the khanate of Khoqand was to be drawn through Suzak (north-east of Turkestan) and Awliya-Ata. Lines of Russian fortifications were built along the Syr Darya and south of the Ili. In May 1864 Russian troops set out from the Syr Darya line and the Trans-Ili region and captured Turkestan and Awliya-Ata. After that the Syr Darya and the Ili lines were connected by a 'New Khoqandian' line, and Major-General M. G. Cherniaev was appointed its commander. Cherniaev continued the offensive, but in July 1864 he was repelled from Chimkent, which was defended by the ruler of Khoqand Mullā ʿĀlim-Qul. But soon after that the Bukharan army invaded the Ferghana Valley, ʿĀlim-Qul had to leave Chimkent, and it was captured by Cherniaev in September. A week later Cherniaev moved against Tashkent, but he was repelled by the Khoqandian garrison. There followed a short period of consolidation of the Russian conquests. In January 1865 all territories captured from Khoqand, from the Aral Sea to Lake Issyk-Köl, were united in one Turkestan Oblast', and Cherniaev became its first military governor. He continued preparations for the capture of Tashkent, taking advantage of the new military campaign of the amir of Bukhara against Khoqand and of the dissent within the population of Tashkent, where a pro-Russian party had been formed led by some influential merchants. In May 1865 the troops of Khoqand were defeated in a battle near Tashkent, in which Mullā ʿĀlim-Qul was killed. Cherniaev stormed the city, and on 29 June it surrendered to the Russians. For a year after this the Russian government was considering the future of Tashkent, until in August 1866 it was formally annexed to the Russian Empire.

Already before the formal annexation of Tashkent, tensions grew between Russia and the khanate of Bukhara. The invasion of Ferghana by Muẓaffar al-Dīn in the summer of 1865 in support of Khudāyār Khan and his occupation of Khojend aroused Russian suspicions about possible joint action of Bukhara and Khoqand against the Russians in Tashkent. The amir demanded that the Russians withdraw from Tashkent, and in response all Bukharan merchants on the territory of the Turkestan Oblast' and the governorate-general of Orenburg were arrested and their goods sequestered. In the autumn of 1865 skirmishes began between Russian and Bukharan troops south of Tashkent. In January–February 1866 Cherniaev crossed the Syr Darya and tried to capture the Bukharan town of Jizak, but failed; he was recalled to St Petersburg and replaced by General D. I. Romanovskii. In May 1866, in the locality of Irjar, the Bukharan army under the command of the amir himself was defeated and fled. After this the Russian army captured Khojend, the key to the Ferghana Valley; it was officially annexed to Russia in August 1866, together with Tashkent, so that the khanate of Khoqand was reduced to the Ferghana Valley. The Russians submitted to Bukhara their conditions for peace, which were deliberately made unacceptable, and when the amir did not comply, the Russian troops resumed the offensive and captured Ura-Tübe and Jizak in October 1866 and Yanï-Qurghan in May 1867. In July 1867 the Russian government created a new governorate-general of Turkestan, with the centre in Tashkent, which comprised all territories conquered in Central Asia since 1847. The first governor-general of Turkestan, who replaced Romanovskii, was General A. P. von Kaufman. He was given almost unlimited authority, including the right to wage wars, conduct diplomatic negotiations, and conclude conventions and treaties with the neighbouring states at his own discretion. In January 1868 Kaufman imposed a commercial convention on Khoqand, which guaranteed various privileges to Russian merchants and symbolized the end of hostilities between Russia and the khanate (no formal peace treaty was concluded). In April 1868 amir Muẓaffar al-Dīn, yielding to militant *mullas* of Bukhara and Samarqand, proclaimed a holy war against Russia. On 1 May Kaufman defeated the Bukharan troops on the Chopan-Ata heights near Samarqand, and the next day Samarqand fell. On 2 June the amir was again defeated at Zirabulaq heights, near Katta-Qurghan, after which he capitulated, and on 30 June he signed the peace conditions dictated by Kaufman. The khanate recognized the loss of all the territories captured by the Russians, agreed to pay a war indemnity, and opened the country to Russian merchants. The capitulation of the amir provoked a rebellion of his son, ʿAbd al-Malik, supported by the chieftains of the Keneges tribe in Shahrisabz, who proclaimed their independence. The rebellion was suppressed by Russian troops in 1870, who returned Shahrisabz to the amir and after this conducted an expedition to the upper course of the Zarafshan, which resulted in the Russian annexation of several small mountain principalities in that area. In 1869–70 amir Muẓaffar al-Dīn (with some assistance from the Russians, who wanted to 'compensate' the amir for his loss of Samarqand) conquered Hisar and Kulab, and in 1876, after the liquidation of the khanate of Khoqand, he annexed Qarategin. The newly acquired territories in the east began to be called 'Eastern Bukhara' or 'Mountain Bukhara'.

After the defeat of Bukhara, Russian attention was focused on Khiva. At the end of 1869 Russian troops from the Caucasus landed in Krasnovodsk Bay, on the eastern coast of the Caspian Sea, where they founded the seaport of Krasnovodsk. In the following three years several reconnoitring expeditions crossed the deserts from the west and from the east in the direction of Khiva. The khan of Khiva, Muḥammad Raḥīm II, was defiant: he claimed the Syr Darya as Khiva's frontier, protested the Russian landing in Krasnovodsk, and supported the Qazaq revolt on the Mangïshlaq. In the spring of 1873 Russian troops under Kaufman set out against Khiva from Tashkent, Orenburg, Mangïshlaq and Krasnovodsk (the latter detachment had to return half-way because of heat). They met with little resistance, mainly by the Turkmens; on 10 June Khiva was captured, and Muḥammad Raḥīm Khan surrendered to the Russians. In mid-July Kaufman launched a punitive expedition against the Yomut Turkmens in the western part of the khanate, slaughtering people and their livestock. On 12 August Kaufman signed a peace treaty with the khan, in which the latter declared himself the 'obedient servant' of the Russian Emperor and renounced his right to conduct independent foreign relations; the khanate lost to Russia all its territory on the right bank of the Amu Darya and had to pay a huge war indemnity.

After the signing of the peace treaty with Khiva, a new peace treaty was signed with Bukhara on 28 September 1873, giving Russia some additional privileges in the khanate, but maintaining its formal sovereignty. The khanate of Khoqand, on the contrary, soon ceased to exist. The reduction of the territory of the khanate with the loss of all regions beyond the Ferghana Valley resulted in a drastic reduction of state revenues. To compensate for this, Khudāyār Khan increased the taxation, which caused great resentment among the population. In the summer of 1875 the Qïrghïz and the Qïpchaqs in the north of Ferghana started a rebellion under an impostor, a certain Mullā Isḥāq, who assumed the name of Pulād Khan, a grandson of ʿĀlim Khan; the Khoqandian troops under ʿAbd al-Raḥmān Aftābachī, son of Musulmān-Qul, joined Pulād Khan, and Khudāyār Khan fled to Khojend, to the Russians (from there Kaufman exiled him to Orenburg). The supporters of Pulād Khan declared the holy war (*ghazavāt*) against the Russians and enthroned a son of Khudāyār, Nāṣir al-Dīn. But the Russian troops, under M. D. Skobelev, had already entered Ferghana and quickly captured Khoqand, Margelan and Osh. On 22 September Nāṣir al-Dīn Khan came to Kaufman in Margelan, where he signed a new treaty; in accordance with it the khanate ceded to Russia the part of Ferghana north of the Syr Darya and had to pay a war indemnity. The treaty had no consequences, because the rebellion in Ferghana continued; in October Nāṣir al-Dīn Khan fled to the Russians in Khojend, and Pulād Khan was enthroned in Khoqand. From the end of October 1875 to the end of January 1876 the Russian troops under Skobelev were fighting the rebels in northern Ferghana, causing huge losses to them. On 20 January ʿAbd al-Raḥmān Aftābachī and several other rebel leaders surrendered to Skobelev; Pulād Khan was captured on 19 January 1876 and executed. On 19 February 1876 the tsar issued a decree abolishing the khanate of Khoqand and annexing its territory to Russia; it was included into the governorate-general of Turkestan as Ferghana oblast'. From Ferghana, Skobelev carried out a raid into the Alay Valley (south of Ferghana) in order to pacify the Qïrghïz of that area.

After the reduction of Bukhara, Khiva and Khoqand the Russian government gave special attention to Turkmenia. By March 1874 it established a 'Transcaspian Military District' (*Zakaspiiskii voennyi otdel*) subordinated to the vicegerent of the Caucasus, with the centre in Krasnovodsk and somewhat vaguely defined borders in the east. In May 1877 Russian troops occupied Qïzïl-Arvat, *c.* 300 kilometres east of Krasnovodsk. The slow Russian advance into the Turkmen land was initially met in friendly fashion by the coastal Yomuts, but soon requisitions of great numbers of camels, tents and food for the Russian army caused growing resistance. In August 1879 a Russian expeditionary force under General A. A. Lomakin moved further east, but it was repelled with heavy losses from the fortress of Gök-Tepe (near modern Ashgabat) defended by the Teke Turkmens. A new campaign against the Teke began in the spring of 1880, under General Skobelev, who in January 1881 stormed Gök-Tepe after a three-week-long siege. About 15,000 Teke Turkmens were killed, and their resistance was broken. The oasis of Akhal was annexed to Russia and, together with the land included in the Transcaspian Military District before, formed the Transcaspian Oblast' subordinate to the vicegerent of the Caucasus. At the end of 1883 a Russian military detachment moved towards Merv, and at the end of 1883 the Teke of Merv decided to accept Russian sovereignty; Merv was occupied in March 1884. The Iolotan and Pende (Panjdeh) oases, up the Murghab River, were occupied later the same year.[19] The last Russian acquisition in Central Asia was the annexation of the Pamir highlands following the expedition to this region by Colonel Ionov in 1891. The end of the Russian expansion in Central Asia was marked by agreements between Russia and China in 1894 and Russia and England in 1895 which established the boundaries in the Pamirs.[20]

19 On the circumstances of the Russian occupation of Panjdeh see Davies, 'Pandjdih (Pendjdeh)', *EI*[2], VIII, pp. 257–8.

20 See D. Balland, 'Boundaries of Afghanistan', *Encyclopaedia Iranica*, IV, pp. 406–10. The boundaries changed again in 1896 with the transfer of the Pamir principalities Rushān, Shughnān and Wakhān to Bukharan authority (see Khalfin, 1975).

Bibliography

ʿAbd al-Razzāq al-Samarqandī. 1993. *Maṭlaʿ saʿdayn wa-majmaʿ baḥrayn*, ed. A. Nawāʾī. Tehran: Muʾassasa-i muṭālaʿāt wa-taḥqīqāt-i farhangī, 1372/1993.
ʿAbdī Beg Shīrāzī. 1990. *Takmilat al-akhbār (Tārīkh-i Ṣafawīya az āghāz tā 978 Hijrī Qamarī)*, ed. Dr ʿAbd al-Ḥusayn Nawāʾī. Tehran: Nashr-i Nay, 1369/1990.
Abdirov, Murat. 1996. *Khan Kuchum: izvestnyi i neizvestnyi*. Almaty: Zhalyn.
Abdullin, Ia. *et al.* 1988. eds. *Istoriia Kazani* I. Kazan: Tatarskoe knizhnoe izdatel'stvo.
Abduraimov, M. A. 1966–70. *Ocherki po istorii agrarnykh otnoshenii v Bukharskom khanstve v XVI- pervoi polovine XIX v.* Tashkent: Fan. 2 vols.
Abel, Wilhelm. 1986. *Agrarian Fluctuations in Europe from the Thirteenth to the Twentieth Centuries*, trans. Olive Ordish, with a foreword by Joan Thirsk. London: Methuen & Co.
Abramowski, Waltraut. 1976. 'Die chinesischen Annalen von Ögödei und Güyük: Übersetzung des 2. Kapitels des Yüan-Shih.' *Zentralasiatische Studien* 10: 117–67.
1979. 'Die chinesischen Annalen des Möngke: Übersetzung des 3. Kapitels des Yüan-Shih.' *Zentralasiatische Studien* 13: 7–71.
Abramzon, Saul M. 1971. *Kirgizy i ikh etnogeneticheskie i istoriko-kul'turnye sviazi*. Leningrad: Nauka.
Abu Ḥayyān (? More probably Ṣalāḥ al-Dīn Khalīl b. Aybeg). *Al-Tuḥfat al-Zakiyya fī'l-Lughat al-Turkiyya*, see Atalay, 1945.
Abu-Lughod, Janet L. 1989. *Before European Hegemony: The World System A.D. 1250–1350*. New York and Oxford: Oxford University Press.
Abuʾl-Ghāzī Bahādur Khan. 1871–4. *Histoire des Mongols et des Tatars*, ed. and trans. Peter I. Desmaisons. St. Petersburg; reprint: Amsterdam and St. Leonards: Philo Press and Ad Orientem Ltd., 1970.
1958. *Shajara-yi Türk: Rodoslovnaia Turkmen. Sochinenie Abu-l-gazi khana khivinskogo*, ed. and trans. Andrei N. Kononov. Moscow and Leningrad: Izdatel'stvo Akademii Nauk SSSR.
1996. *Şecere-i Terākime (Türkmenlerin Soykütüğü)* by Ebulgazi Behadır Han, Turkish trans. Z. Kargı Ölmez. Ankara: M. Ölmez.
Abuseitova, Meruert Kh. *et al.* 2001. *Istoriia Kazakhstana i Tsentral'noi Azii*. Almaty: Daik Press.
Adshead, S. A. M. 1988. *China in World History*. London: Macmillan.
1993. *Central Asia in World History*. New York: St. Martin's Press.
Afshār. 1974. Anonymous, *Bayāḍ-i Tāj al-Dīn Aḥmad Wazīr*, ed. Irāj Afshār and Murtaḍā Taymūrī. Isfahan: Dānishgāh-i Iṣfahān, 1353/1974.

Agadzhanov, Sergei A. 1991. *Gosudarstvo Sel'dzhukidov i Sredniaia Aziia v XI-XII vv.* Moscow: Nauka.

Ağat, N. 1976. *Altınordu (Cuçioğulları) Paraları Kataloğu 1250–1502. Ek olarak şecere ve tarih düzeltmeleri.* Istanbul: Edebiyat Fakültesi Matbaası.

Aka, Ismail. 1991. *Timur ve devleti.* Ankara: Türk Tarih Kurumu Basımevi.

1994. *Mirza Şahruh ve zamanı*. Ankara: Türk Tarih Kurumu Basımevi.

1996. 'The Agricultural and Commercial Activities of the Timurids in the First Half of the 15th Century', in Bernardini, 1996: 9–21.

Äkhmätjanov, Marsel'. 1995. *Tatar shäjäräläre.* Kazan: Tatarstan Kitap Näshriyatï.

2002. *Nughay urdasï.* Kazan: Mägarif.

Akhmedov, Buri A. 1965a. *Gosudarstvo kochevykh uzbekov.* Moscow: Nauka.

1965b. 'Ulugbek i politicheskaia zhizn' Maverannakhra XV v.', in *Iz istorii epokhi Ulugbeka*, ed. A. K. Arends. Tashkent: Nauka: 5–66.

1982. *Istoriia Balkha (XVI-pervaia polovina XVII v.).* Tashkent: Fan.

1985. *Istoriko-geograficheskaia literatura Srednei Azii XVI-XVIII vv., Pis'mennye pamiatniki.* Tashkent: Nauka.

Album, Stephen. 2001. *Sylloge of Islamic Coins in the Ashmolean, 9: Iran after the Mongol Invasion.* Oxford: Ashmolean Museum.

Alektorov, Aleksandr E. 1883. *Istoriia Orenburgskoi gubernii.* Orenburg: Breslin.

Alishan, L. M. 1893. *L'Armeno-Veneto: Compendio storico e documenti delle relazioni degli Armeni coi Veneziani, Primo Periodo: secoli xiii–xiv, i–ii.* Venice: Stab. Tip. Armeno, S. Lazzaro.

Alishev, S. Kh. 1984. 'Sotsial'naia role' i évoliutsiia sluzhilykh tatar vo vtoroi polovine XVI-XVIII vekov', in *Issledovaniia po istorii krest'ianstva Tatarii dooktiabr'skogo perioda.* Kazan: Akademiia Nauk SSSR Kazanskii Filial: 52–69.

Allen, Terry A. 1981. *A Catalogue of Toponyms and Monuments of Timurid Herat.* Cambridge, Mass.: Massachusetts Institute of Technology.

1983. *Timurid Heart.* Wiesbaden: Ludwig Reichart.

Allsen, Thomas T. 1981. 'Mongol Census Taking in Rus', 1245–1275.' *HUS* 5/1: 32–53.

1983. 'The Yüan Dynasty and the Uighurs of Turfan in the 13th Century', in Morris Rossabi, 1983: 243–80.

1985–7. 'The Princes of the Left Hand: An Introduction to the History of the *Ulus* of Orda in the Thirteenth and Early Fourteenth Centuries.' *AEMAe* 5: 5–40.

1987. *Mongol Imperialism: The Policies of the Grand Khan Möngke in China, Russia, and the Islamic Lands, 1251–1259.* Berkeley: University of California Press.

1989. 'Mongolian Princes and their Merchant Partners, 1200–1260.' *Asia Major*, third series, 2/2: 83–126.

1991. 'Changing Forms of Legitimation in Mongol Iran', in Seaman and Marks, 1991: 223–41.

1993. 'Maḥmūd Yalavač', 'Masʿūd Beg', 'ʿAlī Beg', 'Safaliq', 'Bujir', in de Rachewiltz *et al.*, 1993: 122–35.

1994a. 'The Rise of the Mongolian Empire and Mongolian Rule in North China', in *CHChina*, VI: 321–413.

1994b. 'Two Cultural Brokers of Medieval Eurasia: Bolad Aqa and Marco Polo', in *Nomadic Diplomacy, Destruction and Religion from the Pacific to the Adriatic*, ed. Michael

Gervers and Wayne Schlepp. Toronto Studies in Central and Inner Asia, 1. Toronto: Joint Centre for Asia Pacific Studies: 63–78.

1996. 'Spiritual Geography and Political Legitimacy in the Eastern Steppe', in *Ideology and the Formation of Early States*, ed. Henri J. M. Claessen and Jarich G. Oosten. Studies in Human Society, 11. Leiden, New York and Cologne: Brill: 116–35.

1997a. 'Ever Closer Encounters: The Appropriation of Culture and the Apportionment of Peoples in the Mongol Empire.' *Journal of Early Modern History* 1: 2–23.

1997b. *Commodity and Exchange in the Mongol Empire: A Cultural History of Islamic Textiles*. Cambridge: Cambridge University Press.

2000. 'The *Rasūlid Hexaglot* in its Eurasian Cultural Context', in *The King's Dictionary: The Rasūlid Hexaglot, Fourteenth-Century Vocabularies in Arabic, Persian, Turkic, Greek, Armenian and Mongol*, ed. Peter B. Golden. Leiden: Brill: 25–49.

2001a. *Culture and Conquest in Mongol Eurasia*. Cambridge: Cambridge University Press.

2001b. 'Sharing Out the Empire: Apportioned Lands under the Mongols', in *Nomads in the Sedentary World*, ed. Anatoly M. Khazanov and André Wink. Richmond, Surrey: Curzon: 172–90.

2001c. 'Command Performances: Entertainers in the Mongolian Empire.' *Russian History/Histoire Russe* 28 / 1–4: 37–46.

2001d. 'The Cultural Worlds of Marco Polo.' *Journal of Interdisciplinary History* 31 / 3: 375–83.

2002a. 'The Circulation of Military Technology in the Mongolian Empire', in *Warfare in Inner Asian History (500–1800)*, ed. Nicola Di Cosmo. Handbuch der Orientalistik, 8, 6. Leiden, Boston and Cologne: Brill: 265–93.

2002b. 'Technician Transfers in the Mongolian Empire.' The Central Eurasian Studies Lectures, no. 2; Department of Central Eurasian Studies, Indiana University.

2006a. *The Royal Hunt in Eurasian History*. Philadelphia: University of Pennsylvania Press.

2006b. 'Technologies of Governance in the Mongolian Empire: A Geographic Overview', in *Imperial Statecraft: Political Forms and Techniques of Governance in Inner Asia, Sixth–Twentieth Centuries*, ed. David Sneath. Bellingham, Wash.: Western Washington University: 117–40.

Altan Tobchi, see Lubsan Danzan, 1973.

Altaner, Berthold. 1924. *Die Dominikanermission des XIII. Jahrhunderts*. Habelschwerdt: Frankes Buchhandlung.

Amitai-Preiss, Reuven. 1995. *Mongols and Mamluks: The Mamluk Īlkhānid War, 1260–1281*. Cambridge: Cambridge University Press.

1996: 'Ghazan, Islam and Mongol Tradition: A View from the Mamlūk Sultanate.' *BSOAS* 59: 1–10.

2001. 'The Conversion of the Ilkhan Tegüder Aḥmad to Islam.' *Jerusalem Studies in Arabic and Islam* 25: 15–43.

Amitai-Preiss, Reuven and David Morgan. 1999. eds. *The Mongol Empire and its Legacy*. Leiden: Brill.

Amitai-Preiss, Reuven and Michal Biran. 2005. eds. *Mongols, Turks, and Others: Eurasian Nomads and the Sedentary World*. Leiden and Boston: Brill.

al-Andalusī, Saʿīd. 1991. *Science in the Medieval World: Book of the Categories of Nations*, trans. Semaʾan I. Salem and Alok Kumar. Austin, Tex.: University of Texas Press.

Ando, Shiro. 1992. *Timuridische Emire nach dem Muʿizz al-ansāb. Untersuchung zur Stammesaristokratie Zentralasiens im 14. und 15. Jahrhundert*. Berlin: Klaus Schwarz Verlag.

1994. 'The Shaykh al-Islām as a Timurid Office: A Preliminary Study.' *Islamic Studies* 33/2–3 (1415/1994): 253–80.

1996. 'Zum timuridischen Staatswesen: eine Interpretation des Miniaturentwurfs in Diez A. Fol. 74', in *Ẓafar nāme: Memorial Volume of Felix Tauer*, ed. Rudolf Veselý and Eduard Gombar. Prague: Enigma Corp.: 17–33.

Andreev, I. G. 1998. *Opisanie Srednei Ordy kirgiz-kaisakov*. Almaty: Ghylym.

Anonymous, *Bayāḍ-i Tāj al-Dīn Aḥmad Wazīr*, see Afshār, 1974.

Anonymous, *Dede Korkut Kitabı*, see Ergin, 1964.

Anonymous, *Kitab-ı Mecmū-ı Tercüman-ı Türkī ve Acemī ve Mugalī*, see Toparlı, 2000.

Anonymous, *Muʿīzz al-ansāb*, Paris, Bibliothèque Nationale, MS A. F. Pers 67.

Anonymous, *Secret History of the Mongols*, see List of Abbreviations, *Secret History*.

Anonymous, *Shajarat al-atrāk*, Harvard University, MS Pers 6F.

Ao Tegen 2004. 'Menggu shidai de Dunhuang Xining wang Sulaiman [Sulaiman, King of Xining in Dunhuang in the Yuan Dynasty] [*sic*]. *Lanzhou daxue xuebao* 32/4: 35–41.

Apollova, N. G. 1960. *Ekonomicheskie i politicheskie sviazi Kazakhstana s Rossiei v XVIII-nachale XIX v.* Moscow: Izdatel'stvo Akademii Nauk SSSR.

al-Aqsarāyī. 1944. Kerimüddīn Mahmud, *Müsāmeret ül-ahbar: Moğollar zamanında Türkiye Selçukluları Tarihi*, ed. Osman Turan. Ankara: Türk Tarih Kurumu Basımevi.

Armstrong, Terence. 1974. ed. *Yermak's Campaigns in Siberia*. Publications of the Hakluyt Society, series 2, no. 146, London: The Hakluyt Society.

Arnold, Lauren. 1999. *Princely Gifts and Papal Treasures: The Franciscan Mission to China and its Influence on the Art of the West, 1250–1350*. San Francisco: Desiderata Press.

Arslanov, L. Sh. and V. M. Viktorin. 1995. 'Astrakhanskie tatary', *Materialy po istorii tatarskogo naroda*. Kazan: Akademiia Nauk Tatarstana: 336–50.

Asankanov, A. *et al.* 1996. eds. *Kyrgyzy. Etnogeneticheskie i etnokul'turnye protsessy v drevnosti i srednevekov'e v Tsentral'noi Azii*. Bishkek: Kyrgyzstan.

Asım, Ö. 1924–5. ed. ʿAbdulghaffār Qırımī, *Umdet al-tevārīkh*. Istanbul, 1343/1924–5.

Asimov, Mukhamed S. and C. Edmund Bosworth. 1998. eds. *History of Civilizations of Central Asia*, IV/1: *The Age of Achievements: 750 AD to the End of the Fifteenth Century*. Paris: UNESCO.

Atalay, Besim. 1945. *Ettuhfet-üz-Zekiyye fil-Lūgat-it-Türkiyye*. Facs. edn. Turkish trans. Istanbul: s. n.

Atlasi, Hadi. 1993. *Seber tarikhï, Söyenbikä, Qazan khanlïghï*. Kazan: Tatarstan kitap näshriyatï.

Atwood, Christopher P. 2004. ed. *Encyclopedia of Mongolia and the Mongol Empire*. New York: Facts on File.

Aubin, Jean. 1969. 'L'ethnogénèse des Qaraunas.' *Turcica* 1: 65–94.

1976. 'Le khanat de Čaġatai et le Khorassan (1334–1380).' *Turcica* 8/2: 16–60.

1991. 'Le *quriltai* de Sultân-Maydân.' *Journal Asiatique* 279: 175–97.

Ayalon, David. 1963. 'The European Asiatic Steppe: A Major Reservoir of Power for the Islamic World', in *Proceedings of the 25th International Congress of Orientalists*,

Moscow, 1960, ed. Babadzhan Gafurov *et al.* Moscow: Izdatel'stvo Vostochnoi Literatury, 2: 47–52.

Ayātī, ʿAbd Āl Muḥammad. 1967. *Taḥrīr-i Taʾrīkh-i Waṣṣāf.* Tehran: Chāpkhāna-i ʿilmī, 1346/1967.

al-ʿAynī, Badr al-Dīn Maḥmūd b. ʿAlī, *ʿIqd alj-umān fī taʾrīkh ahl al-zamān*. Topkapi Sarayi, MS Ahmet III 2912.

Azamatov, Danil D. 1996. 'Russian Administration and Islam in Bashkiria (18th–19th centuries)' , in *Muslim Culture in Russia and Central Asia from the 18th to the Early 20th Centuries*, ed. Michael Kemper, Anke von Kügelgen and Dmitriy Yermakov. Berlin: Klaus Schwarz: 1: 91–111.

Azimdzhanova, Sabokhat A. 1957. *K istorii Ferghany vtoroi poloviny XV v.* Tashkent: Nauka.

1977. *Gosudarstvo Babura v Kabule i v Indii*. Moscow: Nauka.

Babadjanov, Baxtiyor, Ashirbek Muminov and Jμrgen Paul. 1997. *Schaibanidische Grabinscriften*. Wiesbaden: Dr Ludwig Reichert Verlag.

Babadzhanov, Khadzhi Mukhammed-Salikh. 1861. 'Zametka kirgiza o kirgizakh.' *Severnaia pchela* (4), 5 January, 13–16.

Babajanov, Bakhtiyar. 1999. 'Monuments épigraphiques de l'ensemble de Fatḥābād à Boukhara.' *Cahiers d'Asie Centrale* 7: 195–210.

Babajanov, Bakhtiyar and Maria Szuppe. 2002. *Les Inscriptions persanes de Chār Bakr, nécropole familiale des khwāja Jūybārī près de Boukhara*, Corpus Inscriptionum Iranicarum (Part IV Persian Inscriptions Down to the Early Safavid Period), 31: *Uzbekistan*. London: School of Oriental and African Studies.

Bābur, Ẓahīr al-Dīn Muḥammad. 1943. Reşit Rahmeti Arat, *Vekayi: Babur'un Hatiratı*. Ankara: Türk Tarih Basımevi.

1958. *Babur-Name*, ed. Sabokhat A. Azimdzhanova.Tashkent: Akademiia Nauk.

1969. *The Bābur-nāma in English*, trans. Annette Susanah Beveridge. London, 1922; reprint London: Luzac.

1980. *Le Livre de Babur*, trans. Jean-Louis Bacqué-Grammont. Paris: UNESCO.

1993. *Baburnama. Chaghatay Turkish Text with Abdul-Rahim Khankhanan's Persian Translation, Turkish Transcription, Persian Edition and English Translation*, ed. and trans. Wheeler M. Thackston. Cambridge, Mass.: Sources of Oriental Languages and Literatures, 18, Turkish Sources XVI, 3 vols.

1995. *Bābur-Nāma (Vaqāyiʿ)*, ed. Eiji Mano. Kyoto: Syokado.

1996. *Bābur-Nāma (Vaqāyiʿ)*, ed. Eiji Mano. Vol II: "Concordance and Classified Indexes." Kyoto: Syokado.

Badr al-Dīn b. ʿAbd al-Salām Kashmīrī. *Rawḍat al-riḍwān wa ḥadıqat al-ghilmān*, Tashkent, Institut Sharqshinasliq Uzbekiston, MS inv. no. 2094.

Ẓafarnāma, Dushanbe, IVAN, MS 779.

Bailey, Sir Harold W. 1979. *A Dictionary of Khotan Saka*. Cambridge: Cambridge University Press.

1985. *Indo-Scythian Studies, Being Khotanese Texts*, 8. Cambridge: Cambridge University Press.

Bākharzī, Abuʾl -Mafāḥir Yaḥyā. 1966. *Awrād al-aḥbāb wa fuṣūṣ al-ādāb*, ed. I. Afshār. Tehran: Intishārāt-i dānishgāh-i Tihrān.

Baktygulov, Dzh. 1996. 'Formirovanie kyrgyzskogo naroda', in Asankanov *et al.*, 1996: 164–79.

Balazs, Etienne. 1964. *Chinese Civilization and Bureaucracy*. New Haven and London: Yale University Press.

Balland, D. 'Boundaries of Afghanistan', *Encyclopaedia Iranica*, 4: 406–10.

Bannā'ī (Binā'ī). 1997. 'Kamal al-Din. Shaybānī-nāmah', in *A Synthetical Study of Central Asian Culture in the Turco-Islamic Period*, ed. Kazuyuki Kobo. Kyoto: 5–7.

Barbaro, Josafa, see Lord Stanley of Aldershot, 1873.

Barfield, Thomas J. 1989. *The Perilous Frontier: Nomadic Empires in China*. Oxford: Blackwell; reprint, 1992, Oxford: Wiley-Blackwell.

1990. 'Tribe and State Relations: The Inner Asian Perspective', in *Tribes and State Formation in the Middle East*, ed. Philip S. Khoury and Joseph Kostiner. Berkeley: University of California Press: 153–82.

Barkmann, Udo. 1988. 'Die manjurische Banneradministration in der Qalq-a Mongolei des 18.-19. Jarhunderts.' *Archív Orientální* 56: 27–41.

Barthold, Vasilii V. (see also Barthold, Wilhelm, Bartol'd, Vasilii V.). 1956–62. *Four Studies of the History of Central Asia*, trans. Vladimir and Tatiana Minorsky. Leiden: Brill. 3 vols.

1977. *Turkestan Down to the Mongol Invasion*, trans. Tatiana Minorsky, ed. C. Edmund Bosworth. 4th edn. London: Luzac. Trans. of *Turkestan v epokhu mongol'skogo nashestviia*, see Bartol'd, 1900 and Russian re-edition in Bartol'd, *Sochineniia*, I.

'Abu'l-Khair, *EI*[1]: 95–6.

Barthold, Wilhelm. 1962. *Zwölf Vorlesungen über die Geschichte der Türken Mittelasiens*. Berlin, 1935; reprint Hildesheim: Georg Olms, 1962. German trans. of his *Dvenadtsat' lektsii po istorii turetskikh narodov Srednei Azii*, see Bartol'd below.

Barthold, Wilhelm and György Hazai, 'Ḳazaḳ', *EI*[2], IV: 848–9.

Bartholomaeus de Jano, *Epistola de crudelitate Turcorum*, in Migne, 1857–89, 158: 1055–68.

Bartol'd, Vasilii V. *Sochineniia*, see List of Abbreviations

'Ocherk istorii Semirech'ia', *Sochineniia*, II/1: 23–106.

Istoriia Kult'urnoi zhizni Turkestana, in *Sochineniia*, II/1: 169–432.

'Otets Edigeia', in *Sochineniia*, II/1: 797–804.

Ulugbek i ego vremia, in *Sochineniia*, II/2: 22–196.

Dvenadtsat' lektsii po istorii turetskikh narodov Srednei Azii, in *Sochineniia*, V: 17–192. German trans. Barthold, Wilhelm 1962.

Istoriia turetsko-mongol'skikh narodov, in *Sochineniia*, V: 195–229.

'Obrazovanie imperii Chingiz-khana', in *Sochineniia*, V: 253–65.

1900. *Turkestan v epokhu mongol'skogo nashestviia*. St. Petersburg: Tipografiia imperatorskoi akademii nauk.

1929. *Ocherk istorii turkmenskogo naroda*, in *Sochineniia*, II/2: 547–623; Eng. trans. in Barthold, V. 1962, III: 73–170.

1964. 'Tseremonial pri dvore uzbekskikh khanov v XVII veke', in *Sochineniia*, II/2: 388–99.

Bashir, Shahzad. 2003. *Messianic Hopes and Mystical Visions: The Nūrbakhshīya Between Medieval and Modern Islam*. Columbia, SC: University of South Carolina Press.

Bawden, C. R. 1955. *The Mongol Chronicle AltanTobci: Text, Translation and Critical Notes*. Göttinger Asiatische Forschungen, 5. Wiesbaden: Harrassowitz.

1968a. 'The Mongol Rebellion of 1756–57.' *Journal of Asian History* 2/1: 1–31.

1968b. *The Modern History of Mongolia*. London: Weidenfeld and Nicolson.

Bayat, Fuzulī. 2006. *Oğuz Destan Dünyası*. Istanbul: Ötüken.

Baybars al-Manṣūrī al-Dawādār, Rukh al-Dīn, *Zubdat al-fikra fī ta'rīkh al-hijra*. London, British Library, MS Add. 23325.

Baypakov, Karl M. 2001. 'Culture urbaine de Kazakhstan du sud et du Semiretchie à l'époque des Karakhanides.' *Études Karakhanides* in *Cahiers d'Asie Centrale* 9: 141–75.

Beazeley, Charles Raymond. 1897–1906. *The Dawn of Modern Geography*. London: H. Frowde, [1897?–1906?].

Bell-Fialkoff, Andrew. 2000. ed. *The Role of Migration in the History of the Eurasian Steppe. Sedentary Civilisation vs. 'Barbarian' and Nomad*. Houndmills: Macmillan.

Berend, Nora. 2001. *At the Gate of Christendom: Jews, Muslims, and 'Pagans' in Medieval Hungary, c. 1000-c. 1300*. Cambridge: Cambridge University Press.

Berezin, Il'ia N. 1854. *Jāmiʿ at-tavārīkh*, ed. Qadir ʿAlī Jalāyir. Kazan, 1854. (Biblioteka Vostochnykh Istorikov. Tom II. Sbornik letopisei. Istoriia mongolo-tiurkov, na tatarskom iazyke.)

Bergholz, Fred W. 1993. *The Partition of the Steppe: The Struggle of the Russians, Manchus, and the Zunghar Mongols for Empire in Central Asia, 1619–1758. A Study in Power Politics*. New York: Peter Lang.

Bernardini, Michele. 1996. ed. *La Civiltà Timuride come fenomeno internazionale. Oriente Moderno*. Numero monografico; nuova serie, 15/1–2, 2 vols. Rome: Istituto per l'Oriente.

Bertel's, Evgenii É. 1938. (for F. B. Rostopchin, ed.). *Iz arkhiva sheikhov Dzhuibari*. Moscow and Leningrad: Akademiia Nauk SSSR.

1965. *Izbrannye Trudy, Navoi i Dzhami*. Moscow: Nauka.

Bināʾī, Kamāl al-Dīn ʿAlī. 1997. *Shaybānī-nāma*, ed. Kazuyuki Kubo, in *A Synthetical Study of Central Asian Culture in the Turco-Islamic Period*, ed. Eiji Mano. Kyoto: Ministry of Education.

Biran, Michal. 1997. *Qaidu and the Rise of the Independent Mongol State in Central Asia*. Richmond, Surrey: Curzon.

2002a. 'The Battle of Herat (1270): A Case of Inter-Mongol Warfare', in Di Cosmo, 2002: 175–220.

2002b. 'The Chaghadaids and Islam: The Conversion of Tarmashirin Khan.' *JAOS* 122/4: 742–52.

2004. 'The Mongol Transformation: From the Steppe to Eurasian Empire', in *Eurasian Transformations, Tenth to Thirteenth Centuries. Crystallizations, Divergences, Renaissances*, ed. Johann P. Arnason and Björn Wittrock. Medieval Encounters, 10. Leiden and Boston: Brill: 339–61.

2005. *The Empire of the Qara Khitai in Eurasian History*. Cambridge: Cambridge University Press.

2007. *Chinggis Khan: The Makers of the Islamic World*. Oxford: One World Publications.

Birge, Bettine. 1995. 'Levirate Marriage and the Revival of Widow Chastity in Yüan China.' *Asia Major*, third series, 8: 107–46.

Birtalan, Agnes. 2005. 'The Mongolian Great Khans in Mongolian Mythology and Folklore.' *AOH* 58/3: 299–311.

Blagova, G. F. 1970. 'Istoricheskie vzaimootnosheniia slov *kazak* i *Kazakh*', in *Etnonimy*. Moscow: Nauka: 143–59.

Blake, Robert P. and Richard N. Frye. 1949. 'History of the Nation of the Archers (the Mongols) by Grigor of Akanc, Hitherto Ascribed to Malak'ia the Monk: The Armenian Text Edited with an English Translation and Notes.' *HJAS* 12: 269–399.

Boccaccio, Giovanni. 1949. *The Decameron*, trans. Richard Aldington. New York: Garden City.

Bogatova, G. A. 1970. 'Zolotaia Orda.' *Russkaia rech'* 4/1: 70–7.

Bold, Bat-Ochir. 2001. *Mongolian Nomadic Society: A Reconstruction of the 'Medieval' History of Mongolia*. New York: St. Martin's Press.

Borawski, Piotr and Aleksander Dubiński. 1986. *Tatarzy polscy. Dzieje, obrzędy, legendy, tradycje*. Warsaw: Iskry.

Bosworth, C. Edmund. 1968. 'The Political and Dynastic History of the Iranian World (A.D. 1000–1217)', in *CHIran*, V: 1–202.

1977. *The Later Ghaznavids*. New York: Columbia University Press.

Boyle, John A. 1968. 'Dynastic and Political History of the Ilkhans', in *CHIran*, V: 303–421.

1970. 'The Posthumous Title of Batu Khan', in *Proceedings of the IXth Meeting of the Permanent International Altaistic Conference, Ravello, 26–30 September 1966*. Naples: Istituto Universitario Orientale, Seminario di Turcologia: 67–70.

1977. *The Mongol World-Empire 1206–1370*. London: Variorum Reprints.

Bratianu, George I. 1927. *Actes des notaires genois de Pera et de Caffa de la fin du treizieme siècle, 1281–1290*. Bucharest : Cultură Naţională.

1929. *Recherches sur le commerce genois dans la Mer Noire au xiiie siècle*. Paris: P. Geuthner.

1969. *La mer Noire. Des origins à la conquête ottomane*. Acta Historica IX. Munich: Societas Academica Dacoromana.

Bregel, Yuri. 1961. *Khorezmskie turkmeny v XIX veke*. Moscow: Vostochnaia Literatura.

1982. 'Tribal Tradition and Ethnic History: The Early Rulers of the Qongrats According to Munis.' *Asian and African Studies: Journal of the Israel Oriental Society* 16/3: 357–98.

1983a. 'Bukhara III: After the Mongol Invasion', *Encyclopaedia Iranica*, IV: 515–21.

1983b. 'Abu'l-Ḵayr Khan', *Encyclopaedia Iranica*, I: 331–2.

1991. 'Turko-Mongol Influences in Central Asia', in Canfield, 1991a: 53–77.

1995. ed. *Bibliography of Islamic Central Asia*. Bloomington, Ind.: Research Institute for Inner Asian Studies. 3 vols.

1996. *Notes on the Study of Central Asia: Papers on Inner Asia*, 28. Bloomington, Ind.: Research Institute for Inner Asian Studies.

2000. *The Administration of Bukhara under the Manghïts and Some Tashkent Manuscripts: Papers on Inner Asia*, 34. Bloomington, Ind.: Research Institute for Inner Asian Studies.

2003. *An Historical Atlas of Central Asia*. Leiden: Brill.

'Ersari', *EI²*, Suppl.: 281.

Brockelman, Carl. 1938. *Geschichte der arabischen Literatur.* Zweiter Supplementband. Leiden: Brill.

Brose, Michael C. 2002. 'Central Asians in Mongol China.' *Medieval History Journal* 5/2: 267–89.

Brosset, Marie-Félicité. 1850. trans. *Histoire de la Géorgie*, 1re partie: *Histoire ancienne, jusqu'en 1469 JC*. St. Petersburg: Académie des sciences. Part of Brosse, Marii Ivanovich, 1849–58.

trans. *Histoire de la Georgie depuis l'antiquité jusqu'au XIX siècle, part 1*. St. Petersburg: Imprimerie de l'académie impériale des sciences. 5 vols.

Browne, Edward G. 1964. *A Literary History of Persia*. Cambridge: Cambridge University Press, 1902–29, reprint 1964. 4 vols.

Brunnert, H. S. and V. V. Hagelstrom. 1911. *Present-Day Political Organization of China*. Foochow; reprint Taibei: Ch'en Wen, 1978.

Budge, E. A. Wallis. 1928. trans. *The Monks of Khubilai Khan: The History of Rabban Sawma*. London: The Religious Tract Society.

Buell, Paul D. 1977. 'Tribe, *Qan* and *Ulus* in Early Mongol China: Some Prolegomena to Yüan History.' Ph.D. diss., The University of Washington.

1979a. 'The Role of the Sino-Mongolian Frontier Zone in the Rise of Cinggis-Qan', in Studies on East Asia, 13: *Studies on Mongolia: Proceedings of the First North American Conference on Mongolian Studies*, ed. Henry G. Schwarz. Bellingham, Wash.: Western Washington University: 63–76.

1979b. 'Sino-Khitan Administration in Mongol Bukhara.' *Journal of Asian History* 13: 121–51.

1992. 'Early Mongol Expansion in Western Siberia and Turkestan (1207–1219): A Reconstruction.' *Central Asiatic Journal* 36: 1–32.

2003. *Historical Dictionary of the Mongol World Empire*, Historical Dictionaries of Ancient Civilization and Historical Eras, 8. Latham, Md., and Oxford: The Scarecrow Press Inc.

Buganov, Viktor I. 1976. *Krest'ianskie voiny v Rossii XVII – XVIII vekov.* Moscow: Nauka.

Bukanova, R. G. 1997. *Goroda-kreposti iugo-vostoka Rossii v XVIII veke*. Ufa: Kitap.

Buniiatov, Ziia M. 1986. *Gosudarstvo khorezmshakhov-anushteginidov 1097–1231*. Moscow: Nauka.

Burton, Audrey. 1997. *The Bukharans: A Dynastic, Diplomatic and Commercial History, 1550–1702*. Richmond, Surrey: Curzon.

Caferoğlu, Ahmet. 1964–9. *Türk Dili Tarihi*. Istanbul: Edebiyat Fakültesi Basımevi. 2 vols.

Cai, Jiayi. 1982. 'Shiba shiji zhongye Zhunga'er tong zhongyuan diqu de maoyi wanglai lueshu' in Zhongguo shehui kexueyuan lishi yanjiusuo Qingshi yanjiushi ed., *Qingshi luncong* 4: 241–55. Beijing: Zhonghua shuju.

Cai, Meibiao. 1986. ed. *Zhongguo lishi da cidian: Liao Xia Jin Yuan shi juan*. Shanghai: Shanghai cishu chubanshe.

Canfield, Robert L. 1991a. ed. *Turko-Persia in Historical Perspective*. Cambridge: Cambridge University Press.

1991b. 'Introduction: The Turko-Persian Tradition', in Canfield, 1991a: 1–34.

Carpini, Giovanni del Pian di. 1989. *Ystoria Mongalorum quos nos Tartaros appellamus*, ed. Enrico Menestò *et al.*, *Giovanni di Pian di Carpine. Storia dei Mongoli*. Spoleto: Centro italiano di studi sull'alto medioevo. Trans. in Dawson, 1980: 1–72.

Castagné, Josephe. 1951. 'Le culte des lieux saints de l'islam au Turkestan.' *l'Ethnographie* n.s. 46: 57–65.

Central State Archive of the Republic of Uzbekistan, Fond I–323, no. 55/9.

Cerensodnom, Dalantai and Manfred Taube. 1993. comp. and trans., *Die Mongolica der Berliner Turfansammlung*. Berlin: Akademie Verlag.

Cessi, Roberto, with P. Sambin and M. Brunetti. 1960–61. *Le deliberazioni del Consiglio dei Rogati (Senato)*: Serie 'Mixtorum', Libri i-xiv, 2 vols. Venezia: a Spese della Deputazione.

Chan Hok-lam. 1991. '"Ta Chin" (Great Golden): The Origin and Changing Interpretations of the Jurchen State Name.' *Toung Pao* 77/4–5: 253–99.
ChChina, VI, see List of Abbreviations
CHEIA, see List of Abbreviations
Chekhovich, Olga D. 1954. *Dokumenty k istorii agrarnykh otnoshenii v Bukharskoim khanstve XVII–XIX vv*. Vol. I: *Akty feodal'noi sobstvennosti na zemliu XVII–XIX vv.* Tashkent: Izdatel'stvo Akademii nauk UzSSR.
1965. *Bukharskie dokumenty XIV veka*. Tashkent: Nauka.
1967. 'Bukharskii vakf XIII veka.' *Narody Azii i Afriki* 3: 74–82.
1974. *Samarkandskie Dokumenty xv–xvi vv*. Moscow: Nauka.
1979. *Bukharskii vakf XIII v*. Moscow: Nauka.
Chekhovich, Olga D. and A. B. Vil'danova. 1973. 'Vakf Subkhan-kuli-khana Bukharskogo 1693 g.', in *Pis'mennye Pamiatniki Vostoka*. Moscow: Nauka: 213–25.
Chen, Bangzhan. 1979. *Yuan shi jishi benmo*. Beijing: Zhonghua shuju.
Chen, Dezhi. 1985, 1987, 1990. 'Yuan Lingbei xingsheng jianzhi kao". *Yuan shi ji beifang minzu shi yanjiu jikan* 9: 31–44; 11: 1–18; 12–13: 1–19.
Ch'en Yüan. 1966. *Western and Central Asians in China under the Mongols: Their Transformation into Chinese*, trans. Ch'ien Hsing-hai and L. Carrington-Goodrich. Monumenta Serica Monographs, 15. Los Angeles: University of California Press.
Cherniavsky, Michael. 1959. 'Khan or Basileus: An Aspect of Russian Medieval Political Thought.' *Journal of the History of Ideas* 20: 459–76.
Chernov, Anatolii V. 1954. *Vooruzhennye sily russkogo gosudarstva v XV – XVII vekov. S obrazovaniia tsentralizovannogo gosudarstva do reform pri Petre I*. Moscow: Voennoe Izdatel'stvo.
Chia, Ning. 1993. 'The Lifanyuan and the Inner Asian Rituals in the Early Qing (1644–1795).' *Late Imperial China* 14/1: 60–92.
CHIran, see List of Abbreviations
Christian, David. 1998. *A History of Russia, Central Asia and Mongolia*, I: *From Prehistory to the Mongol Empire*. Oxford: Blackwell.
2000. 'Silk Roads or Steppe Roads?' *JWH* 11/1: 1–26.
Churās, Shāh Maḥmūd. 1976. *Khronika*, Russian trans. by O. F. Akimushkin of Persian text Shāh Maḥmud ibn Mirza Fāḍil Churās *Tarikh*. Includes critical text, commentary and study by O. F. Akimushkin. Pamiatniki Pis'mennosti Vostoka, 45. Moscow: Nauka, Glavnaia Redaktsiia Vostochnoi Literatury.
[Churās, Shāh Maḥmūd] Shah Mähmut Joras. 1988. *Sä'idiyä Khandanliqi tarikhigha da'ir matiriyallar* [Materials Relating to the History of the Saʿidiyya Khanate], Modern Uyghur trans. by Häbibulla Eli from the edition by O. F. Akimushkin (Moscow, 1976), introduction by Qurban Väli. Kashgar: Qäshqär Uyghur Näshriyati.
Clark, Hugh R. 1995. 'Muslims and Hindus in the Culture and Morphology of Quanzhou from the Tenth to the Thirteenth Century.' *JWH* 6/1: 49–74.
Clark, Larry V. 1975. 'On a Mongol Decree of Yisün Temür (1339).' *CAJ* 11/3: 194–8.
Clauson, Sir Gerard. 1972. *An Etymological Dictionary of Pre-Thirteenth-Century Turkish*. Oxford: Oxford University Press.
Clavijo, see González de Clavijo, Ruy.
Cleaves, Francis W. 1949. 'The Sino-Mongolian Inscription of 1362 in Memory of Prince Hindu.' *HJAS* 12: 1–133.
1955. 'The Historicity of the Baljuna Covenant.' *HJAS* 18: 357–421.

1956. 'The Biography of Bayan of the Barin in the *Yuan Shih*.' *HJAS* 19: 185–303.
1959. 'An Early Mongolian Version of the Alexander Romance.' *HJAS* 22: 1–99.
1982. trans. *The Secret History of the Mongols*. Cambridge, Mass.: Harvard University Press.
1992. 'The Rescript of Qubilai Prohibiting the Slaughter of Animals by Slitting the Throat', in *Richard Nelson Frye Festschrift I: Essays Presented to Richard Nelson Frye on his Seventieth Birthday by his Colleagues and Students*, ed. Carolyn I. Cross. Cambridge, Mass.: Harvard University Press = *Journal of Turkish Studies* 16: 67–89.
CMCT, see List of Abbreviations
Codex Cumanicus, see Drimba, 2000 and Kuun, 1880.
Collins, David N. 1991. 'Subjugation and Settlement in Seventeenth and Eighteenth Century Siberia', in *The History of Siberia: From Russian Conquest to Revolution*, ed. Alan Wood. London: Routledge: 37–56.
Conermann, Stephan and Jan Kusber. 1997. eds. *Die Mongolen in Asien und Europa*. Kieler Werkstücke, Reihe F: Beiträge zur osteuropäischen Geschichte, 4. Frankfurt-am-Main: Peter Lang.
Contarini, Ambrogio, see Lord Stanley of Aldershot, 1873.
Crews, Robert D. 2006. *For Prophet and Tsar*. Cambridge, Mass.: Harvard University Press.
Crummey, Robert O. 1987. *The Formation of Muscovy, 1304–1613*. London: Longman.
Csáki, Éva. 2006. *Middle Mongolian Loan Words in Volga Kipchak Languages*. Turcologica, 67 Wiesbaden: Harrassowitz.
Daftar-i Chingīz nāma, see Ivanics and Usmanov, 2002.
Dalai, Ch. 1983. *Mongoliia v XIII–XIV vekax*. Moscow: Nauka.
Dale, Stephen F. 1998. 'The Legacy of the Timurids.' *Journal of the Royal Asiatic Society*, third series, 8 / 1: 43–58.
2004. *The Garden of the Eight Paradises: Bābur and the Culture of Empire in Central Asia, Afghanistan and India 1483–1530*. Leiden and Boston: Brill.
Dalizhabu. 2003. '"Menggu lüli" ji qi yu "Lifanyuan zeli" de guanxi.' *Qingshi yanjiu* 4: 1–10.
2005a. 'Qingdai Chahaer zhasake qi kao.' *Lishi yanjiu* 5: 47–59.
2005b. '"Haerha fagui" zhiding yuanyin ji shishi fanwei chu tan.' *Zhongyang minzu daxue xuebao* 1: 84–91.
Dang, Baotai. 2004. 'Menggu Chahatai hanguo de yizhan jiaotong.' *Xiyu yanjiu* 4: 15–22.
Dardess, John W. 1972–3. 'From Mongol Empire to Yüan Dynasty: Changing Forms of Imperial Rule in Mongolia and Central Asia.' *Monumenta Serica* 30: 117–65.
1973. *Conquerors and Confucians: Aspects of Political Change in Late Yüan China*. New York and London: Columbia University Press.
Darley-Doran, R. E. 1999. "Timurids.' 'Numismatics." *EI*², V. 10, fasc. 177–78. Leiden: Brill: 525–7.
Dashkevich, Iaroslav R. 1988. 'Codex Cumanicus – deistvitel'no li Cumanicus?' *Voprosy iazykoznaniia* 2: 62–74.
Daulbaev, V. D. 1881. 'Razskazy o zhizni kirgiz Nikolaevskogo uezda Turgaiskoi oblasti s 1830 po 1880 god.' *Zapiski Orenburgskogo Otdeleniia Imperatorskago Russkago Geograficheskago Obshchestva* 4: 98–117.
Davidovich, Elena A. 1964. *Istoriia monetnogo dela Srednei Azii XVII–XVIII vv*. Dushanbe: Izdatel'stvo Akademii Nauk Tadzhikskoi SSSR.

1970a. 'Denezhnoe khoziaistvo i chastichnoe vosstanovlenie torgovli v Srednei Azii posle mongol'skogo nashestviia.' *Narody Azii i Afriki* 6: 57–67.

1970b. *Materialy po metrologii srednevekovoi Srednei Azii*. Moscow: Nauka.

1972. *Denezhnoe khoziaistvo Srednei Azii posle mongol'skogo zavoevaniia i reforma Masʿūd-beka (XIII v.)*. Moscow: Nauka.

1983. *Istoriia denezhnogo obrashcheniia srednevekovoi Srednei Azii*. Moscow: Nauka.

1992. *Korpus zolotykh i serebrianykh monet Sheibanidov XVI vek*. Moscow: Nauka.

2001. 'The Monetary Reforms of Muhammad Shībānī Khān in 913–914/1507–08', in DeWeese, 2001: 129–85.

Davidovich, Elena A. and A. H. Dani. 1998. 'Coinage and the Monetary System', in Asimov and Bosworth, 1998: 391–419.

Davies, C. C. 'Pandjdih (Pendjdeh).' *EI²*, VIII: 257–8.

Davydov, A. D. 'Imenie medrese Subkhan-kuli-khana v Balkhe (po vakfnoi gramote XVII v.).' *Kratkie soobshcheniia Instituta Vostokovedeniia* 37. Moscow: 82–128.

Dawson, Christopher. 1980. ed. *The Mongol Mission: Narratives and Letters of the Franciscan Missionaries in Mongolia and China in the Thirteenth and Fourteenth Centuries*. London and New York: Sheed and Ward, 1955; reprinted as *Mission to Asia*, London and New York: Sheed and Ward.

De la Vaissière, Étienne. 2005. *Sogdian Traders: A History*, trans. J. Ward. Leiden: Brill.

De la Vaissière, Étienne and Éric Trombert. 2005. eds. *Les Sogdiens en Chine*. Paris: École française d'Extrême-Orient.

Dede Korkut Kitabı, see Ergin, 1964.

Deér, József. [1938]. *Pogány magyarság keresztény magyarság*. Budapest: A királyi magyar egyetem nyomda, n.d.

Deng, Gang. 1997. *Chinese Maritime Activities and Socioeconomic Development, c. 2100 B.C.–1900 A.D.* Westport, Conn.: Westview.

Desimoni, Cornelio. 1887. 'Trattato dei Genovesi col chan dei Tartari nel 1380–1381 scritto in lingua volgare.' *Archivio Storico Italiano*, quarta serie, 20: 162–5.

Deviatykh, Leonid. 2002. *Iz istorii Kazanskogo kupechestva*. Kazan: Titul.

DeWeese, Devin. 1988. 'The Eclipse of the Kubravīyah in Central Asia.' *Iranian Studies* 21: 45–83.

1993. 'An "Uvaysī" Sufi in Timurid Mawarannahr: Notes on Hagiography and the Taxonomy of Sanctity in the Religious History of Central Asia.' *Papers on Central Asia*, 22. Bloomington, Ind.: Research Institute for Inner Asian Studies.

1994a. *Islamization and Native Religion in the Golden Horde*. University Park: Pennsylvania State University Press.

1994b. 'Bābā Kamāl Jandī and the Kubravī Tradition among the Turks of Central Asia.' *Der Islam* 71: 58–94.

1996a. 'Yasavī shaykhs in the Timurid Era: Notes on the Social and Political Role of Communal Sufi Affiliations in the 14th and 15th Centuries', in Bernardini, 1996: 173–88.

1996b. 'The *Mashāʾikh-i Turk* and the *Khojagān*: Rethinking the Links Between the Yasavī and Naqshbandī Sufi Traditions.' *Journal of Islamic Studies* 7: 180–207.

1999a. 'Khojagānī Origins and the Critique of Sufism: The Rhetoric of Communal Uniqueness in the *Manāqib* of Khoja ʿAlī ʿAzīzān Rāmītanī', in *Islamic Mysticism Contested: Thirteen Centuries of Controversies and Polemics*, ed. Frederick De Jong and Bernd Radtke. Leiden: Brill: 492–519.

1999b. 'The Politics of Sacred Lineages in 19th-Century Central Asia: Descent Groups Linked to Khwaja Ahmad Yasavi in Shrine Documents and Genealogical Charters.' *International Journal of Middle East Studies* 31: 507–30.

2000. 'Sacred Places and "Public" Narratives: The Shrine of Aḥmad Yasavī in Hagiographical Traditions of the Yasavī Ṣūfī Order, 16th-17th Centuries.' *Muslim World* 90/3–4: 353–76.

2001. ed. *Studies in Central Asian History in Honor of Yuri Bregel*. Bloomington, Ind.: Research Institute for Inner Asian Studies.

al-Dhahabī, Shams al-Dīn Muḥammad b. Aḥmad. 1982–96. *Siyar aʿlām al-nubalaʾ*. Beirut: Muʾssasat al-risāla. 25 vols.

1997–2004. *Taʾrīkh al-Islām*, ed. ʿUmar ʿAbd al-Salām Tadmūrī. Beirut: Dār al-Kitāb al-ʿArabī.

Di Cosmo, Nicola. 1998. 'Qing Colonial Administration in Inner Asia.' *The International History Review* 20/2: 287–309.

1999. 'State Formation and Periodization in Inner Asian History.' *JWH* 10/1: 1–40.

2002. 'Military Aspects of the Manchu Wars Against the Čaqars', in *Warfare in Inner Asian History (500–1800)*, ed. N. Di Cosmo. Leiden: Brill: 343–67.

2007. 'Marital Politics on the Manchu-Mongol Frontier in the Early Seventeenth Century', in *The Chinese State at the Borders*, ed. Diana Lary. Vancouver: University of British Columbia Press: 57–73.

Di Cosmo, Nicola and Don J. Wyatt. 2003. eds. *Political Frontiers, Ethnic Boundaries and Human Geographies in Chinese History*. London and New York: Routledge.

Dickson, Martin B. 1958. 'Shah Tahmasb and the Uzbeks (The Duel for Khurasan with ʿUbayd Khan: 930–946/1524–1540)', Ph.D. diss., Princeton University.

Dictionary of Ming Biography. 1976. Ed. L. Carrington Goodrich and C. Y. Fang. New York and London: Columbia University Press. 2 vols.

Dieten, Jan Louis van. 1973, 1979, 1988. Nikephoros Gregoras: *Rhomäische Geschichte. Historia Rhomaike*. I–III: Bibliothek der Griechischen Literatur 4, 9, 24. Stuttgart: Anton Hiersemann.

Dihlawī, Amīr Khusraw. 1953. *Khazāʾin al-futūḥ*, ed. M. Waḥīd Mīrzā. Calcutta: Royal Society of Bengal.

Dmytryshyn, Basil. 1991. 'The Administrative Apparatus of the Russian Colony in Siberia and Northern Asia, 1581–1700', in *The History of Siberia: From Russian Conquest to Revolution*, ed. Alan Wood. London: Routledge: 17–36.

Dobrosmyslov, A. 1900. *Materialy po istorii Rossii* I. Orenburg: F. B. Sachkov.

Dobrovits, Mihály. 1994. 'The Turko-Mongolian Tradition of Common Origin and Historiography in Fifteenth Century Central Asia.' *AOH* 47/3: 269–77.

Dodkhudoeva, Larisa N. 1992. *Epigraficheskie pamiatniki Samarkanda XI–XIV vv.* I. Dushanbe: Donish.

Doerfer, Gerhard. 1963–75. *Türkische und mongolische Elemente im Neupersischen*. Wiesbaden: Franz Steiner Verlag. 4 vols.

Dols, Michael. 1977. *The Black Death in the Middle East*. Princeton: Princeton University Press.

Donnelly, Alton S. 1968. *The Russian Conquest of Bashkiria 1552–1740: A Case Study in Imperialism*. New Haven: Yale University Press.

Dörrie, Heinrich. 1956. 'Drei Texte zur Geschichte der Ungarn und Mongolen. Die Missionsreisen des fr. Iulianus ins Ural-Gebiet (1234/5) und nach Rußland (1237) und der Bericht des Erzbischofs Peter über die Tartaren.' *Nachrichten der Akademie der Wissenschaften zu Göttingen, phil.-hist. Klasse* 6: 125–202.

Dozy, Reinhart. 1968. *Supplement aux dictionnaires arabes*. Leiden: E. J. Brill 1881, reprint: Beirut: Librairie du Liban. 2 vols.

Dreyer, E. L. 1976. 'Toghus Temür', *Dictionary of Ming Biography*, 2: 1293–4.

Dreyer, E. L. and H. L. Chan. 1976. 'Ayushiridara', *Dictionary of Ming Biography*, 1: 15–17.

Drimba, Vladimir. 2000. ed. *Codex Comanicus: édition diplomatique avec fac-similés*. Bucharest: Editura Enciclopedică.

Drompp, Michael R. 1991. 'Supernumerary Sovereigns: Superfluity and Mutability in the Elite Power Structure of the Early Türks', in Seaman and Marks, 1991: 92–115.

Dūghlāt / Ross, see Haydar, Mirza

Dūghlāt / Thackston, see List of Abbreviations

Dūghlāt, Ḥaydar. 1996. *Tarikh-i Rashidi*, ed. and trans. A. Urunbaev *et al.* Tashkent: Fan. See also Dughlāt, in List of Abbreviations.

Dunlop, Douglas M. 1944. 'The Karaits of Eastern Asia.' *BSOAS* 11 / 2: 276–91.

Dunnell, Ruth. 1992. 'The Hsia Origins of the Yüan Institution of Imperial Preceptor.' *Asia Major*, third series, 5 / 1: 85–111.

1994. 'The Hsi Hsia', in *CHChina*, VI: 154–214.

1996. *The Great State of White and High: Buddhism and State Formation in Eleventh Century Xia*. Honolulu: University of Hawai'i Press.

Dzhikiev, Ata. 1991. *Ocherki proiskhozhdeniia i formirovaniia turkmenskogo naroda v epokhu srednevekov'ia*. Ashkhabad: Turkmenistan.

Dzhumagulov, Chetin. 1968. 'Die syrisch-türkischen (nestorianischen) Denkmäler in Kirgisien.' *Mitteilüngen des Institut für Orientforschung* 14: 470–80.

Eberhard, Wolfram. 1970. *Conquerors and Rulers: Social Forces in Medieval China*. Leiden: Brill.

Edel'man, Dzhoi I. 2000. 'Khorezmiiskii iazyk', in *Iazyki mira. Iranskie iazyki*, III: *Vostochno-iranskie iazyki*, ed. N. V. Rogova *et al.* Moscow: Indrik: 95–105.

Edgar, Adrienne L. 2004. *Tribal Nations: The Making of Soviet Turkmenistan*. Princeton: Princeton University Press.

Egami, Namio. 1952. 'Olon-sume et la découverte de l'église catholique romaine de Jean de Montecorvino.' *Journal Asiatique* 240: 155–67.

Egani, A. A. and O. D. Chekhovich. 1981–7. 'Regesty sredneaziatskikh aktov', *Pis'mennye Pamiatniki Vostoka* 1975, 1976 / 7, 1978 / 9. Moscow: Nauka.

Egorov, Vadim. L. 1969. 'Prichiny vozniknoveniia gorodov u mongolov v XII–XIV vv.' *Istoriia SSSR* 4: 39–49.

1985. *Istoricheskaia geografiia Zolotoi Ordy v XIII–XIV vv.* Moscow: Nauka.

Elias, Jamal J. 1994. 'The Sufi Lords of Bahrabad: Saʿd al-Din and Sadr al-Din Hamuwayi.' *Iranian Studies* 27: 53–75.

Elverskog, Johan. 2006. *Our Great Qing: The Mongols, Buddhism and the State in Late Imperial China*. Honolulu: University of Hawai'i Press.

Eminent Chinese of the Ch'ing Period (1644–1912). 1964. Ed. A. W. Hummel. Washington: US Government Printing Office, 1943–4; repr. Taibei, 1964.

Encyclopedia Iranica, ed. Ihsan Yarshater. London and Boston: Routledge, 1982– .

Encyclopaedia of Islam, 1st edn, see List of Abbreviations, *EI*[1]

Encyclopaedia of Islam, 2nd edn, see List of Abbreviations *EI*[2]

Endicott-West, Elizabeth. 1989a. *Mongolian Rule in China: Local Administration in the Yüan Dynasty*. Cambridge, Mass.: Harvard University Press.

1989b. 'Merchant Associations in Yuan China: The *Ortoγ*.' *Asia Major*, third series, 2/2: 127–56.

Ercilasun, Ahmet B. 2004. *Başlangıçtan Yirminci Yüzyıla Türk Dili Tarihi*. Ankara: Ak Çağ.

Erdal, Marcel. 1993. *Die Sprache der wolgabolgarischen Inschriften*. Wiesbaden: Otto Harrassowitz.

Ergin, Muharrem. 1964. ed. *Dede Korkut Kitabı*. Ankara: Ankara Üniversitesi Basımevi.

Ermolaev, I. P. 1982. *Srednee Povolzh'e vo vtoroi polovine XVI–XVII vekov*. Kazan: Kazanskii Universitet.

Études Karakhanides in *Cahiers d'Asie Centrale* 9. 2001. Tashkent and Aix-en-Provence: Editions EDISUD.

Faḍl Allāh b. Ruzbihān-i Īṣfahānī Khunjī. 1962. *Mihmān-nāma-i Bukhārā*, ed. Manochehr Sotoodeh, Tehran.

Fang, C. Y. 1964a. 'Nurhaci', in *Eminent Chinese of the Ch'ing Period (1644–1912)*, ed. A. W. Hummel. Washington: US Government Printing Office, 1943–4; repr. Taibei: 594–9.

1964b. 'Abahai', *in Eminent Chinese of the Ch'ing Period (1644–1912)*, ed. A. W. Hummel. Washington: US Government Printing Office, 1943–4; repr. Taibei: 1–3.

1964c. 'Hsiao-tuan', in *Eminent Chinese of the Ch'ing Period (1644–1912)*, ed. A. W. Hummel. Washington: US Government Printing Office, 1943–4; repr. Taibei: 304–5.

Farquhar, David M. 1968. 'The Origins of the Manchus' Mongolian Policy', *The Chinese World Order*, ed. J. K. Fairbank. Cambridge, Mass.: Harvard University Press: 198–205.

1990. *The Government of China under Mongolian Rule: A Reference Guide*. Münchener Ostasiatische Studien, 53. Stuttgart: F. Steiner.

Faṣīḥ Khwāfī, Muḥammad b. Aḥmad. 1960–1. *Mujmal-i Fāsiḥī*, ed. Muḥammad Farrukh. Mashhad: Kitābfurūshī-yi Bāstān, 1339/1960–1. 3 vols.

Fäyezkhanov, Khösäyen. 2006. 'Qasïym khanlïghï', in *Khösäyen Fäyezkhanov: tarikhi-dokumental' jïyïntïq*, ed. Raif Märdanov. Kazan: Jïyïn.

Fedorov, Michael. 2000. 'On the Attribution of the Anonymous Chaghatayid Coins Minted in 726–7 AH.' *ONS Newsletter* 162: 9–11.

2001. 'On the Exact Date of Yesün Temür's Accession to the Throne, According to the Numismatic Data.' *Iran* 39: 301–2.

2002. 'A Hoard of Fourteenth Century Chaghatayid Silver Coins from North Kirghizstan.' *Numismatic Chronicle* 162: 404–19.

Fedorov-Davydov, German A. 1966. *Kochevniki Vostochnoi Evropy pod vlast'iu zolotoordynskikh khanov.* Moscow: Izdatel'stvo Moskovskogo Universiteta.

1968. '"Anonim Iskandera" i terminy "Ak-Orda" i "Kok-Orda"', in *Istoriia, arkheologiia i etnografiia Srednei Azii*, ed. A. V. Vinogradov *et al.* Moscow: Nauka: 224–30.

1984. *The Culture of the Golden Horde Cities*, trans. H. Bartlett Wells. Oxford: B.A.R.

1994. *Zolotoordynskie goroda Povolzh'ia*. Moscow: Izdatel'stvo Moskovskogo Universiteta.

2004. *Denezhnoe delo Zolotoi Ordy*. Moscow: Paleograf.

Fennell, J. L. I. 1961. *Ivan the Great of Moscow*. London: Macmillan.

Ferguson, R. Brian and N. L. Whitehead. 1997. eds. *War in the Tribal Zone*. Santa Fe: School of American Research Press.

Fine, Jr., John V. A. 1987. *The Late Medieval Balkans: A Critical Survey From the Late Twelfth Century to the Ottoman Conquest*. Ann Arbor: University of Michigan Press.

Firsov, Nikolai A. 1869. *Inorodcheskoe naselenie prezhnego Kazanskogo tsarstva v novoi Rossii do 1762 goda i kolonizatsiia zemel' v éto vremia*. Kazan: Universitetskaia tipografiia.

Fisher, Alan W. 1967. 'Enlightened Despotism and Islam under Catherine II.' *SR* 27: 542–53.

1970, *The Russian Annexation of the Crimea, 1772–1783*. Cambridge: Cambridge University Press.

1978. *The Crimean Tatars*. Stanford, Calif.: Hoover Institution.

Fleischer, Cornell H. 1986. *Bureaucrat and Intellectual in the Ottoman Empire: The Historian Mustafa Âli*. Princeton: Princeton University Press.

Fletcher, Joseph. 1978a. 'Ch'ing Inner Asia c. 1800', in *The Cambridge History of China*, 10: *Late Ch'ing, 1800–1911, part 1*, ed. John King Fairbank. Cambridge: Cambridge University Press: 35–106.

1978b. 'The Heyday of the Ch'ing Order in Mongolia, Sinkiang and Tibet,' in *The Cambridge History of China*, 10: *Late Ch'ing, 1800–1911, part 1*, ed. John King Fairbank. Cambridge: Cambridge University Press: 351–408.

1979–80. 'Turko-Mongolian Monarchic Tradition in the Ottoman Empire.' *Harvard Ukrainian Studies* 3–4 / 1: 236–51; reprinted in Fletcher, 1995.

1986. 'The Mongols: Ecological and Social Perspectives.' *HJAS* 46: 11–50; reprinted in Fletcher, 1995.

1995. 'The Naqshbandiyya in Northwest China', ed. Jonathan Lipman, in Joseph F. Fletcher, *Studies on Chinese and Islamic Central Asia*, ed. Beatrice Forbes Manz. Variorum Collected Studies Series. Aldershot, Hampshire: Variorum, XI: 1–4.

Foltz, Richard. 1996. 'The Central Asian Naqshbandi Connections of the Mughal Emperors.' *Journal of Islamic Studies* 7: 229–39.

1998. *Mughal India and Central Asia*. New Delhi: Oxford University Press: 97–103.

Fraehn, Christian M. 1832 [2001], *Monety khanov Ulusa Dzhuchieva ili Zolotoi Ordy s monetami raznykh inykh mukhammedanskikh dinastii*. St. Petersburg; reprint: Nizhnii Novgorod, 2001.

Frank, Allen J. 1994. *The Siberian Chronicles and the Taybughid biys of Sibir'*, in *Papers on Inner Asia*, 27. Bloomington, Indiana: Research Institute for Inner Asia Studies.

1998. *Islamic Historiography and 'Bulghar' Identity among the Tatars and Bashkirs of Russia*. Leiden and Boston: Brill.

2001. *Muslim Religious Institutions in Imperial Russia: The Islamic World of Novouzensk District and the Kazakh Inner Horde, 1780–1910*. Leiden: Brill.

2003. 'Islamic Transformation on the Kazakh Steppe, 1742–1917: Toward an Islamic History of Kazakhstan under Russian Rule', in *The Construction and Deconstruction of National Identities in Slavic Eurasia*, ed. Hayashi Tadayuki. Sapporo: Slavic Research Center: 261–89.

Frank, Allen J. and Mirkasyim A. Usmanov. 2001. eds. *Materials for the Islamic History of Semipalatinsk: Two Manuscripts by Aḥmad-Walī al-Qazānī and Qurbānʿalī Khālidī*, ANOR 11. Halle and Berlin: Das Arabische Buch.

Frank, Andre Gunder. 1998. *ReOrient: Global Economy in the Asian Age*. Berkeley, Los Angeles and London: University of California Press.

Franke, Herbert. 1962. 'Zur Datierung der mongolischen Schreiben aus Turfan.' *Oriens* 15: 399–410.

1968. 'Ein weiteres mongolisches Reisebegleitschreiben aus Čaghatai (14. jh.).' *Zentralasiatische Studien* 2: 7–14.

1975. 'Ein mongolischer Freibrief aus dem Jahre 1369.' *Ural-Altaische Jahrbücher* 47: 64–72.

1976. 'Toghon Temür', *Dictionary of Ming Biography*, ed. L. Carrington Goodrich and C. Y. Fang. 2 vols. New York and London: Columbia University Press: 2: 1290–3.

1978. *From Tribal Chieftain to Universal Emperor and God: The Legitimation of the Yüan Dynasty*. Bayerische Akademie d. Wissenschaften, Philosophisch-Historische Klasse, Sitzungsberichte, Jahrgang, Heft 2. Munich: Verlag der Bayerischen Akademie der Wissenschaften.

1981. 'Tibetans in Yuan China', in *China under Mongol Rule*, ed. John D. Langlois, Jr. Princeton: Princeton University Press: 296–328.

1990. 'The Forest Peoples of Manchuria: Kitans and Jurchens', in *CHEIA*: 400–19.

1994a. 'The Chin Dynasty', in *CHChina*, VI: 215–320.

1994b. *China Under Mongol Rule*. Aldershot: Variorum Reprints.

Franke, Wolfgang. 1945. 'Yung-lo's Mongolei-Feldzüge.' *Sinologische Arbeiten* 3: 1–54.

Freeze, Gregory L. 1986. 'The *Soslovie* (Estate) Paradigm in Russian Social History.' *American Historical Review* 91 / 1: 11–36.

Fried, Morton. 1967. *The Evolution of Political Society*. New York: Random House.

Frye, Richard N. 1975. *The Golden Age of Persia: The Arabs in the East*. London: Weidenfeld and Nicolson.

Fuchs, Walter. 1946. 'Analecta zur mongolischen Übersetzungsliteratur der Yuan-Zeit.' *Monumenta Serica* 11: 33–64.

Fu-heng, *et al.* 1986. comp. *(Qinding) huangyu Xiyu tuzhi* 1782, repr. Guji shanben congshu, ed. Wu Fengpei. Beijing: Zhongyang minzu xueyuan tushuguan.

1990. comp. *(Qinding) pingding Zhunga'er fanglue* 3 vols. (*qian, zheng, xu*), 1768. Repr. by Xizang Hanwen wenxian huike, 4 vols., Xizang shehui kexue yuan Xizangxue hanwen wenxian bianjishi ed. Beijing: Quanguo tushuguan wenxian suowei fuzhi zhongxin.

Galstian, A. G. 1962. *Armianskie istochniki o mongolakh*. Moscow: Izdatel' stvo vostochnoi literatury.

Gates, Jean M. and C. Y. Fang. 1964. 'Hsiao-chuang Wên Huang-hou', *Eminent Chinese of the Ch'ing Period (1644–1912)*, ed. A. W. Hummel. Washington: US Government Printing Office, 1943–4; reprinted Taibei: 300–01.

Gaziz [Gubaidullin], G. S. 1994. *Istoriia tatar*. Moscow: Moskovskii Litsei.

Geley, Jean-Philippe. 1979. 'L'ethnonyme mongol à l'époque pré-Činggisqanide (XIIe s.). Étude d'ethnologie politique du nomadisme.' *Études Mongoles* 10: 59–89.

Genç, Reşit. 1981. *Karahanlı Devleti Teşkilatı*. Istanbul: Kültür Bakanlığı.

Geng, Shimin and George Hamilton. 1981. 'L'inscription ouïgoure de la stèle commémorative des Iduq Qut de Qočo.' *Turcica* 13: 10–54.

Geraklitov, A. 1926. 'Saratovskaia Mordva (K istorii mordovskoi kolonizatsii v Saratovskom krae).' *Izvestiia Kraevedcheskogo instituta izucheniia iuzhno-volzhskoi oblasti* 1: 135–55.

Ghaffārī, Aḥmad b. Muḥammad b. ʿAbd al-Ghaffār. 1964. *Ta'rīkh-i jahān arā*, ed. Ḥ. Nirāqī. Tehran: Kitābfurūshī-i Ḥāfiẓ. 1343 / 1964.

Gilyazov, Iskander. 1996. 'Die Islampolitik von Staat und Kirche im Wolga-Ural-Gebiet und der Batiršah-Aufstand von 1755', in Kemper *et al.*, 1996: 69–89.

Gökbel. Ahmet. 2000. *Kıpçak Türkleri*. Istanbul: Ötüken.

Golden, Peter B. 1982. 'Imperial Ideology and the Sources of Political Unity amongst the Pre-Činggisid Nomads of Western Eurasia.' *AEMAe* 2: 37–76; reprinted in Golden, 2003.

1987–91. 'Nomads and their Sedentary Neighbors in pre-Činggisid Western Eurasia.' *AEMAe* 7: 41–81.

1990. 'The Karakhanids and Early Islam', in *CHEIA*: 343–70.

1991. 'The Qıpčaqs of Medieval Eurasia: An Example of Stateless Adaptation on the Steppe', in Seaman and Marks, 1991: 132–57; reprinted in Golden, 2003.

1992a. *An Introduction to the History of the Turkic Peoples*. Turcologica, 9. Wiesbaden: Otto Harrassowitz.

1992b. 'The *Codex Cumanicus*', in *Monuments of Central Asia*, ed. Hasan B. Paksoy. Istanbul: Isis Press: 33–63.

1995–7. 'Cumanica IV: The Cumano-Qıpčaq Clans and Tribes.' *AEMAe* 9: 99–122; reprinted Golden, 2003.

2000. '"I Will Give the People unto Thee": The Činggisid Conquests and their Aftermath in the Turkic World.' *JRAS*, third series, 10/1: 21–41.

2001. *Ethnicity and State Formation in Pre-Činggisid Turkic Eurasia*, The Central Eurasian Studies Lectures, 1. Bloomington, Ind.: Department of Central Eurasian Studies, Indiana University.

2003. *Nomads and their Neighbours in the Russian Steppe: Turks, Khazars and Qipchaqs*. Aldershot: Variorum Reprints.

'Sibīr', *EI*², IX: 531–3.

'Tatar', *EI*², X: 370–1.

Golombek, Lisa and Maria Subtelny. 1992. eds. *Timurid Art and Culture*. Leiden: Brill.

Golombek, Lisa and Donald Wilber. 1988. *The Timurid Architecture of Iran and Turan*. Princeton: Princeton University Press.

Gombos, A. F. 1937–43. ed. *Catalogus fontium historiae Hungaricae aevo ducum et regum ex stirpe Arpad descendentium ab anno Christi DCCC usque ad annum MCCCI*, I–IV. Budapest: Szt. István Társulat.

Goncharov, E. Iu. 2003. '"...stradaet sil'noi netochnost'iu" (demonstratsiia nauchnykh fokusov s posleduiushchim ikh razoblacheniem).' *Nizhnevolzhskii Arkheologicheskii Vestnik* 6: 318–28.

González de Clavijo, Ruy. 1928. *Embassy to Tamerlane 1403–1406*, trans. Guy Le Strange. London: Routledge.

Graff, David A. 2002. *Medieval Chinese Warfare, 300–900*. London and New York: Routledge.

Grekov, Boris D. and Aleksandr Iu. Iakubovskii. 1950, 1998. *Zolotaia Orda i ee padenie*. Moscow and Leningrad: Izdatel'stvo Akademii Nauk; new edition with different pagination: Moscow: Bogorodskii Pechatnik.

Grigor of Akanc (Akner), see Blake and Frye, 1949.

Grigor'ev, Arkadii P. 1981. 'Ofitsial'nyi iazyk Zolotoi Ordy XIII–XIV vv.' *Tiurkologicheskii Sbornik 1977*. Moscow: Nauka: 81–9.

1983. 'Zolotoordynskie khany 60–70-kh godov XIV v.: khronologiia pravleniia.' *Istoriografiia i istochnikovedenie istorii stran Azii i Afriki* 7. St. Petersburg: Izdatel'stvo Sankt-Peterburgskogo Universiteta: 9–54.

2004. *Sbornik khanskikh iarlykov russkim mitropolitam*. St. Petersburg: Izdatel'stvo Sankt-Peterburgskogo Universiteta.

Grigor'ev, Arkadii P. and Vadim P. Grigor'ev. 2002. *Kollektsiia zolotoordynskikh dokumentov XIV veka iz Venetsii*. St. Petersburg: Izdatel'stvo Sankt Peterburgskogo Universiteta.

Gross, Jo-Ann. 1988. 'The Economic Status of a Sufi Shaykh: A Matter of Conflict and Perception.' *Iranian Studies* 21/1–2: 84–104.

2001. 'Naqshbandī Appeals to the Herat Court: A Preliminary Study of Trade and Property Issues', in DeWeese, 2001: 113–28.

Grupper, Samuel. 1984. 'Manchu Patronage and Tibetan Buddhism During the First Half of the Ch'ing Dynasty: A Review Article.' *The Journal of the Tibet Society* 4: 47–75.

1992–4. 'A Barulas Family Narrative in the *Yuan Shih*: Some Neglected Prosopographical and Institutional Sources on Timurid Origins.' *AEMAe* 8: 11–97.

Gulbadan, Begim. 1972. *The History of Humūyūn (Humāyūn Nāma)*, ed. trans. Annette S. Beveridge. Delhi: Idārah-i Adabiyat, reprint.

Haenisch, Erich. 1943. *Die Kulturpolitik des mongolischen Weltreichs*, Preussische Akademie der Wissenschaften, Vorträge und Schriften, 17. Berlin: Walter de Gruyter.

1969. trans. *Zum Untergang zweier Reiche: Augenzeugen aus den Jahren 1232–33 und 1368–70*. Abhandlungen für die Kunde des Morgenlandes, 38/4. Wiesbaden: Franz Steiner.

Ḥāfiẓ-i Abrū. 1938. *Dhayl-i Jāmiʿ al-tawārīkh-i Rashīdī*. Tehran: Chāpkhāna-i ʿilmī, 1317/1938.

1970. *Jughrāfiyā-yi Ḥāfiẓ-i Abrū: qismat-i rubʿi Khurāsān*, ed. Māyil Haravī. Tehran: Bunyād-i Farhang-i Irān.

1993. *Zubdat al-tawārīkh*, ed. Sayyid Kamāl Ḥājj Sayyid Jawādī. Tehran: Nashr-i Nay, 1372/1993. 2 vols.

1997–9. *Jughrāfiyā-i Ḥāfiẓ-i Abrū*, ed. Ṣādiq Sajjādī. Tehran: Bunyād-i Daftar-i Nashr-i Mirāth-i Maktūb, 1375–8/1997–9. 3 vols.

Ḥāfiẓ-i Tanīsh. 1983. *Sharaf-nāma-i shāhī (ʿAbd Allāh-nāma)*, partially ed. and trans. M. A. Salakhetdinova, 2 vols. (of four projected), Moscow: Nauka; British Library (India Office Library Collection), MS no. 574.

Hagen, Arne. 2003. *The Establishment of National Republics in Soviet Central Asia*. Harlow, London and New York: Longman.

Haider, Mansura. 1976. 'The Sovereign in the Timurid State.' *Turcica* 8/2: 61–82.

Halasi-Kun, Tibor. 1985 [1987]. 'Kipchak Philology X: The *At-Tuḥfah* and its Author.' *AEMAe* 5: 167–78.

1986 [1988]. 'Some Thoughts on the Hungarian–Turkish Affinity.' *AEMAe* 6: 31–9.

Halman. Talât. 2006. ed. *Türk Edebiyatı Tarihi*. 2nd edn. Istanbul: T. C. Kültür ve Turizm Bakanlığı Yayınları.

2007. ed. *Türk Edebiyatı Tarihi*. 2nd edn. Istanbul: T. C. Kültür ve Turizm Bakanlığı Yayınları. 4 vols.

Halperin, Charles J. 1985. *Russia and the Golden Horde: The Mongol Impact on Medieval Russian History*. Bloomington, Ind.: Indiana University Press.

1986. *The Tatar Yoke*. Columbus, OH: Slavica Publishers, Inc.

Hambis, Louis. 1945. *Le chapitre CVII du Yuan Che*. Supplement to *T'oung Pao*, 38. Leiden: Brill.

1954. *Le chapitre CVIII du Yuan Che*. Leiden: Brill.

1970. 'L'histoire des Mongols avant Gengis-khan d'après les sources chinoises et mongoles, et la documentation conservé par Rašīdu'd-Dīn.' *CAJ* 14: 125–33.

von Hammer-Purgstall, Joseph. 1840, *Geschichte der Goldenen Horde in Kiptschak, das ist: der Mongolen in Russland*. Pesth: C. A. Hartleben's Verlag.

Han, Rulin. 1985. ed. *Yuan shi*. Beijing: Zhongguo dabaike quanshu chubanshe.

1986. ed. *Yuan chao shi*. Beijing: Renmin chubanshe. 2 vols.
Hansen, Valerie. 2005. 'The Impact of the Silk Road Trade on a Local Community: The Turfan Oasis, 500–800', in *Les Sogdiens en Chine*, ed. Étienne De la Vaissière. Paris: École française d'Extrême-Orient: 283–310.
Harawī, Sayf b. Muḥammad b. Yaʿqūb. 1944. *Taʾrīkh-nāmah-i Harāt*, ed. Muḥammad Z. al-Ṣiddiqī. Calcutta: The Baptist Mission Press and the Imperial Library.
Hauer, Erich (Trans). 1926. *Huang-tsing k'ai-kuo fang-lüeh. Die Gründung des mandschurischen Kaiserreiches*. Berlin and Leipzig: Walter de Gruyter.
Haw, Stephen G. 2006. *Marco Polo's China: A Venetian in the Realm of Khubilai Khan*. London and New York: Routledge.
Hawting, Gerald R. 2005. ed. *Muslims, Mongols and Crusaders*. London: Routledge Curzon.
Hayashi, Toshio. 1990. 'The Development of a Nomadic Empire: The Case of the Ancient Turks (Tuque).' *Bulletin of the Ancient Orient Museum* (Tokyo) 11: 164–84.
Haydar, Mirza. 1898. *The Tarikh-i-Rashidi of Mirza Muhammad Haidar, Dughlāt; a history of the Moghuls of Central Asia being the Tarikh-i-Rashidi of Mirza Muhammad Haidar, Dughlāt. An English version edited, with commentary, notes and map by N. Elias. The translation by E. Denison Ross.* London: Curzon Press; reprint New York: Barnes and Noble, 1972.
Hayton, Frère. 1906. *La Flor des estoires de la terre d'Orient*, in Recueil des historiens des croisades, Documents arméniens, II. Paris: L'imprimerie nationale.
He, Tianming. 2003. 'Shilun Yuan chao yu Chahetai, Wokuotai hanguo de guanxi.' *Heilongjiang minzu congkan* 72: 83–8.
Heissig, Walter. 1953, 1954. *Neyici Toyin. Das Leben eines lamaistischen Mönches (1557–1653)*, Sinologica 3 (1953), 4 (1954).
1976. '"Die Čaghadai "Bilig" und ihre Historizitat"', in *Tractata Altaica*, ed. Walter Heissig *et al.* Wiesbaden: Harrassowitz: 277–90.
1979. *Die Zeit des letzten mongolischen Grosskhans Ligdan (1604–1634)*. Rheinisch-Westfälische Akademie der Wissenschaften, Vorträge G 235. Opladen: Westdeutscher Verlag.
Heller, Michel. 1997. *Histoire de la Russie et de son Empire*. Paris: Flammarion.
He-ning. 1966. ed. *Huijiang tongzhi* [Comprehensive Gazetteer of Altishahr], original 1804; reprint Zhongguo bianjiang congshu, 67. Taibei: Wenhai chuban.
Henthorn, William Ellsworth. 1963. *Korea: The Mongol invasions*. Leiden: Brill.
Het'um (Hayton / Hetoum). 1906. 'La Flor des estories de la Terre d'Orient', in *Receuil des historiens des Croisades: Documents Armeniens*. Paris: Imprimerie nationale, 2: 111–253.
Heuschert, Dorothea. 1998. 'Legal Pluralism in the Qing Empire: Legislation for the Mongols.' *International History Review* 20/2: 310–24.
Hevia, James. 1993. 'Lamas, Emperors, and Rituals: Political Implications in Qing Imperial Ceremonies.' *Journal of the International Association of Buddhist Studies* 16/2: 243–78.
Holcombe, Charles. 2001. *The Genesis of East Asia, 221 B.C.–A.D. 907*. Honolulu: University of Hawai'i Press.
Honda, M. 1958. 'On the Genealogy of the Early Northern Yüan.' *Ural-altaische Jahrbücher* 30/3–4: 232–48.
Hong, Jun. 1990. *Yuan shi yiwen zhengbu jiaozhu*, ed. Tian Hu. Shijiazhuang: Hebei renmin chubanshe.
Hori, Sunao. 1997. 'Jūhachi-nijū seiki uiguru joku jinkō shiron.' *Shirin* 60/4: 111–28.
Hosking, Geoffrey. 1997. *Russia: People and Empire, 1552–1917*. London: Harper Collins.

Howorth, Henry H. 1880. *History of the Mongols, Part II The So-called Tartars of Russia and Central Asia, Division I*. London: Longman, Green & Co.

Hsiao Ch'i-Ch'ing. 1978. *The Military Establishment of the Yüan Dynasty*. Cambridge, Mass.: Harvard University Press.

1993. 'Bayan', in de Rachewiltz *et al.*: 564–607.

1994. 'Mid-Yuan Politics', in *CHChina*, VI: 490–560.

Hua Li. 1994. *Qingdai Xinjiang nongye kaifa shi*. Bianjiang shidi congshu, 5. Harbin: Heilongjian jiaoyu chubanshe.

Huang, H. T. 2000. 'Fermentations and Food Sciences', in *Science and Civilization in China, 6: Biology and Biological Technology*, ed. Joseph Needham *et al.* Cambridge: Cambridge University Press, 1954– .

Song Xian, ed. 2000. *Huihui yaofang kaoshi*. Zhongwai jiaotong shiji congkan, 17. Beijing: Zhonghua shuju. 2 vols.

Ḥudūd al-ʿālam. 1970. *The Regions of the World*, trans. Vladimir F. Minorsky. Second rev. edn, ed. C. Edmund Bosworth. E. J. W. Gibb Memorial New Series, 11. London: Luzac.

Ḥudūd al-ʿālam. 1962. ed. Minūchihr Sutūdeh. Tehrān: Danishgāh-i Tehrān, 1340/ 1962.

Ḥusayn b. Amīrkhān. 1883. *Tawārīkh-i Būlgharīya*. Kazan: Viacheslav.

Huttenbach, Henry J. 1988. 'Muscovy's Penetration of Siberia: The Colonization Process 1555–1689', in *Russian Colonial Expansion to 1917*, ed. Michael Rywkin. London and New York: Mansell: 70–102.

Hyer, Paul. 1982. 'An Historical Sketch of Köke-Khota City.' *Central Asiatic Journal* 26: 54–61.

Iakovlev, I. A. 1916. *Zasechnaia cherta Moskovskogo gosudarstva v XVII veke*. Moscow: Tipografiia I. Lisnera.

Ibn ʿArabshāh, Aḥmad. 1936. *Tamerlane or Timur, the Great Amir*, trans. J. H. Sanders. London: Luzac.

Ibn al-Athīr, see List of Abbreviations

Ibn Baṭṭūṭa, see List of Abbreviations

Ibn al-Dawādāri, Abū Bakr b. ʿAbdallāh. 1960–94. *Kanz al-durar wa-jamīʿ al ghurar. Die Chronik des Ibn ad-Dawādarī*, see individual volumes:

1971. Vol. VIII: *al-Durra al-kanziyya fī akhbār al-dawla al-turkiyya* [*Der Bericht über die frühen Mamluken*], ed. Ulrich Haarmann. Quellen zur Geschichte des islamischen Ägyptens. Freiburg and Cairo: Maṭbaʿat ʿIsā al-bābī.

1960. Vol. IX: *al-Durr al-fākhir fī sīrat al-malik al nāṣir* [*Der Bericht über den Sultan al-Malik an-Nāṣir Muḥammad ibn Qalāʾūn*], ed. Hans R. Roemer. Freiburg and Cairo: Maṭbaʿat ʿIsā al-bābī.

Ibn al-Furāt, Nāṣir al-Dīn. 1942. *Taʾrīkh al-duwal waʾl-mulūk*. vol. VII, ed. Costi K. Zurayk. Beirut: al-Maṭbaʿa al-amīrikāniyya.

Ibn al-Fuwaṭī, Kamāl al-Dīn Abūʾl-Faḍl. 1962–5. *Talkhīṣ majmaʿ al-ādāb fī muʿjam al-alqāb*, ed. Muṣṭafā Jawwād. Damascus: Wizārat al-thaqāfa wa'l-irshād al-qawmī. 3 vols.

1995. *Majmaʿ al-ādāb fī muʿjam al-alqāb*, ed. Muḥammad al-Kāẓim. Tehran: Vizārat-i Farhang va Irshād-i Islāmī, 1415/1374/1995.

Ibn Ḥajar al-ʿAsqalānī. 1966. *Al-Durar al-kāmina*. Cairo: Dār al-kutub al-ḥadītha.

Ibn Khaldūn, see List of Abbreviations

Ibn Taghrībirdī, Abuʾl-Maḥāsin Yūsuf. 1929–72. *Al-Nujūm al-zāhira fī mulūk Miṣr waʾl-Qāhira*. Cairo: al-Muʾasasa al-Miṣriyya al-ʿĀmma lil-Ṭaʾlīf waʾl-Ṭibāʿah waʾl-Nashr. 16 vols. (noted by volume).

1942. *Al-Nujūm al-zāhira fī mulūk Miṣr wa'l-Qāhira* vol. IX. Cairo: Dār al-kutub al-Miṣriyya.

Ibragimov, S. K. *et al.* 1969. eds. *Materialy po istorii kazakhskikh khanstv XV–XVIII vekov (izvlecheniia iz persidskikh i tiurkskikh sochinenii)*, comp. by S. K. Ibragimov, N. N. Mingulov, K. A. Pishchulina and V. P. Iudin. Alma-Ata: Akademiia Nauk Kazakhskoi SSR, Institut istorii, arkheologii i etnografii.

Inal, Günar. 1976. 'Artistic Relationship between the Far and Near East as Reflected in the Miniatures of the *Jāmiʿ al-Tavārīkh*.' *Kunst des Orients* 10: 108–43.

Inalcik, H. 1979–80. 'The Khan and the Tribal Aristocracy: The Crimean Khanate under Sahib Giray I.' *HUS* 3–4/1: 445–66.

Iṣfakhānī, Fazlallākh ibn Rūzbikhān. 1976. *Mikhmān-nāme-ii Bukhārā (Zapiski bukharskogo gostia)*, trans. R. P. Dzhalilova. Moscow: Izdatel'stvo 'Nauka', Glavnaia redaktsiia vostochnoi literatury.

Isfizārī, Muʿīn al-Dīn, Muḥammad Zamchī. 1959–60. *Rauzāt al-jannāt fī auṣāf madināt Harāt 897–899 a.h.* [1491–93], ed. Sayyid Muḥammad Kāzim Imām. Tehran: Tehran University. 2 vols.

Isin, A. 2004. *Kazakhskoe khanstvo i Nogaiskaia Orda vo vtoroi polovine XV–XVI v.* Almaty: n.p.

Iskandar Beg Munshi. 1978–86. *Tārīkh-i ʿālam-ārā-yi ʿAbbāsī*, ed. Īraj Afshār. [Tehran], n.d. 2 vols.; trans. Roger M. Savory as *History of Shah ʿAbbas the Great*. Boulder, Colo.: Westview Press. 3 vols. including separate index vol.

Iskhakov, D. M. 1997. *Seidy v pozdnezolotoordynskikh tatarskikh gosudarstvakh*. Kazan: Iman.

2002. 'O rodoslovnoi khana Ulug-Mukhammeda', in *Tiurkologicheskii sbornik 2001: Zolotaia Orda i ee nasledie*. Moscow: Vostochnaia Literatura: 63–74.

2004. *Tiurko-tatarskie gosudarstva XV–XVI vv*. Kazan: Institut Istorii imeni Merdzhani.

2006. *Vvedenie v istoriiu Sibirskogo khanstva*. Kazan: Institut Istorii imeni Merdzhani.

Islam, Riazul. 1982. ed. *Calendar of Documents on Indo-Persian Relations*, vol. II. Karachi: Institute of Central and West Asian Studies.

Istoriia Chuvashskoi ASSR. 1966. Vol. I: *S drevneishikh vremen do Velikoi Oktiabr'skoi sotsialisticheskoi revoliutsii*. Cheboksary: Chuvashskoe knizhnoe izdatel'stvo.

Istoriia Kazakhstana III. 2000. Almaty: Ata-Mura.

Istoriia Mordovskoi ASSR. 1981. Vol. I: *S drevneishikh vremen do Velikoi Oktiabr'skoi sotsialisticheskoi revoliutsii*. Saransk: Mordovskoe knizhnoe izdatel'stvo.

Istoriia Sibiri s drevneishikh vremen do nashikh dnei. 1968. Vol. III: *Sibir' v sostave feodal'noi Rossii*. Leningrad: Nauka.

Istoriia Tatarskoi ASSR. 1955. Vol. I. Kazan: Tatknigoizdat.

Iudin, Veniamin P. 1965. 'O rodoplemennom sostave mogulov Mogulistana i Mogulii i ikh etnograficheskikh sviaziakh s kazakhskimi i drugimi sosednimi narodami.' *Izvestiia Akademii Nauk Kazakhskoi SSR, seriia obshchestvennykh nauk* 3: 52–65.

1983. 'Ordy: belaia, siniaia, seraia, zolotaia', in *Kazakhstan, Sredniaia Aziia i Tsentral'naia Aziia v XVI–XVII vv.*, ed. B. A. Tulepbaev. Alma-Ata: Nauka: 106–65. Reprinted with different pagination in Iudin, Baranova and Abuseitova, 1992: 14–56.

2001a. *Tsentral'naia Aziia v XIV–XVIII vekakh glazami vostokoveda*. Almaty: Daik Press.

2001b. Review of B. A. Akhmedov, *Gosudarstvo kochevykh uzbekov*, in Iudin, 2001a: 261–70.

2001c. 'Istoriograficheskaia kontseptsiia avtora "Tarikh-i Rashidi"', in Iudin, 2001a: 179–221.

2001d. 'K étimologii étnonima *kazakh (qazaq)*', in Iudin, 2001a: 137–66.

Iudin, Veniamin P., Iu. G. Baranova and Meruart Kh. Abuseitova. 1992. Eds. *Utemish-hadzhi, Chingiz-name.* Alma-Ata: Gylym.

Ivanics, Mária and Mirkasym A. Usmanov. 2002. *Das Buch der Dschingis-Legende (Däftär-i Čingiz-nāmä).* I. Szeged: Department of Altaic Studies, University of Szeged.

Ivanov, N. S. 1895. *Dzhanger Khan Vnutrennei Kirgizskoi Ordy.* Astrakhan: Rosliakov.

Ivanov, P. P. 1954. 'Issledovanie', in *Khoziaistvo Dzhuibarskikh Sheikhov*. Moscow: Izdatel'stvo Akademii Nauk SSSR: 7–83.

Ivanova, Margarita G. 1994. *Istoki udmurtskogo naroda.* Izhevsk: Udmurtiia.

Izmailov, Iskander. 1992. 'Idegei', *Tatarstan* 1: 51–9; 2: 63–71.

Jackson, Peter. 1975. 'The Mongols and the Delhi Sultanate in the Reign of Muhammad Tughluq (1325–1351).' *CAJ* 19: 118–57.

1978. 'The Dissolution of the Mongol Empire.' *CAJ* 22: 186–244.

1992. 'Chaghatayid Dynasty.' *Encyclopedia Iranica* V: 343–7.

1999a. *The Delhi Sultanate: A Political and Military History.* Cambridge: Cambridge University Press.

1999b. 'From *Ulus* to Khanate: The Making of the Mongol States, *c.*1220–*c.*1290', in Amitai-Preiss and Morgan, 1999: 12–38.

2005a. *The Mongols and the West, 1221–1410.* Longman's Medieval World Series. Harlow, London and New York: Pearson, Longman Press.

2005b. 'The Mongols and the Faith of the Conquered', in Amitai-Preiss and Biran, 2005: 245–90.

2006. 'World-conquest and Local Accommodation: Threat and Blandishment in Mongol Diplomacy', in *History and Historiography of Post-Mongol Central Asia and the Middle East: Studies in Honor of John E. Woods*, ed. Judith Pfeiffer and Sholeh A. Quinn. Wiesbaden: Harrassowitz: 3–22.

Jagchid, Sechin. 1978. 'Traditional Mongolian Attitudes and Values as Seen in the *Secret History of the Mongols* and the *Altan Tobchi*', in *Aspects of Altaic Civilization*, ed. D. Sinor, II. Indiana University, Uralic and Altaic Series, 134. Bloomington, Ind.: Asian Studies Research Institute: 89–114; reprinted in Jagchid, 1988: 52–66.

1981. 'The Kitans and their Cities.' *CAJ*, 25/1–2: 70–88; reprinted in Jagchid, 1988: 21–33.

1988. *Essays in Mongolian Studies.* Provo, UT: Brigham Young University Press.

Jagchid, Sechin and Charles R. Bawden. 1965. 'Some Notes on the Horse Policy of the Yuan Dynasty.' *CAJ* 10: 247–68.

Jahn, Karl. 1956a. 'Kamālashri – Rashīd al-Dīn's Life and Teaching of Buddha.' *CAJ* 2: 81–128.

1956b. 'A Note on Kashmir and the Mongols.' *CAJ* 2: 176–80.

1970. 'Some Ideas of Rashīd al-Dīn on Chinese Culture.' *CAJ* 14: 134–47.

Janhunen, Juha. 1996. *An Ethnic History of Manchuria.* Helsinki: Finno-Ugrian Society.

2003a. ed. *The Mongolic Languages.* London and New York: Routledge.

2003b. 'Para-Mongolic', in Janhunen, 2003a: 391–402.

Jansen, Johannes J. G. 1986. *The Neglected Duty: The Creed of Sadat's Assassins and Islamic Resurgence in the Middle East.* New York: Macmillan.

Jaubert, Amédée M. 1833. ed. 'Precis de l'histoire des khans de Crimée, depuis l'an 880 jusqu'à l'an 1198 de l'hégire.' *Journal asiatique,* second series, 12: 341–80.

al-Jazarī, Shamsh al-Dīn Abū ʿUbaydallāh Muḥammad b. Ibrāhīm. 1998. *Taʾrīkh ḥawādith al-zamān wa-anbāʾihā wa-wafayāt al-akābir waʾl-aʿyān min abnāʾihā*, ed. ʿUmar A. Tadmūrī. Beirut and Saida: al-Maṭbaʿa al-baṣariyya. 2 vols.

Jenkinson, Anthony. 1886. *Early Voyages to Russia and Persia by Anthony Jenkinson and other Englishmen with some account of the first intercourse of the English with Russia and Central Asia by way of the Caspian Sea*, ed. E. Delmar Morgan and C. H. Coote. London: Hakluyt Society.

Jing shi dadian, zhan chi. 1960. in *Yongle da dian*, chs. 19420–1, facs. edn. Beijing: Zhonghua shuju.

al-Juvainī, see List of Abbreviations, English trans.

Jūzjānī, see List of Abbreviations

Kabuzan, Vladimir M. 1971. *Izmeneniia v razmeshchenii naseleniia Rossii v XVIII-pervoi polovine XIX v. po materialam revizii*. Moscow: Nauka.

Kadyrbaev, Aleksandr Sh. 1990. *Tiurki i irantsy v Kitae i Tsentral'noi Azii XIII–XIV vv.* Alma-Ata: Gylym.

1993. *Ocherki istorii srednevekovykh uighurov, dzhalairov, naimanov i kireitov.* Almaty: Rawan.

Kafalı, Mustafa. 1976. *Altın Orda Hanlığının kuruluş ve yükseliş devirleri*. İstanbul: İstanbul Üniversitesi Edebiyat Fakültesi.

2002. 'The Chagatay Khanate', in *The Turks*, Vol. II, ed. Hasan C. Güzel *et al.* Ankara: Yeni Türkiye: 805–15.

Kafesoğlu, İbrahim. 1956. *Harezmşahlar Devleti Tarihi*. Ankara: Türk Tarih Kurumu.

Kahar, Barat and Yingsheng Liu. 1984. 'Yiduhu Gaochang wang shixun bei Huihu bei wen zhi jiaokan yu yanjiu [Regarding the Uighur Inscription of the Stele of the Family Achievements of the Iduq Qut Gaochang Wang]', *Yuan shi ji beifang minzu shi yanjiu jikan* 8: 57–106.

Kakhovskii, Vasilii F. 2003. *Proiskhozhdenie chuvashskogo naroda*. Cheboksary: Chuvashskoe Knizhnoe Izdatel'stvo.

Kämpfer, Frank. 1969. *Die Eroberung von Kasan 1552 als Gegenstand der zeitgenössischen russischen Historiographie*. Forschungen zur osteuropäischen Geschichte, 14. Wiesbaden: Harrassowitz.

Kantakuzenos, Johannes. 1982, 1986. *Geschichte*, I–II, trans. G. Fatouros and T. Krischer, in Bibliothek der Griechischen Literatur 17, 21. Stuttgart: T. Anton Hiersemann.

Kappeler, Andreas. 1976. 'L'éthnogénèse des peuples de la moyenne Volga (Tatars, Tchouvaches, Mordves, Maris, Oudmourtes) dans les recherches soviétiques.' *Cahiers du monde russe et soviétique* 17 / 2–3: 311–34.

1982. *Russlands erste Nationalitäten. Das Zarenreich und die Völker der Mittleren Wolga vom 16. bis 19. Jahrhundert*. Cologne: Böhlau.

1992. *Russland als Vielvölkerreich. Entstehung, Geschichte, Zerfall*. Munich: Beck.

2003. 'Formirovanie Rossiiskoi imperii v 15 – nachale 18 veka. Nasledstvo Rusi, Vizantii i Ordy', in *Rossiiskaia imperiia v sravnitel'noi perspecktive*. Moscow: Novoe izdatel'stvo: 94–112.

Karaev, Omurkul. 1995. *Chagataiskii ulus. Gosudarstvo Khaidu. Mogulistan*. Bishkek: Muras.

Karmysheva, B. Kh. 1976. *Ocherki etnicheskoi istorii iuzhnykh raionov Tadzhikistana i Uzbekistana (po étnograficheskim dannym).* Moscow: Nauka.

Karryev, A., V. G. Moshkova, A. N. Nasonov and A. Iu. Iakubovskii. 1954. *Ocherki iz istorii turkmenskogo naroda i Turkmenistana v VIII–XIX vv.* Ashkhabad: Akademiia nauk Turkmenskoi SSR, Institut istorii, arkheologii i etnografii.

Karypkulov, Amanbek K. *et al.* 1984–5. eds. *Istoriia Kirgizskoi SSR.* Frunze: Kyrgyzstan. 5 vols.

al-Kāšγarī, Maḥmūd, see List of Abbreviations

Kasymbaev, Zh. K. 1990. *Goroda vostochnogo Kazakhstana v 1861–1917 gg.* Alma-Ata: Nauka.

Kasymbaev, Zh. K. and I. Agubaev. 1998. *Istoriia Akmoly.* Almaty: Zheti Zharghï.

Kataoka Kazutada. 1991. *Shinchō Shinkyō tōji kenkyū* . Tokyo: Yû San Kaku.

Kato, Kazuhide. 1991. 'Kebek and Yasawur: The Establishment of the Chaghatai Khanate.' *Memoirs of the Research Department of the Toyo Bunko* 49: 97–118.

Kauz, Ralph. 2001. 'Hormuz in Yuan and Ming Sources.' *Bulletin de l'École française d'Extrême-Orient* 88: 28–75.

2005. *Politik und Handel zwischen Ming und Timuriden: China, Iran und Zentralasien im Spätmittelalter.* Wiesbaden: Reichert.

Kazakov, B. A. 1987. *Dokumental'nye pamiatniki Srednei Azii.* Tashkent: 'Uzbekistan'.

Ke, Shaomin. 1979. *Xin Yuan shi* [The New Official History of the Yuan]. Beijing: Zhongguo shudian chufan.

Keenan, Edward L. 1967. 'Muscovy and Kazan: Some Introductory Remarks on the Patterns of Steppe Diplomacy.' *SR* 26/4: 548–58.

Keep, John. 1985. *Soldiers of the Tsar: Army and Society in Russia, 1472–1874.* Oxford: Clarendon Press.

Kemper, Michael. 1998. *Sufis und Gelehrte in Tatarien und Baschkirien, 1789–1889. Der islamische Diskurs unter russischer Herrschaft.* Berlin: Klaus Schwarz.

Kemper, Michael, Anke von Kügelgen and Dmitriy Yermakov. 1996. eds. *Muslim Culture in Russia and Central Asia From the 18th to the Early 20th Centuries,* Vol. I. Berlin: Klaus Schwarz.

Kempiners, Russell G. 1985. 'The Struggle for Khurāsān: Aspects of Political, Military and Socio-economic Interaction in the Early 8th/14th Century', Ph.D. diss., University of Chicago.

1988. 'Vaṣṣāf's *Tajziyat al-amṣār wa tazjiyat al- aʿṣār* as a Source for the History of the Chaghadayid Khanate.' *Journal of Asian History* 22: 160–86.

Ken'ichi Isogai. 1997. 'Yasa and Shari'a in Early 16th century Central Asia.' *Cahiers d'Asie centrale* 3–4 (L'Héritage timouride: Iran-Asie centrale Ince XVe–XVIIIe siècles): 91–103.

Keppen, Petr. 1869. *Khronologicheskii ukazatel' materialov dlia istorii inorodtsev evropeiskoi Rossii.* St. Petersburg: Imperskaia akademiia nauk.

Kern, A. 1938. 'Der "Libellus de Notitia Orbis".' Archivum *Fratrum Praedicatorum* 8: 82–123.

Kervran, Monique. 2002 'Un monument baroque dans les steppes du Kazakhstan: Le tombeau d'Orkina Khatun, princesse Chaghatay?' *Ars Asiatique* 57: 5–32.

Khafizov, M. Z. 1998. *Nizhegorodskie tatary.* Nizhnii Novgorod: Nizhpoligraf.

Khalfin, N. A. 1975. *Rossiia i Bukharskii emirat na Zapadnom Pamire (konets XIX – nachalo XX v.).* Moscow: Nauka.

Khalidov, A. B. and Maria E. Subtelny. 1995. 'The Curriculum of Islamic Higher Learning in Timurid Iran in the Light of the Sunni Revival Under Shāh-Rukh.' *JAOS* 115/2: 210–36.

Khanykov, Ia. V. 1847. 'Ocherk Vnutrennei kirgizskoi ordy v 1841 godu.' *Zapiski Russkago Geograficheskago Obshchestva*: 27–60.

Khazanov, Anatolii (Anatoly) M. 1975. *Sotsial'naia istoriia skifov*. Moscow: Nauka.

1983. 'The Early State Among the Eurasian Nomads.' *Oikumene* 4: 269–83.

1984, 1994. *Nomads and the Outside World*, trans. J. Crookenden. Cambridge: Cambridge University Press, 1984; 2nd edn. Madison, Wisc.: University of Wisconsin Press, 1994.

2003. 'Nomads of the Eurasian Steppes in Historical Retrospective', in *Nomadic Pathways in Social Evolution*, ed. N. N. Kradin *et al.* Moscow: Center for Civilizational and Regional Studies: 25–49.

Khodarkovsky, Michael. 1997. 'Ignoble Savages and Unfaithful Subjects: Constructing Non-Christian Identities in Early Modern Russia', in *Russia's Orient: Imperial Borderlands and Peoples, 1700–1917*, ed. D. Brower and E. Lazzerini. Bloomington, Ind.: Indiana University Press: 8–32.

2002. *Russia's Steppe Frontier: The Making of a Colonial Empire, 1500–1800*. Bloomington, Ind.: Indiana University Press.

Khudiakov, M. G. 1991. *Ocherki po istorii Kazanskogo khanstva*. 3rd edn. Kazan, 1923, reprint Moscow: Insan.

Khunjī (Iṣfahānī), Fazlullāh ibn Rūzbihān. 1976. *Mihmān-nāma-i Bukhārā*, ed. Manuchihr Sutūdeh. Tehran: BTNK.

1983. *Sulūk al-mulūk*. Tehran: Intishārāt-i Khwārazmī.

Khuzin. Faiaz Sh. 1997. *Volzhskaia Bulgariia v domongol'skoe vremia (X- nachalo XIII vekov)*. Kazan': Fest.

Khvāndamīr, Ghiyāth al-Dīn b. Humām al-Dīn. 1954. *Ḥabīb al-siyar fī akhbār afrād al-bashar.* Tehran: 4 vols.

Khwāfī, see Faṣīḥ Khwāfī.

Khwāja Samandar Termezi (Tirmidhī). 1971. *Dastūr al-mulūk (Nazidanie gosudariam)*, ed. M. A. Salakhetdinova, Moscow: Nauka.

Khwāndamīr, Ghiyāth al-Dīn. n.d. *Ḥabīb al-siyar fī akhbār afrād al-bashar*. Tehran: Kitābkhāna-i Khayyām. 3 vols. in 4.

Kim, Hodong. 1996. 'Muslim Saints in the 14th to the 16th Centuries of Eastern Turkestan.' *International Journal of Central Asian Studies* 1: 285–322.

1999. 'The Early History of the Moghul Nomads: The Legacy of the Chaghatai Khanate', in Amitai-Preiss and Morgan, 1999: 290–318.

2004. *Holy War in China: The Muslim Rebellion and State in Chinese Central Asia, 1864–1877*. Stanford: Stanford University Press.

Kirakos Ganjakecʿi, *Patmutʿiwn Hayocʿ*. 1986. *Kirakos Ganjakets'i's History of the Armenians*, trans. Robert Bedrosian. New York: Sources of the Armenian Tradition.

Kireev, F. N. 1964–8. ed. *Kazakhsko-russkie otnosheniia* I-II. Alma-Ata: Akademiia Nauk Kazakhskoi SSR.

Kirmānī, Nāṣir al-Dīn Munshī. 1949–50. *Simṭ al-ʿulā li'l-haḍra al-ʿulyā*, ed. Iqbal ʿAbbās. Tehran: AHS, 1328/1949–50.

Kiselev, S. V., *et al.* 1965. *Drevnemongol'skie goroda*. Moscow: Nauka.

Kitapçı, Zekeriya. 2004. *Doğu Türkistan ve Uygur Türkleri Arasında İslāmiyet*. Konya: Yedi Kubbe.

Kljaštornyj, Sergei G. 1992. 'Das Reich der Tataren in der Zeit vor Čingis Khan.' *CAJ* 36 / 1–2: 72–83.

Kliashtornyi, Sergei G. and Tursun I. Sultanov. 1992. *Kazakhstan. Letopis' trekh tysiacheletii*. Alma-Ata: Rauan.

Kliashtornyi, Sergei G. and Dmitrii G. Savinov. 2005. *Stepnye imperii drevnei Evrazii*, 2nd edn. St. Petersburg: Filologicheskii Fakul'tet Sankt Peterburgskogo Gosudarstvennogo Universiteta.

Klein, Wassilios. 2000. *Das nestorianische Christentum an den Handelswegen durch Kyrgyzstan bis zum 14. Jh*. Silk Road Studies, 3. Turnhout: Brepols.

Kluchevski, V. O. 1960. *A History of Russia* I. New York: Russell & Russell.

Kochekaev, B.-A. B. 1988. *Nogaisko-russkie otnosheniia v XV–XVIII vv*. Alma-Ata: Nauka.

Kōdō, Tasaka. 1957. 'An Aspect of Islam[ic] Culture Introduced into China.' *Memoirs of the Research Department of the Toyo Bunko* 16: 103–18.

Kolmaš, Josef. 1994. *The Ambans and Assistant Ambans of Tibet (A Chronological Study)*. Archív orientální Supplementa 7. Prague: The Oriental Institute.

Komaroff, Linda. 1986. 'The Epigraphy of Timurid Coinage: Some Preliminary Remarks.' *American Numismatic Society: Museum Notes*, 31: 207–32.

Kononov, Andrei N., see Abu'l-Ghāzī Bahādur Khān.

Köpeev, Mäshhür-Zhüsip. 2003–7. *Shïgharmalarï* 1–10. Pavlodar: Pavlodar memlekettik universiteti.

Kotchnev, Boris D. 2001. 'La chronologie et la généalogie des Karakhanides du point de vue de la numismatique', in *Études Karakhanides* in *Cahiers d'Asie Centrale* 9: 49–75.

Kotwicz, Władysław. 1950. 'Les Mogols, promoteurs de l'idée de paix universelle au début du XIII siècle.' *Rocznik Orientalistyczny* 16: 428–34.

Kozlov, S. Ia. and L. V. Chizhova. 2003. eds. *Tiurkskie narody Kryma*. Moscow: Nauka.

Kozlova, K. I. 1978. *Ocherki étnicheskoi istorii mariiskogo naroda*. Moscow: Izdatel'stvo Moskovskogo Universiteta.

Kradin, Nikolay. 2002. 'Nomadism and World Systems: Pastoral Societies in Theories of Historical Development.' *Journal of World Systems Research* 8 / 3: 368–88.

Kradin, Nikolay *et al*. 2003. eds. *Nomadic Pathways in Social Evolution*. Moscow: Center for Civilizational and Regional Studies.

Krause, F. E. A. 1922. *Cingis Han. Die Geschichte seines Lebens nach den chinesischen Reichsannalen*. Heidelberg: Carl Winters Universitätsbuchhandlung.

Krawulsky, Dorothea. 1989. *Mongolen und Ilkhâne – Ideologie und Geschichte. 5 Studien*. Beirut: Verlag für Islamische Studien.

Krippes, Karl. 1991. 'Sociolinguistic Notes on the Turcification of the Sogdians.' *CAJ* 35 / 1–2: 67–80.

Kroeber, A. L. 1952. 'The Ancient Oikoumenê as a Historic Culture Aggregate', in his *The Nature of Culture*. Chicago: University of Chicago Press: 383–93.

Kryczyński, S. 2000. *Tatarzy litewscy. Próba monografii historyczno-etnograficznej*. 2nd edn. Gdańsk: Rada Centralna i Oddz. w Gdańsku Związku Tatarów Polskich; 1st edn: Warsaw: Rada Centralnej Związku Kulturalno-Oświatowego Tatarów Rzeczypospolitej Polskiej, 1938.

von Kügelgen, A. 2002. *Die Legitimierung der mittelasiatischen Manggitendynastie in den Werken ihrer Historiker (18.–19. Jahrhundert)*. Istanbul: Ergon Verlag Würzburg.

Kumekov, Bulat E. and A. K. Muminov. 2005. eds. *Istoriia Kazakhstana v arabskikh istochnikakh*, vol. I. Almaty: Daiks Press. Contains reprint of Tizengauzen, 1884.

Kusber, Jan. 1998. 'Um das Erbe der goldenen Horde: Das Khanat von Kazan' zwischen Moskauer Staat und Krimtataren', in *Zwischen Christianisierung und Europäisierung. Beiträge zur Geschichte Osteuropas in Mittelalter und früher Neuzeit. Festschrift für Peter Nitsche zum 65. Geburtstag*, ed. Eckhard Hübner *et al.* Stuttgart: Steiner: 293–312.

Kuun, Géza. 1880. ed. *Codex Cumanicus*. Budapest: Editio Scientiarum Academiae Hungaricae.

Kuzeev, Rail' G. 1960. *Bashkirskie shezhere*. Ufa: Bashkirskoe Knizhnoe Izdatel'stvo.

1974. *Proiskhozhdenie bashkirskogo naroda*. Moscow: Nauka.

1992. *Narody Srednego Povolzh'ia i Iuzhnogo Urala*. Moscow: Nauka.

Kuzeev, Rail' G. and R. V. Ovchinnikov. 1975. eds. *Krest'ianskaia voina 1773–1775 gg. na territorii Bashkirii*. Ufa: Bashkirskoe Knizhnoe Izdatel'stvo.

Kychanov, Evgenii I. 1968. *Ocherk istorii tangutskogo gosudarstva*. Moscow: Nauka.

1980. 'Mongoly v VI-pervoi polovine XII v.' *Dal'nii Vostok i sosednie territorii v srednie veka*. Novosibirsk: Nauka, Sibirskoe Otdelenie: 136–48.

1997. *Kochevye gosudarstva ot gunnov do man'chzhurov*. Moscow: Vostochnaia Literatura RAN.

Kyzlasov, Leonid R. 1984. *Istoriia iuzhnoi Sibiri v srednie veka*. Moscow: Vysshaia Shkola.

Lambton, Ann K. S. 1999. '*The Āthār wa aḥyā*' of Rashīd al-Dīn Faḍl Allāh Hamadānī and His Contribution as an Agronomist, Arboriculturist and Horticulturalist', in Amitai-Preiss and Morgan, 1999: 126–54.

'Tiyūl.' *EI*², X, fasc. 171–2: 550–1.

Lane, Edward W. 1968. *An Arabic–English Lexicon*. London and Edinburgh: Norgate and Williams, 1863–93, reprint: Beirut: Librairie du Liban.

Lane-Poole, Stanley. 1875–91. *Catalogue of Oriental Coins in the British Museum*: III, *Coins of the Turkomans* [1877]; VI, *Coins of the Mongols* [1881]; IX and X, *Additions to the Collections, 1876–1888* [1890–1]. London: British Museum.

Langlois, John D., Jr. 1981. ed. *China Under Mongol Rule*. Princeton: Princeton University Press.

Lantzeff, George V. 1972. *Siberia in the Seventeenth Century: A Study of the Colonial Administration*. New York: Octagon Books.

Lantzeff, George V. and Richard A. Pierce. 1973. *Eastward to Empire: Exploration and Conquest on the Russian Open Frontier, to 1750*, Montreal: McGill-Queen's University Press.

Larner, John. 1999. *Marco Polo and the Discovery of the World*. New Haven and London: Yale University Press.

Lattimore, Owen. 1934. *The Mongols of Manchuria*. New York: The John Day Company.

1940. *The Inner Asian Frontiers of China*. New York: American Geographical Society; reprint, Hong Kong: Oxford University Press, 1988.

Lăzărescu-Zobian, Maria. 1984. 'Cumania as the Name of Thirteenth Century Moldavia and Eastern Wallachia: Some Aspects of Kipchak-Rumanian Relations.' *Journal of Turkish Studies* 8: 265–72.

Lebedev, Vladimir I. 1937. 'Bashkirskoe vosstanie 1705–1711.' *Istoricheskie zapiski* 1: 81–102.

Lemercier-Quelquejay, Chantal. 1967. 'Les missions orthodoxes en pays musulmans de Moyenne et Basse Volga, 1552–1865.' *Cahiers du Monde Russe et Soviétique* 8: 369–403.

Lentz, Thomas W. 1996. 'Memory and Ideology in the Timurid Garden', in *Mughal Gardens*, ed. James Wescoat, Jr., and Joachim Wolschke-Bulmahn. Washington, DC: Dumbarton Oaks: 31–57.

Lentz, Thomas W. and Glenn D. Lowrey. 1989. *Timur and the Princely Vision*. Washington, DC, and Los Angeles: Arthur Sackler Gallery and The Los Angeles County Museum of Art.

Lessing, Ferdinand D. *et al.* 1982. *Mongolian–English Dictionary*, Bloomington, Ind.: The Mongolia Society.

Levi, Scott. 1999. 'India, Russia and the Eighteenth-Century Transformation of the Central Asian Caravan Trade.' *Journal of the Economic and Social History of the Orient* 42/4: 519–48.

Levshin, A. I. 1996. *Opisanie kirgiz-kazach'ikh ili kirgiz-kaisatskikh ord i stepei*. Almaty: Sanat.

Li Baowen. 1997. ed. *Arban doloduɣar jaɣun-u emün-e qaɣas-tu qolbuɣdaqu Mongɣol üsüg-ün bičig debter / Shiqi shiji Menggu wen wenshu dang'an (1600–1650)*. Dongliao: Neimenggu shaonian ertong chubanshe.

Li Wenqi. 2007. 'Qingdai Lifanyuan zhineng de fazhan yu wanshan.' *Wenjiao ziliao* 5: 130–1.

Li, Yixin. 1995, 1996. 'Menggu san da hanguo yisilan jiaohua shulun shang.' *Nanjing gaoshi xuebao* 11/2: 43–8; second Part (xia) 12/2: 38–46.

'Chahatai hanguo de Iselanhua.' *Xibei minzu yanjiu* 23: 56–84.

Li Zhichang. 1983. *Chang Chun xi you ji* In *Wang Guowei yi shu*, ed. Wang Guowei. Shanghai: shanghai guji shudian, vol. XIII (see Waley).

Liao shi, see Wittfogel and Feng, 1949.

Ligeti, Louis [Lajos]. 1972. *Monuments préclassiques XIII et XIV siècles*. Budapest: Akadémiai Kiadó.

Lin Enxian. 1988. *Qingchao zai Xinjiang de Han Hui geli zhengce*. Taibei: Taiwan shangwu yinshu guan.

Lin Yongkuang and Wang Xi. 1991. *Qingdai xibei minzu maoyi shi*. Beijing: Zhongyang minzu xueyuan chubanshe.

Little, Donald P. 1970. *An Introduction to Mamluk Historiography*. Wiesbaden: Franz Steiner Verlag.

Litvinskii, Boris A. 1992. ed. *Vostochnyi Turkestan v drevnosti i rannem srednevekov'e. Étnos, iazyki, religii*. Moscow: Nauka.

Liu Dan. 1978. 'Lun Nuerhachi yu Mingchao de guanxi.' *Liaoning daxue xuebao* 5: 56–66.

Liu Mau-tsai. 1958. *Die chinesischen Nachrichten zur Geschichte der Ost-Türken (T'u-Küe)*. Göttinger Asiatische Forschungen, 10. Wiesbaden: Otto Harrassowitz. 2 vols.

Liu, Mingzhong. *Zhong'an ji*. Yuan edn, Beijing tushuguan guji zhenben congkan, 92, facs. edn. Beijing: Shumu wenxian chubanshe, n.d.: 247–529.

Liu Weixin, *et al.* 1995. *Xinjiang minzu zidian*. Urumchi: Xinjiang renmin chubanshe.

Liu, Yingsheng. 1984. 'Ali Buge zhi luan yu Chahatai hanguo de fazhan' *Xinjiang daxue xuebao* 2: 29–37.

1985a. 'Yuan dai Menggu zhuhanguo de yuehe ji Wokuotai hanguo de miewang. *Xinjiang daxue xuebao* 2: 31–43.

1985b. 'Zhiyuan chu nian de Chahatai hanguo' *Yuan shi ji beifang minzu shi yanjiu jikan* 9: 45–56.

1986. 'Shiji's Wokuotai hanguo monian jishi buzheng.' *Yuanshi ji beifang minzu shi yanjiu jikan* 10: 48–59.
1992. 'Lun Talasi.' *Yuan shi lun cong* 4: 256–65.
1993. 'Chahatai Hanguo jiangyu yu lishi yange yanjiu.' *Zhongguo bianjiang shidi yanjiu* 3: 30–44.
1995. 'Meng-Yuan shidai Zhongya shehui jingji yanjiu,' *Zhongya xuekan* 4: 184–211.
2006. '*Chahatai hanguo shi yanjiu*. Shanghai: Shanghai guji chubanshe.
van Lohuizen-de Leeuw, J. E. 1970. 'India and its Cultural Empire', in *Orientalism and History*, ed. Denis Sinor, 2nd edn, Bloomington, Ind.: Indiana University Press: 35–67.
Lopez, Robert S. and Irving W. Raymond, 1955. *Medieval Trade in the Mediterranean World: Illustrative Documents Translated with Introductions and Notes*. New York: Columbia University Press.
Lord Stanley of Aldershot. 1873. trans. *Travels to Tana and Persia by Josafa Barbaro and Ambrogio Contarini*. London: Hakluyt Society Publications.
Lü Wenli. 2007. 'Qingdai dui Menggu diqu shixing de piaozhao zhidu falü fagui chu tan.' *Lanzhou xuekan* 2: 172–5.
Lubsan, Danzan. 1973. *Altan Tobchi*, trans. Nina P. Shastina. Moscow: Nauka.
Luo Yunzhi. 1983. *Qing Gaozong tongzhi Xinjiang zhengce de tantao*. Taibei: Liren zhuju.
Lupprian, Karl E. 1981. *Die Beziehungen der Päpste zu islamischen und mongolischen Herrschern im 13. Jahrhundert anhand ihres Briefwechsels*. Vatican City: Biblioteca apostolica Vaticana.
Luvsandendev, A. and Ts. Tsedendamba. 2001. *Bol'shoi akademicheskii mongol'sko-russkii slovar'*. Moscow: Academia. 4 vols.
Ma, Zuchang. 1985. *Ma Shitian wenji*, ed.Wang Deyi, IV. Taibei: Xin wenfeng chubanshe: 509–681.
Maḥmūd b. Amīr Valī. 1977. *More tayn otnositel'no doblestei blagorodnykh (geografiia)*, ed. and trans. Buri A. Akhmedov. Tashkent: Fan.
Maḥmūd b. Amīr Walī. *Baḥr al-asrār fī manāqib al-akhyār*, vol. VI, part 3, Tashkent, Institut Sharqshinasliq Uzbekiston (IVAN Uzbekistana), MS no. 1375; vol. VI, part 4, London, British Library (India Office Library Collection), MS no. 575.
Makkai, L. 1936. *A milkói (kún) püspökség és népei*. Debrecen.
'Malīḥā', Muḥammad Badīʿ Samarqandī. *Mudhakkir al-aṣḥāb*, Tashkent, Institut Sharqshinasliq Uzbekiston (IVAN Uzbekistana), MSS nos. 4270, 58.
Mandeville, Sir John. 1983. *The Travels of Sir John Mandeville*, trans. S. W. R. D. Moseley. New York: Penguin.
Mano, Eiji. 1964. 'Jûgo seiki shotô no Mogûrisutân.' *Tōyōshi kenkyū* 23 / 1: 1–24.
1978. 'Moghulistan.' *Acta Asiatica of the Institute of Eastern Culture* 3–4: 47–53.
Manz, Beatrice F. 1978. 'The Clans of the Crimean Khanate, 1466–1532.' *HUS* 2: 282–309.
1983. 'The Ulus Chaghatay Before and After Temür's Rise.' *CAJ* 27: 79–100.
1988. 'Tamerlane and the Symbolism of Sovereignty.' *Iranian Studies* 21 / 1–2: 105–22.
1989. *The Rise and Rule of Tamerlane*. Cambridge: Cambridge University Press.
1992. 'The Development and Meaning of Čagatay Identity', in *Muslims in Central Asia: Expressions of Identity and Change*, ed. Jo-Ann Gross. Durham, NC: Duke University Press: 27–45.
2001. 'Mongol History Rewritten and Relived', in *Figures Mythiques des mondes musulmans*, special issue of *Revue du monde musulman et de la Méditerranée*: 129–49.

2007a. *Power, Politics and Religion in Timurid Iran*. Cambridge: Cambridge University Press.

2007b. 'Ulugh Beg, Transoxiana and Turco–Mongolian traditions', in *Iran und iranisch geprägte Kulturen: Studien zu Ehren von Bert G. Fragner; überreicht an seinem 65. Geburtstag*, ed. Birgitt Hoffmann, Ralph Kauz and Markus Ritter. Beiträge zur Iranistik. Wiesbaden: Reichert.

'Ulugh Beg', *EI*²: 812–14.

al-Maqrīzī. 1934–73. *Kitāb al-sulūk li-maʿrifat duwal al-mulūk*, vol. II. Cairo: Maṭbaʿat dār al-kutub.

Marjānī, Shihāb al-Dīn b. Bahāʾ al-Dīn. 1885–1900, *Mustafād al-akhbār fi aḥwāli Qazān wa Bulghār* I–II. Kazan: Karimov.

Markov, A. K. 1896. *Inventarnyi katalog musul'manskikh monet Érmitazha (i dopolneniia)*. St. Petersburg: s. n.

Martin, H. Desmond. 1950. *The Rise of Chingis Khan and his Conquest of North China*. Baltimore, Md.: The Johns Hopkins University Press; reprint New York: Octagon Books, 1971.

Martin, Janet. 1986. *Treasure of the Land of Darkness: The Fur Trade and its Significance for Medieval Russia*. Cambridge: Cambridge University Press.

1988. 'Russian Expansion in the Far North, X to mid XVI Century', in *Russian Colonial Expansion to 1917*, ed. Michael Rywkin. London and New York: Mansell: 23–43.

Martinez, Arsenio P. 1984. 'Regional Mint Outputs and the Dynamics of Bullion Flows Through the Il-Khanate.' *Journal of Turkish Studies* 8: 121–73.

1986 [1988a]. 'The Third Portion of the History of Ghazan Khan in Rashidu 'd-Din's *Taʾrīkh-e Mobarak-e Ghazani*... The Narrative Sections Concerning the Military Establishment Together with Ghazan Khan's Decree Conceding Cleruchies to the Mongol Army.' *AEMAe* 6: 41–127.

1986 (1988b). 'Some Notes on the Īl-Xānid Army.' *AEMAe* 6: 129–42.

1987–91. 'Changes in Chancellery Languages and Language Changes in General in the Middle East, with Particular Reference to Iran in the Arab and Mongol Periods.' *AEMAe* 7: 103–52.

Marvazī. 1942. *Sharaf al-Zamān Marvazī on China, the Turks and India*, trans. V. Minorsky. London: Royal Asiatic Society.

Mas Latrie, L. de. 1868. 'Privilèges commerciaux accordés à la république de Venise par les princes de Crimée et les empereurs mongols du Kiptchak.' *Bibliothèque de l'école des chartes* 29. 6 série, 4: 583–95.

Masaki, Horie. 1986. 'On the Xuanwei Inscriptions and the Xuanwei Jun Fortress', in *Papers Contributed to the Symposium for the History of the Yuan Dynasty – Abstracts*. Nanjing: s. n.: 68–74.

Masevich, M. G. 1960. ed. *Materialy po istorii politicheskogo stroia Kazakhstana* I. Alma-Ata: Akademiia Nauk Kazakhskoi SSR.

Maṣʿūd b. ʿUthmān Kūhistānī, *Tārīkh-i Abu'l-Khayr Khānī*. St. Petersburg, Institute of Oriental Studies, MS C-480.

al-Masʿūdī. 1861–77. *Murūj al-dhahab wa'l-maʿādin al-jawhar*, ed. and trans. C. Barbier de Meynard. Paris: L'imprimerie nationale. 9 vols.

Materialy po istorii kazakhskikh khanstv XV–XVIII vekov, see Ibragimov, S. K. *et al.* 1969.

Matsui, Dai. 2005. 'Taxation Systems as Seen in Uighur and Mongol Documents from Turfan: An Overview.' *Transactions of the International Conference of Eastern Studies* 50: 67–82.

Mayer, Tobias. 1998. comp. *Sylloge Nummorum Arabicorum Tübingen: Nord und Ostzentralasien, XVb Mittelasien II*. Tübingen: Ernst Wasmuth Verlag.

McChesney, Robert D. 1983. 'The Amīrs of Seventeenth-Century Muslim Central Asia.' *Journal of the Economic and Social History of the Orient* 26: 33–70.

1991. *Waqf in Central Asia: Four Hundred Years in the History of a Muslim Shrine, 1480–1889*. Princeton: Princeton University Press.

1993. 'The Conquest of Herat 995–6 / 1587–8: Sources for the Study of Ṣafavid / Qizilbāsh–Shībānid / Uzbek Relations', in *Etudes safavides*, ed. J. Calmard. Paris and Tehran: Institut français de recherche en Iran: 69–107.

1996a. *Central Asia: Foundations of Change*. Princeton: The Darwin Press: 109–14.

1996b. 'Shībānī Khān', *EI²*, IX: 426–8.

1996c. 'Shībānids', *EI²*, IX: 428–31.

1999. 'Bukhara's Suburban Villages: Juzmandun in the Sixteenth Century', in *Bukhara: The Myth and the Architecture*, ed. Attilio Petruccioli. Cambridge, Mass.: Aga Khan Program for Islamic Architecture: 93–119.

2000. 'Zamzam Water on a White Felt Carpet: Adapting Mongol Ways in Muslim Central Asia: 1550–1650', in *Religion, Customary Law and Nomadic Technology: Papers Presented at the Central and Inner Asian Seminar, University of Toronto, 1 May 1998 and 23 April 1999*, ed. M. Gervers and W. Schlepp. Toronto: Joint Centre for Asia Pacific Studies: 63–80.

Mel'nikov, S. 1859. ed. *Akty istoricheskie i iuridicheskie i drevniia tsarskiia gramoty Kazanskoi i drugikh sosedstvennykh gubernii* I. Kazan: Dubrovin.

Melville, Charles. 1990. '*Pādshāh-i Islām*: The Conversion of Sultan Maḥmūd Ghāzān Khān.' *Pembroke Papers* 1: 159–77.

1999. *The Fall of Amir Chūpān and the Decline of the Ilkhanate, 1327–37: A Decade of Discord in Mongol Iran*. Papers on Inner Asia, 30. Bloomington, Ind.: Indiana University, Research Institute for Inner Asian Studies.

2006. 'The *Kesig* in Iran: The Survival of the Royal Mongol Household', in *Beyond the Legacy of Genghis Khan*, ed. Linda Komaroff. Leiden: Brill: 135–64.

Meng Da beilu, see List of Abbreviations

Meserve, Ruth. 1982. 'The Inhospitable Land of the Barbarians.' *Journal of Asian History* 16: 51–89.

Migne, (L'Abbe) Jacques-Paul. 1866. ed. *Michaelis Glyca, Opera Omnia, post Philippi Labbei, Johannis Lamii, Francisci Fontani, Joannis [sic] Leunclavii, C. Fr. Matthcii, Leonis Allatii, Angeli Mali curas in unum corpum nunc primum collecta, accedunt Josephi Constantinopolitani Patriarcae, Johannis Diaconi Adrianopolitani et aliorum Epistolae, Opuscula Historica, Fragmenta accurate et de novo recognoscente*, in *PatrologiaGraeca*, 158, Paris: J.-P. Migne, 1857–89.

Mikhaleva, G. A. 1982. *Torgovye i posol'skie sviazi Rossii s sredneaziatskimi khanstvami cherez Orenburg*. Tashkent: Fan.

Miller, Gerard F. 1937–40. *Istoriia Sibiri*. Vols. I-II. Moscow: Izdatel'stvo Akademii Nauk SSSR.

Miller, Roy A. 1976. 'Batu Möngke', in *Dictionary of Ming Biography*, 2 vols., ed. L. Carrington Goodrich and C. Y. Fang. New York and London: Columbia University Press. 1: 17–20.

Millward, James. 1998. *Beyond the Pass: Economy, Ethnicity and Empire in Qing Xinjiang, 1759–1864*. Stanford: Stanford University Press.

2004. 'The Qing Formation, the Mongol Legacy, and the "End of History" in Early Modern Central Eurasia', in *The Qing Formation in World Historical Time*, ed. L. A. Struve. Cambridge, Mass., and London: Harvard University Asia Center: 92–120.

2007. *Eurasian Crossroads: A History of Xinjiang*. New York: Columbia University Press.

Millward, James and Laura J. Newby. 2006. 'The Qing and Islam on the Western Frontier', in *Empire at the Margins: Culture, Ethnicity and Frontier in Early Modern China*, ed. Pamela Crossley, Helen Siu and Donald Sutton. Berkeley: University of California Press: 113–34.

Mingshi (Official Ming Dynasty History). 1996. Comp. Zhang Tingyu. Repr. Changsha: Yuelu shushe: Hunan sheng xin hua shu dian.

Minorsky, Vladimir and Mojtaba Minovi. 1964. 'Nasiru'd-Din Tusi on Finance.' *Bulletin of the School of Oriental and African Studies*, 10/3 (1940): 755–89; reprinted in *Iranica: Twenty Articles/Bīst maqāla-yi Minorski*, Publications of the University of Tehran no. 775: pp. 64–85 Hertford: J. Austin and Son, Ltd.

Mīrkhwānd, Muḥammad b. Khwāndshāh. 1959–61. *Rawḍat al-ṣafā*. Tehran: Payrūz. 10 vols.

Mitroshkina, A. G. 1968. 'Termin "Zolotaia Orda".' *Trudy Irkutskogo Gosudarstvennogo Universiteta im. Zhdanova* 65/4: 25–32.

Miyawaki, Junko. 1984. 'The Qalqa Mongols and the Oyirad in the Seventeenth Century.' *Journal of Asian History* 18: 186–73.

1995. *Saigo no Yūboku Teikoku: Jungaru bu no kōbō* [The Last Nomadic Empire: the Rise and Fall of the Zunghar *Ulus*]. Tokyo: Kodansha.

1997. 'The Khoyd Chief Amursana in [*sic*] the Fall of the Dzungars: The Importance of the Oyirad Family Trees Discovered in Kazan', in *Historical and Linguistic Interactions Between Inner-Asia and Europe*, ed. Árpád Berta. Szeged: John Benjamins Publishing Company: 195–205.

1999. 'The Legitimacy of Khanship Among the Oyirad (Kalmyk) Tribes in Relation to the Chinggisid Principle', in *The Mongol Empire and Its Legacy*, ed. Reuven Amitai-Preiss and David O. Morgan. Leiden: Brill: 319–31.

Morgan, David O. 1982. 'Who Ran the Mongol Empire?' *JRAS* 2: 124–36.

1986a. *The Mongols*. Oxford: Blackwell.

1986b. 'The "Great *Yāsā* of Chingiz Khān" and Mongol Law in the Īlkhānate.' *BSOAS* 49/1: 163–76; reprinted in Hawting, 2005: 198–211.

1989. 'The Mongols and the Eastern Mediterranean', in *Latins and Greeks in the Eastern Mediterranean after 1204*, ed. Benjamin Arbel, Aryeh Graboïs and David Jacoby. London: Frank Cass = *Mediterranean Historical Review* 4/1: 198–211.

2005. 'The "Great *Yasa* of Chinggis Khan" Revisited', in Amitai-Preiss and Biran, 2005: 291–308.

Mote, F. W. and L. Carrington Goodrich. 1976a. 'Chu Ti', *Dictionary of Ming Biography*, 2 vols., ed. L. Carrington Goodrich and C. Y. Fang. New York and London: Columbia University Press. 2: 1035–7.

1976b. 'Chu Ti', *Dictionary of Ming Biography*, 2 vols., ed. L. Carrington Goodrich and C. Y. Fang. New York and London: Columbia University Press. I: 356.

Mouminov, Achirbek. 2001. 'Le rôle et la place des jurists hanafites dans la vie urbaine de Boukhara et de Samarcande enttre le XIe et le début du XIIIe siècle.' *Études Karakhanides*: 131–40.

Mufaḍḍal b. Abī al-Faḍāyil. 1919–28. *al-Nahj al-sadīd wa'l-durr al-farīd fīmā ba'da ibn al-'amīd (Histoire des sulatans mamlouks)*, ed. and trans. Edgar Blochet. *Patrologia orientalis*, vols. XII, XIV, XX. Paris: Firmin-Didot.

1973. *Ägypten und Syrien zwischen 1317 und 1341 in der Chronik des Mufaḍḍal b. Abī al-Faḍāyil*, ed. and trans. Samira Kortantamer. Islamkundliche Untersuchungen, 23. Freiburg: Schwarz.

Muginov, A. M. 1958. 'Persidskaia unikal'naia rukopis' Rashīd al-Dīna.' *Uchenye zapiski Instituta vostokovedeniia* 16: 352–75.

Muḥammad Amīn b. Mīrzā Zamān Bukhārī. 1957. *Ubaidulla-name*, Russian trans. A. A. Semenov. Tashkent: Izdatel'stvo Akademii nauk Uzbekskoi SSR.

Muḥammad Amīn b. Mīrzā Zamān Bukhārī Ṣufiyānī. *Muḥīṭ al-tawārīkh*, Paris, Bibliothèque Nationale, MS no. 472.

Muḥammad Ṭālib b. Tāj al-Dīn Ḥasan Jūybārī. Maṭlab al-ṭālibīn, Tashkent, Institut Sharqshinasliq Uzbekiston (IVAN Uzbekistana), MS inv. no. 80; Berlin, Staatsbibliothek zu Berlin-Preussischer Kulturbesitz, MS Or. oct. 1540.

Muḥammad Vafā Karmīnagī. *Tuḥfat al-khānī*, St. Petersburg, Institute of Oriental Studies, MS C-525.

Muḥammad Yūsuf Munshī. *Tārīkh-i Muqīm Khānī (or Tadhkira-i Muqīm Khānī)*, London, Royal Asiatic Society, MS no. 160.

Mu'īn al-Fuqarā', Aḥmad b. Muḥammad. 1960. *Kitāb-i Mullāzāda - Mazārāt-i Bukhārā*. Tehran: Kitābfurūshī-i Ibn Sīnā, 1339/1960.

Mu'izz al-ansāb fī shajarat al-ansāb. Paris, Bibliothèque Nationale, MS no. 67.

Mukanov, M. S. 1974. *Étnicheskii sostav i rasselenie kazakhov Srednego Zhuza*. Alma-Ata: Nauka.

Mukminova, R. G. 1976. *Ocherki po istorii remesla v Samarkande i Bukhare v XVI veke*. Tashkent: Fan.

1966. *K istorii agrarnykh otnoshenii v Uzbekistane XVI v. Po materialam 'Vakf-name'*. Tashkent: Akademiia Nauk UzSSR.

Müller, Gerhard Friedrich. 2003. *Nachrichten über die Völker Sibiriens, 1736–1742*. Hamburg: Institut für Finnougristik der Universität Hamburg.

Mullie, E. P. J. 1964. *De mongoolse prins Nayan*. Mededelingen van de Koninklijke Vlaamse Academie voor Wetenschappen, Letteren en Schone Kunsten van België, Klasse der Letteren, Jaargang 26, 3. Brussels: Paleis der Academiën.

Muminov, Aširbek. 1998. 'Die Qožas: Arabischen Genealogien in Kasachstan', in *Muslim Culture in Russia and Central Asia from the 18th to the Early 20th Centuries. Vol. II: Inter-Regional and Inter-Ethnic Relations*, ed. Anke von Kügelgen, Michael Kemper and Allen J. Frank. Berlin: Klaus Schwarz: 193–210.

Müneccimbaşı, Ahmet ibn Lutfullah. 1868–9. *Ṣaḥā'if al-akhbār*, I-III. Istanbul, 1285/1868–9.

Munis, Shir Muhammad Mirab and Muhammad Riza Mirab Agahi. 1999. *Firdaws al-iqbāl: History of Khorezm*, trans. from Chaghatay and annotated by Yuri Bregel. Leiden: Brill.

Munkuev, Nikolai Ts. 1977. 'Zametki o drevnikh mongolakh', in Tikhvinskii, 1977: 377–408.

Muraoka, Rin. 1986. 'Haidu yu Tu'ersitan: lun Talasi hulitai dahui', in *Papers Contributed to the Symposium for the History of the Yuan Dynasty: Abstracts*. Nanjing: s. n.: 189–92.

Murguliia, Melita P. and Vladimir P. Shusharin. 1998. *Polovtsy, Gruziia, Rus' i Vengriia v XII–XIII vekakh*. Moscow: Rossiiskaia Akademiia Nauk, Institut Slavianovedeniia i Balkanistiki.

Muslimov, Il'iaz B. 1996. ed. *Na styke kontinentov i tsivilizatsii . . . Iz opyta obrazovaniia i raspada imperii XV–XVI vv*. Moscow: Insan.

MWLD, see List of Abbreviations

Nagel, Tilman. 1993. *Timur der Eroberer und die islamische Welt des späten Mittelalters*. Munich: C. H. Beck.

Nalivkin, V. 1886. *Kratkaia istoriia Kokandskogo khanstva*. Kazan: Tipografiia Imperatorskago Universtiteta.

Namka, Midong. 2004. 'Lun Menggu tongyi Xiyu de yingxiang.' *Nei Menggu daxue xuebao* 36 / 2: 115–20.

al-Nasafī, ʿUmar b. Muḥammad. 1955. *Qandiyya (dar bayān-i mazārāt-i Samarqand)*, ed. Irāj Afshār. Tehran: Tahurī.

al-Nasawī, see List of Abbreviations

Naṭanzī, Muʿīn al-Dīn. 1957. *Extraits du Muntakhab al-tavārīkh-i Muʿīnī (Anonym d'Iskandar)*, ed. Jean Aubin. Tehran: Khayyām, sh. 1336 / 1957.

Navāʾī, ʿAbd al-Ḥusayn. 1977. Ed. *Asnād wa makātibāt-i tārīkhī-yi Īrān*. Tehran: Bungāh-i Tarjuma wa Nashr-i Kitāb.

Necef, Ekber N. 2005. *Karahanlılar*. Istanbul: Selenge Yayınları.

Neff, John U. 1987. 'Mining and Metallurgy in Medieval Civilization', in *Cambridge Economic History of Europe*, ed. Michael Postan *et al*. 2nd edn. Cambridge: Cambridge University Press: II: 693–762.

Németh, Julius [Gyula]. 1952. 'Wanderungen des mongolischen Wortes *Nökür* "Genosse".' *AOH* 3: 1–23.

1991. *A honfoglaló magyarság kialakulása*. Budapest, 1930; 2nd rev. edn, Budapest: Akadémiai Kiadó.

Newby, L. J. 1998. 'The Begs of Xinjiang: Between Two Worlds.' *Bulletin of the School of Oriental and African Studies, University of London* 61 / 2: 278–97.

2005. *The Empire and the Khanate: A Political History of Qing Relations with Khoqand c. 1760–1860*. Brill's Inner Asian Library, 16. Leiden and Boston: Brill.

Niu, Ruji. 2007. 'Xinjiang Alimali gucheng faxian de Xuliya wen jingjiao beiming yanjiu.' *Xiyu yanjiu* 1: 74–80.

Nizami, A. K. 1998. 'The Ghurids', in Asimov and Bosworth, 1998: 170–90.

Noack, Christian. 2000. 'Die sibirischen Bucharioten. Eine muslimische Minderheit unter russischer Herrschaft.' *Cahiers du monde russe* 42 / 2–3: 263–78.

Nogmanov, Aidar. 2002. *Tatary Srednego Povolzh'ia i Priural'ia v rossiiskom zakonodatel'stve vtoroi poloviny XVI–XVIII vv*. Kazan: Fen.

Nolde, Boris. 1952–3. *La Formation de l'Empire Russe. Études, notes et documents*, 1–2. Paris: Institut d'Études Slaves.

Nolte, Hans-Heinrich. 1969. *Religiöse Toleranz in Russland, 1600–1725*. Göttingen: Musterschmidt.

Nongsang jiyao. 1965. Sibu beiyao ed. Taibei: Taiwan Zhonghua shuju.

al-Nuwayrī, Shihāb al-Dīn Aḥmad b. ʿAbd al-Wahhāb. 1984. *Nihāyat al-arab fī funūn al-adab*, vol. XXVII, ed. F. ʿAshūr. Cairo: al-Hayʾa al-miṣriyya al-ʿāmma li-l'kitāb.

Obolensky, Dimitri. 2000. *The Byzantine Commonwealth: Eastern Europe 500–1453*. London: Phoenix Press.

Ocherki po istorii Bashkirskoi ASSR. 1956. Vol. I. Ufa: Institut Istorii, Iazyka i Literatury.

Okada, Hidehiro. 1966. 'Life of Dayan Qaghan.' *Acta Asiatica* 11: 46–55.

O'Kane, Bernard. 2004. 'Chaghatai Architecture and the Tomb of Tughluq Temür at Almaliq.' *Muqarnas* 21: 277–87.

Olbricht, Peter. 1954. *Das Postwesen in China unter den mongolischen Herrschaft im 13. und 14. Jahrhundert*. Wiesbaden: Otto Harrassowitz Verlag.

Olschki, Leonardo. 1960. *Marco Polo's Asia*. Berkeley: University of California Press.

1969. *Guillaume Boucher. A French Artist at the Court of the Khans*. Baltimore, Md., 1946; reprint New York: Greenwood Press.

Ostrogorski, Georgije. 1963. *Geschichte des Byzantinischen Staates*. Munich: C. H. Beck.

Ostrogorsky, George. 1969. *History of the Byzantine State*, trans. Joan Hussey. 3rd rev. edn. New Brunswick: Rutgers University Press; English trans. of Ostrogorski, 1963.

Ostrowski, Donald. 1998. *Muscovy and the Mongols: Cross-cultural Influences on the Steppe Frontier, 1304–1589*. Cambridge University Press: Cambridge.

Ötemish Ḥajjī, *Chingīz nāma*, see Iudin *et al.*, 1992.

Özyetgin, A. Melek. 1996. *Altın Ordu, Kırım ve Kazan Sahasına ait Yarlık ve Bitiklerin dil ve üslûp İncelemesi*. Ankara: Atatürk Dil ve Tarih Yüksek Kurumu.

Pachymérès, Georges. 1984. *Relations historiques*, ed. Albert Failler, trans. V. Laurent in Corpus Fontium Historiae Byzantinae, Series Parisiensis 24/1, 2. Paris: Belles Lettres.

Paksoy, Hasan B. 1991. ed. *Central Asian Monuments*. Istanbul: Isis Press.

Pallavicino, Eleonora. 2001. ed. *I* Libri Jurium *della Repubblica di Genova*, 1/7, in Ministero per i Beni e le Attivita Culturali: Pubblicazioni degli Archivi di Stato: Fonti 35, Fonti per la Storia della Liguria, 15, Genoa.

Pamiatniki russkogo prava. ed. Aleksandr A. Zimin, Lev V. Cherepnin *et al.* 1952–63. Moscow: Gosudarstvennoe izdatel'stvo iuridicheskoi literatury. 8 vols.

Papas, Alexandre. 2005. *Soufisme et politique entre Chine, Tibet et Turkestan: étude sur les Khwajas Naqshbandis du Turkestan oriental*. Paris: Librairie d'Amérique et d'Orient, Jean Maisonneuve successeur.

Pashuto, Vladimir T. 1966. 'Poloveckoe episkopstvo', in *Ost und West in der Geschichte des Denkens und der kulturellen Beziehungen. Festschrift für Eduard Winter zum 70. Geburtstag*, W. Steinitz, P. N. Berkov, B. Suchodolski and J. Dolansky. Berlin: Akademie-Verlag: 33–40.

Paul, Jürgen. 1990. 'Scheiche und Herrscher im Khanat Čagatay.' *Der Islam* 67/2: 278–321.

1991. *Die politische und soziale Bedeutung der Naqšbandiyya in Mittelasien im 15. Jahrhundert*. Berlin and New York: W. De Gruyter.

1997. 'La propriété foncière des cheikhs Juybari.' *Cahiers d'Asie centrale* no. 3–4 (L'Héritage Timouride: Iran-Asie centrale XVe–XVIIIe siècles): 183–202.

1998. *Doctrine and Organization: The Khwājagān/Naqshbandīya in the First Generation after Bahā'uddīn*. ANOR 1, Halle and Berlin: Das Arabische Buch.

Paviot, Jacques. 2000. 'England and the Mongols.' *JRAS*, third series, 10: 305–18.

Pegolotti, Francesco Balducci. 1936. *La pratica della mercatura*, ed. Allan Evans. The Mediaeval Academy of America, Publication, 24. Cambridge, Mass.: The Mediaeval Academy of America.

Pelensky, Jaroslaw. 1974. *Russia and Kazan: Conquest and Ideology, 1438–1560s*. Paris: Mouton.

Pelliot, Paul. 1922–3. 'Les Mongols et la papauté.' *Revue de l'Orient Chrétien* 23: 3–30.

1924. 'Les Mongols et la papauté.' *Revue de l'Orient Chrétien* 24: 225–335.

1925. 'Note sur Karakorum.' *Journal Asiatique* 206: 372–5.

1927. 'Une ville musulmane dans Chine du Nord sous les Mongols.' *Journal Asiatique* 211: 261–79.

1932. 'Les Mongols et la papauté.' *Revue de l'Orient Chrétien* 28: 3–84.

1949. *Notes sur l'histoire de la Horde d'Or*. Paris: Librairie d'Amerique et d'Orient. Adrien-Maisonneuve.

1959–73. *Notes on Marco Polo*. Paris: Imprimerie Nationale. 3 vols.

Pelliot, Paul and Louis Hambis. 1951. *Histoire des campagnes de Gengis Khan*. Leiden: Brill.

Peng, Daya and Xu, Ting. 1937. *Heida shilüe* ed. Congshu jicheng. Reprint: Changsha.

Perdue, Peter. 1996. 'Military Mobilization in Seventeenth- and Eighteenth-Century China, Russia, and Mongolia.' *Modern Asian Studies* 30 / 4: 757–93.

2005. *China Marches West: The Qing Conquest of Central Eurasia*. Cambridge, Mass.: Belknap Press of Harvard University Press.

Pershits, Abram I. and D. Traide. 1986. eds. *Svod étnograficheskikh poniatii i terminov. Sotsial'no-ékonomicheskie otnosheniia i sotsial'no-normativnaia kul'tura*. Moscow: Nauka.

Petech, Luciano. 1976a. 'bSod-nams-rgya-mts', *Dictionary of Ming Biography*, 2 vols., ed. L. Carrington Goodrich and C. Y. Fang. New York and London: Columbia University Press: vol. I: 22–3.

1976b. 'Yon-tan-rgya-mts'o', *Dictionary of Ming Biography*, 2 vols., ed. L. Carrington Goodrich and C. Y. Fang. New York and London: Columbia University Press: II: 1604–06.

1983. 'Tibetan Relations with Sung China and with the Mongols', in Rossabi, 1983: 173–203.

1990. *Central Tibet and the Mongols: The Yüan–Sa-skya Period of Tibetan History*. Serie Orientale Roma, 65. Rome: Istituto Italiano per Il Medio ed Estremo Oriente.

Petrukhin, Vladimir Ia. and Dmitrii S. Raevskii. 2004. *Ocherki istorii narodov Rossii v drevnosti i rannem srednevekov'e*. Moscow: Znak.

Petrushevskii, Il'ia P. 1949. 'K istorii instituta soiiurgala', in *Sovetskoe Vostokovedenie*, ed. V. V. Struve *et al.* Moscow and Leningrad: Akademiia Nauk: 227–46.

Pfeiffer, Judith. 1999. 'Conversion Versions: Sultan Öljeytü's Conversion to Shi'ism (709 / 1309) in Muslim Narrative Sources.' *Mongolian Studies* 22: 35–67.

2003. 'Conversion to Islam Among the Ilkhans in Muslim Narrative Traditions: The Case of Ahmad Tegüder.' Ph.D. diss., University of Chicago.

Pfeiffer, Nikolaus. 1913. *Die ungarische Dominikanerordensprovinz von ihrer Gründung 1221 bis zur Tatarenverwüstung 1241–1242*. Zurich: Gebr. Leemann.

Phillips, Eustace D. 1969. *The Mongols*. Ancient Peoples and Places. London: Thames and Hudson.

Pikov, Gennadii G. 1989. *Zapadnye kidani*. Novosibirsk: Izdatel'stvo Novosibirskogo universiteta.

Pishchulina, Klavdiia A. 1969. 'Prisyrdar'inskie goroda i ikh znachenie v istorii kazakhskikh khanstv v XV–XVII vekakh', in *Kazakhstan v XV–XVIII vekakh*. Alma-Ata: Nauka: 5–49.

1977. *Iugo-vostochnyi Kazakhstan v seredine XIV-nachale XVI vekov*. Alma-Ata: Nauka.

Pokotilov, D. 1949. *History of the Eastern Mongols During the Ming Dynasty from 1368–1634, Part II*, Addenda and Corrigenda by W. Franke. Studia Serica, Monographs, Series A, no. 3. Chengtu: Chinese Cultural Studies Research Institute and West China Union University.

Polo, Marco. 1903. *The Book of Sir Marco Polo*, trans. and ed. Henry Yule. London: John Murray. 2 vols.

1931. *The Travels of Marco Polo. Translated into English from the Text of L. F. Benedetto* by Aldo Ricci. London: Routledge.

1935–38. *The Description of the World*, trans. and ed. Antoine C. Moule and Paul Pelliot. London: George Routledge and Sons. 2 vols.

1982. *Le divisament dou monde*, ed. Gabriella Ronchi, *Milione. Le divisament dou monde. Il Milione nelle redazioni toscana e franco-italiana*. Milan: A. Mondadori.

1986. *Il Milione*, introduzione, edizione del testo toscano ('Ottimo') note illustrative, esegetiche, linguistiche repertori onomastici e lessicali a cura di Ruggero M. Ruggieri. Florence: L. S. Olschki.

Poluboiarinova, Marina D. 1978. *Russkie liudi v Zolotoi Orde*. Moscow: Nauka.

Portal, Roger. 1950. *L'Oural au 18e siècle, étude d'histoire économique et sociale*. Paris: Institut d'Études slaves.

Postan, M. M. and H. J. Habakkuk. 1966–89. eds. *The Cambridge Economic History of Europe*. Cambridge: Cambridge University Press.

Potter, Lawrence G. 1994. 'Sufis and Sultans in Post-Mongol Iran.' *Iranian Studies* 27: 77–102.

Predelli, Ricardo. 1876, 1878, 1883, 1896. *I Libri Commemoriali della Repubblica di Venezia: Regesti*, i-iv, in Monumenti Storici publicati dalla Deputazione Veneta di Storia Patria, 1; Serie Prima, Documenti, I. Venice.

Pritsak, Omeljan. 1950. 'Āl-i Burhān.' *Der Islam* 30: 81–96 reprinted in Pritsak, 1981.

1952. 'Stammesnamen und Titulaturen der altaischen Völker.' *Ural-Altaische Jahrbücher* 24/1–2: 49–104.

1968.'Two Migratory Movements in the Eurasian Steppe in the 9th –11th Centuries', in *Proceedings of the 26th International Congress of Orientalists, New Delhi, 1964*. New Delhi: A. K. Ghosh: 2: 157–63; reprinted in Pritsak, 1981, VI.

1981. *Studies in Medieval Eurasian History*. London: Variorum Reprints.

1988. 'The Distinctive Features of the Pax Nomadica', in *Popoli de delle Steppe* in *XXXV Settimana di Studio del Centro Italiano di Studi sull'Alto Medioevo*. Spoleto: Pressa La Sede del Centro, 2: 747–88.

Privratsky, Bruce. 2001. *Muslim Turkistan*. Richmond, Surrey: Curzon.

Ptak, Roderich. 1995. 'Images of Maritime Asia in Two Yuan Texts: *Daoyi zhilue* and *Yiyu zhi*.' *Journal of Sung-Yuan Studies* 25: 47–75.

al-Qalqashandī, Aḥmad b. ʿAlī. 1962. *Ṣubḥ al-aʿshā fī ṣināʿat al-inshāʾ*. Cairo: al-Maṭbaʿa al-amīriyya, 1913–19; reprint: Cairo: al-Muʿassasa al-Miṣriyya al-ʿĀmma lil-Taʾlīf wa-al-Tarjama wa-al-Ṭibāʿa wa-al-Nashr, 1383/1962. 14 vols.

Qarshī, Jamāl, *Mulkhaqāt al-ṣurāḥ*, in Bartol'd, 1900: I: 128–52.

Qāshānī, Abuʾl-Qāsim ʿAbdallāh b. ʿAlī. 1969. *Taʾrīkh-i Uljaytū*, ed. Mahin Hambly. Tehran: Bungāh-i tarjuma wa-nashr-i kitāb.

Qazwīnī, Ḥamdallāh b. Abī Bakr Mustawfī. 1913. *Taʾrīkh-i guzīda*, ed. Edward G. Browne. Leiden and London: Brill and Luzac.

1915. *Nuzhat al-qulūb*, ed. Guy Le Strange. Leiden and London: Brill and Luzac.

Qidan guozhi: Istoriia gosudarstva kidanei (tsidan' gochzhi) see List of Abbreviations, *QGZ*/ Taskin.

Qi-shi-yi (Chunyuan). 1835. *Xiyu wenjian lu*, original 1777; reprint Qingzhao tang congshu, 95.

Qozha, Mukhtar. 2000. *Iasï-Türkistan tarikhï-Istoriia Iasy-Turkestana*. Almaty: QAZaqparat.

QTZWHSL, see List of Abbreviations

Quinn, Sheila A. 1989. 'The Muʿizz al-Ansab and Shuʿāb-i Panjgānah as Sources for the Chaghatayid Period of History: A Comparative Analysis.' *CAJ* 33: 229–53.

al-Qurashī, ʿAbd al-Qādir b. Muḥammad. 1993. *al-Jawāhir al-muḍiyya fī ṭabaqāt al-ḥanafiyya*, ed. ʿAbd al-Fattāḥ M. al-Ḥilw. Cairo: Hajar. 5 vols.

Qurbān ʿAlī Khālidī. 1910. *Tawārīkh-i khamsa-yi sharqī*. Kazan: Kazakov.

2005. *An Islamic Biographical Dictionary of the Eastern Kazakh Steppe: 1770–1912*, ed. A. Frank and M. Usmanov. Leiden: Brill.

de Rachewiltz, Igor. 1962. trans. 'The Hsi-yu lu by Yeh-lü Ch'u-ts'ai.' *Monumenta Serica* 21: 1–128.

1966. 'Personnel and Personalities in North China in the Early Mongol Period.' *Journal of the Economic and Social History of the Orient* 9: 88–144.

1971. *Papal Envoys to the Great Khans*. London: Faber.

1971–81. trans. *The Secret History of the Mongols* published serially in *Papers in Far Eastern History*.

1973. 'Some Remarks on the Ideological Foundations of Chingis Khan's Empire.' *Papers on Far Eastern History* 7: 21–36.

1983. 'Turks in China Under the Mongols: A Preliminary Investigation of Turco-Mongol Relations in the 13th and 14th Centuries', in Rossabi, 1983: 281–310.

1989. 'The Title Činggis Qan/Qaγan Re-examined', in *Gedanke und Wirkung: Festschrift zum 90. Geburtstag von Nikolaus Poppe*, ed. Walther Heissig and Klaus Sagaster. Asiatische Forschungen, 108. Wiesbaden: Harrassowitz: 281–98.

1993. 'Some Reflections on Činggis Qan's *Jasaγ*.' *East Asian History* 6: 91–104.

Chan Hok-lam, Hsiao Ch'i-ch'ing and Peter W. Geier. 1993. eds. *In the Service of the Khan: Eminent Personalities of the Early Mongol-Yüan Period*. Wiesbaden: Harrassowitz.

de Rachewiltz, Igor and May Wang. 1988. *Repertory of Proper Names in Yuan Literary Sources*. Taibei: Oriental Book Store. 3 vols.

2004. *The Secret History of the Mongols. A Mongolian Epic Chronicle of the Thirteenth Century*. Brill's Inner Asian Library, 7. Leiden: Brill. 2 vols.

Raeff, Marc. 1971. 'Patterns of Russian Imperial Policy Toward the Nationalities', in *Soviet Nationality Problems*, ed. Edward Allworth. New York: Columbia University Press: 23–42.

Rakhmatullin, U. Kh. 1988. *Naselenie Bashkirii v XVII–XVIII vv.: voprosy formirovaniia nebashkirskogo naseleniia*. Moscow: Nauka.

Rall, Jutta. 1960. 'Zur persischen Übersetzung eines *Mo-chüeh*, eines chinesischen medizinischen Textes.' *Oriens Extremus* 7: 152–57.

Rásonyi, László. 1981. *Hidak a Dunán*. Budapest: Magvető Kiadó.

Rashīd al-Dīn, Faḍlallāh Abuʾl-Khayr, see List of Abbreviations and below

Shuʿāb-i panjgāna, Topkapi Sarayi Ahmet III, MS no. 2937.

1945. *Mukātabat-i Rashīdī, yaʿnī rasāilī ki wazīr-i dānishmand, Khwāja Rashīdu 'd-Dīn Faḍlu 'Llāh Tabīb bi pesarān wa ʿummāl wa dūstān wa dīgirān siwāʾ-i īshān niwishta wa Maulānā Muḥammad-i Abarqūhī an-rā jamʿ namūda*, ed. Muhammad Shāfiʿ. Lahore: Panjab University Oriental Publications.

1971a. *Die Chinageschichte des Rašīd al-Dīn*, ed. and trans. Karl Jahn. Vienna: Herman Böhlaus.

1971b. *The Successors of Genghis Khan*, trans. John A. Boyle. New York: Columbia University Press.

1972. *Tanksūq nāma yā ṭibb ahl-i Khitā*, ed. Mujtabā Minuvī. Tehran: University of Tehran.

1980. *Die Indiengeschichte des Rašīd al-Dīn*, ed. and trans. Karl Jahn. Vienna: Verlag der Österreichischen Akademie der Wissenschaften.

1989. *Āthār va Aḥyā*, ed. M. Sutūdah and I. Afshār. Tehran: Tehran University Press.

Ratchnevsky, Paul. 1966. 'Les Che-wei étaient-ils des Mongols?' in *Mélanges de Sinologie offerts à Monsieur Paul Demiéville*, I. Bibliothèque de l'Institut des Hautes Études Chinoises, 20. Paris: Presses universitaires de France: 225–51.

1966. 'Zum Ausdruck "Touhsia" in der Mongolenzeit', in *Collectanea Mongolica. Festchrift für Professor Dr. Rintchen zum 60. Geburtstag*, ed. Walther Heissig. Asiatische Forschungen, 17. Wiesbaden: Harrassowitz: 173–91.

1970. 'Rašid al-Din über die Mohammedaner-Verfolgungen in China unter Qubilai.' *CAJ* 14: 163–80.

1992. *Genghis Khan: His Life and Legacy*, trans. Thomas Nivison Haining. Oxford: Blackwell, 1991; US edn, 1992. First published in German as *Čiggis-Khan. Sein Leben und Wirken*. Wiesbaden: Franz Steiner, 1983.

1993. 'Jurisdiction, Penal Code, and Cultural Confrontation under Mongol-Yüan Law.' *Asia Major*, third series, 6: 161–79.

Reichert, Folker E. 1992. *Begegnungen mit China. Die Entdeckung Ostasiens im Mittelalter*. Beiträge zur Geschichte und Quellenkunde des Mittelalters, 15. Sigmaringen: Jan Thorbecke.

Ren Chongyue. 1996. 'Cong liang tong Yuan dai beiwen kan "Haidu zhi luan" de xingzhi.' *Zhongzhou xuekan* 5: 115–20.

Ren, Rongkang. 1990. 'Yuan chu de Yuan-Yi lianmeng yu Zhongya jioatong.' *Zhongya xuekan*3: 184–93.

Richard, Jean. 1967. 'La conversion de Berke et les débuts d'islamisation de la Horde d'Or.' *Revue des études islamiques* 35: 173–84.

1977. *La Papauté et les missions d'Orient au moyen age (XIIIe–XVe siècles)*. Rome: Ecole Française de Rome.

1979. 'Les causes des victoires mongoles d'après les historiens occidentaux du XIIIe siècle.' *CAJ* 23: 104–17; reprinted in Richard, 1983.

1983. *Croisés, missionnaires et voyageurs. Les perspectives orientales du monde latin medieval*. London: Variorum Reprints.

Riḍā al-Dīn b. Fakhr al-Dīn. 1900–08. *Āsār* I-II. Ufa and Orenburg: Karimov.

Roemer, Hans R. 1986. 'The Successors of Timur', in *CHIran*, VI: 98–146.

Roerich, George N. 1949–53. trans. and ed. *The Blue Annals*. Royal Asiatic Society of Bengal. Monograph series, 7. Calcutta: Royal Asiatic Society of Bengal. 2 vols.

Rogers, Greg S. 1996. 'An Examination of Historians' Explanations for the Mongol Withdrawal from East Central Europe.' *East European Quarterly* 30: 3–26.

Romaniello, Matthew P. 2000. 'Controlling the Frontier: Monasteries and Infrastructure in the Volga Region, 1552–1682.' *Central Asian Survey* 19: 429–43.

Rossabi, Morris. 1972. 'Ming China and Turfan, 1406–1517', *CAJ* 16/3: 206–25.

1976a. 'Arughtai', *Dictionary of Ming Biography*, 1: 12–15.

1976b. 'Mahmūd', *Dictionary of Ming Biography*, 2: 1035–7.

1976c. 'Esen', *Dictionary of Ming Biography*, 1: 416–20.

1976d. 'Ibrahim', *Dictionary of Ming Biography*, 1: 683–5.

1979. 'Khubilai Khan and the Women in his Family', in *Studia Sino-Mongolica: Festschrift für Herbert Franke*, ed. Wolfgang Bauer. Wiesbaden: Franz Steiner Verlag: 153–80.

1981. 'The Muslims in the Early Yuan Dynasty', in Langlois, 1981: 257–95.

1982. *The Jurchens in the Yüan and Ming*. Cornell University East Asia Papers, 27. Ithaca: Cornell University China–Japan Program.

1983. ed. *China Among Equals*. Berkeley: University of California Press.

1988. *Khubilai Khan: His Life and Times*. Berkeley and Los Angeles: University of California Press.

1992. *Voyager from Xanadu: Rabban Sauma and the First Journey from China to the West*. Tokyo and New York: Kodansha.

Roux, Jean-Paul. 1997. *L'Asie Centrale: Histoire et civilizations*. Paris: Fayard.

Rubruck, William of, *Itinerarium*, in Wyngaert, 1929: 145–332.

1990. *The Mission of Friar William of Rubruck: His Journey to the Court of the Great Khan Möngke 1253–1255*, trans. Peter Jackson and ed. Peter Jackson with David Morgan. Hakluyt Society, second series, 173. London: Hakluyt Society.

Rūmlū, Hasan-i. 1978. *Aḥsan al-tawārīkh*, ed.ʿAbd al-Ḥusayn Navāʾī. Tehran: Intishārāt-i Bābik.

Ruotsala, Antti. 2001. *Europeans and Mongols in the Middle of the Thirteenth Century: Encountering the Other*. Helsinki: The Finnish Academy of Science and Letters.

Ryan, James D. 1998. 'Preaching Christianity Along the Silk Route: Missionary Outposts in the Tartar "Middle Kingdom" in the Fourteenth Century.' *Journal of Early Modern History* 2/4: 350–73.

Rywkin, Michael. 1988. 'Russian Central Colonial Administration. From the Prikaz of Kazan to the XIX Century, a Survey', in *Russian Colonial Expansion to 1917*, ed. Michael Rywkin. London and New York: Mansell: 8–22.

al-Ṣafadī, Ṣalāḥ al-Dīn, Khalīl b. Aybak. 1981–2004. *Al-Wāfī biʾl-wafayāt*. Beirut: Orient Institut der Deutschen Morgenländischen Gesellschaft. 31 vols.

1998. *Aʿyān al-ʿaṣr wa-aʿwān al-naṣr*, ed. ʿAlī b. Abū Zayd. Beirut and Damascus: Dār al-fikr. 6 vols.

Safargaliev, Magamet G. 1960. *Raspad Zolotoi Ordy*. Saransk: Mordovskoe Knizhnoe Izdatel'stvo; reprinted with different pagination in Muslimov, 1996: 277–526.

Sagaster, K. 1976. *Die Weisse Geschichte. Eine mongolische Quelle zur Lehre von den beiden Ordnungen Religion und Staat in Tibet und der Mongolei*. Asiatische Forschungen, 41. Wiesbaden: Harrassowitz.

Saguchi Tōru. 1963. *18–19 saeki Higashi Torukisutan shakai shi kenkyû*. Tokyo: Yoshikawa Kōbunkan.

1986. *Shinkyō minzoku shi kenkyū*. Tokyo: Yoshikawa Kōbunkan.
Sakhāwī, Muḥammad b, ʿAbd al-Raḥmān. 1966. *Al-Dawʾ al-lāmiʿ li-ahl al-qarn al-tāsiʿ*. Beirut: Dār maktabat al-ḥayāt. 12 vols.
Samarqandī, ʿAbd al-Razzāq. 1941–9. *Maṭlaʿ al-saʿdayn wa majmaʿ al-baḥrayn*, ed. Muḥammad Shafīʿ. Lahore: Kitābkhāna-i Gīlānī, 1360–68/1941–9. 2 vols.
Sandag, Sh. 1977. 'Obrazovanie edinogo mongol'skogo gosudarstva i Chingiskhan', in Tikhvinskii, 1977: 23–45.
Sanutus dictus Torsellus, Marinus. 1611. *Liber secretorum fidelium Crucis super Terrae Sanctae recuperatione et conservatione*, ed. Jacques Bongars, Hanau (Prelum Academicum Universitatis Torontonensis, MCMLXXII).
Sapabekulï, S. 1996. 'Türkistandaghï tarikhï ziyarat', in *Yasawi taghïlïmï*. Turkistan: Mura: 123–32.
Sato Tsugitaka. 2004. 'Sugar in the Economic Life of Mamlūk Egypt.' *Mamlūk Studies Review* 8/2: 87–107.
Saunders, Jay J. 1971. *The History of the Mongol Conquests*. London and New York: Routledge.
Savel'ev, P. S. 1858. *Monety dzhuchidskie, dzhagataiskie, dzhelairidskie i drugie, obrashchavshiesia v Zolotoi Orde v épokhu Tokhtamysha. Zapiski Imperatorskogo Arkheologicheskogo Obshchestva* XII. St. Petersburg.
Savinov, Dmitrii S. 1984. *Narody Iuzhnoi Sibiri v drevnetiurkskuiu épokhu*. Leningrad: Izdatel'stvo Leningradskogo Universiteta.
Savory, Roger M. 1964. 'The Struggle for Supremacy in Iran After the Death of Timur.' *Der Islam* 40/1: 36–65.
Sayılı, Aydın. 1988. *The Observatory in Islam and its Place in the General History of the Observatory*. 2nd edn Ankara: Türk Tarih Kurumu Basımevi.
Sayyid-Muḥammad Riḍā. 1832. *As-sabʿ as-sayyār*. Kazan: Tipografiia Kazanskago Universiteta.
Sazonov, A. A. *et al.* 1992. eds. *Pod stiagom Rossii: Sbornik arkhivnykh dokumentov*. Moscow: Russkaia Kniga.
Schamiloglu, Uli. 1984. 'The *Qaraçi* Beys of the later Golden Horde: Notes on the Organization of the Mongol World Empire.' *AEMAe* 4: 283–97.
1991. '*The Umdet ül-ahbar* and the Turkic Narrative Sources for the Golden Horde and the Later Golden Horde', in Paksoy, 1991: 81–93.
Schamiloglu, Uli and Timur Kocaoğlu. 2009. Eds. *The Golden Horde and its Successors/Altın Orda ve Varisleri*. Istanbul: Ayaz-Tahir Türkistan Idil–Ural Vakfı Yayınları (in press).
Schmidt, Isaac Jacob. 1961. *Geschichte der Ost-Mongolen und ihres Fürstenhauses*. St. Petersburg and Leipzig: N. Gretsch, 1829; reprint The Hague: Europe Printing, 1961.
Schmieder, Felicitas. 1994. *Europa und die Fremden. Die Mongolen im Urteil des Abendlandes vom 13. bis in das 15. Jahrhundert*. Sigmaringen: Jan Thorbecke Verlag.
Schmieder, Felicitas and Peter Schreiner. 2005. Eds. *Il Codice Cumanico e il suo Mundo*. Rome: Edizioni di storia e letteratura.
Schmitz, A. 1996. *Die Erzählung von Edige. Gehalt, Genese und Wirkung einer heroischen Tradition*. Turcologica, 27. Wiesbaden: Harrassowitz.
Schönig, Claus. 2005. 'Türkische-Mongolische Sprachbeziehungen.' *Ural-Altaische Jahrbücher*, N. F. 19: 131–66.
Schorkowitz, Dittmar. 1992. *Die soziale und politische Organisation bei den Kalmücken (Oiraten) und Prozesse der Akkulturation vom 17. Jahrhundert bis zur Mitte des 19. Jahrhunderts*. Frankfurt am Main: Peter Lang.

Schuh, Dieter. 1977. *Erlasse und Sendschreiben mongolischer Herrscher für tibetische Geistliche. Ein Beitrag zur Kenntnis der Urkunden des tibetischen Mittelalters und ihrer Diplomatik*, Monumenta Tibetica Historica Abtlg. III, Bd. 1. St. Augustin: VGH Wissenschaftsverlag.

Schurmann, Herbert F. 1956a. 'Mongolian Tributary Practices of the 13th Century.' *HJAS* 19: 304–89.

1956b. *Economic Structure of the Yuan Dynasty*. Harvard-Yenching Institute Series, 16. Cambridge, Mass.: Harvard University Press.

Schwarz, Florian. 1999. 'Bukhara and its Hinterland: The Oasis of Bukhara in the Sixteenth Century in the Light of the Juybari Codex', in *Bukhara: The Myth and the Architecture*, ed. Attilio Petruccioli. Cambridge, Mass.: Aga Khan Program for Islamic Architecture: 79–92.

Schwarz, Henry G. 1976. 'The Khwâjas of Eastern Turkestan.' *Central Asiatic Journal* 20/4: 266–96.

Seaman, Gary and Daniel Marks. 1991. Eds. *Rulers From the Steppe: State Formation on the Eurasian Periphery*. Ethnographics Monograph Series, 2. Los Angeles: Ethnographics Press.

Sebes, Joseph. 1962. *The Jesuits and the Sino-Russian Treaty of Nerchinsk (1689): The Diary of Thomas Pereira*. Rome: Institutum Historicum S. I.

Secret History, see List of Abbreviations

Sela, Ron. 2003. *Ritual and Authority in Central Asia: The Khan's Inauguration Ceremony*. Papers on Inner Asia, 37. Bloomington, Ind.: Research Institute for Inner Asian Studies.

Semenov, Aleksandr A. 1954a. 'K voprosu o proiskhozhdenii i sostave uzbekov Sheibani-khana', in *Materialy po istorii tadzhikov i uzbekov Srednei Azii*, Vypusk I. Stalinabad: Izdatel'stvo Akademii Nauk Tadzhikskoi SSR: 3–37.

1954b. 'Pervye Sheibanidy i bor'ba za Maverannakhr', in *Materialy po istorii tadzhikov i uzbekov Srednei Azii*, Vypusk 1, Stalinabad: Izdatel'stvo Akademii Nauk Tadzhikskoi SSR: 109–50.

1954c. 'Sheibani-khan i zavoevanie im imperii Timuridov', *Materialy po istorii tadzhikov i uzbekov Srednei Azii*, Vypusk 1, Stalinabad: Izdatel'stvo Akademii Nauk Tadzhikskoi SSR: 39–83.

1978. 'Ocherk kul'turnoi roli uigurov v mongol'skikh gosudarstvakh', in *Materialy po istorii i kul'ture uigurskogo naroda*, ed. Gozhakhmet S. Sadvakasov *et al.* Alma-Ata: Nauka: 22–48.

Sen, Tansen. 2000. *Buddhism, Diplomacy and Trade: The Realignment of Sino-Indian Relations, 600–1400*. Honolulu: University of Hawai'i Press.

Serruys, Henry. 1955. *Sino-Jürčid Relations During the Yung-lo Period (1403–1424)*. Göttinger Asiatische Forschungen, 4. Wiesbaden: Harrassowitz.

1958. *Genealogical Tables of the Descendants of Dayan-Qan*. 's-Gravenhage: Mouton.

1960. 'Four Documents Relating to the Sino-Mongol Peace of 1570–1571.' *Monumenta Serica* 19: 1–66.

1963. 'Early Lamaism in Mongolia.' *Oriens Extremus* 10: 181–216.

1967. *Sino-Mongol Relations During the Ming II: The Tribute System and Diplomatic Missions (1400–1600)*. Brussels: Institut Belge des Hautes Etudes Chinoises.

1972. 'A Manuscript Version of the Legend of the Mongol Ancestry of the Yung-lo Emperor', *Analecta Mongolica, Dedicated to the Seventieth Birthday of Professor Owen*

Lattimore, ed. John G. Hangin and Urgunge Onon The Mongolia Society Occasional Papers, 8. Bloomington, Ind.: Mongolia Society: 19–61.

1975. 'Two Remarkable Women in Mongolia: The Third Lady Erketü Qatun and Dayicing Beyiji', *Asia Major* 19.

1976a. 'Mar-körgis', *Dictionary of Ming Biography*, 2 vols., ed. L. Carrington Goodrich and C. Y. Fang. New York and London: Columbia University Press: 2: 1054–6.

1976b. 'Altan-qaghan', *Dictionary of Ming Biography*, 2 vols., ed. L. Carrington Goodrich and C. Y. Fang. New York and London: Columbia University Press: 1: 6–9.

1976c. 'Qutughtai Secen-qung-tayiji', 2 vols., ed. L. Carrington Goodrich and C. Y. Fang. New York and London: Columbia University Press: 2: 1128–31.

1978. 'The Čaqar Population during the Qing.' *Journal of Asian History* 12: 58–79.

1980. *The Mongols in China During the Hung-wu Period (1368–1398)*. Brussels: Institut Belge des Hautes Etudes Chinoises.

Sevim, A. 1998. 'The Origins of the Seljuqs and the Establishment of Seljuk Power in the Islamic Lands up to 1055', in Asimov and Bosworth, 1998: 145–55.

Sevortian, Ervand V. 1966. 'Krymsko-tatarskii iazyk', in *Iazyki narodov SSSR*. Vol. II: *Tiurkskie iazyki*. ed. V. Vinogradov *et al.* Moscow: Nauka: 234–59.

Shabānkāraʾī, Muḥammad b. ʿAlī. 1984. *Majmaʿ al-ansāb*, ed. Mirhashim Muḥaddith. Tehran: Muʾasasat-i intishārāt-i amīr kabīr, 1363/1984.

Shāmī, Niẓām al-Dīn, see List of Abbreviations

Shāniyāzov, Karim. 2001. *O'zbek khalqining Shaklanish Jarayāni*. Tashkent: Sharq.

Shao, Yuanping. 1968. *Yuanshi leibian*. Taibei: Guangwen shuju.

Sharaf al-Dīn b. Nūr al-Dīn Andijānī. Tārīkh-i Mīr Sayyid Sharīf Rāqim (or Tārīkh-i Rāqimī), London, Royal Asiatic Society, MS no. 163.

Sharifullina, Farida. 1991. *Kasimovskie tatary*. Kazan: Tatarskoe Knizhnoe Izdatel'stvo.

Shaw, Dennis J. B. 1983. 'Southern Frontiers of Muscowy, 1550–1700', in *Studies in Russian Historical Geography*, ed. James H. Bater and Richard A. French, vol. I. London: Academic Press: 117–42.

Shaw, R. B. 1897. 'The History of the Khojas of Eastern-Turkestan, summarised from the 'Tazkira-i-khwajagan of Muhammad Sadiq Kashghari', edited with introduction and notes by N. Elias. Published as a supplement to the *Journal of the Asiatic Society of Bengal*, 66/1.

Shekin, V. P. 1985. 'Klad serebrianykh dinarov i dirkhemov Chagataidov XIV v.' *Épigrafika Vostoka* 23: 60–2.

Shengwu qinzheng lu (*Sheng-wu ch'in-cheng lu*), see Pelliot and Hambis, 1951.

Shimo, Hirotoshi. 1977. 'The Qaraunas in the Historical Materials of the Ilkhanate.' *Memoirs of the Research Department of the Toyo Bunko* 35: 131–81.

al-Shujāʿī, Shams al-Dīn. 1985. *Taʾrīkh al-malik al-nāṣir Muḥammad b. Qalāwūn al-ṣāliḥī wa-awlādihi*, ed. Barbara Schäfer. Wiesbaden: Franz Steiner Verlag. 2 vols.

Siddiqi, Iqtidar H. 1988. 'Sultan Muhammad bin Tughluq's Foreign Policy: A Reappraisal.' *Islamic Culture* 62/4: 1–22.

Sima Qian. 1993. *Records of the Grand Historian. Han dynasty*, trans. Burton Watson. Rev. edn. New York: Renditions-Columbia University Press. 2 vols.

Sinor, Denis. 1970. ed. *Orientalism and History*, 2nd ed. Bloomington: Indiana University Press.

1972. 'Horse and pasture in Inner Asian history.' *Oriens Extremus* 19: 171–84. Reprinted in Sinor, 1977.

1975. 'On Mongol strategy', in Ch'en Chieh-hsien 1975. ed. *Proceedings of the Fourth East Asian Altaistic Conference* (Tainan, Taiwan: 238–49. Reprinted in Sinor, 1977.

1977. *Inner Asia and its Contacts with Medieval Europe*. London: Variorum Reprints.

1988. 'Diplomatic practices in medieval Inner Asia' in C. Edmund Bosworth, Charles Issawi, Roger Savory and Abraham L. Udovitch, eds. *Essays in honor of Bernard Lewis: The Islamic world from classical to modern times*. Princeton, NJ: Darwin Press: 337–55. Reprinted from Sinor, 1977.

1989. 'Notes on Inner Asian Bibliography IV: History of the Mongols in the 13th Century', *Journal of Asian Studies*, 25/1: 28–79.

1997. *Studies in Medieval Inner Asia*. Aldershot: Ashgate.

al-Sirhindī, Yaḥyā, *Taʾrīkh-i Mubārak Shāhī*. 1931. ed. M. Hidayat Hosain [sic]. Bibliotheca Indica, vol. 254. Calcutta: Asiatic Society of Bengal.

Slezkine, Yuri. 1994. 'Naturalists versus Nations: Eighteenth-Century Russian Scholars Confront Ethnic Diversity', *Representations* 47: 170–95.

Smirnov, Nikolai A. 1946. *Rossiia i Turtsiia v XVI–XVII vv.* vol. I–II (Uchenye Zapiski Moskovskogo gosudarstvennogo universiteta, Vyp. 94). Moscow: MGU.

Smirnov, Vasilii D. 2005. *Krymskoe khanstvo pod verkhovenstvom Ottomanskoi Porty do nachala XVIII veka*, Vol. I–II (St. Petersburg: Tipografiia Suvorina, 1887, Reprint Moscow: Rubezhi XXI).

Smirnova, Ol'ga I. 1970. *Ocherki iz istorii Sogda*. Moscow: Nauka.

Smith, John Masson, Jr. 1970. 'Mongol and nomadic taxation.' *HJAS* 30: 46–85.

1994. 'The Mongols and world conquest.' *Mongolica* 5: 206–14.

2000. 'Dietary Decadence and Dynastic Decline in the Mongol Empire.' *Journal of Asian History*, 34/1: 35–52.

Sneath, David. 2007. *The Headless State. Aristocratic Orders, Kinship Society and Misrepresentations of Nomadic Inner Asia*. New York: Columbia University Press.

Soloviev, Sergei M. 1976ff. *History of Russia*. Gulf Breeze: Academic International Press.

Song, Lian. *Yuan shi*, see *YS*, in List of Abbreviations

Song-yun, Wang Tingkai, Qi Yunshi and Xu Song, comps. 1821. *(Qinding) Xinjiang zhilue* (Imperially commissioned gazetteer of Xinjiang). Beijing: Wuying Dian.

Soucek, Priscilla. 1980. 'The Role of Landscape in Iranian Painting to the 15th Century' in William Watson, ed., *Landscape Style in Asia*, Percival David Foundation Colloquies in Art and Archaeology of Asia, London: 86–109.

Spuler, Bertold. 1965. *Die Goldene Horde: Die Mongolen in Russland 1223–1502*. Leipzig: Otto Harrassowitz Verlag, 1943, 2nd edn. Wiesbaden: Otto Harrassowitz Verlag.

1972. *History of the Mongols based on Eastern and Western Accounts of the Thirteenth and Fourteenth Centuries*. Berkeley: University of California Press.

1985. *Die Mongolen in Iran*, 4th ed. Leiden: Brill.

Stary, Giovanni. 1974. *I primi rapporti tra Russia e Cina. Domumenti e Testimonianze*. Napoli: Guida.

Stary, Giovanni. 1984. 'The Manchu Emperor "Abahai": Analysis of an Historiographic Mistake.' *CAJ* 28/3–4: 196–9.

Standen, Naomi. 2003. 'Raiding and Frontier Society in the Five Dynasties' in Nicola Di Cosmo and D. J. Wyatt eds. 2003. *Political Frontiers, Ethnic Boundaries and Human Geographies in Chinese History*. London and New York: Routledge.

Steingass, Francis. 1970. *A Comprehensive Persian-English Dictionary*. London: Routledge & K. Paul, 1892, reprint: Librairie du Liban.

Stevens, Carol B. 1995. *Soldiers on the Steppe. Army Reform and Social Change in Early Modern Russia*. DeKalb, Illinois: Northern Illinois University.

Stoianov, Valeri. 2006. *Kumanologiia. Opiti za rekonstruktsiia*. Sofia: Akademichno Isdatelstvo 'Prof. Marin Drinov'.

Su, Tianjue. 1916. *Zixi wen gao*. Shiyuan congshu ed.

comp. 1936. *Yuan wen lei*, Guoxue jiben congshu ed. Shanghai: Shangwu yinshu guan.

1962. *Yuan chao ming chen shilüe*. Beijing: Zhonghua shuju.

Subtelny, Maria Eva. 1984. 'Scenes from the Literary Life of Timurid Herat', in Roger M. Savory and Dionisius A. Agius eds., *Logos Islamikos: Studia Islamica in honorem Georgii Michaelis Wickens*. Toronto, Canada: Pontifical Institute of Medieval Studies: 137–55.

1988. 'Socioeconomic Basis of Patronage under the later Timurids.' *International Journal of Middle East Studies* 20/4: 479–505.

1991. 'The Vaqfīya of Mīr ʿAlī Shīr Navāʾī as Apologia.' *Journal of Turkish Studies* 15: 9–19.

1997. 'Agriculture and the Timurid Chahār Bāgh: the Evidence from a Medieval Persian Agricultural Manual', in Attilio Petruccioli ed., *Gardens in the Time of Great Muslim Empires*: 110–28.

Su-er-de, *et al.* 1968. *Xinjiang Huibu zhi* (gazetteer of the Muslim region of Xinjiang), Qianlong period manuscript; repr., Zhongguo fangzhi congshu, xibu difang, no. 10. Taibei: Chengwen.

Suleimenov, R. B. and V. A. Moiseev. 1988. *Iz istorii Kazakhstana XVIII veka (o vneshnei i vnutrennei politike Ablaia)*. Alma-Ata: Nauka.

Sultan, Izzat. 1985. *Kniga priznaniī Navoi*. Tashkent: Gafur Gulyam.

Sulṭān Muḥammad (al-)Aṣamm 'Muṭribī' Samarqandī, Nuskha-i zībā-yi Jahāngīrī, ed. Ismāʿīl Begjānūf and Sayyid ʿAlī Mūjānī, Tehran, 1377/1998. The khātima of this work, pp. 267–344, has been separately published by A. M. Mirzoev as Khāṭirāt-i Muṭribī Samarqandī, (Karachi, 1977) and translated by Richard C. Foltz as *Conversations with Emperor Jahangir* (Costa Mesa: Mazda, 1998); Mirzoev also took selections from it and published it under the title *Tadhkirat al-shuʿarā* (Karachi, 1976).

Sultanov, Tursun I. 1982. *Kochevye plemena Priaral'ia v XV–XVII vv.* Moscow: Nauka.

2001. *Podniatye na beloi koshme. Potomki Chingiz-khana*. Almaty: Daik-Press.

2002. 'Rod Shibana, syna Dzhuchi: mesto dinastii v politicheskoi istorii Evrazii.' *Tiurkologicheskii Sbornik 2001 (Zolotaia Orda i ee nasledie)*. Moscow: 11–27.

Sümer, Faruk. 1980. *Oğuzlar.* 3rd rev. ed., Istanbul: ANA Yayınları.

Szentpétery, E. 1937–38. ed. *Scriptores Rerum Hungaricarum tempore ducum regumque stirpis Arpadianae gestarum*, I–II. Budapest.

Szuppe, Maria. 1992. *Entre Timourides, Uzbeks et Safavids*. Studia lranica 12. Paris: Association pour l'advancement des études iraniennes.

Taagepera, Rein. 1978. 'Size and Duration of Empires: Systematics of Size.' *Social Science Research* 7: 108–27.

Tafel, G. L. Fr. and G. M. Thomas. 1856–7. *Urkunden zur alteren Handels- und Staatsgeschichte der Republik Venedig mit besonderer Beziehung auf Byzanz und die Levant*, III (1256–1299) in Fontes rerum Austriacarum, 2. Abt. Diplomataria et acta, 12–14, Vienna: Wien, Hof- und Staatsdruckerei.

Ṭāhir Muḥammad b. ʿImād al-Din Sabzawārī. *Rawḍat al-ṭāhirīn*, vol. II, Hyderabad, Salar Jung Library, MS no. HIST. 291.

Tan, Qixiang . 1982. Ed. *Zhongguo lishi ditu ji*. Vol. VII. Shanghai: Guji chubanshe.

Tanīsh, see Ḥāfiẓ-i Tanīsh, 1983.

Tardy, Lajos. 1980. *A tatárországi rabszolgakereskedelem és a magyarok a XIII–XV. Században*. Budapest: Nauka.

Taskin, Vsevolod S. 1984. *Materialy po istorii drevnikh kochevykh narodov gruppy dunxu*. Moscow: Nauka.

Teng, S. Y. 1976. 'Chu Yüan-chang', *Dictionary of Ming Biography*, 2 vols., ed. L. Carrington Goodrich and C. Y. Fang. New York and London: Columbia University Press: 1: 381–92.

Tenishev, Edgem R. 1997. ed. *Sravnitel'no-istoricheskaia grammatika tiurkskikh iazykov. Leksika*. Moscow: Nauka.

Tezcan, Semih. 2006. 'Oğuznameler', in Halman, 2006: 607–20.

al-Thaʿālibī. 1968. *The Book of Curious and Entertaining Information: The Laṭāʾif al-maʿārif of Thaʿālibī*, trans. C. E. Bosworth. Edinburgh: The University Press.

Thackston, W. M. 1996. 'Editor's Preface', in *Mirza Haydar Dughlat's, Tarikh-i-Rashidi: A History of the Khans of Moghulistan,* Persian text ed. W. M. Thackston, English trans. and annotation by W. M. Thackston. Sources of Oriental Languages and Literatures, 37 and 38. Cambridge, Mass.: Harvard University, Dept. of Near Eastern Languages and Civilizations: vii–x.

Thirsk, Joan. 1967–2000. ed. *The Agrarian History of England and Wales*, H. P. R. Finberg, London: Cambridge University Press.

Thomas, Georg M. and Riccardo Pedrelli. 1880, 1899. eds. *Diplomatarium Veneto-Levantinum, sive Acta et Diplomata res Venetas Graecas atque Levantis illustrantia*, I-II. Venice.

Tikhvinskii, Sergei L. 1977. ed. *Tataro-mongoly v Azii i Evrope*. 2nd rev. edn. Moscow: Nauka.

Tizengauzen, Vladimir G. 1884, 1941, 2004. *Sbornik materialov, otnosiashchikhsia k istorii Zolotoi Ordy*. I: St. Petersburg, 1884; II, sobrannye V. G. Tizengauzenom i obrabotannye A. A. Romaskevichem i S. L. Volinym: Moscow and Leningrad, 1941. New edition of the Russian translations, without the original Arabic and Persian texts: Moscow: Tsentr po izucheniiu voennoi i obshchei istorii, 2004. See also Kumekov and Muminov, 2005 for reprint of vol. I with Arabic texts.

Togan, İsenbike. 1998. *Flexibility and Limitations in Steppe Formations: The Kerait Khanate and Chinggis Khan*. Leiden, New York and Cologne: Brill.

Togan, Zeki Velidi. 1958. 'Timurs Osteuropapolitik.' *Zeitschrift der Deutschen morgenländischen Gesellschaft* 108: 279–98.

1959–60. 'Kazan hanlığında islâm türk kültürü.' *İslam Tetkikleri Enstitüsü Dergisi*, 3/3–4: 179–204.

Tolybekov, S. E. 1971. *Kochevoe obshchestvo kazakhov v XVII-nachale XX veka*. Alma-Ata: Nauka.

Tomilov, N. A. 1981. *Turkoiazychnoe naselenie Zapadno-Sibirskoi ravniny v kontse XVI-pervoi chetverti XIX vv.* Tomsk: Izdatel'stvo Tomskogo Universiteta.

Toparlı, Recep *et al.* 2000. eds. Anonymous, *Kitab-ı Mecmū-ı Tercüman-ı Türkī ve Acemī ve Mugalī*. Ankara: Türk Dil Kurumu.

Tremblay, Xavier. 2001. *Pour une histoire de la Sérinde*, Österreichische Akademie der Wissenschaften, Philosophisch-historische Klasse, Sitzungsberichte, 690. Vienna: Verlag der Österreichischen Akademie der Wissenschaften.

2007. 'Kanjakî and Kâšγarian Sakan.' *CAJ* 51 / 1: 63–76.

Trepavlov, Vadim V. 1993. *Gosudarstvennyi stroi Mongol'skoi imperii XIII v.* Moscow: Nauka.

2001a. 'Saraichuk: pereprava, nekropol', stolitsa, razvaliny', *Tiurkologicheskii sbornik 2001: Zolotaia Orda i ee nasledie*. Moscow: Vostochnaia Literatura: 225–44.

2001b. *Istoriia Nogaiskoi Ordy*. Moscow: Vostochnaia literatura RAN.

Tu Fang, L. C. and C. Y. Fang. 1976. 'Chu Ch'i-chen', *Dictionary of Ming Biography*, 2 vols., ed. L. Carrington Goodrich and C. Y. Fang. New York and London: Columbia University Press: 1: 289–94.

Tu, Ji. 1962. *Mengwuer shiji*. Taibei: Shijie shuju.

Tuimebaev, Zhanseit K. 2005. *Kazakhsko-mongol'skie leksicheskie paralleli. Materialy k etimologicheskomu slovariu kazakhskogo iazyka*. Moscow: Parad.

Tulepbaev, B. A. 1983. ed. *Kazakhstan, Sredniaia Aziia i Tsentral'naia Aziia v XVI–XVII vv.* Alma-Ata: Nauka.

Tulibaeva, Zhyldyz M. 2001. *Kazakhstan i Bukharskoe khanstvo v XVIII–pervoi polovine XIX v.* Almaty: Daik Press.

Tumanovich, Nataliia N. 1989. *Gerat v XVI–XVIII v.* Moscow: Nauka.

Tumanshin, K. M. 1961. 'Osnovanie i razvitie goroda Petropavlovska i ego uezda vo vtoroi XVIII–pervoi polovine XIX vv.' *Uchenye zapiski Kustanaiskogo Gosudarstvennogo Pedinstituta* 6: 39–84.

Turan Fikret. 2007. 'Doğu Türk Yazı Dili Edebī Çevresi: Harezm-Kıpçak, Mısır-Suriye Çağatay Sahası', in Halman, 2007: 1: 681–96.

Ṭūsī, Muḥammad ibn Muḥammad Nāṣir al-Dīn. 1969. *Tansūkh-nāma-yi Īl-Khānī*, ed. Mudarris Raḍawī. Tehran: Intishārāt-i Bunyād-i Farhang-i Īrān, 1348 / 1969.

Twitchett, Dennis and Herbert Franke. 1994. eds. See List of Abbreviations, *CHChina*, VI

Tynyshpaev, Mukhamedzhan. 1998. *Istoriia kazakhskogo naroda*. Almaty: Sanat.

Uljitokto. 2004. 'Jindai Menggu sifa shenpan zhidu de yanbian.' *Zhongyang minzu daxue xuebao* 5: 68–74.

al-ʿUmarī / India, see List of Abbreviations

/ Lech, see List of Abbreviations

1988. *al-Taʿrīf bi'l-muṣṭalaḥ al-sharīf*. Beirut: Dār al-Kutub.

Usmanov, A. N. 1960. *Prisoedinenie Bashkirii k russkomu gosudarstvu*. Ufa: Bashkirskoe Knizhnoe Izdatel'stvo.

Usmanov, Kh. F. 1996. ed. *Istoriia Bashkortostana s drevneishikh vremen do 60-kh gg. XIX veka*. Ufa: Kitap.

Usmanov, Mirkasym A. 1972. *Tatarskie istoricheskie istochniki XVII–XVIII vv*. Kazan: Izdatel'stvo Kazanskogo Universiteta.

1979. *Zhalovannye akty Dzhuchieva Ulusa XIV–XVI vv*. Kazan: Izdatel'stvo Kazanskogo Universiteta.

Ustiugov, Nikolai V. 1947. 'Bashkirskoe vosstanie 1662–1664 gg.' *Istoricheskie zapiski* 24: 30–112.

1950. *Bashkirskoe vosstanie 1737–1739 gg*. Moscow: Akademiia Nauk.

Valeev, Fuat T. and Nikolai A. Tomilov. 1996. *Tatary Zapadnoi Sibiri. Istoriia i kul'tura*. Novosibirsk: Nauka.

Valikhanov, Chokan. 1985. *Sobranie sochinenii v piati tomakh* I–V. Alma-Ata: Kazakhskaia Sovetskaia Entsiklopediia.

Vásáry, István. 1976. 'The Golden Horde Term *daruġa* and its Survival in Russia.' *AOH* 30: 187–97.

1978. 'The Origin of the Institution of *Basqaqs*.' *AOH* 32: 201–6.

1990. 'History and Legend in Berke Khan's Conversion to Islam', in *Aspects of Altaic Civilization III*, ed. Denis Sinor. Bloomington, Ind.: Indiana University, Research Institute for Inner Asian Studies: 230–52.

2005. *Cumans and Tatars: Oriental Military in the Pre-Ottoman Balkans, 1185–1365*. Cambridge and New York: Cambridge University Press.

2007. 'Immunity Charters of the Golden Horde Granted to the Italian Towns Caffa and Tana', in István Vásáry, *Turks, Tatars and Russians in the 13th–16th Centuries*. (Variorum Collected Studies Series). Aldershot, Hampshire and Burlington, VT: Ashgate Publishing Ltd.: XII: 1–13.

2009. 'The Beginnings of Coinage in the Blue Horde', in U. Schamiloglu and T. Kocaoğlu, (forthcoming).

Vasil'ev, A. V. 1898. *Materialy k kharakteristike vzaimnykh otnoshenii tatar i kirgizov s predvaritel'nym kratkim ocherkom etikh otnoshenii*. Orenburg: Zharinov.

Veinstein, Gilles. 1999. 'À l'arrière-plan de la conquète de Sibir: Moscou et la Grande Horde nogaye', in *Siberie. Histoire, cultures, literature*, ed. B. Chichlo. Paris: Institut d'Études slaves : 49–58.

Veit, V. 1986a. 'Die mongolischen Völkerschaften vom 15. Jahrhundert bis 1691', in *Die Mongolen. Beiträge zu ihrer Geschichte und Kultur*, ed. M. Weiers. Darmstadt: Wissenschaftliche Buchgesellschaft: 379–411.

1986b. 'Qalqa 1691–1911', in *Die Mongolen. Beiträge zu ihrer Geschichte und Kultur*, ed. M. Weiers. Darmstadt: Wissenschaftliche Buchgesellschaft.

Vel'iaminov-Zernov, V. V. 1855. *Istoricheskie izvestiia o kirgiz-kaisakakh i snosheniiakh Rossii s Srednei Aziei* II. Ufa: Gubernskaia tipografiia.

1859. 'Monety bukharskie i khivinskie.' *Trudy Vostochnogo otdeleniia Imp. Russkogo Arkheologicheskogo obshchestva* 4: 328–456.

1864–8. *Izsledovanie o kasimovskikh tsariakh i tsarevichakh* I–IV. St. Petersburg: Tipografiia Imperatorskoi Akademii Nauk.

Vernadskii, Georgii [Vernadsky, George]. 1927. 'Zolotaja Orda, Egipet i Vizantiia v ikh vzaimootnosheniiakh v tsarstvovanie Mikhaila Paleologa.' *Seminarium Kondakovianum* 1: 73–84.

1953. *The Mongols and Russia*. New Haven: Yale University Press; Russian trans.: G. V. Vernadskii, *Mongoly i Rus'*. Tver' and Moscow: LEAN-AGRAF, 1997.

Veselovskii, N. I. 1922. 'Khan iz temnikov Zolotoi Ordy Nogai i ego vremia.' *Zapiski Rossiiskoi Akademii Nauk po otdeleniiu istoricheskikh nauk i filologii* 13: 1–58.

Viatkin, M. P. 1939. 'Zhurnal Orenburgskogo Muftiia.' *Istoricheskii arkhiv* 2: 117–220.

1940. ed. *Materialy po istorii Kazakhskoi SSR* IV. Moscow and Leningrad: Akademiia Nauk Kazakhskoi SSR.

1947. *Batyr Srym*. Moscow and Leningrad: Akademiia Nauk.

1948. ed. *Materialy po istorii Kazakhskoi SSR* II. Alma-Ata: Akademiia Nauk Kazakhskoi SSR. ch. 2.

Viktorova, Lidiia L. 1980. *Mongoly. Proiskhozhdenie naroda i istoki kul'tury*. Moscow: Nauka.

Vil'danova, A. B. 1970. 'Podlinnik Bukharskogo traktata o chinakh i zvaniiakh', *Pis'mennye Pamiatniki Vostoka 1968*. Moscow: Nauka: 40–67.

Vladimirtsov, Boris Ia. 1922. *Chingis-khan*. Berlin, Prague and Moscow: Z. I. Grzhebin, reprinted and repaginated in his *Raboty*, 2002: 141–207.

1934. *Obshchestvennyi stroi mongolov. Mongol'skii kochevoi feodalizm*. Leningrad: Izdatel'stvo Akademii Nauk SSSR; reprinted and repaginated in his *Raboty*, 2002: 295–488.

1948. *Le regime social des Mongols: Le feodalisme nomad*. Paris: Publications du Musée Guimet, Bibliothèque d'Études. French trans. of his *Obshchestvennyi stroi mongolov*, see above.

2002. *Raboty po istorii i etnografii mongol'skikh narodov*. Moscow: Vostochnaia Literatura.

Voegelin, Eric. 1941. 'The Mongol Orders of Submission to European Powers, 1245–1255.' *Byzantion* 15: 378–413.

Vogelsang, Willem. 2002. *The Afghans*. Oxford: Blackwell.

Voll, John Obert. 1992. 'Islam as a Special World System.' *JWH* 5/2: 213–26.

Vorob'ev, N. I. and G. M. Khismatullin. 1967. Eds. *Tatary Srednego Povolzh'ia i Priural'ia*. Moscow: Nauka.

Vorob'ev, Mikhail V. 1975. *Chzhurcheni i gosudarstvo tszin'*. Moscow: Nauka.

Vostrov, Veniamin V. and Marat S. Mukanov. 1968. *Rodoplemennoi sostav i rasselenie kazakhov*. Alma-Ata: Nauka.

Waley, Arthur. 1931. Trans. *Travels of an Alchemist; the journey of the Taoist, Ch'ang-Ch'un, from China to the Hindukush at the summons of Chingiz Khan/recorded by his disciple, Li Chih-Ch'ang*. London: G. Routledge & Sons.

Wang, Deyi *et al.* 1879–82. *Yuan ren zhuanji ziliao suoyin*. Taibei: Xin wenfeng tushu gongsi. 5 vols.

Wang, Puren *et al.* 1985. *Meng-Cang minzu guanxi shilüe*. Beijing: Zhongguo shehui kexue chubanshe.

Wang Xiangyun. 2000. 'The Qing Court's Tibet Connection: Lcang skya Rol pa'I rdo rje and the Qianlong Emperor.' *HJAS* 60/1: 125–63.

Wang Xilong. 1990. *Qingdai Xibei tuntian yanjiu*. Lanzhou: Lanzhou Daxue chubanshe.

Wang Zhonghan. 1956a. *Mingdai Nüzhen de fenbu*. s. l.: Zhongguo minzu wenti yanjiu jikan.

1956b. *Manzu zai Nuerhachi shidai de shehui jingji xingtai*. s.l.: Zhongguo minzu wenti yanjiu jikan.

1984. 'Shilun Lifanyuan yu Menggu.' *Qingshi yanjiuji* 3: 166–79. Chengdu: Sichuan renmin chubanshe.

Waṣṣāf, see List of Abbreviations

Wāṣifī, Zayn al-Dīn. 1961. *Badāʾiʿ al-waqāʾiʿ*, ed. A. N. Boldyrev. Moscow: Nauka. 2 vols.

Watanabe, Hiroshi. 'An Index of Embassies and Tribute Missions from Islamic Countries to Ming China (1368–1466) as Recorded in the Ming *Shih-lu* Classified According to Geographic Area.' *The Memoirs of the Toyo Bunko* 33: 285–347.

Watt, James C. Y. and Anne E. Wardell. 1997. eds. *When Silk Was Gold: Central Asian and Chinese Textiles*. New York: Metropolitan Museum of Art in cooperation with the Cleveland Museum of Art.

Wei, Liangtao. 1994. *Yererqiang hanguo shigang*, Bianjiang shidi congshu. Harbin: Heilongjiang jiaoyu chubanshe.

1996. 'Di jiu bian: Mingdai ji Qingchu zhi Xiyu', ed. Yu Taishan. Zhengzhou: Zhongzhou guji chubanshe.

Wei, Su. 1985. *Wei Taipu wen xu ji*, in *Yuan ren wenji zhenben congkan*, ed. Wang Deyi. Taibei: Xin wenfeng chubanshe, 7: 486–604.

Wei, Yuan. 1990. *Yuanshi xinbian*. Yangzhou: Yangzhou guji shudian.

Weiers, Michael. 1967. 'Mongolische Reisebegleitschreiben aus Čaghatai.' *Zentral-Asiatische Studien* 1: 1–53.

1979a. 'Die Kuang-ning Affäre, Beginn des Zerwürfnisses zwischen den Mongolischen Tsakhar und den Mandschuren.' *Zentralasiatische Studien* 13: 73–91.

1979b. 'Mandschu-Mongolische Strafgesetze aus dem Jahre 1631 und deren Stellung in der Gesetzgebung der Mongolen.' *Zentralasiatische Studien* 13: 137–90.

1979c. ed. *Die Verträge zwischen Russland und China, 1689–1881*. Bonn: Wehling.

1983. 'Der Mandschu-Khortsin-Bund von 1626', *Documenta Barbarorum: Festschrift für Walther Heissig zum 70. Geburtstag*, ed. K. Sagaster and M. Weiers. Societas Uralo-Altaica, 18. Wiesbaden: Harrassowitz: 412–35.

1986a. 'Die Mandschu-Mongolischen Strafgesetze vom 16. November 1632.' *Zentralasiatische Studien* 19: 88–126.

1986b. ed. *Die Mongolen. Beiträge zu ihrer Geschichte und Kultur*. Darmstadt: Wissenschaftliche Buchgesellschaft.

1987. 'Die Vertragstexte des Mandschu-Khalkha-Bundes von 1619/20', in *Aetas Manjurica*, 1. Wiesbaden: Harrassowitz: 119–65.

1996. 'Zum Mandschu-Kharatsin-Bund des Jahres 1628.' *Zentralasiatische Studien* 26: 84–121.

2001. 'Die drei Amtshöfe des Schriftwesens im späten Aisin-Staat.' *Zentralasiatische Studien* 31: 65–88.

2002. *Die Siegel des Ayushiridara, die politischen Ideologien der Mongolen, und ihre Geschichtsschreibung*. Stipes Philologiae Asiae Maioris (S.P.A.M.). Contributions on Philology and History of Eastern Inner Asia, 4. www.zentralasienforschung.de/spam/spam042002.pdf

2003 'Moghol', in Janhunen, 2003a: 248–64.

2004. *Geschichte der Mongolen*, Urban Taschenbücher, 586. Stuttgart: Kohlhammer.

Werth, Paul W. 1999. 'Armed Defiance and Biblical Appropriation: Assimilation and the Transformation of Mordvin Resistance, 1740–1810.' *Nationalities Papers* 27/2: 247–70.

2002. *At the Margins of Orthodoxy: Mission, Governance and Confessional Policy in Russia's Volga-Kama Region, 1827–1905*. Ithaca and London: Cornell University Press.

Wessels, C. 1924. *Early Jesuit Travellers in Central Asia, 1603–1721*. The Hague: Martinus Nijhoff.

William of Rubruck, see Rubruck.

Wittfogel, Karl A. 1963. 'Russia and the East: A Comparison and Contrast.' *Slavic Review* 22/4: 627–43.

Wittfogel, Karl A. and Feng Chia-sheng. 1949. *History of Chinese Society: The Liao (907–1125)*. Philadelphia: American Philosophical Society.

Woods, John E. 1984. 'Turco-Iranica II: Notes on a Timurid Decree of 1396/798.' *Journal of Near Eastern Studies* 43/4: 331–7.

1987. 'The Rise of Tīmūrīd Historiography.' *Journal of Near Eastern Studies* 46/2: 81–108.

1990a. 'Timur's Genealogy', in *Intellectual Studies on Islam: Essays Written in Honor of Martin B. Dickson*, ed. Michel M. Mazzaoui and Vera B. Moreen. Salt Lake City: University of Utah Press: 85–126.

1990b. *The Timurid Dynasty*. Papers on Inner Asia, 14. Bloomington, Ind.: Indiana University, Research Institute for Inner Asian Studies.

Wylie, Turrel V. 1977. 'The First Mongol Conquest of Tibet Reinterpreted.' *HJAS* 37: 103–33.

Wyngaert, Anastasius van den. 1929. ed. *Sinica Franciscana I: Itinera et relationes fratrum minorum saeculi XIII. et XIV*. Ad Claras Aquas. Quaracchi and Florence: Collegium S. Bonaventurae.

Xiao, Gongqin. 1981. 'Lun Da Menggu guo de han wei jicheng weiji.' *Yuan shi ji beifang minzu shi yanjiu jikan* 5: 48–59.

Xiao Jinsong. 1977. 'Qingdai zhu Zang dachen de zhiquan.' *Bulletin of the Institute of China Border Area Studies* 8: 241–90.

Xu, Lili. 1998. 'Chahetai hanguo yu Wokuotai hanguo guanxi shuping.' *Xiyu yanjiu* 2: 29–37.

Yan, Fu. 1985. ed. *Jingxuan ji*, in Wang Deyi, *Yuan ren wenji zhenben congkan*. Taibei: Xin wenfeng chubanshe 2: 541–70.

Yang Qiang. 2006. 'Qingdai dui Mengguzu fazhi gaige de yingxiang.' *Tianshui xingzheng xueyuan xuebao* 5: 99–101.

Yang Qiang and Shi Yu. 2005. 'Lun Qingdai dui Mengguzu de lifa.' *Liaoning jingzhuan xuebao* 3: 35–7.

Yao, Dali. 1983. 'Naiyan zhi luan kao.' *Yuan shi ji beifang minzu shi yanjiu jikan* 7: 74–82.

Yao, Jing'an. 1982. *Yuanshi ren ming suoyin*. Beijing: Zhonghua shuju.

Yao, Sui. 1919–36. *Mu'an ji*, ed. Sibu Congkan. Also available electronically.

Yazdī, Sharaf al-Dīn ʿAlī, see List of Abbreviations and below

1972. *Muqaddima-i Ẓafar nāmah*, ed. Asom Urunbaev. Tashkent: Academy of Sciences of the Uzbek SSR.

Ye Zhiru. 1986. 'Cong maoyi aocha kan Qianlong qianqi dui Zhunga'er bu de minzu zhengce', *Xinjiang daxue xuebao* 1: 62–71.

Yelü, Zhu. 1999. *Shuangxi zuiyin ji*. Siku quanshu electronic edition.

Yong-bao. 1990. *Zongtong Yili shiyi*, original *c*.1795; repr., *Qingdai Xinjiang xijian shiliao huiji*. Zhongguo bianjiang shidi shiliao congkan, Xinjiang volume. Beijing: Quanguo tushuguan wenxian suowei fuzhi zhongxin: 125–76.

Yong-bao *et al*. 1950. *Wulumuqi shiyi*, original 1796; reprint Bianjiang congshu xubian, ed. Wu Fengpei, no. 6. Beijing: n.p.

Yong-bao and Xing-zhao. 1950. *Ta'erbahatai shiyi*, original 1805; reprint Bianjiang congshu xubian, ed. Wu Fengpei, no. 4. Beijing: n.p.

Yu, Ji. 1937. *Daoyuan xue gu lu*, ed. Wanyou wenku. Shanghai: Shangwu yinshu guan.

Yu Taishan. 1996. ed. *Xiyu tongshi*. Zhengzhou: Zhengzhou guji chubanshe.

Yuan, Jue. n.d. *Baizhu yuanshuai chushi shishi*, in *Qingrong jushi ji*, Yuan facs. edn, ch. 34. Shanghai: Shangwu yinshuguan.

Yuan, Mingshan. 1968. *Qinghe ji*, in Miao Quansun, ed Ou xiang ling shi, vols. III–IV. Taibei: Guangwen shuju.

Yuan Senpo. 1996. 'Qingchao zhili Meng Zang fanglüe.' *Zhongguo bianjiang shidi yanjiu* 4: 43–8, 108.

Yuan Shih, see Abramowski, 1976, 1979; Krause, 1922 and in List of Abbreviations, *YS*

Yuanshi. 1978. Beijing: Zhonghua shuju.

Yücel, Bilal. 1995. *Babur Dīvānı*. Ankara: Atatürk Kultur Merkezi.

Yule, Henry. 1863. trans. *The Wonders of the East by Friar Jordanus*. Works Issued by the Hakluyt Society, first series, 31. London: Hakluyt Society; reprint New York: Burt Franklin, n.d.

1967. trans. and comp. *Cathay and the Way Thither*, see Yule / *Cathay*, in List of Abbreviations

Yule, Henry and A. C. Burnell. 1903. *Hobson-Jobson: A Glossary of Anglo-Indian Words and Phrases*. London: John Murray.

Yunggui (Yong-gui), Gu Shiheng and Se-er-de. 1968. *Huijiang zhi* [Gazetteer of the Muslim Frontier], original 1772; reprint, Zhongguo fangzhi congshu, xibu defang, 1. Taibei: Chengwen.

al-Yūnīnī, Quṭb al-Dīn Mūsā b. Muḥammad. 1954–61. *Dhayl mira'ʾt al-zamān fī ta'rīkh al-aʿyān*. Hyderabad and Deccan: Dairat al-Maʿārif al-ʿUthmāniyya, 1374–80 / 1954–61. 4 vols.

Zagorovskii, Vladimir P. 1969. *Belgorodskaia cherta*. Voronezh: Gosudarstvennyi universitet.

1980. *Iziumskaia cherta*. Voronezh: Gosudarstvennyi universitet.

Zahidullin, Ildus. 1997. 'La conversion à l'orthodoxie des Tatars de la région volga-oural, aux XVII–XVIIIe siècles, et ses causes économiques et sociales', in *L'Islam de Russie. Conscience communautaire et autonomie politique chez les Tatars de la Volga et de l'Oural, depuis le XVIIIe siècle*, ed. Stéphane A. Dudoignon, Dämir Is'haqov and Räfyq Möhämmätshin. Paris: Maisonneuve et Larousse: 27–64.

Zaitsev, I. V. 2002. 'Istoriografiaia istorii otnoshenii postordynskikh 'iurtov' s Rossiei i Osmanskoi imperiei', in *Istochnikovedenie istorii ulusa Dzhuchi (Zolotoi ordy) ot Kalki do Astrakhani, 1223–1556*. Kazan': Master Lain: 269–313.

2004. *Astrakhanskoe khanstvo*. Moscow: Vostochnaia Literatura.

Zajączkowski, Ananiasz. 1966. ed. *La chronique des steppes Kiptchak, Tevārīkh-i dešt-i Qipčaq*. Warsaw: Państwowe Wydawnictwo Naukowe.

Zākānī, ʿUbaid-i, Niẓām al-Dīn. 1999. *Kullīyāt-i ʿUbaid Zākānī*, ed. Mohammad Jaʿfar Maḥjūb. New York and Winona Lake, Ind.: Bibliotheca Persica Press.

Zakiev, Mirfatykh Z. 2003. *Proiskhozhdenie tiurkov i tatar*. Moscow: Insan.

Zakirov, Salikh. 1966. *Diplomaticheskie otnosheniia Egipta s Zolotoi Ordoi (XIII–XIV vv.)*. Moscow: Nauka.

Zambaur, Eduard K. M. von. 1968. *Die Münzprägungen des Islams. I. Der Westen und Osten bis zum Indus mit Synoptischen Tabellen*. Wiesbaden: Franz Steiner Verlag.

Zarcone, Thierry. 1995. 'Sufism from Central Asia Among the Tibetans in the 16–17th Centuries.' *The Tibet Journal* (Dharamsala, India) 20 / 3: 96–114.

1996. 'Soufis d'Asie centrale au Tibet aux XVIe et XVIIe siècles', in *Cahiers d'Asie Centrale*, special issue on 'Inde-Asie centrale: Routes du commerce et des idées', Aix-en-Provence: Ed. Edisud, 1–2: 325–44.

Zeng Wenwu. 1986. *Zhongguo jingying Xiyu shi*. Shanghai: Shangwu, 1936; reprint Xinjiang Weiwu'er zizhiqu zongbian shi.

Zettersteen, Karl V. 1919. *Beiträge zur Geschichte der Mamlukensultane in den Jahren 690–741 der higra nach arabischen Handschriften*. Leiden: Brill.

Zhandarbek, Zikiriya. 2000. *Türkistan qïsqasha tarikhï*. Turkistan: Yasavi University.

Zhanaev, B. T. *et al.* 2002. eds. *Istoriia Bukeevskogo khanstva, 1801–1852 gg.* Almaty: Daik Press.

Zhang, Yan. 1996. 'Alimali gucheng de lishi yanbian.' *Xinjiang daxue xuebao* 24 / 1: 68–72.

Zhang Yuxin. 1986, 1987. 'Suzhou maoyi kaolue' parts 1–3. *Xinjiang daxue xuebao*, 1986, 3: 24–32; 1986, 4: 48–54; 1987, 1: 67–76.

Zhao Hong. 1975. *Mengda beilu*, in *Menggu shiliao sizhong*, ed. Wang Guowei. Taibei: Zhengzhong shuju.

Zhao Yuntian. 1994. 'Qingchao zhili Meng Zang diqu de jige wenti.' *Zhongguo shekui kexue* 3: 175–92.
Zhou, Lingxiao. 1986. *Hubilie*. Jilin: Jiaoyu chubanshe.
Zhou, Qingshu. 2001. 'Wanggubu tongzhi jiazu', in *Yuan-Meng shizha*. Hohhot: Nei Menggu daxue chubanshe: 48–88.
Zhou Yuanlian. 1979. 'Guanyu 16 shiji 40–80 niandai chu jianzhou Nuzhen he zaoqi manzu de shehui xingzhi wenti.' *Qingshi luncong* 1: 158–76.
Zhouli. 1991. 'Qiu Guan Sikou', in *Shisan jing*. Beijing: Yanshan chubanshe, vol I.
Zhu, Feng and Wang, Lu. 1981. 'Hubilie de dingxin gegu', in *Menggu zu lishi renwu lunji*, ed. Lu Minghui. Beijing: Zhongguo shehui kexue chubanshe: 57–67.
Zhu, Xinguang. 1997. 'Dong Chahetai hanguo yu Tiemuer diguo zhi zhan ji yingxiang.' *Zhongguo bianjiang shi di yanjiu* 3: 112–18.
Ziiaev, Kh. Z. 1983. *Ekonomicheskie sviazi Srednei Azii s Sibir'iu v XVI–XIX vv.* Tashkent: Fan.
Zlatkin, I. Ia. 1965. 'The History of the Khanate of Dzhungaria.' *Central Asian Review* 13/1: 17–30.
1983. *Istoria Dzhungarskogo khanstva, 1635–1758*. 2nd edn. Moscow: Nauka.

Index

Note on alphabetization: All Mongol and other Asian personal names are listed in the fullest form in which they appear in the text, without inversion, except in a few cases of major literary or religious figures who are well known under the last element of their names.
n = footnote.

Abadai Khan (of the Khalkha) 172
Abahai *see* Hung Tayiji
Abaqa (son of Hülegü) 50, 52, 130
ʿAbbasid Caliphate 33, 122, 129, 142
ʿAbd al-ʿAzīz b. Nadhr Muḥammad (Togha-Timurid Khan) 300–1
ʿAbd al-ʿAzīz Sulṭān b. ʿUbayd Allāh Khan 279*n*
ʿAbd al-Karīm (Astrakhan Khan, d. 1514) 254, 257
ʿAbd al-Karīm (Moghul Khan, d. 1591/2) 266
ʿAbd al-Karīm b. Baltay (Ṣūfī Shaykh, fl. 1750s) 390
ʿAbd al-Karīm Biy (Khoqand founder, fl. 1740) 400–1
ʿAbd al-Laṭīf b. Ibrāhīm (Kazan Khan) 248
ʿAbd al-Laṭīf b. Küchkünji (Abu'l-Khayrid Khan) 285
ʿAbd al-Laṭīf b. Ulugh Beg (Timurid descendant) 197, 200
ʿAbd al-Malik b. Muẓaffar (Bukharan leader) 409
ʿAbd al-Muʾmin b. ʿAbd Allāh (Abu'l-Khayrid Khan) 297–8
ʿAbd al-Mūʾmin b. Abu'l-Fayẓ (Bukhara Khan) 395
ʿAbd al-Quddūs b. Iskandar (Abū'l Khayrid Khan) 295
ʿAbd al-Raḥmān Aftābachī (Khoqand leader) 410
ʿAbd al-Raḥman al-Ūtiz-Īmānī (theologian) 389
ʿAbd al-Razzāq Samarqandī (historian) 223
ʿAbd Allāh Anṣārī, Shaykh 196
ʿAbd Allāh b. Ibrāhīm Sulṭān (Timurid descendant) 197
ʿAbd Allāh b. Iskandar (Abū'l Khayrid Khan, r. 1583-98) 197, 281, 283, 287–8, 289–90, 295–9, 300
ʿAbd Allāh b. Küchkünji (Abū'l Khayrid Khan, r. 1540) 285, 287
ʿAbd ar-Raḥman al-Ūtiz-Īmānī (religious leader) 389
ʿAbd as-Salām b. ʿAbd ar-Raḥīm (religious leader) 377
ʿAbdallāh b. Ulugh Beg (Timurid descendant) 223
Abdul-Rashid b. Saʿīd (Moghul Khan) 266*n*
ʿAbdullāh b. Muslim, Imām 376–7
ʿAbdullāh Khan 9, 80, 131, 183
Abishqa (Chaghadaid descendant) 49
Ablay Khan b. Walī Sulṭān (Qazaq leader) 370–1
Abu Bakr, Caliph 242*n*
Abū Saʿīd b. Küchkünji (Abu'l-Khayrid Khan) 281, 285
Abū Saʿīd b. Muhammad Mīranshāhī (Timurid ruler) *see* Sulṭān-Abū Saʿīd
Abū Saʿīd (last Ilkhanate ruler) 57, 79, 93
Abū Saʿīd Qara Qoyunlu 191
Abū Yazīd Bisṭāmī 123
Abu'l-Fayẓ (brother of ʿUbaydallāh , Bukhara Khan) 393, 394, 395
Abu'l-Ghāzī b. ʿArab Muḥammad (Khwārazm Khan) 301
Abu'l-Ghāzī b. Ilbārs (Khiva Khan) 394
Abu'l-Ghāzī Bahādur Khan (historian) 221, 221*n*, 222, 224*n*, 225*n*, 226, 230, 231, 233, 234

Abu'l-Ghāzī (Bukharan puppet khan) 395
Abu'l-Ghāzī Sulṭān (Arabshahi leader) 234
Abū'l-Khayr Khan (Qazaq leader, d. 1748) 368–9
Abū'l-Khayr Khan (Uzbek leader, d. 1468) 191, 194, 201, 237–8, 251
 death 226, 291, 369
 expansionist campaigns 222–6, 291
Abu'l-Khayrids line 277, 278–82, 286–94
 internal conflicts 294–6, 297–8
 military tactics 296–7
Abū'l-Mambat Khan (Qazaq leader) 368, 369–70
Abū'l-Qāsim Bābur b. Baysunghur (Timurid descendant) 197–8, 200–1
Abūlak b. Yādigār (Jochid descendant) 227
Abunai (Chakhar Khan) 342
Achaemenid Empire 141
Adai (descendant of Temüge) 163
Adaqlï(-Khïzïr) (Türkmen tribe) 233–4
Adshead, S.A.M. 4
Āfāq Khwāja (and followers) 268–9, 271, 275
Agalak (Kazan claimant) 251
Aghbarji Jinong (brother of Toghto-bukha) 164, 165
agriculture 35, 61, 63, 179, 404
 failing yields 91
 manuals 137–8
 Qing 273, 274, 335–6
 relocation of colonies / specialists 136
 taxation 98–100, 205
 unsuitability of terrain 265
Ahacu 334
Aḥrārī family 295
Aḥmad Ḥājjī Beg Duldai 209
Aḥmad Jalayir (Turko-Mongolian leader) 185
Aḥmad Kāsānī *see* Makhdum-i A'zam
Aḥmad Khan b. Kichī-Muḥammad (Great Horde leader) 253
Aḥmad Khan (Jochid descendant) 222, 251
Aḥmad Tegüder (son of Hülegü) 123–4
Aisin (Jurchen) state 157, 158
 Aisin Gioro (clan), 333, 334, 359
Akbar, (Mughal) Emperor 216, 287
ʿAlā' al-Dawla b. Baysunghur (Timurid descendant) 192, 197
ʿAlā' al-Dawla Simnānī *see* Simnānī
Alan Gho'a (legendary figure) 20–1, 20*n*
Alan people 136
Alaqush (Tegin Quri) (Önggüt leader) 24
Alash (Qazaq ancestor) 365–6
alban 'tax' 97
albatu 'taxable private property' 97
alcoholic beverages, production / consumption 150
Alcu Bolud (offspring of Dayan Khan) 166
Aldï Er ('Forest People' leader) 18
Alghu (grandson of Chaghadai) 49, 50–1, 52, 61, 129
Alghui Temür (rebel prince) 42
ʿAlī b. Ibrāhīm (Kazan Khan) 248
ʿAlī Quli Khan (Qïzïlbash governor) 296–7
ʿAlī Sulṭān b. Ürük Temür (Ögödeid usurper) 59, 65
ʿAlīka Kükeltash (Timurid Emir) 190, 192
ʿĀlim-Qul (Qïrghïz / Khoqand leader) 402, 407
ʿĀlim "The Tyrant" (Khoqand Khan) 401
Allāh-Quli b. Muḥammad Raḥīm (Qongrat Khan) 399
Allāh-Yār (Kasimov Khan) 258
Almalïq 31, 51
 as Chaghadaid capital 47, 59
Altai Mountains 370
Altan (Golden) *Khan*, title of 9–10, 19, 346
Altan Khan (grandson of Dayan Khan) 5, 169–72, 176, 338
Amīnak b. Yādigār (Jochid descendant) 227
Amīr Ḥusayn (grandson of Qazghan) 131, 183–4
Amīr Khusrau Dihlavī 210
 Hasht Bihisht (Eight Paradises) 211–12
Amīrānshāh (son of Temür) 185, 186, 189
amirs
 duties 289–90
 political significance / activism 189–90, 301–2, 392, 393, 398–9
 relations between 286–9
 relations with government 298
 use of title 279, 396–7
Amu Darya (Khwārazm) region 277, 282, 393, 400
Amursana (Khoyd chief) 352
An Tong, General 51
Ananda (grandson of Qubilai) 41
Andijan, building of 62
Anna Ivanovna, Empress 368–9
Anūsha Khan b. Abu'l-Ghāzī (Khwārazm Khan) 301, 392
appanage, system of 37–9, 280–2, 294, 302
Aq Orda ('White Horde') 81, 82
Aq Qoyunlu people 202
Aq-Sarāyī (historian) 98
Ara Bolud (son of Dayan Khan) 166
Arabs 96
ʿArabshāh (Jochid descendant) 224

ʿArabshāhī line 224, 233–4, 277, 279, 282, 300–1, 392–3
Ardabīl (Ṣafavid ancestor) 123
Arghun (tribe) 202
Arghūn Khan (son of Hülegü) 90, 101–2*n*, 123, 130
Arigh Böke (son of Tolui) 39–40, 49, 76, 129
Arshad ad-Dīn, Shaykh 262
Arsk (city) 309, 310
Arsu Bolud (offspring of Dayan Khan) 166
art 149–50, 212
artisans 335
  relocation 136–7, 147–8, 192–3, 269
Arughtai (post-Yuan chieftain) 162–3
Ashina (Türk Qaghan) 110*n*
Ashtarkhanids 393–5, 398
Astarabad 223
Astrakhan 298
  conflicts over 238, 239, 240, 244
  Khanate 247, 253–5, 257
  Russian conquest / rule 306, 317–18, 325–6, 374, 380, 387, 405
astronomy 138–9, 149, 195
Atsïz (Khwārazm leader) 14
Awrangzeb, (Mughal) Emperor 300
Āy-Chuvāq b. Abū'l-Khayr (Qazaq Khan) 369
ʿAyn Jālūt, battle of 39
Ayuki (Qalmaq Khan) 316, 320–1
Ayushiridara (son of Toghan Temür) 159
Azerbaijan 76, 79, 111–12, 119, 190
Azov (fortress) 320, 322

Bābā Kamāl Jandī (Ṣūfī leader) 65–6
Baba Tükles, Saint 242
Babadzhanov, Muḥammad-Ṣāliḥ 378
Bābur, (Moghul) Emperor (Ẓahīr al-Dīn Muḥammad) 199, 203, 205–6, 212–17, 262*n*, 401
  conflicts with Abu'l-Khayrid 285, 291, 293
  historical reputation 216
  literary tastes / theory 212, 213
  memoirs 208–9, 212–14, 215–16
  military theory / practice 213–15
Badakhshan 296
Badr al-Dīn Maydānī (Ṣūfī jurist) 130
Baghdad, capture of 76
Bahāʿal-Dīn Naqshband (Ṣūfī leader) 59, 196, 268
Baibars, (Cuman) Prince 69
Baibars, Sulṭān *see* Baybars
Baidar (Tatar commander) 70
Baikal, Lake 18, 23, 313
Bakhchesaray, as Russian administrative centre 322
bakhshi 'commissary clerk, administrator' 99, 209
Bakrids 242
Balazs, Étienne 94–5
Baljuna, Lake / Covenant 29
Balkh, Khanate of 393, 405
Bannāʾī (historian) 291
Banners (Qing military / administrative units) 339, 340–2, 348; *see also* Eight Banners
Bāqī Muḥammad b. Jānī Muḥammad (Uzbek amir) 289, 298–9
Bāqī Muḥammad b. Jānī Muḥammad (Uzbek Khan) 289
Baraba (steppe) 252
Barāq b. Suyunjuq (Abu'l-Khayrid) 285, 293
Baraq (Chaghadai Khan) 50–1, 129–30
Baraq (Oghlan) b. Quyurchaq (Golden Horde Khan) 193–4, 222, 240–1, 363, 366
Barāq Sulṭān b. Tursun (Qazaq leader) 285
Barfield, Thomas J. 174
Barlas tribe 183–4, 195–6
Barsu Bolud (offspring of Dayan Khan) 166
Bartol'd, V.V. 193, 230*n*
Bashkir people / Bashkiria 244, 247, 308, 314–17, 325–6, 327, 329, 383
basqaq 'tax official' 99
Batïr Shah (anti-Russian insurrectionist) 317, 329
Batu Möngke Dayan Khan *see* Dayan Khan
Batu "Sa'in" Khan (son of Jochi) 32, 42, 48, 67–8, 93, 127, 232
  contemporary / posthumous reputation 74–5
  European invasion 69–72, 74
  role in determining succession 72–3
Batur Hongtayiji (Zunghar leader) 269, 344, 345–6, 352
Bawden, C.R. 172
Bayan Möngke (father of Dayan Khan) 165
Bayan-Quli (Bukhara Khan) 64
Baya'ut (Bayawut) people 11, 14–15
Baybars, (Mamlūk) Sulṭān 76, 103
Baysunghur b. Shāhrukh (grandson of Temür) 190, 191–2, 195, 197
Beazeley, Chales Raymond 106
Beijing 9
Bekovich-Cherkasskii, Prince 406
Béla IV of Hungary 70, 71–2
Benedict XII, Pope 44
Berdibek Khan (son of Janïbek) 79, 104
Berke Khan 39, 49–50, 65–6, 103
  accession 75
  conversion to Islam 126–7, 129
  personality / abilities 75

Bessarabia 245
Beveridge, Lord 107*n*
Bayezit, (Mamlūk) Sulṭān 186
Bihzād (miniaturist) 212
Bingke Bureau (Qing administrative department) 354–5
birth rates 92
bitichki 'clerk' 99
Black Death 91, 105
Black Sea 102–4, 322
Blue Horde 80, 81–2, 81*n*, 114, 221, 224*n*, 238; *see also* Kök Orda
  conflicts with Timurids 193–4
Bodi Alagh (post-Yuan Khan) 167
Bodonchar (legendary figure) 20*n*
boghol / bo'ol 'slave' 97; see also *ötegü boghol*
Böjek (son of Tolui) 71
Bolad Agha 3–4, 110–11, 137–8, 142–3
Boqa-Temür (grandson of Büri) 50–1, 55, 56–7
Börte (wife of Chinggis Khan) 28–9, 31, 67, 114
Bratianu, Georges 103
Breslau, destruction of 70
brigands 96
Browne, E.G. 210
bSod-nams rgyamts'o, Dalai Lama 170, 171–2
Buchholtz, Lt.-Col. 406
Bucher, Guillaume 43
Buddhism 5, 11–12, 64, 131, 170–3, 320
  adoption by Zunghars 269–70, 345, 346–8
  communications network 145–6
  missionaries 172
  political ideology 171–2
  relations with Qing government 345, 350–1, 355–6
  revival amongst Mongols 170–3, 179, 181
Buell, Paul 38
Bujaq Horde (Noghay subdivision) 245
Büкäy b. Nūr-ʿAlī (Qazaq Khan) 371
Bukhara region / Khanate 9, 15, 111, 289
  conflicts for possession of 285, 301, 393–8, 401–2
  diplomatic relations with Russia 405–6
  economy 404
  ethnic composition 402–3
  as religious centre 65–6, 207, 388–9
  Russian conquest 408–10
  socio-political structure 403–4
Bulavin, Kondratii 319
Bulghar (city) 77, 239–40, 246
  as Islamic centre 390–1
Bulghar (Islamic identity), 390–1
Bulghars
  absorption into Mongol state 73
  conflicts with Mongols 32, 69, 80
  language 115
Bulghars (Volga Bulghars, people) 11, 69, 73, 80, 83, 92, 115, 126, 146
Bulughan, Empress (wife of Abaqa) 41
Bürge Sulṭān b. Yādigār(Jochid descendant) 227
Burhān ad-Dīn Khwāja 271
Burhān al-Dīn ʿAlī Qïlïch al-Marghīnānī 205
Buriats (people) 327
Büri b. Mö'etüken (grandson of Chinggis Khan) 51
Burni b. Abunai (Chakhar Khan) 342
Burni (grandson of Ligdan) 181
Burunduq b. Kiray (Qazaq Khan) 227, 228, 363
Buyān Qulï 131–2
Buyan Tayiji Sechen (post-Yuan Khan) 167
Buyruq (Buyiruq, Naiman leader) 23
Buzan b. Döre Temür (grandson of Du'a) 58
Byzantine Empire 9, 78, 142

Caffa (trade centre) 102–5, 108
canonization, posthumous, of emperors 159
cartography 138
Catherine II 'the Great' of Russia 258, 312, 330, 371, 377, 385–7
Central Asia
  Chinggisid takeover / rule 3, 46, 53–4, 278–82
  geographical features 277–8
  political / strategic significance 278
  Russian conquest 405–11
  south-western desert 404–5
  treatment of subject peoples 47
  see also names of regions / dynasties
Central Khanate *see* Mongolia
Chaghadai (Chaʿadai, Chaghatay) (son of Chinggis Khan) 184
  death 72
  harshness to subject peoples 43, 47, 63–4
  interests / skills 47, 63
  relations with brothers 31–2, 40, 47–8
  religion 64
  territory granted to / controlled by 38–9, 46–7, 67, 114, 278
Chaghadaid dynasty / territory
  administration 61–3
  conflict / accommodation with Timurids 189, 193, 198, 262–3, 279
  conflict with Abu'l-Khayrids 293–4
  conflicts with other branches of family 52–60, 143, 262, 363

Chaghadaid dynasty/territory (*cont.*)
genealogy 45
geographical extent 114, 278
institutional development 89
internal divisions 182–3, 261–2
languages/ethnicity 116–17, 119
military role within Empire 60
religion/culture 64–6, 122, 128–33
Ulus Chaghatay (Transoxania) 60, 66
Chaghan (interpreter/translator) 137
Chakhar people 179, 181
Banners 341–2
conflicts with Qing 333, 341
Chakhundorji (Khalkha Khan) 346
Chakrī and Chingīz Oghlān (Golden Horde Khan) 239
Chala-Qazaqs 384
Changshi Khan (grandson of Du'a) 58–9, 64
Chao Hung (Song diplomat) 27, 28
Chapar (son of Qaidu) 40, 54–6, 130
Cheboksary (city) 309–10
Chekü, Amīr (supporter of Temür) 184
Chengzong, Emperor *see* Temür Khan
Cherniaev, M.G., Maj.-Gen. 407–8
Chimgi-Tura (city) 227, 250
Chimkent 371
China
alcoholic beverages 150
art 149–50
economy 89–90, 94–5
foreign relations/trade 140–1, 266, 270–1
independence of Mongol Empire 73–4
languages 9
(management of) trade routes 260–1
medicine 148–9
military technology 34, 150–1
Mongol takeover/rule 3, 89–93, 141, 147
movement of Mongol capital to 76
natural disasters 91
relations with Mongolia 5–6
relations with 'Qara Khitai 12–13
relations with Temür/Timurids 187, 189, 263
reputation for intelligence/learning 152–3
rule in Eastern Central Asia 261
twelfth-century politics 9
see also Ming dynasty; Qing dynasty; Yuan dynasty
Chinggis Khan 1–2, 137, 171
ancestry 20–1, 21*n*, 28, 122
(claimed) descent from 186, 195–6, 401
conquests 18, 30–1, 46
court protocol 284
death/burial 31, 42
duplicity 29
legacy 184–5, 338–9, 344–5
legislation 34–5, 67, 97
marital alliances 24
marriage 28–9
military/political objectives 3, 113
political manoeuvres 25, 29
religion 134
rise to power 19, 22, 28–30, 157, 177
sons: conflicts over succession 31–3; grants of territory 37–9, 46–7, 67, 113–14
will 94
Chinggisid House, Qazaq Chingisids 366, 373, 398
control of Empire/portions thereof *see* Chaghataids; Chinggis Khan; Golden Horde; Ilkhanate; Mongol Empire; Ögödeids; Yuan dynasty
legitimacy 95–6, 120–1, 171
return to Mongol leadership 165–8, 227–8, 277–8, 283–4
Chingünjav (Khalkha rebel leader) 352
Chowdur (Turkmen tribe) 392
Christians/Christianity
conversions to 69, 310, 328
governmental enforcement 381
missionaries 22, 24, 44, 78–9
persecution 59, 65
spread in Mongol regions 24, 42, 44, 65
see also Russian Orthodox Church
Chū bān (military commander) 90
Chuvash people/language 115*n*, 249, 328, 381–2
Cisoxania 282, 285
Clement V, Pope 44
climatic conditions, economic impact 91
clothing, religious/prestigious 388–9
see also textile industry
Coleridge, Samuel Taylor, *Xanadu* 40
colonization (Russian) 309, 326–7, 375
communications systems 144–6
Constantinople, fall to Crusaders 102
Cossacks
conquest of Siberia 257–8, 312–13
raids on other neighbouring states 315, 319, 322
settlements 370, 375
see also Qazaqs
Crimea 73, 77, 102–3, 115*n*, 239–40
Crimean Khanate 246, 255–8, 307, 321–2
influence in neighbouring Khanates 247–8, 255
Ottoman control 256–8, 321–2

relations with Russia 304, 306, 316, 321–2
socio-political structure 249–50, 255–6
Crimean War (1853-6) 407
cultural exchange 3–4, 35–6, 111–12, 135–54
agency 146–9
by appropriation 149, 153–4
direction 142–3
fine arts 149–50
global / historical significance 153–4
resources 141–2
scientific / technological 138–40, 150–1
Cuman people / Cumania 68–9, 70–1, 116*n*
currency 61–2, 76–7, 80, 82, 90–1, 238, 239, 253–4, 293
paper 91
Timurid 195–6

Da Qing dynasty 157
Daftar-i Chingīz Nāma (anon.) 259
Daghestan, as centre of Islamic study 245, 388
Dalai Lama
creation / nature of office 171–2
political role 338, 347–8, 350, 351
relations with Zunghars 268–9, 338, 345, 346–8
see also names of incumbents
Daniil, Prince of Galich 75
Dāniyāl Biy Atalïq (Bukharan leader) 395–6
Dāniyār b. Qāsim (Kasimov Khan) 258
Danyal Bi Mangghït (Uzbek amir) 302
Darayisun (post-Yuan Khan) 167
Dasht-i-Qïpchaq *see* Qïpchaq steppe
Dastūr al-jumhūr (hagiography) 123
Dastūr al-kātib (administrative manual) 122
Dawachi (Zunghar leader) 352
Dawlat-Berdī b. Tāsh-Tīmūr (Crimean Khan) 256
Dawlat-Girāy b. Mubārak-Girāy (Kazan Khan) 257
Dawlat Shaykh Oghlan (Jochid descendant) 222
Dayan Khan (Batu Möngke) 165–8, 176, 338
descendants / legacy 166, 168
historical assessment 167–8
Dayicing Tayiji (grandson of Altan Khan) 169
Dayisung Khan *see* Toghto-bukha
De Weese, Devin 241*n*
debt slavery 94–5
Dede Qorqut (epic cycle) 118, 118*n*
Delbeg (post-Yuan khan) 161, 163
Delhi 52–3, 54, 213
Dénes, Palatine 71
deportations 94
Dge-lungs-pa sect 338
Dīn-Aḥmad b. Ismāʿīl (Noghay Khan) 244
Dīn Muḥammad Sulṭān (Uzbek leader, fl. 1539) 234
Dīn Muḥammad (Togha-Timurid Khan, d. 1598) 282, 298–9
disease
social / economic impact 91, 105
spread of 4
Dmitrii Ivanovich, Prince (Dmitrii Donskoi) 80–1, 82, 307
Dobruja 245
Dominican Order 68–9
Don (river) 245
Döregene (wife of Ögödei) 72
Döre Temür (son of Du'a) 58
Dost Muḥammad Khan of Afghanistan 398
dowager princesses, numbers / accommodation 91
Du'a (Duwa) b. Baraq (Chaghadaid Khan) 51–2, 53, 54–5, 64, 130
Dughlat people 182, 184, 193, 194, 262, 268
Durmān people 288–9

Eastern Europe, Mongol conquests in 32
Edigü (White Horde / Manghit leader) 84, 85, 115, 118, 222, 237–40, 241–2
education, religious 65, 207
Egypt *see* Mamlüks
Eight Banners 340–1
Eight White Tents (Chinggisid icon) 166, 181
Elbeg (post-Yuan khan) 161, 162, 163
Eljigidei (son of Du'a) 58, 64
Eltüzer Ināq (Qongrat Khivan Khan) 399
Emba (river) 241, 244–5
emir *see* amir
Engke Jorigtu (post-Yuan khan) 161
Engke Temür of Hami, murder of 162
enthronement ceremony 283–4, 291–2, 295
envoys, reception of 286
Er-ʿAlī b. Abū'l-Khayr (Qazaq Khan) 369
Erdeni Juu, temple of 172
Erke Khonggor Eje b. Ligdan (Chakhar Khan) 341–2
Erketü Khatun (wife of Altan Khan) 176
Ersarï (Türkmen ancestor) 231
Ersarï tribe 231, 234
Esen-Boqa (son of Du'a) 56
Esen Bugha Khan (of Moghulistan) 225
Esen-eli (Türkmen tribal grouping) 232, 235
Esen Khan (Oirat leader) 163–5, 176, 336, 338

estate, role in Russian ethos 382, 383–4
Euclid 138
Euphrosyne, (Byzantine) Princess 78
Europe / European powers
cultural influence 64
medicine 139–40
Mongol invasions 68–75, 141–2
New World conquests 4
relations with Chinggisid Empire 43–4
respect for Chinese learning 152–3
trade with Mongol states 100–8
travellers from *see individual names especially* Polo, Marco
Evstratov, I.V. 74*n*
explosives *see* gunpowder

Fāẓil Töre (Bukharan puppet khan) 395
Faḍlallāh b. Ruzbihan Isfahani (historian) 226–7
Fakhr al-Dīn ʿAlī (Rum-Seljukid statesman) 90
Faraj, (Mamlūk) sulṭān 186
Farīdūn Ghāzī Khan 235*n*
Farmer, David L. 107*n*
Fars (Timurid city)
conflicts over 200–1
as cultural centre 195
Fayẓ-Khan al-Kābulī (Ṣūfī Shaykh) 390
Fedor I, Tsar 310, 313, 324
Ferghana Valley 393–4, 400–1
as trading centre 205–6
Finno-Ugric peoples / languages 119, 249, 380–2
firearms, (military) use of 214–15
Fīrūzshāh (Timurid Emir) 190–1, 192
fish, trade in 104, 104*n*
Fiyanggū, General 349
food / drink, ceremonial use 284–5
'forest peoples' 18, 30
furs, trade in 146, 252, 313–14, 316, 336

Galdan (Zunghar leader, d. 1697) 268–9, 270, 339, 344, 346–8, 349
Galtantsering (Zunghar leader, d. 1745) 271, 351–2
Gaozu, (Han) Emperor 161
Gauhar Shad *see* Gawarshad
Gawharshād (wife of Shāhrukh) 190–1, 192, 196, 202
Genghis Khan *see* Chinggis Khan
Genoa 103–4
geography, study / collection of information 138, 151–2
Geresenje (son of Dayan Khan) 166, 168, 170
Ghāyib Khan (Qazaq leader) 398
Ghāzān Khan (son of Arghun) 52, 62, 90, 96, 119
conversion to Islam 123–5, 145
economic reforms 95, 97, 98, 137–8
Ghazna, struggles for control of 52–3, 57
Ghiyāth al-Dīn Pīr Aḥmad Khwāfī (Timurid governor) 191
Ghiyāth al-Dīn Tarkhan (Timurid Emir) 190–1
Ghūrid dynasty 15
Giano, Bartolomeo di 106*n*
Girāy dynasty 255–7, 258, 322
Goes, Bento de, SJ 267
gold *see* precious metals
Golden Horde 5, 48, 68–85, 114–15, 246, 249, 256, 304
administration of captured territories 68, 72–5, 93
conflicts with other Mongol peoples 49, 50, 53, 55, 56, 143, 221–2
conflicts with Temür 83–5, 221
currency 76–7, 80, 82
disintegration 79–81, 85, 93, 237, 240–1
European invasions 68–72, 82–3
extent of territory 73–4
importance in European power struggles 78, 79, 95
interest in Central Asia 58–9
naming 68
religion 78–9, 122, 125–8, 390
reunification 82
trade / revenues 97–8, 99–100, 101, 102–4
Gömbodorji Khan(of Khalkha) 168, 172
Goncharov, E. Iu. 74*n*
Gonzáles de Clavijo, Ruy 187
goods, movement of 140–1
grain, trade in 374–5
Great Horde 240, 242–3, 304, 319
Great Wall of China 158
guardianship 24, 24*n*
Grekov, Boris D. 81*n*
Grey Horde 114
Guangning (Chinese city), conflict over 179
Güchülük (Qara Khitai Khan) 13, 23–4, 30–1, 33, 37, 47
Gulbadan Begim (daughter of Bābur) 214
Gün Bilig Mergen (brother of Altan Khan) 169, 170
Güng Temür (post-Yuan khan) 161, 162
gunpowder, invention / development 34, 150–1

Gurii (Grigorii Rigotin), Archbishop of Kazan 310
Güüshi Khan (Khoshut leader) 350
Güyük, Great Khan (son of Ögödei) 32, 43, 48, 55, 139
election 72–3

Ḥabash (ʿArabshahid descendant) 234
Ḥāfiẓ-i Abrū (historian) 195, 204
Ḥāfiẓ (Persian poet) 210
Ḥāfiẓ al-Dīn al-Kabīr (religious scholar) 65
hagiographies 123, 132–3
Haixi dynasty (division of Jurchen) 334–5
Ḥājjī Beg Barlas 183
Ḥājji-Giray b. Ghiyās ad-Din (Crimean Khan) 256
Ḥājji-Muḥammad Khan 240–1, 242, 251–2
Ḥakīm Ātā, Saint 250
Hambaghai (early Mongol leader) 21, 22*n*
Hammer-Purgstall, Joseph von 81*n*
Ḥammūyī, Saʿd al-Dīn (Ṣūfī leader) 123, 124
Ḥammūyī, Ṣadr al-Dīn Ibrāhīm 124–5
Han dynasty 261, 333
Ḥanafī legal school 207
Ḥaqq-Nażar b. Qasim Khan (Qazaq leader) 244, 364
Ḥaydar, Mīrzā Muḥammad (historian) *see* Mīrzā Muḥammad Ḥaydar Dughlat
Ḥaydar b. Shāh Murad, Amīr (Bukharan leader) 284, 396–7
Hayton (Hetʿum), Prince of Armenia 153
heir apparent, office / title of 280, 293
Helin province *see* Mongolia
Henry II, Duke, of Silesia 70
Herat, as Timurid capital 190, 198, 200, 205–7
architectural development 211
conflicts over 203, 212, 223, 291, 293–4, 296–7
as cultural centre 208–12
Heʿtum *see* Hayton
Hö'elün (mother of Chinggis Khan) 28
Hong Li, Emperor *see* Qianlong Emperor
Hong Taiji (Qing Emperor), 333, 337–8, 339, 340, 342, 344–5, 357, 359: *see also* Hung Tayiji
Hongwu Emperor (Zhu Yuanzhang / Ming Taizu) 91, 160, 174–5
horses
role in Chinese economy 334
role in Mongol aims / strategy 112–13
Huizong, Emperor *see* Toghan Temür
Hülegeid dynasty *see* Ilkhanate
Hülegü 39, 40, 49–50, 76, 79, 90, 98, 114, 127, 136
conflict with ʿAbbāsids 142
conflict with family rivals 143
scientific interests 138–9
Humāyūn, (Moghul) Emperor 213, 216
Hung Tayiji, (Qing) Emperor 157, 180–1; *see also* Hong Taiji
Hungary 9
Mongol invasion 69, 70–2
religion 68–9
Ḥurūfī sect 191, 196
Ḥusām ad-Dīn b. Sharaf ad-Dīn al-Bulghārī (religious writer) 390
Ḥusayn b. Janïbek (Astrakhan Khan) 254
Ḥusām Bayqara (Timurid ruler) *see* Sulṭān-Ḥusām Bayqara

Iakubovskii, A.I. 81*n*, 84
ʿIbād Allāh b. Iskandar (Abū'l-Khayrid Khan) 295
Ībāq Khan (Shibanid descendant) 226, 242, 251–2, 253
Ibn al-ʿAlqamī (Caliphate statesman) 90
Ibn al-Fuwaṭī (historian) 122–3
Ibn al-Nafīs (Egyptian polymath) 133
Ibn Baṭṭūṭa (historian) 59, 130
Ibn Khaldūn (polymath) 91
Ibn Taymīya (religious scholar) 125
Ibrāhīm b. Maḥmūd (Kazan Khan) 247
Ibrāhīm b. Muḥammad-Tulāk, Imām 376–7
Ibrahim (Oirat leader) 167
Ibrāhīm Sulṭān b. Shāhrukh (grandson of Temür) 190, 191–2, 195
Ikhtiyār al-Dīn b. Ghiyāth al-Dīn al-Ḥusaynī 207
İl-Arslan (Khwārazm leader) 14*n*
Ilbārs (ʿArabshahid descendant, d. 1622) 234
Ilbārs Khan (of Khiva, d. 1740) 394
Ilchi Temür *see* Taishi Oghlan
Ilkhanate
conflicts with ʿAbbāsids 142–3
conflicts with other Mongol states 52, 55, 56–7, 143
disintegration 93, 102, 185
founding 114, 127
institutional development 89
rebel groups 96
religion 122–5
scientific / medical interests 138–9
Timurid claim to 185
trade / revenues 97–8, 102, 103–4

Imām Qulī b. Dīn Muḥammad (Togha-Timurid Khan) 282, 299–300
Inanch Bilge Bögü Khan (Naiman leader) 23
India
languages 16–17
Mongol incursions 54
Timurid invasion 214–15
Inner Horde (Qazaq migrants to Russia) 371–2, 375
Innocent IV, Pope 36–7, 43
Iran
independence of Mongol Empire 73–4
inter-tribal relations 288–9
mints 101–2*n*
Mongol rule 3, 90
occupation of Mongol/Central Asian territory 394–6
trade 90, 101–2*n*, 140–1
see also Ilkhanate
Iraq, Mongol rule 90
Irbit 385
Īrdāna Biy (Khoqand leader) 401
Irtysh (river) 244, 313, 363, 368, 370
ʿIsā Kelemachi (ʿIsā the Interpreter') 139
Isen Bugha (Moghul Khan) 264–5
Isfandiyār Sulṭān (Arabshāhi leader) 234
Ishim (Qazaq Khan, d. 1628) 364, 367
Ishim Sulṭān (Qazaq Khan, d. 1797) 369
Ishterek Biy (Noghai leader) 319
Iskandar b. Janïbek (Abū'l-Khayrid Khan) 281, 295
Iskandar b. ʿUmar Shaykh (grandson of Temür) 189, 190, 195
Iskandar Qaraqoyunlu 191
Islam
attitudes towards unbelievers 94, 106, 107–8
communication networks 145–6
conventional scholarship on 121–2
conversions to 15*n*, 41, 62, 65–6, 75, 120–1, 123–5, 130–1, 132, 221–2*n*, 230, 252, 262
education/scolarship 65, 129, 207, 376, 385, 387–91; significant trends 389
European diasporas 84–5
imposition in Mongol territories 58, 78, 127–8, 130–1, 132–3
legitimising role 121, 242, 252–3
political ideology 280
political influence 290–1
pre-existence in Mongol-occupied territories 128–9
resistance to 131–2
in Russian territories 310, 375–9, 381–91; revival 377–9, 387–91; Spiritual Assemblies 377, 386–7
Shīʿī *vs.* Sunnī 125, 207
slavery under 94
spread in Mongol territories 4, 64, 65–6, 115, 116–17, 120–34, 252–3, 280
Sunnī 216–17
suppression 42–3, 63–4, 133–4, 328–9, 381; calls for 378
survival in conquered territories 310
in Timurid empire 196
see also Hanafi; Shariʾa; Sufism
Islām-Girāy b. Muḥammad-Girāy (Crimean Khan) 255
Ismāʿīl Biy b. Mūsā (Noghay Khan) 243–4, 306
Ismāʿīl (Chaghadayid Khan) 268
Issyk-Kul, Lake/region 57, 407–8
Christian community 65
Italy
slave trade 105–6, 108
surnames 106*n*
Iurii Vsevolodovich, Grand Prince 69–70
Ivan III, Grand Prince of Muscovy 248, 253, 304, 307–8
Ivan IV 'the Terrible', Grand Prince/Tsar 31, 246, 303, 304–6, 308, 311, 380, 405
Ivan Kalita, Prince 79
ʿIzz al-Dīn Kai Kāʾūs II 98

Jabbār-Bīrdī (son of Toqtamïsh) 239
Jagiello, Grand Duke, of Lithuania 81
Jahāngīr, (Mughal) Emperor 287, 300
Jahāngīr (Qazaq Khan, d. 1652) 364, 367
Jahāngīr (son of Temür) 186
Jahāngīr b. Bükäy (Qazaq Khan, d. 1845) 373, 377
Jalāl ad-Dīn (son of Toqtamïsh) 237, 238–9
Jālāyirī, Qādir-ʿAlī-Bek (historian) 251–2, 259, 390
jam (postal relay system) see *yam*
Jamāl ad-Dīn, Shaykh 262
Jamāl al-Dīn (astronomer) 138
Jamāl Qarshī (Muslim writer) 130
Jāmī, ʿAbd al-Raḥmān 208, 210–11
Jamuqa (blood-brother of Chinggis Khan) 29
Jān-ʿAlī b. Allāh-Yār (Kazan Khan) 249, 258–9
Jān-Törä b. Āy-Chuvāq (Qazaq Khan) 369
Jan Wafa Biy (associate of Shïbānī Khan) 289
Jānī Muḥammad b. Yār Muḥammad (Togha-Timurid Khan) 298–9
Janïbek b. Baraq (Qazaq leader) 224–5, 227, 243, 363, 366, 368

Janībek b. Khwājah (Abu'l-Khayrid Khan) 282
descendants of, conflicts with family rivals 294–5, 296, 299
Janībek b. Maḥmūd (Astrakhan Khan) 254
Janībek Khan (son of Özbek) 79, 93, 104–5, 107, 231, 231*n*
Jao Modo, battle of (1696) 349
jasagh (local Mongol official, under Qing) 342–3, 351, 356, 357–8
jasagh (jasaq)/yasa (Mongol legal code) 34–5, 47, 63, 64, 67, 97, 195, 198, 280
compatibility with Islam 286, 290
Jasaghtu Khan (Khalkha title) 345–7
Jayiq River *see* Ural (river)
Jebe, General 30–1, 47
Jebtsundamba Khutukhtu (Buddhist authority figure) 347–8, 358
Jemboyluq Horde (Noghay subdivision) 244, 245
Jenkinson, Anthony 405
Jete people 117, 182
Jianzhou Jurchen 334–5, 339
Jihān Khwāja 271
Jīn dynasty *see* Jurchen dynasty (Jīn)
Jochi Qasar (brother of Chinggis Khan) 40–1
Jochi (son of Chinggis Khan)
death 32, 47, 67
legitimacy 31
military exploits 18, 30, 161–2
offspring 67–8
territory granted to 67, 114, 221
Jochid dynasty/territory 114–16, 221–3, 250–1, 278–82
struggles for control of 237–41
see also Blue Horde; Golden Horde; White Horde
John, Prince (of the Önggüt) 44
judiciary, appointment/function 35
Julian, Brother 36, 37, 68–9
Jumaduq (Jochid Khan) 222
Junior Zhüz 245, 364–5, 367–71, 373, 376–7, 398
Jurchen dynasty (Jin) 3, 9–10, 19, 22, 26, 27 29, 94
conflicts with Mongols 21, 22*n*, 25, 30, 32, 33–4
Jurchen people
alliance with Mongols 169, 180, 181
allies/subject peoples 23, 24
conflicts with Mongols 178–81
internal conflicts 336
return to power/renaming 157, 158, 169, 175, 177, 178, 181, 333, 337–8
social structure 336–7
subdivisions 334–5, 336
see also Da Qing dynasty; Manchu dynasty
Justinian, Roman Emperor 95
Juvainī (historian) 34–5, 99, 124, 126
Jūybārī family 295
Jūzjānī (historian) 127

Kābul-shāh (Timurid puppet khan) 132
Kama (river) 243, 247, 314
Kangxi, Qing Emperor (Aisin Gioro Xuanye) 339, 342, 347–9, 351, 355, 360
Karakorum *see* Qaraqorum
Karīm-Bīrdī (son of Toqtamïsh) 238, 239
Kashgharia 9, 116–17, 193, 262–3, 353
Kasimov, city/Khanate 247, 258–9, 305, 324, 326, 380
Kaufman, A.P. von, General 408–9, 410
Kazan (city) 246, 309
Kazan Khanate 245–50, 256
administration (from Moscow) 309
geopolitical situation 247
incorporation into Russian state 308–10
internal conflicts 247–8
resistance to Russian rule 308, 310–11
Russian conquest/rule 303–9, 324, 326–7, 329–30, 380, 387, 405
social structure 249–50
territorial extent 246–7, 247*n*
Kebek Khan (son of Du'a) 55–8, 60, 62, 63, 130
Kebek (son of Toqtamïsh) 239
Kel-Aḥmad (Kazan leader) 249
Keldibek (Golden Horde Khan) 80
Keneges tribes 393–4, 397
Kereyit people 21–2, 23, 24, 27, 42, 113
alliances/conflicts with Mongols 29
Khalīl Sulṭān b. Amīrānshāh (grandson of Temür) 189–90
Khalīl Sulṭān b. Yasawur 59, 131
Khalkha, Tribal Camps of 166, 168, 170, 172, 180
conflicts with Zunghar 347–8, 351
internal conflicts 346–7
Qing legal code 358–9
relations with Qing 269–70, 339, 344–6, 352
submission to Qing 348–9
Khanbaligh (Chinggisid capital) 40, 41, 43, 44
Khanzāda (daughter-in-law of Temür) 186, 189
Kharachin people 180
Khazar Empire 2
Khiḍr Khwāja(Chaghadayid Khan) 186, 262–3

Khitan dynasty 2, 9, 20, 111
alliance with Mongols 33–4, 37
overthrow 26
Khitay (Uzbek tribe) 397
Khiva, Khanate of 371, 393, 398–400
conflicts with Bukhara 397
diplomatic relations with Russia 405–6
economy 404
Iranian invasion 394–5
language / culture 403
Russian conquest 409–10
socio-political structure 403–4
Khmel'nitskii, Bogdan 257–8
Khoqand, Khanate of 370–1, 400–4
conflicts with Bukhara 397, 398, 401–2
economy 404
ethnic composition 403
expansionist policies 401–2
language / culture 403
Russian conquest 408–10
socio-political structure 403–4
Khorchin people 180, 340*n*, 341, 356, 358–9
Khorezm *see* Khwārazm
Khoshut people 350
Khoyd people 352
Khudāyār b. Shīr ʿAlī (Khoqand Khan) 402, 408, 410
Khudāydād Dughlat, Emir 189–90, 190, 193, 263, 264
Khudiakov, M.G. 247*n*
Khurasan 183–4, 196, 230, 404–5
Chinggisid / Uzbek rule 298
conflicts over 52, 56–7, 96, 197, 200, 227–8, 281, 293–4, 296–7
Timurid rule / economy 205–6
Turkmen migrations to 235–6, 392–3
Khutukhtai Sechen Khung Tayiji (great-nephew of Altan Khan) 170
Khwajas *see sayyids*
Khwāndamīr (historian) 226
Khwāndamīr, Ghiyas ad-Dīn Muḥammad 204
Khwārazm (Khorezm) state / territory 10, 13, 14–15, 47, 73, 80, 126, 129, 184, 230, 398–400
conflicts with Bukhara 397–8
conflicts with Mongols 30–1, 33, 37, 46, 301
internal conflicts 392–3
language 16, 114*n*
Timurid attacks / rule 184–5, 186, 190, 238–9
Turkmen migrations to 233–5
Uzbek attacks / rule 227–8, 232, 233–5, 291
see also Amu Dayra
Kichi Muḥammad b. Temür Khan (Great Horde founder) 240, 242–3, 245–6, 248, 253, 256
Kiev, Mongol capture of 69–70
Kim Ho-dong 262, 262*n*
Kirāy b. Baraq (Qazaq leader) 224–5, 227, 243, 363, 366
Kish (Timurid capital) 192
Kök Orda ('Blue Horde') 81, 82
Könchek (son of Du'a) 55
Körgüz (George), Prince (of the Önggüt) 44
Körgüz (governor of Khurasan) 48
Körgüz (son of Temür Khan) 53
Köten, Prince (of the Cumans) 71
koumiss (ceremonial drink) 150, 284–5
Kubak (son of Toqtamïsh) 238
Kublai Khan *see* Qubilai Khan
Kubraviyya (Ṣūfī order)
Küchkünji (Abu'l-Khayrid Shibanid Khan) 281, 282, 285, 287, 288, 293, 294
Küchüm (Siberian Khan) 250, 251–3, 313, 315

Lamaism 95
Latter Jin (Jurchen) dynasty 337, 339; *see also* Aisin state
Lazhang Khan (Khoshut leader) 350
legitimacy, efforts to establish
Manchu / Qing 338, 344–5
Mongol 95–6, 120–1, 242, 344–5
Timurid 195–6
Zunghar 345, 346–7
Liao people 9–10, 11–12, 19, 20, 113
Liegnitz, battle of (1241) 70
Lifan Yuan (Qing institution) 342–3, 349, 350–1, 353, 354–61
Ligdan (Chakhar Khan) 167, 178–81, 333, 337, 338, 339–40, 341
linguists, administrative use / value 137–40
literacy, introduction / spread 24, 35
Lithuania 80–1, 84–5, 238, 239–40
see also Poland-Lithuania
Liu Bingzhong 161
livestock, trade in 374
Livonian Wars 311, 313
Lixing (Punishment) Bureau (Qing administrative department) 355, 356–8
Lobzang Tayiji (Khalkha Khan) 346
Lomakin, A.A., General 410–11
Lu Jia 161
Luqmān b. Taghay Temür (Timurid puppet khan) 185
Luxun Bureau (Qing administrative department) 354–5

Maḥbūbī *ṣadrs* 65
Maḥmūd b. Amīr Walī (historian) 226, 283–6
Maḥmūd b. Kichi Muḥammad (Astrakhan Khan) 253–4
Maḥmūd b. Ulugh Muḥammad (Kazan Khan) 247, 258
Maḥmūd Bi Qaṭaghān (Uzbek amir) 302
Maḥmūd (Chaghadayid Khan, d. 1402) 195–6
Maḥmūd Kāshgharī (scholar / lexicographer) 16–17
Maḥmūd Khiḍr (Golden Horde Khan) 80
Maḥmūd Khoja Khan (Jochid descendant) 222
Maḥmūd Mīrzā (Timurid descendant) 203
Maḥmūd of Ghazna 80
Maḥmūd (Oirat leader) 162–3
Maḥmūd Sulṭān (brother of Shībānī Khan) 288
Maḥmūd Ṭarabī (Bukharan rebel leader) 48
Maḥmūd Yalawāch / Yalavach (Mongol administrator) 35–6, 48, 99, 129
Maḥmūtak (brother of Ībāq) 251–2
Maidiribala (son of Ayushiridara) 159–60
Makata, Princess 181
Makhdūm-i Aʾẓam (Naqshbandī master) 268
Mamai, Emir (Golden Horde) 80–1, 84
Mamat (descendant of Taybugha) 251
Mamich-Berdei (Tatar leader) 308
Mamlüks
  conflicts with Temür 186
  relations with Golden Horde 76, 103, 126
  trade with European powers 102
Māmuq (Kazan Khan) 248, 251
Manchu dynasty 5–6, 151, 181, 261, 333–4
  conflicts with Mongols 339–40
Manchuria 33–4
  conflicts over 41–2, 334–5
Mandughul (post-Yuan khan) 165–6
Mandukhai Sechen Khatun 165–6
Mandulai Aghulkhu (Ordos chieftain) 167
Mangghala (son of Qubilai) 41
Manghït dynasty 394–8
Manghït tribe 84, 221, 222, 224, 225, 229, 241, 283–4, 289, 301
Mangïshlaq (peninsula) 222, 232–3
Mann, Thomas, *Buddenbrooks* 209
Mano, Eiji 213
Mansur (Moghul Khan) 264, 265–6, *266n*, 267, 268
Mansūr (son of Edigü) 242
manufactured goods, trade in 374–5
Mar-körgis (post-Yuan khan) 165
Marghuz (early Mongol leader) *22n*
Mari (Cheremis) people 328, 381–2
Marignolli, Giovanni di 44
marriage, laws / customs 359
  see also polygyny
Marvazī, Sharif al-Zaman 152
Masʿūd Yalawāch (Masʿūd Beg) 36, 48, 50, 51, 61, 65, 129
Maʿṣūma Sulṭān Khānum (wife of Yār Muḥammad) 298
Mawarannahr *see* Transoxania
McKnight, Brian 95
medicine 139–40, 148–9
Menglī-Girāy (Crimean Khan) 248, 254, 256–7, 258
Mengü-Temür *see* Möngke Temür
Menzelinsk 315
merchants, privileges of 384–5
Mergit (Merkit) people 22–3, 24, 33
  conflicts with Mongols 29–30
Merv, conflicts for possession of 396, 399–400, 405, 411
Meshsherskii Goroders *see* Kasimov
Middle Zhüz 35, 368–72, 377
Mihrjān Khānum (wife of ʿAbd Allāh) 298
military strategy
  Chinggisid 33, 34, 296–7
  Russian 305–6, 311, 313
  Timurid 213–15
military technology
  Chinese 34, 150–1
  Russian 317–18
Millward, James 338
Ming dynasty 91, 151, 173–7, 263, 289, 334–6
  alliances / agreements with Mongols 169
  collapse 158, 333
  conflicts with Mongols 159–60, 161, 167, 169, 174–7, 334
  foreign relations / trade 266–7
  frontier policy 157–8
  tribute system 173, 266–7
Ming Taizu, Emperor *see* Zhu Yuanzhang
Ming (Uzbek tribe) 400–1
mints 101–*2n*
Mīr ʿAlī Shīr (poet) 211
Mīr Ḥusayn *see* Amīr Ḥusayn
Mīrkhwānd (historian) 226
Mīrzā Muḥammad Ḥaydar Dūghlāt (historian) 132, 194, 214, 225, 226–7, 228, 263–4, *263n*, 265, 272–3, 286
Mö'etüken (son of Chinggis Khan) 48, 51
Moghul, Mughūl 110–11, 114

Moghul Khanate 261–7, 363–4
  'culture clash' 264–5
  distinguished from Moghulistan 262*n*
  neighbouring races' disdain for 263–4
  political instability 265
  political significance 263
  trade / diplomatic relations with China 266–7
Moghulistan 116, 117, 182, 184, 200, 224–5, 262, 262*n*, 365
  geographical extent 260
  see also Moghul Khanate; Xinjiang
Moldova, Mongol invasion 71
Molon (post-Yuan khan) 165
Möngke, Great Khan (son of Tolui) 32, 39, 43, 75–6, 94, 113, 126
  conflicts with rival claimants 48–9
  death 143
  election 73
  wife of, religious endowments 65–6
Möngke Temür (Nurhaci's ancestor) 335
Möngke Temür Khan (grandson of Batu) 50, 53, 76–7, 103
Mongol Empire(s) 1–2
  administration 34–6, 37, 89–100, 135–7
  atlases 138
  capital(s) 35, 40, 144, 285
  ceremonial traditions 283–6
  communications 144–6
  contribution to world history 135
  cultural exchange within 35–6, 111–12, 135–54 *see separate main heading*
  cultural resources 141–2
  economy 2–3, 36, 60–3, 89–93, 96–108
  emergence 19
  emergence of new tribes 118–19
  expansion(ism) 36–7, 111
  fragmentation 73–4, 113–14, 237, 261; reasons for 161
  geographical extent 1, 43, 73, 141, 261
  hierarchy (military / political) 2, 94, 112, 118–19, 147, 280, 284
  influence on later empire-builders 157–8, 184–5, 194, 195–6, 283–6, 338–9
  intelligence gathering 151–2
  internal power struggles 31–3, 38–42, 48–60, 91, 117, 143
  languages / ethnicity 111–12, 114–19, 137
  legal system 34–5, 42–3
  legitimacy 95–6, 120–1
  military resources / transport 135–6, 142
  officials: distribution / relocation 3–4, 35–6, 119; payment 147
  origins 21, 26–7
  political legacy 4–6
  reasons for success 33–4
  rebellions 91, 95–6
  relocation of officials / population *see separate main heading*
  revenues 96–100 (*see also* taxation)
  subject peoples, treatment of *see separate main heading*
  succession, rules of 280–1
  titles 279*n*, 280–1
  trade regulation 3
  see also Chaghataids; Golden Horde; Ilkhanate; Ögödeids; Yuan dynasty
Mongol people(s) 19–21
  conflicts with Timurids 199, 201
  'dark' age 157–65
  genealogy 20–1
  (hopes of) reunification 166, 345–7
  internal conflicts 160–5
  language 92*n*, 111
  nomadic lifestyle 61, 63
  origins 19–20, 20*nn*, 26–8
  Qing rule 340–3, 354–62
  return to homeland (1368) 157–8
  social organization 27–8, 96–7, 109–11
  social structure 109–11
  in Temür's army / administration 187–8
  tribal divisions 168–9, 340*n*
  see also names of dynasties / peoples
Mongolia
  civil wars 160–5, 167
  conflicts over 41–2
  economy 97–8
  post-Chinggisid history 5–6, 157–81
  pre-Chinggisid peoples 18–25
  Qing rule 340–3
  return of Yuan to 157–8
  social structure 96–7
Montecorvino, Giovanni da 44
Mordvin people 328, 382
Morgan, David 37
Moscow 79
  conflicts for possession of 238
  Mongol capture 69, 82
  political / economic rise 80–1
  see also Muscovy
mosques
  construction 377
  destruction 329
Mubārak-khoja (Blue Horde Khan) 82
Mubārak Shāh (son of Hülegü) 48–9, 50, 52, 129–30

Mughal *see* Mughal Empire *and* Moghul Khanate Moghul
Mughal Empire 60
  conflicts with Togha-Timurids 300
  derivation of name 110–11, 262*n*
  ethno-religious composition 216–17
  foundation 216–17
  literary / cultural patronage 217
Muḥammad, the Prophet 286, 390
  (claimed) descent from 250, 290
Muḥammad II, (Ottoman) Sulṭān 253, 256–7
Muḥammad, the Prophet, claimed descent from 250
Muḥammad al-Jazarī (religious scholar) 196
Muḥammad ʿAlī (Khoqand Khan) 401–2
Muḥammad-Amīn b. Ibrāhīm (Kazan Khan d. 1519) 248
Muḥammad Amīn b. Muḥammad Raḥīm (Qongrat Khan, d. 1855) 399–400
Muḥammad Amīn Inaq (Qongrat leader, fl. 1770) 399
Muḥammad b. Pulād b. Könchek b. Du'a 59
Muḥammad b. Tughluq, (Delhi) Sulṭān 65
Muḥammad Dost (Moghul Khan) 264
Muḥammad-Girāy b. Menglī-Girāy (Crimean Khan) 254–5, 257
Muḥammad Ḥakīm (Biy Manghït) Ataliq (Bukhara leader) 394–5
Muḥammad Jahāngīr b. Muḥammad Sulṭān (great-grandson of Temür) 189, 193
Muḥammad-Jān al-Ḥusayn (religious leader) 377
Muḥammad Jūkī Mīrzā (grandson of Ulugh Beg) 224
Muḥammad Jūkī b. Shāhrukh (grandson of Temür) 192, 193–4
Muḥammad Khān (Moghul Khan) 266, 267, 268
Muḥammad Khwārazmshāh 14–15, 15*n*, 30–1
Muḥammad Nūrbakhsh (religious leader) 191
Muḥammad Raḥīm b. Muḥammad Ḥakīm (Bukhara Khan, d. 1758) 394–5, 398
Muḥammad Raḥīm II (Khivan Khan, r. 1864-73) 409
Muḥammad Raḥīm (Qongrat Khan, d. 1825) 399
Muḥammad Shāh-Bakht / Muḥammad Shïbānī *see* Shïbānī Khan, Shibānī Khan, Shaybānī Khan, Shaybaq Khan
Muḥammad Sulṭān b. Jahāngīr (grandson of Temür) 186, 188
Muḥammad Temür b. Shïbānī Khan (Abu'l-Khayrid Khan) 293
Muhi, battle of (1241) 70, 71–2
Muḥsin al-Dīn Muḥammad Turkistānī (Ṣūfī) 130
Muʿīn al-Dīn Naṭanzī (historian, fl. 1410s) 81*n*
Muʿīn al-Dīn Suleiman, the Parvānah (statesman, fl. 1260s-70s) 90
Mukmikova, R.G. 221*n*
Munis (historian) 224, 224*n*
Muqali, Viceroy 30, 34
Muqan (Türk Qaghan) 110*n*
Murid (Golden Horde Khan) 80
Mūsā Biy b. Waqqas (Noghay Horde leader) 224, 227, 242, 243, 253
Muscovy
  conflicts with Khanates 247–9, 253, 303–30
  ethnic composition 382
  see also Moscow; Russia
Muṣṭafā ʿÂli (historian) 208
Muṣṭafā Khan (Jochid descendant) 222–3
Musulmān-Qul (Qïpchaq leader) 402
Muṭribī (Sulṭān Muḥammad Samarqandī) (poet) 287–8
Muẓaffar al-Dīn b. Naṣrallāh , Amīr (Bukharan leader) 398, 402, 408–9

Nadhr Muḥammad b. Dīn Muḥammad (Togha-Timurid Khan) 282, 283, 299–300
Nādir Shah of Iran (Nādir Khan Afshar) 302, 394–5, 396, 398
Nagyvárad, destruction of 72
Naiman people 22, 23–4, 27, 288–9
  conflicts with Mongols 29–31, 33, 47
Najm al-Dīn Kubrā 65, 129
Nalighu (Chaghadaid) 130
Naliqo'a (Nalighu) 55, 130
Naqshbandiyya (Ṣūfī order) 196, 206–7, 210–11, 216, 268, 290, 295, 390, 400
  internal conflicts 268
Nārbūta Biy (Khoqand leader) 370, 401
Nāṣir al-Dīn b. Khudāyār (Khoqand leader, dep. 1876) 410
Nāsir al-Dīn Ṭūsī (polymath, d. 1274) 90, 97–8, 138–9
Naṣrallāh b. Ḥaydar "The Butcher," Amīr (Bukharan leader) 397–8, 401–2
natural disasters 91
  Qing aid system 359–60
Nauruz *see* Nawruz (Emir, Ilkhanid governor)
Navāʾī, ʿAlī Shīr (poet) 205, 208, 209–11, 212
Nawruz (Emir, Ilkhanid governor) 52, 90, 123–4, 222
Nawrūz, Emir (military commander) 90, 123–4, 222

Nawrūz Ahmad *see* Baraq (Suyunjuqid Khan)
Nayan (descendant of Temüge) 41, 51
Negübei b. Sarban (Chaghadaid Khan) 50–1
Negüderi (Nigūdārī) (lit. 'nomad') *see* Qara'unas
Nerchinsk, Treaty of (1689) 348
Nestorians *see* Christianity
Neyici Toyin (Buddhist missionary) 172
Nikonian Chronicle 238
Ni'matullāhī (Ṣūfī order) 196
Niyāz-Qul al-Turkmānī (Ṣūfī Shaykh) 390
Nizhnii Norgorod 385
Noghai Khan (Golden Horde) 53, 77–8, 84, 127
Noghay Horde 5, 115, 118, 238, 241–5, 249, 364, 383
  disintegration 244–5, 319–20, 363
  influence in neighbouring Khanates 247–8, 251–2, 255, 258
  internal conflicts 243–4
  relations with Russia 305–6, 308, 315
  studies 241*n*
  territorial extent 243
  see also Manghïts
nöküd (Emperor's 'boon companions', 'retainers') 2 , 94, 97
Nomuqan (son of Qubilai) 51
Nūr ad-Dīn (son of Edigü) 243
Nūr-ʿAlī b. Abū'l-Khayr (Qazaq Khan) 369
Nūr-Dawlat b. Ḥajjī-Giray (Kasimov Khan) 258
Nurhaci, Manchu Emperor 157, 177, 333, 335, 339, 344–5, 359
  conflicts with Mongols 179–80, 339–40
  rise to power 177–8, 337–8

oases, socio-political significance 278
Ob-Ugrians 252, 313, 328
Ocir Bolud (offspring of Dayan Khan) 166
Oghuric (language) 115*n*
Oghuz Khan (mythical figure) 127, 230
Oghuz tribe 230, 232
Ögödei, Great Khan (son of Chinggis Khan) 31–3, 35, 40, 43, 71, 99, 148, 161, 184
  death 72
  grant of territory 67, 114
  succession to Qaghanate 38–9, 47–8
Ögödeid dynasty
  conflicts with other branches of family 52–60, 103, 143
  institutional development 89
Oirat (Qalmaq) people 24, 96, 136, 267, 269–70, 316
  conflicts with Mongols 161–5, 167, 169–70
  conflicts with Qazaqs 367–8
  conflicts with Uzbeks 224
  control of Mongolia 161, 164–5
  destruction 352–3
  divisions under Qing 352
  internal conflicts 346–8, 352
  relations with Ming dynasty 164–5, 176
  relations with Qing dynasty 344–8, 352–3, 367–8, 370
  relations with Russia 319–21
  treaty with Khalkha 345–6
Oleg, Prince, of Riazan' 81
Öljei Temür (post-Yuan khan) 161, 162
Öljeitü Khan (son of Arghun) 56, 57, 104*n*, 123, 130
  religious conversions 125
Omsk 371–2
Ong Khan (To'oril) (ally of Chinggis Khan) 22, 23, 29, 36
Önggüt people 24, 27, 33
  religion 42, 44
Orda (son of Jochi) 53, 67–8, 82, 93, 221
Ordos (area of Mongolia) 166–7
Ordu-Melik (Golden Horde Khan) 80
Örebek Digin ('Forest People' leader) 18
Orenburg (fortress) 316–17, 369, 373, 375, 376–7, 379, 406
  as Islamic centre 377, 379, 386–7
Orghina (wife of Yesü Möngke) 48–9, 50
Örög-Temür b. Ananda (descendant of Qubilai) 41
ortaq ('merchant partner') 62, 99
Orus (son of Qaidu) 54–5
Osmanlï (Ottomans) 118, 119
Ostyakes *see* Obollgrians
Otchigin *see* Temüge Otchigin
Ötegü boghol (*bo'ol, bo'ul*) ('long-standing serfs', 'bound vassals') 28, 97, 113
Ötemish-Girāy (Kazan Khan) 249
Ottoman Empire
  administration 273
  Chinggisid vassals 5
  conflicts with Temür 186
  conquests 108
  histories 208
  influence in Crimean Khanate 256–8
  military strategy/technology 214–15
  relations with Russia 306, 316, 317, 318
  rise in power 119
Özbek Khan 56, 59, 78–9, 104, 115, 118*n*
  religion 127–8, 221
Özbek people *see* Uzbek people

Palaeologus, Michael 102–3
Panipat, battle of 214
papacy
ban on Eastern trade 102
dealings with Mongol states 36–7, 43–4
'Pax Mongolica' 135
Pegolotti, Francesco Balducci 98, 104, 106
Perovskii, Governor 406
Persia *see* Iran
Persian (language) 92*n*
literature 210, 211–12, 217
Pest, destruction of 71–2
Peter I 'the Great' of Russia 316, 320, 324, 325, 328, 348, 405–6
Petrarch (Francesco Petrarca) 103
Petropavlovsk 374–7
'Phags-pa, Lama 5, 63, 171
Pian del Carpine, Giovanni del (John of Plano Carpini) 43, 44, 68, 72–3, 74*n*
pietism 389
Pīr Muḥammad b. Jahāngīr (grandson of Temür) 188–9
Pīr Muḥammad b. Janïbek (Abu'l-Khayrid Khan) 281, 285
Pīr Muḥammad b. 'Umar Shaykh (grandson of Temür) 186, 189
Poland
Mongol invasion 70–2
Tatar settlements 84–5
Poland-Lithuania
alliance with Great Horde 304
conflict with Russia 95, 320
decline 318
Polo, Maffeo 44, 101–2
Polo, Marco 27, 40, 44, 101–2, 104, 144, 150
Polo, Niccolò 44, 101–2
polygyny 92
Porto Pisano 102–3
postal system 144–6, 360–1
introduction of 35
resricted access to 90
pottery, manufacture / trade 140–1
Pozdneev, A.M. 157
precious metals
mints 101–2*n*
trade in 100, 105, 107
'Prester John' 12
Pugachev, Yemelian 317, 329, 371
Pulād Khan (Khoqand leader) 410
Pūlāt (son of Shādī-Bek) 238
Punishments, Bureau of *see* Lixing
qa'alghah see heir apparent
Qabūl Khani (early Mongol leader) 21, 21*n*
Qachi'un (brother of Chinggis Khan) 40–1
Qadan (son of Ögödei) 70, 71–2
Qādir-Bīrdī (son of Toqtamïsh) 239–40
Qaghan (Emperor), title of 1–2
dispute / non-recognition 39–40
Qaidu Khan 40, 49–54, 63
administration 60–1
conflicts with Qubilai 41–2, 50, 51–2, 130
currency 61–2
European invasion 70
rebellions against 50–1
religious tolerance 130
Qaishan (Wuzong), Yuan Emperor (nephew / heir of Temür Khan) 41–2, 53, 58
qaran 'corvée, personal duty' 97
Qalmaqs *see* Oirats
Qamar al-Dīn, Emir 184–6, 193, 262
qara Hülegü (grandson of Chaghadai) 48
Qara Khitai 10, 11–13, 23–4, 27, 130
creation 26
dealings with Mongols 30–1, 33, 46
extent of rule 12, 26, 47
influence 12*n*, 35
overlordship / vassals 15, 17, 18, 23, 26
relations with neighbours 12–13, 14*n*
Qara Khojo (Uighur capital) 56
Qara Qalpaqs 115–16, 403
Qara Yūsuf Qaraqoyunlu 190
Qarachar Barlas (Timurid ancestor) 195–6
qaraju 'commoners' 97
Qarakhanids 10, 13–14, 127
Qaramanlï people 118
Qaraqorum (Mongol capital)
as centre of communications network 144
Chinggisid rule from 23, 35, 37, 158
conflicts for possession of 41–2, 51–2, 169–70
post-Chinggisid reestablishment 159
Qaraqoyunlu people, conflict with Timurids 189, 190–1, 197–8, 201–2
Qara'unas 52, 58, 60, 96, 182, 184
Qāsim b. Ulugh Muḥammad (Kasimov Khan) 247, 258
Qāsim Khan b. Janïbek (Qazaq leader) 227, 228, 243, 363–4
Qayalïq 31, 47, 49, 129
Qazan b. Yasawur (Chaghadaid Khan) 59, 182
Qazaq people / Khanate 5, 96, 115, 117, 117*n*, 223, 224–9, 231, 243, 266, 267, 271, 312, 320, 363–79
ancestry / social hierarchy 365–7

Qazaq people / Khanate (*cont.*)
conflicts with Noghay Horde 243, 244
conflicts with Oirats / Zunghars 349–50, 367–8
dealings with Qing 351, 370
increase of power / territory 363–4
migrations to Russia 371
naming 225–6, 225*nn*, 228–9
new setttlements 375, 384
numerical strength 227, 228
relations / integration with Russia 367–71
religion 375–9
Russian adminstration 371–9
split from Uzbeks 224–5, 226–7
trade with Russia 374–5, 406
tribal groupings 229, 364–7
Qazghan Khan 59–60, 131, 182, 183
Qianlong Emperor (Hong Li) 352, 355, 360
Qing dynasty / Empire 6, 261, 271–6, 333–62, 370
administration 272–3, 274, 275–6, 343, 347–8, 350–1, 352–3, 354–62
agreements with Russia 348
conflicts with Zunghars 270–1, 339, 346–8, 349–50, 351–2
cultural / religious policy 274, 274*n*
economy / revenues 273–4, 275–6
frontier strategy 338, 361–2
geographical extent 333–4
indirect rule 343, 353
Inner Asian expansion 333–4, 338–53, 361–2
legal system 356–9
marriage alliances 359
military organization 339, 340–3, 356–7
penal code 358
political tutelage 361–2
postal system 360–1
reasons for success 361–2
rebellions against 274–5, 352
(state control of) religion 345, 350–1, 355–6
studies 271*n*
Qïpchaq steppe / people 10–11, 14, 15, 67, 277, 410
conflicts with Mongols 32
exodus from 228
Golden Horde occupation 73, 81–2
language 114–16, 119
Uzbek control / conflicts 221–9, 402
Qïrghïz state / people 17–18, 23, 117, 146, 265, 267, 372*n*, 402, 410
Qïrïm (city) 239
Qïzïlbash tribes 288–9, 296, 299, 396
Qonghrat (dynasty) 398–400
Qongrat (Uzbek tribe) 223
qopchur / qobchi'ur / qob[i]chūr 'levy, tax' 97, 98
Qoshila (son of Qaishan) 58
Qubilai Khan 5, 39–40, 44, 49–50, 92, 94, 129, 150, 161, 171
conflicts with rival claimants 41–2, 49, 50, 76, 129–30, 143, 261
(post-Imperial) descendants 161, 163
religious practice / legislation 43, 145
relocation to China 76
scientific / technological interests 138, 139, 150
Qul Baba Kökeltash (Uzbek amir) 289–90, 297–8
Qul-Sharīf (Kazan leader) 250
Qurjaquz Buyruq Khan 22, 22*n*
al-Qūrṣawī, Abū'n-Nāṣir (religious scholar) 389
qurultai (clan conclave) 29–30, 32, 34, 269–70, 280, 291
Qutlugh Nigar Khanim (mother of Babur) 262*n*
Qutlugh Khwāja(son of Du'a) 53
Qutula Khan (early Mongol leader) 21, 21*n*
Qutuqa Beki (Oirat leader) 24, 30

Rabbān Ṣawma 44
Rabīʿa Sulṭān Begum (daughter of Ulugh Beg) 223
Raḥīm-Quli b. Muḥammad Raḥīm (Qongrat Khan) 399
railroads, construction of 374
Rajab Sulṭān (Bukhara Khan) 393
Rashīd ad-Dīn 4, 18, 20, 22–3, 28, 35, 39, 41, 67*n*, 68, 95, 99, 110–11, 124, 125, 137–8, 139, 145, 148, 195
Razin, Stepan 315, 319, 325
religion
legitimising role 121, 242, 252–3, 346–7
Mongol 4, 42, 63–6, 120–34, 170–3
Qing 345, 351
repressive policies 42–3, 328–9
Russian 11, 327–9, 375–9, 385–7
Timurid 191, 196
tolerant policies 64, 78, 130, 135, 327, 386–7
Zunghar 269–70, 346–7
see also Buddhism; Christianity; Islam; Russian Orthodox Church
relocation, within Mongol Empire 113–14, 118–19, 135–7
populations 94, 136
public officials 3–4, 35–6, 119
skilled personnel 136–7, 147–8, 192–3
troops 112, 119, 135–6
retreat(s), religious, rulers' resort to 132

Riasanovsky, Nicholas V. 94
Riazan', Mongol capture of 69
Ricci, Matteo 44
Riḍā-Quli b. Nādir Shah 394
Robert, Archbishop of Esztergom 69
Rogerius (historian) 70–2
Roman law 95
Romanovskii, D.I., General 408
Rouyuan Bureau (Qing administrative department) 355–6
Rubruck, William of 43–4, 126
Rudakov, V.G. 74*n*
Rukn al-Dīn Qïlïch Arslan IV 98
Rūm (Anatolia) 9, 90, 111–12, 118
as trading centre 98, 103–4
Rūmī, Jalāl al-Dīn 134
Russia
administration (of conquered territories) 309, 313–14, 315–16, 322–6, 329–30, 371–9
agreements with China 348
Central Asian expansion 405–11
construction / upkeep of fortresses 309, 311, 313, 316–17, 323
cultural resources 143
demography of conquered territories 326–7
foreign relations / trade 11, 313–14, 316–17, 405–6, 407
languages 10–11
military organization / strategy 305–6, 323, 323*n*
Mongol invasions 69–70, 82–3, 141–2
Mongol rule 3, 73–4, 78–9, 93–4, 95–6, 98
political / military involvement in neighbouring Khanates 244–5, 246, 247–8, 254, 257–8, 270, 303–6, 321–2, 367–71, 402, 405–11
post-Chinggisid politics 5–6
pre-Mongol political situation 9, 10–11
rebellions in subject territories 308, 310–11, 315, 317, 319, 325–6, 329, 380–1, 409, 410
religious policy 11, 327–9, 385–7 (*see also* Russian Orthodox Church)
'Time of Troubles' 311, 312, 326
trade within / between territories 374–5, 384–5
Russian Orthodox Church 78–9, 306–8, 310, 314, 323, 327–9

Saʿd al-Dīn al-Taftazānī 196
Saʿdī (Persian poet) 210
Gulistān 211–12
Ṣafā-Girāy b. Fātiḥ-Girāy (Kazan Khan) 249, 305
Ṣafavī, Shah Ismāʿīl 207
Ṣafavid dynasty / empire 123, 282, 291, 299
Ṣafī al-Dīn, Shaykh 123
Sagang Sechen (Ordos nobleman) 97, 344–5
Ṣāḥib-Girāy b. Menglī-Girāy (Kazan Khan) 248–9, 257
Salors (Türkmen tribal grouping) 232, 234–5
Samāghār (military commander) 90
Samarqand 9, 15, 136
conflicts for possession of 285, 291
Russian capture 409
as Timurid capital 184, 192, 200–1, 206–7, 285
as Togha-Timurid capital 299
Samur, Princess 163
Sarai (Golden Horde capital) 74, 74*n*, 114, 186
struggles for possession of 80
Saray Malik (wife of Temür) 184
Saraychiq 242, 242*n*, 243, 244
Sariq Khan (early Mongol leader) 22*n*
Sart 'Central Asian Muslims' 99
people 398, 402–3
Sartaq (son of Batu) 42, 75
Satuq Bughrā Khan (early Islamic convert) 127
Sayf al-Dīn Aḥmad (religious scholar, d. 1510) 207
Sayf al-Dīn Bākharzī (Ṣūfī leader) 65–6, 126–7, 132
Sayram 363, 367
Sayyid-Aḥmad b. Aḥmad Khan (Great Horde leader) 253
Sayyid Alī Hamadānī (Ṣūfī leader) 196
Sayyid Alī Jurjānī (religious scholar) 196
Sayyid-Muḥammad Riẓā (historian) 255*n*
sayyids (descendants of the Prophet) 250, 290, 366, 378
Sechen Khan (Khalkha title) 346, 347–8
Secret History of the Mongols (Mongghol'un niucha tobcha'an) 20, 27–8, 30, 36, 37, 161
Seitovskii Posad, as commercial / Islamic centre 385
Selim II, (Ottoman) Sulṭān 257
Seljuk state 9, 13, 230
conflict with Qara Khitai 12
Semënov, A.A. 221*n*
Semipalatinsk 374–6
Semirech'e 224–6, 363–4, 368, 370
Sengge b. Batur (Zunghar leader) 346
Senior Zhüz 364–5, 368, 370–1
Sergei of Radonesh 81

Serruys, Henry 173
Shādī-Bek b. Küchik (nephew of Temür-Qutlugh) 238
Shāh ʿAbbās (Ṣafavid leader) 299
Shāh ʿAlī b. Allāh-Yār (Kazan Khan) 248, 249, 258–9, 305
Shāh b. Manṣūr (Moghul Khan) 266*n*
Shāh Budaq b. Abu'l-Khayr 282, 285, 293, 294
Shāh Jahān, (Mughal) Emperor 300
Shāh Murād b. Dāniyāl Biy, Amīr (Bukharan leader) 395–7
Shāh Oghul (son of Qaidu) 130
Shāhrukh (son of Temür) 186, 188–92, 193–4, 202, 223, 238–9, 265
  achievement / legacy 198, 199–200
  cultural / religious interests 195, 196, 208
Shāhrukh Biy Ming (Uzbek leader) 400
shamanism 42
Shams al-Aiʾmāʾ Kārdārī (religious scholar) 65
Shangdu (Xanadu) (Mongol capital) 40
Sharaf al-Dīn Alī Yazdī 211, 265
Sharīʿa (Islamic law) 290
  compatibility with *jasagh* 286, 290
Shaybaq Khan *see* Muḥammad Shāh-Bakht, Muḥammad Shïbānī, Shïbānī Khan, Shibānī Khan, Shaybānī Khan
Shaykh Ḥaydar (son of Abu'l-Khayr) 226, 227, 253
Shaykh Nūr al-Dīn, Emir 189, 190
Shaykh Sharaf 231
Shiban (son of Jochi) 67
Shïbānī Khan (grandson of Abu'l-Khayr Khan) 134, 227–8, 233, 285, 288, 289, 291–3, 295, 363
Shibanid line 221–2, 224, 240–1, 250–1
  rule in Central Asia 278–82, 291
Shigi Qutudu (adopted son of Chinggis Khan) 35
Shigü 24
Shīr ʿAlī (Khoqand Khan) 402
Shīr-Ghāzī b. Āy-Chuvāq Khan 373
Shīr Ghāzī Khan (Turkmen leader) 235, 393
Shīr Muḥammad Khan (Chaghadaid leader) 193–4
Shirin (tribe) 239, 255
Sholoi Khan (of Khalkha) 168
Siberian Khanate 250–3
  attempted restoration 315
  Russian conquest / rule 312–14, 324–5, 326, 328, 330, 384–5
Sighnaq (Sïghnaq) 11, 65, 193
sigüsün 'tax on food and *koumiss*' 97
silk, trade in / Silk Route 62, 103, 104*n*, 205–6, 273
silver *see* precious metals
Simnānī, ʿAlāʾ al-Dawla (Ṣūfī writer) 123, 130
Sinie Vody, battle of (1362) 80
siqagha 'jury duty' 97
skilled personnel
  exchange between leaders 147–8
  identification / preservation 147
  redistribution 136–7, 192–3
Skobelev, M.D., General 410–11
slaves / slavery
  European 43
  impact on modern names 105–6, 106*n*, 108
  role in Mongol societies 28, 94–5, 110, 307
  trade in 104, 105–6, 106*nn*, 307, 322
Soghdian (language) 16–17
Soldaia / Sudak / Sughdaia / Sughdaq 69, 97, 104
Solov'ev, S. 84
Song dynasty 27, 51, 146
Sorqaqtani (wife of Tolui) 38
soyurghal ('semi-autonomous military fief') 204, 205
Soyurghatmïsh b. Shāhrukh (grandson of Temür) 191
Soyurghatmïsh (Chaghataid Khan) 184
Spuler, Bertold 81*n*
steppe
  geopolitical characteristics 9, 112–13, 147, 278, 313, 317–19
  new setttlements 375
  trade 374–5
  see also names of specific areas, e.g. Qipchaq
Subadi Khan (of Khalkha) 168
Sube'etai, General 31, 68, 71
Subḥān Qulī b. Nadhr Muḥammad (Togha-Timurid Khan) 300–1
subject peoples, Mongol treatment of 42–3, 47, 112
  appropriation of cultural assets 149, 153–4
  assimilation with (*see also names of regions / dynasties*)
  distribution of spoils 147
  repressive / punitive measures
  suppression of (religious) traditions 42–3, 63–4, 133–4
Ṣūfī Allāh-Yār (religious writer) 388
Ṣūfī Oghlan (Jochid descendant) 222
Sufism 65–6, 123, 132, 134, 196, 206–7, 264, 389–90
  political / military influence 268, 400
  see also Naqshbandiyya

Ṣufyān Khan (Uzbek leader) 233–4
sugar, manufacture 150
Sulṭān-Abū Saʿīd b. Muḥammad Mīran-Shāhī (Timurid ruler) 201–3, 206, 223–4, 225, 226
Sulṭān Aḥmad b. Abū Saʿīd (Timurid descendant) 203, 291
Sulṭān ʿAlī Mashhadī (calligrapher) 209
Sulṭān ʿAlī Tarkhan (Arghun amir) 290–1
Sulṭān Ḥusayn Bayqara (Timurid ruler) 202, 203, 214, 226, 279*n*
  cultural patronage 205, 208–12, 213
Sulṭān Maḥmūd (Chaghatayid Khan, r. 1488) 291
Sulṭān Malik Kāshgharī 209
Sulṭān Muḥammad b. Baysunghur (Timurid descendant) 192, 197, 200
Sulṭān Muḥammad "Mutribi" Samarqandi (poet) *see* Mutribi
Sulṭān-Saʿīd (Moghul Khan) 265–6, 266*n*
Sulṭānov, T.I. 228
Suyunjuq b. Abu'l-Khayr (Shibanid Khan) 282, 288, 291, 293, 294
Suzdal' (city) 247
Suzdal', Principality of 69
Sviiazhsk, as Russian administrative centre 305, 309, 310, 326, 328
Syr Darya valley 363, 367, 371, 379, 393

al-Taftazānī, Saʿd al-Dīn Masʿūd b. 'Umar b. Abd Allah 207
Ṭaghāchār (military commander) 90
taghar 'donative in trade goods' 99
Ṭāhir Khan (Khiva Khan, d. 1740/1) 395
Ṭāhir Khan (Qazaq leader, d. 1526) 364
Taishi Oghlan (Yuan pretender) 187
Tāj ad-Dīn b. Yālchīghul al-Bashqordi (religious writer) 388, 389
Tajuddin Khwāja 268
Tamerlane *see* Temür
tamgha ('tolls, customs duties, commercial tax') 97–8, 205
Tana ('on River', 'name of trade center') 104, 106
Tang dynasty 26, 261, 333
Tangut people 3, 9–10, 26, 30
Tarim Basin 260–1, 262, 265–6, 268, 272–3, 334, 353
Tarmashirin (son of Du'a) 57–8, 60, 61, 63, 130–1, 182
  religion 58, 62, 64, 130–1, 262
Tash-Temür (Golden Horde Khan) 256
Tashkent 363, 368, 371, 402, 407–8
Tatar people 19, 27, 110–11
  commercial activities 385
  conflicts with Mongols 21, 22*n*, 25, 28
  conflicts with other races 22
  European invasion/rule 69–72, 73–4, 75
  general application of name 27, 111*n*
  religion 42
  Russian conquest/rule 303–11, 325–6, 385
  Russian use of term 383
Tatar Tonga (Uighur scribe/teacher) 24, 35
Tawakkul b. Shïghāy (Qazaq Khan) 364
Tawke (Qazaq Khan) 364, 367
taxation 36, 60–1, 75, 93, 97–100, 205, 275–6
  disaster relief 359–60
  exemptions 64
Tayang (Naiman leader) 23
Taybugha/Taybughids 251, 312–13
Taydūla Khātūn (wife of Özbek) 104
technology 150
  military 150–1
Teke (Turkmen tribe) 235–6, 392, 400, 404–5, 411
Tekish (Khwārazm ruler) 14*n*
Temüge Otchigin (brother of Chinggis Khan) 32, 40–1, 51, 163
Temüjin (Temüchin) *see* Chinggis Khan
Temür, Emir (Tamerlane) 4–5, 60, 82, 118, 182–8
  administration 187–8, 285
  conflicts with Golden Horde 83–5, 185–6, 237
  conquests 183–7, 192–3, 198, 213, 262–3
  cultural/religious policy 195, 196
  death 85, 187, 221, 263
  Islamization programs 131, 133
  legacy 198
  literary depictions 211, 265
  provisions for succession 186, 188–9
  rise to power 182, 183–5, 262, 279
  title 279
  see also Timurid Empire
Temür Khan b. Temür Qutlugh 238–9
Temür Khan (Chengzong), Emperor (grandson of Qubilai) 40, 53, 54
Temür-khoja (Golden Horde Khan) 80
Temür Qutlugh Khan (of Golden Horde) 84, 238
Timūr Shāh of Afghanistan 396
Tengri, cult of 149
Tergen Khatun (wife of Tekish) 14–15, 15*n*
textile industry/trade 140
texts, transmission of 137–40
al-Thaʿālibī 152

Thomas, Archdeacon of Spalato 70–2
Tibet 349, 350–1
Tīmūr Ghāzī Sulṭān (Togha-Temürid descendant) 398
Tīmūr / Timurid empire *see* Temür / Temürid empire
Timurid Empire / dynasty
  administration 187–8, 204–5
  (claimed) heritage 195–6
  conflicts with (restored) Chinggisids 291–2, 295–7
  continuance of Mongol traditions 184–5, 194, 195
  cultural / scientific patronage 194–5, 207–12, 217
  decline 277
  economy 205–7
  geographical extent 193, 198
  internal power struggles 197–8, 199–201
  legacy 198
  military strategy / technology 213–15
  religion / religious policy 191, 196, 206–7
  titles 279, 279*n*
  see also Shāhrukh; Temür
Tiumen' (city) 238, 251, 313
Tiumen (khanate) 247
Tobol'sk (city) 313, 371–2, 374
Togh Temür (Wenzong) (Yuan Emperor 1328-32) 94, 101–2*n*
Togha-Temür (son of Jochi) 67, 224–5, 298
Togha-Temürid line 256, 278–9, 282, 393
  control of Khurasan 298–302
  internal conflicts 299–300
Toghan (Oirat leader) 163–4
Toghan Temür (Huizong) (Yuan Emperor 1333-70) 42, 44, 159
Toghto-bukha (Dayisung Khan) 163–5
Toghus Temür (son of Toghan Temür) 159–60, 163, 175
Tokharian (language) 17
Töle-Bugha (Golden Horde Khan) 77
Tolui (son of Chinggis Khan) 32–3, 38, 67, 114
Toluid dynasty *see* Ilkhanate; Yuan
Tom' (river) 252
Tomsk (city) 313
To'oril *see* Ong Khan
Toqtamïsh 81–3, 93, 104, 222
  conflicts with Edigü 237–8
  conflicts with Timür 83–5, 185–6, 237, 238
  death 85, 238
Toqto'a Beki (Merkit leader) 23, 30
Toqto'a (descendant of Temüge Otchigin) 41
Toqto'a (Golden Horde Khan) 53, 77–8, 127
Töregene (wife of Ögödei) 48
törü (body of legal practice) 2
Törü Bolud (son of Dayan Khan) 166
Törültü, Princess (daughter of Dayan Khan) 166
trade 3, 62–3, 100–8, 266–7, 374–5, 406, 407
  centres 205–6, 384–5
  commodities 100–1, 103–4, 106–7, 140, 252, 270–1, 273–4, 313–14, 336, 374–5
  Golden Horde 74–5, 77
  importance to Mongol economies 89–90
  within Mongol Empire 140–1
  relationship with postal system 144–6
  routes 62, 84, 95, 101–3, 104*n*, 144–5, 205–6, 260–1, 266, 270–1, 316–17, 374
Transcaucasia 9
Transoxania (Mawarannahr) 31, 33, 47, 50, 54–5, 56–7, 59–60, 63, 82, 99, 126, 129, 182, 192, 193, 199, 200, 201, 212
  conflicts over 201, 212, 223, 392
  geopolitical situation 260
  language 111, 117
  religion 132–3, 196
  Timurid conquest / redevelopment 185–6, 192–3, 198, 205–6
  Togha-Timurid Khanate 282, 285
  Uzbek migration to 288
Transylvania, Mongol invasion 70–2
travels, and flow of information 151
  see also relocation
Trepavlov, Vadim V. 241*n*
Tsewang Rabdan (Zunghar leader) 269, 348, 349–50, 351
Tsong kha pa, Lama 171
Tudä-Mengü (Golden Horde Khan) 77
Tugha Temür *see* Togh Temür
Tughluq Temür Khan 59–60, 116, 182, 183
  conversion to Islam 60, 64, 132, 262
tümen (fiscal / military unit) 60–1
Tümen Jasaghtu (post-Yuan Khan) 167, 169
Tura (city) 250–1, 313
Türk Empire 1–2, 15–16, 37
  Mongolian states 18–19
Turkestan
  ethno-linguistic characteristics 15–17, 116–17
  Mongol invasion (1219-21) 31, 142
  Qing invasion 351
Turkestan (city) 367, 370, 379
Turkic (language) 111–12, 114, 114*n*, 119, 252, 382–3
  literature 213, 215–16

Mongol influence on 119*n*
vocabulary of genealogy 109*n*
Turkic peoples / communities 15–17, 110
assimilation of Mongol elements 73
groupings 111*nn*
heroic ethos 118
in Mongolia 18–19, 22
rebel bands 96
in Temür's army / administration 187–8
westward migrations 111–12
Türkmen people 96, 229–36, 398, 402–3
conflicts with Timurids 199, 201–2
desert settlements 404–5
early history 229–31
migrations 230–1, 233–6, 392–3, 400
relations with Uzbeks 233–5
Russian conquest 410–11
social structure 231
tribal divisions 231–3
Tüsiyetü Khan (Khalkha title) 346–8, 358

ʿUbaid-i Zākānī (satirist) 98
ʿUbaydullah Ahrār, Khwāja (Ṣūfī Shaykh) 202–3, 206–7
Ubashi (Qalmaq viceroy) 321
ʿUbaydallāh Khan (of Bukhara, d. 1711) 234, 279*n*, 281, 285, 291, 293–4, 393
ʿUbaydallāh (Khiva Khan, d. 1756) 395
Üch El (Türkmen tribal grouping) 233, 234
Udmurt (Votiak) people 328, 382
Ufa (city) 313–14
Uighur state / people 1, 2, 17, 24, 26, 27, 99
alliance with Mongols 30, 35, 37, 47
language / script 35
later conflicts over territory 56, 57
Mongolian states 18–19, 22
population 275, 275*n*
religion 64, 117
Ükek 83
Ulaghchi (son of Batu) 75
ulema (religious scholars) 107–8, 206–7, 264, 290–1, 391
Ulan Budung, battle of (1690) 348
Ulugh Beg b. Shāhrukh (grandson of Temür) 192, 193–4, 197, 223, 264, 287–8, 293
achievement / legacy 199–200
cultural / religious interests 195, 208, 213
Ulugh Beg Kābulī (Timurid descendant) 203
Ulugh Muḥammad (Kazan Khan) 240–1, 245–6, 247, 248, 256
ulus (appanages, state, people), defined 37–9
for individual ulus *see names of tribes / royal houses*

Ulus Bolud (son of Dayan Khan) 166, 167
ʿUmar Shaykh Mīrzā (Timurid descendant) 203, 205–6
'Umar Shaykh (son of Temür) 184, 188
'Umar "The Tyrant" (Khoqand Khan) 401
al-ʿUmarī 130–1
Ura-Tübe (city) 397
Ural (river) 221, 241–2, 244, 316, 319, 363, 369, 371
Uran Temür (relative of Möngke Temür) 103
Uraz Bi Ming (Uzbek amir) 302
Urgench
destruction of 84, 185, 186
(Ürgench, capital of Khwārazm) 80, 83, 239
Ürük Temür (Ögödeid Khan) 59
Urus Khan (of the Golden Horde) 82, 84, 222
Uz Temür Tayshi (Oirat leader) 224
Uzbek people 115–16, 118, 118*n*, 191, 221–9, 237–8, 286–90, 398
alliance with Timurids 223
conflicts with Bukhara 397
conflicts with Jochids 221–3
conflicts with Oirats 224
conflicts with Timurids 199, 201, 203, 212–13, 214, 216, 223–4, 227–8
increasing independence / territorial attachment 301–2
inter-tribal relations 288–9
internal divisions 224–8, 398–400
naming 221–2*n*, 228–9, 287–8
relations with Türkmen 233–5
tribal composition 228, 229, 286–8, 402–3
Uzboy (Türkmen tribe) 231
Uzun Hasan Aq Qoyunlu 202, 203

Vaisov, Bahā' ad-Dīn 389
Valikhanov, Chokan 378
Vaqqāṣ Biy (grandson of Edigü) 222, 224
Vasilii II, Grand Prince of Muscovy 246, 247
Vasilii III, Grand Prince of Muscovy 248, 258
vassalage, system of 93–4
Venice, trade with Mongol states 102–3, 104–5
Vitautas (Witold / Vitovk, Grand Duke of Lithuania) 84–5, 238–249
Vladimir (city / principality) 79
Mongol capture of 69–70
Vladimirtsov, Boris Ia. 97, 109*n*
Voguls *see* Ob-Ugrians
Volga region 11, 69, 74–5
language / culture 114*n*, 115–16, 119
Russian occupation / control 317–18, 323, 325, 326, 330, 380–91

Walī b. Ablay Khan (Qazaq leader) 370
Walī Muḥammad b. Jānī Muḥammad (Uzbek amīr) 282, 298–9
Wālid b. Muḥammad-Amīn al-Qārghālī (Walī-Muḥammad Īshān) (Ṣūfī Shaykh) 390
Wallachia, Mongol invasion 71
Wang Anshi 90
Wang Chonggu 169
Wanli Emperor (Zhu Yijun) 335
Wenzong, Emperor *see* Togh Temür
White Horde *see* Aq Orda
Wuzong, Emperor *see* Qaishan

Xiaozhuang Wen Huanghou, Empress 180
Xinjiang
- geopolitical situation 260–1, 272–3
- Moghul rule 261–7, 278
- naming 272*n*
- Qing conquest / rule 271–6, 339, 351–3
- Zunghar rule 267–71

Xiongnu people 1, 2
Xi Xia empire *see* Tangut people

Yādigār b. Qāsim Khan (Kazan Khan) 227, 249
Yādigār Biy (Taybughid leader) 251, 312
Yādigār Sulṭān b. Tīmūr Shaykh (Jochid descendant) 224, 227
Yadgar Muḥammad (Timurid descendant) 202, 203, 208
Yaghmurchï Biy (Noghay Horde leader) 253
Yakuts (people) 327
yam 'imperial post system' 97, 144
Yanchichar (son of Qaidu) 55
Yār Muḥammad (Togha-Timurid Khan) 289, 298
Yarkand Khanate 266*n*
yarligh 'decree' 97
yasa see *jasagh*
Yasariyya (Ṣūfī order) 196
Yasawur (Chaghadaid prince) 56–7, 130, 131
Yasï *see* Turkestan (city)
Yayïq River *see* Ural (river)
Yazdi *see* Sharaf al-Dīn Ali Yazdi
Yazïr tribe 231*n*
Yedi Inal ('Forest People' leader) 18
Yedisan Horde (Noghay subdivision) 245
Yedishkul Horde (Noghay subdivision) 245
Yehe people 178
Yelü Ahai (Khitan leader) 35
Yelü Chacai (Chinggisid minister) 34, 35*n*, 161
Yelü Dashi (Qara Khitai founder) 11
Yelü Liuge (Khitan leader) 34
Yelü Mian-Sige (Khitan leader) 35
Yelü Zhilugu (Qara Khitai leader) 13
Yenisei (river) 327
Yermak Timofeev (Cossack leader) 250, 312–13
Yesü Möngke (son of Chaghadai) 48–9
Yesün-Temür (grandson of Du'a) 59, 64
Yisügei (Yesügei) Ba'atur (father of Chinggis Khan) 21*n*, 22, 28
- death 27, 28

Yomut (Turkmen tribe) 392, 398–9, 409, 410–11
Yon-tan rgyamts'o, Dalai Lama 172
Yongle Emperor (Zhu Di) 160, 175–6, 193, 334
Yongzheng Emperor (Yinzhen) 360
Yuan dynasty
- aftermath 158, 166
- claims to Ming throne 158, 160
- conflicts with Central Asia 51–2, 54–6, 143
- decline / fall 157, 159, 334
- extinction 181
- institutional development 89
- inter-regional trade 62, 89–90
- scientific / acadcemic interests 138

Yūnus Khan (of Moghulistan) 225, 262*n*, 264–5, 268
yurt (capital city) 285
Yūsuf Biy b. Mūsā (Noghay Khan) 243
Yūsuf Khaṣṣ Ḥājib, *Qutadhghu Bilig* 10
Yüz (Uzbek tribe) 393, 395

Zahir al-Dīn Muḥammad Babūr *see* Babūr
Zaitsev, I.V. 254
Zaya Pandita (Buddhist monk) 269
Zhaozong *see* Ayushidara
Zhengtong Emperor 164
Zhu Di, Emperor *see* Yongle Emperor
Zhu Yuanzhang, Emperor *see* Hongwu Emperor
zhüz (Qazaq tribes) 229, 364–5, 406
Zunghar people 267–71, 338–9, 345
- conflicts with Qing 270–1, 339, 346–8, 349–50, 351–3
- control of trade routes 270–1
- destruction 352–3
- economy / social structure 269
- internal conflicts 352
- religion 269–70, 345
- rise to power 268–70, 345

For EU product safety concerns, contact us at Calle de José Abascal, 56–1°, 28003 Madrid, Spain or eugpsr@cambridge.org.

www.ingramcontent.com/pod-product-compliance
Ingram Content Group UK Ltd.
Pitfield, Milton Keynes, MK11 3LW, UK
UKHW022239220326
469255UK00018B/267
* 9 7 8 1 1 0 7 4 9 2 0 5 9 *